MW00783915

AN IRISH PASSION FOR JUSTICE

An Irish Passion for Justice

The Life of Rebel New York Attorney Paul O'Dwyer

ROBERT POLNER AND MICHAEL TUBRIDY

Three Hills

CORNELL UNIVERSITY PRESS   ITHACA AND LONDON

First published 2024 by Cornell University Press

Printed in the United States of America

Library of Congress Cataloging-in-Publication Data

Names: Polner, Rob, author. | Tubridy, Michael (Michael Joseph), 1959– author.
Title: An Irish passion for justice : the life of rebel New York attorney Paul O'Dwyer / Robert Polner, Michael Tubridy.
Description: Ithaca : Three Hills, Cornell University Press, 2024. | Includes bibliographical references and index.
Identifiers: LCCN 2023045868 (print) | LCCN 2023045869 (ebook) | ISBN 9781501773051 (hardcover) | ISBN 9781501775345 (pdf) | ISBN 9781501775352 (epub)
Subjects: LCSH: O'Dwyer, Paul, 1907–1998. | Lawyers—New York (State)—New York—Biography. | City council members—New York (State)—New York—Biography.
Classification: LCC KF373.O38 P65 2024 (print) | LCC KF373.O38 (ebook) | DDC 974.7/1043092 [B]—dc23/eng/20231010
LC record available at https://lccn.loc.gov/2023045868
LC ebook record available at https://lccn.loc.gov/2023045869

The ideals should always come first.
—Paul O'Dwyer (quoted in Clines, 1998)

CONTENTS

Photographs follow pages 124 and 222

AN IRISH PASSION FOR JUSTICE

INTRODUCTION

A S THE 1991 St. Patrick's Day parade in New York got under way, Paul O'Dwyer marched with the aid of a cane alongside members of the Irish Lesbian and Gay Organization (ILGO). Out of the thousands of spectators on Manhattan's Fifth Avenue, some screamed antigay slurs, and two older women shrieked, "AIDS, AIDS, AIDS!" O'Dwyer, the white-pompadoured spokesman for Irish America, continued for eight blocks before his wife, Patricia Hanrahan, guided him to higher ground. But epithets and brickbats flew fast from the sidewalk when Mayor David Dinkins, a longtime O'Dwyer ally, joined up with the small ILGO parade contingent a few blocks on.

Luckily, O'Dwyer, who was then eighty-three, missed getting nicked by one of the beer cans hurled at the progressive group and the mayor. But having participated in decades of left-wing activism as a Democratic politician, civil rights lawyer, and social agitator, the elderly activist was familiar with the front lines of protest politics. On the day of the big parade, he stayed long enough to show which side he was on: that of gay men and lesbians, just the latest in a long line of US minority groups to draw enmity and suppression. Known in the United States and Ireland for his radical egalitarian spirit, the County Mayo–born O'Dwyer battled for most of the twentieth century for scapegoats and outcasts of all types.

O'Dwyer's remarkably consistent work for the causes of liberals and the left began during the Great Depression, but he only became very well known in 1968, when, improbably, he captured the Democratic nomination for US senator from New York on the coattails of the presidential hopeful Eugene McCarthy. Like the Minnesota dove, O'Dwyer declined until days before the general election to endorse the Democratic Party's nominee Hubert Humphrey, the vice president, because of his equivocations over how and when to end what Paul called America's "grossly immoral" war in Vietnam.[1] Rarely uncomfortable in the role of Democratic establishment conscience and critic, O'Dwyer refused to disappoint his own followers, including tens of thousands of college students, even if it contributed to his reputation among conservative Irish Americans as a contrarian. But constancy in his beliefs was an O'Dwyer signature, even when it jeopardized his Senate race or the liberal Humphrey's chances of defeating Richard Nixon.

In the last third of his life, all the same, O'Dwyer emphasized compromise over confrontation with regard to the Troubles, the brutal conflict born of centuries of British misrule in Ireland. Using the skills he accrued as a defense attorney in American courthouses and a tirelessness often noted by friends and associates, he proved integral to grassroots Irish American efforts to enlist the White House as an international peace broker in Northern Ireland, a role that successive US presidents had hesitated to assume in light of America's "special relationship" with, and deference to, Great Britain, and which the Irish Republic, too, was often hesitant to disrupt. O'Dwyer and his fellow Irish American lawyer-activists in New York City managed to strap Bill Clinton to Paul's lifetime cause, starting the then Arkansas governor on the path that led during his presidency to the Good Friday Agreement of 1998. Quelling three decades of sectarian violence, the multiparty pact was signed and sealed shortly before Paul's death.

Because of this contribution, among many others, O'Dwyer's life and times are relevant to understanding America's, and the world's, polarization in the twenty-first century, representing an example of how to remain true to one's beliefs in a reactionary era, amass allies across ideological lines, and both defy and negotiate with the status quo. Believing strongly that the Democratic Party must focus more on opening doors for marginalized groups, O'Dwyer linked his passion for change to facts and argumentation, never denunciation, and his liberalism to unionism. While in the Cold War period he quit the National Lawyers Guild, the alternative association with many Marxist members, he did so without animosity and continued to represent individuals blacklisted, jailed, or deported during Congress's anti-communist witch hunts. But under the category of unfairly pilloried he included, at the deepest and most personal level, his older brother Bill, who worked under the shadow of rumor and scandal as a gangbusting Brooklyn district attorney, as New York's midcentury mayor, and as President Harry Truman's ambassador to Mexico.

While Paul lacked the crowd-pleasing temperament of Bill, he cultivated warm feelings in both major parties and among left-wing sects, though he was often too extreme for Democratic Party regulars in New York and not extreme enough for Young Turks of the Democratic Reform movement who—with his active participation—challenged boss rule in New York City from the late 1950s to the early 1970s.

If O'Dwyer perplexed conservative Irish Americans with left-wing advocacy on a wide range of issues affecting the working class and the poor and legal representation of radicals like Father Phil Berrigan of the New Catholic Left, he also puzzled officials in the Irish Republic later by refusing either to endorse Irish Republican Army (IRA) attacks against security forces in Northern Ireland or to condemn the equally lethal handiwork of the loyalist paramilitaries. Indeed, he came to be viewed from London and Dublin during the Troubles as one of the most enigmatic stalwarts of Irish American republicanism. While he strongly loathed the British hand in the six-county north, he flatly refused to play one Irishman in Ulster against another, whether Catholic or Protestant. His targets instead were the economic and political imbalances he felt most responsible for driving a wedge between the two communities since Ireland's unfortunate 1921 partition. Whenever possible, he marshaled resistance and outcry against the British-dominated security, political, and legal apparatus in Ulster, along with its gerrymandering, hiring discrimination, and many other factors that weighed heavily on the Catholic minority in particular.

O'Dwyer was born to humble circumstances in 1907 in Bohola, a hamlet that would be difficult to find on a map of Ireland even today. As he grew up, British police auxiliaries known as the Black and Tans rampaged through the countryside in the Irish War of Independence. His family was among many who opposed a peace treaty establishing an Irish Free State under British dominion and the partition of Ireland, north from south. But the atmosphere of dread, anger, and disappointment he experienced in his native land as a child conditioned in him a lifelong identification with the victims of injustice as well as a deep distrust of clerical and state authority.

After arriving in New York in 1925 at age seventeen, Paul gravitated toward people and neighborhoods beyond the tight-knit Irish world, aided by his four older brothers, who preceded him in the huge and inexplicable metropolis. Enrolling at Brooklyn's newly opened St. John's Law School, he made friends with Jewish classmates and found, much to his surprise, that they too were offshoots of a world of strife, persecution, and hardship. His friendships contributed to his decision, uncommon for an Irish immigrant, to aid Jewish activists smuggling weapons and medical supplies to Zionist paramilitaries in British Mandatory Palestine during and after World War II. His empathy for underdogs linked him, too, to the trade union movement in New York during the Great Depression and to the city's interracial civil rights movement in the 1940s. The same set of shared concerns precipitated in the summer of 1966 his inspired defense of Ernest Gallashaw, an African American teenager railroaded for a child's shooting amid racial turmoil on the streets of Brooklyn.

In the early 1970s, O'Dwyer organized legal and political support for a group of lower-middle-class New York Irish Catholics subpoenaed to testify before a Texas grand jury investigating IRA gunrunning from south of the Mexican border—the celebrated "Fort Worth Five" case. He had recently completed his work on the successful defense of Berrigan and the imprisoned clergyman's associates in a case initiated by the Nixon Justice Department, as well as repeated trips to support the civil rights movement to end racial segregation and disenfranchisement in the American South. When friends in the Irish American community—one he saw as increasingly comfortable and even complacent—asked why he cared so much about the mistreatment of Black people in the former Confederacy, his answer characteristically traced back to his upbringing amid the Irish War of Independence: "The Black and Tans used to drive through the town, shooting it up. It was not too different from Mississippi."[2]

We will never know how the kindly radical, as the *New York Post* columnist Murray Kempton characterized him, would have fared in an era of social media–lofted outrage and accusation.[3] But O'Dwyer, whose highest public office was New York City Council president, was neither drawn to nor intimidated by reactionaryism, scandal, or racism. Principle, not a thirst for power, drove him, along with the pursuit of what he called "fair play over the period of a lifetime," without regard to race, gender, class, origin, religion, or—though it only became a major focus of contention in his later years—sexual orientation.[4]

Deeply connected to his experience as an early twentieth-century immigrant, he remains a model for those who look for ways, as he did, to improve fallible democracies. His guiding instinct was not to foster contrarian opposition to authority for its own sake but rather to seek to compel the United States to live up its founding ideals and Great Britain to allow all of Ireland to achieve an enduring condition of justice and self-determination.

THE BOY FROM BOHOLA

STARTING IN THE TUDOR PERIOD, England used Ireland as a kind of laboratory for the colonial system that gave rise to the far-flung British Empire. By the time Paul was born, the legacy of these experiments in Ireland was plain: the enfeeblement of native industry, the near obliteration of the Irish language, a lack of elementary political autonomy for most residents, and bitter sectarian divisions fostered by an occupying power. What the historian F. S. L. Lyons termed "the long-standing and deep-rooted hatred of the English connection" had contributed to a massive, multidecade exodus to the United States, Canada, Australia, New Zealand, and Britain itself, hotbeds of Irish republican movements that ensured that "the Irish question became and remained an international question."[1]

Paul O'Dwyer joined that exodus as an adolescent in the middle of the 1920s, and his activism in America proved never-ending: working on behalf of the formative trade union movement in New York City, campaigning for votes as an anti–Vietnam War candidate for the US Senate in New York, confronting all-white juries in the Deep South, and joining rallies for women's equality, Soviet Jewry, and almost every other liberal humanitarian cause of the twentieth century. But his consistent outrage at injustice and his willingness to defy convention sprang from an early source: what he saw and absorbed as a child in Bohola, a tiny community in rural County Mayo in the west of Ireland.

O'Dwyer's paternal grandfather, John O'Dwyer, of Tullylease, County Cork, set the pattern by breaking with the then prevalent custom of arranged marriages in Ireland as a young man: he married Catherine Norcott, a member of the class of English and Scottish settlers whose receipt of land confiscated from Catholics had put them at the heart of the "Protestant Ascendancy" that had held sway in Ireland since the mid-seventeenth century. Catherine's decision to not just marry a Catholic but also convert to his faith led to disinheritance and alienation from her family.[2]

The couple set up a trading shop in Tullylease and had nine children, but by 1887, with the population of John's hometown having dwindled to only a few hundred, economic opportunity was limited for their offspring. Forsaking two other available options—the military and emigration—one of the nine, twenty-seven-year-old Patrick, chose education instead. A year later, having completed his studies at St. Patrick's College at Drumcondra, Dublin, the only teacher-training school for men in Ireland, he answered an ad in the newspaper for a teaching job and, with his belongings in a cardboard suitcase, took the train to Tuam, County Galway. From there he walked 35 miles to a County Mayo parish 150 miles west of Dublin: Bohola, where he not only began his career but also started a family and spent the remainder of his life.[3]

It was in Bohola that Patrick O'Dwyer, Paul's father, met Bridget McNicholas, a local schoolmistress three years his junior with hair that was "dark as night and went down to her waist," as Paul recalled. Though her formal education was more limited than Patrick's and she had qualified as a teacher simply on the OK of the local pastor, her efforts at bettering herself were unstinting. Like John O'Dwyer, Bridget's father Pat McNicholas, too, had defied custom by marrying his wife without resort to a dowry. Nor would he accept money from any suitor of his daughter's. McNicholas looked with approval on the courtship of his daughter with the teacher from Cork.[4]

Patrick married Bridget in 1889. The couple's toehold was a boggy three and a half acres. They chose one of the seventeen cottages spread over three hundred acres in Lismirrane. The village lay within Bohola, a place that, with its Catholic church, three pubs, and post office, was "not even a dot on the map," as Paul recalled as a grown man. It might as well have been "the other side of the moon" (as his middle son, Rory, came to describe it).[5]

Like the rest of County Mayo, Bohola had been devastated by the Great Famine that began in 1845, a blight that brought with it staggering levels of hunger, disease, and evictions. Bohola's population dropped from 4,301 in the 1841 census to 2,907 a decade later, mirroring the national wave of death and exodus. The mournful migration that ensued at the height of the Potato Famine in 1847—the infamous "Black '47"—became an established pattern, with the population dropping further, reaching 2,580 by the 1911 census.[6] Early in the twentieth century, the scars of deprivation remained on the Bohola landscape, seen in "the ruins of abandoned dwellings—mute evidence that hunger, the battering ram, the landlord's dreaded demolition machine, had overcome these occupants during famine and eviction," as Paul wrote.[7]

Unlike so many others in the region, Pat and Bridget O'Dwyer would stay. But little had changed by the time their first child, William, was born in 1890 into "an atmosphere of confusion and utter despair," as Paul starkly described it, "with no hope for Ireland but a continuation of tyranny, and in Mayo little to look forward to but the immigrant ship, the army or the clergy."[8]

William was followed by another nine children who survived to maturity. (One other died soon after birth.) The last-born—Peter Paul O'Dwyer (Paul, as he was known)—showed up on June 29, 1907. It was the feast day of Saints Peter and Paul, so he was named in honor of the two pioneering missionaries of the Roman Catholic Church. Once in America, he dropped the first name. Oddly enough, William and Paul would not lay eyes on each other for the first time until nearly eighteen years later, in America. But in their adopted country the oldest and youngest O'Dwyer sons would form a bond of such tenacious loyalty that it did not dissolve even amid the crucible of mid-twentieth-century New York politics and scandal, or their periodic quarrels and estrangements.

Paul was born into "an already overcrowded five-room house," he recalled seven decades later in his spare memoir, *Counsel for the Defense*; "and while I know my deeply religious mother proclaimed me to be a gift from heaven, I doubt that the other members of the family subscribed to this view."[9] The feeling encompassed more than just the housing arrangements (which had already been enlarged, with two new rooms and a slated roof joining the original thatched cottage in 1899).[10] His birth meant another mouth to feed—just one more burden in a household that, like many others in this and other rural communities in Ireland, had to juggle debts.[11]

After giving birth a seventh time, Bridget was fired from her teaching job by the dominating parish priest, Canon John O'Grady, who may have seen it as a means of reminding her husband who was boss. The loss of her forty-pound annual salary represented "near economic disaster," Paul recalled.[12]

At all times, though, physical labor on the O'Dwyer farm was intense. Starting with William, who went by Willy as a youngster, all the O'Dwyer sons were expected to sow seed, feed and shelter livestock, thrash and winnow oat sheaves, and harvest turnips and cabbage. In perhaps the most necessary but vexing chore, they used a spraying machine to halt the longtime dread of farmers, the potato blight, even if it inevitably resulted in them getting thoroughly wet and sick from the fumes. A barefooted Paul would enter nearby bogs, where he loaded turf needed for winter fuel and hauled it back home with a donkey and cart, usually borrowed from a neighbor.[13] This tedious regimen would be relieved from time to time in those prewar years by dancing to the sounds of melodeons, flutes, and fiddles in the kitchens of country houses.[14]

Hazards in the surrounding countryside also had to be contended with. Fishing for salmon entailed poaching, as the local stream was owned by a London-based absentee landlord. Villagers had little to no contact with the medical profession. An injury would not be treated by an osteopath, a chiropractor, or a physical therapist but by a "bone-setter," a local practitioner whose skill in manipulating joints was regarded as an instinctual gift rather than the result of training. As for other illnesses, some women with knowledge of herbs—including both Paul's mother, Bridget, and his maternal grandmother, Penelope McNicholas—might be called on for assistance.[15]

Above almost all other dangers, villagers were at the mercy of "consumption"—tuberculosis. "In those days, if you had TB, it would have been easier for the people who had a child to say that they had immigrated, that they had gone, rather than acknowledge that there was somebody with TB in the house," said Paul's nephew, Adrian Flannelly, the son of Paul's sister Linda and Padraic Flannelly.[16] TB struck with particular force among the O'Dwyers and McNicholases: three of Bridget O'Dwyer's eight siblings contracted it at an early age and died. Yet Bridget was "one of the first to take a strong hand in the anti-tuberculosis drive, cleanliness around the homes and things of that kind," her eldest child Bill recalled in one interview.[17] "Up to the time of her death, she was very active on these things."

Despite her strenuous efforts, Bridget could only mitigate the spread of TB in Bohola, and it penetrated even her own household as an adult. Bill was shocked to discover upon entering the US Army Air Forces in 1942 that he had scar tissue on his left lung, revealed in an X-ray. He speculated that he had contracted it when he was less than a year old, while staying in a house in which three aunts had come down with it. The disease exacted a toll on the nation's psychology, and Irish emigrants found it to be part of the emotional burden they carried to the New World. A slur entered the mainstream: "tubercular Irish." It became shorthand for the belief that emigrants were the cause of TB epidemics.[18]

In spite of such worries, the O'Dwyer children possessed a significant advantage over their Mayo neighbors: although they lived in a remote rural townland with parents who were in hock to many mercantile establishments, theirs was a literate household that valued culture.[19] Even with little to no money coming in, Patrick and Bridget managed to scrape together enough to purchase a harmonium. Under the watchful eyes of Bridget, the girls—Mary Rose (or May), Kathleen, Josephine, and Linda—took lessons in the piano and singing, while Bill received instruction in the melodeon. As adults, all four daughters would, before marriage, follow their mother into teaching. (Kathleen earned a master's degree from Dublin's Trinity College, one of the first women west of the Shannon River to earn that distinction.)[20]

Unlike the four O'Dwyer daughters, who spent most or all of their lives in Ireland, the four O'Dwyer sons emigrated in sequence to the United States. Patrick O'Dwyer impressed on them that the limited opportunities available in Bohola practically dictated that they needed to go. But his sense of independence also gave them the self-confidence they needed to strike out for a new country. With Patrick's tutelage in the classroom and presence at home, the O'Dwyer boys—but Bill and Paul especially—turned out more learned than many of the fellow Irish Americans they came to encounter on the docks, on construction sites, and in the New York City Police Department. In addition to providing overall direction for the three-room school, located just a few hundred feet from the family's home, Patrick taught academic subjects such as mathematics, to which he added expertise born of his experience as a surveyor and his studies of Euclid. Each of his sons passed through his classroom. He was, remembered Bill, a "patient, helpful and insistent teacher."[21] Furthermore, Great Britain's difficulties in World War I furnished Patrick with a contemporary demonstration of geography as students discovered how the narrow Dardanelles Strait led to disaster in the 1915 Gallipoli campaign. Both Bill and Paul, under their father's tutelage, read Shakespeare's *The Merchant of Venice*. But since the population of Bohola included no Jews (and just one Protestant), the only member of the Jewish faith whom Paul would come to "know" in any sense until he reached America was the character of Shylock, the play's principal antagonist.

Three formative Irish movements beyond the confines of Bohola shaped the schoolmaster's mindset about Ireland's history and current events, in education, labor, and republicanism. Patrick O'Dwyer's belief in the importance of these forces of reform affected how he and his family came to regard the dominant element in Irish life: the Roman Catholic Church.[22]

Irish republicanism had played a part in Patrick's life even before he set foot in the townland. Paul's father strongly supported Michael Davitt's agitation for the Land League. His embrace of the principles of the socialist revolutionary and land reformer went a long way toward smoothing his way to acceptance as a trustworthy outsider in County Mayo, Paul remembered.[23] In the classroom, he would invoke the aid of the Almighty against those he saw as the country's oppressors, ending with the hope that God would "look kindly on Ireland's struggles and bring confusion to our enemies."[24]

Athletics provided another outlet for nationalists like Paul's father, within County Mayo and across Ireland as a whole. The Gaelic Athletic Association, established in 1884, quickly became not only a means of encouraging interest in Irish football and hurling but also "a recruiting ground for republican activists," according to historian J. J. Lee.[25]

Bohola cheered the exploits of local athletic hero Martin Sheridan, who, after emigrating to the United States, won much glory for his adopted country in track and field events in three different Olympics in the early 1900s—five gold medals, three silver medals, and one bronze, such that, more than a century after his death in the 1918 flu pandemic, many still regarded him as the greatest athlete ever born in Ireland.[26] For the most part the O'Dwyer boys shared this fascination, with Bill—his friend, both in Ireland and America—excelling as a youth in football, handball, and hurling.[27]

But Paul, perhaps because of his short stature, mirroring that of his mustachioed father, did not participate in athletic pursuits, nor did he become an avid fan. Coming to the United States during the golden age of sports that featured Babe Ruth, Red Grange, and Jack Dempsey, he paid little attention to the games that consumed the attention of so many other New Yorkers. In later years he dealt with the legal and commercial affairs of the Gaelic Athletic Association of New York, but this was in support of Bill's involvement with the organization rather than the result of any intrinsic interest of his own.[28]

Education was more than just Patrick's occupation: it also enabled the Bohola schoolmaster, as Bill noted a half-century later, "to spread his learning and extend his influence"—not just through his work with the young but also through teaching an after-hours adult learning class and reading to farmer neighbors, many of whom could not read.[29] Through good schooling, Patrick believed Ireland might improve economically and even achieve its rightful place among the nations of the world. Throughout the eighteenth century, despite proscriptions by England against teaching by the two chief dissenting religions, Catholicism and Presbyterianism, schools were maintained in secret, often outdoors, moving from place to place. A common surreptitious setting gave rise to the name of such institutions: "hedge schools."[30] Opposition to English authority expressed by such secret schools culminated in a rebellion aided by Napoleon Bonaparte in 1798—the so-called Year of the French. In its wake, successive British prime ministers resolved at first to weld Ireland closer to the rest of the British Isles. Multidenominational "national schools" were established starting in 1831 to help the British muffle Irish public resentment against colonial rule. The efforts took on even greater urgency during Ireland's unrest over the British government's tragically misbegotten approach to dealing with the Great Famine in Ireland. Britain gave denominational schools, including those operated by the Roman Catholic Church, a freer and more open hand in educating the young.[31]

The education reforms, in turn, afforded wide latitude to local pastors acting as the schoolhouse overseers and managers. They were the bane of anyone, like Patrick O'Dwyer, who had to work under the likes of Bohola's Canon John O'Grady, who wielded his powers heavy-handedly and dourly. Patrick, unlike the two teachers under his own supervision, had undergone training at Drumcondra, so he was more self-confident and less pliable than the cleric seemed to prefer.

A collision between the well-educated schoolmaster and the cleric was inevitable once Patrick became a secret organizer of the Irish National Teachers' Organisation, a union established in 1868. Early in the twentieth century, when young Paul's father was well along in his teaching career, discord with the church hierarchy led the organization to plead, not always successfully, for wage and pension reforms from the much-despised British government.

It was bad enough that teachers were reduced to paltry salaries; it was even worse that they had to contend with arbitrary dismissals. The formative teachers' union of Ireland and its rebellious foot soldiers, including Patrick, fought to change all of that.

Patrick and Canon O'Grady came to loathe each other. Their continuous conflict was worsened by the O'Dwyer family's suspicion that the priest would replace Patrick with a nephew of his once the younger relative passed his tests to qualify as an instructor. O'Grady came to embody for the entire O'Dwyer family an unholy mixture of natural nastiness and institutional conservatism, "a relentless tyrant, a sworn enemy of the Land League, the Fenians and all those opposed to the Crown," Bill recalled.[32]

The schoolmaster was among many who yearned for change in the old order in Ireland. In the political realm, that desire became increasingly clear in the early twentieth century as the Irish Parliamentary Party, under its leader John Redmond, pressed for "Home Rule," or limited self-government.

At that point, Redmond and his followers appeared on the brink of achieving the aim of Irish moderates since the peak of Charles Stewart Parnell's influence in the 1880s, as Irish nationalists held the balance of power in the British Parliament, pressing the Liberal Party to enact a bill calling for Home Rule. But Ulster Unionists rallied under the intransigent Edward Carson to oppose the measure by "all means necessary," even calling for the setting up of a provisional government for "the Protestant province of Ulster."[33]

With the outbreak of war in Europe, Redmond agreed to defer settlement of "the Irish question" until after the guns fell silent. But that opened the way for others who wanted a complete break with Great Britain, including Patrick Pearse. In a fiery graveside oration for the venerable Fenian Jeremiah O'Donovan Rossa in August 1915, the barrister turned teacher proclaimed, "The Defenders of this Realm have worked well in secret and in the open. They think that they have pacified Ireland. They think that they have purchased half of us and intimidated the other half. They think that they have foreseen everything, think that they have provided against everything; but the fools, the fools, the fools!—they have left us our Fenian dead, and while Ireland holds these graves, Ireland unfree shall never be at peace."[34]

Redmond had hoped to secure British backing for Irish Home Rule by pledging the support of the paramilitary Irish Volunteers. Instead, his backing of the war effort led to a schism with the more militant members of the Irish Volunteers, including Pearse. In April 1916, from the steps of the General Post Office in Dublin, Pearse read the Proclamation of the Irish Republic. Within days, another schoolteacher, Patrick O'Dwyer, would be reading to Mayo farmers newspaper accounts of the Easter Rebellion in which Pearse played a leading role. Patrick's eight-year-old son Paul, listening gravely, would never forget how these men absorbed the news and headed out of his home in solemn silence.[35]

2

SECOND-CLASS PASSENGER

L IKE MANY OTHER CHILDREN in Bohola, Paul O'Dwyer grew up assuming he would likely have to emigrate. This was not a comforting thought for a dutiful boy with no deep resentments concerning his home life. From his earliest memories, he was a contented child, blissfully unaware of how tenuous his family's circumstances were. He got along well with the farmers who were his neighbors, none of whom were unkind to him despite long days colored by toil and subsistence. The canon of the parish was, as previously noted, the one exception. Echoing his older brother Bill, Paul said later that Bohola's Canon O'Grady wielded the authority bestowed by his clerical collar like a "petty tyrant."[1]

The family's difficulties with the cleric, who held the highest status in the community, may help one understand O'Dwyer's lifelong difficulties with the institution of the Roman Catholic Church. But because it would not have occurred to Paul or perhaps any youngster to openly disobey an elder, especially one with the imprimatur of the Church, he could only stand idly by as his father contended, sometimes bitterly, with his boss. But his father's burden seeded in Paul a skepticism of those with religious authority, at least when that authority was not placed in the service of comforting congregants or achieving national self-determination for Ireland.

Living under the stern gaze of adults and the Church, Paul regularly rode a bicycle into town to conduct his errands. The onus brought no complaint from him, in part because it brought a brief respite from the high and heavy expectations concerning his school performance, the carrying out of farm chores, and his moment-by-moment behavior.

Bohola was home to a small number of subsistence farmers who spent half of every year away from their seven-to-twenty-acre plots of land and typically large families, earning extra shillings as migrant agricultural or construction laborers in Scotland or England. They returned (though not in every case, as when a husband went missing it was called an "Irish divorce") to renew their marital bond and greet slightly taller offspring and, perhaps, a new child born during the father's seasonal absence.

Like the predictable cycle of the seasons, the Bohola surroundings seemed much as they had a half-century in the past. The landscape remained verdant and rocky, the running brooks clear, the mornings often misty, and the nights often damp. The cow bell and the church bell competed with the deep rural quiet, as the automobile was still a rarity. Paul took his devout mother (who used to have her children kneel and say the rosary) to church on Sundays using a horse and two-wheeled cart, so he had less time than his peers to be carefree, to ensnare a fish or brain a fleeing hare (food for the table). He waited for his mother without complaint outside her favorite public house. She and a girlfriend liked to have a post-homily pint, "her only compensation," as he related years later.[2]

Bohola was spread over the broad green crest of a hill, fifteen miles from anywhere else in the coastal Connaught region, barnacled with the ruins of a fifth-century Christian monastery. To the occasional stranger who trundled in on foot or mule, some to sell simple wares or to beg for a shilling, the hamlet could be differentiated from similar crossroads by its stately, late-Gothic St. Mary's Church. The sizable house of worship dominated its surroundings, which included a blacksmith's shop, a general store, and a trio of pubs. The commercial buildings numbered about fifteen in all. There were some fifty thatched residential cottages. The O'Dwyer house, while modest by American measures, was the largest in the seventeen-cottage Lismirrane subsection of Bohola proper, about a mile from the church.[3]

Ireland was endowed with a storied natural beauty and deep connections to the Gaelic language and culture, literature, music, art, folklore, and love of sport. But young people were still leaving for better economic prospects than the 750-year-old colonial holding promised. As during the era of famines great and small, the Irish diaspora in New York—more than half as large as the entire population of Ireland—beckoned continuously. The burgeoning, almost mythic American metropolis was looked upon as a place of refuge and opportunity, though life there was typically much harder than many imagined.

Shortly before the outbreak of World War I in July of 1914, the British government was at last on the verge of granting Ireland its own parliament. Although, under this planned extension of Home Rule, Ireland would continue to be under the thumb of the British Empire, the prospect of a greater degree of self-rule satisfied the majority of Irish nationalists at the time. However, impediments remained: Protestant unionists, who made up a majority in Ulster in the north, resisted any lessening of the political welding of Ireland and Great Britain. Their militant opposition kept Britain from instituting Home Rule for the entire island. Nationalist and unionist paramilitary organizations, each seeing the use of violence as the principal way to ensure their aims, coalesced in the south and in the north amid pitched tensions over Ireland's political future. Then World War I erupted, scuttling the implementation of Home Rule arrangements.

WITH ITS NEARLY four million people, Ireland avoided the atrocious losses suffered by England and Germany in the Great War because trade unions, nationalist parties, and clergy had long resisted the Crown's plan to conscript tens of thousands of Irishmen for service in Her Majesty's trenches. Instead, the watershed events within Ireland that Paul experienced as a youngster were set in motion by a single week of tumult encompassing the Easter Rising of 1916, when fewer than two thousand ill-prepared Irish republicans occupied the heart of Dublin and held out for the next six days against a far larger number of British troops.

Causing the deaths of 480 people, more than half of whom were civilians, the rebellion ended with a bust. But in the aftermath the British government made a gross miscalculation, executing sixteen of the insurrection's leaders—poets, diplomats, and intellectuals among them. Far more than their revolutionary gesture to take up arms, which most Irish people thought ludicrous, the executions touched off nearly countrywide outrage and support for independence. And they conditioned in the then nine-year-old Paul similar sympathies, starting him on a path toward defending individuals and movements resisting state-sanctioned oppression on both sides of the Atlantic.

As World War I ended, in November 1918, not long after Britain finally decided to impose conscription in Ireland, the island stood on the brink of revolution, the "terrible beauty" whose advent William Butler Yeats gleaned in his poem "Easter, 1916."

In January 1919, the Irish republican party Sinn Féin (Gaelic for "Ourselves" or "We Ourselves")—emboldened by a landslide victory in the general election a month before—formed a breakaway government, Dáil Éireann. Soon after, the Third Tipperary Brigade of the Irish Volunteers ambushed and killed two members of the Royal Irish Constabulary, a newly militarized British police and intelligence force composed primarily of Irish natives. Thus the Anglo-Irish War was joined on January 21, 1919, with the British government, having signed the Treaty of Versailles between the world's great powers, able now to turn greater attention to the rebellion just across the Irish Sea.

To the task of suppressing the Irish insurrection, the British Army, decimated by World War I, recruited murderers and thieves serving prison sentences, some Irish-born (about one-fifth, by scholars' estimates). They became known in Ireland as the Black and Tans due to the colors of their makeshift uniforms. Just as poorly supervised as their clothing made them appear, the paid recruits employed arson, torture, shootings, and rape starting in the spring of 1920, though recent research has found that British soldiers were much more likely to commit atrocities in Ireland.[4] Working with many former British soldiers, the Black and Tans met resistance from an agile, highly motivated guerrilla army consisting of thousands of young Irish volunteers. In a sign of the latter's progress, the Royal Irish Constabulary abandoned rural police barracks, including in Mayo. The county harbored forty-seven barracks in 1920, but a year later the total was down to twenty-three.[5]

Paul first translated his nationalist ideals into a bit of action a year earlier, when he supported Eamon de Valera's successful East Mayo candidacy in parliamentary elections by hammering a sign bearing the Sinn Féin leader's name to a tree in front of his Bohola home. When the Anglo-Irish War broke out, most in Ireland felt that the time had come to break away, and that the moment was a once-in-a-lifetime opportunity for national self-rule in the spirit of the 1920 post–World War I formation of the League of Nations.

The O'Dwyer family was no different. Although Paul's father was un-usually well educated for a teacher of his generation, Paul remembered hearing no high-sounding talk of freedom and liberty from him or from the illiterate farmers who were their neighbors, nor from the local news-papers. "The British were there. They had no business being there. They had persecuted us all this time and they ought to get out." To the average person, "that was the gist of it. It didn't mean anything more than that," he said.

When the War of Independence reached the outskirts of Bohola, Paul carried messages on a bike to Irish Volunteers grouped in the hills, thread-ing through civilian police, who, also riding bicycles, were despised as British informers. Paul's older brother Jack was with the Bohola branch of the Irish Volunteers. Inspiring his younger sibling to look up to him, Jack taught himself how to use a rifle and to signal messages with flags to rebels waiting at a distance.

The rebel bands included many young men eluding conscription by the British Army, including Paul's other brother Francis, or Frank, who had been working in England at the outbreak of World War I. The tallest of the five O'Dwyer boys, Frank could pass for a nineteen-year-old though he was only sixteen at the time. Stout and five foot eleven, he landed work as a migrant laborer because of his stature, but it meant he also faced the risk of being inducted by the Brits. So he made the quick crossing back to Ireland.[6] Meanwhile, Paul's family, by virtue of having a remote house, accommodated some of the fighters, giving them a place to lie low. His mother at times rousted her children from their sleeping places to allow tired young volunteers to catch a few winks.[7]

After returning from mass one overcast afternoon, Bridget O'Dwyer was met by a British Army sergeant searching for Jack, referring to him as a "tramp," or military deserter. "My mother shouted to the sergeant to get out if he valued his life, and ran to where she knew the gun [belong-ing to Jack] was hidden," remembered Paul, who described her concen-trated fury sending the sergeant clambering backward on his boot heels and then away on his bike.[8]

The British security forces inspired great loathing. Paul attended a funeral for a man who had been taken out of his building and shot.

Looking back on it with worldlier eyes in a 1987 interview, he also recalled seeing the charred remains of torched houses. "Seeing the house of a merchant who was not political but who had his name over the house in Gaelic . . . [was] sufficient to burn his house down. We had incidents like that that we knew."[9]

"As kids, we were in the middle of it," he wrote in his 1979 memoir, *Counsel for the Defense*. "The Black and Tans were going up and down the roads in open-throttled Crossley Tenders, rifles poised on both sides." Children were told to be cautious on their walk to school since the Tans took potshots while speeding through unsympathetic townlets. In a discussion of the British gendarmerie's impact on the Irish countryside beyond Bohola, Paul added, "They rode roughshod over the populace, burning homes of suspected patriots, killing, destroying and hunting. Young people with ideals took to the hills."[10]

VIEWING THE STORIED Irish revolutionary Michael Collins as perhaps his most formidable rival for power during the aroused Irish independence movement, Eamon de Valera, a New York City–born survivor of Britain's death row after participating in the Easter Rising, worked to cement his popularity as one of the preeminent leaders of the Sinn Féin Party. Employing Machiavellian methods, he sent Collins to lead treaty negotiations in London, aware that the inevitable agreement to end the war could bring a backlash against the negotiators of a compromise—as well as, therefore, a political opportunity for himself. Collins, the founder of the infamous squad that assassinated British military and security officials, had long lived as a hunted man when he secured the Anglo-Irish Treaty at the end of 1921, concluding the War of Independence.

But the Irish people's divide over the treaty ran deep. The country descended into nearly a year of internecine savagery. Collins led the pro-treaty army faction into this chasm of killings and reprisals, while de Valera, claiming he had not been properly consulted before Collins signed the deal, waved the banner of the anti-treaty forces. In New York, the eighty-year-old Irish republican journalist and activist John Devoy bemoaned his native country's full-on civil war. Though a champion of a united Irish republic, and one who had contributed personal savings to the Easter Rising, Devoy assailed the descent into bloodshed for "devastating Ireland, ruining her economic life, breaking the morale of the people, and filling the world with the idea that the old English theory is correct, that when England's firm hand was removed, the Irish would start to cut each other's throat."[11]

Collins, addressing the multitudes in the Dublin streets and elected legislators in the transitional legislature, urged his countrymen to accept the new Irish Free State arrangements despite their more distasteful aspects, like Ireland's newly defined status as a dominion of the British Empire (comparable to Canada) and an oath of allegiance to the British King. More controversially, the treaty he worked on stipulated Ireland's partition, establishing six Ulster counties in the north as a separate, Protestant-majority polity, distinct from the majority-Catholic south of Ireland. (Three years later, a three-member commission for setting the boundary between the north and south disappointed Irish negotiators who had hoped to undermine the viability of Ulster by including nationalist/Catholic populations from two counties in the province.) The creation of two discrete political entities would long embitter Irish nationalists, Paul among them. "Protestants and Catholics," recalled O'Dwyer, "had always found it difficult to get along with each other in the North, but the partition institutionalized their hate."[12]

Despite the obstacles to wide acceptance, the "Big Fellah," as Collins was known, asked his countrymen to see the newly established Free State provisional government as a "stepping stone" to a united, independent republic. But that was too much of a compromise for many Irish people, like the O'Dwyers, who traced their ideological lineage to the teachings of the original Irish revolutionary, Wolfe Tone (a Protestant), of 1798. The treaty seemed to many of them to amount to betrayal of the centuries-old hope of achieving a single Irish republic that was free of any deference to the Crown. The record of British betrayals had galvanized the Easter Rebellion and the War of Independence, and so had centuries of British misrule typified by tenant evictions, the Great Hunger, and recently the rampages of the Black and Tans and British soldiers.[13]

That Ireland itself was excluded from Woodrow Wilson's principle of self-determination for the world's smaller nations—part of the president's rationale for committing American troops and airplanes to the European conflagration—only added salt to these wounds and disillusionment for anti–Free State families like the O'Dwyers. The most favored O'Dwyer son, Jimmy, spent eleven months in an army uniform during World War I for the United States and the Allied forces, which of course included Great Britain itself, and the irony of that was not lost on the family. A further source of vexation, including for Paul, was the sight of Irish priests handing out bags of flour during the 1924 parliamentary elections in order to influence his neighbors to vote for pro–Free State candidates. Paul's own attempt to vote in the election, his first, was thwarted when, adding to the picture of liberty denied, a poll worker turned him away because his correct name could not be found in the registration rolls. Inexplicably, only an unknown and likely nonexistent O'Dwyer appeared, with the first name of "Austin."[14]

Father O'Grady was also grating to the young rebel because the Bohola cleric in Paul's eyes was effectively an agent of the English imperial scepter and its Irish subjects. Few young people dared to question his God-given authority, not even Paul. "In those years, the canon of my village was condemning the Irish Republican Army," O'Dwyer later said, "and of course denying absolution to its soldiers—all the bishops did that—they excommunicated all of them." Yet those young men were "engaged in what we considered to be the fight for freedom. You have no idea how important the clergy's reaction was: you've got a young man who is taught, as I was, that if you die and you are not in a state of grace, you will go to hell for all eternity, and there is no punishment imaginable like the punishment of hell—ever consuming, always constant, and forever. And it boggles the mind to know what forever was. And we believed it. Deep down we believed it."[15]

Irish families felt impelled to choose sides, and the O'Dwyers made no secret of their hostility to a *partially* independent Ireland and the partition (i.e., the so-labeled Free State). Paul's sisters, however, worried over their school jobs since Irish teachers from families who opposed the treaty with London faced increased chances of dismissal by their clerical employers. And it could not have been reassuring that the O'Dwyer home was temporarily used to hide armaments and revolutionaries. "There seemed to be enough explosives in our backyard to blow up half of Ireland," Paul later remembered.[16]

———

MICHAEL COLLINS, having conducted his campaign of assassination, was himself ambushed and killed amid the civil war. The Free State provisional government to which he had signed on remained alive, however, as the Irish Republican Army under de Valera's leadership laid down its arms in May 1923, bringing the crossfire to a halt. The British government continued to have a hand in Ireland's governance.

It is true that the limitations on Ireland's sovereignty would one day be chipped away, as Collins promised. But the erosion of British influence in Dublin occurred slowly, over the next quarter-century. It would not be gone until an independent republic was established in 1949, at least south of the line of partition. At the helm throughout most of this halting and contested period of maturation stood de Valera. A mathematician, the gangly "Long Fellow," who had conferred his national prestige on the anti–Free State movement, remained the partitioned Éire's most prominent leader for decades.[17]

Paul as a youngster had not only hammered de Valera signs onto trees outside his home but also took the politician's first name at his Catholic confirmation rites. But he came to regret the latter choice, lamenting, once in America, what he called de Valera's inconsistent record on civil liberties—especially de Valera's decision to intern and even execute some of his own former associates in the Irish Republican Army (IRA) in the mid-1930s. The IRA had remained wedded to the goal of a countrywide thirty-two-county republic. It campaigned with violence and bombings that threatened de Valera's efforts to establish his control over the twenty-six counties of the south through his Fianna Fáil ("Soldiers of Destiny") party, founded in 1926.[18]

AND SO PAUL would carry the aroused grievances and dichotomies of the Irish experience with him to America as a bona fide Irish republican who glimpsed parallels with the Irish experience wherever he went in his adoptive country.

His point of reference differed from that of his eldest sibling, Bill, as Bill had not experienced the Anglo-Irish War or its aftermath with any immediacy, having left home almost a decade before the Easter Rebellion—in 1907, the year Paul was born. In some ways, these two brothers, meeting for the first time upon Paul's arrival in New York, were a study in contrasts. One of the first to notice this would be the New York attorney Oscar Bernstien, who became Paul's professional mentor and law partner over a forty-year period. Unlike Paul, Bill, according to Bernstien, did not carry the world's problems on his shoulders nor evince a strong desire to change it. While showing relatively little interest in the Irish republican movement beyond the disinterested intellectual sort, Bill nevertheless exhibited no great feeling against any race or people. To Bernstien, who was Bill's contemporary, and to Paul, this marked him as decent and cosmopolitan, to go along with their respect for his quick wit and intelligence. Bill was simply one who settled for taking the world as it is, according to Bernstien, understanding what made it tick and noting other people's all too human foibles with a wry appreciation: "He wasn't trying to change it, he wasn't trying to reform it, he wasn't trying to make people better than they were."[19]

Having arrived in New York on the *Philadelphia*, a weathered old tub, in 1910, Bill missed not only Ireland's intense political violence and drama of the 1910s and '20s but also his family's private upheavals. Most significantly of all, in January 1921, when Paul was thirteen, their father died of pneumonia, meeting his end only seven months after Paul's taller, athletic eighteen-year-old brother, Tommy—Patrick's favorite son—died from appendicitis. The double tragedy represented "one of the most devastating incidents of his [Paul's] young life," according to Paul's nephew Frank Durkan.[20]

The grief a young teenager still living at home might feel over losing two family members in so short a period of time was compounded by the response of O'Grady to the death of his longtime schoolmaster and underling: the aged priest ordered that the school open the day after the late schoolmaster's funeral, a transparent sign of disrespect that did not go unnoticed in the small community. Paul never forgot or forgave it.

The other O'Dwyer children, too, seethed. Bridget O'Dwyer, while seemingly more forgiving, refused to put her youngest son's education directly into the hands of O'Grady's teacher-nephew, whom the cleric could now install in Patrick's place; the canon had long made little secret of his desire to do so, making the union-friendly Patrick uncomfortable. Promptly, Bridget sent her bright-eyed son to another school three miles away operated by a friend of Patrick's and his wife. In the coming year, they prepared him for secondary school, mainly in math, English, and religion. In his memoir, Paul could not help but relish the irony of receiving the class prize in the last of these subjects from an archbishop, given the anticlerical sentiments of his late father.[21]

With Patrick's salary gone and her children living at home or in America, the widowed Bridget resorted to a painful expedient to clear the way for her youngest child's education. Under heavy rain, she and Paul headed out to the town of Ballaghaderreen in County Roscommon and the closest secondary school for boys, St. Nathy's. In those years, an education in an Irish secondary school had to be paid for, and Bridget told the president of the school that she could in no way come up with the forty-pound annual fee. Luckily, he reduced it to thirty pounds. But even that amount was "a tremendous burden on my mother and my two working sisters," Paul would later say.[22]

A onetime military barracks before conversion to a training school for Catholic priests, St. Nathy's was twenty miles from Bohola and the only high school in the diocese. Bill would recall his earlier experience at the same school as placing him among "the poorer middle class . . . in between the poor and the rich." Paul himself disliked the Dickensian environment—little time allowed outside, a minimum of five hours of homework each day under close supervision, and gruel served at mealtimes, along with the humiliations heaped upon him by instructors. In a comment that could just as well have come from Frank McCourt's memoir of growing up destitute in County Limerick in the 1930s and '40s, *Angela's Ashes*, Paul observed, "In Ireland, poverty is a crime for which there is no defense."[23]

During his three years in this institution that at worst echoed Dotheboys Hall in *Nicholas Nickleby*, the schoolteacher's son received many reminders that he was not among the wealthier families who could pay the full freight. His resentment may have been retrospective, but his feeling of rebellion was not. Chafing at the restrictions on his freedom of movement, Paul underwent a behavior change: "I was punished quite often—an angry box on the ears—for what seemed to me trivial infractions, and I learned to fight back in my fashion," including complaining to the unsympathetic school president about the "abominable" food.[24] Though an above-average student, and receiving a rigorous education, he regarded himself as "by no means the pride of my family."[25]

He finished up and went on to a single term at the University of Dublin, where he found it hard to connect with a more erudite stable of professors and, surprisingly enough, was ill at ease with the comparatively lax disciplinary atmosphere. He performed rather poorly in his academic subjects there, he recalled. Many years later, Paul—as a successful lawyer, but still smarting from these memories—wrote out a check to the school for the dollar equivalent plus interest of his modest tuition break, which had represented an unflattering reflection of his family's lack of means. He was "getting rid of pent-up resentment" by paying it back later in life, not wanting the university administration to feel that he remained in its debt in any way.[26]

———————

THE SURVIVING BROTHER closest in age to Paul, Frank, who was seven years his senior, decided after relocating to New York and working on the docks and in a wholesale produce market that Paul was becoming an unnecessary weight on their mother, who was no longer working as a teacher in the Bohola parish school. The bills for Paul's education and upkeep were falling to his low-paid schoolteacher sisters to pay, holding them back from building families of their own.

In a 1925 letter to Paul, Frank stated that the time had come for him to join him and his three brothers (Bill, Jack, and Jimmy) in New York, where he would be able to work by day and study to be a lawyer at night. The letter presumptuously enough included a paid boarding ticket for the White Star line, arranging for Paul to travel in second class to avoid having his thick head of hair deloused at boarding, as was required of third-class, or steerage, passengers.[27]

Frank advised that it would be best if Paul headed out straight from the University of Dublin and avoided telling their mother, whom he assumed would oppose his leaving. Paul thought that part over and decided against it, as it would have left his sisters and mother exposed to intrusive questions from their neighbors. He promptly told them of his plans, and the strong-willed Bridget McNicholas O'Dwyer took in the news. She reminded her son that he could remain with her—they would all manage, somehow. But she said she did not ever want it said after she was dead and buried that she had tried to keep her youngest boy from seeking a better future for himself.[28]

The traditional farewell gathering was held, with Paul's farmer neighbors pressing coins into his palm at his "American wake," as the rite was sometimes known. The gifts at such fleeting rites of passage were meager yet generous considering none of Paul's Lismirrane neighbors had a shilling they could comfortably afford to give away. But this was a traditional way of bidding another young one to safe passage and a new life with the knowledge that they might not see them ever again.

Paul accepted the coins or "luck payments." He looked much younger than his age, seventeen, his dark mane swept back, his eyes a pale blue, and his eyebrows as thick and bristly as push brooms. Standing five foot five, still two inches shy of his full adult height, he was slight, weighing a bit short of nine stone, or 125 pounds, and his skin was pale.

He packed light for the expected six-day journey, bringing a razor and his only substantial article of clothing: the heavy green wool suit his mother gave him for protection against the Atlantic's winds. He climbed into the suit the morning after the "wake" and wore it all the way to the other side of the ocean. Paul's mother and sisters accompanied him to the rail station at Claremorris, exchanging few words as they arrived.

The morning train rumbled into the station soon enough and collected the sole waiting passenger. Paul climbed aboard with his one satchel, and after a spell the railroad engineer sounded the steam whistle. Slowly gathering speed as it departed, the locomotive carried him on an easterly course for three hundred kilometers to the seaport at Cobh (its name changed from Queenstown with the 1922 founding of the Irish Free State) in his late father's native County Cork.

Out on his own with twenty-five dollars' worth of gifted shillings in his pockets, he arrived to scout the pungent seaport, noticing the British troops and clusters of emigrants waiting to board transatlantic ships operated by the Cunard and White Star lines. The lines had long profited from the want that impelled Ireland's poor to emigrate. In the little time left before boarding, Paul felt as if everyone nearby wanted a piece of him—the "prostitutes, the old women selling tin shamrocks, mottoes and shillelaghs to take to relatives and friends, the man wearing half a uniform who insisted on taking my bag whether I liked it or not."

His mood lightened when he bumped into an acquaintance of the same age named Pat Shannon. The night before, Shannon told him excitedly, a girl had entered his room after the gaslights at his hotel in Dublin (where he had been sent by his travel agent to get a visa) were extinguished for the night. For reasons she did not explain, she climbed into his bed with him. He had screamed, he recounted, and the stranger had fled down a dingy hallway.

After comparing notes on their traveling experiences thus far, the two ticket holders separated. Paul boarded the ship to New York, while Pat was bound for a different sea route, to Chicago. But each was headed for the world far beyond the horizon, a world of which the two young men knew practically nothing.[29]

———

ALTHOUGH THE SUPPERS in second class on the SS *Doric* were decent, Paul enjoyed slipping below deck to the more crowded and lively third-class section and staying there until late in the night. One evening, as the ship pitched and rocked in ungentle swells, Paul swayed gaily as a Galway girl played a vivacious folk song on a melodeon. A boy from Sligo taught his fellow passengers a siren's tune of mid-nineteenth-century vintage, and Paul crooned the popular emigrant ballad "I'm Off to Philadelphia" with the rest of the jubilant choir. With someone playing a fiddle, the human cargo of post–civil war Ireland, some looking exhausted and others tending their wee ones, raised their voices in unison: "I must leave the place, I tried to keep a cheerful face. . . ." And then, when Paul was up on the main deck again and leaning against the ship's railing, he may have looked into the distance. The wool suit he wore offered somewhat less comfort than his mother hoped against the strong, frigid ocean breezes of April 1925.

When the ship reached New York Harbor, Paul paid no heed to the great Statue of Liberty; if he did notice it, he said later, he knew almost nothing then of its historical significance. Having had his travel papers checked at Sandy Hook, New Jersey—an onboard visit from the uniformed immigration officers—he simply waited for the chance to disembark, and soon enough did.

To all the fast-talking brokers who haunted the lower Manhattan pier, proffering jobs, meals, and rooms, the young Paul may have appeared as easy pickings. But his brother Frank claimed him at the dock and, with Jack, steered him clear of their habitual entrapments. After giving him a quick embrace, the pair led Paul to the subway, which carried them north and west under the streets in a city of 7.7 million. Plying Paul with advice, Frank said he would take him to Hester Street for some up-to-date duds as, he and Jack explained, Paul needed to find work and look less like a greenhorn, with little or no delay.[30]

Reunited, the brothers soon emerged topside on the Upper West Side of Manhattan and walked past a row of handsome, roseate brownstones with smooth stone stoops to a three-story rooming house located on West

103rd Street, between Amsterdam and Columbus Avenues. Frank and Jack, the older of the two, lived in a furnished room and received, from its Galway-born operator, Mrs. Maguire, their breakfasts and dinners in the dining room. She kept ten Irish boarders in all and provided a room to Paul, too, for the weekly rent of ten dollars. The wife of one of the two Irish brothers who owned the house, she made her own watery beer, along with a gritty whiskey, offering the latter for fifty cents a bottle. She found Paul polite, as he obeyed the rules and caused no general upset. But she forced him to give up an initial, short-lived job as a stable hand at the Van Cortlandt Riding Academy because he was returning home smelling of manure with the bottom of his shoes and pants caked with mud.[31]

Jack warmed to Paul, whom he had not seen for several years. Perpetually restless, by Paul's description, and something of a "wiseacre," Jack was earning his keep as one of the thousands of nameless, faceless dockworkers at Bush Terminal in Brooklyn. While accepted within the insular world of the port, he wanted to manage prizefighters, which he would soon come to do, co-opening, with a former IRA man, a speakeasy a few steps down from the sidewalk at Sixty-Fifth Street and Broadway. After Prohibition, Jack opened another place, where Tom Tunney, the brother of the famous boxer Gene Tunney, "the Fighting Marine," was a regular. (The Tunney family, like Bill's late friend and Olympic star Martin Sheridan, had Bohola roots.)

Next into Mrs. Maguire's Irish rooming house to greet Paul came Jimmy, an amiable, slight fellow who immigrated to New York in 1912, two years after Bill. While working in 1914 aboard a German commercial vessel, Jimmy came close to being conscripted as a British subject, as he was not yet a naturalized US citizen at the time. He ended up being conscripted by the US Army, though he scribbled in the margins of his draft card that he needed to continue working at a Manhattan bar to support his siblings back in Ireland. As might well have been expected, his handwritten appeal fell on deaf ears.[32] But the appeal was not without truth, as Jimmy's weekly letters home invariably included money from his pay envelope.

Trained at Camp Upton on Long Island, Jimmy was shipped to the western front. For eleven months he was assigned as a private in the twenty-thousand-member Seventy-Seventh Infantry Division of the US Army, known as the "Metropolitan" division because most of the soldiers were drawn from tough working-class streets in New York, and later known as the "Statue of Liberty" division because of the insignia on the patch worn on their uniforms. While Jimmy himself may not have experienced combat, his luck would have been relatively rare, given the timing of his conscription. More than 550 men from his division made up a subset that were to be remembered as the "Lost Battalion" after the contingent became isolated from Allied lines in October 1918 and suffered dearly for it. The incident precipitated an intense battle in the Argonne Forest involving the survivors and other American battalions sent to relieve them. It became one of the most talked-about episodes in the Meuse-Argonne offensive begun a month before—the largest combat mobilization in US military history, with 1.2 million soldiers participating, 26,777 American lives lost, and roughly an equal number of Germans and an unknown number of French killed.

When he returned from war-torn Europe, Jimmy joined the heavily Irish ranks of the New York Fire Department and began to plan for his future, all before reuniting with his brother Paul on a memorable day.

––––––––

THE LAST BROTHER to rendezvous with Paul in New York was Bill. A former hotel barman, trolley-car ticket puncher, riverboat furnace tender, and construction laborer, Bill had an American-style swagger to go along with his sturdy build. Wed in 1917 to Catherine ("Kitty") Lenihan, a former hatcheck girl he met while working as a bar assistant at the Vanderbilt Hotel, he had recently completed a seven-year stint as a Brooklyn policeman, during which he shot and killed a drunk and armed Long Island Rail Road worker invading the home of his estranged wife. Determined to move on from policing, Bill as a cop entered Fordham in Manhattan and took night classes in law. Thirty-four years old when Paul arrived, he investigated accident claims for an insurance firm to fulfill the requirement of a clerkship in order to practice law. The only one of the O'Dwyer sons who was then married, Bill made friends as easily as he would subsequently make enemies in politics and became one of the most important people in his youngest brother's life. But at their initial encounter, Paul was apprehensive.[33] He knew of the great hopes their parents had invested in Bill's seminary education and how those hopes had been dashed by Bill's decision to drop out of the venerable Pontifical University of Salamanca, Spain. Perhaps they should have known that it would take Bill, who by his own account was something of a hellion as a teen, little more than a year to realize that the priestly path was ill-suited to his worldly ambitions. Bill dropped out and made his way to Cherbourg in Normandy and on to a new life in New York. But unlike Jimmy, he did not send money home from New York, a fact of which Paul was aware.

To Paul, getting his initial look at his eldest sibling, Bill seemed alien—he was "too old" and "too fat." What was more, he had a gold tooth, and it flashed when he grinned.[34]

––––––––

AS BILL HEADED out from Mrs. Maguire's, he promised to return with some job leads for the new arrival. Still wet behind the ears, Paul did not take too well to his new environment, though it included, just around the corner, a subway station for the Ninth Avenue Elevated and a drugstore where Jack bought him his first strawberry ice cream soda, hailing it as "this great American drink." The frothy pink confection was Paul's compensation for his homesickness and disorientation, as was the occasional eight-hour scenic boat ride up the Hudson with Frank, which offered Paul a chance to flirt with Irish girls and test his awkwardness.

Paul also took in an occasional vaudeville act during what would later be dubbed the Roaring Twenties; the venue was a theater on Riverside Drive. And on Thursday nights—the night off for Irish housemaids—he ventured out to Irish music halls like the Tuxedo Ballroom on Fifty-Ninth Street or the Mayo Ballroom on Eighty-Fourth Street.

He meanwhile weighed the limited paths to self-sufficiency. First he imagined trying to become a doctor, but Bill advised that a medical education took longer and cost more money than law school and thus was not available to him. A more promising route, the eldest brother suggested, went through the Irish-built Democratic political machine in New York. At the time, the machine was in charge at city hall, and the mayor was the carrot-topped John Francis "Red Mike" Hylan, a former railway engineer preoccupied with acquiring privately owned subway lines and maintaining the fare at five cents. Lawyers were not highly paid, but the work required brains, not brawn, of which Paul had discernibly little. Though the modern era was busting out all over—with skyscrapers rising, radio waves carrying disembodied voices, and Times Square ablaze in white light—the Irish immigrant was still the subject of much exploitation, fielding some of the most physically challenging and dangerous jobs with little recourse to compensation of any kind in the event of disabling injury. Some 60 percent of residents of Celtic ancestry in the city's sprawling patchwork of ethnic enclaves held jobs as menial laborers, while the remainder worked in low-level white-collar occupations or skilled trades.[35] Tammany Hall, the Democratic organization, helped many an Irish immigrant gain a foothold, with more than half the Irish working for municipally-owned or -subsidized subways, street railways, waterworks, and port facilities. Most city government employees, too, were of Irish descent, as were the majority in the police and fire departments. Many others with Irish roots worked at commercial construction sites. While only the rare Irish immigrant family had a breadwinner who worked in a white-collar profession, the signs of economic mobility were gathering strength by the 1920s. Irish-born Americans had been climbing the ladder for more than a generation. They were now beginning to enter the ranks of a nascent US middle class.

Paul decided on a law degree as the clearer road to a stable, though not necessarily well-paid, career. His two years of secondary school studies at St. Nathy's College prepared him for his new life more than he realized, as he was better educated than the average Irish American immigrant he met. His school record, including geography, math, English, Latin, and Greek, was at least the equivalent of an American high school diploma. What was more, admission to law school in the United States did not require him to have a college degree.

———

WHILE THINKING ABOUT becoming a lawyer, he went to work as a stock clerk in a mechanic's garage, a job Bill found for him through a police station house commander. In this role he discovered that threats of violence—do what I say or "I'll tan your ass," a coworker once warned him—were fairly common forms of verbal abuse in the city and not to be taken literally.[36] But the job was temporary, ending in only a matter of weeks, and Paul was soon sorting gaskets for Pure Oil Company instead.[37] Nodding off at 4 p.m. became a habit, attributable, he told himself, to the dramatic change in climate from that with which he was familiar in Ireland. He was again let go, providing his first experience with occupational failure.[38]

His next job to pay Mrs. Maguire her ten-dollar rent and to put some money aside for himself entailed operating a passenger elevator in an apartment building on Riverside Drive near 157th Street. He found out about this open position through a help wanted ad in the *New York World* and landed it simply because he fit into the uniform worn by the previous man charged with riding people up and down.[39] But captaining the lift precluded his going to law school at night due to the job's late hours. So, he changed positions anew in June 1925, opting for a higher-paying post (sixty cents an hour) with the American Express Company. He kept watch as packages arrived at the depot by truck and sometimes horses. The hours suited him, but one day he had words with a teamster. His supervisor, far from taking his side, told him to pack it in.

Jim and Frank covered Paul's first semester's tuition of seventy-five dollars. His Fordham prelaw night courses met downtown on the twenty-third floor of the Woolworth Building, then the tallest building in the country, which Bill had coincidentally worked on the construction of in 1913, hauling steel beams and hod (and reading aloud to coworkers on breaks, he said, in order to improve his American diction). At the suggestion of a police captain from Tipperary whom Bill knew, Paul soon tried to land a paid internship with a corporate law firm, but the partner he met told him that he needed to lose the brogue, so he did not follow up.[40]

Still, as a result of his prelaw classes, he felt he was getting some traction. Responding to Paul's ready curiosity, one of his instructors handed him a copy of *Common Sense*, Thomas Paine's plainspoken argument for launching the American War of Independence. The child of Irish nationalists devoured it repeatedly in the years to come, sold on the forty-seven-page paean to the history-changing potential of democratic self-governance.

Paul gained enough credits at Fordham to qualify for a state certificate to go on to law school and was thinking of attending the more affordable, newly opened St. John's Law School, located on Court Street in Brooklyn. So he soon checked out of Mrs. Maguire's rooming house for good, renting, in the summer of 1926, an upstairs bedroom in a Norwegian family's two-family house in Brooklyn. The heavily Scandinavian Sunset Park section in which the house was located was accessible by subway and close to the massive warehouses, twenty-four-hour loading piers, and street-embedded freight lines along the waterfront. The area also included a small Greek eatery where he liked to stop coming back from school for two pork chops and a slice of bread ("the dessert," he called it).[41] It cost a manageable forty-five cents plus a nickel for coffee.

With help from his brother Jack, Paul got into the International Long-shoremen's Association (ILA) and landed a job as a cargo checker at Brooklyn's Bush Terminal; this required he report early each morning to a loading boss.[42] The work consisted of calculating the correct weight of cargo, inspecting the shipments, and helping ensure that the huge crates were stacked safely. It left the heavy lifting to others on one of the busiest and most lucrative harbors in the world. Stretching hundreds of miles along the city's industrial shoreline, the Port of New York and New Jersey's bustling piers extended like thick fingers into the heavily trafficked waters off poor and working-class Brooklyn and Manhattan neighborhoods. During the first half of the twentieth century, before the advent of a full-service aviation industry and interstate highway system, more than half of all goods bound for the American interior traveled through the port.[43] While in the nineteenth century the workforce had been predominantly made up of Irish immigrants, it was more diverse when Paul showed up, including immigrants from Italy, Poland, and Scandinavia and African Americans. Some of the early hazards of the work had been ameliorated by mechanized cranes.

Some union locals, including Paul's Checkers Local 975, were democratically run, allowing longshoremen to elect their representatives honestly, Paul later remembered, but the Brooklyn waterfront of 1926–30—his tenure on the loading docks—was on the whole "highly *racketeered*." Pilferage flourished, with gangster enforcers and Tammany district leaders taking their illicit cut on every dock. Paul recalled one such scheme: the hiring of three- or four-day laborers fewer than the contractually required nineteen men per hatch. A hiring boss, he said, pocketed the missing men's pay.[44]

Local Democratic politicians saw no reason to interfere with the day-to-day corruption, that is if they hoped to get ILA members' votes and the union's financial support. Shippers, too, benefited from leaving well enough alone, assured of minimal work stoppages and of keeping their labor costs down through the collusion of ILA loading bosses and union honchos. As for the dockworkers, they remained dependent on this system for a day's wage and were never heard questioning dangerous conditions or pressing their union chapters for job security. Outsider reformers who voiced concerns about the health and welfare of longshoremen were often viewed as suspect by the workforce and were as rare as dissident insiders.[45]

On his very first day inside the block-long Pier 3 shed, Paul was handed a copy of management's book of rules by his Italian supervisor. Workers advised him to take its dos and don'ts with a grain of salt. He did not heed this advice, however. Instead he called attention to a few minor violations of the union contract as a newly minted member of the Local 975 of the ILA. The act of whistleblowing landed him on the wrong side of the supervisor. While his transgression was overlooked, it confirmed for Paul the symbiotic relationship that prevailed between the loaders' union bosses and the shipping and stevedore companies.

It also was clear that kickbacks were not occasional but every day.[46] Payments were extracted from almost everyone who encountered the ILA—for example, the truck drivers who wanted goods loaded or unloaded without costly delays. Like almost everyone else, Paul did learn, eventually, to keep his mouth shut, realizing that nothing would be done in response to the filing of a grievance and that bucking the routine arrangements could be fatal to one's job, if not one's person; the New York Harbor was notorious for "floaters," whether accidental or intended victims. At the same time, the waterfront was one of the few places where someone coming out of prison, or fresh off the boat, could find work.

While he did not last long in this initial dock posting, O'Dwyer landed other dockside assignments with his ILA union membership card. The better-known Jack O'Dwyer vouched for him with loaders. Paul also turned to Bill, who seemed to know everybody in Brooklyn of any importance.[47]

Yet as a novice longshoreman Paul found himself enthralled by the sight of unsavory characters on the docks, one of them a gruff-spoken dandy in a derby hat and spats, Chesterfield overcoat, and diamond stickpin who answered to the name Johnny Spanish. Paul encountered him at Pier 44 while Spanish was soliciting "donations" to help a "sickly" worker. His audience consisted of men who hoped he might favor them with a day's wages. They stood around him in a semicircle, Paul recalled, literally with hat in hand.[48]

Earning a not insubstantial six dollars a day, Paul would delay his development into a social activist. Looking back to those years much later, he acknowledged that he paid scant attention to the African Americans working in the most hazardous and strenuous jobs on the docks and knew next to nothing about America's history of slavery and racism. Instead, he held tightly to his Irish identity; his survival instincts signaled that the gearwheels of upward mobility turned more easily for some ethnic groups than for others:

> All I knew about America was what I had picked up between April, when I arrived, and September, when I started school. I understood that all kinds of people lived here—blacks and whites, Jews and Gentiles, Catholics and Protestants, Italians and Irish—and that more often than not they didn't get along. I myself had conflicted feelings. I found myself clinging to my Irish identity because it gave me an edge over an Italian, and to my Catholic identity because it gave me a favored position over a Jew. I was aware too that being white put me in a class in which I was, even as a noncitizen, ahead of a black American of long standing.[49]

Yet on one broiling day in August 1927, he did notice when Italian-speaking longshoremen were pelted with insults by Irish, Polish, and Scandinavian workers as the immigrant anarchists Bartolomeo Vanzetti and Nicola Sacco were to be put to death in a Massachusetts state prison for the murder of a guard and a paymaster during the armed robbery of a shoe company. Following the case in the press, O'Dwyer believed that Sacco and Vanzetti were victims of bias—against Italians, against anarchists, against any and all foreigners—after the failure of appeals based on disavowed witness testimony and clashing ballistics evidence.

"The country was then at the apex of one of its periodic repressive binges," Paul later wrote, referring to national events before the pair's indictment, trial, and execution, which took seven years in all, "and the Commonwealth had not had more satisfying victims since the Salem (witch) trials."[50] For when Sacco and Vanzetti's indictment first came out in 1920, Woodrow Wilson's attorney general, A. Mitchell Palmer, was arresting—without warrants—thousands of people in raids merely under general suspicion of radicalism; coming amid exaggerated fears of a Bolshevik Revolution in America, the sweeps (facilitated in part by J. Edgar Hoover, then a young Justice Department official), became known as the Red Scare.

Before Sacco and Vanzetti were put to death, going after so-called revolutionists and labor radicals had been shown to be good politics, equated in the popular mind with preserving order. When Massachusetts Governor Calvin Coolidge rebuked the American Federation of Labor president Samuel Gompers and thousands of low-paid police officers seeking unionization in Boston, the stage was set for Coolidge to gain the GOP nomination for vice president in 1920 and then, upon the death of Warren Harding in 1923, the presidency itself. Sacco and Vanzetti's case epitomized for the American left the government's willingness to use unrestrained powers to quash dissent and intimidate the foreign-born. That is how O'Dwyer came to see it. "No one today doubts," he wrote, "that those gentle idealists were convicted and executed for a crime they did not commit." Today, scholars believe that at least one of the pair was likely guilty, and possibly both, but that they were unfairly tried.

Yet in the shack at the head of Pier 3 in Brooklyn, Italian immigrant men who showed up for work when Sacco and Vanzetti went to the electric chair suffered "every kind of vengeful epithet" that Irish, Polish, and Scandinavian coworkers could dish out, said O'Dwyer.[51] Looking back at the racist bullying with regrets, he said neither he nor any of the other occupationally insecure dockhands showed the presence of mind or courage to defend the Italian workmen from threats and vilification.

————

ST. JOHN'S LAW SCHOOL classrooms overflowed with students in the institution's first full academic year, 1925–26, prompting it to expand soon into another building. Part of a university conducted by the priests of the Venetian Fathers, the school filled a need for children of immigrants, and immigrants themselves, who found its $180 annual tuition more affordable and accessible than Brooklyn or Fordham law schools, while exclusionary admissions quotas at Columbia, Harvard, and Yale kept them away. The school opened with night classes alone, and the inaugural graduating class comprised "every nation, creed, cult, age, and section of the country," as a local newspaper enthused. Though part of a Catholic university, it mainly drew Jewish students, and it graduated its first Hispanic student in 1929, its first African American student in 1931, and one of the first Chinese American law school enrollees in the state. The New York State Court of Appeals' chief judge Benjamin Cardozo, a Sephardic Jew who would soon be placed on the Supreme Court, delivered the school's first commencement address in the spring of 1928.

Paul graduated the next year in a commencement ceremony held at the Brooklyn Elks Lodge with US Senator Robert Wagner. The Prussian-born American champion of labor delivered the address to the predominantly

Jewish American class, whose 170 Bachelors of Law in total included three women.

O'Dwyer went on from commencement to sit for the bar exam, passing it even before naturalizing in 1931—he garnered a waiver to do so from Cardozo himself. Here, too, Bill was most helpful with his contacts, speaking to a state senator, Phil Kleinfeld, an Orthodox Jew from Coney Island. Kleinfeld went to see the eminent jurist when Paul felt ready to take the bar exam, and the judge suggested Kleinfeld have Bill present him with a petition on Paul's behalf. He did, and the great jurist readily granted Paul a special waiver.[52]

Paul was lucky not to have sought a judge's help in earlier years, during the Red Scare; given the climate at that time, it is unlikely that the offices of the state's highest court would have entertained the application of an Irishman who had not yet gained his citizenship. Instead, he benefited from his timing, and from the growth and strength of immigrant cultures that preceded his arrival in the city. The possibilities for immigrants like Paul were not lost on him or his fellow St. John's law students; the paeans to American pluralism voiced by Senator Wagner and Judge Cardozo at the school's early commencement ceremonies carried more of the ring of truth than of platitude for this postwar generation.

Still, the years of Paul's matriculation occurred against a backdrop of anti-Catholic hostility, whether in the South, the Midwest, or even parts of the New York area. Though the Ku Klux Klan's strength had lately dimmed due to scandals, much of the latent prejudice it had awakened remained intact. (The legion's hostility toward and physical intimidation of Roman Catholics were perhaps only exceeded by its deep hatred for and lynching of their Black neighbors, including uniformed veterans of World War I.) Coupled with Americans' unease in a time of urbanization and technological change, intolerance proved insurmountable to the presidential hopes of a progressive product of Tammany Hall, New York's Democratic governor Al Smith. Indeed, Smith had three strikes against him in the eyes of xenophobic Americans: he was Catholic, opposed Prohibition, and epitomized all things urban. The attacks against his religion made obvious the gulf of distrust between Protestants and Roman Catholics, one many had thought was going the way of the pony and trap.[53] "I don't want any Catholic to vote for me . . . because I am a Catholic," said Smith, a practiced stump speaker with an unmistakable

New York accent, in Oklahoma City, where his campaign train was greeted by burning crosses along the tracks. Ku Klux Klan rallies also flared on Long Island and in New Jersey that year. "But on the other hand, I have the right to say that any citizen of this country [who] votes against me because of my religion, he is not a real, pure, genuine American." Frances Perkins, who campaigned with Smith in 1928 and became the first female cabinet member under President Franklin D. Roosevelt, commented, "We were not prepared in the least degree with the prejudice we encountered . . . and were surprised and shocked by the way in which our opponents appealed to the basest passions and lowest motives of the people."[54]

Smith, while in the state assembly and with then state senator Robert Wagner, had conducted a high-profile investigation of assembly line conditions around the state after a fire in 1911 at the Triangle Shirtwaist Factory Company near Manhattan's Washington Square Park trapped and killed 146 young workers, predominantly teenage girls. The garment workers leaped from window ledges to their deaths because of locked doors and other safety hazards. Smith and Wagner's investigation helped transform the nation's labor laws and launched the two Tammany figures onto the national stage. Although he never won the presidency—and was eclipsed by his protégé, Roosevelt—Smith embodied the aspirations of Irish Americans of the 1920s. And like him, they deeply resented the prejudice and condescension they came up against based on their religion and ethnic lineage.[55]

PAUL FOR HIS own part was called "Pat" and "Paddy" as a new immigrant.[56] Despite such commonplace belittlements for the Irish greenhorn, he was fortunate, too, that his move to America followed (by eight months) the imposition of the Johnson-Reed Act of 1924. Though the first widely restrictive immigration law strengthened a wall keeping immigrants from Asia out of the United States, it also curtailed new entries from European countries. With visas afforded to just 2 percent of the total number of people of each nationality in the United States as of 1890, Congress's measure promulgated the ideology and myth of America's white homogeneity. While the flow from Ireland to the United States averaged 20,000 annually in the 1920s (with the Irish quota set at 28,000 a year, compared to 5,900 for Poland, 3,800 for Italy, and 2,200 for Russia), it reduced to a trickle overall—less than 400 annually—from 1932 to 1945 and did not pick up again until after World War II, and even then only modestly.[57] In New York, the many decades of Irish demographic dominance owing to immigration, rivaled by the more recent and massive influx of Jews and Italians, were at an end. O'Dwyer, as it happened, avoided the clampdowns.

If it added up to a good omen of sorts, this did not extend to Paul's brother, Jimmy, for the 150-pound firefighter and military veteran died in 1926 in an accident as he and his wife, Mildred, were anticipating the birth of their first child. The tragedy took place on Paul's birthday, June 29, when Jimmy stayed in his West Side firehouse past the end of his regular shift to hear from his sibling how he had fared on a prelaw examination. When a fire alarm was pulled near the station, Jimmy climbed onto the truck with other men and the rig sped out of the firehouse. The rescuers were unaware that the smoky fire under a commuter bus's hood had already been extinguished. A motorcycle driven by a young man slammed into their fire truck at an intersection, and Jimmy and another firefighter lost their lives.[58]

On both sides of the Atlantic, the O'Dwyer family was plunged into grief, burying a brother whom Bill called "their counsel, their family worrier, their consolation."[59] The shock was exacerbated by Mildred's pregnancy. She was just weeks from giving birth, and they were in love, their dreams of a future together hinted at in a gentlemanly letter Jimmy penned to her in July 1921 from his home on West Twenty-Ninth Street during their courtship. "Dear Mildred," he wrote in a refined hand reminiscent of his mother's penmanship. "Received your letter this morning and also your card's [sic]. Needless to say how glad I was to get them."[60]

"He was regarded as the kindest and gentlest of the O'Dwyer brothers," said Liam O'Neill, who exhumed the letter from his late grandfather's few extant belongings. "He was known for always sending money home to Ireland and never forgot about the family." Thankfully, the baby girl was born healthy, and Joan O'Dwyer—later a mother of three, including Liam—would go on to become the first woman to serve on the bench in Queens County, New York. Paul and Bill doted over her during her childhood and young adult years, all the more so after her mother died in her early teens, leaving her in the care of her mother's sister, Mika.[61]

But Paul carried guilt over Jimmy's death, as Jimmy had stayed late at the firehouse on his account. He felt untethered as well. "Jimmy was the force that kept us together," he said.[62]

————

SINKING HIS ROOTS in Irish New York, Paul joined the Mayo Men's Patriotic and Benevolent Society, a conventional choice. His St. John's law education meanwhile opened him to the experiences of other immigrant cultures beside his own, chiefly the Yiddish- and Russian-speaking community from which his Jewish classmates hailed. Some 85 percent of his class were Jews, and he grew keenly interested in these poor, communal, often religiously oriented, and much-discriminated-against Eastern European transplants. Their world was something of a parallel universe to his own experiences and heritage, he felt.[63] He had never spoken to a Jewish person before.

Eager to get out of town for a spell, Paul worked as an ordinary seaman during the summer after his first year at law school, traveling all the way to Buenos Aires as a deckhand on the cargo ship *Coldbrook*. On one leg of the adventure, Paul, wearing a tweed cap, ended his seaborne duties at San Pedro, California, where he hopped onto boxcars for the free ride and checked out areas of the West, memorably Salt Lake City. He sat around a campfire with former cowboys who were making their living as performers in a traveling Old West show.

On his way back to New York in August, the twenty-one-year-old got off a train in Chicago to visit one of his mother's sisters, Bonnie, who lived in Oak Park, Illinois. He had his first alcoholic drink in her home, a brew distilled by his uncle Barney Rourke (his aunt's third husband, following the deaths of the first two). To have turned down Rourke's offer would have been inconsiderate, to be sure. So sip the heady concoction the young scholar did—and very much liked it. There would be many, many more sips to come, until finally Paul opted in middle age to go cold turkey, worried that his well-ingrained habit of imbibing socially interfered with his courtroom performance.

Still, his introduction to Jewish life back in Brooklyn impressed him more than his intoxicating first taste of alcohol. Though he never developed a liking for Russian Jewish cuisine, he was touched by the hospitality of his classmates' poor parents, some of whom, he sensed, had suffered unspeakable depredations in the now vanquished czarist Russian Empire.

Bowing to memorizing case law and poring over class notes, Paul and some friends formed a study group, and he picked up not only their thoughts on members of the opposite sex—a constant subject of conversation—but also a smattering of quaint Yiddish expressions (like *haimisher*, *goy*, and *mensch*). A Jewish classmate, Ben Shor, invited him one day to attend the debut meeting of a student club he had just started. Paul thought his friend meant a social club or another study group, but this was to be a club for students interested in influencing Democratic politics in Brooklyn. At the initial meeting in a Jewish neighborhood in Brooklyn, there were thirty-five students, an impressive number. The first order of business was the election of officers. Paul eked out election as treasurer and immediately began overseeing the organization's thirty-five-dollar budget.

But his first experience with Democratic reform, as it were, did not last long. The confident but inexperienced scholars invited themselves to meet the well-known district boss of Coney Island, Ken Sutherland. But, to their innocent surprise and amazement, he was decidedly uninterested in, if not offended by, their suggestions for solving the problems of his district and the candidates they recommended to run for state assembly. Sutherland "had us shown out of his office so fast, the wind nearly gave us pneumonia," Paul remembered in a 1979 interview. "I knew then I could never go to the club and wait for the boss to anoint me."[64]

Through Bill, however, Paul met someone who would look after his interests and development and become his law partner and friend: Oscar Bernstien, "a small man with the brightest blue eyes," in Bill's description.[65] Bill himself had begun working at the Court Street offices of the law firm of Holmes & Bernstien after a police detective introduced him to George Joyce, a city alderman and lawyer from the Gowanus section. With Bernstien's OK, Joyce brought over Bill to meet his new friend, and Bill made an impression, displaying a surprising—to Oscar—knowledge of literature and theater. While the transition from cop to lawyer was rare—at least as unusual as female or Black lawyers and politicians then in Brooklyn—what was equally exceptional was hearing a former policeman discussing a Shakespearean sonnet. Bill was a well-schooled and winsome storyteller, or so Bernstien would comment years later.

The Gowanus alderman and the former cop formed a partnership enduring only until Joyce went on the bench six months later. During the time they worked together, the pair represented cops indicted for casual crimes. Bill, showing an early knack for garnering newspaper coverage, also navigated a Coastal Airways Inc. pilot to acquittal of charges of culpable negligence in 1929. The former World War I aviator named William Alexander went on trial after his emergency landing on the Coney Island shore on a foggy early September afternoon resulted in the death of two children and injuries to ten other people. To build a case for Alexander's innocence, O'Dwyer convinced the judge to go for a spin in a seaplane with Alexander at the helm. With interest in aviation especially intense two years after Charles Lindbergh's solo trip across the Atlantic, reporters on the boardwalk gawked as the aircraft took off and sailed high over the rolling surf. The judge observed firsthand how the navigation stick might have gotten stuck and led to the lethal crash. Won over, he acquitted Bill's client of the manslaughter charges.[66]

With Bill working the courthouse and the reporters stationed there, his youngest brother dropped by the law office on occasion to hit the law books in a quiet corner. The avuncular Bernstien gave Paul and his classmates permission to use the office as long as the students stayed out of his way and studied quietly. It was Paul's first introduction to Bernstien and a law firm.[67]

Oscar emigrated from Russia with his parents and six siblings in the latter years of the nineteenth century, joining the massive exodus of Jews fleeing pogroms, impoverishment, and antisemitic codes. He spoke Yiddish before he mastered English and got a job as an office boy with Caldwell & Holmes. The two partners, Everett Caldwell and Frank Wing Holmes, were lifelong Republicans who handled real estate litigation. The firm was renamed Holmes & Bernstien after Caldwell, who was then first assistant Brooklyn district attorney, fatally shot himself on Christmas Eve in 1921 after party leaders dropped him from consideration for district attorney.[68] By this time, Bernstien was a lawyer in the small Court Street firm near Borough Hall.

He was "a man of great culture, a devotee of literature, theater, science and math," as Paul later described him. He got married in 1915, and, with his spouse, Rebecca (Becky) Drucker, frequented the opera, ballet, and Broadway shows. After living in a series of small Manhattan apartments, they found a barn-like one at 121 Madison Avenue, so cavernous it came to be known by their artist, activist, and writer friends as Boyle's 30 Acres, after the wooden Jersey City boxing palace that served as the site of Jack Dempsey's world-famous bout against Georges Carpentier. The apartment, though, was only for combat of the intellectual kind, with much flourishing of cigars and opinions, and savoring of cocktails. Drucker was then working as a secretary and reader for the *American Magazine*, where she met the socially conscious writers Ida Tarbell, John Reed, and Walter Lippmann. Later, at the *New York Tribune*, she was a reporter and assistant to columnist Heywood Broun. She became acquainted, too, with critics and thespians who gathered at the Algonquin Roundtable for champagne and bon mots. By the 1930s, she was working steadily as a theatrical publicist.[69]

Though not nearly as famous as the Roundtable, the Bernstien-Drucker living room drew columnists, artists, and poets to talk about the latest novels and stage dramas. Between sips and puffs, another guest, the American labor activist John L. Lewis of the United Mine Workers, decried industrial capitalism's brutal excesses and the latest headline-making miscarriages of racial injustice, like the 1931 Alabama trial of the Scottsboro Boys—nine Black teens and young adults falsely accused of raping two white girls on a train (and defended by the skilled Brooklyn lawyer Sam Leibowitz, known to Bernstien for his unbroken string of courthouse victories). As Broun, the syndicated columnist, was a close friend of Bernstien and Drucker, it so happened that the first union ever created for the era's abysmally paid newspaper employees germinated in their apartment. The Newspaper Guild was Broun's 1933 brainchild.

Becky Drucker helped found the League of Women Shoppers, a consumer group that picketed department stores in support of workers walking the line for better pay. She assisted Broun's first wife, Ruth Hale, in the founding of a group advocating for married women keeping their last names. Drucker helped carry the banner for many such pioneering forays in women's equality.[70]

While Bill worked at Bernstien's law office in the late 1920s and early 1930s, he showed up one evening at the Bernstiens' home only after repeated invitations in those years, for he was apparently shy around Manhattan sophisticates. It turned out, however, that he need not have been. Bernstien and Drucker and their guests welcomed him, and Becky in particular grew enamored of his stem-winders about guileless New York cops and Bohola old-timers and never failed to be struck by the former cop's knowledge of poetry and novels. She tried to get him to compose some of his stories on a typewriter for the *American Magazine*, but she was unsuccessful.[71]

Holmes & Bernstien was then looking for law clerks, and Paul was chosen. He found he could withstand Oscar's impatience with professional imperfection—Oscar did not suffer fools gladly, even fresh-faced law clerks, and once fired his own son-in-law—for Bernstien had a reputation for brilliance and concision in legal brief-writing. And with the strong lean of a liberal humanist toward the creed of individual rights, he cottoned to the precocious Paul and his interest in American political ideals. The older man was not a courtroom lawyer, so the job of arguing cases before judges and juries in the criminal courts fell in large part to Holmes and Paul, giving the latter the courtroom experience he desired.

———

FIRST, THOUGH, AFTER PASSING the New York bar exam and giving up his job on the waterfront in 1929, O'Dwyer addressed another hurdle in becoming a lawyer, the requirement of undergoing a clerkship. That inglorious stint took place in an unglamorous law office above a theater out on Church Avenue in the Flatbush section of Brooklyn, the firm of Cohen & Lieberman. "Mr. Cohen," as Paul described him in his memoirs, was a hard-headed businessman and Mr. Lieberman a *yeshiva bucher*, meaning unmarried and unsettled.

Paul's posting consisted of taking dictation from the ill-matched duo (the law firm didn't last too much longer) and running out to a corner lunch counter to fetch sandwiches for the partners. But his five-dollars-a-week posting took an interesting turn when he was sent to the offices of one Hyman Schorenstein to serve him a summons.

Paul knew bupkis about Schorenstein, but Schorenstein was in fact the Democratic district leader of the largely Jewish neighborhood Brownsville, a powerful, and down-to-earth, power broker to whom even the likes of Franklin Roosevelt and Herbert Lehman paid heed in election years because of his influence over Jewish voters. Wearing a suit and tie, O'Dwyer walked over to the appointed address and climbed the stairs to Schorenstein's unexalted second-floor headquarters. It was located on Pitkin Avenue, a bustling street of commerce filled with stores, pushcarts, and shopper-hagglers.

Having arrived from Eastern Europe as a child, Schorenstein rose to be the borough's first prominent Jewish leader and quelled, at the 1928 Democratic National Convention in Houston, a last-minute rebellion in the Ohio delegation, ensuring that Al Smith won the nomination for president. Among the numerous hats Schorenstein donned, he was the commissioner of records for Brooklyn, though he could not write or read in English with any fluency. (That was no problem, a judge ruled—and the ruling surprised few observers, since Schorenstein, as district boss, appointed local judges to the bench.)

The summons that Paul held in his hands was connected to yet another role Schorenstein had: owner of the Brownsville Bus Company. One of his buses had struck the pushcart of a peddler on Pitkin Avenue and destroyed an estimated thirty dollars' worth of random merchandise, known as "notions." The street peddler in question was the uncle of Cohen's wife!

Paul turned left at the top of the stairs and found Schorenstein at his desk. The political boss waved him in, peering up at the youngster through the top half of his round eyeglasses and snapping, "What do you want?" Paul extended the summons in front of him, and, since Schorenstein could not read it, related the circumstances that lay behind it—the victim's thirty-dollar loss.

"Thirty dollars in notions?" Schorenstein gasped. He said that there was not even thirty dollars of notions on *all* of hardscrabble Pitkin Avenue. Call your boss, demanded the businessman-politician.

When Paul dialed his office, Lieberman answered.

"Find out if he'll accept a reduction down to a $5 fine," Lieberman said, after a pause.

Paul always remembered what happened next.

"So I said, 'Mr. Schorenstein, if you'll make it five dollars, this case is settled.' He says, 'Look, you're a *goy mit a yiddshe kop*'"—a gentile with a Jewish head. He handed Paul a crisp five-dollar bill.[72]

O'Dwyer headed out the door and down the stairs, thrilled at having successfully resolved the first legal dispute of his career.

3

AMONG THIEVES

THE GALES of the Great Depression of 1929–39 beleaguered New Yorkers as much as countless other Americans. Most commonly but not exclusively working-class men, the jobless waited on the city's scattered breadlines as their dreams, and savings accounts, went up in smoke. Little "Hoovervilles" dotted the city, gathering the dislocated and the destitute. Years later Paul recalled one of many poverty-stricken encampments, at Riverside Park and Seventy-Second Street, remarking that the gaunt denizens often looked bewildered rather than angry. An economic collapse was never supposed to happen in industrially burgeoning twentieth-century America, much less the financial capital of the world.[1] It was impossible for its victims, willing to accept *any* job to feed themselves and their families, to comprehend.

Starting with the Wall Street panic of October 1929, the windfall profits that had accrued from a decade's worth of unchecked financial speculation were wiped out. The collapse touched off mass strikes, aggressive strike-breaking, and social protest. In the Bronx, panicked depositors mobbed the Bank of the United States, demanding entrance to the institution to withdraw their hard-earned savings. The scene was repeated the next day outside the bolted doors of the savings and loan's monumental branch on the Lower East Side of Manhattan. Thousands of small factories and stores in the city shuttered for lack of anyone who could still afford their wares. The municipal government, too, floundered in red ink.[2]

The city government's incapacity was paralleled by Washington's re-calcitrance in the face of fast-spreading destitution. The Republican president Herbert Hoover appeared determined to view the economy's downward spiral as greatly exaggerated and transitory, retaining a near ironclad faith in the free market system. In the end, his ideological cer-tainties were no match for reality. By January 1930, the total number of unemployed workers nationwide had increased to 4,065,000 from 429,000 in October 1929. By October 1931, more than a year before Hoover was voted out of office in a landslide, nine million workers sat idle.[3]

In New York City, the unemployment figure reached 800,000, with many of the victims no longer able to support their wives and children, who had no other means to buy food or pay their rent.

The truth was that even before the crash nearly a third of New York-ers, a fraction representing more than two million, lived down at the heels, their "distressful" and "disgraceful" condition underscored by a 1927 city government report that pointed to neglected and decaying New York City streets, parks, and hospitals.[4]

While the pain and dread of New Yorkers varied widely by household during the Depression decade, effects were acute in areas already long fa-miliar with destitution, such as the Red Hook area of Brooklyn, an Ital-ian immigrant enclave where redbrick row houses lacked even basic plumbing. When shipping slowed after the crash, men and women wan-dered Red Hook's streets in search of a day's wages, shining shoes, swab-bing floors, hauling crates, or selling cheap wares. Out-of-work sailors shacked up in a flimsy "Tin City" at the edge of Upper New York Bay.[5] It was a typical scene, emblematic of the era.

Harlem, meanwhile, was conveniently viewed by many white people who possessed political and legal authority as a world of its own. Ab-sorbing African Americans from the Jim Crow South, the northern Man-hattan community's reputation as a center of cultural and artistic renaissance—jazz and blues, performance, fine arts, and poetry—was more and more contested by crumbling and overcrowded apartment buildings. According to a 1935 report that Mayor Fiorello La Guardia suppressed, Harlem experienced not only poverty but also "shocking bar-barity" from the white police force.[6] Paul, writing in later years, took the view that the degradation suffered by Black Americans, then and histori-cally, was far worse than any subjugation suffered by his Irish immigrant

forbears. And it was poverty and discrimination, he argued, that were
the main drivers of social problems and street disturbances that urban
ghettos experienced, both before and after the Depression.

In the infamous 1863 Draft Riot, he noted, a heavily Irish mob, many
from the disease-ridden Five Points slum, stormed through the better pre-
cincts of Manhattan with knives, clubs, and broken bottles. Faced with
Union Army conscription, which the wealthy were gallingly able to buy
their way out of, these marauders trashed government buildings as well
as Brooks Brothers, attacked African American waterfront workers, and
set fire to the Orphanage for Colored Children on Fifth Avenue. At least
119 people were killed. "The Draft Riot of 1863," Paul wrote pointedly in
the 1980s, "still hovers over our head when we tend to put on airs of
righteousness."[7]

WHEN O'DWYER graduated from St. John's Law School at age twenty-
four and apprenticed under Oscar Bernstien's physically imposing senior
partner, Frank Holmes, the city's social distress ironically presented Paul
with opportunities for court experience. The tides of immiseration from
all quarters brought with them a surfeit of casual crime and indigent wrong-
doers. "Whatever came, I took—whatever I could get," Paul later said of
his Depression-era client list.

So, along with other legal eagles starting out in Brooklyn during the
Depression, Paul opted to stay late at the state court every Thursday when
the sitting grand jury handed down indictments and a judge parceled out
defendants to hungry lawyers. "It was pro bono, but it was giving us experience," Paul remarked. Over time, he received more serious cases and
represented three cops accused in 1936 of terrorizing a suspect in the basement of their Bath Beach station house. In another notable case, he defended a truck driver indicted for the brutal murder of his girlfriend, a
mother of two children.[8]

He found that some of the older lawyers he worked with from other
firms could be lethargic: some were not even willing to head over to the
dilapidated Raymond Street jail to meet with clients or to go into strange
neighborhoods in search of witnesses. Bill, his brother, was somewhat in
the latter camp. Working then at Holmes & Bernstien, Bill delegated scut
work to office assistants, Bernstien said. He detected in the elder O'Dwyer
brother what he branded "a lazy streak."[9]

But Bill was in a hurry in his own way, and so was Paul. The latter circulated among the fraternal and county-based Irish societies to raise his profile and perhaps gain clients. He gained his US citizenship in November 1930 but, in the act of doing so, retained his rebellious edge. When asked at the naturalization ceremony if he renounced his allegiance to George VI, Paul said, "I had never had any in the first place."[10]

He was soon enough seen in Brooklyn pubs waving a lit cigar and imbibing into the wee hours, trading courthouse gossip and news of home. In May 1932, the *Brooklyn Daily Eagle* published a page-one profile of "the youngest man practicing law in the Brooklyn criminal courts," describing the rising young barrister as "given to understatements." By O'Dwyer's own fantastical reckoning (or perhaps that of an imaginative reporter), he could speak five foreign languages and had once "dropped in" on Africa's Gold Coast and traded a pipe for "eight miles of Africa waterfront," which, the writer asserted, "he still owns."[11]

In a more sober moment shortly after the laudatory article appeared, Paul received an unexpected opportunity to return to Bohola for the first time since his departure seven years earlier, a fortuitous development at least as interesting as the *Eagle* profile—if merely factual. It arose because Bill was organizing a tournament at New York's Polo Grounds between the Gaelic football team of County Mayo—champions in their province that season—and a select New York team. With Frank Holmes's OK, Bill sent Paul across the ocean to work out final arrangements for the coming tournament with the Gaelic Athletic County Board.

The serendipitous Bohola homecoming for the youngest O'Dwyer was surely an intense one. Upon arriving in the hamlet, he found his mother Bridget looking "much older," though carrying her usual authority. The houses "seemed small." But the farmers, many more stooped with age, greeted Bridget McNicholas O'Dwyer's and Patrick O'Dwyer's youngest son with enthusiasm and warmth, gathering around to hear stories about his new life. Paul listened more than he talked, however, letting the old-timers' anecdotes wash over him (he had lost sight of how much he missed hearing their winding stories), as it was "good manners for the one who had seen a large piece of the world to keep quiet about it."

When the visit, measured in days, not weeks, came to an end, he left his mother and sisters as once before at the nearby train station, harboring perhaps a heightened awareness of the passage of time and transience of life, as well as the stark differences between his former life in Ireland and his new existence in America.

His work for his brother done, Paul returned to New York uneventfully by sea to find Bill—who had himself visited Bohola in 1927 with his wife, Kitty, and his brother Frank—short of the funds to cover the much-promoted tournament. Becoming concerned about the prospect of insolvency, Bill had turned to the hardworking Frank, who had managed to save some $6,500 at his job loading fruits and vegetables onto trucks (and who was on his way to becoming a better-paid buyer for Harry Kelly & Sons in lower Manhattan's Washington Market). Though the middle brother was wary of Bill's business acumen, he contributed his hard-won savings, caught by Bill's enthusiasm.

The games began, drawing heavy newspaper coverage from Damon Runyon of the Hearst syndicate and other sports writers. While the gate receipts from the first two days went to the Milk Fund charity for slum children founded by William Randolph Hearst's wife Millicent, rain dampened attendance at the third, and final, match. The final game's ticket revenue was supposed to pay for the entire tournament, but it fell well short, and Frank's risky investment was used by Bill to cover the losses.[12]

LIKE FRANK, Paul scratched his head at the juxtaposition of Bill's initial brashness with the flow of red ink. He decided, in any event, that he was ready to move on from Holmes & Bernstien at 26 Court Street, no longer content to continue working in his more charismatic and successful older brother's shadow. He experimented with launching his own practice in a small office on Fifth Avenue in Manhattan, "in the center of the world." Supported with a $300 loan from his brothers, the experiment also proved unsuccessful—Paul realized in short order that he was not yet well known enough around the Irish community to attract an adequate number of paying clients; he returned after a few months to Holmes & Bernstien. But by this time, happily so for Paul, Bill was no longer working there. And as with many other things that involved Paul's complicated eldest sibling, the reasons behind Bill's departure from the firm had been complex: to begin with, Mrs. Hearst had put in a word on Bill's behalf to the interim mayor John McKee, knowing of Bill's interest in gaining appointment as a Brooklyn magistrate. Her recommendation nicely complemented the references Bill drummed up from the Coney Island district leader Kenneth Sutherland, the editors of three Irish weeklies, and the head of the city patrolmen's union. The former mayor Jimmy Walker's first interim successor McKee was looking around for an independent Democrat not unlike himself to fill a vacancy on the magistrates' bench. McKee's interim term was four months and was to be followed by a special city election for someone to complete the twelve months that remained of Walker's scandal-abbreviated second term as mayor.

The New York political and legal world, at that juncture, was still reeling from the resignation of Walker, an icon of American possibility for New York's Irish like his mentor, Governor Al Smith. Walker's talents extended from writing the Tin Pan Alley hit song "Will You Love Me in December as You Do in May?" to pushing, as the state senate majority leader under Smith and the Tammany Hall boss Charles Murphy, popular legislation that opened baseball parks and boxing arenas on Sundays, the working man's traditional day off. The press dubbed him "Beau James" when, as mayor, he painted the Manhattan nights red with a Broadway showgirl mistress who would become his second wife. Smith called him a "candy stick," uncomfortable with his protégé's sartorial and personal flamboyance. But Walker was a savvy negotiator and unrivaled in the art of disarming critics who questioned his Prohibition-era indulgences. When he was called out during his successful 1929 reelection campaign against Republican Fiorello La Guardia and Socialist Norman Thomas for having received a raise—from $25,000 to $40,000—the clotheshorse mayor parried the reporters' questions, quipping to uproarious laughter, "Think what it would cost if I worked full-time!"[13]

When the stock market derailed and hard times set in, Walker's charms wore thin.[14] An investigation by Judge Samuel Seabury produced evidence that transport moguls had kept Walker close with drinks, meals, and cash totaling as much as $1 million. Other findings showed the human consequences of corruption: Vivian Gordon, a surprise witness, told of how immigrant women were arrested on trumped-up charges of prostitution and forced to buy their way out of jail. Their predators in blue were hardly punished—instead, they received boosts in pay. After Gordon was found strangled to death in a park in the Bronx, no less a moral authority than Patrick Joseph Hayes spoke out: the New York archbishop and cardinal suggested Walker's cavalier character allowed proliferation of "girlie magazines," illegal casinos, and perhaps the economic spiral itself. Tammany, too, gave up on Walker, who resigned on September 1, 1932, after failing to make a convincing case that he was capable of looking a gift horse in the mouth. As he departed for Europe, New York Governor Franklin D. Roosevelt, who oversaw Walker's administrative tribunal, began the final stretch of his own campaign for the White House, promising to address the Great Depression far more forcefully than Herbert Hoover—and then doing so in his first hundred days in office.[15]

A Walker antithesis, McKee was a former schoolteacher who had been promoted to the role of head alderman with the backing of the powerful Bronx Democratic leader and Roosevelt confidant Edward Flynn. As he looked to fill the Brooklyn magistrate's opening, he had to consider questions of probity—the Manhattan magistrates' bench had recently been the target of press allegations that two judges had purchased their seats. He also felt his arm pulled by the Brooklyn Democratic boss John McCooey, who let it be known that he supported a Polish American attorney from the Greenpoint section of his borough.

In the end, though, McKee chose Bill O'Dwyer. According to Bill, Flynn was out of town, or the judgeship would almost certainly have gone to McCooey's man. But by luck or connections, Bill's brashness paid dividends for him this time. After seven years with Holmes & Bernstien, representing a man tried for abducting an eight-year-boy, a burglary defendant, a person claiming the $6,500 estate of a retired police officer, and an applicant for a license to run a dance hall over the objections of a Methodist church, he gave up lawyering for the Brooklyn bench, rising "right out of the ruck," as he put it. His reputation for independence was such that he even came to the favorable attention of Walker's ultimate successor, La Guardia, who, after becoming mayor at the start of 1934, named Bill as one of four magistrates to preside in a rehabilitation-oriented Brooklyn Adolescents Court for first offenders between the ages of sixteen and nineteen.[16]

And Paul, for his part, finally had some breathing room at Holmes & Bernstien, able to make a mark without fear of eclipse by his far better-known, and faster-rising, sibling.

———

RETURNING TO THE DAY-TO-DAY (and nightly) work of becoming better known himself, it was helpful to Paul's career that he had been elected—a year before Bill's departure from the Court Street firm—as president of the New York Mayo Men's Patriotic and Benevolent Association. But the position as the head of a voluntary organization whose members were older and usually conservative did not keep him from making his opinions known. At one Sunday afternoon meeting, he revealed his opposition to a clampdown in Ireland by Eamon de Valera on civil dissent and disorder, disappointing many in the group. At another gathering, O'Dwyer voiced concern over sectarian overtones he alleged were behind the Mayo County Council's suspension of a Protestant librarian, the subject of newspaper stories in Irish weeklies in New York. The association's Catholic chaplain agreed with the suspension. Paul did not.[17]

Despite his outspoken liberal opinions, some of his fellows referred friends and family members in need of a sympathetic lawyer to Paul. "Joining fraternal organizations for business reasons is not always successful, but for a young lawyer without wealthy friends, it was the only way to succeed," he later explained.[18]

In 1934, weekly contact with fellow immigrants from his native land gave rise to a far more fruitful and lasting outcome when Paul attended the Mayo Men's Association's St. Patrick's Day beauty pageant, an annual fete at the Lexington Avenue armory immediately following the parade. There he joined a crowd of seven thousand revelers. Although asked to help judge the beauty contest, O'Dwyer declined, reluctant, he later explained, to arouse the enmity of the disappointed boyfriends and parents of the runners-up.[19] But the pageant's winner, the fair-skinned, blue-eyed Kathleen O'Connor Rohan, looked resplendent, and Paul was immediately smitten, so he asked to be introduced.

Seventeen years old, Miss Rohan resided at the time with her hard-working parents in the Yorkville section of the East Side, near Jacob Ruppert's Knickerbocker Brewery, a complex of thirty-five buildings responsible for brewing the country's best-selling beer. Her mother hailed from a "dirt-poor" family from Galway.[20] Like the millions of other young women who left behind the rural poverty and confining social arrangements of their homeland to haul tin pails laden with coal and scrub floors in the homes of wealthy Americans in the nineteenth and early twentieth centuries, Kathleen's mother traveled across the ocean to work—in her case for the Twomleys, a titled aristocratic family that employed sixty servants in their mansion on Fifth Avenue near East Fifty-Fourth Street. Kathleen's mother met her father during her service there. Pinching their pennies, the couple came to move on from housework and operated a corner store in Yorkville,[21] a German and Irish community where, as liberal newspaper columnist Jimmy Breslin later put it, describing the era of the 1930s, "if a black were ever able to get a drink in a bar, the bartender immediately took out a hammer and smashed the glass."[22] Paul was nearly a decade older than Kathleen. On their first date he took her for a night out to a mostly Black dance hall in Harlem. "She went out on the dance floor and enjoyed herself and never mentioned that there was anything different about the night," O'Dwyer later recounted.[23]

For Kathleen, it seemed, Paul was something of a catch. Irish and handsome, he had a subdued charm, was quietly eloquent, and worked hard and had a promising career. After Kathleen graduated from Julia Richmond High School, the two were wed in a quiet Catholic ceremony in Brooklyn. They selected St. Casimir's, a Polish church likely because its Irish priest had nationalist sympathies.[24] It was August 1935.[25]

The next year Kathleen gave birth to the first of the couple's four children, Billy. After Kathleen's father died some years on, her mother Mary moved in to assist her daughter with the children, the youngest of whom, Brian, was then in diapers.[26]

At first, the newlyweds resided in Paul's small apartment on Plaza Street, Brooklyn, within walking distance of the law firm. To make room, Paul's roommate, his brother Frank, graciously cleared out; he would wed Mary Sweeney of Bayonne, New Jersey, in 1941 and moved with her to El Centro, California, where he became an Imperial Valley lettuce grower on a sizable scale.[27]

Sadly, however, Paul's mother did not live to share in the news of Bill, Frank, and Paul's milestones—she died in Ireland of a sudden heart attack in 1935, prior to Paul and Kathleen's marriage. She was sixty-five.[28]

In Bohola, as Paul was to learn, her funeral sparked a bitter confrontation between her grieving daughters and the town's then reigning conservative cleric, Father Higgins, as had happened after her husband Patrick died. When the oldest O'Dwyer sister, Kathleen, went to the church to arrange Bridget's funeral, Higgins, "being, somewhat, under the influence of John Barleycorn, said he was not in any position to do anything to her communist brother, but that he did have control over his family," Paul recalled. Kathleen "tore him apart, and told him what kind of person he was." However well justified, her response made matters difficult for another O'Dwyer sister, Mary Rose (known as May), as she was still dependent on the cleric for her teaching job—the one previously held by Patrick.

It was only after their aging mother had appealed on bended knee to the bishop at Ballaghaderreen in the chancery office that Higgins's objections to granting May the post after Patrick's death had been overruled.

May, even more than the rest of the family, was sensitive to the risk that could arise from having an opinionated brother speaking his liberal mind in faraway New York. After Bridget's funeral, she wrote to Paul, imploring him to tone down his radical sentiments for the sake of his sisters and their livelihoods. "We really can't tell you how to conduct your life, that would be inappropriate," she wrote, "but for God's sake can't you keep out of all this stuff that's getting back to Ireland? Our life is being made miserable here."[29] (May held on to her job until retiring at seventy, becoming the last family member to live in the family home, along with her husband, Bernard Durkan, with whom she brought up three sons.)[30]

Tragically, Bridget O'Dwyer's death may have been precipitated by another family loss in the same way that the death of her son Tommy may have hastened the end of her husband Patrick O'Dwyer's days in 1921. In January 1934, John ("Jack") O'Dwyer was with off-duty police detective Bill Donnell at the Terminal Bar and Grill on Brooklyn's Fourth Avenue, capping off a double date with sisters Mae and Josephine King of Flatbush Avenue, when three men entered the premises and held up the counterman. Jack's friend reached for his police sidearm and fired. One of the intruders, twenty-year-old Harold Seaman, who was two years out of work and had a third-grade education, squeezed off a shot. The bullet tore a hole in Jack's back. As he slumped in his chair, the robbers ran off. An ambulance arrived and took Jack to Holy Family Hospital. Paul, Frank, and Bill converged within hours at his hospital bed. They watched helplessly as he languished for ten desultory days before expiring.[31]

The charges faced by the three alleged stickup men, who were detained and arraigned, included a possible sentence of capital punishment. After a trial, Harold Seaman of Brooklyn drew a death sentence, though the public defender claimed Seaman was "mentally retarded" and not in control of his actions the night he allegedly acted as the gunman. At one point in the trial, a taxi driver retracted an eyewitness account related to the incident, which had been instrumental in the conviction of one of Seaman's accomplices (the driver said Donnell forced him, with threats, to lie to prosecutors). As the proceedings continued, both of Seaman's accomplices were saved from the electric chair—Brooklyn District Attorney William Geoghan asked Governor Herbert Lehman to commute their respective death sentences, maintaining that they were only "vicariously guilty" of causing Jack's death, as compared to Seaman, who was found to have pulled the trigger.[32]

In his autobiography, Paul called the loss of Jack a "tragedy hideously compounded by the judicial aftermath in which the gunman was tried, convicted, and executed."[33] But at that point he had not yet thought long and hard about capital punishment, nor had he yet come to see it, as he later did, as an unwarranted and unconstructive use of state power. He and his surviving brothers Bill and Frank chose not to attend hearings over Seaman's death sentence, neither requesting that Seaman's life be spared nor calling for it to be cut short. Apparently, to try to save the life of the troubled and by some accounts mentally defective young man who had robbed his brother of the rest of his life was simply a bridge too far.

On the morning before Seaman was electrocuted, his three sisters took a train up to the state prison in Ossining, New York, to see him for the last time. They greeted him in his cell, finding him resigned to his fate after back-to-back sentences, the first for manslaughter in an earlier case and the second and prevailing one for firing the shot that killed Jack.

"I've got to do it for the O'Dwyer case," the doomed man was quoted saying.[34]

———

THE CONJUNCTION of major family-related events in the mid-1930s—Paul's return home after several years away on Bill's behalf, Jack's fatal shooting, his mother's subsequent decline and demise, and Paul's ensuing marriage—nudged the conscientious youngest O'Dwyer son toward the position of unofficial patriarch of his far-flung relations. After becoming a father and tending to his career on a more than full-time basis, Paul became increasingly well connected in New York. He carried an ever-expanding network of clients and friends who could assist any new transplant from Ireland with finding an apartment or a job, and he also maintained an active transatlantic correspondence. On a personal level he was approachable, founded on what one of his nephews, Adrian Flannelly, described as "a rock bed of sense."[35]

During Paul's earlier days as a legal apprentice at Holmes & Bernstien, the Depression-era clients he reeled in could barely afford to pay.

One story Paul later told his kids involved a Fulton Fish Market fish peddler who compensated him with lobsters pulled from a wooden trap. "He put them in the drawer and forgot about them," Brian said when asked what his father did with his crustaceous legal fee.[36] But Paul took home more cash than he had as a freight checker and unburdened himself of more than $1,100 in various IOUs to the firm and his brothers.

It was still a struggle to keep afloat in those days—court-assigned defendants, the basis of Paul's initial court experiences, did not pay anything for representation, except in a murder trial. In these more coveted cases, his firm would receive $1,000, a flat fee, of which, as the practicing lawyer, he would receive a small share.

In 1936, still on this road to coming into his own, Paul received a significant court appointment to defend a trio of police detectives charged with torturing a "confession" from a suspect named Benedict Parmigiani. The cops, who had allegedly strapped the twenty-one-year-old to a steam pipe in the cellar of the Bath Beach station house after arresting him, were indicted for second-degree assault after Parmigiani showed a jury the scars on his arms and wrists, the result of burns and the skin graft operations he underwent over four months in hospital after his mistreatment. Parmigiani was in the end absolved of armed robbery charges. On the cops' behalf, O'Dwyer argued not the facts but the law (i.e., whether grand jury procedures had been technically violated in their indictments). With the aid of Paul's footwork, the officers were exonerated. They were put back on duty after a three-week departmental suspension. A blurb buried in the *Brooklyn Daily Eagle* reported this outcome, its obscure placement and the lack of public outcry the signs that police brutality was routine or at least tolerated in the borough.[37]

Judge Algernon Nova also assigned Paul to serve as the public defender in a 1937 murder case and sent him over to the Raymond Street jailhouse to meet the accused individual, George Grubee, who was languishing there after having been grazed by a police officer's bullet as he fled across the backyard of his former lover's home and hopped over a fence. Grubee waved away the bow-tied visitor to his jail cell, apparently thinking he was a detective. But with no other lawyer available to him, Nova had to settle for O'Dwyer.

Paul must have known the odds of acquittal for the twenty-eight-year-old Mr. Grubee were long and ominous. During the 1930s, New York

State laws gave judges wide berth to mete out the death penalty, and they did, executing a total of 153 people in the Depression decade, more than any other state.[38] In this instance, the criminal defendant had signed his confession to police, and the statement was read aloud to the jury at Judge John Fitzgerald's behest. In the confession, Grubee admitted shooting his girlfriend in the belief she entertained other men while he was on the road.

Declared sane by two court-appointed psychiatrists, he endured a trial lasting several days. When the jury deliberated, a single juror—an Irish American who wore tailored clothes—balked at convicting the defendant. Off hours, Paul picked up from a mutual acquaintance that this juror had been jilted by a former girlfriend, and it was this unlucky experience, rather than the juror's Catholic faith or any opposition to the death penalty, that caused him to be the holdout. Though Paul was not aware of it, he was insisting in the jury room on a reduced charge of murder in the second degree, saying the killing was a crime of passion and not, as the prosecution contended, premeditated.

Paul stayed awake all night in the vacant courtroom with the aid of coffee.

Finally, after twenty-six hours of deliberation, the door to the jury room swung open and the twelve jury members filed in, led by a court officer.[39]

"Has the jury reached a verdict?" Fitzgerald asked.

"Yes, your honor."

"How do you find?"

"Guilty of murder in the *second* degree," the jury foreman declared.

Paul did not betray his elation. If nothing else, he had saved his client from a likely one-way ticket to the Sing Sing death house.

Judge Fitzgerald, however, was anything but delighted. He scolded jury members for their failure to find Grubee guilty of *first*-degree homicide. The thirty-one-year-old victim—a mother, he reminded them—was brutally murdered in her home.

"On last Wednesday I was asked by attorneys for the defense to accept a plea of murder in the second degree [on] behalf of the defendant. I refused," Fitzgerald said, smoldering, in the account published by the *Brooklyn Daily Eagle* the next day. "On Thursday before this murder was committed, this defendant made up his mind that he would kill her, and on Saturday night he carried out his determination and murdered her. If that is not murder in the first degree, there is no such crime." Fitzgerald dismissed the jurors without so much as the customary "Thank you for your service."[40]

The prosaic and necessary duties of a 1930s criminal defense lawyer in Brooklyn were one thing, but O'Dwyer was too sensitive to walk away from each and every jury decision without feeling. Appearing before Judge Fitzgerald in another case, in late 1937, for example, Paul became certain that the evidence fell short of justifying a conviction of his nineteen-year-old client—Vincent Forte—for the fatal shooting of a grocery store owner in a robbery in which Forte and his alleged accomplices were said to have netted $703.[41] And of course a conviction, right or wrong, almost invariably meant death by execution.

O'Dwyer felt betrayed by the system when Forte was sentenced to death at Sing Sing; it was the sole case in which O'Dwyer lost a client to the electric chair, out of the seven murder cases he handled in all. He long remembered how the hard-of-hearing Fitzgerald rebuffed Forte's plea to undergo a lie detector test, along with his own motion to that effect. "We have no such apparatus here," was Fitzgerald's terse reply. Not two years before, however, a different judge had permitted an O'Dwyer client to take a lie detector test in an armed robbery case, contributing to his acquittal.

Paul took Forte's case up to the court of appeals but did not prevail. The legality of the device's use in a court of law was still a subject of legal controversy at the time.

Fitzgerald, recalled O'Dwyer many years later, "took a fiendish delight in sending people to the electric chair." According to O'Dwyer's cousin Michael McNicholas (who changed his first name to Mychal in 2001), Paul felt that Forte's conviction and electrocution stemmed from anti-Italian and anti-immigrant prejudice not unlike the atmosphere that had sealed Nicola Sacco and Bartolomeo Vanzetti's fates in 1927.

FOR GENERATIONS, the visible center of civic life in Brooklyn was not situated at New York City Hall, across the East River, but at Borough Hall. The building sat in the heart of downtown Brooklyn, a Greek Revival edifice announced by six fluted columns, a massive staircase, and the figure of Justice standing atop a cupola. Brooklyn became a city of its own in 1834, and the administrative hub opened its doors in the mid-nineteenth century. Part of the courthouse district, Borough Hall remained central even well after the city's five boroughs were consolidated as one great metropolis after 1898. Like Manhattan, with its Tammany Hall, Brooklyn had its own Democratic machine. The two apparatuses competed, shared, or fought over the spoils of municipal dominance.

As later investigations dramatized, the world in which Paul was learning his craft was lousy with gangsterism. From 1910 to 1934, the leader of the Brooklyn Democratic organization was the plump, mustachioed McCooey, whom one writer of the era, Niven Busch, described as "The Emerald Cherub."[42] The career of Bill O'Dwyer's first law associate, George Joyce, from the poor, industrial Gowanus section, reflected the benefits of deferring to the McCooey-led Brooklyn Democratic machine. As Joyce recalled, McCooey held sway not with threats and punishments but rather with "maple syrup." In order to gain a dollop of power of his own, Joyce decided against contesting a close race for Gowanus alderman, though he believed the election was stolen right out of the ballot box. The next time Joyce ran, after completing his navy service in World War I "without doing appreciable damage to either side, the Germans or the Americans," he ran as an organizationally endorsed candidate and won.[43]

In this post, Joyce helped people to get public relief or a job on the city payroll. He also attended political meetings of aldermen from all the boroughs. He became a lawyer—Bill's friend and associate—and a judge. But for all his experience with rough-and-tumble politics and gaming the machine, he may have neglected, when he and Bill were working as lawyers together in the Brooklyn courts, to impress upon Bill the importance of "clearing it with McCooey." Bill's unilateral maneuvers to gain the interim mayor McKee's appointment to the magistrate's bench so unsettled the Brooklyn Democratic boss that they appeared to contribute to McCooey's decision not to back the Bronx boss Ed Flynn's pick—McKee—in the special election for mayor held in November 1932. Instead of backing McKee, McCooey endorsed the Manhattan surrogate justice John O'Brien. O'Brien went on to win the election to serve the final year of what had been Jimmy Walker's second term. But at his postinaugural news conference for the single-year term as mayor, he answered a question about who the new police commissioner would be by saying, "I don't know—*they* haven't told me yet." Even if the remark suggesting he was a political hack was said in jest, which was quite possible, it marked him as a Tammany puppet, and so he attracted a third-party challenge from his immediate predecessor, McKee. This split in the Democratic Party created the path to victory for La Guardia the following November—he was Samuel Seabury's reformist choice and ran on an anti-Tammany and anti-corruption platform. Although impossible to imagine at the time Bill was seated as a magistrate, the Democrats' exile would end with his election as mayor in November 1945. He would be the last New York City mayor to have been born in Ireland.

———

PERHAPS THE MOST lucrative position in Borough Hall during Paul's tenure as a young attorney in the Brooklyn courts was that of public administrator. This official was appointed by the borough's surrogate justice, whom the party in power selected. The administrator also named legal guardians to look after orphaned babies, incompetents, and widows, setting the fees; he was not required to be a lawyer.

In one measure of the position's—and the machine's—clout, local banks competed to be chosen as the repositories of the unclaimed inheritances, and whenever party leaders held a testimonial dinner in the ballroom of the St. George Hotel the bankers could be counted on to purchase several tables' worth of seats.[44] This was a reflection of the symbiotic nature of business and politics and what helped to make the borough fertile territory for shakedown artists and Prohibition-enriched gangsters. Louis ("Lepke") Buchalter and Jake ("Gurrah") Shapiro, two of the most successful Depression-era gangsters, were among dozens of criminals who operated both in Manhattan and Brooklyn as well as the Bronx. Each was targeted by Tom Dewey after Governor Lehman appointed him as special prosecutor to supersede the complacent Manhattan District Attorney William Dodge in 1935. Zealous in pursuit of gangland's bosses and their associates, Dewey brought indictments in more than one hundred industries, from trucking to baking to restaurants. His foot soldiers even brought Lucky Luciano out of his Waldorf Astoria apartment to face charges of running a prostitution ring, making him the highest-ranking mob boss ever prosecuted to that date. Luciano drew a prison term of thirty to fifty years from Philip J. McCook, the justice who swore La Guardia into office.[45]

La Guardia suspected that the Brooklyn machine might be even more felonious than Manhattan's Tammany Hall. To the extent that illegality thrived in the borough during the Depression—with gambling rings, loan-sharking, and protection rackets omnipresent—it was attributable in part to law enforcement officials' history of complacency. The climate was characteristic of the Depression years, a time when, according to labor historian Joshua Freeman, "gangsters and petty criminals were a daily presence, selling jobs and protection, stealing goods, taking bets, making loans, running racketeer unions, and acting as management goons."

"Murder is safe in Brooklyn," the Republican Dewey said in November 1938 as he competed, unsuccessfully, to succeed Governor Lehman, a Democrat. "Two of every three murders remain unsolved. Two out of every three murderers are never indicted . . . [and] walking the street, free men."[46]

Brooklyn's shortage of reform fervor was evident when a judge suspended the sentence of the leader of the "Affiliated Laundry Owners Club" in 1933. The club was a front for a multimillion-dollar racket that induced laundry owners to become paying members with vandalism and assault, including blinding attacks with battery acid. A jury in County Court found the leader, Jacob Mellon, guilty of racketeering, but another judge called off the sentencing and let him go free. The judge later claimed that Geoghan asked him to do it. The district attorney denied it.

Then, in March 1935, a group of Brooklyn cops responding to a report of a disturbance found the garroted body of Samuel Druckman in a Williamsburg garage. They also found three men with their hands and clothes stained by blood, along with murder weapons. Druckman, it emerged, worked for a mob-linked trucking firm from which he was siphoning funds to cover gambling losses. Taken away by the police, two of the blood-splattered men were owners of the firm. But when the case went before a grand jury, Geoghan found the evidence inadequate, and Druckman's alleged killers were let go. With other crimes going unprosecuted, La Guardia sent Police Commissioner Lewis Valentine over the Brooklyn Bridge to sniff around. Valentine went on to inform Geoghan that an acting detective sergeant had served as the "go-between" in the collection and disbursement of graft. Geoghan declined to seek a new indictment, with or without Valentine's demands for counts of complicity and bribery. This made Valentine steam. "What kind of crime do you have to commit in Brooklyn to obtain an indictment?" he commented to reporters—he later testified, "I urged him [Geoghan], I pleaded with him. I threatened him, I did everything but physically assault him."[47]

That December, Lehman took the rare step of appointing a special prosecutor to supersede Geoghan, and it took the special prosecutor—the decidedly mild-mannered and punctilious Hiram Todd—just six weeks to launch a murder trial that brought the convictions of Druckman's two killers. Todd also secured the indictment of ten local and state functionaries and an assistant district attorney's son. Todd's grand jury unilaterally went further, demanding Geoghan's removal for what it called his incompetence, negligence, and association with known crooks, particularly Leo Byck, whom authorities called the czar of the slot machine racket, as well as the professional gambler, mobster, and bookmaker Frank Erickson. The governor declined to remove Geoghan.[48] The latter never seemed too perturbed, even jesting during Todd's investigation that Brooklyn was so safe that his staff did not have enough to do.

Maybe it was possible to ignore the dark side of Brooklyn civic life. The borough was better known for half-sour pickles, Ebbets Field, and the Coney Island roller coaster than for crime and corruption. But Mayor La Guardia was not willing to turn a blind eye to what he quite correctly saw as an atmosphere of malfeasance-as-usual in the rival Democratic Party. The report of a special Citizens Committee on the Control of Crime in New York City, which the mayor had requested, showed prevalent irregularities based on a review of fourteen thousand cases. So, once again, Lehman superseded Geoghan, appointing Grover Cleveland's son-in-law, John Harlan Amen of Manhattan's Park Avenue, to investigate official malfeasance in the borough on an interim basis.[49] Though denounced as an aristocrat and unwarranted muckraker by at least two Brooklyn state judges, and bringing heat from Rev. Edward Lodge Curran, the editor of the closely read and influential borough diocesan newspaper *The Tablet* ("Why is Kings County picked out for attack?" he asked at a public event with District Attorney Geoghan), the Ivy League graduate and former Marine Corps Reserve Flying Corps pilot won 193 racket convictions. Amen was helped by a staff of sixty-eight lawyers on the second floor of Borough Hall, the former home of the appellate division.[50] In more than four years of investigations and trials, he secured convictions implicating cops, local magistrates, appellate court judges, assistant district attorneys, bookies, loan sharks, and a host of professional racketeers. The special prosecutor's attempts to prosecute the organized crime boss and businessman Joe Adonis for a 1932 abduction, extortion, and assault fell apart, however, when successive juries failed to convict the mobster's alleged accomplice, whom the prosecutor had hoped to turn into a cooperative witness.[51]

In his final report, investigator Amen named one of the chapters after a revealing remark made by District Attorney Geoghan after La Guardia first directed a city investigations commissioner to investigate every city agency: "Why pick on Brooklyn?"[52]

"Corruption was hardly corruption, it was tradition," Amen summed up. "It wasn't organized. It was patronized. . . . Everybody of the small group that controlled Brooklyn civic and legal interests knew everybody else. Irregularity was based upon precedent."[53]

BEFORE AMEN'S PROBE had even begun, Bill O'Dwyer was deriving special satisfaction from his service as a magistrate in the local courthouse in Brownsville and later Coney Island. He invoked the spirit of populism that President Roosevelt was then investing in the New Deal, mixed with the folksiness of a small-town justice of the peace. His Solomon-like use of his gavel made a favorable impression on Paul, who still "clung to my Irish clannishness." Bill excused poor Russian Jewish and Italian peddlers hit with police summonses while also asking them to accept that cops were not harassing them, as they claimed, but just doing their job.

Bill also distinguished himself, much to Paul's liking, by refusing to levy fines against working men ticketed for wearing topless bathing attire on the Coney Island beach. Magistrate O'Dwyer asked why those coming before him should be held to outmoded standards of Victorian propriety when the pugilists in the ring were permitted to fight shirtless before boxing fans. Not everyone cheered the judge's sentiments. "Judge O'Dwyer, I hope, would not be happy to find his near and dear relatives among those who voluntarily attend prize fights, burlesque shows or near-nudist exhibitions such as a certain element of the population are fond of enjoying," wrote L. E. O'Toole of Brooklyn in a letter to *The Tablet*, which had an outsize role in New York politics as the house organ of the Brooklyn-Queens Diocese.[54]

The magistrate also earned the gratitude of striking *Brooklyn Daily Eagle* reporters and the displeasure of the publisher M. Preston Goodfellow, not to mention the owners of the nine Manhattan dailies, by showing leniency toward these picketers. A key avenue to the judge was Clifford Evans, an *Eagle* reporter making three dollars a week after a few years at the paper. He had gotten to know Bill personally while writing for a community weekly in Bay Ridge, where Bill lived in one-half of a two-family brick house with Kitty, his wife. During the 1937 strike, a deputy police inspector had allowed cops on horseback to charge the strike line outside the *Eagle* building at Johnson and Adams Streets. Evans did not hesitate to feel out Bill, at the request of some of his colleagues, about receiving the cases of those who daily were pulled off the picket lines and arrested.

"There was a feeling that Bill O'Dwyer would have the measure of courage and would be sympathetic to a labor situation of this sort, and would I call him at home, as his friend, and because his telephone number was unlisted? I called him and he immediately said, 'Yes,'" recalled Evans. Bill, it turned out, believed Goodfellow had the strikers arrested in anticipation of the fines that judges typically meted out to pickets. He did not require the reporters to pay a fine and released them to the custody of their attorney. The reporters promptly returned to the picket line, with their union's scant resources remaining intact. The newspaper strike lasted sixteen weeks, forcing Goodfellow to come to terms with Heywood Broun and his guild.[55]

One day, a group of picketers who were brought before Bill included none other than Oscar Bernstien's wife, Becky, a member of the League of Women Shoppers. She and several other female consumer activists were placed in a lockup after supporting workers at May's Department Store picketing for higher pay. Bill, draped in his judicial robe, forgave the exercise of free citizens' First Amendment rights. Another time, the judge cooperated with one of the earliest labor law firms of the era, Boudin, Cohn & Glickstein, which represented many labor cases in Brooklyn's magistrates' courts, in devising a plan to cut out the role of the often-corrupt courthouse bondsman. The judge began accepting the signature of defendants as insurance that they would return for trial, with their bail amount determined ahead of time based on the nature of the offense.[56]

Like Paul, reporter Evans became an admirer of Bill O'Dwyer. After graduating to political columnist at the *Eagle*, he bumped into Bill near the Fourth Avenue precinct station house and Bay Ridge magistrate's court, a popular spot for cops, reporters, judges, and politicians. The judge, he recalled, waxed fulsome about a prizefighter who had been his favorite, Packey McFarland, a boxer he described as graceful on defense, capable of slipping in punches out of nowhere. "And the next thing I know, there was O'Dwyer on his feet, and O'Dwyer was not sylph-like, ever, and yet, amazingly enough, on the balls of his feet he could move very quickly and very gracefully—and then O'Dwyer had his hands out, and he was showing me, and doing it with his left and right and with legwork, how Packey used to fight . . . and with grace which I'd never seen in him."[57]

BY 1937, as Paul worked as a criminal defense lawyer, Magistrate O'Dwyer hoped to advance up the judicial ladder. He was making a comfortable $12,000 a year when his wife, Kitty, at home in Bay Ridge, began to suffer more and more from what would be diagnosed as an incurable neurological disorder; she needed operations and nursing care beyond the day-to-day help and companionship provided by a young African American woman named Edna Davis, who became an employee and a friend of the family.

Bill discussed his future prospects with the public administrator turned Democratic leader Frank Kelly, the late Democratic boss McCooey's successor. The borough's Republican boss, John Crews, whom Bill knew better, had encouraged him to get in touch with Kelly. With the scandals surrounding District Attorney Geoghan's office weighing on his mind, Kelly met Bill at his office. A few weeks later, at the Venetian-style Montauk Club off Brooklyn's Grand Army Plaza, Kelly disclosed that he had decided to recommend O'Dwyer for a vacancy on the county court and to sponsor him for election to the seat's fourteen-year term of office. But Bill would first have to agree to turn right around and run, in 1939, to succeed Geoghan, the continuing target of La Guardia's anti-corruption crusade. "An independent these days seems to have an edge," Kelly indicated. That was certainly true if the independent had the backing of the leader of the Democratic machine.[58]

Bill accepted these arrangements. (When, come 1949, *Mayor* Bill O'Dwyer told President Harry Truman that he would run for reelection despite health problems—and again in 1950, when he abruptly resigned as mayor and became the US ambassador to Mexico—it may have been preceded by a handshake deal similar to the one he consummated with Kelly.) By Bill's own account, in any case, Kelly and himself came to this understanding: Bill would leave the $25,000-a-year county judge's seat as the handpicked candidate for Brooklyn district attorney, a $20,000-a-year position of prominence. "I knew I was a pawn, but Oscar Bernstien said it was the only way for me," Bill remembered.[59] He would soon be named the grand marshal of the 1938 St. Patrick's Day parade and Brooklyn Citizen of Year, further eclipsing, and even awing, his youngest sibling.

Of course, the political and legal world in Brooklyn depended on unstated hierarchies and private handshakes, as both Bill and, by now, Paul understood. But the elder O'Dwyer could not help but signal his aversion to being someone's—or anyone's—servant. He made clear his feelings in the 1938 regular election for the county justice seat by arranging through a friend in the GOP organization to induce the Gowanus Republican district leader Harold Turk to enter the GOP primary in order to help his own chances. Turk agreed to square off against the La Guardia–endorsed labor lawyer Louis Waldman for the GOP nomination. Waldman was one among a number of left-wing assemblymen who were prevented from assuming their seats in Albany in 1919 because of their Socialist Party affiliation. Turk defeated Waldman on the GOP line in the judicial primary, so Waldman could only use the American Labor Party line in the general election, in which Bill prevailed over his two opponents.[60] In other words, Bill's unilateral electoral machinations worked. But there was a problem: the machinations were conducted without the knowledge or approval of Appellate Division Justice John Johnston, who, while virtually unknown by Brooklyn voters, was the chief strategist of the Brooklyn machine and the power behind the thrones of McCooey and Kelly. The one thing Johnston apparently could not abide was insubordination. "You will be advised to leave the political decisions to those who know them best," the jurist scolded Bill. Mortified, Bill turned to Bernstien and Paul. His informal advisers told him to hold his tongue. He followed this instruction, though, as he later put it, "one of the two who had offered that sage advice could hardly be considered a successful practitioner of the art."[61]

After gaining front-page attention for some big cases in which he presided, County Judge O'Dwyer ran as promised for election to district attorney and won easily, assuming the post in January 1940 and going on to garner national acclaim prosecuting and sending to the electric chair the members of a predominantly Jewish gang of mobster-hired killers that the press dubbed "Murder Incorporated." His celebrated smashing of the slum-area murder ring would serve as his successful launchpad to the New York City mayoralty in 1945. But in failing to have prosecuted or even questioned Albert Anastasia, one of the era's most feared organized crime figures, Bill as district attorney would stir up a cloud of ethical questions about himself that shadowed him for the rest of his days. Paul, who in contrast maintained a seldom-questioned reputation for integrity, would rally to his brother's defense at this juncture, as in others.

———

BY THE TIME he was married, Paul had a handful of labor unions as his clients, representing hod carriers, who hauled bricks for bricklayers; "sand-hogs," who bored the underwater tunnels deep underground; dock grain loaders; and warehouse workers, who made up the only racially integrated union on the waterfront. To the extent his services were needed for increasingly active and progressive American Federation of Labor (AFL) unions and their political work, he gravitated to them and to left-wing politicians who supported New York's trade union movement.[62] He was making about $20,000 a year, a very respectable and comfortable income.

The fiercer elements of New York's trade labor movement were attracted to the American Labor Party (ALP), the country's only significant labor party before or since. Created in 1936, the ALP ballot line allowed unionists to vote for both the Democratic Roosevelt for president and the Republican-Fusion La Guardia for mayor at the same time.[63] Behind the party's formation were labor leaders Max Zaritsky of the United Hatters, Cap, and Millinery Workers International Union, David Dubinsky of the International Ladies Garment Workers' Union, and Sidney Hillman of the Amalgamated Clothing Workers of America—all household names in the working-class firmament of New York. Behind *them* were the Roosevelt operatives Ed Flynn of the Bronx and Democratic Party Chairman James Farley, who saw the benefits of a third-party line for the president's reelection.

Alex Rose of the hatmakers' union became the party secretary and main political strategist of the ALP, helping it capture, in that first year, 275,000 votes for Roosevelt's reelection in New York. The ALP line also helped Lehman defeat the Republican crime-buster and GOP gubernatorial candidate Dewey in 1938. The ALP pulled the Democratic Party to the left as it struggled with the effects of the Great Depression and kept far-left voters within the larger New Deal fold. For Paul, the ALP's focus on economic insecurity for immigrants and the working class squared with his own developing point of view.

In time, however, the ALP found itself split into two factions. One was left-wing and tolerant of Communists, a force in the labor movement; the other was right-wing and unwilling to accept what they regarded as influence by Moscow. Paul was still taking the left-wing, and Communist-tolerant, position when, by the mid-1940s, it was wholly unwelcome in socially conservative Irish American circles. At a Sunday afternoon meeting of the Ancient Order of Hibernians division he had started in the Park Slope section, where he then lived after moving with Kathleen from their first apartment together on Plaza Street, he voted against a resolution to condemn the Irish-born leader of the Transport Workers Union, Michael Quill, as being too closely allied with the Communist Party (in light of the strong role played by Communists in the union). Paul was not only defending free speech but also speaking up for someone who, as a young man during the Irish War of Independence, carried a gun as a volunteer for the Irish Republican Army. After the war, Quill immigrated to America and found work as a New York subway changemaker, earning an appalling seventy cents an hour. But the republican physical-force movement in Ireland had introduced him to the concept of militant industrial labor unions, especially that of James Connolly, who went from helping to organize the Industrial Workers of the World (or Wobblies) in the United States to cofounding, with James Larkin, the Irish Labor Party in 1912 and finally helping to lead the Easter Rising, for which Connolly was executed, bound and seated, by British guns.[64]

Becoming a major labor activist in New York, Quill was high-spirited, blunt, and as quick with ridicule as Mayor La Guardia himself, especially when it came to parsimonious traction company executives and conservative, anti-labor politicians. Like New York itself, the massive bus and subway workers' union Quill organized in collusion with other transit workers in the secretive Clann na Gael amounted to a rough-hewn kettle of Irish nationalists, Communist activists, and militant laborers. O'Dwyer became Quill's lifetime personal lawyer and friend, the two bound not only by their shared Irish past but also by mutual belief that a person's political affiliation or activities should never be allowed to interfere with the right to speak out or organize working people.[65]

A second motion that same Sunday gave O'Dwyer a chance to express his mortification over the increasingly antisemitic broadcasts of Father Charles Coughlin, the American "radio priest" of Royal Oak, Michigan, who was bent on keeping the Roosevelt administration from intervening against Adolf Hitler. While the anti-Quill resolution had brought one other dissenting vote in addition to his own, this time Paul was alone in dissent. "The liberalism I was espousing had become embarrassing even to my friends," Paul wrote in his memoirs. His willingness to defend the constitutional rights of radicals opened the door to his involvement with the prolabor left of New York. By the 1940s—more than a year before Roosevelt wore down the Coughlin-cheered isolationists in Congress and the forces of Imperial Japan attacked Pearl Harbor, setting the stage for US intervention in World War II—Paul was fully swept up by the trade union movement and its socialist underpinnings.

Aggressive trade unions such as those in Manhattan's Garment District—the square-mile hub of most US clothing and textile manufacturing—had long fought against being marginalized but were thwarted by the power of industry to sway Congress and by judges whose rulings served to curb unionism on behalf of commerce and trade. But when unregulated industrial capitalism foundered in America and worldwide, Roosevelt brought federal relief and governmental action to suffering Americans on an unheard-of scale. Cornered by the worsening Depression, Congress passed and Roosevelt signed the National Industrial Recovery Act. Critically, for labor, the 1933 measure made it clear that employees, predominantly immigrants and women, had the legal right to organize and bargain collectively through representatives of their own choosing.

Two years later, the National Labor Relations Act, known as the Wagner Act after its sponsor, US Senator Robert Wagner of New York, created enforcement machinery to safeguard labor rights. Under the measure, the National Labor Relations Board certified unions as collective bargaining agents. It was a "Magna Carta of Labor," clearing the way for hundreds of new unions and millions of new rank and file to arise, unchallenged until a Republican-led Congress passed the Taft-Hartley Act of 1947 over President Truman's veto.[66]

But not even the landmark New Deal legislation of 1935 was enough to protect labor leaders against the power of big business and Americans' ready fear of the equivalent of the Bolshevik Revolution on US soil. They needed the help of constitutional lawyers such as Louis Boudin, the author of studies on the US Supreme Court's history of First Amendment rulings and the applicability of Marxist theory to American law. The aging and almost blind Boudin liked and respected Oscar Bernstien and, in 1940, hired his young partner on Bernstien's suggestion to assist his firm's defense of the radical Fur and Leather Workers Union. Paul was given the job of defending the president of the union, Ben Gold, an avowed Communist, in a case that in some ways presaged the anti-communist witch hunts of the coming Cold War, the period that would involve O'Dwyer even more heavily in the defense of lawyers, union leaders, and others who became the targets of government suppression and public hysteria.

The son of a jeweler, Gold emigrated with his parents in 1910 from czarist Russia, where Jews suffered pogroms, were forced to pay higher taxes, and were barred from serving in government posts or owning farms. Starting out in the New World as a twelve-year-old machine operator in a leather and fur manufacturing shop, he became two years later a member of the Furriers Union of the United States and Canada (which later changed its name to the International Fur Workers Union of the United States and Canada, or IFWU), as well as the Socialist Party of America (SPA). He was part of a group that broke off from the SPA to form the Communist Labor Party of America in 1919 and rose to a position of influence in the party and his union.

Before Louis Boudin brought O'Dwyer over to the defense table for the furriers' union, and even before the Great Depression, the furriers' union had distinguished itself with strikes in 1926 and 1927. Its thousands of members worked for the small and large sweatshops that crowded the Garment District. When the workers poured into the streets to protest their insecure seasonal peonage, they were perhaps the best-dressed picketers in the history of labor activism in their trim overcoats and fedoras, suits, and ties, and some of the most aggressive as well. The furriers were initially challenged by resistance to their massive strikes by the more conciliatory AFL and Calvin Coolidge's thoroughly probusiness US Department of Labor. The union also drew violent attacks from gangsters hired by garment manufacturing employers. To fend off the thuggery, it invented a self-defense squad composed of union members—not gangsters, who other unions sometimes employed for dirty work. But picketers were nevertheless arrested en masse, targeted with harassment by the New York City Police Department's Industrial Squad under Mayor Jimmy Walker. The police squad's violence was noticed by the *New York Times* reporter A. C. Sedgwick, who was covering a rally by thousands of furriers' union members in mid-Manhattan. "One detective," he reported, "takes a piece of rubber hose, which is part of the equipment of the detectives' bureau and is favored because it leaves no marks. Another takes out his blackjack. Others grab for anything—blackjacks and night-sticks. The prisoners fall to the floor. The blood pours from their faces. They spit and cough blood."[67]

In February 1940, intertwined forces seeking to upend Gold's union came to a head—Gold was indicted in federal court in Manhattan along with two dozen other furriers' union officers under the Sherman Anti-Trust Act, a statute dating back to 1890 aimed at big business, not labor unions. At the time the case was brought, the furriers' union was no longer in the AFL; it had become part of the far more aggressive Congress of Industrial Organizations (CIO), led by John L. Lewis.

The government's case against the union's Communist leaders was an outgrowth of strike-related violence of the 1930s. However, while indictments against the leaders were handed down initially in 1933, prosecutors in the Roosevelt administration's Justice Department did not bring the case to trial until 1939, alleging that the New York union had engaged in a conspiracy to thwart interstate commerce by organizing a manufacturing shop in Newark, New Jersey. The trial lasted for weeks. During the proceedings, a witness testified under questioning by O'Dwyer that an assistant US attorney had sworn falsely to testimony implicating Gold—a win for the defense. O'Dwyer also elicited testimony on the Newark shop's working conditions, including hourly wages as low as twenty-five cents and electrical hazards requiring women to wear rubber boots. The judge, however, struck the comments from the record, calling them "irrelevant."[68] In all, the defense called seventy-five witnesses, and the government brought sixty to the stand.

"Throughout the trial, it became evident that the government authorities were determined to use the anti-trust laws to deprive trade unions of their constitutional right to strike and to organize," according to a laudatory and comprehensive history of the union by Philip Foner, published in 1950. In all, eleven union leaders were found guilty in the trial and sentenced to jail time. Gold drew a prison term of one year and a

$2,500 fine, comparable to the sentences incurred by his associates.[69] Still dissatisfied, the Justice Department issued a new indictment six days later, charging the union leaders with obstruction of justice and influencing government witnesses. O'Dwyer remained with the defense team. This time, Gold was not convicted, while four other defendants from the union were.[70] The rank and file hailed all of them for their militancy and returned them to office. For O'Dwyer, they were noteworthy. Although the Roosevelt administration was prolabor, Paul may have regarded the trial of leaders in the Communist-led union as politically motivated, since the Communist Party opposed Roosevelt and US involvement in the war during its early stages, starting with the signing of the Soviet-German nonaggression pact in August 1939.

Paul's participation in the federal trial brought him to the attention of J. Edgar Hoover at the FBI. That was not known to him at the time, and in fact he was caught up with planning his move to Manhattan. The provincial atmosphere of Brooklyn's Irish enclaves and political culture had come to feel stultifying, and his and Kathleen's first two children, Bill and Eileen, would soon be starting school. Kathleen began looking for an apartment near a good Catholic school, zeroing in on a building on the Upper West Side of Manhattan.

Coincidentally, Holmes & Bernstien had suffered a shock when Frank Holmes died in a fall from his Court Street office twenty-three stories up. The tragedy—in October 1938—occurred on a morning in which the senior partner had conferred with Paul about the Forte death penalty case, and his secretary had observed him breezing through the office with what she described as a cheerful demeanor. Whether or not his death was accidental was never determined. Married but childless, Holmes was dead at sixty-seven.[71]

The firm was renamed O'Dwyer & Bernstien after his funeral, marking a professional milestone for Paul.

In still another point of transition in Paul's life, Bill's election as Brooklyn district attorney came in November 1939. Bill's high-profile role brought with it a conflict of interest concern for O'Dwyer & Bernstien in the Brooklyn state courts with regard to the immediate prospect of representing clients prosecuted by the office of Paul's brother. The partners therefore relocated—to the fifty-sixth floor of 40 Wall Street. Paul began his work there on the defense of Ben Gold and the other furriers. "I had no wish to be engaged in practice across the street from the district attorney's office," he explained.[72]

Nor did it make sense for him to continue making Brooklyn his home. For a tireless lawyer with deepening progressive ideas and political ambitions of his own, recentering himself and his family across the Brooklyn Bridge was liberating.

4

Tests of Loyalty

O N NOVEMBER 24, 1940, some 2,500 people in New York answered the call to attend a gathering on the future of Ireland in World War II. The meeting, held at the Tuxedo Ballroom on Madison Avenue and Fifty-Ninth Street, was meant to show a united front of support for the fledgling state's position of neutrality in the face of growing British pressure to bring Ireland into the battle against Nazi Germany's forces. But the opposite of comity resulted, surprising the event sponsor, the American Friends of Irish Neutrality (AFIN).

Indeed, the late afternoon event got off on the wrong track, with extremists of one stripe or another flowing in, including supporters of the pro-Hitler American Bundists, and using their voices to drown out the Irish republicans and nationalists also in attendance. Supporters of the antisemitic "radio priest" Father Charles Coughlin were also on hand, hellbent on being heard.

The AFIN president was James O'Brien, a Fordham professor. Paul was the chair of the group and the event. The meeting's organizer, Charles Connolly, the founding publisher and editor of the *Irish Echo*, had promoted the meeting with house ads quoting the prime minister of Ireland Eamon de Valera's statement that "all people interested in assisting Mother Ireland in preserving her neutrality" should attend given Winston Churchill's efforts to convince US leaders to pressure Ireland to lend her southern ports to the war effort. England was mobilizing 250,000 troops in the wake of the September 1939 invasion of Poland by German troops that prompted France, and Britain, to declare war on Germany.[1]

The question was brought home to a New York ballroom usually known for swing orchestras: Connolly was not able to quiet the audience, and nor was O'Dwyer. With anti-Jewish comments flying all around, Paul shouted that everyone had a right in America to express their individual point of view but must do so respectfully. Throwing up his hands, he turned the floor over to a Catholic priest named Father O'Leary, but the cleric insulted the Jewish religion and Great Britain, saying both were "at the bottom of the barrel," and had harsh words, too, for the pro-British deference of the *New York Times*.[2]

Finally, O'Dwyer summoned ten former Irish Republican Army (IRA) men, members of the Transport Workers Union, from the back of the room. These toughs, who were on hand at the request of Paul's friend, the North Cork–born Sean Keating—an AFIN founding member—walked toward the dais, glaring at the jeerers as if daring them to try something.[3]

When the mayhem ended, Paul and his AFIN cohorts seriously doubted their ability to make an impact on American public opinion with the new organization. On top of that, Paul wanted nothing to do with the anti-Jewish strains in the American isolationist movement vocalized that evening. So, with the bombing of Pearl Harbor over a year later and the US mobilization, Paul's AFIN faded to dark—and his focus and that of most Irish Americans turned toward US patriotism and direct participation in the Allied forces, Britain included.[4] In a controversial juggling act, de Valera kept the Irish government neutral even after the German bombardment of London between September 1940 and May 1941.[5] Remaining on the fence was not only critical to the republic's security, as the prime minister and his majority Fianna Fáil party saw it, but also an assertion of Ireland's sovereignty.

For all the German aerial bombings de Valera may have saved Ireland from, Franklin D. Roosevelt and Churchill resented what they saw as Ireland's accommodation of the Third Reich, and this would long complicate Washington's relations with Dublin. The damage to US-Irish ties took decades to unknot for Irish Americans seeking Washington's help for their divided ancestral land. Like de Valera, O'Dwyer saw southern Ireland's wartime posture as an unavoidable matter of national survival.

"One raid from the Luftwaffe would have made a shambles of all of Ireland," he wrote.[6]

––––––––––

IN 1942, Paul responded to a draft board notice that came in the mail to the family's Upper West Side apartment, where they had just moved after leaving their former home on Prospect Park West in Brooklyn; their eldest son, Bill, was six, Eileen was four, and Rory was one. (Brian, the fourth and last child, would arrive before the end of 1945 and was the favorite of his maternal grandmother, Mary Rohan, who was living with the family after the death of her husband.) On St. Patrick's Day, Paul underwent a physical ordered by the draft board and passed it. But a few weeks after the physical, the army lowered the maximum draft age to twenty-five. Paul's induction was derailed, as he was thirty-four. "Rejection produced mixed emotions in me and a sigh of relief from Kathleen," he recalled.[7] As an eventual total of three million GIs began shipping out from New York, the able-bodied O'Dwyer signed up with the Sixty-Ninth Regiment of the National Guard, the Manhattan regiment known as the "Fighting 69th" due to its acclaimed engagement in the US Civil War. But his attachment to the regiment lasted just a "very short period" before he and his fellow trainees were discharged without being called up for service—yet not so briefly as to preclude his receiving, several years later, an official military letter in the mail "thanking me for winning the war." The perfunctory letter aroused in him a chuckle.[8]

Paul in the war years threw himself into new battles to shape public opinion, representing, for example, the grandson of Jeremiah O'Donovan Rossa, the revolutionary Irish political leader of the late nineteenth and early twentieth centuries. Having filled a rotation as the president of the United Irish Counties Association, which coordinated social and cultural activities of the thirty-two counties in New York, O'Dwyer helped organize a letter-writing campaign to free young Jeremiah from a four-year prison sentence for military insubordination. The campaign marked a rare success, as General Dwight Eisenhower downgraded Jeremiah's death sentence and the clemency board freed the court-martialed soldier. O'Donovan Rossa III had landed in the clink for disobeying an order to dig ditches in the North African theater of conflict following verbal scrapes with superiors.[9] Paul viewed his release as remarkable, saying it was the first time the army had ever set aside a soldier's dishonorable discharge.

The episode also demonstrated for him that Irish America harbored political clout when it worked in unison.

The attorney's clients during the war included ardent IRA supporters in New York who did not want to serve in the Allied forces due to their feelings about Great Britain. But he also represented a pair of affluent New York men who had no apparent reason for resisting their induction notice other than the instinct to steer clear of the battlefield. Relying on his wiles rather than facts or the law, O'Dwyer won their case with an outpouring of humor and humility, mollifying a justice of the United States District Court for the Eastern District whom he had likely previously encountered. In Justice Robert Inch's wood-paneled chambers, Paul pleaded guilty to the crime of hubris for having advised his clients that their conviction for draft evasion in a lower court was flawed and likely the result of wartime hysteria. The defendants faced the possibility of up to a year in prison—so what, then, was their lawyer to say or do now except admit that he had gone too far?

"Pride goeth before a fall," O'Dwyer told the judge.

Turning around to face the window, Paul remembered, Inch could be heard "barely controlling his laughter." The jurist placed the two shirkers on probation.[10]

THROUGHOUT THE DEPRESSION, the New York Jewish American community viewed President Roosevelt as well as Mayor Fiorello La Guardia as dual champions in a country awash with antisemitism. La Guardia's denunciations of the Nazi führer compensated, in a way, for Roosevelt's strategic incrementalism in seeking to overcome an anti-Jewish isolationist wing in Congress often given to thinly veiled antisemitism, and his attendant reticence over the growing persecution of German Jewry.

Roosevelt made no secret of his fondness for the bane of corrupt Tammany officials and mob bosses in New York. For La Guardia, the feeling was mutual.

"Our mayor is probably the most appealing person I know," Roosevelt once enthused. "He comes to Washington and tells me a sad story. The tears run down my cheeks, and tears run down his cheeks, and the first thing I know, he has wangled another fifty million dollars."[11] With the addition of hundreds of new schools, hospitals, cultural venues, and parks, La Guardia was tirelessly laying the groundwork for modern New

York and making provisions for its poorer citizens in this most challenging of eras.

The pugnacious, pint-sized La Guardia pitched public works projects and made regular pleas for a larger share of New Deal largesse, citing the enormous needs of his depleted 7.5-million-person metropolis, the nation's largest city. As a result, New York became the only large city, in the hands of an ally, that the president allowed to administer its own federal Works Progress Administration public works programs to foster employment. The city also drew a much larger slice of Washington's assistance than any other. "At the start of his administration, La Guardia had to beg for home rule from Albany to straighten out a $30 million budget crisis," the La Guardia biographer Thomas Kessner wrote. "Two years later, he was negotiating directly with Washington for ten times that amount."[12]

One of the first major public figures in America to denounce Hitlerism, La Guardia stayed close to the more cautious and calculating White House as Hitler's military aggression and scapegoating of Jews grew more pronounced and diabolical. After the German war machine rolled into Czechoslovakia in the spring of 1939, La Guardia inveighed against isolationists in Congress, whom he called backers of Nazi Germany, and strongly endorsed Roosevelt's proposal to relax US neutrality on Great Britain's behalf, though the initial measure was rejected by the Senate Foreign Relations Committee by a vote of 12–1. After the German invasion of Poland on September 1, 1939, La Guardia openly broke with Republicans who were seeking a "peace candidate" to prevent Roosevelt's election to a third term.[13]

While Paul, also an admirer of Roosevelt, might have been expected to be simpatico with the president's progressive and pluralistic city hall ally, he often was not. For one thing, O'Dwyer was a progressive Democrat, whereas La Guardia was a progressive Republican, albeit supported by the left-wing American Labor Party (ALP). Paul also was put off by La Guardia's endless streams of invective and bombast against foes real or perceived. He resented La Guardia's opposition to letting the city government recognize the collective bargaining rights of public employees.

For O'Dwyer, too, the mayor's clampdown on the city's burlesque houses, Italian American organ grinders, and church bingo games smacked of grandstanding and infringements on constitutionally protected rights. That the La Guardia administration police force failed to break up the wartime harassment of Jewish New Yorkers along Eastern Parkway in

Brooklyn, upper Manhattan, and parts of the Bronx by the Christian Front was just as irksome. Not only did La Guardia shy away from calling out Benito Mussolini for fear of alienating fellow Italian New Yorkers, but he also ignored the young fascists who unnerved Jewish New Yorkers in their own backyards.

Paul, in contrast, spoke out unequivocally against the Christian Front after a mob smashed windows of Jewish-owned shops and chanted about hanging Jews from Brooklyn lampposts. Moreover, he helped convince his politician brother to do the same, enabling the county judge turned Brooklyn district attorney to differentiate himself from the sitting mayor he hoped one day to succeed.

The deeper reason Paul failed to appreciate La Guardia was undoubtedly related to Bill's decision to be the county Democratic bosses' candidate to run against La Guardia in the 1941 mayoral contest. Paul jumped in as a volunteer operative to help his brother's long-shot mayoral campaign, most significantly by trying to convince the ALP to endorse the Democrat nominee and to drop the Republican-Fusion incumbent.

As an important third party since 1936, the ALP had proven vote-getting ability and was the electoral spearhead for labor leaders like Sidney Hillman and David Dubinsky closely tied to Roosevelt and the New Deal. But Bill's links to the Brooklyn Democratic organization and Tammany Hall made ALP officials somewhat uneasy—many did not want a role in putting Tammany back in the saddle at city hall. It fell to Paul, who counted several trade unions in New York among his clients, to win the ALP over.

Paul began the uphill effort by approaching a group of political operatives from the ALP and the Congress of Industrial Organizations (CIO). His entrée was Eugene Connolly, a left-wing city councilman whom Paul had represented the year before in addition to the Transport Workers Union president Austin Hogan and nine taxi drivers. The drivers, who were then trying to establish a union for hacks, were charged with beating up another driver in a Bickford's cafeteria-style restaurant. No weapons were brandished, no serious injuries sustained. O'Dwyer's arguments in their criminal case were largely successful.[14]

For that reason, in part, Connolly felt comfortable welcoming Paul to an unofficial gathering with party officials in the summer of 1941. While most ALP supporters, including its pro-Communist wing, said they were satisfied with La Guardia—their appreciation for his support of US intervention in the war had only deepened when the Soviet Union was invaded by Germany that June—O'Dwyer stressed that the mayor was "less than helpful" to municipal unionism, a conclusion difficult to dispute. He raised other local concerns, such as poor housing conditions, in urging the party to drop Fiorello and get behind Bill. But only Mike Quill, who believed Bill would be more likely to negotiate a wage contract with his Transport Workers Union, was willing to consider it. Paul had recently set up the Irish Citizens Committee to Support Collective Bargaining for Transit Workers to push for collective bargaining for thirty-two thousand bus and train workers on the public payroll. But the La Guardia protégé US Rep. Vito Marcantonio of East Harlem, among other ALP leaders present, indicated that he was not on board with Paul.

Bill, well known to city residents for breaking up "Murder Incorporated," a band of mob-directed killers-for-hire in the slums of Brooklyn, faced an even larger obstacle to his election: the city's Democratic bosses were giving his candidacy lip service and little help. President Roosevelt was the all-but-announced backer of La Guardia's reelection, and the Democratic bosses on both sides of the East River fully expected the incumbent to capture a third term. Still, a Democratic president's indifference to the *Democratic* nominee bothered Paul, striking him as a matter of disloyalty to their party. The bosses' behavior was just as bad.

As La Guardia went through the motions of declaiming "boss rule"—a dependable campaign-season bugaboo—he also secured the backing of Thomas Dewey, of Democratic Party reformers, and of many prominent labor leaders. In the contest's final weeks, Bill's punches, unlike those of Packey McFarland, the prizefighter admired by the district attorney, failed to make an impact. The Democrat criticized La Guardia for his failure to act against the Christian Front (for which antisemites branded Bill a "Jewish Irishman"). Bill also pointed out that La Guardia had illegally required city workers and welfare relief recipients to collect the voter signatures needed to appear on the ballot and had bottled up a report on the influence of Communist union organizers in the welfare department, all to little effect.[15]

Paul's advice to Bill was brushed aside as often as accepted, but Bill at least knew he could be trusted and he accepted some of his kid brother's suggestions and referrals into his campaign. Still, he was never as free to speak out as Paul. "Paul, of course, was 20 years [*sic*] younger than me," the elder O'Dwyer said years later, after retiring from public life, "and he had little patience for me because of compromises that I may have made. . . . Paul would not compromise. That's perhaps the difference between a successful politician and one who had to learn some things yet."[16]

For their own purposes, public figures and politicians periodically painted Paul as more influential than he actually was. Robert Moses, the baron of city reconstruction, had first encountered Paul in 1938, lacerating a grassroots plan for new housing for families of longshoremen dwelling in the ramshackle Brooklyn Navy Yard locale put forth by a citizen panel that Paul chaired.[17] Moses told the *Christian Science Monitor* in mid-1946 that the "radical side" in New York politics used Paul as a "lever" to influence Bill at city hall, adding in reference to Bill, "He had that family tie. It was a big temptation for him to waver toward the Left."[18]

In the subsequent Cold War years, New York officials approached by FBI agents dropped hints that Bill and Paul were surreptitiously disloyal to the United States. But a "high New York City official," also cited anonymously in FBI papers, threw cold water on this, saying Paul wielded no Svengalian influence over his brother or the mayor's appointees. For example, the interviewee said, the left-wing Paul Ross, though referred to Bill by Paul, was not particularly influential at city hall.

Another unidentified official the FBI interviewed said that Paul and Oscar Bernstien made up a "board of strategy" for Bill.[19] This, too, much overstated matters. As when Brooklyn's countywide Democratic leader Frank Kelly had Bill run with the party's backing for county judgeship on the condition he made the race for Brooklyn district attorney the following year, Bill conferred with Paul and Bernstien about important personal and even personnel considerations. But that was as far as it went when it came to Paul's supposed left-wing hold on his brother.

As loyal as the siblings were to each other, they were not immune to argument as Bill climbed the political ladder and wielded greater influence, with their periodic fallings-out sometimes lasting for months.[20] For Paul, the sore points that arose between them typically had to do with municipal labor issues or social legislation, or questions "on which," he said, "I felt he was not living up to the mandate of the forces that had elected him, in not going along with it."[21]

An instance of perhaps the sharpest policy divergence was Bill's decision as mayor to double the long-standing five-cent city subway fare to cover raises for Mike Quill's transit workers. The decision was made despite opposition from the ALP, which had endorsed Bill's second and successful bid for mayor. The 1948 fare hike proposal sparked liberal and left-wing fury, including from Paul, who, while supporting Quill's goal of higher wages for the bus and subway workers, saw the hike as a regressive tax: it asked the poorer classes to spend an average of $60 more of their $2,000 yearly household income.[22] Paul signed citizen petitions and flocked with hundreds of demonstrators to Albany to seek approval of a real estate tax increase from legislators and Governor Dewey (to no avail) in order to make a hike unnecessary. Ross resigned from the mayor's cabinet, drawing castigation from Bill. The New York chapter of the National Lawyers Guild (NLG; with Paul then serving as the chapter president) came out against the hike, too. In a public statement, the NLG chapter called for a 40 percent city-assessed rise in business taxes to cover needed transport-worker raises. But Bill got his way.[23]

THE ALP'S DECISION not to get behind Bill's candidacy in 1941 despite Paul's pleading was almost as disappointing to the younger O'Dwyer as what both siblings saw as Tammany Hall's two-facedness. Paul sensed that wooden speeches drafted by Judge John Johnston of the Kelly machine for Bill to deliver were leaked in advance to La Guardia, so he advised Bill to start delivering his own addresses, to much livelier effect.[24] But it was of little use, for as the 1941 election neared, Roosevelt delivered the clincher for La Guardia, declaring that the Little Flower had given the city "the most honest . . . most efficient municipal government of any." La Guardia responded with a single-word telegram: "Merci."[25] Bill knew his own campaign was finished. He told friends that while he could defeat Fiorello, he could not defeat *both* Fiorello and Roosevelt at the same time.[26] What was surprising, though, including to Paul, was how close Bill came to winning anyhow. It was not because of anything he did but rather because the irascible La Guardia went on the attack against a favorite son, Governor Lehman.

The puzzling onslaught began after Lehman delivered a pro forma endorsement of Bill. La Guardia confused the Democratic governor's gesture of partisanship toward his opponent with a power play, saying, "A politician will always remain a politician," and bemoaned Lehman's willingness to "lend his name to re-establish the 'tin box' politicians," harkening to Tammany's corruption under his predecessor, Jimmy Walker. "You have heard of gonifs stealing from gonifs," La Guardia railed. "Well, now you have the double crossers double-crossing the double crosser!"

Specifically, La Guardia alluded to a recent decision from a state appeals court panel whose members included Governor Lehman's brother, Irving, the panel's presiding judge. The court nullified the governor's appointment of an ALP official as acting state controller and ordered a special election. "Who's loony now?" asked La Guardia, though Lehman was not only exceedingly popular with Jewish voters but close with President Roosevelt, too. "Lehman or [Bronx Democratic boss Edward] Flynn or both? Boy oh boy, have I got them groggy." The mayor's unbalanced tirade drove Lehman supporters straight into the Democratic column, and La Guardia won the election by just 5.8 percentage points, one of the tightest finishes in a New York City mayoral contest since 1905. Bill's surprising finish set him up for his second try for mayor four years hence.

Paul was vexed rather than relieved, all the same. During his summer talks with the ALP, the party's leaders had allowed that they might be willing to let Bill compete in a primary contest for a spot on their ballot line—it would not simply be handed to him. So Paul went directly to Bill, getting him to ask Kelly and Democratic legislative leader Irwin Steingut for a $35,000 grant to pay for a third-party primary. However, Steingut and Kelly rebuffed Bill, and Bill put up no resistance.[27]

"I am convinced that, had he proceeded with the plan, Bill would have been elected mayor of New York in that year," Paul said long after his brother lost the election—or, as he put it in an oral history interview, "That year we could have knocked it over just like that."[28]

Perhaps. But the way the Democratic bosses treated his brother left a bad taste in his mouth that would linger much longer than his immediate frustration. "I didn't really know then that they were just pushing him up and really had no hopes of his winning," he said.[29]

———

DURING 1941, Bill, in anticipation of the mayoral race, declared, "I believe that the place for all crooks, whether pickpockets or politicians, is in jail."[30] But his handling of a major investigation by his district attorney's office into the brutal murder of Peter Panto—a dockworker who vanished while leading a dissident movement to clean up his violence- and graft-beset longshoremen's union—raised disturbing questions about the district attorney's willingness to solve the case or prosecute union officials and the mobster suspected in Panto's killing. The problematic aspects of Bill's investigation of the 1939 disappearance might have been expected to complicate Paul's personal policy of never criticizing Bill publicly, then or even after Bill's death following a heart attack in 1964. But when asked in a Columbia University oral history interview about this highly controversial phase of Bill's career—and whether Bill might have pulled punches to accommodate murderous gangsters tied to the Democratic Party—his unstintingly loyal younger brother, looking back, seemed to talk around the still-sensitive subject.[31]

Bill's actions as district attorney were in fact more suggestive of an opportunistic politician placing his own career advancement over the public interest than of the prosecutorial zeal of a Thomas Dewey or the professional resolve of Governor Lehman's special prosecutor in Brooklyn, Harlan Amen. The immigrant former construction worker seemed determined not to let the mystery surrounding the brutal silencing of a dissident longshoreman get in the way of his political career.

————

IN THE WAKE of Panto's disturbing 1939 disappearance on the Brooklyn waterfront, Bill took office as district attorney and began his remarkable 1940–41 probe of gangland murders that had taken place in the Jewish and Italian neighborhoods of Brownsville, East New York, and Ocean Hill.

The famous spate of gangbusting began when a gravely ailing inmate in the Rikers Island prison in Queens, Harry Rudolph, penned a note stating that Abe Reles, a little-known Brownsville hoodlum, and two of Reles's buddies, Martin Goldstein and Tony Maffetore, had murdered Rudolph's friend Alex Alpert back in 1933. Hearing that police were looking for them, Reles and Goldstein walked in voluntarily to the district attorney's office and began spilling the beans. They were followed by Maffetore, a criminal whom one of Bill's old friends from his days as a cop, the storied police detective John Osnato, had worked on in a Bronx jailhouse. (Osnato was known for having arrested a young Al Capone after a Christmas shooting of Irish criminals in Red Hook in 1925.) The detective reportedly had several talks with Maffetore, using his fluency in Italian and extensive knowledge of gangs around the city to bring him over.

The first of the Brownsville miscreants to cooperate with the district attorney's investigation, Maffetore implicated cohort Abe "Pretty" Levine in several murders. In turn, Levine was brought in and started talking, too. But only when Reles offered many particulars on dozens of older and recent killings was the picture of a large murder-for-hire enterprise discerned by investigators. Bill held a press conference to announce his discovery, revealing what he called a mob hit squad brought into existence by Louis "Lepke" Buchalter in 1929. He said it was responsible for hundreds of murders in his borough and beyond. The hit squad was the low-rent killing service of the notorious Garment District racketeer and his aides-de-camp in the field of terror-driven extortion, and was used, too, by some of Buchalter's high-ranking allies. A member of the press branded the operation "Murder Incorporated."

Louis Capone (unrelated to the Chicago Capone), who would later be pictured smiling en route to death row, was identified early by the O'Dwyer team as Buchalter's go-between to Murder Incorporated. Other law enforcement officials linked Meyer Lansky and Benjamin "Bugsy" Siegel to ordering the services of the squad, but it was Albert Anastasia who was said to be its immediate supervisor.

Lepke and other mob honchos paid for killings with cash and pinball machine concessions. But their payroll had too many poorly paid incorrigibles for the identity of the paymasters to remain a secret forever. Reles's steel-trap memory yielded up evidence against Buchalter, showing that he and several of his associates were involved in the 1936 murder of Joseph Rosen, a former garment trucking firm owner. Reles also testified that Irving ("Puggy") Feinstein, an ex-prizefighter involved in illegal gambling and labor racketeering, was murdered in 1939 on orders from Anastasia, his corpse set afire. Reles alleged Anastasia cued up the hit as a courtesy to Vincent Mangano Sr., who was thought to be in league with six nefarious longshoremen's union locals in Brooklyn operated by Emil Camarda. Anastasia allegedly took orders from the mob "Boss" Joe Adonis.

Throughout the proceedings, Reles was the prosecution's linchpin witness, uncannily recalling for the O'Dwyer probers the pervasive gangland violence and official corruption plaguing the borough, its waterfront piers and shipyards, political culture, and halls of justice. At the same time, Assistant District Attorney Burton Turkus, the estimable attorney whom Paul recommended to Bill for his legal team, drove a stunning series of guilty verdicts.[32] By the time the prosecutions were finished and the appeals knocked back, seven Murder Incorporated thugs went to the electric chair and—with the involvement of federal prosecutors and Thomas

Dewey—so did Buchalter himself, the first and only mob boss ever executed in the United States.

The gusher of courthouse wins arising from Abe Reles's uncanny powers of recollection and loose lips allowed District Attorney O'Dwyer to close the books, in all, on eighty-five Depression-era murders committed in Brooklyn and various other parts of the United States, many by Reles himself.

While the district attorney's investigation revealed the existence of a kind of nationwide "syndicate" or "combination" of mob bosses for the first time, Bill's handling of the mystery of Panto's disappearance was troubling and drew investigation after he left office by George Beldock— his August 1945 interim successor named by the then governor Dewey— as well as by Senator Estes Kefauver of Tennessee, Dewey's New York State Crime Commission, and other government panels. The problem for Bill was that despite Reles's statements linking Albert Anastasia to the vanishing and, he claimed to Bill, the murder of Panto, as well as to the fatal shooting of Morris Diamond, a trucking union official, Anastasia was never arrested nor even brought in for questioning in the eighteen months that Bill's star witness, Reles, remained in protective custody.

So when Bill resigned from the district attorney's office in the summer of 1945 to run for mayor for the second time, this time successfully, Acting District Attorney Beldock promptly empaneled a grand jury to consider the question of Bill's alleged laxity vis-à-vis the fearsome Anastasia. The suggestion to investigate Bill's tenure had apparently begun with Assistant District Attorney Burton Turkus (or so recalled Beldock's son, Myron, a noted New York criminal defense attorney, speaking about it many years later in his Manhattan law office while calling Turkus a "straight shooter in a minefield of cronyism.")[33]

Days before the mayoral election on November 6, 1945, the grand jury's findings were leaked, charging Bill with "gross laxity," "inefficiency," and "maladministration" of the district attorney's office. A wealthy businessman and former La Guardia assistant with aspirations to be mayor, Clendenin Ryan Jr., taped the grand jury presentment to an iron fence outside city hall. But the bombshell list of charges was too late to keep the high-flying O'Dwyer from winning his race and a record-setting plurality of 685,000 votes.

Beldock, a Republican, was running for a full term as district attorney when the presentment came out. When he lost his race, he returned to the grand jury and it handed down still another scathing presentment on Bill's record as district attorney.

Having refused to appear before the Beldock grand jury during the campaign, Bill turned up as the mayor-elect. In ten hours of testimony, he acknowledged that his district attorney's office was remiss for not having prosecuted Anastasia. But he did not accept blame for the lapse. He instead laid responsibility at the feet of Thomas Craddock Hughes, the assistant district attorney he chose to fill in for him temporarily when he left office on army leave in 1942. Hughes naturally did not take the criticism well, saying he had never heard from Bill about Anastasia, either before his leave of absence or after. The deputy asserted that Bill never indicated that taking down the alleged mob underboss whom reporters labeled as "the Lord High Executioner" was a priority.[34]

Paul kept his moral blinders on. When asked about the Beldock grand jury investigation in his Columbia University oral history interview, conducted in the early 1960s, he said Abe Reles might have been involved in Diamond's killing (some investigators in the district attorney's office had believed it so). Paul noted that it would not have been permissible for Reles to have taken the stand against Anastasia if that were true.

At the same time, Paul offered, Bill's departure for military service may have understandably blurred his recollections of the Murder Incorporated prosecutions. Paul noted, too, that Franklin Taylor, a Brooklyn judge, ordered the grand jury's initial presentment expunged after it was leaked on the 1945 election's eve. But the signature skepticism that O'Dwyer was known for was missing as he discussed his older brother's problematic probe—and possible cover-up—in connection with the brutal silencing of the dissident Panto and with the corrupt union leaders he had dared to criticize.[35]

While Panto was dead, and Anastasia free, Reles met his maker, shockingly and violently. On November 12, 1941, just after Bill lost his initial bid against La Guardia, the original mob stool pigeon leapt, slipped, fell, or, as some speculated, was hurled in predawn hours from a sixth-floor window at the Half Moon Hotel on Coney Island while under twenty-four-hour watch by a district attorney police squad. His clothed body was found on the kitchen roof extension of the seashore hotel, where the remaining state's witnesses slept in their locked rooms.

Bill excused the police officers assigned to watch Reles and would later attribute Anastasia's escape from prosecution or punishment for the killing of Morris Diamond to the death of his star witness. The case against the Lord High Executioner, he insisted, simply went out the window with Reles.

———

THOUGH PAUL'S LAW firm moved in late 1939 to a new address, on Wall Street, he could not keep from becoming involved, glancingly, in the corrupt Brooklyn political fabric and its waterfront cornerstone—the six International Longshoremen's Association (ILA) locals operated by the longshoremen's officer Emil Camarda. The ILA vice president Camarda worked in an office at the water's edge at 33 President Street. His inner circle included union cronies who were related to him or to one another by blood or marriage.[36]

Far from shying away from publicity, the pistol-packing leaders of Camarda's so-called Pistol Locals, which oversaw some fourteen thousand dock workers, flexed their muscle through the City Democratic Club; the club, formed in 1929, operated in a Clinton Street building owned by an Anastasia associate, Vincent Mangano. While Bill O'Dwyer was serving as a magistrate, a county judge, and the Brooklyn district attorney, the club was where "longshore union figures could do business with local mobsters under friendly cover of pinochle games," wrote Nathan Ward in his narrative history *Dark Harbor: The War for the New York Waterfront*. It hosted the yearly Columbus Day ball, held in Hotel St. George, Brooklyn Heights. In addition to drawing local politicians, judges, and businessmen, the event featured a program with full-page welcomes from Anastasia, Adonis, and other dishonorables. Decadent by Depression-era standards, the ballroom banquet was underwritten by the sale of thousands of useless tickets to more dockworkers than the five-hundred-person ballroom could possibly have accommodated. The dockers' purchases were a required down payment for regular pier work, lifted straight from the workers' pay envelopes.[37] The "tribute" extended to mandatory overpaying at selected barber shops, bars, and loan-sharking operations, while the work gang on the piers also shouldered extra physical burdens and risks to make up for "ghost" employees whose wages went into the pockets of union agents and hiring bosses.[38]

By the spring of 1939, Panto, an immigrant from southern Italy, had marshaled hundreds of rank-and-file members of the ILA to the cause of democratically reforming their union; he gave speeches demanding fair and honest union elections, inspired perhaps by Harry Bridges, the aggressive longshoremen's union leader of the West Coast. Bringing out as many as 1,100 rank-and-file longshoremen for stump speeches at the foot of Brooklyn Heights, Panto was allegedly summoned by Camarda for a sit-down with himself and fellow ILA local officials Constantino "Gus" Scannavino (Vincent Mangano Sr.'s brother-in-law) and Anthony "Tony Spring" Romeo. Camarda, whose own life would be cut short by a bullet in about a year's time, allegedly gave Panto some ominous-sounding advice: drop the rebel act, which the ILA president Joseph Ryan had labeled a Communist plot. "Some of the boys are unhappy," Camarda supposedly said.[39]

Panto lived with his fiancée and her brother in Fort Greene, opposite the sprawling Brooklyn Navy Yard. Though a hiring boss, he was driven by a desire for justice and fairness for the workers and not so easily cowed. Leaving home on July 14, 1939, he told his twenty-year-old wife-to-be, Alice Maffia, that he was going to see some unsavory people.

He was last seen climbing into Romeo's car after the confrontational meeting.[40]

Within days of the report of his disappearance, the Italian phrase "Dov'è Panto?" ("Where's Panto?") could be seen scrawled all over the waterfront. The Hearst syndicated columnist Walter Winchell, whose sources had helped reel in Buchalter after the mob boss had spent two years in hiding, wrote, "Police fear Pete is wearing a cement suit at the bottom of the East River." The *Daily Worker* reported that Panto was replaced on the docks by a subservient hiring boss and that workers were living in fear.[41]

Reles told Bill's investigators that Anastasia arranged Panto's silencing and, about a year and a half after the abduction, led the district attorney's diggers to the location of the activist-longshoreman's body, along the banks of the Passaic River near Lyndhurst, New Jersey. Panto's trussed-up corpse was coated in quicklime, a substance that the mob often used to disguise its victims. He had been strangled to death.[42]

Murder Incorporated's killings had transpired largely on La Guardia's watch, as Bill took pains to point out. But La Guardia was not oblivious to the lasting bewilderment that Panto's abduction created in Italian American enclaves while his body still lay undiscovered. A preliminary probe by the city Department of Investigation underscored the shadowy presence of Anastasia and associates Anthony Romeo and Gioacchino

Parisi. Evidence pointed to Parisi as having been Panto's hands-on "mugger."[43] But another Murder Incorporated informant, Albert "Tick Tock" Tannenbaum, stated that Mendy Weiss, a Buchalter associate, told him during a stroll around Prospect Park Lake after the discovery of Panto's body that the 165-pound longshoreman-activist—"some guy Albert had a lot of trouble with down in the waterfront"—had struggled fiercely with him to try to save his own life. Tannenbaum's account of this conversation with his "Combination" partner was taken down by investigators from Bill's office and placed in a filing cabinet. The transcript remained in a file drawer until the New York State Crime Commission fished it out thirteen years later.[44]

———

ONCE THE LA GUARDIA ADMINISTRATION'S Department of Investigation finished an initial probe of Panto's disappearance, it turned over its leads to Lehman special investigator Harlan Amen in early 1940. Amen went to work, subpoenaing the ledgers and records of the six waterfront locals led by Camarda.

This was the point when the Brooklyn Bridge proved too short a span to keep Paul O'Dwyer removed from the waterfront drama. Camarda, wanting to fight Amen's subpoena, sought out the kid brother of the district attorney. Advisedly or not—and very likely *not*, considering Paul was later summoned before the grand jury assembled by Bill's interim replacement to explain the reason behind the meeting—the younger O'Dwyer met the patriarch of the piers on President's Street on his way home from Foley Square and the Ben Gold trial.[45] The attorney had encountered Camarda before. When they spoke that evening, the union business agent showed him the subpoena of March 14, 1940, from Amen. Camarda asked Paul to represent him on behalf of the six locals with whom he was associated.

"I had a perfect right, if I cared to, to represent him in connection with it in any effort to quash the subpoena or to represent him for it," Paul recalled when asked about it in the Columbia University oral history interview. "But I had felt that even that was something I didn't care to do. I told him that I wasn't going to be involved in any criminal case in Kings County at all." Paul insisted he merely referred Camarda to another attorney—"and that was the end of it."[46] But, with his background as criminal defense lawyer, he had managed to let himself interact with one of Brooklyn's more nefarious characters.

Perhaps Paul let Bill know about this encounter, one sibling to another. "President-for-life" Joseph Ryan's ILA was a powerful union, one no Democratic mayoral hopeful could afford to alienate. But then again, perhaps not, as Paul long insisted on keeping his professional life removed from the district attorney's business. Bill in any case sprang into action and opposed what he no doubt saw as an incursion on his jurisdiction by the governor's office and Amen.

The state supreme court nonetheless upheld the Amen subpoena in late April 1940. However, before the special investigator could get his hands on the Camarda locals' business records, Bill landed them—or what he might have thought were authentic union records. According to Beldock's later grand jury presentment, the locals substituted the originals with cleaned-up versions, providing falsified documents to Joe Hanley, who was Bill's chief assistant, and Ed Heffernan, an assistant district attorney.[47]

Down at the docks, Bill's investigators swooped in, arresting over one hundred union flunkies, jailing some of them, and empaneling a grand jury. Amen, satisfied that the Brooklyn district attorney was doing his job, turned over all of his evidence to him, including testimony, exhibits, and the city Department of Investigation's spade work.[48] But the evidence against the ILA locals was whitewashed by Bill: the grand jury he assembled heard the testimony of just one witness. And on May 15, the district attorney's investigation of Camarda's "Pistol Locals" was closed—just as hurriedly as it began. The investigation's plug was pulled after Bill sat down with Camarda and the ILA president Joseph Ryan, according to a subsequent investigation by the New York State Crime Commission. Ryan announced that he would revoke the charters of three of the six suspect waterfront locals and ordered new elections for union officers. But as a result of Ryan's intervention, only the numerical designations of the corrupt locals were changed, while the corrupt officers were reshuffled rather than removed.

AFTER NARROWLY LOSING the 1941 mayoral election, Bill returned to the district attorney's office. When Imperial Japanese forces attacked Pearl Harbor, he shifted gears, enlisting in military service through a telegram he sent to President Roosevelt and going on leave from the district attorney's office in June 1942. In the military, O'Dwyer held a series of posts investigating fraud and waste in military contracts. He was moved up by Roosevelt to brigadier general and administered the Allied powers' hunger relief efforts in Rome, depriving Undersecretary of War Robert Patterson of his investigative services. Patterson, who was enamored of Bill's work, which had included feisty appearances before Missouri senator Harry Truman's congressional committee on fraud in wartime contracting, sent the president a letter, stating, "In a nation of 135 million, why deprive me of Bill O'Dwyer?"[49]

After being reelected in absentia as district attorney in 1944, Bill was named the head of the War Refugee Board in the federal board's waning months, contributing to its mission of rescuing as many Holocaust survivors as possible. The assignments helped endear him to New York's sizable Jewish and Italian American voting blocs. La Guardia's health was faltering and he announced that he would not seek a fourth term, effectively leaving the field wide open for Bill to succeed him.

PAUL'S CAREER was veering off in new left-wing directions. Eschewing the all-male, lily-white, and corporate-oriented American Bar Association, he became active in the National Lawyers Guild. This pioneering, alternative bar organization contained many left-wing members, and it had a significant influence on his development as an attorney in the field of labor and civil rights. The NLG had held its first national meeting in the New Deal year of 1937. By the early 1940s, when Paul served as chair of its civil rights committee, it included nearly 5,000 of the total 175,000 attorneys in practice nationwide (of whom 35,000 belonged to the mainstream bar association).[50] Notably, the NLG became a target of the FBI and the House Un-American Activities Committee (HUAC), empaneled in 1938 and chaired initially by the Texas Democrat Martin Dies. Among other things, the NLG assailed and contested the Hatch Act of 1939, which allowed the federal government to deny a government job to anyone who belonged, then or in the past, to any organization propounding the overthrow of the state. It also took on the Smith Act of 1940, which required all adult noncitizens to register with the government and be fingerprinted. And it opposed Congress making it easier to deport foreign-born labor leaders for alleged support of the Communist Party.[51]

An illiberal spirit was infecting many quarters of the United States when Paul joined the NLG. The government's crackdown on civil liberties was not simply a reaction to Soviet communism's aversion to free market capitalism and competitive elections, or even Josef Stalin's emergence as a personification of what, from a Brooklynite's perspective, looked almost like Murder Incorporated–style cruelty writ large. It was also a symptom of the public's dread of wartime subversion on the home front.

"The same way the Jew embodied for Hitler a psychotic fear of the alien and the un-Aryan, so the Communist was for American xenophobes and their political bedfellows a threat to the status quo and to patriotism itself," wrote the Cold War historian Larry Tye.[52] And there was no shortage of politicians willing to exploit this fear, even when the United States paradoxically became a wartime ally of Stalin following Nazi Germany's surprise invasion of the Soviet Union in June 1941.[53]

The president of the NLG from 1940 to 1948 was Robert Kenny, who started as a young Republican state senator in California who fought Prohibition, supported Roosevelt's "Supreme Court-packing move," and ran successfully for attorney general of his state. Becoming a Democrat, Kenny became the lead defense counsel in the 1947 "Hollywood Ten" case, in which Dies's HUAC successor, J. Parnell Thomas of New Jersey, pressured film artists to inform against their colleagues under threat of government imprisonment or the studios' subsequent blacklisting.[54] Martin Popper, someone Paul greatly admired in the NLG in New York, was the executive director under Kenny. After also defending members of the Hollywood Ten, he was cited for contempt of Congress for refusing to cooperate with HUAC. Paul kept him out of prison with the help of the constitutional lawyer Leonard Boudin, the nephew of Louis Boudin.

Paul's membership placed him within the fold of a national fraternity that included many New Deal liberals and left-wingers who used their skills as legal advocates to pressure for anti-lynching bills, defend hunger marchers, promote public works jobs, and lobby for legislation in workers' right to organize, housing integration, and low-cost legal services for the poor.[55]

Becoming president of the guild's important New York chapter, O'Dwyer smithed friend-of-the-court briefs in cases brought by the Justice Department under the anti-subversives Smith Act, while going on, well into the early 1950s, to spearhead briefs supporting legal challenges to anti-union laws in Florida and Alabama, racial segregation in the military, and the dismissal of New York teachers for supposedly treasonous leanings (about fifty public school instructors in the city lost their jobs under a state statute known as the Feinberg Law of 1949).[56]

As a fledgling constitutional lawyer himself, O'Dwyer took the First Amendment at face value, with its guarantees of freedom of religion, expression, assembly, due process, and the right to petition the government for redress, as did his NLG cohorts. His work for unions was consistent with this framework. If an employee could be dismissed for advocating the formation of a union, then their constitutional rights were worth nothing in America. So Paul acted on the belief that in a democracy any exception to the liberties enshrined by the Bill of Rights endangered the freedom of all. His weddedness to this elemental principle could sometimes come off as self-righteous. John Keenan, who served as a Manhattan assistant district attorney and a federal judge, said, not without affection, that "Paul was charming—right as could be."[57] But Paul's bedrock was the Bill of Rights, and so it would remain.

O'Dwyer's stance also ran afoul of attorneys who, during the Cold War, prioritized national security over individual rights, most notably Morris Ernst. Close with lawyers who advised the Roosevelt White House on the New Deal, Ernst was an NLG cofounder and prominent attorney with the American Civil Liberties Union (ACLU). But he tried, unsuccessfully, to rid the NLG of members of the Communist Party. With equal fervor, Ernst tried to drum out of the ACLU the storied radical Elizabeth Gurley Flynn, a former leader of the Industrial Workers of the World who had first joined the American Communist Party in 1937.[58] He went so far as to inform on the guild's activities to the FBI's J. Edgar Hoover in the 1940s, though the revelation of Ernst's snitching would only emerge years later as a result of the guild's litigation over the FBI's secret campaign of break-ins and wiretapping of its offices in Washington, DC.

Chilled by the passage of the Smith Act and government efforts to discredit the NLG, guild members quit in large numbers in the early 1940s, with membership falling even more precipitously at the turn of the next decade when the attorney general and HUAC tarred it with broad strokes. Paul remained an active member of the guild, however, and represented a number of lawyers and union leaders accused by elected and government officials of harboring Communist leanings and ties. In light of his involvement with the guild as well as the ALP, the New York City mayor's younger brother was attacked as "Pink Paul," a label that became even more pronounced when he decided to run for Congress in 1948 in a northern Manhattan district centered in the largely Irish Inwood neighborhood. The red-baiting continued, on and off and in one context or another, for much of his public career. But it never caused O'Dwyer to denounce either Communists or Jews—whatever their politics—nor did it distract him from an agenda that placed individual rights over national security prerogatives as defined by the US government.

5

IRISH ZIONIST

O N A CHILLY November day in 1990, the *Newsday* columnist Jim Dwyer boarded a flight to Israel from New York City to cover the East Jerusalem funeral of Meir Kahane. The Jewish Defense League founder and advocate of the use of violence to restrict democratic rights in Israel to Jewish citizens only was assassinated after speaking at the New York Marriott East Side Hotel on Lexington Avenue in Manhattan.

After touching down, Dwyer donned a yarmulke from a friend's wedding. With his natural beard, he felt safer appearing more Jewish than Irish after riding in a taxi from the Tel Aviv airport to the funeral. Sensing belligerence from some of those gathered, Dwyer stayed back, avoiding punches and slurs thrown at foreign journalists by "extremist, racist, asshole supporters" of the late militant, as he put it years later. When the rites closed, Dwyer went to a small office leased by *Newsday* and typed up his piece. It was dark out when he finished. Finding the door to the building at the bottom of the stairs locked, he retraced his steps and called his newspaper on Long Island, asking a news desk assistant to contact the East Jerusalem authorities for help. The American-born police official who showed up questioned Dwyer through a small window in the front door, telling him finally to stay put until the building owner could be found. The officer turned suddenly more helpful, however, when Dwyer pushed his press pass against the window, facing out. "Dwyer," the man in uniform said, squinting to read the ID. "Are you related to *Paul Dwyer?*"

"Uncle Paul!" the columnist responded, using the endearment with which the then New York mayor David Dinkins and other African American politicians enjoyed addressing the Irish American community's elder statesman. The officer, who looked to be about sixty years old, saw to it that Dwyer was released sooner than expected.[1]

The O'Dwyer name, precisely rendered or not, still resonated with at least one older Israeli more than four decades after the nation's founding. The reason, in part, was Paul's visible work after World War II as a "shill"— by his own description—for militant Zionists in New York known as the Bergson Group. At that time, these activists were aiding the Irgun Zvai Le'umi, the underground Zionist "National Military Organization" that fought the British Mandate for Palestine, as well as pushing American leaders to support the establishment of a Jewish homeland. O'Dwyer heard in the Bergsonites' support of the Irgun underground an echo of the nationalists who had fought the British during the Irish War of Independence in his boyhood.

A right-wing paramilitary outfit, the Irgun was founded in 1931 by followers of Ze'ev (Vladimir) Jabotinsky along with Jewish settlers of longer standing in Palestine, among them Hillel Kook, the nephew of the chief rabbi in Palestine. In 1940, Kook, adopting the American alias Peter Bergson, led his initially small, highly determined mission to New York. In its first phase, it sought to cultivate public support for creating a Jewish army of self-defense in Europe, something that never came to fruition. Paul decided to join this growing circle of Zionist activists after reading a full-page *New York Times* ad for Bergson's American League for a Free Palestine in 1945. By this time, the Bergson Group consisted of hundreds of American Jewish and non-Jewish supporters, liberals as well as conservatives, and Democrats and Republicans. It had completed its second phase, a press for decisive military action in place of calculation by President Franklin Roosevelt to rescue Jews trapped by Hitler. Its adherents were now involved in aiding the Irgun and terminating the British role in Palestine.

In assisting with fundraising, O'Dwyer helped the Bergson Group's work to evade the US embargo on arms shipments to the Irgun and other forces of Jewish defense and insurrection in Palestine. Their work included the smuggling of weapons and medical supplies to both Irgun and Haganah fighters. Like the Irgun, Haganah (Hebrew for "Defense") was a significant Zionist defense force in the embattled Jewish community in Palestine and carried European Jews into harbors beyond Europe on unauthorized passenger ships. Like the United States, the British authorities allowed but a tragically tiny fraction of desperate Jewish refugees to enter the ports under their control.

Paul's enthusiasm for the Bergson Group was partly an extension of Bill's support of Jewish causes in New York. Most well-remembered, by the time the war was won and Bill had won election as mayor, was the elder O'Dwyer's appointment in the closing months of World War II to head the Roosevelt administration's War Refugee Board; he helped the temporary agency direct food rations and trucks to decimated victims of newly liberated concentration camps, contributing to the saving of as many as two hundred thousand Jewish lives, by some historians' estimates. Bill also added his voice to a campaign to allow 982 Jewish refugees who had endured a twenty-day journey by sea to make the United States their home. Interned at Fort Ontario in Oswego, New York, the survivors were permitted in 1946 to remain in the United States, the result of an order by President Harry Truman that defied anti-refugee, and antisemitic, sentiment in Washington and around the country.

Both O'Dwyer brothers also participated in the pressure campaign that Zionist organizational leaders and ordinary Jews in America exerted to overcome the Truman administration's surprising eleventh-hour hesitation to accord US recognition of the Jewish State. For Jews, the birth of Israel was the preeminent goal, a culmination of a nearly two-thousand-year-old quest. While Paul's support of the Irgun through the Bergson Group's grassroots pursuit of that goal may have dismayed a few socialist friends who viewed the Irgun as a vigilante group unconnected to the egalitarian ideals of the labor movement, he was nonetheless in step with the majority of Americans who supported, in the aftermath of the Holocaust, the founding of an independent Jewish country. The extent to which Bergson and his followers had been at odds with mainstream American Zionist organizations during the war because of their typically confrontational approach to Washington and London was no longer at issue by the time Paul offered his Irish voice to militant Zionists after the war.

Paul's sympathies had begun to form during law school, when he had many Jewish friends and classmates. Peering beyond his provincial background, he glimpsed for the first time the wider world far from Ireland.

His visits to the homes of his law school classmates, he reflected later, helped him understand that the Irish story of state subjugation and exile was not unique, nor uniquely horrible. In addition, he noted, many of his associates in the National Lawyers Guild in the 1940s were Jews, and so was his law firm partner, Oscar Bernstien, who was responsive to Paul's pluralistic and humanitarian impulses.[2]

While it became known as a diverse movement in the 1920s, militant Zionism sunk some of its earliest roots as a result of a single horrifying pogrom on Easter 1903 in Kishinev (later called Chisinau, the capital of the Republic of Moldova). The episode, four days and nights of anti-Jewish rioting in which forty Jews were killed, was carried by William Randolph Hearst's *New York American* after the publisher sent the Irish republican activist and journalist Michael Davitt out of the country to investigate reports of antisemitic fanaticism in the Pale. His reports filtered shtetl persecution through an Irish republican mindset, with dispatches likening Kishinev henchmen in the Russian Empire to the British government's Royal Irish Constabulary in Ireland. Davitt wrote of how Russian Jews were "hemmed in and hedged about by penal laws."[3]

When the British in 1917 announced support for an eventual Jewish national home in Palestine, the declaration was made in a letter from British Foreign Secretary Arthur Balfour to Lord Lionel Rothschild, an eminent member of London's Jewish community. Paradoxically, Balfour was Britain's former chief secretary for Ireland, nicknamed "Bloody Balfour" for his ruthlessness in suppressing nationalist insurrections there. The British invaded Palestine soon after the "Balfour Declaration," capturing it from the Ottoman Empire and providing what David Lloyd George called "a Christmas present to the British people."

Still, when the wrapping paper came off, antagonism toward British policies—as in Ireland itself at the time—was revealed, led by Jewish pioneers like the Russian Jabotinsky (born in territory that is part of today's Ukraine). Arab resistance to British policies and brutal attacks against Jewish villagers accelerated as well, leading to the establishment of Haganah in 1920. In that particularly fractious and violent year, British authorities brought in Hugh Tudor, a Boer War and World War I veteran who had held senior military posts in the Anglo-Irish War; some of his Royal Irish Constabulary troops were known in England as "Tudor's Toughs" after opening fire in a crowded Dublin stadium in 1920 in a search for Irish Republican Army (IRA) assassins, killing or wounding dozens of Gaelic-football fans. These soldiers followed their conflict-hardened captain to the Holy Land for additional military service.

Like his police adviser post and his promotion to lieutenant general for English rule in Dublin, Tudor's assignment to Palestine stemmed from his friendship with the future prime minister Winston Churchill, whom he had met in Bangalore in 1895. His role in the Palestine Mandate was to train England's colonial police, and he ordered the gunning down of Adwan Bedouins as they marched on Amman, the capital of Transjordan (later Jordan), to protest higher taxes set by their emir (though Tudor at the time made clear that he knew the tribe to be friendly to Great Britain).

Another British official exported to Palestine would also have been familiar to O'Dwyer and other Irish republicans: Douglas Duff. He was trained in Ireland with the Royal Irish Constabulary that Tudor—or "Hughie," as Churchill called him—helped command. While Tudor left Palestine before the end of 1924, Duff remained for ten years, policing Arab villages.[4] British authorities in search of manpower were known to press many Black and Tan veterans into service. But for all their experience in suppressing insurrections, Great Britain lost control in Palestine during the Arab uprisings of 1936–39, a period of popular rebellion that the Israeli historian Tom Segev has described as "Ireland in Palestine."[5]

As in Ireland, militant opposition to British rule encompassed many different permutations, reflected by differences and overlaps in the tactics and philosophies of the Irgun and the Stern Group, the Palestine underground more prone at times to violent acts of resistance and provocation than the Irgun. While Jabotinsky's followers pushed for Jewish solidarity based on sectarianism and nationalism in the 1920s and 1930s, the foundational Histadrut trade union and employer under the British Mandate in Palestine espoused a working-class, socialistic program. Meanwhile, the Hebrew University president and former American Zionist leader Judah Magnes proposed, with few takers and relatively little notice at the time, a binational Palestine with an Arab-Jewish parliament.[6] The Reform rabbi Stephen Wise of New York, the head of the Zionist Organization of America, also evoked Hebraic strains of social justice and peace, asking, "Shall we have a sharecropper Palestine or shall we have a Palestine of Jewish freemen?"[7]

At the end of the 1930s, when the British under Neville Chamberlain issued the "MacDonald White Paper" that reversed the government's previously declared support of Zionism—set out in the 1917 Balfour Declaration and serving as a component of the British Mandate for Palestine that the League of Nations approved in 1922—the followers of Jabotinsky, or Zionist Revisionists, had expanded. Jabotinsky died in 1940 from a heart attack while visiting a self-defense training camp in Hunter, New York. And Kook, a.k.a. Bergson, took the cause of European Jews directly to the American public that same year. For as if intended to worsen the plight of Jewry, the 1936–39 Arab revolts in Palestine had prompted the Chamberlain government to issue a statement of guidance that restricted future Jewish immigration to Palestine to only seventy-five thousand people over five years to reduce the chances of further Arab insurrection.

In the British calculus, the Arabs in Palestine needed placating to discourage the surrounding Arab countries from enlisting in the Nazi war effort. As for the Jewish people, no matter what happened to their half-million or so pioneers living in Palestine, or to those suffering under the Nazis, the British clearly considered them as dependents—dependent, that is, on Great Britain's (and France's) armies to counter Nazi Germany's aggressions. As in the case of the US government, the grave perils ensnaring the Jews of Europe, and their problems with the British supervision of Palestine, were treated as secondary to the necessity of winning the struggle against Hitler's war machine.

———

THOUGH HE HAD NOT RESEARCHED Jabotinsky extensively, O'Dwyer undoubtedly sympathized with the late Zionist's public outrage over the British use of internment without trial, flogging, and hanging to quell insurrection in Mandatory Palestine. His awareness of Peter Bergson, though, did not come until he spied the 1945 *New York Times* ad for the American League for a Free Palestine.

Bergson's search for American followers and contributions had begun in 1940 as soon as the "shrewd and unpredictable" twenty-five-year-old had arrived in the United States after traveling directly behind a ship torpedoed by Nazi war boats.[8] It was then a year and a half since *Kristallnacht*, when Nazis sacked hundreds of German Jewish homes and synagogues, a night of destruction that did little to soften American isolationist sentiments in Congress or harden those arguing for sending US troops to assist the British in the fight to defeat the Nazis. While Bergson's initial effort—for funds to create a Jewish army to fight alongside Americans and their allies—went nowhere, it raised awareness of the plight of the Jewish people and forcefully made the case for a more militant and vocal Zionist organizational response to the widening cataclysm.

By the time Paul lent his Irish American voice to Bergson, supporters of the American League for a Free Palestine included scores of notable Jewish and non-Jewish actors, entertainers, scientists, and athletes, among them Barney Ross, Groucho Marx, Bob Hope, Marlon Brando, and William Randolph Hearst, a novel and bipartisan coalition putting pressure on Roosevelt and then Truman to aid the Jews of Europe. Boycotts of German products were conducted and rallies against the British Mandate staged. They stood in contrast to mainstream Zionists such as those under Stephen Wise. The rabbi had been first to boycott German goods and call for mass demonstrations, but, like other Jewish leaders, he exempted Britain and the US government from complaint, given their crucial importance in confronting Nazi Germany militarily.

Bergson and his uniquely diverse coalition extended well beyond New York, forming new chapters from Scranton, Pennsylvania, to South Bend, Indiana. His most important recruit, though, was Ben Hecht, the prolific, acidic Hollywood scriptwriter whom O'Dwyer said he found to be tactless when they later approached prospective donors together but who had written the newspaper ad that first attracted him to the movement.[9] Hecht initially came to Bergson's attention after shouting against what he called the listless American Jewish push for US military action to save the lives of millions of Jews. Working together, Hecht and Bergson were ephemerally different—the stormy and bull-headed Hecht and the driven and mustachioed Bergson, who squeaked when excited.[10] But they shared a powerful desire to challenge cautiousness and recalcitrance by American and British government leaders at one of history's most horrifying junctures.

At the start of 1943, Hitler's systematic annihilation of Jews was still little mentioned in the American media but for a few small-circulation liberal publications like *The Nation* (one of the journals Paul kept abreast of), and the term *Holocaust* had not yet been coined to describe the Nazi genocide. The Nazis' diabolical deeds gained their most widespread attention in America, at long last, from the staging of the theatrical production *We Will Never Die*. Underwritten by the Bergson Committee for a Jewish Army, scripted by Hecht, produced by Billy Rose, directed by Moss Hart, and scored by Kurt Weill, the grand pageant led audiences on a tour of Jewish history from biblical times to the nightmarish present, with a "cast of thousands." After two highly successful performances in Madison Square Garden, the show went on the road and helped arouse consciences and pressures for Jewish rescue. Its heartrending final segment, "Remember Us," punctuated the unfolding horror of two million Jews murdered as of that time with reminders that the Jews of Europe would be homeless and stateless should any of them actually manage to survive the ordeal. "The massacre of two million Jews is not a Jewish situation," the narrator intoned. "It is a problem that belongs to humanity. It is a challenge to the soul of man."[11]

At Bergson's request, the Iowa senator Guy Gillette and the California representative Will Rogers Jr. (both Democrats) introduced, with the Ohio senator Robert Taft (Roosevelt's bitter partisan enemy) and the New York representative Joseph Baldwin as Republican cosponsors, a joint congressional resolution calling for a US government rescue agency. The White House at first opposed creation of the agency. The State Department official Breckinridge Long, widely suspected of being an antisemite, responded to the resolution with wildly inflated statistics on the number of Jewish refugees granted entry to the United States, stirring outcry from Jewish leaders. Meanwhile, by late 1942, Roosevelt's political rivals, the Republicans Wendell Willkie and Thomas Dewey, had already voiced their sympathy for European Jewry and called for greater government action in response.[12] Prodded by Treasury Secretary Henry Morgenthau Jr., Roosevelt's sole Jewish cabinet secretary—and in the wake of Bergson organizing four hundred rabbis to march to the White House in March 1943 to demand a special board—the president established the War Refugee Board in January 1944. The Gillette-Rogers resolution, the rabbis' demonstration, and the We Will Never Die production had all created a groundswell that gave rise to the board, the only US government entity ever designated to save the lives of foreign nationals.[13] Despite scant resources and bureaucratic resistance from high offices of the State Department, the staff members assigned from Morgenthau's Treasury who ran the board helped save the lives of thousands of the persecuted (some historians estimate two hundred thousand, though the precise number is impossible to know) over the final fifteen months of the war.[14]

More than three months before he died while in office, Roosevelt named Brigadier General William O'Dwyer to the novel and important wartime board on January 27, 1945. Never to forget his tête-à-tête with the great man, by that point weary, bone-thin, and wispy-voiced, Bill assumed the mantle as executive director until the agency's dissolution on September 15, 1945. Less than two months later, he was elected as mayor of New York.

After the war, the American League for a Free Palestine was working out of Times Square's Hotel Astor. Moving beyond Peter Bergson's initial goals, the league revised its charter with words that sounded as if Paul could have written them (and indeed, O'Dwyer would lend his name to subsequent advertising appeals from 1946 to 1948, cosigning them along with dozens of other Bergson Group supporters):

> We, the people of America, ourselves a free and mighty nation, born in a revolution against oppression and tyranny, have joined in an American League for a Free Palestine . . . in the mortal struggle of the Hebrew people of Europe and Palestine for life and liberation. It is not the first time that oppressed and subjugated people of a foreign land have appealed in America for help, and whenever such a call reaches our shores, it echoes in our ears and we respond with compassion and humanity. Free Czechoslovakia and Free Ireland are living examples of our response.[15]

"My primary job was to extract money from people who had given previously to other Jewish charities," Paul explained later. "Our purpose was to get arms and ammunition and skilled manpower to Palestine so that the Irgun could conduct the fight against Britain. The fact that I had had waterfront experience helped."[16]

Paul's fundraising and speechifying continued until the end of the British Mandate on May 14, 1948, with the incipient Jewish State's declaration of independence coming immediately after and United Nations approval of the State of Israel finally following on May 11, 1949.

The huge celebrations in the streets of New York and other cities had barely subsided when the fragile new state was plunged into a war, attacked by five neighboring Arab countries. This, the Arab-Israeli War, became known by Jews as the Israeli War of Independence of 1948–49.

More than 6,300 Israeli civilians and fighters were killed in the ten-month conflict. Arabs, in contrast, referred to the *Nakba*, "the catastrophe," with more than half a million Arabs fleeing their homes of their own accord to escape Arab-Israeli crossfire, at least 100,000 forcibly expelled (by some historical estimates), and as many as 7,000 Arab fighters and 13,000 Arab civilians killed.[17]

In New York and internationally, the newly born Israel was embraced across virtually the entire political spectrum. No great power in 1947–48 had been more supportive than the Soviet Union and Soviet bloc countries such as Poland and Czechoslovakia. In comparison, the US government under Truman had supported a UN arms embargo on Palestine during the formative period of November 1947–May 1948 and switched at a crucial time from supporting a Jewish State to backing instead a UN trusteeship over Palestine, and then back again.

While today it may be difficult for many on the American left to look back at the Israeli War of Independence and not see it, at least in part, as *Nakba*, that was not how the American left or right was looking at it at the time. The most widespread view was that if there was one lesson to be learned from the horrors and convulsions of World War II and the Holocaust, it was that the Jews should have their own country.

The Bergsonites sought to attract as many supporters as possible, embracing, on the American left, for example, such well-known cultural and political figures as the singer-activist Paul Robeson and Ben Gold of the International Fur and Leather Workers Union, whose support of the Soviet Union held strong despite geopolitical tensions between the United States and the USSR after the war. Although the Irgun's godfather Jabotinsky was right-wing by the standards of the American left in the 1930s, and while the Irgun moved further to the right when the Polish-born Menachem Begin emerged as its leader in 1943, Paul's public involvement *as a non-Jew* was relatively unusual only for its wellspring—his strongly anti-British attitude. The paramilitary's attacks on British installations reminded him of the Irish War of Independence of 1919–21, not to mention the American patriotic War of Independence.

———

ON A FRIGID January night in 1947, it was not Paul but Bill who backstopped New York smugglers working at the water's edge in Jersey City to ship arms and medical supplies to Jewish defense services in Palestine, in this instance Haganah. The mayor's quiet action consisted of ordering a contingent of New York police to leave the New Jersey pier they had attended (along with federal and local authorities) because of shippers' concerns about potential disruptions from a longshoremen's picket line. Bill acted after the Haganah organizer and lawyer Nahum Bernstein buttonholed him in his city hall office about the situation, in a meeting hastily convened at the request of Bernstein's law associate Edward Silver, a colleague of the mayor and the chief assistant district attorney for Brooklyn. Bernstein told His Honor he feared that seventy-seven wooden crates filled with weapons for the Haganah could be found out as a result of the police presence, emphasizing that the Zionist military organization was preparing for a possible invasion by Arab countries. Bill picked up the phone and asked the police commissioner why city cops were working in Jersey City when there was more than enough crime for them to contend with in New York. With that, the police soon departed from the Jersey City docks, along with FBI and Customs agents. The supplies destined for Palestine were safely smuggled into the hold of a cargo ship in the port.[18] The mayor had acted as if heedless of possible ramifications—whether disbarment, federal prosecution, or merely awkward headlines.[19]

Another occasion when the O'Dwyer brothers responded to pressing Jewish concerns followed the statement by US Ambassador to the United Nations Warren Austin on March 19, 1948, declaring that the UN Assembly's November 1947 partition of Palestine between Arabs and Jews (setting the stage for the establishment of Israel)—enacted over the opposition of Arab countries—was no longer viable. Secretary of State George Marshall confirmed the quietly hatched Truman administration position, saying that only a temporary UN trusteeship to defuse the Arab-Jewish violence in Palestine would be considered. Dismayed by the White House's about-face, the Zionist leadership and ordinary citizens inundated the White House with postcards and letters of protest.

For President Truman, the fear that the Soviets might enter the Middle East under the pretext of keeping the peace weighed heavily, as did the need to find safe harbor for hundreds of thousands of Holocaust survivors stranded in Europe. Already saddled with other postwar worries, from fears of the Soviets gaining an atomic bomb to growing Soviet pressures on Czechoslovakia, he equivocated, decrying Austin's apparently unilateral move. To help him see the light, Bill himself put in a call to the White House, saying, "I know that next year I will have the utmost difficulty in getting cooperation here for a party that does not support the people of New York."[20] Edward Flynn, the Bronx County Democratic boss, went to Washington and told the president to "give in" on Palestine or to expect New York's opposition to his nomination at the July convention. Paul, meanwhile, led 150 members of the National Lawyers Guild, within which he chaired the Lawyers Committee for Justice in Palestine, to the UN temporary headquarters in Flushing, New York, and presented a petition and lawyers' statement to Ambassador Austin demanding "steadfast adherence" to Palestine's partition under a 1947 UN map and "effective UN measures to enforce it."[21] The Jewish congressman Emanuel Celler of Brooklyn vowed that anything less than full US recognition of an independent Jewish State would spell a certain end to Truman's career, while Eleanor Roosevelt offered to tender her resignation as a UN delegate if he did not act.

Amid the widespread protests arising from the Austin statement, police happened upon a typical local arms-smuggling operation, arresting two young Jewish men. They were apprehended when a patrolman noticed them placing a bulky duffel bag in a freight elevator in an industrial loft at 223 West Twenty-Eighth Street. When alerted by the building's superintendent, police arrived and found canvas bags holding hundreds of pistols, rifles, machine guns, and grenades, thousands of rounds of ammunition, and an assortment of knives.[22]

Paul was alerted to the incident quickly at his law office at 40 Wall Street by a call from Esther Untermeyer, the national treasurer for the American League for a Free Palestine. Her own nineteen-year-old son, Joseph, she said, was being held along with Isaiah Warshaw, a thirty-year-old watchmaker and member of the New Zionist Organization of America political party. The weapons confiscated had been bound for Irgun fighters, or so Mrs. Untermeyer was given to understand. With that, Paul calmed her, saying he would handle it.

Untermeyer and her husband, Louis, a well-known poet, were on hand in the magistrate's courtroom the next morning as Paul represented their son at the young men's arraignment before Judge Peter Horn. The defendants faced felony violations of the Sullivan Act. O'Dwyer called the 1911 law immaterial, noting that the state legislature's intent was to curb the transportation of rifles by gangsters then known to shoot at each other from speeding roadsters on the streets of the city. O'Dwyer converted the court proceeding into a political forum of sorts, declaring that by defying the US arms shipment embargo for Palestine the two young men "were only doing what every freedom-loving person should be doing." Horn patiently listened to Paul's oratory and the prosecutor's counterarguments. He adjourned, releasing the young men into the custody of their attorneys.[23]

Paul next appeared for the pretrial hearing, held before another magistrate, Frederick Strong, a month later. He moved for dismissal of all the charges, likening the two alleged smugglers to the American patriots who fought for independence during the American Revolution. No fair-minded court, he said, "could declare it a crime to help people gain their freedom." While he said that "somebody should be indicted," he offered that "it should not be these two defendants but rather Glubb and Abdullah and Bevin"—a British officer helping to lead Arab forces against Israel, the king of Jordan, and the British foreign minister, respectively. Amid the public atmosphere that, in New York, was often deeply sympathetic to the plight of Jews and the cause of an independent haven and homeland, the declamation seemed to hit its intended target. This was not immediately clear when Strong delivered his final ruling from his courtroom perch. He said the defense lawyer's argument might have been persuasive "in Boston in 1776," but not so much in 1948, and added that he did not consider the case relevant to the Sullivan law. However, Strong said the defendants' presence where the contraband was found was insufficient proof that they had "exclusive possession" of it, which the judge termed an important distinction when it came to culpability. While the Manhattan assistant district attorney Richard Denzer objected, Strong approved O'Dwyer's motion and tossed the charges out.[24]

IN MARCH 1948, the month before Paul went into court for the two young smugglers, ten thousand New Yorkers who were angered by the Truman administration's wavering support for the establishment of a Jewish State paraded in favor of that objective. Ben Gold was the grand marshal. Jewish voters in New York City were making themselves heard, and, as history showed, could not easily be ignored by elected officials. Earlier in the twentieth century, Charles Murphy had been the first pragmatic Tammany boss to respond to the influx of Jews from Eastern Europe, freeing Al Smith to champion the cause of the worker and the immigrant as assemblyman and governor. As the Jewish community became more educated and middle class, and as it grew to be one of the city's largest voting blocs, it influenced elections numerically and through active collaboration with other groups. The state of New York represented forty-seven electoral votes in presidential elections, the most of any state in the country, and was evenly split between Democrats and Republicans.

When Truman in Washington was drawing heat, Paul attended a rally organized by the Bergson Group at New York's Madison Square Garden on May 13—the day before the scheduled end of the British Mandate. The boisterous rally included dozens of elected officials and religious leaders seeking to put pressure on the president. Sitting next to Paul on the long dais, US Rep. Adam Clayton Powell of Harlem listened to the speakers' less-than-inspired-sounding fundraising appeals with a sinking feeling. Paul felt much the same, especially after hearing the British major Samuel Weiser, who had helped Jabotinsky form the Jewish Legion in Palestine during World War I, deliver a decidedly lackluster pitch. "This guy's blowing it," Powell whispered to Paul in the lawyer's remembrance. "This calls for a Baptist minister and an Irish revolutionary." O'Dwyer's rolling brogue was joined to the Christian cleric and civil rights tribune's fiery oratory. The two reeled in $75,000 (the equivalent of more than $864,000 in purchasing power in 2022).[25]

The next day, Truman, in the middle of an election campaign that many Democrats predicted he would lose, acceded to the pressure, according de facto US recognition of Israel just hours after it had declared its independence based on the UN-approved partition map. The Soviet Union followed up with de jure recognition. The US gesture was "everything this country should represent," the Truman aide Clark Clifford had said at the most decisive White House meeting on the matter.[26]

There was rejoicing in the streets of Brooklyn and the Bronx. And in Manhattan, a capacity crowd squeezed into Madison Square Garden under the auspices of the American Zionist Emergency Council to celebrate the new Zion and cheered speeches by Rabbis Abba Hillel Silver and Stephen Wise, Henry Morgenthau, Sen. Robert Taft of Ohio, Herbert Lehman, and Bill O'Dwyer, with a message of support sent by Chaim Weizmann, the Russian-born biochemist who had long had the ear of

British and American statesmen as leader of the World Zionist Organization and who would become the first president of Israel.[27]

———

PAUL OCCASIONALLY FOUND himself in the middle of ideological cross-fire because of his Bergson Group ties. In March 1948, he heard from David Wahl, the executive director of Americans for Haganah, that his continuing involvement with the Bergsonites was "rendering a real disservice to the cause" as Menachem Begin and the Irgun were "disruptive and detrimental to the efforts of the vast majority of the Jews in Palestine" and to the rescue of the remnants of Europe's Jewish community. Wahl's letter to O'Dwyer dealt chiefly with Paul's attendance at a dinner earlier that month honoring Guy Gillette, a major congressional supporter of the Bergson Group. O'Dwyer reacted primarily to the implication that he was a well-meaning goy who had possessed no idea of what he was doing or the potential ramifications. "I was well aware of exactly what I was doing," O'Dwyer wrote to Wahl. "The cause of freedom in Palestine has too many enemies here and abroad, and its friends are few. Do you have to attempt to discourage the few that are around?"[28]

Later that year, verbal flak caught O'Dwyer again when he was criticized for participating in a December dinner at New York's Waldorf Astoria to honor Begin, the leading Irgun figure, also attended by Jabotinsky's widow, Johanna. A student of the Irish War of Independence and the methods of Michael Collins, the Irgun militant was at the time a pariah to the British government for having ordered the bombing of the English military and administrative headquarters at Palestine's King David Hotel. The 1946 attack, preceded by a thirty-minute warning, destroyed the hotel's southern wing and caused the deaths of at least ninety Britons, Arabs, and Jews. The explosion followed a British crackdown in which 2,700 were arrested and documents revealing the identities of underground Jewish resistance leaders were seized.[29]

Shortly before the December 1948 fete at the Waldorf, Harvey Rosen, a fire department official in the O'Dwyer administration and trade union leader, passed along to Paul a letter from Harry Avrutin, the field director of the American Trade Union Council of the National Committee on Palestine, that voiced shock about Paul's role in helping to organize the dinner. "Mr. Begin," wrote Avrutin, "is the leader of a dissident group in

Israel known as Irgun, and is the head of the most reactionary anti-labor elements in Israel." Avrutin had asked Rosen to try to convince O'Dwyer to boycott the dinner for the Irgun leader. Instead of complying, Paul delivered a riposte—with relish.

"The Irgunists are good boys," Paul wrote back to Avrutin, "and they did a very intelligent job of chasing the British out of Israel. If Israel were to wait for freedom to come from the conference table, Harvey Rosen would be getting Social Security before the matter would come up for a second reading. To ask me to turn my back on the Irgunists would be like asking me to denounce the Irish Republican Army. I have been not merely a name on an ad, but I have been working actively to help them and support them for a number of years."[30]

O'Dwyer was similarly unfazed when the Waldorf dinner prompted a strong objection from Albert Einstein, Hannah Arendt (a critic of Zionism), Sidney Hook, and other prominent intellectuals in a letter in the *New York Times*. Their letter asserted, "Within the Jewish community" the Herut ("Freedom") party, formed from the Irgun and led by Begin, "has preached an admixture of ultra-nationalism, religious mysticism, and racial superiority" and is "a political party closely akin in its organization, methods, political philosophy and social appeal to the Nazi and Fascist parties." Begin's supporters, Paul among them, felt strongly, however, that without the grit and determination of Jewish pioneers who fought in the Jewish Legion in World War I and resorted to militancy against the British, Israel would never have come into being. He did not disguise his gratitude when Begin referred to him, in his 1951 memoir, *The Revolt*, as "that prince."

O'Dwyer later recalled,

I got many times challenged by very good friends who said, "How can you support these fascists [Begin and the Irgun]?" and I would say, "Well, one of the things that you have to learn is that while you're engaged in a war of revolution, you don't question the ideology of your compatriots, of your comrades in arms. And then when it's all over and the victory is won, you can make your decision whether you bring back the kin of David and make them kings of Israel or you want a workers' republic or whatever else it is. You make the decision later."[31]

A question about O'Dwyer would linger for years nonetheless: For all the ideological skirmishes he weathered, and all the enthusiasm he showed for the militant Zionist underground after the war, did he ever really run guns for the Irgun, as many assumed, both then and after?

"That's kind of a legend," Paul answered convincingly when questioned by an interviewer years later. "If I were to say no, that would not be accurate. If I were to say yes, it might imply that I was over on the piers and I was handing up the boxes of guns over to someone, and that wasn't so. We, the American League for a Free Palestine, had the job of getting immigrants into Israel . . . people who could take a rifle apart or be able to be of some value . . . in their war of independence."[32]

Still, Paul's activities for the Irgun were not confined to New York—they also extended to Dublin and Lord Mayor Robert Briscoe, a onetime revolutionary in the Irish War of Independence who at the time was printing propaganda for Irgun. At the suggestion of the veteran Jabotinsky ally, Paul paid a visit after the war to the Irgun's Paris office, which Briscoe had warned was then a target of French surveillance (though, O'Dwyer soon learned, it was actually the Stern Group that concerned the French authorities). Briscoe, a Jew, had desperately sought Irish visas for family relations as a member of the Irish ruling party. His efforts were tragically unavailing; 150 members of his extended family were murdered by the Nazis, including his aunt and her daughter. Having been early to warn of the storm clouds forming over the Jewish community of Europe in the early 1930s, he had gone on to serve as an emissary for Jabotinsky. As such, he visited Poland and, in January 1939, the United States, seeking a meeting with Roosevelt to urge transferring to British-controlled Palestine as many as one million Jews of Hungary, Poland, and Romania. Though closely allied with Eamon de Valera, Briscoe was unable to get a meeting with Roosevelt, and organizations like the United Jewish Appeal opposed making resettlement a focus of Zionist pressure in Washington.[33] One of the New York political figures who readily embraced Briscoe, however, was the then Brooklyn magistrate Bill O'Dwyer. In April 1939, while the Dubliner was visiting the United States to raise funds for the Irgun's *Ha'apalah* project, under which some forty thousand European Jews were illegally ferried from death's door to Palestine from 1937 to 1939, O'Dwyer and US Postmaster General James Farley introduced him to New York Governor Herbert Lehman, a close Roosevelt ally, and helped open the way to Briscoe meeting other prominent Jewish leaders as well, including Supreme Court Justice Felix Frankfurter and the newly retired Justice Louis Brandeis.[34]

———

LONG AFTER ISRAEL'S heady founding, Paul did not insert himself in Israeli politics or the activities of Begin's rightist political party. Nor did he involve himself in Israeli politics much beyond Israel's founding year. He continued to reaffirm his commitment to Israel's long-term survival in his political campaigns of the 1960s and '70s but did not join those on the left, including his former New York City Council chief of staff John McGettrick, at rallies for Palestinians of the West Bank and Gaza territories that Israel controlled as a consequence of the 1967 Six-Day War. As evidenced when Paul challenged Daniel Patrick Moynihan, Bella Abzug, Ramsey Clark, and others for an open US Senate seat for New York in 1976, aspirants for public office in the state realized that there was no future in taking issue with the policies of the Israeli government or supporting Arab Palestinian rights. This held true for Paul as well, though he would not refrain from assailing other US-backed governments, whether South Africa, Chile, or Britain.

———

WHILE HUMANITARIANS the world over were coming together to support the founding of Israel, the struggle for dominance over the New York City government remained as testy and fierce as ever. Bill O'Dwyer had first won election in the wake of the huge Fifth Avenue parades celebrating the victories over Nazi Germany and Imperial Japan. As he took office, the triumphal mood was giving way to creeping fears of another Great Depression. Bill drew editorial praise for purposefully confronting a terrific shortage of housing for returning veterans, an avalanche of labor strikes, and a municipal budget so depleted it surprised even him. As Cold War tensions heated up during his first term, he spurned the Communist-pervaded American Labor Party (ALP), which had endorsed him. By the time his 1949 reelection campaign was to start, he had positioned himself just to the right of the ALP and its leader US Rep. Vito Marcantonio and just to the left of the Republican-Liberal Newbold Morris, a former city council president and Republican who supported the New Deal. Both Marcantonio and Morris challenged Mayor O'Dwyer in 1949 after he announced, with characteristic abruptness, that he was too taxed and worried about his health to run for reelection; Paul and Frank urged him strongly to call it quits, but Bill changed his mind at the request of the leading Democratic bosses, including Flynn, and prevailed that November at the polls, handily.

Paul was keenly familiar with the double-crossing political arena by this time, as he made his first run for office in 1948 as the official Democratic candidate in the Twenty-First Congressional District in the Inwood and Washington Heights sections of northern Manhattan. His maiden turn for office had occurred against the backdrop of Bill's perpetual first-term conflicts with Tammany Hall's unstable and often furtive directorate over questions of patronage. One particular dispute gave rise to Paul's candidacy, stemming from a fatal attack on a Republican poll watcher, Joseph Scottoriggio, during East Harlem US Representative Marcantonio's successful bid for reelection to Congress two years before. Thought to have been ordered by mobsters, the 1946 Election Day assault evoked public concern about a possible reassertion of underworld influence in city elections. Following the attack, Mayor O'Dwyer replaced the Tammany Hall chief Edward Loughlin, an Irish figurehead for the party's dominant Italian wing influenced by the reputed crime syndicate leader Frank Costello, with an Irish district leader who was more to Bill's liking: Frank Sampson. In doing so, he publicly asserted his independence from nefarious Tammany influences.

As Bill burnished a reputation for independence, Louis Valente announced plans to retire from his seat as Manhattan surrogate court judge, a traditional plum. The Tammany board nominated Valente's nephew to replace him. Mayor O'Dwyer promptly objected, accusing Tammany of "gutter politics," which earned him praise from newspaper editorial pages.[35] He recommended instead an ally, City Council President Vincent Impellitteri, while the well-regarded Manhattan district attorney, Frank Hogan, whom O'Dwyer had supported for reelection in 1946, opened an investigation into whether Manhattan Democratic district leaders were bribed to give their blessings to the younger Valente.

Finally, under a truce that ended the two-week knock-down, drag-out fight, the Tammany board dropped Valente's nephew in favor of John Mullen, a judge in the New York Court of General Sessions who, in 1942, had helped Hogan succeed Thomas Dewey as Manhattan district attorney.[36] In return, Tammany won leeway to choose one of its own as party chairman, selecting Manhattan Borough President Hugo Rogers. And, for good measure, Tammany agreed to back the mayor's youngest brother, Paul, for the Twenty-First Congressional District race in northern Manhattan, shouldering out Albert Wald. (Wald was a state senator who had cosponsored a 1933 law creating a board to fix "fair wages" for working women and minors, a forerunner of a statewide minimum wage.)[37]

SO ANOINTED BY TAMMANY, albeit by way of a circuitous route, Paul entered the 1948 congressional race in the Inwood and Washington Heights sections of Manhattan. But the novice candidate faced sizable hurdles in the first of seven electoral quests he would seriously pursue through 1977, when he retired from city politics.

By far the biggest obstacle was the broad popularity of his opponent, the incumbent US Rep. Jacob Javits, a moderate. Almost as significant as Javits's wide appeal was that, in insecure eras especially, voters tended to give the benefit of the doubt to one of their own: Javits was the only Jewish Republican in the House or Senate.[38]

Even so, O'Dwyer, while Irish, was also popular in the Jewish community, and he secured the ALP ballot line to supplement his Democratic endorsement. But the labor party's cosupport of his candidacy proved as problematic to moderate Jewish voters as it was repellent to more conservative Irish voters such as the Catholic War Veterans. For such Irish Democrats in the district, O'Dwyer was soft on Communism and even a "renegade," in his remembrance.[39] The labor party also came out for the Progressive Party's presidential candidate, Henry Wallace, who was calling for conciliatory US policies toward the Soviet Union.

MUCH OF THE JEWISH population of the Twenty-First Congressional District had followed the northward trail of the Independent Subway System (IND) subway line, which opened in 1932, out of the overpopulated Lower East Side of Manhattan. Most of these Jewish families were clustered in the apartment buildings west of Broadway, while a larger census of Irish Americans resided east of Broadway. The nearby George Washington Bridge provided a striking visual landmark for both as of 1931. Irish and Jews were the two most numerous and engaged ethnic voting blocs of Inwood and Washington Heights when the congressional election campaign started. As of the 1940 federal census, Irish numbered

23,900, or 11.7 percent of the total population, and Jews constituted 73,100, or 35.8 percent. The remainder of the district was made up of white Protestants, African Americans, and Puerto Ricans. (Religious data were reported by the Census Bureau at the time.)[40]

Overall, New York was a working-class city of distinctive ethnic neighborhoods, and within the most insular and protective enclaves the range of a typical inhabitant's social life might be a five- or six-block radius from his or her home and house of worship. Invisible boundaries demarked the neighborhood turfs but could not always keep interethnic hostilities to a minimum. Such tensions arose in part from cultural differences and from competition for housing as residency widened, encompassing new German refugees, Black people from the Jim Crow South, and migrants from the recently mechanized Puerto Rican agricultural economy. Irish-Jewish differences over US foreign policy were also a source of resentment some voters expressed toward both candidates. During the Spanish Civil War, many Irish Catholics backed Francisco Franco, while many Jews supported the Loyalist opposition. Irish and Jews in the district were also on different pages in another way: Great Britain was admirable to Jewish voters for fighting Hitler, whereas to many Irish in the district Britain remained chiefly Ireland's oppressor. Irish gangs meted out violence and vandalism against Jews and others. At one point, the pane-glass windows of the O'Dwyer-for-Congress headquarters were shattered, but the culprits were never identified.

Paul's campaign staff was small but determined. The campaign manager was Leon Hershbaum, Paul's law associate, then and for decades to come. Invariably dapper in dress, Hershbaum spoke in an accent that identified him as a Russian Jewish immigrant and a Brooklyn contemporary of Oscar Bernstien, his longtime friend.[41] Colleagues would recall Hershbaum's habit of keeping his desk clear except for a single lined notepad; he drove to work in a pink Cadillac and specialized in cases involving people who took their doctors and hospitals to court under the 1965 Medicare law.

Helping Paul raise contributions was John Francis ("Chick") Meehan, the former football coach at Manhattan College and New York University. A onetime collegiate quarterback, Meehan was the campaign's director. (He would get a contract during Bill's second term to place and operate hot-tea vending machines in subway stations.) Sean Keating, another friend of both brothers, also pitched in—sans formal title. The onetime IRA prisoner of war and hunger striker had previously helped Paul start the American Friends of Irish Neutrality and held an appointment in Bill O'Dwyer's administration.

Their common rival, Jacob Javits, was elected to Congress two years earlier in a three-cornered race for the seat with the former state assemblyman Daniel Flynn, a Democrat whom Jewish residents had judged an inadequate foe of antisemitism, and the ALP's Eugene Connolly. Javits was carried into office on the coattails of Governor Thomas Dewey, reelected that year in a landslide. With thoughts of giving Javits a run for his money, Paul had first approached Connolly and other friends in the ALP who "figured they had nothing to lose and seemed glad to have a willing candidate."[42] The potential advantage of coupling ALP's backing to his Democratic endorsement made some sense—party backing, not the size of a candidate's war chest, was the principal factor in determining the outcome of elections.

The Liberal Party, consisting of former ALPers who broke with the labor party over its refusal to oust its Communist members, backed Javits. The party was then the New York linchpin of the Truman presidential campaign, not the New York Democratic Party. Bill and other local leaders had publicly tried to convince Dwight Eisenhower to run on the party's ticket in place of Truman, fearing the often-underestimated president had little chance of winning.

"My debut as a candidate for public office could not have come at a worse time, for red-baiting was at its peak, and all its techniques were practiced on me," Paul wrote, looking back on the race. His endorsement by the ALP made many voters wonder whether Paul was a supporter of Wallace (he was not, he insisted—he was for Truman). Voters' doubts were epitomized by a telegram from a local Democratic captain to Paul, which read, "Democrats demand to know if you're for Wallace or Truman or for communism or against it. Irish greatly agitated at two inconsistent roles. Better declare—great resentment and uprising against you—carrying water on both shoulders."[43]

O'Dwyer and Javits actually agreed on many issues, the campaign demonstrated. Both opposed the 1947 Taft-Hartley Act, unquestionably supported opening Palestine and US ports wide to Holocaust survivors, and resisted the 1948 Nixon-Mundt bill to force all members of the Communist Party—including members of ill-defined "front groups"—to register with the US Attorney General's office (a step that would have gone beyond Truman's "loyalty oaths" for federal employees). Paul was left to differentiate himself from the Republican Javits and even Dewey, Roosevelt's former rival for the presidency who in his first term as governor signed a rent control measure that appealed to liberals, as well as the pioneering state Ives-Quinn law, which barred hiring discrimination based on race.[44] The Javits supporter George Meany of the American Federation of Labor (AFL) pointed out, correctly, that O'Dwyer did not live in the congressional district. In response, O'Dwyer sought to define the congressman as not a friend of the district, like himself, but rather of the wealthy. He pointed to Javits's votes for a tax-cut measure helpful to high earners.[45]

Going further, the thick-maned O'Dwyer, forty-one, described the baldish Javits, forty-four, as a "phony liberal" at a late October public debate sponsored chiefly by the German-language newspaper *Aufbau*. He chided him for having supported a federal law that allowed railroads to set ticket prices without strictly adhering to the Sherman Anti-Trust Act. Javits was a World War II veteran who served in the Pacific. As a member of the House Foreign Affairs Committee, he had proposed lifting the embargo on refugees to Palestine and giving loans to Israel. At the debate, the congressman suggested that O'Dwyer's support of the nascent Jewish State, then fighting an invasion by five Arab countries, was politically motivated.

The two rivals took to the streets with campaign trucks fitted with large loudspeakers. Javits's truck, dubbed the "Dreamboat," catalyzed antisemitic heckling but made stops where he read aloud from the Nixon-Mundt bill and expounded on why its stipulations against membership in communist front groups were to his mind unenforceable (a clear attempt to mollify those who saw his vote against the bill as evidence of a dangerous tolerance of godless communism on his part). Javits also distanced himself from America's "Mr. Republican," Robert Taft, given the Ohio senator's slap at the Nuremberg trials of Nazi war criminals as "ex post-facto" American justice. While Governor Dewey mildly criticized the Cincinnatian's statement, Javits objected strongly.[46]

Paul was hemmed in—on all sides. He realized that, given the district's demographics, it was pointless to inveigh too much about his liberal-leaning Jewish incumbent. He also felt it to be fruitless to deny accusations that he was a Communist; that would have only brought further attention to the falsehood and perhaps made him seem defensive.

The conservative New York clergyman Edward Lodge Curran urged Paul to abandon the ALP line, all the same. "Your brother Bill O'Dwyer, mayor of New York, has charged the American Labor Party with being controlled by Communists," fumed the Coughlin of the East in a telegram.[47]

Paul's brother, though he had gained the mayoralty with the help of the ALP, was then making his estrangement from the labor party and the Communists known. Escaping August's heat, he took a late afternoon boat ride with the anti-communist Cardinal Francis Spellman and the labor leader George Meany during the annual AFL convention, where Spellman gave a speech calling for labor-management concord and Meany offered an address rippling with anti-communist phrasing and calling for Democrats to support Representative Javits in his reelection campaign against Paul. Bill left Meany's endorsement of Javits unremarked upon and merely took aim at the Republican Party over its support of the anti-labor Taft-Hartley Act passed over Truman's veto.[48]

Paul's reputation meanwhile suffered an untimely slap from the Hearst newspaper chain's syndicated right-wing columnist George Sokolsky two weeks before Election Day: a confidant of J. Edgar Hoover, Sokolsky lumped Paul in with the Wallace-for-President campaign, warning that if he beat the Republican he would become part of a "pernicious quartet" with US Representative Marcantonio, the Congress of Industrial Organizations counsel Lee Pressman (a House Un-American Activities Committee [HUAC] target), and the left-wing US Rep. Leo Isaacson of the Bronx.[49]

In the final two weeks before voters went to the polls, Paul and Javits traded newspaper op-eds over J. Parnell Thomas and HUAC, which had made its splash conjuring pervasive Red influence in Hollywood; Javits called for the replacement of Thomas, while Paul stated that the panel should be abolished. At the same time, O'Dwyer drew up a list of facts for campaign volunteers to use in response to what he viewed as the rising "neurosis" of anti-communism in American life. "I assume," it stated, "that people believe that a Communist would not have his kids baptized or that he would not have them confirmed. Here are the facts: my kids were baptized Catholics, and the ones who are old enough are confirmed Catholic, and here are the churches where it happened."[50] A colleague and supporter of O'Dwyer was so impressed by the document, he distributed hundreds of copies to voters. In response, Javits supporters opportunistically distributed it around the predominantly Jewish west side of Broadway, accusing O'Dwyer of seeking to appeal to Catholics at the expense of Jews.

"I was being attacked by the Irish for being a Communist," Paul recalled. "The same label was applied to me by the Liberals, Christian Mobilizers and Catholic War Veterans, while in Jewish sections of the district I was accused of running a campaign catering to the very crypto-Nazis who were the most active workers against me."[51]

Before an overflow crowd of four hundred residents at the *Aufbau*-sponsored debate at the Royal Manor at 157th Street and Broadway, O'Dwyer struggled to defend himself, insisting that he would have been one of the first to be sent to a labor camp had he lived in a communist country, given his unflagging support of freedom of speech and individual rights. "The reactionaries and moneyed class . . . make deals with the Communists; it is the liberals who suffer," he declared. But Americans, he went on, should be different and "fight for the right of a Communist to be a Communist in the United States if he felt like it."[52]

―――――

AT HIS JANUARY 1946 inauguration ceremony at New York City Hall, Bill O'Dwyer had celebrated to the song "It's a Great Day to Be Irish." But Paul's congressional campaign more than two and a half years later showed that being Irish was no longer a certain ticket to winning an election, at least in most districts of the city. Irish New York, like the city's Jewish community, had matured—it was on average more educated and had become even more discerning politically since Bill began climbing the ladder. Paul's difficulties as a candidate in 1948 turned out to be a preview, of sorts, of future Republican success at peeling away many white and Catholic voters from the New Deal coalition, a trend that became more pronounced after the 1963 death of President John F. Kennedy. The peel had begun with the fierce red-baiting of a frightening new atomic age. Fear and denunciation would carry the California representative Richard Nixon and the Wisconsin senator Joe McCarthy to prominence. The issues that Paul flagged—labor, racial fairness, antitrust legislation, a higher minimum wage—lost ground to the politics of fear, racism, and anti-communism, as he learned the hard way.

When the polls closed on election night in 1948, Paul, like Dewey in his simultaneous challenge to Truman, was projected as the apparent winner. The news came across on the radio. But the early prediction was premature. Like the *Chicago Tribune*'s front-page headline trumpeting an illusory Dewey victory over Truman, the appearance of Paul's possible win yielded to a more sobering light after dawn. In the final count, Javits defeated O'Dwyer by a sliver, 1,873 votes—just .014 percent of the 130,372 votes cast.

"I'm surprised that I lost by so little, thinking back on it," O'Dwyer said, in an interview for a *New York Times Magazine* profile two decades later. "Some of my people thought I would have won anyway had I not taken time off to help the brewery workers in a wildcat strike."[53]

Paul took some consolation from postelection letters sent by voters like Ralph Nunberg of Riverside Drive. "It is unbelievable that even your opponent had to concede how many voters cast their ballots for you," Nunberg wrote, urging Paul to seek a recount.[54] But he had no interest in dragging things out. All the same, he realized, there was no denying that a switch of a mere handful of votes "would have made me a congressman and Javits running for, you know, the bus."[55]

Instead of asking that the final tallies be checked, Paul returned to his busy law firm, a job he enjoyed far more than giving speeches, touting himself, or shaking hands for votes. He fit as comfortably as ever in the multiracial fabric of left New York, whose pressing for the racial integration of baseball had culminated in Jackie Robinson's signing by the Brooklyn Dodgers. Paul also befriended Percy Sutton, a Harlem politician and for the rest of his days one of his closest friends. They met on a picket line outside the newly constructed all-white Levittown, a sprawling, tic-tac-toe housing development on Long Island catering to returned veterans.[56] In collaboration with the National Lawyers Guild, Paul joined with ten other organizational leaders in assailing a New York City Board of Education vote (6–1) in favor of banning a best-selling book on Tom Paine whose author, Howard Fast, was a Stalinist who refused to provide the names of like-minded comrades and served three months in prison for contempt of Congress.

The book-censoring board included several appointees of the then mayor O'Dwyer, including Maximillian Moss, who provided the sole vote of dissent. While Paul's positions were to the left of Bill's, he harbored no resentment over Bill's failure to do more for him in the congressional race. In fact, he had discouraged his older brother from giving his endorsement for fear it might expose him to potentially crippling red-baiting, he said.[57]

Bill, at the same time, was not comfortable that Paul maintained many friendships in the ALP. A month before insisting to reporters he hoped Paul would win, he had denounced the labor party as "Communist-controlled."

When he gave Paul's candidacy his somewhat tardy and tepid blessing two weeks before the election, his words of support were merely occasioned by the publication of a mischievous article suggesting he was helping Paul raise campaign funds in secret. That simply was not true, the mayor told the press.

"I had hoped to stay out of all local political fights, but when I read this I feel that I have been dragged into it," he said. "I had nothing to do with Paul's nominations and I have done nothing to help Paul's campaign. However, since I am dragged into it, it is only fair to say that I hope every Democratic candidate is elected, including President Truman."

In the Cold War minefield of guilt-by-association that was growing omnipresent, the mayor restricted himself to casting aspersions on Javits's voting record and endorsing his brother's *character* rather than his positions or record.

"Paul O'Dwyer is blessed with a good strong mind, and he makes it up for himself without any help," Bill declared that day. "All his life he has been intuitively on the side of the underdog. When he gets to Congress, the little people of the neighborhood will have a true friend and that covers the whole field of Democratic thinking—civil rights for every race, color and creed and decent living conditions for all the people."[58]

The Liberal Party jumped all over the mayor's somewhat circumspect comments, branding them a "flip flop."[59] The major dailies' endorsements leading up to Election Day tilted decidedly toward Javits, including that of the *Daily News*, with its huge Catholic readership. The conservative *News* editorial board did at least allow that Paul should not be confused with a Communist despite his ALP nomination.[60]

———

A MONTH AFTER the election, Paul stood beaming on the Waldorf Astoria dais to welcome Menachem Begin to New York. Though Paul had lost his first election, the close finish—and his usually optimistic nature—left him feeling hopeful; he told friends he would one day try again for public office. But while many Democratic candidates around the country would capitalize on the improving postwar economy, the red-baiting that O'Dwyer attracted on the campaign trail was destined to become a more pronounced and successful part of the GOP playbook against outright supporters of civil rights and civil liberties on the left.

Faded family photo of Paul as a boy sitting between his parents and with siblings in Bohola, County Mayo. Many children of his age were destined to leave Ireland in search of better economic prospects. In 1925, at age seventeen, Paul would follow the path of four older brothers to a city of more than 7.7 million souls.
(NYC Municipal Archives.)

Lawyer Paul (left) and his spouse, Kathleen O'Dwyer, with the then Brooklyn county judge Bill O'Dwyer in 1939, the year the latter ran successfully for district attorney of the borough. (Brooklyn Library/Brooklyn Eagle.)

Paul looks over Mayor Bill O'Dwyer's shoulder, a frequent role in their long and close relationship. They are returning to New York from a family trip with Paul's wife, Kathleen, and their two elder children, Bill and Eileen.
(NYC Municipal Archives.)

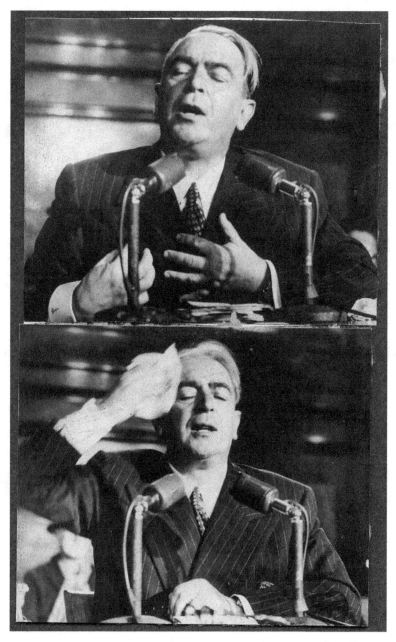

After quitting the mayoralty in the first year of his second term, Bill O'Dwyer returned voluntarily to New York in March 1951 to field questions from a committee chaired by the first-term Democratic senator Estes Kefauver of Tennessee to investigate the role of organized crime in interstate commerce. Then the US ambassador to Mexico, Bill endured an accusation-laced grilling, with the Senate hearing broadcast on the new medium of television. Photos in the
Brooklyn Eagle *portray Bill mopping his brow during two days of questioning.*
(Brooklyn Library/Brooklyn Eagle.)

In 1957, the year after John Kennedy (right) was disappointed in his bid for the vice-presidential nomination, the Massachusetts senator was guest of honor at the annual dinner of O'Dwyer's Irish Institute on the West Side of Manhattan, where he was introduced by an associate of the O'Dwyer brothers as a future president of the United States. (NYC Municipal Archives.)

Serving as Manhattan councilman-at-large, on October 10, 1964, Paul visits the shaft of the subway tunnel at Thirteenth Street and Sixth Avenue with members of the sandhogs' union coming off their shift.
(Photo by Arthur Brower/*New York Times*/Redux.)

Paul (seated) at a fundraiser at the New York Hilton Hotel in early October 1968.
(Photo by © Jefferson Siegel.)

Senator Eugene McCarthy of Minnesota (at lectern) discusses prospects for peace in Vietnam within the deeply divided Democratic Party at New York Hilton Hotel fundraiser, as 1968 Senate hopeful O'Dwyer (sitting) listens.
(Photo by © Jefferson Siegel.)

Paul shaking hands with union members during New York City's Labor Day parade, September 2, 1968. (Photo by © Jefferson Siegel.)

Paul marching with members of the sandhogs' union during New York City's Labor Day parade, September 2, 1968. (Photo by © Jefferson Siegel.)

Paul, who nearly defeated Jacob Javits in a 1948 race for Congress in northern Manhattan, speaks on October 24, 1968, at a Garment Center rally attended by about eight thousand people in his second effort to unseat the broadly popular Republican-Liberal in 1968.
(Photo by Carl T. Gossett Jr./*The New York Times*/Redux.)

The night before the 1968 election, Paul reprises a candlelight march he and fellow anti-war delegates held outside the tumultuous Democratic National Convention in Chicago. Helping him get out the vote are the Long Island congressman Allard Lowenstein and Kathleen O'Dwyer. (Photo by © Jefferson Siegel.)

6

BROTHER'S KEEPER

WHATEVER DIRECTION Paul had hoped to take his political career in was inevitably affected by Bill's abrupt exit from Gracie Mansion at the start of the 1950s. Some of the negative impact on Bill's political standing was self-inflicted—not least of all the then mayor's denunciation, which he eventually retracted, of the Democratic Brooklyn district attorney Miles McDonald's investigation of protection payoffs to high- and low-ranking cops. The mayor's defensive swipe at McDonald immediately followed the funeral of one of the hundreds of officers implicated in the district attorney's wide-ranging probe, who had killed himself.

The headline-making outburst represented an even more acute source of embarrassment to the Bronx political boss Edward Flynn, who set in motion a secret effort to move Bill far away from press inquiries about the probe. And after Bill gave up Gracie Mansion to become the US ambassador to Mexico with President Truman's OK, questions and rumors about his brother were a source of continuing worry for Paul, distracting him from his need to shore up and expand his small legal practice. At stake was not only his future political potential but the O'Dwyer family name itself.

Bill had arrived at, but not yet acclimated to, the American embassy in Mexico when its legal attaché, a clandestine FBI agent, opened a memorandum sent to him in October 1950 by J. Edgar Hoover. The document reviewed how the new ambassador had dealt with the FBI method of crime reporting while mayor of New York, how the charge of support by underworld figures had been raised in his last election, and how the former mayor had been supported by the Communist-infused American Labor Party as well as radical labor unions. Hoover concluded the memo by telling the attaché to keep a close eye on the American diplomat, further stating, "It is desired that your contacts with the new Ambassador be courteous but cautious."[1]

As absurd as it was to consider Bill O'Dwyer a secret ally of Josef Stalin's Soviet Union or a cog in a worldwide communist plot, the former mayor was assuming control of an important American embassy amid the intensifying Cold War, during which paranoia mixed with rank opportunism to raise new charges, revive old ones, and blur ethical distinctions and constitutional rights. By the time these forces had finished darkening the 1950s and pitching the world toward nuclear Armageddon in the Cuban Missile Crisis of 1962, Bill had seen his already sullied political reputation battered almost beyond repair. Paul, as in the past, felt compelled to try to rescue him.

———

WHILE BILL WAS HOSPITALIZED in May 1949 for exhaustion, Paul and Frank, deeply concerned about his increasing health problems, persuaded him not to run for reelection—a decision, later reversed, that he even made public. He had been publicly vacillating about running again when, at the behest of Edward Flynn in particular, he went through with the race and, as expected, handily won another four years. But the second term was cut short when Flynn changed gears and eased Bill out of office as of September 1, 1950, less than a year in.

As Bill made his sudden exit from New York, he could not have foreseen the intense political and personal fallout that was to follow, nor could his second wife Sloane Simpson (Kitty, his wife of thirty years, died at fifty-four in his first year as mayor) or even Frank and Paul. Sitting in an open-air automobile at the head of a formal cavalcade on lower Broadway as ticker tape fluttered down, Bill and Sloane waved to three hundred thousand spectators in hundred-degree heat. There were questions yet to be answered, but the newspapers were largely positive, for the moment. Even the recently more critical *New York Times* sent Bill off as "an experienced executive who had a close knowledge of municipal affairs" and as a public servant who had displayed "warm sympathies for the underprivileged and the sick."[2]

Obscured by the blizzard of ticker tape was the behind-the-scenes maneuvering to spirit him to Mexico City—to a posting with a $15,000 cut in pay—in the belief this would open electoral possibilities for the party that fall. By setting up the need for a special election for mayor in November, it was hoped that Democratic voter turnout would rise in the simultaneous gubernatorial election. Flynn and other Democratic bosses apparently figured that this might help them regain control of Albany from the Republican Party and the incumbent governor Thomas Dewey, a perennial presidential candidate. Getting Bill out of the way was necessary to control damage from the mushrooming scandal involving a Brooklyn bookie's payoffs to cops. Flynn likely thought that the results of a grand jury investigation into the organized system of cash payoffs to hundreds of members of the police department to safeguard an illegal gambling operation could prove calamitous to the party's chances for maintaining control of city hall, and to the party's reputation. In one sense, the political boss resembled Bill in having a reputation for competence largely removed from the historically corrupt image of Tammany Hall. He had long worked effectively with the dominant New York City political machine for shared electoral purposes and was "like Jesus Christ" when it came to the awesome power he wielded, in the remembrance of one former Bronx judge, Louis Fusco Jr., many years later.[3]

Yet for the past decade Flynn had periodically nettled both Bill and Paul: by his not-so-subtle support of Mayor Fiorello La Guardia in Bill's bid to unseat him in 1941, for instance, and his 1945 statement that Bill would not make a good mayoral candidate because of his ties to the American Labor Party and Communist activists within it. Bill was irked, too, by Flynn thwarting, on behalf of Truman, with whom he was close, the efforts of Bill and other national party leaders to deny the president the Democratic nomination in 1948.

The O'Dwyer brothers could not have been faulted for feeling especially angry with Flynn and the Democratic machine in New York in September 1950. Only a year after convincing an openly indecisive Bill to run for reelection, he had helped push him out the door—for reasons neither Flynn nor Bill ever explained.[4]

Although the Senate confirmed Bill as ambassador, suspicions about possible legal jeopardy stemming from his years as an elected official did not abate. Under ordinary circumstances, the questions might have passed with time, but together with the witch-hunting atmosphere in Washington and the investigation of police payoffs in New York, Bill's once soaring popularity suffered irreparable damage.

The first faint hint that Bill's reputation was in serious trouble had come just a month after his 1949 reelection when Brooklyn District Attorney McDonald decided to extend a sitting grand jury in order to investigate a fast-talking bookie at the center of the payoffs to police—one Harry Gross, the Flatbush laundry man's son who parlayed a nickel-and-dime operation out of the back door of candy shops into a sophisticated network that ran thousands of weekly bets with the help of four hundred bookies, runners, and accountants in thirty-five betting parlors across the city, Long Island, and northern New Jersey.[5]

With its epicenter in the Dug Out tavern near Ebbets Field, home of baseball's Brooklyn Dodgers, Gross's operation dished out $1 million a year to crooked cops (or almost $12.7 million in 2023 purchasing power). But there were consequences. Ensnaring everyone from junior patrolmen all the way up to Police Commissioner William O'Brien, the exposure of the extensive police role in protecting the betting ring turned into the largest municipal scandal since the Samuel Seabury investigation. Gross was arrested two weeks after Mayor O'Dwyer left office, and as the tale of endemic police corruption hit the front pages, it evoked for many the Jazz Age indulgences that sent the then mayor Jimmy Walker out of the country shortly before the 1932 presidential election.[6]

As the full dimensions of the police department's flagrant corruption became more apparent, a tragedy involved Bill more deeply in the investigation's fallout. The police captain John Flynn turned his gun on himself after being called before the McDonald grand jury. At his funeral, six thousand policemen turned their backs on the district attorney. Afterward, Bill told reporters that the investigation targeting the police force had turned into a "witch hunt," implying Captain Flynn was an innocent victim of the prosecutor's zealousness. But the decision to attack the investigation backfired in no small way. Sympathetic toward a department to which he once belonged, and in charge as mayor of its management, Bill understood all too well the temptations besetting the underpaid cop patrolling amid ubiquitous illegal gambling. But the criticism from Bill only led McDonald, who had once worked under him in the Brooklyn district attorney's office, to press on, while Bill came across as more interested in covering up the bookie payoffs to cops than addressing a phenomenon of long standing in New York and many other cities. McDonald would tell a *Times* reporter toward the end of his career, "No one has asked me to do anything that wasn't right—except O'Dwyer."[7]

The backlash against the mayor was bad enough that a decade later, in retirement from public life, Bill noted in his own defense that not a single policeman was ever convicted as a result of the scandal, though he rued what he called his political miscalculations: "I had, with poor wit, placed myself in the position of being about the only casualty of the investigation." Less apparent than his self-pitying tone, Bill's recollection of the scandal dovetailing with the demise of his New York political career was misleading: while Gross's refusal to testify at a criminal proceeding after doing so before a grand jury may have forced the dismissal of eighteen cases against indicted policemen, the bookie's sudden case of cold feet at the trial earned him a sentence of seventeen years in prison—twelve for his bookmaking activities, five for contempt of court. Even so, his testimony at a departmental trial in 1952, when he was assured of some clemency, resulted in twenty-three policemen being removed from the New York City Police Department.[8] By the end, nearly five hundred cops had resigned, retired to protect their pensions, or been fired.[9]

The attention of state investigators to the O'Dwyer administration swung toward someone with whom Bill had felt a particular affinity: his two-hundred-pound, six-foot-tall cohort James Moran. Like Bill, Moran, forty-nine, was the oldest child from a large family who traced his ancestry to County Mayo. After taking a civil service test, Moran (known as "Red" due to his hair) went to work at the county criminal courts in Brooklyn. It was at the Fourth Avenue courthouse that he came to the attention of Bill while serving as a judicial attendant and legal secretary who thoroughly knew the workings of the building. A "fatherly" assignment official in the county court, Dan Corrigan, advised the local magistrate O'Dwyer, "Everybody knows you have a sick wife"—Kitty O'Dwyer was suffering the early effects of Parkinson's—"and this court is full of gossip. I would get a male rather than a female stenographer/secretary."[10] Bill agreed.

Moran impressed Bill with his ability to assign cases, move the calendar efficiently, and perform menial tasks that the judge invariably preferred to fob off on underlings. Not unexpectedly, Bill brought Moran along as his chief of staff when he won election to Brooklyn district attorney; when he became mayor, Bill appointed him as deputy fire commissioner. A strong personal bond adhered between the two working-class Irishmen. Bill was grateful for Moran helping him during the war: "Big Jim" not only attended to his boss's financial affairs after he went on leave in the army but also looked in daily on Mrs. O'Dwyer. He was the district attorney's right arm, including during Bill's military enlistment.[11]

Had Bill not gone back on his original intention to resign from the mayoralty in his reelection year, he would almost certainly have become a less tempting piñata for political opponents and investigators. But according to several reports, Moran forcefully argued that Bill should continue in office.[12] According to one unconfirmed account, in the hospital room Moran burned the retirement papers the ailing mayor had quietly filed, accidentally setting fire to the wastepaper and bringing firefighters up to the room.[13] Whether true or apocryphal, the rumor depicted a Bill given to changing his mind, unable to say no for fear of making an enemy instead of a friend. That, at least, rang true.[14]

In his final hours at city hall, Bill rewarded Moran for his loyalty by naming him as a commissioner on the Board of Water Supplies, a paid appointment with no end date. The appointment raised eyebrows, as did other eleventh-hour gestures for cronies. But Moran found himself drowning in a miasma of corruption charges. He gave up the position as Manhattan District Attorney Frank Hogan homed in on his career in the O'Dwyer administration. Press reports began to circulate that Moran had allegedly served as a conduit for illicit contributions that may have found their way into private pockets and campaign treasuries during Bill's mayoral races in both 1945 and 1949. Moran became legally vulnerable with the discovery of bribes he was accused of having demanded from city oil-burner inspectors—a surreptitious fire department practice that some believed to be of long standing, but one that amounted to a reported half a million dollars a year.[15]

Those who were forced to pay the kickbacks may not have known the ultimate recipient of the arrangements, which could have been Moran, Bill's campaigns, or, as press reports suggested, Bill himself. What *was* important, and immediately apparent, was that if the fire department inspectors had wanted to stay in the good graces of the O'Dwyer administration, they had needed to please the mayor's right-hand man.

Though known as a straight shooter, Hogan was upset that Bill had dangled and then withheld support for a 1949 mayoral run in place of him. The district attorney took an unusual step—visiting Moran in New York's forbidding holding cell, the Tombs, after his February 1952 conviction in the extortion scheme. In the chapel of the jail, Hogan disclosed that his real target was Bill. He offered Moran a suspended sentence if he cooperated with the investigation. But Moran spurned the offer, reportedly saying, "I came into this world a man—and I'm going out a man."[16]

Still protesting his innocence, Moran was sentenced to twelve and a half to twenty-five years in prison. (His cause was not helped by his earlier testimony before the Kefauver Committee that he had only received the Brooklyn police bookmaker Louis Weber in his office a few times—an assertion flatly contradicted by the office receptionist's memory that the number of visits was closer to one hundred.) Looking back many years later, Myron Beldock, a noted New York defense attorney and the son of the Dewey-appointed successor to Bill as Brooklyn district attorney, attributed what he called the sentence's harshness to the notoriety of the case and the need for a scapegoat. Beldock questioned why prosecutors had not "followed the money" up the political ladder to learn the identity of the main culprits, potentially including one or more powerful men holding office and their election campaigns.[17]

Said Moran's son, Robert, "They wanted something on O'Dwyer. They wanted O'Dwyer in the worst way. They thought they'd get it from my father. He didn't have it to give them. It's that simple. And he wouldn't make it up. . . . He paid a tough price."[18]

After nine years, Moran's sons, acting as his attorneys, succeeded in winning his release from the federal penitentiary in Danbury, Connecticut, where he had been sent to serve an additional sentence for perjury and income tax evasion. He returned to the once familiar job from which he had begun his climb: stenographer, in this case for his lawyer son Eugene. In January 1968, riding on a subway train in Brooklyn with his wife, Josephine, he suffered a fatal heart attack.[19]

In the years between Moran's 1952 conviction and 1968 death, Bill never reached out to his former friend. However, Paul sought to acknowledge what Moran's friendship had meant to Bill by going to his wake—"the only public man" in attendance, according to New York Times reporter Sidney Zion.[20]

The magnanimity of Paul's gesture was not lost on the Moran family. As Robert Moran noted, nearly fifty years later, "Paul was a wonderful man, a real prince." Robert pointed to O'Dwyer's extensive pro bono representation in civil rights cases. "He gave away more business than most lawyers would get in a lifetime. He was a true believer for the downtrodden. That was not an act."[21]

Still another appointee of concern for the mayor was Frank Bals, a retired police captain whom Bill, shortly after becoming mayor, had appointed "seventh" deputy police commissioner—a newly created position. Bals, who had been roundly criticized as the head of the detail in charge of Abe Reles's protective custody when the star mob witness plunged to his death from a window of the Half Moon Hotel in Coney Island in 1941, was assigned responsibility for a plainclothes unit investigating organized crime. But Bals only lasted about four months in the mayoral assignment, as Bill eased him out after accusations were made that Bals had tipped off bookmakers to possible arrests, interfered in police operations, and crossed bureaucratic lines. The appointment, while enlarging Bals's pension, diminished Bill's reputation as a crime-fighter, particularly once Gross alternated between referring to the unit of corrupt cops as "Bals's squad" and "the Mayor's squad." Bill conceded after his mayoralty that he had made a "boner" with this appointment. All in all, it only added to the perception that Bill had been at best negligent and at worst complicit in the corruption clinging to the police, and fire, departments.[22]

PAUL AND BILL did not fully grasp how the political and media landscapes were shifting beneath their feet in the months after the dramatic conclusion of the O'Dwyer administration. Even with his penchant for delegating authority, Bill still had to pay more than a modicum of attention to day-to-day embassy tasks. The situation with Paul was more complicated: he lacked Bill's direct experience in the political arena, and there were long stretches when, due to a quarrel or his own activities, he had not consulted with Bill.

In a 1962 oral history interview for Columbia, Bill left no doubt that he had felt overwhelmed by his responsibilities as mayor, using words like "big," "colossal," and "terrifying" to describe the job. His personal woes in his first term left him positively miserable about the burdens. "There was no glamor in it, I had a sick wife at home. I had a million headaches in City Hall and they continued with me when I was there."[23]

In contrast, an ambassador's life offered a welcome distraction.[24] Bill's elegant second wife, the Texas-born Simpson, made the cover of *Life* magazine in May 1950, looking relaxed under a wide-brimmed hat in lipstick and pearls, and Bill basked in the warm climate and even warmer relationships with the Mexican people and their US-friendly government.

The new ambassador's command of Spanish was smooth; his manner was genial; his Catholicism was appreciated by the churchgoing public; his acquaintance with three of six living former Mexican presidents was useful; and his interest in the issues affecting US-Mexican relations was genuine.

Bill thrived in the social environment in which department heads at the embassy handled the administrative niceties while he waited for more sensitive, higher-level points in negotiations to make use of his friendship with the Mexican president Miguel Alemán; it dated back to Alemán's visits to Gracie Mansion and the advent of Mexico's assiduous courting of US corporations and foreign aid. Meanwhile, Acapulco brought a steady flow of Hollywood movie stars and the nascent "jet set."[25] The punchbowl parties in the ambassador's Mexico City residence were glittering, with a cultured and convivial host and his glamorous wife at their center. The O'Dwyers made a point of including everyday Mexicans, not just those with access to cash and clout. Bill made trips to virtually all thirty-two Mexican states.

US embassy staffers were well aware of the allegations back home about their new boss. "The contemporary explanation," said Smith Simpson, who was first secretary and labor attaché in Mexico City at the time, was "to get him out of the country in a sufficiently official position so that nobody would try to subpoena him."

Nevertheless, no matter why President Truman and Secretary of State Dean Acheson appointed him or the Senate handily confirmed him, Bill by most accounts acquitted himself well. The rumors about corruption emanating from New York did not concern representatives of the Mexican government, Simpson observed: "The Mexicans didn't feel there was anything wrong about sending an ambassador there who was under a cloud—many of their politicians were under clouds, so it made no difference to them that our ambassador was." The new Irish-born diplomat was "friendly, outgoing, unpretentious"—a far cry from "many Norte Américanos [who] come down there with a superior air."[26] "I think and I know many people, including some Republicans, feel that Bill was one of the best ambassadors we ever had in Mexico, certainly up to that time," recalled David Stowe, who was an administrative assistant to Truman.[27]

Ambassador O'Dwyer negotiated a settlement of Mexico's lend-lease account, expedited the Truman administration's "Point Four" aid for farm education, public health nursing, and mining, and oversaw the consolidation of American embassy offices from all over the city into a new chancery building. The ex-mayor had "a solid list of accomplishments in the year since [he] presented his credentials Nov. 23, 1950," summarized the United Press reporter Laurance Stuntz. "In fact, diplomacy has not given the ambassador any trouble."[28]

Bill was especially proud of negotiating the Migratory Labor Agreement, the first international pact to protect braceros, the seasonal Mexican farmhands who crossed the border to work in the United States. He had been aware that the workers were exploited through meager wages, substandard housing and food, and backbreaking labor under the scorching sun, as well as their arbitrary treatment by US authorities—who conveniently overlooked the lapsing of their legal status during labor shortages, arresting and placing them in detention camps for shipment back home when they were no longer so needed.[29]

The agreement, however, expired after only six months, as the Mexican government refused to extend it or negotiate a new one until the US government passed legislation aimed at ensuring fairer treatment by the employers of the undocumented workers. Bill urged renewal of the accord.[30]

Like others in the State Department, Bill said he hoped that a report from the President's Commission on Migratory Labor would lead Congress to pass legislation protecting domestic farm laborers in the United States and reducing reliance on foreign workers, especially the Mexicans. But the increasingly powerful postwar conservative movement stymied any changes in the existing labor arrangements benefiting large-scale growers.[31]

In his later years at city hall, when multiple crises weighed on him, Bill had found the weather and hospitality at his brother Frank's large commercial produce farm in El Centro in California's Imperial Valley to be salubrious. By the early 1950s, the continuing visits raised the suspicions of federal agents, who subjected this most apolitical of the O'Dwyer brothers to nine examinations of his books and—to no avail—searches of the property for Bill's "buried" cash.[32]

New Yorkers back home may have wondered why Bill was going out of town so often. No single event, however, would prove as damaging as his testimony before the US Senate's Special Committee on Organized Crime in Interstate Commerce—popularly known as the Kefauver Committee. It took its moniker from its chair, Senator Estes Kefauver, a Tennessee Democrat who had drafted the resolution creating the five-man investigative panel.[33] While not the first televised congressional hearing, it became the first to garner all-consuming national attention, the product of both the growing new mass communications medium and a constant fascination since the beginning of Prohibition: mobsters in America. For Kefauver, who had won his Senate race after adopting a coonskin cap as his trademark, the hearing on organized crime would encourage presidential ambitions.[34]

In its formative stages, the committee reached out to Paul about sending a representative to meet with Bill in Mexico, with the possibility that he might later come north to testify. Acquainted with committee counsel Louis Yavner from his days as the commissioner of investigation for La Guardia, Bill initially saw little reason to worry, conversing with the investigator informally in the embassy-issued car and at the embassy residence, where Yavner stayed as a guest in February 1951.[35]

By the end of the month Bill was concerned about the steady attention he was receiving from the feds. Another investigator, Irving Saypol, the US attorney for the Southern District of New York, arrived in Mexico City to speak with him. This latest visitor bluntly informed him that "the situation was worse than he knew and that the entire public was against him"; noticing a large soft-drink sign near the embassy, he snickered, "I suppose by now you're a part owner in that company," as if to imply that Bill was using his contacts in Mexico to make money on the side.[36]

The unappreciated attention of Washington probers brought Paul to Mexico to speak to Bill and to communicate on his behalf to the committee staff. The defensiveness Bill had manifested in his last months at city hall returned in full measure. He angrily told Paul—whose picture had appeared in a local paper among a group at the embassy—"to remain out of photographs in the future."[37]

A national audience for Kefauver's true-crime traveling show had been building for over a month, with the first hearings held in New Orleans and Detroit, when it reached New York in March 1951. The hearings then became a public obsession: "Kefauver block parties" sprang up spontaneously, while attendance at Broadway productions dropped as people stayed home, went to a bar, or stood outside one of the new stores selling

TVs to gawk.[38] In the climactic moments of the hearings, two men whose paths had crossed nine years before in a Central Park West apartment were separately questioned before thirty million TV viewers nationwide: Frank Costello and William O'Dwyer.

Known in the press as the "Prime Minister of the Underworld," Costello had objected to testifying because microphones would interfere with his ability to consult privately with his attorney. But Kefauver's compromise—only permitting cameras to focus on the Tammany Hall–associated mobster's hands—ironically seemed to do Costello's reputation more harm than good; his hand-wringing under questioning encouraged viewers to link his hands, rather than his hidden-from-view mug, to all sorts of underworld venality.

Juxtaposed with an unsavory character, Bill did not leave a much more positive impression when he voluntarily took questions. Having already spoken to Senator Kefauver and the committee counsel Rudolph Halley before being interviewed by a committee emissary at the Mexican embassy, he regarded the probe as a "rehash" liable to produce "nothing which had not been already known by the New York prosecutors." All the accusations had indeed been flagged before grand jury members and newspaper readers again and again in his mayoral years. Paul felt the same.

So—with his brother Paul's concurrence—he came north voluntarily to clear the air.[39]

But he faced a drastically different atmosphere than either brother anticipated—a visceral, firsthand experience of what Saypol had warned him about, that the situation back in New York was "worse than he knew." In place of the thousands of people clapping and cheering in a ticker tape parade, he encountered a gaggle of news reporters as he stepped off the plane at Idlewild Airport. A few platitudes later he found his way to a waiting black car, as arranged by Paul.

The sense of Bill having being forsaken by his party only intensified downtown. Shaky from a bout with the flu and running a temperature, he withered under the glare of multiple cameras in the crowded hearing room in New York's Federal Courthouse. His testimony over two days was long on bristling exchanges with one panel member in particular, the moralistic Charles Tobey, a Republican from New Hampshire, and short on specifics. He mopped his brow as Tobey asked about his visit with Jim Moran to the Central Park West apartment of Frank Costello during an Army Air Force investigation of one of Costello's associates, a supplier named Joe Baker.[40] Though a number of Tammany's regulars were also present, sipping cocktails, this was an investigatory mission, Bill insisted. Critics forever doubted him, believing that he sought Costello's, and Tammany's, endorsement in anticipation of his race for mayor three years hence.

Bill proved himself a combative witness when responding to Tobey's finger-wagging.

TOBEY: "Why did Moran go to the apartment with you, to carry a bag or what? Was he an errand boy, a companion, an advisor?"

O'DWYER: "Senator, if the answer is intended to be anything other than sarcastic, I will answer it."

TOBEY: "When you were there, were you conscious that he was a gangster?"

O'DWYER: "I was conscious that he had a reputation as a very big book-maker."

TOBEY: "It seems to me you should have said about Costello, 'Unclean, unclean!' And that you should have left him alone, as if he were a leper. But instead you trotted up to his place—"

O'DWYER: "I had *business* with him. They say there is a lot of it in your home state of New Hampshire—30 million dollars a year ... I wonder who the bookmakers in Breton Woods support for public office in New Hampshire?"

TOBEY, TURNING CRIMSON: "I hate a four-flusher!"

When the hearing-room audience, bestirred, settled down, Tobey resumed questioning O'Dwyer about his visit to the underworld figure's apartment in 1942.

"You were not embarrassed?" the senator asked.

"Nothing embarrasses me that happens in Manhattan," came Bill's terse reply.[41]

———

IN AGREEING TO APPEAR before the committee, Bill, with Paul's okay, had unwittingly stepped on a live grenade, bringing no defenses other than his wit and folksiness. Both had served him well in a less conspiratorial era but now made him appear evasive or simply out of touch.

Although organized crime encompassed a wide variety of activities—"protection," prostitution, murder, blackmail, and gambling, according to the committee's mission statement—it was the last of these that drew the Kefauver Committee's continuing attention, for it exerted a pervasive influence on politicians and law enforcement in city and state governments nationwide.

But with the Kefauver Committee hearings highlighting the symbiotic connections between the mob and the machines, New York's political bosses and their long and colorful history of scandals came under intense scrutiny by the panel. Viewed through the midcentury lens of conspiracy, even Bill's past appeal to Governor Dewey to relax restrictions related to gambling—a vice, the then mayor noted, that was at least as old as Western civilization—was portrayed as a sop to underworld figures. It was no wonder Dewey himself, the great rackets-buster of the 1930s, declined to appear before the committee to answer questions about an annual underworld gathering held at the Saratoga racetrack with the apparent acquiescence of the state superintendent of police.

The issue of organized crime had exploded into the nation's consciousness in an environment shaped by Cold War exigencies. Just as communists sought to erode the international appeal of democracy following World War II, so the mob world's lucre was subverting democracy from within, the new zeitgeist went. Senator Joe McCarthy's description of the danger posed by communism—"a conspiracy on a scale so immense as to dwarf any previous such venture in the history of man"—evoked the same kind of secretive, sprawling enterprise. Much of the Kefauver Committee's findings were furthered by separate hearings before Dewey's New York State Crime Commission, where latter-day Abe Reles types drew a picture of a post-Prohibition criminal syndicate that grew highly centralized—a cooperating syndicate with a kangaroo court for those accused of endangering the Mafia's code of conduct. While paralleling the growing specter of international communism, it simplified a more complex reality, relying partly upon uncorroborated statements by insider witnesses.

So, what once had been regarded as a local problem for cities and states to contend with, and something unworthy of sustained FBI attention since the 1930s, was now seen as a grave threat to democracy, insidious, pervasive, and national in scope. As a consequence, Bill would not be looked at as someone who may have pulled punches on behalf of loosely tied gangsters and other characters then plaguing New York—serious though the accusation was—but rather as a figure who abetted an "alien" conspiracy with a large cast of Italian American criminals that had destabilized the American experiment from within, just when it needed to be strongest.[42]

The hearings were devastating for Bill. Paul, who endured them, felt instantly that Bill was the victim of a political ambush. The feeling that he had erred badly in letting Bill appear was impossible to deny.

In the end, the committee's summary report slammed Bill's service both as Brooklyn district attorney and as New York City mayor, stating, "Neither he nor his appointees took any effective action against the top echelons of the gambling, narcotics, waterfront, murder, or bookmaking rackets. In fact, his actions impeded promising investigations of such rackets. His defense of public officials who were derelict in their duties, and his actions in investigations of corruption, and his failure to follow up concrete evidence of organized crime, particularly in the case of Murder Inc., and the waterfront, have contributed to the growth of organized crime, racketeering and gangsterism in New York City."[43]

"In a few paragraphs, they had distorted a lifetime of accomplishment in the public domain," Bill lamented in the wake of the document's release. He called it "a crushing blow."[44] Paul certainly concurred. Other defenders of Bill's public record might have agreed with the first part of his lament. Virtually no one who had ever encountered the ebullient O'Dwyer, however, could argue with the second.

The assassination of "Bill-O's" character, and spirit, was described vividly over a decade later by Clifford Evans, a onetime *Brooklyn Eagle* reporter who regularly relied on Bill as a source and came to view him as a friend.

"Suddenly, it was as if the world were coming to an end," Evans remembered the moments when Bill, facing increasingly hostile questions, realized he was the panel's target rather than friendly witness. "And what made it so horrible was that, with things going bad for him, there was yet nothing that one could put a finger on. And yet things had gone bad."

The sense of deflation and dejection exhibited by Bill was palpable in the room at the Roosevelt Hotel where he stayed during the hearings. Evans continued,

Suddenly he looked old. Suddenly this very proud man . . . who had gone from bartender here in N.Y. all the way up to being the No. 1 citizen as Mayor, and then during the war, had become a General and had been given the rank in our State Department of minister—a man who, single handedly, on assignment from Roosevelt, had negotiated with dollars and in secrecy for the saving of thousands of Jews from Hitler's Germany—a man who had done so much to make us feel good, and suddenly, everything just crashed. The grayness about him and the open window there—it was kind of a difficult moment.[45]

Bill saw his prospects for any further elective, appointive, or even advisory roles in government vanish. His reputation had fallen from crusading crime-buster and effective mayor to one of the most hounded figures ever to have lived at Gracie Mansion. Shadowed by rumors that he would have to resign because of the hearings, he faced inquiries by two district attorneys, a US attorney, two state attorneys general, the New York State Crime Commission, and the Internal Revenue Service.[46]

Under enormous pressure, Bill buckled. An account by Lester Velie in *Collier's* told of how, upon returning to Mexico from the Kefauver hearings, Bill had "collapsed at the airport. At the Embassy he locked himself in the library and it took literally days of persuasion by his doctor to bring him out." Bill, discussing it a decade later, did not confirm the details in Velie's account but said, "I was in shock."[47]

As time went on, tensions developed with Sloane, reportedly fueled by Bill's jealousy and increased drinking and Sloane's sense, as his term as ambassador neared its end, that life outside the United States for an increasingly indefinite period was not what she had had in mind when she married him.

The rumors of trouble between the two, at first denied, became reality with the granting of a temporary separation by Mexico City's archbishop near the end of 1953 and their divorce in Cuernavaca the next year.[48]

Long after he had seen the demoralizing impact of the hearings on Bill, Paul still regretted that he had not heeded the warning by his brother's doctor that he might be unable to stand the strain of the televised Kefauver Committee spectacle; this was the same physician who had warned him to slow down while mayor due to concern about his heart.

"I felt his [Bill's] appearance was imperative because he should not let his detractors say they had frightened him from coming to a town over which he had presided with such distinction for five years. It was immature reasoning, and in retrospect, I believe I would not have given that advice to a client not related to me but otherwise under the same circumstance,"[49] Paul later wrote. Well after the furor caused by Bill's appearance before the Kefauver Committee had died down, Paul showed still-persistent committee probers the door at his Manhattan law office, refusing to answer still more questions about his brother because of the way the panel had treated him.

Paul's anger and dismay were compounded by his belief that the Kefauver Committee had deliberately steered away from those in office whose careers might not have withstood such a grilling, such as Governor Dewey, Interim Mayor Vincent Impellitteri, the five city district attorneys, and even the panel's own Charles Tobey of New Hampshire and Herbert O'Conor of Maryland. But mostly he regarded the interrogation as a "rank injustice." At a congressional hearing, he noted, witnesses did not enjoy any of the legal protections the Constitution afforded a defendant in a court of law, such as the rules of evidence or right of appeal. More particularly, Bill had never profited financially from his positions, according to Paul. "Money had never been his god, and the suggestion that in the office he sought to serve with such dedication he had fouled his nest was infuriating to me,"[50] he said. In fact, in the back of Paul's mind must have been the memory of how Bill had asked for financial assistance from Paul, Frank, and his closest associates before leaving New York for Mexico City.[51]

WHILE BILL WAS MAYOR, Paul found himself often irritated by Bill's consistent foibles—the difficulty keeping appointments, the lack of regret for inconveniencing others, the deficient sense of obligation to family members in Bohola, and the political flip-flopping.[52] But all such ambivalence about Bill's conduct seemed to evaporate when Kefauver made a spectacle of him. Though Paul could have benefited, as an aspiring politician, from distancing himself from Bill, the thought did not appear to occur to him—then, before, or after.

"William O'Dwyer's career was shadowed at its end by scandals of the sort that are more gossip than substance but which are still enough to reduce any public man to being one of the circus animals of our profession," wrote the New York columnist Murray Kempton. "Paul O'Dwyer was proud of his brother when it was useful to him; and he remained not just proud but fiercely proud when it was a handicap."[53]

Bill continued, all the same, to be plagued by whispers of considerably less substance. The FBI, CIA, State Department, Treasury Department, and Passport Division fed each other scraps of gossip and, no doubt, planted tips with reporters. A front-page report in August 1951 in the *Daily News* raised the question of whether his personal account at Chase National Bank had received a $1 million letter of credit transferred from Banco de Mexico—as if he might have been caught red-handed receiving a massive payoff.

Within days, a State Department spokesman and even an internal Hoover memo pointed out that the transfer was a payment for lend-lease goods made by the Mexican government and a legitimate government transaction. None of this discouraged the Eisenhower administration's undersecretary of the Treasury, Marion Folsom, from rehashing the allegation not long after the Republicans took over the White House, in a memo to Secretary of State John Foster Dulles.[54]

A subsequent memo from Hoover to the State Department's Office of Security even more absurdly flagged a Bill-and-Paul tie to Cuba's Fidel Castro, based on the sketchiest of reports and assumptions.[55]

One story in the press made Bill livid more than any other: that he intended to renounce US citizenship and remain in Mexico City beyond the end of the ambassadorship. Paul phoned from New York with this news, saying that it had "hit every paper." His besieged older sibling called a press conference at the embassy, where he denounced the United Press reporter Robert Prescott before his news colleagues as a "lying bastard" and ordered him out of the building.[56]

———

WITH AN INCOMING Republican Party administration poised to make its own appointments, Bill resigned as ambassador in December 1952. His successor, Francis White, irritated Mexico's diplomats by removing Bill's portrait from among those of other former ambassadors (while simultaneously speaking of his "corruption"). But White's act of pettiness enlisted a measure of sympathy for Bill among Democrats who had sought to distance themselves from him after the Kefauver hearings. White's suc-

cessor, Robert Hill, received some strong advice from the then Democratic
Senate majority leader Lyndon Johnson, according to Ben Stephansky, the
labor attaché at the Mexico City embassy: "The first thing I want you to
do is put that picture right back up." He did so.[57]

Oscar and Becky Bernstien's friendship with a prominent Mexico City
lawyer allowed O'Dwyer & Bernstien to establish a branch there staffed
by the lawyer's son and Bill. The former ambassador used the opportunity
to entertain visiting actors, journalists, and politicians in his three-room
penthouse apartment, where a butler prepared his meals. O'Dwyer, Bernstien & Correa never fulfilled the hopes of its founders in attracting the
patronage of Mexican and American commercial interests. After eight
years of sporadic business, it would close in 1960.[58]

But as far as many New Yorkers were concerned, during this period
Bill remained "The Man Who Won't Come Home," as a two-part *Collier's* series on his rise and fall put it in 1953.[59]

At the height of his popularity and power, Bill had personified all the
possibilities for advancement that Gotham offered to a hardworking immigrant. After his downfall, he instead represented the urban politician's
temptations for unsavory compromise. Had he given up on the American dream?

He confessed to his Columbia University interviewer that he had not.

"If you can't stand up to a little tragedy once in a while, you'll end
up in a saloon, like *The Iceman Cometh* indicated, and you give up the
fight," Bill O'Dwyer replied. "This is no world for weaklings, unless
they're satisfied with mediocrity. And that's all I have to say."[60]

7

"A VERY PECULIAR TIME"

B
Y 1953, Paul was "feeling very vulnerable because we were living in a very peculiar time," as he put it.[1] Although the postwar economic boom was under way, and his small law firm was stable, he was feeling compelled to parachute into his ambassador brother's unsteady professional life and marriage in Mexico City. He was at the same time navigating the political landscape of Cold War America, something of a danger zone for someone who defended radical unionists associated with the American Labor Party and joined civil rights activists to challenge rampant housing and employment discrimination in New York.

O'Dwyer's years of involvement in the National Lawyers Guild (NLG) were equally conspicuous by the time the House Un-American Activities Committee (HUAC) branded the guild, in a scathing 1950 report, as the "Legal Bulwark of the Communist Party." He had served as president of the NLG's New York chapter in 1947 and 1948 and on the national executive board from 1948 to 1951. J. Edgar Hoover first noticed him in 1940 when he was part of the defense team for the International Fur and Leather Workers Union, one of the country's most radical unions.

The work of defending individual rights was riskier once the Cold War began in earnest five years later. Principled lawyers devoted to the Bill of Rights took on the task, contending that whenever constitutionally protected freedoms of expression, assembly, or religion were threatened, so too was American democracy. As Bill was a continual subject of surveillance, Paul could never be sure that right-wing opportunists would refrain from accusing the brother of the former US ambassador of disloyalty to their adopted country.

The FBI, however, did not appear to notice Paul's departure from the front lines of NLG engagement in 1953; it was the last year of the Korean War and the height of Joe McCarthy's anti-communist crusade. But Paul's cohorts in the guild certainly did.

The resignation was unexpected. Looked at superficially, O'Dwyer leaving a group that included disciples of Marx and Engels could have signaled a retreat from the intensifying struggle over democratic values, the very ones that thousands of Americans had recently been killed or maimed trying to protect. While delivered orally—not in writing—his NLG resignation did not, in fact, mark a withdrawal from the struggle for democratic principles in the United States in the McCarthy years and atomic age. O'Dwyer continued, outside the auspices of the guild, to represent accused Communists and so-called fellow travelers, most conspicuously Martha Dodd Stern, the daughter of the former American ambassador in Hitler's Berlin—she turned to O'Dwyer in 1957 when, as a Soviet agent and major financial contributor to the American Communist Party, she was facing extradition by Mexico, to be followed in the United States by charges of espionage. Paul quickly grew convinced that the ex-Chicagoan, who had been under FBI watch since the late 1940s, would incur the same fate as Julius and Ethel Rosenberg if forced to return, together with her husband, the millionaire New York investor Alfred Stern Jr. Paul intervened to help the couple fight extradition, lasting until the Sterns fled from Mexico to Soviet-controlled Prague.

Similarly, O'Dwyer teamed up with Leonard Boudin to defend the guild's executive director, Martin Popper, in 1961–62, though Paul had long before quit the NLG. Popper served as a consultant to the United States delegation at the San Francisco conference that organized the United Nations, a legal observer for the American Bar Association at the Nuremberg trials of Nazi war criminals, and the lawyer for Dalton Trumbo and John Howard Lawson of the "Hollywood Ten." After declining to answer certain questions from a HUAC subcommittee in 1959, he was cited for contempt of Congress and convicted in federal court. O'Dwyer and Boudin got the finding reversed, and Popper returned to a senior role with the NLG.

So, while not intending to duck the "Red Scare" hysteria, Paul wanted his resignation from the NLG to be as little noticed as possible. In fact, his departure may have been one of the rare NLG internal developments since its founding in 1937 that did not receive governmental scrutiny. Formed as an alternative to the racially segregated American Bar Association, which supported Supreme Court decisions overturning New Deal legislation, the NLG aimed, according to a preamble to its constitution, to be "a professional organization which shall function as an effective social force in the service of the people to the end that human rights shall be regarded as more sacred than property interests." What was more, it emerged as an outgrowth of the controversy over Franklin D. Roosevelt's controversial "court-packing" scheme to tilt the balance away from the hidebound right-wing majority on the Supreme Court.[2]

During the Great Depression, the NLG had been appealing to a recent law school graduate drawn to championing the rights of the working class after his initial sojourn as a criminal lawyer. One of the developing unions that Paul got hooked into was the Transport Workers Union, formed by a group of seminal municipal-labor activists, including Mike Quill, who had channeled his youthful service as an anti–Free State volunteer for the Irish Republican Army (IRA) into organizing New York's woefully underpaid bus and subway workers. Paul modeled his own guiding principles as a lawyer partly on NLG founders like Frank Walsh of Kansas City, Missouri, a fierce defender of labor. Another founder, Louis McCabe of Philadelphia, represented union and government targets. For O'Dwyer, it was notable, too, that Walsh and McCabe were champions of Irish freedom during the 1920s, while the grandfather of the guild pioneer and inaugural president Robert Kenny had emigrated from Ireland in the Famine era a century before.[3]

In defending political dissidents, the NLG members were the descendants of the early twentieth century's "attorney for the damned," Clarence Darrow, who, in a ringing 1920 defense of twenty members of the Communist Labor Party, said, "I know that the Constitution is a delusion and a snare if the weakest and the humblest man in the land cannot be defended in his right to speak and his right to think as much as the greatest and the strongest in the land. I am not here to defend their opinions. I am here to defend their rights to express their opinions."[4]

By 1946, the NLG membership topped 2,500 lawyers plus more than 500 nonvoting law students, a thorn in Hoover's side just when Cold War tensions and paranoia about homegrown communism began to accelerate. One month after Winston Churchill's speech warning of an "Iron Curtain" descending in Europe, Harry Truman's attorney general, Tom Clark, sounded the alarm against homegrown revolutionaries who used "every device in the legal category to further the interests of those who would destroy our government by force, if necessary." Though Clark stopped short of listing the NLG as a Communist front, HUAC picked up his cudgel four years later and branded it with its "Legal Bulwark" report—featuring extensive input from the FBI—and the guild's membership fell by one-third. The association managed to survive this battering since it had distinguished itself by taking the cases of the Hollywood Ten and the longshoremen's union organizer Harry Bridges, as well as other strong union leaders who faced expulsion in the wake of the anti-labor Taft-Hartley Act of 1947.[5]

Not only the NLG's steadfast left-wing members but also its policy of welcoming lawyers of any race, gender, or affiliation left it out of step with the climate of fear and accusation and the politicians who, for their own reasons, grossly exaggerated the size and influence of the small American Communist Party. The NLG was out of step, too, with those seeking to narrow the ideological spectrum and strip out voices of the left from culture, education, and politics. Paul, of course, said a healthy democracy required a broad and unrestricted bandwidth of opinions and ideas, and understood that "many of the people in the New York chapter [of the guild] were members of the Communist Party, or if they weren't members, they were espoused to the same cause"—economic rights for the working class in the face of wealth and reaction, as well as the hope, despite evidence to the contrary, that the Soviet experiment in socialism represented a step toward a fairer society. Many who had lived through the Great Depression wrought by unregulated capitalism remained inspired by the Soviet constitution, with its guarantees of ethnic, religious, and gender equality. Paul felt no enthusiasm for the Soviet state, but he generally liked the older Marxist lawyers who had helped found the group—interesting, passionate, worldly men, and, typically, Jews of Eastern European extraction who argued heatedly with one another about such subjects as how to end lynching in the South, economic equities in the workplace, and the causes of the two world wars in their lifetime.

Still, Paul pointed out, the Marxists "didn't represent the majority" of the group in the 1940s when he was most active. Hoover, too, understood this: a 1950 internal memo informed him that a random check of the NLG's membership lists, purloined in a black bag job at the guild's headquarters in Washington, DC, had revealed that only 6.6 percent of guild members were members of the Communist Party.[6]

Yet Hoover remained determined to clip the NLG's wings. One plausible target lay behind this goal: Leonard Boudin, who associated with the guild as he came into his own as a constitutional attorney on the left in the late 1940s. Boudin made the FBI's legally dubious investigative practices the core of a successful 1951 appeal of the conviction on espionage charges of Judith Coplon, a New York–based Department of Justice employee who, later evidence suggested, was indeed a spy. The defense lawyer's focus on constitutionally questionable FBI evidence and machinations forced Hoover to shift to pressuring his investigative targets to compromise themselves or others before congressional committees.[7] He could no longer make their radical beliefs or the circles in which they traveled the grounds for successful prosecution. As a result, Boudin became the bane of Hoover, and so were lawyers at the NLG who represented many hauled before congressional inquisitors based on dirt turned up by the nation's top G-man.

———

DURING O'DWYER'S term as president of the NLG's active New York chapter, the Justice Department tended to view the city as a veritable hive of subversion. The department's mindset was rarely more evident than in 1949, the year of the successful Communist revolution in mainland China and the disclosure of the Soviet Union's infiltration of the top secret "Manhattan Project." Tom Clark, a future Supreme Court justice, prosecuted the "New York Twelve" under the Smith Act, which made it a crime to advocate the violent overthrow of the government. The dozen defendants were alleged to have associated with the enemy nation. They included several individuals Paul admired and associated with in civil and labor rights, such as the Harlem city councilman Benjamin Davis, the furriers' union official Irving Potash, and the Communist Party leader Gus Hall. The New York chapter of the NLG, with Paul's involvement, filed a friend-of-the-court brief on their behalf.

On the trial's first day, four hundred cops, some on horseback, kept a far greater number of demonstrators and the curious away from the doors of the federal courthouse in Manhattan's Foley Square. Inside, five defense lawyers began to engage in heated clashes with Justice Harold Medina. A forerunner of the "Chicago Seven" government conspiracy trial a generation later because of attorneys' disruptions, the ten-month trial unfolded as President Truman provided Americans with shocking and transformative revelations, including that the Soviets had tested their first A-bomb. Soon, duck-and-cover announcements over school loudspeakers, civil safety drills, and home fallout shelters grew routine. Against that backdrop, the proceedings twice made the cover of *Time*.

Federal prosecutors relied on informants who, at one point, were goaded on the witness stand to distill sinister motivations from a passage by Karl Marx despite the witnesses' lack of familiarity with the text. The defense, shooting for a mistrial, frequently interrupted to protest the kangaroo court atmosphere. But the jury in the end found all of the defendants guilty, and Medina not only sentenced the notorious twelve (all, that is, except the Communist Party USA general secretary William Foster, cut loose due to a serious illness), but he sent their lawyers to prison, too—for contempt of court. The NLG pounced, saying the punishment of lawyers jeopardized "the people's right to effective representation, and the attorney's right and duty of vigorous advocacy." [8]

One person who incurred Medina's wrath was McCabe, the NLG cofounder. He was forced to spend five months behind bars. When he finally walked free from the West Eleventh Street jailhouse, O'Dwyer and a few other colleagues, including Elizabeth Gurley Flynn, were gathered to greet him. [9]

———

THE TERM *WITCH HUNT*, adopted by the left to signify intense political suppression, was an inexact metaphor for the flow of investigations into Communist infiltration. While there were no covens of witches in Salem Village, Massachusetts, in 1692, another episode of scapegoating by powerful men, there were certainly Communists in twentieth-century America, even if only a handful proved to have engaged in espionage. [10] But what "witch hunt" did accurately represent was the anti-communist mania that engulfed American life in the first decade after the end of World War II as Eastern Europe fell under Soviet control. In the new Red Scare, featuring right-wingers waving lists and flinging charges, the channels for constitutionally protected freedoms were severely narrowed. Most famously, a New York Jewish couple, the Rosenbergs, went to the electric chair in 1953 after their conviction on charges of passing military secrets to the Soviet Union.

At the same time, the left's blanket condemnation of prosecutions of accused collaborators only seemed to fuel political reaction. When, for example, the former State Department official Alger Hiss was convicted of perjury charges related to his denial of knowing the American Communist Party member and Soviet spy Whittaker Chambers, "one of the anticommunist right's endless and amorphous charges about treachery in government had been proven," wrote Richard Gid Powers, a historian of the FBI and the anti-communist movement, and Truman's contention that the case was a hoax (or, in Truman's phrasing, a "red herring") was undermined. This created "a power vacuum in Washington that ambitious politicians . . . hastened to fill."[11] The anti-subversion baton passed from successive HUAC chairs Martin Dies, Edward Hart, and J. Parnell Thomas, who wielded it for publicity and power for a total of ten years, to an even more unscrupulous demagogue: Joe McCarthy.

Before his rise to nationwide prominence, McCarthy was a first-term Republican senator with an unexceptional record and what promised to be a difficult reelection campaign two years hence when he addressed local GOP stalwarts at the annual Lincoln Day fundraising dinner in Wheeling, West Virginia, in February of 1950. In his briefcase were two speeches of vastly different subject matter and tone. The first dealt with housing policy; in the second, prepared by a journalist friend, he claimed to have a list of Communists working in the State Department. McCarthy went with the second, and the nonskeptical press coverage launched "Tail Gunner Joe" from relative obscurity in Wisconsin.[12]

As it was, Paul already had his hands full at the New York City NLG chapter due to Truman's 1947 executive order mandating that all federal employees take a "loyalty oath" to protect the government from Communist infiltration. After a debate on this constitutionally dubious presidential fiat at a Detroit meeting of the NLG, Paul sent a sharply worded message to the American Civil Liberties Union (ACLU), as the national organization had deeply disappointed him and others by declining to challenge the loyalty oath or even to represent alleged Communists "on the ground that they were believers in . . . the overthrow of the country by violence."[13] It mattered little to O'Dwyer that President Truman was casting himself as a prolabor, pro–civil rights Democrat who was skeptical of the domestic anti-communist furor, or that the ACLU had a distinguished history of fighting for civil liberties. Paul only saw former allies giving in to reactionism. "Unless all persons interested in civil liberties are heard now to protest against this order in its entirety, the memorable happenings in the days of the infamous Mitchell Palmer shall undoubtedly be paled into insignificance by the reign of terror soon to come," he wrote in a private message to the ACLU's acting director, Clifford Forster.[14]

In an ideal world O'Dwyer would have been preaching to the already converted, but in the dynamics of the Cold War—when communism incurred enemies not just from the right but, as shown by the ACLU, from the left as well—he simply was not. The conservative American Bar Association consistently resisted the fight to protect individuals' civil liberties, while the ACLU retreated. So, the onus to fill the vacuum fell heavily on overmatched groups like the NLG and the parallel Emergency Civil Liberties Committee, an organization formed in 1951 to advocate for the Bill of Rights, especially freedoms of speech, religion, travel, and assembly.

WHILE O'DWYER'S 1948 run for Congress in northern Manhattan attracted a barrage of red-baiting, his appetite for politics had not diminished when, almost a year later, anti-communist tensions and racism boiled over with violence at a civil rights benefit concert featuring Paul Robeson near Peekskill, New York. Paul drew a potentially volatile chiding from the columnist Ed Sullivan for speaking out on behalf of those who were attacked.

Robeson, the African American bass-baritone concert artist and stage actor, was a Communist sympathizer though not a member of the party. He frequently wielded his fame and powerful intellect to fight for Black equality. His three prior appearances at this venue had gone off without a hitch. This time, however, a white mob turned out for the African American artist, spurred by an Associated Press story falsely quoting the performer as comparing US government policy to that of the Nazis. Concertgoers were attacked with rocks and baseball bats as police, arriving late, did little to stop them. The concert came to a sudden halt, and the sponsors rescheduled it for Labor Day, when an enlarged turnout of twenty thousand attendees (now including more union members on hand to cheer and protect Robeson in light of police reluctance) braved hurtling rocks and ugly taunts from rioters, including many members of the American Legion who were charged for their part in the disruptions.[15]

While many pundits and politicians (including Governor Thomas Dewey) blamed Robeson's supporters for the unrest, *Daily News* columnist Ed Sullivan gratuitously jabbed O'Dwyer for denouncing the white rioters and, in Sullivan's words, exploiting "the opportunity to rush into print and peddle the same bill of goods which voters rejected, when he last ran for office."[16]

In an intolerant climate in which even Sullivan, in his other role as the host of a television variety show on CBS, felt compelled to clear guests with notorious red-baiter Theodore Kirkpatrick of *Counterattack*, Paul hesitated to allow the well-known entertainment impresario's comment to stand unchallenged, lest it damage not just Paul's political future but even his ability to represent clients. Relying on a tactic he used to deal with fierce opponents (such as Metropolitan Life Insurance's Fred Ecker), O'Dwyer went to see Sullivan in the writer's office in the Hotel Delmonico on Park Avenue. Sullivan must have been "misinformed" about his views, O'Dwyer told him. In the nasal twang that would become familiar to millions of TV viewers for nearly the next quarter-century, the columnist offered a nonspecific response. O'Dwyer soon realized Sullivan was being defensive; it was pointless to continue. Sullivan did not apologize or publish a retraction.[17]

The Delmonico encounter at least gave O'Dwyer the opportunity to take the measure of Sullivan, which was helpful for later clients dealing with the sometimes touchy personality. One of them ran a particularly strong risk: African American folksinger and actor Leon Bibb, who was so close to Robeson that the performer-activist became godfather to Bibb's twins. The reliably anti-Red American Legion pressed Sullivan to stop Bibb from appearing on his show. In response, Paul drafted a letter for Bibb to sign that adroitly played to Sullivan's pride in advancing the careers of many African American entertainers. While disavowing any Communist affiliation, the letter concluded, "I don't want you to be in any way embarrassed by my presence on your show. You have been too fine and too decent for me to forget that. What happens to me is not that important."[18] The contrite and self-sacrificing tone worked: Bibb continued to sing on the show through the mid-1960s.

Many Truman Democrats of the conformist early 1950s (known as Cold War liberals) followed the ACLU tack, finding it far easier to express outrage about Communists than to defend their right to express themselves, as did many moderate Republicans, who privately found McCarthy's accusations unfair and distasteful. It was safest to wait him out: drawing an accusation of being friendly to "Reds" and their "fronts" could be akin to stepping on a third rail.

The suspicion-filled political atmosphere was reflected in *The Tablet*, the influential weekly newspaper of the Catholic Diocese of Brooklyn, then led by Bishop Thomas Edmund Molloy. Bill's waning days at city hall saw the paper publish an investigative series that, in part, cited the NLG's links to what it described as the treasonous underbelly of the nation. The series darkly depicted Paul's official role in the guild, and, in response, a reader wrote that for all his Irish republican bona fides, Paul was one of *them*—a Communist Party fellow traveler. "What I would like to know is how a man with the name of Paul O'Dwyer is spokesman for a pro-Communist group," fumed Timothy O'Shea.[19] Though the series' suspicions and the reader's acid response hit close to home, Paul could not have been surprised. He had already inspired adverse attention from *The Tablet* for an NLG survey he conducted of guild members in New York, seeking their opinions on whether the legal grounds for divorce should be expanded to include a husband's alleged instances of cruelty and non-support. (Until 1966, spouses could obtain divorces in the state only because of adultery.) This kind of threat to the church's moral jurisdiction probably engendered about as much approval from the New York Catholic hierarchy as had the refusal by then magistrate Bill O'Dwyer to fine men for going topless at the Coney Island shore in violation of priggish mores.[20] In an interview years later, Paul recalled his divergence from "a very aggressive church and a very intolerant church"—and from many of "my own kinsmen"—on such social issues as the grounds for seeking a divorce. "When they condemned me, I couldn't complain about it because I had left them and I stayed on the path that I thought was appropriate," he said. "Many times it was very uncomfortable, but there were many friends of mine in the Irish community that continued to disagree with me, but, nevertheless, felt I was alright anyway."[21]

Still, by the time of the scathing *Tablet* articles discussing the NLG and Paul's prominence within the left-wing group, the fifty-page report issued by HUAC had recommended that the Justice Department place the guild on its list of subversive groups and that its members be excluded from federal positions of all kinds. Fear of the blacklist had driven the sharp falloff in NLG membership. Only after the eleven-year lawsuit by the guild, filed in 1977, did the FBI admit that it had twice conducted warrantless searches of the guild's national headquarters in 1947 and 1951 and had broken into these offices at least seven times from 1940 to 1951 to steal records.[22]

Those still willing to remain in the guild after 1950 were, admirably, prepared to pay the price—potential curbs on their ability to make a living and their freedom. Paul would not have had to look too far to see the psychological scarring that could result from representing the left.[23] In New York, his NLG colleagues Phil Sipser, Martin Popper, and Abe Unger each spent several years trying to get out from under accusations and blacklisting.[24] Paul felt certain that he himself lost potential clients because of his associations, though he was rarely short of them or at a loss for legal clientele of one sort or another. For Sipser, a father of four, some ten years passed, consuming the 1950s, before unions felt comfortable enough about the political climate to hire him again.[25]

No such perils seemed to surround Richard Nixon. The California congressman became a sensation after championing the writer, editor, and onetime Communist Party member Whittaker Chambers's 1948 allegations that Hiss, from an upstanding Baltimore family, had committed espionage at the State Department. Two years later, the ambitious politician's Senate campaign pitted Nixon against another Californian in the House of Representatives: Helen Gahagan Douglas, the former opera singer, actress, and liberal Hollywood activist. Nixon's tactics, leading to his victory, featured a new low in postwar American politics, an attack fusing red-baiting with chauvinism: Douglas, Nixon said, was "pink all the way down to her underwear." (Douglas's campaign countered with a nickname that would dog Nixon for the rest of his career: "Tricky Dick.")[26]

Nixon and McCarthy were the new Dies and Thomas. With their five-o'clock shadows and glowering visages hinting at darker impulses behind their smiles, the pair inspired savage satire from the Washington editorial cartoonist Herbert Block, a.k.a. "Herblock." However, McCarthy's four-year torrent of brazen bullying and falsehoods was buoyed by his Republican Senate colleagues, who either relished the damage he wreaked on Democrats, as in Nixon's case, or remained silent for fear he would turn on them (anticipating how a later GOP would deal with President Donald Trump).[27] President Dwight Eisenhower, a decorated general, also erred on the side of political timorousness. Ultimately, the wild-firing tail gunner would be undone by the badgering of top US Army brass, finally compelling Eisenhower (long reluctant, as he told the speech-writer C. D. Jackson, to "get in the gutter with that guy") to support the convening of televised hearings in 1954 by a Senate subcommittee to look into the clashing accusations of the US Army and McCarthy.

With the TV cameras rolling, a nationwide audience—and not just colleagues and reporters who had already tired of his show—had a full-immersion experience of McCarthy's habit of browbeating, sneers, and smears until the proceedings reached a climax: McCarthy's targeting of Fred Fisher, an associate of the army chief counsel Joseph Welch, for his having once joined the NLG. Welch's pointed response—"Have you no sense of decency, sir, at long last?"—turned public opinion against the senator's reign of terror and error. With the cooperation of the White House's congressional liaisons, a bipartisan coalition voted 67–22 to censure the legislator who had ridden roughshod over the Senate's norms and traditions as well as the constitutional rights of citizens.[28] McCarthy died three years on, an isolated drunk. The more chameleonic Nixon endured, as did the aroused spirit of paranoia about Communism, for two additional decades. In the second half of his political career, yet to begin, Paul would have disagreed with Daniel Moynihan's assertions about many aspects of politics but not with the New York senator's contention that "Communism—as an indigenous force, as yet another manifestation of diaspora politics, or as an instrument of Soviet policy—achieved astonishing influence not in its own right, much less on its own behalf, but as an agent for poisoning American politics. The ghoulish side-effects were felt for a generation or more; the reverberations are felt even today, after the collapse of the Soviet Union."[29]

O'Dwyer would always remember how Nixon urged the HUAC probe into the NLG starting in 1949. When that on-the-make politician finally became president, Paul was immediately alarmed, for Nixon now had at his disposal the full resources of the federal government to harass political enemies, including some of his own clients.[30] In the calculating mind of J. Edgar Hoover, only left-wing radicals and the Communist Party USA—men and women the highly popular FBI director described as "masters of deceit"—possessed the size, international influence, and ideological commitment to lead an insurrection against American democracy. Paul, at least, was more suspicious of the right-wing than of the much-demonized left, with one side embodying the interests of the wealthy and powerful and the other those of the poor, recent immigrants, workers, and the marginalized, as he saw it.

———

IN THE MOST IMMEDIATE SENSE, O'Dwyer's decision to withdraw in 1953 from the National Lawyers Guild was catalyzed by disagreement with the organization on a singular issue of principle—antisemitism in the Soviet sphere—and a notorious instance of it: that of Rudolf Slansky, the general secretary of Czechoslovakia's Communist Party, and thirteen other defendants accused in November 1952 of instigating an "anti-State conspiracy." Their confessions were extracted by means of imprisonment and torture. In the swiftness of Soviet-bloc "justice," meted out to leaders who had been loyal Communists throughout the convulsions of World War II, just one week transpired from indictment to execution, with the tribunal instantly evoking comparisons with the Moscow 1937–38 show trials. In its unmistakable antisemitic overtones (all but three of the defendants were listed in the indictment as being "of Jewish origin"), the show trials also foreshadowed the preposterous "Doctors' Plot" to murder Kremlin leaders that the aging, paranoid Josef Stalin unveiled at the start of the next year.[31]

The Slansky affair in Prague posed a dilemma for Paul given his deep commitment to an organization so closely tied to his work and thinking about freedom of expression, and which refused to bar any lawyer committed to its ideals, including Communists. For one thing, he was put off by the Soviet Union's interference with free and fair elections in Eastern and Central Europe in the mid-to-late 1940s. And as someone who, from childhood, resented Britain's attempt to limit Irish independence, the prospect of Soviet electoral interference in Czechoslovakia was also disturbing, though he reminded people that the Soviets had been most responsible for the Nazi defeat, suffered the heaviest losses by far in the world war, and were naturally determined to gird against another. But when some of his fellow NLG members soft-pedaled the Slansky affair, he was not prepared to overlook their obliviousness to Soviet antisemitism, or how far the USSR had strayed from its founding ideals of socialism and equality. He had, in 1947, participated in the Second Congress of the International Association of Democratic Lawyers, where his group of six US delegates—all NLG members—applauded speeches by Czech delegates, both Jews and non-Jews, about the danger of another world war in a nuclear age.[32]

The pattern of Soviet authoritarianism that was in evidence in 1947 was borne out with a vengeance six years later in the Slansky case, with the verdicts decided in advance to solidify Soviet domination of Czechoslovakia. (The geopolitics surrounding Arab lands were also in play: in the spring of 1952, Ana Pauker, the first female foreign minister of Romania, was purged from her office and from the Communist Party for supporting Zionism and Israel—her stances were anathema to Stalin, who, after initially backing Israeli independence, grew enraged by the Jewish State's tilt toward the West.)[33] Paul told a New York University interviewer years later that the prosecution in Prague used "trumped-up charges" and that he was sure of it because some copies of the trial transcript were immediately available and translated into four languages.[34] "We now had so much proof, there was no question what the Soviet government was up to." He may have assumed the NLG executive board, with its large Jewish component, would denounce the travesty of justice. Instead, the board declined to do so. The defendants, according to his apologist colleagues in the guild, were prosecuted for "taking strong positions against the Soviet government," not for being Jews. Despite Paul's threat to quit the executive board "unless they charged that Soviet Russia was involved in genocide," the debate went no further—"so I quit."[35]

Two friends of his on the board, Murray Gordon and Sipser, also wanted to quit to show that the NLG was "not a satellite of the U.S.S.R." Gordon even went so far as to draft a resignation letter, stating his objections. O'Dwyer, however, persuaded them not to go through with it. While during the Depression informing, or "ratting," had a negative connotation in neighborhood life, on the waterfront, and in the movies, during the Cold War the tinge seemed to lessen. Now those who pointed a finger at friends and colleagues for holding Communist sympathies were often extolled, both by men in power and average anti-communist Janes and Joes, even if the information they provided to government investigators to save their own skin sent someone they knew to prison or, in the worst possible scenario, death row.

In this perverse climate in which personal betrayal was seen as a virtue instead of a character stain, O'Dwyer did not want himself or anyone else to have to tell HUAC or McCarthy "what my objection to the Guild was—which would place [me] in a position of an informer." Further-more, "as an Irishman, I'd have particular difficulty with that role."[36]

———

THE IRISHMAN HAD DIFFICULTY, too, with the government's mistreat-ment of Michael Obermeier, a client. The president of a branch of the Hotel and Club Employees' Union in New York City, Obermeier had wrung gains over a period of a decade for poor, immigrant, minority, and female workers in the hospitality industry and had sidelined formerly dominant mobster elements. But because he had entered the United States illegally in his early twenties from his native Germany in 1913, his at-tempts to gain citizenship rendered him vulnerable at the end of World War II, leading to an arrest on a charge of perjury in 1947. In applying to naturalize, he had falsely denied a past Communist Party affiliation.

By the time of his arrest, Obermeier was captaining twenty-seven thousand union members in a combative affiliate of the American Fed-eration of Labor. He was one of forty-one labor organizers targeted in an initial wave of clampdowns based on yellowing immigration paper-work and their status, in the eyes of the Justice Department, as "undesir-able aliens," to use terminology the department invoked during the Red Scare of 1919–20. The number of arrestees ballooned to 135 by the time Obermeier was charged, while US Attorney General Tom Clark main-tained a list of 2,100 foreign-born communists he wanted to kick out of the country. The guiding law, a kind of twentieth-century version of the late eighteenth century's Sedition Act, was passed by Congress in 1940—the Alien Registration, or Smith, Act.[37]

O'Dwyer sought to have the charges against the hotel workers' union chief dismissed on the grounds of the statute of limitations expiring and lack of authority of the person who administered the citizenship oath to him. He was forced to stipulate at Obermeier's 1950 trial that his client had been a party member from 1930 to 1939. But Obermeier was con-victed and sentenced to two years in prison. During the war, Obermeier had made broadcasts in German for the US Office of Strategic Services. His son fought in the army and his daughter was an American college professor. None of that seemed to matter to the court, and O'Dwyer was incensed that he was unable, finally, to protect him from expulsion from the United States in December 1952. Eight years after his forced return to Germany, the trade union leader died. He was sixty-eight.[38]

AFTER ENDING HIS INVOLVEMENT with the guild, O'Dwyer "more or less dropped out of public life for a while," he wrote in his memoirs. He was still dealing with the fallout from his brother's disastrous appearance before the Kefauver Committee. The hearings damaged Bill principally but also complicated Paul's own ambitions in politics, while necessitating increased attention to his brother's difficulties. He felt, for personal reasons, that it was time to take a break. "My law practice had suffered for lack of attention during five rather exciting years, and the business of providing for a family of four children and a few nephews and nieces, who had become all but stepchildren of Kathleen and me, was pressing."[39]

He turned his attention more and more to Irish culture. Midway through Bill's mayoralty, Paul had started inviting people encountered through his legal and political activities to his Central Park West apartment for meetings to form a new organization "for the promotion of cultural pursuits in the United States and for extending some financial assistance to newly formed cultural groups in Ireland." The gatherings culminated in the incorporation, in 1950, of the Irish Institute of New York. Two years later, with Paul himself providing $5,000 for the down payment, the group purchased a four-story building on West Forty-Eighth Street from the Hispanic Masonic Society and began its work in earnest.[40]

For Paul, the Irish Institute had an advantage over the traditional county organizations that had offered emigrants from Ireland the opportunity to maintain friendships or create new ones among like-minded transplants. The money that these organizations raised from dances was usually only enough to secure meeting places and organize gatherings, not to disperse elsewhere. In contrast, the institute "had money, and we had huge fundraisers," recalled Kevin Morrissey, who became president of the association at Paul's urging in 1982.[41]

As the writer of the group's constitution and bylaws, Paul was wary of domination by one individual or faction, so he set term limits for presidents. Nevertheless, after serving as its first president in the 1950s as the

Cold War raged, he came by his influence naturally, Morrissey said. "He automatically got reverence from people in the Institute. He didn't have to act bossy. I don't remember him talking people down. People allowed him to direct from his experience, knowledge, capabilities and the things he had produced. They respected him. They could disagree [with him]." For Dan Tubridy, another institute board member, Paul was simply "the godfather," he noted.[42]

Like those in southern Ireland who were seeking to revive the Gaelic language to foster a greater sense of national identity, the Irish Institute saw culture as a means of greater historical awareness and cohesion in Irish America. Over the years, the institute contributed funds for the library at Dublin's Trinity College, the restoration of the ancient Ballintubber Abbey, the John F. Kennedy Memorial Park in the family ancestral homeland of County Wexford, Ireland, and, in gratitude for Jewish contributions to the institute at the time of its founding, a history of Irish Jews.[43] The list of grants for small groups sponsoring playwrights, poets, painters, dancers, and historians grew long. But the highlight of the organization in those early years was not a cultural outreach but a political one. In 1957, the year after John F. Kennedy was defeated for the vice-presidential nomination at the Democratic National Convention, the senator was guest of honor at the Irish Institute's annual dinner at the suggestion of O'Dwyer. Paul's friend Sean Keating, who served in Bill's administration and as the toastmaster that night, introduced the handsome Kennedy to the gathering of seven hundred as "the next president of the United States," believed to be the first time anyone along the Eastern Seaboard had ever done so.[44] Three years later, O'Dwyer would serve as the state chair for the Kennedy-Johnson presidential campaign.

———

THE FIRST CASE to bring Paul back into the thick of Cold War politics after leaving the NLG began in January 1957 when Bill was contacted at his law office in Mexico City by Alfred Stern Jr. The New York millionaire and his wife Martha Dodd Stern needed legal advice, not on politics and commerce in Mexico, where they were then living, but rather on a subpoena to appear before a Manhattan grand jury on charges of passing information to the Soviets.[45]

The daughter of William Dodd, the former US ambassador to Hitler's Germany, the vivacious Martha had veered over the four years of her father's posting and the intensification of Nazi brutality from wide-eyed acceptance of the Third Reich to skepticism to loathing. She described this trajectory in a memoir written after her return home, *Through Embassy Eyes*, as well as a postwar novel, *Sowing the Wind*. She married Stern, a decade her senior, in 1938.

In the early Cold War, gossip about their stylish life and friends would have been enough to spark suspicion about their loyalty. Two swans adorned the private waters at the couple's estate in Ridgefield, Connecticut, which were named after Vladimir Lenin and his wife, Nadezhda Krupskaya. The evening salons at their Central Park West pad attracted Paul Robeson and the playwrights Lillian Hellman and Clifford Odets. Artists and intellectuals mingled with Soviet and Eastern European diplomats.[46]

The impetus for the federal government's interest in the couple was, true to form, an informant: Boris Morros, a short, baldish American Communist Party member, Paramount Pictures producer, and, starting in 1947, counterspy for the FBI. After meeting Morros in 1943, the Sterns had invested in the Boris Morros Music Company, an intended front for Soviet intelligence in the western hemisphere. Before long, the Sterns had grown distrustful of Morros, and within a year the business had collapsed. Though the FBI investigated the Sterns for three years after Morros turned double agent, it could not develop a case that it felt would stand up in court.[47]

Still, acting against the Sterns became more complicated with their 1953 move to Mexico, then a haven for blacklist victims that, like Canada, did not require a passport for traveling around the Americas. The couple found a cultural circle not unlike the one they had left behind in Connecticut and Manhattan.[48]

Their idyll south of the border was interrupted when, fearing imminent exposure as a double agent to his Soviet handlers, Morros came in from the cold in January 1957. In short order Jack Soble, an operative with the Soviet People's Commissariat for Internal Affairs (NKVD), his wife, Myra, and another spy, Jacob Albam, were arrested and pleaded guilty. A Manhattan grand jury now wanted to hear from the Sterns themselves, and within a month, consular officials in Mexico served them with a subpoena. O'Dwyer delayed their court date—successfully arguing irregularities in the delivery of the subpoena—but he could not stop it because, as he knew, the Justice Department could invoke Article 33 of the Mexican Constitution, which "permits a government agent to drop an American alien over the border and into the waiting hands of American authorities." Convinced that extradition awaited them, and hearing from alarmed friends and family members about FBI calls to their homes and offices, the Sterns used black-market Paraguayan passports to flee abroad under assumed names in July 1957, ultimately settling in Czechoslovakia. Paul, who had left for a vacation in Ireland two days before the Sterns quit Mexico, found out about their flight from justice when he opened a newspaper the next day. They were indicted in absentia in early September on three counts of conspiracy to commit espionage.[49]

Given the involvement of Justice Irving Kaufman, who had sentenced the Rosenbergs to death, and the Sterns' fear that they could be indicted if any of their testimony differed from that of Morros, the couple had been right to worry. "I certainly wouldn't have persuaded them not to [flee]," O'Dwyer told the writer Katrina Vanden Heuvel for a 1991 *Vanity Fair* article about the Sterns. "Their lives were at stake. I am firmly of the belief that knowing how Boris Morros was acting, that if the government had taken the Rosenbergs and electrocuted them, they would have electrocuted Martha and Alfred." He noted with satisfaction that the US government was forced to drop its indictment in 1979.[50]

While the Sterns feared American agents might kidnap them in Mexico, as O'Dwyer suggested, it was less certain that they would have been punished with the same severity as other high-profile individuals accused of espionage. The couple did not pass along atomic bomb secrets like Julius Rosenberg, nor military plans that might endanger American lives in the Korean War, as Britain's Cambridge spy ring did. Their activities were circumscribed, instead, by their Soviet handlers, who scorned Martha as "a typical representative of American Bohemia, a woman who has become sexually depraved, ready to sleep with any handsome man." The Sterns were limited to recruiting more emotionally stable spies from their circle of intellectuals and entertainers, such as Jane Foster Zlatovski, who allegedly provided details of American diplomacy with Indonesia and information on US intelligence agents. It seems likely that the FBI was less interested in prosecuting the Sterns than in their publicity value as socialites, and in pressing them for more incriminating information about their contacts and Soviet intelligence methods.[51] However, to O'Dwyer and much of the left, the Stern case, along with the Alger Hiss and Rosenberg trials, represented an egregious example of government overreach to quell domestic dissent. Such certainties would be complicated, albeit many years later, by intelligence intercepts declassified in 1995—the so-called VENONA transcripts—along with FBI documents obtained by scholars through the Freedom of Information Act. With these sources in hand, historians disclosed that, even while her father was serving in the US embassy in Berlin, the NKVD, the Soviet predecessor of the KGB, informed the operative Boris Winogradov that Martha's anti-Nazi sentiments and affair with him had "fully ripened for her to be recruited once and for all to work for us."[52] By March 1942, Vasily Zubilin, the chief Soviet intelligence officer in the United States, had recruited Martha—code-named "LISA" and "LIZA" in the VENONA transcripts—to persuade Alfred (already a member of the Communist Party and a Marxist study group) to join them in their espionage.[53]

The federal government's interest in the O'Dwyers and the Sterns nonetheless remained intense for a year after the couple's renunciation of their American citizenship, while the State Department and FBI wondered about Bill's connection to the case, as well as Paul's. Robert Johnson, who took over as the chief of the State Department's Passport Division, left a record in the summer of 1957 in the "Passport Files" about a phone call from a "Mr. Chase" indicating that "the subject . . . has engaged in activities which are inimical to the interest of the U.S. He says that [William] O'Dwyer is mixed up somehow with the Alfred Kaufman Stern matter." Chase felt Bill could be stripped of his citizenship and pointed to a looming anniversary: Bill would "*soon complete 5 years residence in Mexico.*"[54]

At this time, John Speakes, the FBI's legal attaché in Mexico City, advised the FBI's R. R. Roach that Bill "reportedly furnished some information to the Ambassador [Robert C. Hill] concerning Alfred and Martha Stern," and added that Bill "also indicated that he wished to furnish additional details." Nevertheless, Bill claimed he was "unaware of the Sterns' espionage connections until he read [of] them in the newspapers." A year later, after a lead article in the Mexican newspaper *La Prensa* alleged that local investigations might show that Bill had prepared "false documents for entrance of prominent Communists into Mexico," the ex-ambassador stormed into Hill's office to deny the charge and stated his intention to request an FBI investigation to disprove "charges he has befriended Communists and been their lawyer."

Paul, assuming a familiar posture toward Bill, told him to take his foot off the gas pedal for his own sake. He said it was the height of naivety to imagine that Hoover's FBI would work fairly and diligently to clear the Truman-appointed ambassador's name. Reasonable advice, but, perhaps thanks to Bill's loose lips, Paul's skepticism of the FBI got back to the agency, provoking suspicion of the younger brother. ("Of interest," noted Speakes, "was [William] O'Dwyer's remark that his brother Paul had told him he was foolish to ask [the] FBI to interest itself in his case.")[55]

————

THE TREPIDATIONS PAUL FELT about incurring potential legal jeopardy were also borne out by the case of his friend and former NLG colleague Martin Popper. In addition to serving as a lawyer for the Hollywood Ten, Popper had visited clients behind the Iron Curtain in Poland and Czechoslovakia; he had also served as an observer at the 1948 Prague conference of the International Association of Democratic Lawyers. These and other activities put him in the crosshairs of the House Un-American Activities Committee, which had expanded its investigative writ to cover passports issued to citizens traveling outside the United States. Called to testify before a House subcommittee on passport controls in 1959, Popper challenged the panel's jurisdiction and refused to answer a question about whether he had been a Communist Party member when he applied for a passport, citing his rights under the First Amendment right of free speech and association (a defense more likely to lead to a prison sentence for contempt of Congress, he realized, than the more common one invoking the Fifth Amendment protection against self-incrimination).[56] Judge John Sirica presided at his trial in court. A longtime Republican who had been appointed District Court judge in Washington, DC, during the Eisenhower administration, Sirica's history suggested that he was not well disposed toward a defendant who was tarred by leftist activities. Even before he would later gain a reputation as "Maximum John" for meting out unusually long sentences, Sirica struck Paul as a "tense and nervous man, frightened by the atmosphere of the times," an impression that lingered until he expertly oversaw the trials of the Watergate defendants in 1973–74.[57]

O'Dwyer's and cocounsel Boudin's firm contention that passport legislation was not the province of HUAC met its match in Francis Walter, the Pennsylvania Democratic congressman and subcommittee chair, who served as a hostile witness for the prosecution. O'Dwyer and Boudin had faced an equally daunting obstacle during jury selection. Simply finding impartial jurors in the District of Columbia, where government employees were subject to surveillance, was "virtually impossible." Paul blamed the guilty verdict, returned in less than an hour, on what he perceived as jurors' fears for their own jobs.

After this initial setback, the US Circuit Court of Appeals set the verdict aside in 1962. The government chose not to pursue the matter further. Free of the shadow of imprisonment, Popper—though receiving no compensation for the harassment and legal fees he incurred—returned to his legal career, subsequently representing the New York family of Andrew Goodman, one of the three civil rights workers murdered in Mississippi in the summer of 1964. He returned to being a forceful voice with the NLG.[58] In appreciation for O'Dwyer charging no fee for representing him, Popper sent over to the family their first TV, particularly delighting Paul's young son Brian.[59]

———

ALWAYS GRATEFUL for ways to shore up the firm's balance sheet since he increasingly represented civil rights clients on a pro bono basis, O'Dwyer's firm handled major entertainers with long ties of friendship to Oscar and Rebecca Bernstien. Paul himself represented several in their divorces, including the Broadway musical star Ethel Merman, the model-actress Suzy Parker, and the blond ingenue Nancy Valentine.[60] A subsequent client, Jackie Mason, sued Ed Sullivan for libel in 1964 after the powerful TV host accused the comedian of flipping him the bird on the set; Sullivan apologized, citing a misimpression, and allowed him back on the show.

These bold-faced names (or they appeared as such in tabloid gossip columns like the one Sullivan used to author in New York) represented a source of revenue, and publicity, for Paul and his firm, but more mundane ones may have given him greater satisfaction because they entailed helping ordinary people—with their personal injury suits and, later, worker's compensation claims. In 1953, O'Dwyer won $37,500 for a $45-a-week handyman whose left foot was crushed under a power press being installed by an auto accessory manufacturing firm. Months later, he pulled off a $50,000 settlement for a client in Brooklyn Supreme Court in a testament to his powers of persuasion; the jury returned the financial verdict even though the city's corporation counsel played film footage in court showing the client doing a jig in the street after filing his disability claim.[61]

Another even more satisfying client was Harry Barrett. In November 1958, amid the IRA's futile 1956–61 campaign in Ulster, Barrett was arrested after New York police, in a search of his Bronx home, found in the cellar enough guns and ammunition "to fight a 10-year war," according to a *New York Herald Tribune* column by Jimmy Breslin. O'Dwyer was successful in defending Barrett against gunrunning charges by comparing him to Hungarian revolutionaries who fought in 1956 against domestic policies imposed by the Soviet Union. "If the freedom fighters in the streets of Budapest had had the kind of support that Harry Barrett is giving his brothers in Northern Ireland, perhaps they would be free men today, your honor," Paul said.[62]

————

PAUL'S FAMILY LIFE was far more conventional than his public life might have suggested to outsiders. His four children were growing up under the day-by-day oversight of Kathleen. Their eldest, Billy, was fourteen when Uncle Bill gave up Gracie Mansion in 1950. Eileen attended the private Columbia Grammar, around the corner from their apartment, though it bothered Paul that no Black children were enrolled, and he wrote repeatedly to the headmistress to complain about it.[63]

"One of his biggest things was education—everybody had to have an education," remembered Billy, who went to medical school at University College in Cork. Paul had not only been "very generous, obviously" in paying his son's way through medical school but also provided tuition for many of the children's cousins. After a residency abroad, "Dr. Billy" returned to the United States, serving for two years in the navy in Buford, South Carolina, during the Vietnam War as part of the medical corps. He spent the rest of his career as a pediatrician in the Albany area.[64]

Eileen graduated from Beaver College (now Arcadia University) in eastern Pennsylvania. She earned an MBA from Columbia Business School, an unusual distinction for a woman in the early 1960s, before marrying the New York assistant district attorney Thomas Hughes in 1962. Hughes later entered private practice at O'Dwyer & Bernstien.[65]

The O'Dwyer child who came to resemble most his father in schooling and choice of career was Brian. A graduate of George Washington
University with a BA in Spanish-American literature, he earned his MA
degree in Spanish literature from Middlebury College in Madrid and received his juris doctor degree and a master's in law from Georgetown.
He joined O'Dwyer & Bernstien and, like his father, represented labor
unions, eventually taking his place as senior partner. He was a Democratic
fundraiser and stump speaker and advocated for human rights for Northern Ireland. He also extended his Northern Irish advocacy efforts to
Mexican migrants in the xenophobic climate after September 11, 2001,
and beyond.[66]

Rory, the third O'Dwyer child, took a different path to an education.
Paul was advised by a pediatrician that a change of climate might help
alleviate young Rory's asthma. "I think the doctor meant a change to Ari-
zona, where it was dry," Rory wryly remembered. "But my father took it
to mean Ireland." He sent Rory to live with his sister, May Durkan, in
Mayo. Through age fourteen, he attended Lismirrane National School, a
three-room institution with no indoor toilets and heating supplied by turf
required from all students at the start of the school year. The school's
headmaster, Dudley Solan, had also taught Paul.

He returned to Central Park West from Lismirrane for a couple of
years, then went back to Ireland and attended Black Rock Academy, a
Dublin boarding school. "My father's theory was, if you're not going to
school and you're not working, you can't live in this house. So, he got me
into the International Brotherhood of Electricians, which involved five
years of apprenticeship," said Rory.[67]

Still, constantly on the go as his children grew up, Paul "was mostly
an absent father," related Brian. With the children heading off for school
and Paul constantly leaving home to work late, they "never knew him to
come home when we were awake," according to Rory. The exception
was Sunday night, when everyone had to be home and the children could
talk about their readings and teachers at school at the dining room
table.[68]

———

PAUL'S EMPHASIS on education and responsibility spilled over to his
extended family. Ten days after Bill was inaugurated as mayor in 1946,
for example, Paul wrote to warn their sister May not to get her hopes up

that Bill would visit Bohola again soon despite rumors of a great home-coming: "Don't pay any attention to these talks, even when Bill is in a serious mood," he stated, for Bill often talked about "things that are ut-terly impossible." The problem was that Bill's new job had "more com-plications and more difficulties in it than you can imagine, and it is a nuisance from early morning until late at night," Paul counseled.[69]

Three years later, he took issue with May's concerns about Bill's up-coming marriage to the slender fashion model Sloane Simpson. Paul stated that he was "totally in disagreement with your viewpoint" and that even though Sloane had been married (and divorced) once before, he "wouldn't interfere no matter who or what the person is. It is so personal a matter that I wouldn't presume to influence anyone on the question. . . . I am fully conscious of the fact that you are living in a locality which is medieval in its thinking and presumes to be more Catholic than the pope, and any act on the part of its natives is the subject of acclaim or censure."[70]

Paul used his union contacts with New York's Irish dance halls to launch the musical career of Adrian Flannelly, the son of his closest sister, Linda, when the seventeen-year-old emigrated to the United States in 1959. Phone calls from Paul quickly enabled Flannelly, an accordionist, to play the halls his well-connected uncle represented. At Paul's recom-mendation, Adrian applied to Local 802 of the American Federation of Musicians. "I made more in my first weekend than I had in a month," said Flannelly, who by the end of the 1960s launched a weekly radio show that would lead the *Daily News* to call him "Dean of Irish Radio in the United States."[71]

O'Dwyer formed especially close professional associations with an-other nephew and a niece—Frank Durkan and Joan O'Dwyer. The older of the cousins, Joan O'Dwyer, was born three months after the death of her fireman father, Jimmy, in 1926, and became an orphan at thirteen when her mother died of a heart ailment resulting from scarlet fever contracted during childhood. Joan went to live in a private home in the Bronx with her aunt Mika, another aunt, and her grandmother. Bill, Frank, and Paul pooled their money to pay the tuition at her Catholic school, Bill let her have a party at Gracie Mansion, and Paul showed up at the Beaver Col-lege annual father-daughter dance as her "date."[72] Joan abundantly re-turned her uncles' goodwill. And after graduating from Columbia Law in 1950, Joan became involved in managing O'Dwyer & Bernstien and its cash-only payroll.[73] Durkan, meanwhile, joined the firm as a clerk, rising to copartner along with Brian when Paul retired.

———

MAYOR ROBERT WAGNER JR. weighed naming Joan—who by this time had cut her long hair on Paul's advice and married John O'Neill—as a magistrate in March 1960. The Association of the Bar of the City of New York, however, issued an adverse report on her qualifications, with some members complaining she lacked sufficient trial experience for the $16,000-a-year post. That was bad, but an editorial in the *New York Post*, at that time a liberal newspaper, especially incensed Paul with its charge that her nomination would be "a wrong appointment that has the right connections." (Wagner had risen to prominence through successive appointments in Bill's administration as commissioner of housing and buildings and chairman of the City Planning Commission.) Outraged by the aspersions being cast on Joan's qualifications, Paul telegrammed a protest to the *Post* publisher Dorothy Schiff, accusing her of "a misuse of the editorial page to work over old grudges." He forwarded recommendations from twenty-eight judges who had worked with Joan over the prior decade to the chair of the Criminal Courts Committee of the New York County Lawyers Association and to Wagner, who could be exasperating with his habit of slow, delayed appointments.

Paul's campaign carried the day, as Wagner appointed Joan in May to the desired position; she would become the first ever female criminal court judge in Queens. Twenty years later, she was appointed as an acting supreme court justice, and in 1985 Governor Mario Cuomo named her to the state court of claims. When she retired in 1996, she was the longest-serving senior judge in New York City.[74]

If Paul served as a protector of sorts for his beloved Joan, he became a professional partner of his sister May's son, Frank Durkan. Four years younger than Joan, Durkan followed in the courts a career closer to his uncle's as an independent immigrant son of two schoolteachers who took menial jobs while working his way through Columbia College, earned a law degree, and began litigating for labor and immigration clients. He would become a well-known counsel, along with his uncle, to Irish republican gunrunners arrested in America.

Paul's expectation that Frank would start out as a common laborer, as Bill and he himself had done, was thrown into question as soon as the

youngster traveled to New York at seventeen. The teenager was met at
the dock by a chauffeur and driven to Gracie Mansion, where Uncle Bill
promised to put him up in style. Paul, having gotten wind of the situation, the next day headed straight for the mansion and took his nephew
to an apartment building on Ninety-Seventh Street in Manhattan, arranging for him to start work immediately as a janitor. What Frank would
remember as a "harsh dose of reality in 24 hours" after his arrival in
America was followed by other jobs to help pay for his education, including as a liquor store clerk and parking attendant at the Saratoga Race
Course.[75]

After earning his law degree from New York Law School and reaching the end of his clerkship, Frank handled negligence and malpractice
suits with O'Dwyer & Bernstien. Over time, as Bernstien slowed with age
and more of his younger partner's time was consumed by political campaigns and pro bono civil rights cases, Frank served as a legal associate
and "workhorse," gradually assuming Bernstien's responsibilities in managing the office, along with Brian O'Dwyer. Paul and Frank would constantly confer through the adjoining doors of their offices.[76] Paul himself
could at times seem notoriously oblivious to the nuts and bolts of running
the firm.

In habits and style, though, differences between uncle and nephew
were evident. Whereas Paul tended to be direct and concise in court, Frank
was more "the orator," as recalled by Sean Downes, who worked at the
firm as a young attorney in the 1980s. During a summation in a case involving a construction worker who went in for stomach surgery and
came out blind, Durkan halted and simply read to the jury a poem "by a
blind person who's never seen, and he wrote about what it would be like
to see a flower. And it was, like, Virgil. Just word for word. And I remember, a $3 million verdict later, one construction guy comes out of the jury
room and says, 'That was fuckin' beautiful, Mr. Durkan. Beautiful,'" said
Downes.

Both uncle and nephew were "down-to-earth, smart—they were not
full of themselves," added Downes. "They wouldn't be seen in *People*
Magazine and wouldn't *want* to be in *People* Magazine."[77]

WITH THE SAME SPIRIT in which he helped his extended family, Paul
tried to save Bill from stresses unusual for an O'Dwyer of his mature

years. The younger sibling felt that, despite his best efforts, he had failed to safeguard the former mayor's reputation adequately by allowing him to appear at the disastrous Kefauver hearings.[78]

In battling with the Internal Revenue Service over his brother's finances, he was determined not to repeat that mistake—and, in the process, put his shoulder against what he considered the arbitrary power of the federal government and the continued harassment of his more famous, and more vulnerable, sibling.

Before the IRS dunned Bill for taxes for an alleged bribe of $10,000 by the head of the firemen's union, never proven, prompting Paul to serve as his lawyer at a tax tribunal, Bill had asked him for advice on how to handle reimbursement for miscellaneous expenses as ambassador.

"All items of expense that you undoubtedly will have are deductable [*sic*] and very large amounts have been allowed. It is necessary, however, that you keep some accounting of the various items of expense," O'Dwyer advised in response. "For example, if you had a reception, some note should be made of the general nature of it and the number of people and the expense involved. Necessary items of clothing, for instance, would be deductable [*sic*] and hotel expenses in Washington. If the deductions are established, the Treasury Department is not in the habit of questioning whether it is reasonable or not. The only thing to establish is whether they were made."[79] The former mayor no doubt had seen the need to be scrupulous about money, but his younger brother's suggestions fell on deaf ears. The convivial Bill was seldom inclined to economize or account for every dollar used. More than a decade on, after Bill died, Paul raged at his nephew Adrian over an instance of ill-advised spending, bursting out, "Goddamn it, Bill O'Dwyer never died!" ("That was not a compliment to me," Flannelly related.)[80] Financial imprudence might have been excused in the immediate postwar years, when campaign contributions were not as important as the backing of party bosses, nor well accounted for. But as Truman's presidency drew toward a close and Republicans glimpsed the chance to reclaim the White House, financial errancy was a riskier pitfall. Long after Truman had okayed hearings by his fellow Democrat Estes Kefauver, an ensuing dispute with the IRS dogged Bill. Paul represented him, fearing another blow to his reputation and the furthering of the public perception that Bill profited from his extensive public service. What should have put to rest such fictions, he felt, was that, with so many opportunities for cash having been within his reach as a magistrate, county-level judge, district attorney, mayor, and even ambassador, Bill had demonstrably little money for himself. In fact, he owned no real estate, nor had significant savings for retirement.

The IRS case flowed from the Kefauver hearings. John Crane, the president of the Uniformed Firemen's Association (UFA), testified to the congressional panel that he had contributed $10,000 in a brown envelope to Bill's 1949 reelection campaign, two years before. Bill denied the charge to the committee.

At the request of the New York office of the IRS's Intelligence Unit, Bill, following his disastrous questioning by the Kefauver panel, answered questions for part of two days under oath without legal counsel and submitted a sworn statement of his financial worth. After a year, the IRS advised him and Paul that "everything checked out satisfactorily."[81] That seemed to settle it. But the family's relief was short-lived: the election of Dwight Eisenhower, succeeding Truman, brought a new head of the IRS, Coleman Andrews, a conservative Democrat who in three years' time would mount a third-party campaign for president based on the proposition, "The Income Tax Is Bad." During his two years at the helm of the IRS, Andrews sympathized with taxpayers' confusion over the forms they had to fill out annually. His private comments indicated he took a dim view of judicial leniency toward tax cheats and was particularly cynical about the fine and prison sentence meted out to Bill's longtime aide Jim Moran for perjury and income tax evasion arising from his participation in a fire department extortion scheme.[82] "It'll be interesting to see who springs him when things quiet down," he cynically remarked.[83]

The Bill O'Dwyer tax matter was reopened. With the IRS chief taking an equally jaundiced view of Moran's former boss, government agents descended on Frank O'Dwyer's California ranch, attempting to discover if he was concealing money on Bill's behalf (to no avail). Joan O'Dwyer was asked to submit an affidavit attesting that she was not holding any money for Bill or Paul, but the request was sufficiently galling that Paul told a federal agent visiting his office about the matter to leave, threatening to remove him bodily.[84]

In addition to the alleged firemen's union contribution of $10,000 in an envelope (which the IRS unilaterally ruled was income received), the tax agency sought payment for more than $36,000 spent during 1950 and 1951—the cost of items for which Bill claimed he was not reimbursed as ambassador and therefore had sought to deduct on his taxes. Also alleged was a failure by Bill to report to the IRS an unexplained deposit of $1,500 made by Sloane from Mexico to a joint account in a New York bank that she shared with her mother. Fighting the case in the United States Tax Court not only prolonged media attention to Bill's difficulties but also posed a greater downside: Paul had never handled a case in that venue. Yet he felt he had no choice, for the IRS had rendered what he called a "corrupt decision."[85]

The case was heard in June 1956. An affidavit filed by Paul charged that the IRS pursuit of his brother was motivated by "ulterior political purpose or advantage, particularly in this Presidential year" and had thus far cost the taxpayers $100,000. Mindful of the IRS's interrogations of Frank, Joan, and Bill's longtime friend and political ally, the hotelier David Martin, O'Dwyer's affidavit also complained that "friends and relatives of the petitioner were harassed, bullied, threatened and annoyed."[86]

Three decades later, Paul understood that the tax court judge, Arnold Raum, "would never side against the government in this most political of cases." Nor did Paul expect an offer of a settlement from the IRS. Instead, he told the court, he only wanted an opportunity to review the Treasury Department file on his brother and to cross-examine Crane.[87] The case, he explained, involved an elemental issue of fairness: "When the government slaps a tax on a citizen, it should then at least accord the citizen the information on which the Tax Commissioner acted, and . . . a denial of such information was the denial of a constitutional right which should be reviewed by the United States Supreme Court, if necessary."[88]

Raum did not grant Paul's request to produce the IRS file, which he suspected would show that Andrews's "animosity and bias" were behind the case. But the judge did grant the right to cross-examine Crane, giving the defense lawyer access to what he considered "the greatest and most effective device ever invented for the discovery of the truth and the testing of any narrative." Paul's goal was to expose the accuser's contradictory accounts, through questions such as, Who exactly was Crane traveling with? What circumstances led him to hand $10,000 to Bill outside of Gracie Mansion? What did Bill do when he received it?[89]

When appearing before the Kefauver Committee, Crane had testified under oath that there were no witnesses watching when he handed the envelope to Bill. But after testifying five times before grand juries from

January 1951 to July 1952, he claimed that his memory had been refreshed and that he had been accompanied on his trip to Gracie Mansion by the UFA treasurer Terrence Dolan and the firefighter Victor Wilders. Now, under Paul's aggressive questioning, Crane acknowledged the inconsistency—a glaring one, and one of several to be surfaced by Paul. Paul also accused Crane of "looting" the UFA's funds, as the union leader had been unable to produce any written approval from the union's trustees for the use of the rank and file's moneys as a political donation, purportedly to win pension sweeteners from the state legislature.

Paul did not put his brother on the stand, saying his prior sworn testimony before the Bureau of Internal Revenue demonstrated that the tax assessment was "erroneous, arbitrary and capricious." But Judge Raum's refusal to allow Bill's sworn testimony to be introduced as evidence—along with Paul's insistence that Bill's appearance in court would "serve no useful purpose to swear to the same thing twice"—furnished the judge with the basis for his June 1957 decision that Paul had not met the heavy burden of proof. Bill himself was "the one person who could throw the most light on this matter. Yet he deliberately chose not to take the witness stand and subject himself to cross-examination. This is a circumstance that cannot be lightly ignored," the judge stated. The court ruled against Bill, as well as against Sloane for the unexplained $1,500 deposit in the New York account.[90]

A year and a half later, Paul appealed Raum's ruling in the US Court of Appeals, Fourth Circuit, arguing that the revenue agents' confidential reports should have been disclosed to determine whether Coleman Andrews's move against Bill and Sloane had been politically motivated, but the court only affirmed its decision.[91] The Supreme Court did not take the case.

At least Bill's tax debt had been reduced through his brother's efforts—from $20,532 to $8,242. But the IRS did not let the matter drop. Instead, the agency "came back and said we want the money," Paul remembered angrily three decades later. It "made the claim he has money hidden in the Caribbean, that he owns a gambling house, so and so—go get it."

The government ended up taking it out of Bill's pension.[92]

———

THE CONCLUSION OF BILL'S TAX fight removed the last legal danger in front of him. The former ambassador returned to Mexico City and the three-room penthouse apartment he rented in the Prince Hotel, where he was served by a butler called Pishta whose broken English he teased but whose cooking he cherished. Bill entertained a diverse stream of visitors. While on amicable terms with Sloane, he initiated relationships with other women, including the Scottish-born lead in the Broadway musical *Finian's Rainbow*, the blacklisted singer-actress Ella Logan, who was also friends with Paul and Frank.

A friendly journalist, Philip Hamburger, stopped by and profiled Bill for the *New Yorker* and for his book, *Mayor Watching and Other Pleasures*. The intelligence, charm, and wit that had captivated those who encountered Bill when he was a new immigrant continued to impress guests now, but those qualities were now mingled with open resentment against "bluenoses" and hypocrites. Along with his bitter feelings, Bill displayed wistfulness for the city he once mastered, pulling out, for Hamburger's benefit, a trunk with a few treasured keepsakes, including his magistrate's robe, a photograph of him as a cop holding his nightstick, and what he called his "Mayor's Badge," "given to me by my friends in the Police Department after I became Mayor."[93]

In 1960 he agreed with his partners in the short-lived, slackening Mexico City branch of O'Dwyer & Bernstien to close the office and returned to New York after ten years away, initially staying at the luxurious Hotel St. Moritz. He picked up the tab at meals with visitors there, evidently for fear of leaving lunch companions with the impression that he lacked adequate income, no matter how exorbitant the bill. With Paul's help, he found an apartment courtesy of the Rudin real estate management firm, which had benefited from an O'Dwyer administration zoning compromise that enabled it to construct an apartment building near Washington Square Park. The founder's son, Lew, was surprised when the ex-mayor did not request a special rate. World-weary, perhaps, and wary of even the slightest appearance of impropriety, he asked the younger Rudin to fill it in according to his best judgment.[94]

Bill shook his head whenever anyone wondered why he had not been arrested or served a subpoena the moment he returned. From his opening of the firm's Mexico office to the end of the decade, he had not only been in the United States some twenty times but had also been interviewed on the radio and TV. But the perception of corruption lingered, starting with the cabbie who, failing to recognize his once famous passenger, blurted out, "That crook! That thief!" Tipping the taxi driver fifty cents on a dollar fare, Bill said quietly, but sadly, "I'm O'Dwyer. I don't find a bit of fault for you not liking me. Many people exposed to the press feel like you do. But I have never been charged with a crime, let alone convicted."[95]

The former ambassador took a desk at O'Dwyer & Bernstien, and he enjoyed the camaraderie of relatives and old friends. In 1964, at the St. Patrick's Day parade, the march he had led as grand marshal twenty-six years before, he was "anything but an aging man that nobody recognizes," one columnist (Jimmy Breslin, then with the *New York Herald Tribune*) wrote.[96] The rainy parade turned out to be Bill's last. On November 24, he died at seventy-four of a heart attack while in Beth Israel Hospital. He had not discussed with Paul his funeral arrangements, but the sight of the dog tags from Bill's World War II service in his New York apartment convinced Paul to have him buried with full military honors in Arlington National Cemetery.

Nearly 1,700 mourners filled St. Patrick's Cathedral for the funeral mass celebrated by family friend Father Sean Reid. Afterward, forty-six friends and family members (except Joan, who was pregnant) flew to Arlington in a chartered plane to see him laid to rest on the hill overlooking John F. Kennedy's gravesite. The ceremony included a horse-drawn caisson and the presentation of a folded American flag to Paul by the army as the next of kin of the retired brigadier general.[97]

In the years to come, Paul continued his efforts to vindicate his brother's memory, endeavoring without success to have a city memorial erected to him, belaboring old grudges against party bosses, whether dead or alive, and wrestling with his own personal and policy divergences from his brother, who had both actively helped and indirectly hindered his political career. But the two had already acknowledged their differences. Asked in an oral history interview two years before his death if he saw Paul as a "left-winger," Bill responded, "I'd consider him a good thinker, just as I'd consider all good thinkers. You can call them any dirty name you like but they remain good thinkers, and so long as they keep within the Constitution of the U.S. they have an absolute right to think and to say what they think. I'd consider Paul one of the best thinkers that I know of." Many of their policy disagreements, he said, could be ascribed to their wide difference in age. "Paul, of course, was 20 years [*sic*—17 years] younger than me. He was impetuous, and he had very little patience for me, because of compromises that I may have made. . . . Paul would not compromise."[98]

Paul's own assessment of his brother, inserted into Bill's posthumous memoir, acknowledged the debt he owed the sibling who guided him "beyond the golden door" in America. Despite Bill's "many" shortcomings, "his vast store of knowledge of history and his capacity for recounting even minute details . . . gave one the feeling that there was a depth to him, which was far beyond what might be expected from his earlier, or even later, environment."[99] Whatever else one might say about Bill, that was certainly true. As for Paul, it would be difficult to find a sibling more dutiful to a powerful elder brother—except perhaps Robert Kennedy.

8

Middle-Aged Reformer

ON THE MORNING of the New York primary in September 1960, Paul bumped into an old-school West Side district leader, Gene McManus. McManus was seething because a group of young Democrats—part of the nascent Democratic Reform movement opposing political bosses like him—were supporting a liberal, issues-oriented challenger in his Hell's Kitchen district's primary election. Paul, whose involvement in the Democratic Party in New York went back to the Great Depression, was aligned with the younger reformers and on hand to assist them. McManus did not hide his view that party disloyalty of any kind amounted to disrespect, even a betrayal.

"What *issues*? Paul, tell me what *issues* I was against," McManus, a Tammany Hall regular if ever there was one, said gruffly. "Was I against Worker's Compensation? Was I ever against Widow's Pension? Was I against Social Security?"[1] He said he did not have patience for those dedicated to destroying the machine simply because leaders rewarded loyalists with jobs, for that was how it got *results*.

He had a point. Something of a throwback, McManus was the product of a political dynasty dating to the late 1800s and based at his family's brownstone at Forty-Ninth Street near Tenth Avenue. McManus enjoyed a patronage job in the city's courts and, in his spare time, shared his father's love of betting on horse races. His West Side district was steeped in Irish immigrant lore, in which, early in the century, if an Irishman's life was not cut short by extreme poverty, he might have seen a child with no park to play in crushed under the wheels of the New York Central Railroad trains that traversed the surface of Tenth and Eleventh Avenues, or felled by one of the many rival street gangs.

By 1960, the year John F. Kennedy defeated Richard Nixon for president, many of Hell's Kitchen's tenements, warehouses, churches, and neon-lit bars were still as ramshackle and grimy as they had been in the harsh days of old. The frayed McManus brownstone itself resembled a tenement. But to Paul, the McManuses were a gear in a great wheelwork that had long dispensed city jobs, bags of coal, and holiday poultry in return for votes from New York's poor immigrants, bringing them into the political system instead of ignoring them or castigating them for their indigence or Catholicism. The Tammany machine was, in fact, responsible to at least some degree for ensuring economic security. But in the modern age, with the government providing Social Security, public assistance, and bank deposit insurance, Tammany was no longer relevant. The New Deal had made a well-oiled political machine less central to the lives of ordinary citizens and less and less needed or even justifiable for the new college-educated generation of political reform activists.

Although the reform movement had helped William Fitts Ryan win a seat in Congress for Manhattan's West Side in the recent years, McManus was not in any present danger of losing his perch, as the movement represented a small proportion of the district's voters. But the participants made up for their size with hard work; for his part, Paul remained true to one of the earliest of the new generation of New York City reform clubs, the FDR–Woodrow Wilson Independent Democrats, founded in 1959, the product of a merger of three West Side factions (Woodrow Wilson, Hudson, and FDR Independent Democrats) in opposition to a long-Tammany-backed assemblyman's reelection. Pressing contemporary social issues and supporting new blood for office to undermine the party bosses, the movement would grow to include eighteen clubs during the 1960s, most in Manhattan. Membership peaked at about twenty-five thousand.[2]

To Paul, his fellow members of the FDR-Wilson Club and other reform satellites were "the kids," middle-class recent college graduates who

admirably harnessed their education to their ideals and energetically can-
vassed for candidate-petition signatures on street corners and door-to-
door in apartment buildings. Like himself, they were not bomb-throwers
but purely political.[3] Still, for all his support, some "found it difficult to
understand me and questioned my motives in joining the movement," Paul
later wrote,[4] in part due to his old-fashioned courtliness—he was known
for holding open the door for women, noted Gail Collins, a historian of
American women and *New York Times* op-ed columnist.[5] There were also
his friendships with, and respect for, many of the Tammany old-timers.
Plus, it was difficult for some in the largely Jewish reform movement to
accept that an Irish American could really be liberal.

What united the younger reformers and O'Dwyer, though, was a
shared interest in electing liberal and left-wing outsiders who took the
electoral process seriously and felt an urgency to make it more accessible
and open, especially the tightly controlled delegate candidate-nominating
procedures. They cared about issues rather than merely getting elected—
for example, better housing for Black and Latino residents suffering the
brunt of the city's chronic shortage of decent, affordable homes for the
lower and working classes. Within a few years, Democratic activists
were early to the barricades of protest against American military involvement in Southeast Asia, whereas many regulars were initially reluctant to criticize a Democratic administration in Washington as it ramped
up US engagement in Vietnam. (Before the anti-war movement ignited
on college campuses nationwide, thousands of all ages traveled from
New York City to Washington, DC, in April 1965 for the first major
rally against the war, and the FDR-Wilson Club came out with a statement against US military engagement in Southeast Asia the same year.)[6]
With their potluck dinners, street canvassing, and contentious meetings
that often extended well past midnight, they could hardly be ignored by
ward heelers.

"I had been out front on civil rights issues before most of them were
born," Paul wrote of his more youthful counterparts—and he might
have added, in his own defense, that he had been one of the first to inaugurate the party's reform wing, launched in 1959 (though there were some
earlier clubs formed to support Adlai Stevenson for president) by the
former US senator and ex-governor Herbert Lehman, then seventy-
nine; Eleanor Roosevelt, seventy-four; and the former secretary of the Air

Force Thomas Finletter, sixty-four.[7] O'Dwyer was the youngest among them. He was then fifty-one.[8]

————

AT THAT TIME Tammany was headed by Carmine DeSapio, who had succeeded Hugo Rogers as leader of the Tammany executive committee during Bill O'Dwyer's mayoralty. Having served as the New York County boss for more than a decade, DeSapio could disarm his critics with surprising courteousness. He held frequent press briefings (unusual for a political boss) and even gave learned-sounding speeches to college audiences, wearing finely cut suits. In other ways, however, he was more typical of the long line of Tammany Hall bosses who preceded him, routinely placing toadies in city jobs and arranging judgeships and municipal contracts, some of which he profited from personally. The dark sunglasses he invariably wore due to an eye condition lent him something of a sinister appearance.

After wielding legitimate power in state and city Democratic strongholds, DeSapio's political instincts finally gave out in 1958, when voters rejected the entire Democratic slate of major state candidates he put together except for one candidate, Arthur Levitt for state comptroller. Mayor Robert Wagner Jr. and Governor Averell Harriman led the opposition to the Tammany boss's choice of Manhattan District Attorney Frank Hogan to run for Lehman's Senate seat after the longtime Roosevelt ally announced plans to retire. Reacting to DeSapio's heavy-handedness, voters elected Kenneth Keating as senator and Nelson Rockefeller as governor—both Republicans.[9]

Two years after the DeSapio-authored election debacle, the Riverside Democratic Club helped elect its own leader, William Fitts Ryan, to Congress, the first big win for this coalition. The Riverside Democrats were the original reform club, and the reliably liberal Ryan went on to Washington, DC. The same year, 1960, O'Dwyer went to court to challenge the constitutional validity of the state board of elections' English-language literacy requirement for becoming a voter, a longtime provision he viewed as a blatant hindrance to Spanish-speaking voters.[10]

Though Ryan and O'Dwyer were on the same page ideologically, Paul had tried to snag reform club support from Ryan during the run-up to the latter's nomination to carry the movement's banner in the 1960 race for Congress on the West Side.[11] But Paul quickly abandoned this unavailing maneuver.[12]

His intra-reform-wing jockeying, though, was not unusual, and it reflected, too, his tendency to fish with a wide net for a seat to run for. O'Dwyer would cast the net widest to try to succeed Mayor Wagner in the 1965 Democratic primary, with Ryan also among the challengers. Again taking on a like-minded candidate for higher office, Paul ran for the US Senate in 1976, getting in the way of US Rep. Bella Abzug of Manhattan, who was just as closely linked as he to the National Lawyers Guild, support for Israel, and organized labor. Bad blood was the result.

Before becoming known in the 1970s as verifiably fratricidal, New York Democrats often engaged in a less contentious game of musical chairs. Borough presidents ran for comptroller, councilmen for mayor, and congressmen for governor. Paul wanted badly to gain a seat in Congress, in part to advance his ideas for a more active US role in reuniting the partitioned Ireland. But his decisions to run against like-minded liberal Democrats seemed to come, too, from his view that elections were supposed to be competitive. If he had a less than strong chance of winning most of the ones he entered, or if he complicated other left-wingers' chances, he felt it his right, or anyone's, to run.[13]

Paul was also not without ego; he had a subdued yet insistent temperament. On a trip to Ireland he turned to Kathleen, his full-time supporter and occasional driver (her husband alarmed family and colleagues with his habit of careless driving and periodic accidents), to ask her how many "great men" she thought there were.[14]

"I don't know, Paul," she replied, patting the back of his hand, "but I can tell you there's at least one *less* than you think."[15]

———

WHEN IT CAME to the "great men" most admired by the young Democrats, few could compare to Adlai Stevenson. Here, they felt, was an American politician of intellect who carried himself with nobility. The Minnesota senator Eugene McCarthy reflected this admiration when he exhorted delegates at the Democratic convention held in Los Angeles in 1960, "Do not leave this prophet"—a twice-failed presidential candidate—"without honor in his own party." And John F. Kennedy, after winning the nomination and becoming president, appointed Stevenson as United States ambassador to the United Nations.

Curiously or not, proponents of the new grassroots politics seemed to believe that virtue adhered to those who *lost* elections if they had run campaigns focused on important issues and had not insulted the voters with cheap applause lines—especially those voters questioning the traditional route to office, by way of the smoke-filled room. Like Stevenson, O'Dwyer spoke his own mind and espoused his own deeply felt principles without regard for the calculations of Democratic leaders. Come 1968, Paul would attach himself to Eugene McCarthy, the subdued former college professor of the US Senate, and in 1988, his preference for president would be still another insurgent, Jesse Jackson, the rousing Baptist minister and former aide to the Reverend Martin Luther King Jr. But for Paul's young counterparts in the early 1960s, it was the erudite Stevenson who fit the bill.

The glory of a political campaign, be it for sheriff or president, was in the end the preserve of the winner, however. As in professional sports, runners-up are not much remembered. Who, besides perhaps Murray Kempton, the gentlemanly columnist for the *New York Post*, would bother to visit the losers' locker room after a World Series clincher to interview defeated teammates, or go looking for the politician who lost an election for the right reasons (he once referred to O'Dwyer in a column entitled "How to Lose" as a "candidate who has proved often that he is too good for the Democratic Party")?[16]

"Stevenson was smart, so smart," said Sarah Schoenkopf, a Democratic Reform movement strategist who in 1964 married Victor Kovner, a noted First Amendment lawyer, and took his surname. "He wasn't of the old school, and he was really intelligent. If you ever read any of his speeches, he was brilliant. Most of us couldn't believe that he could lose because he was clearly the smartest guy."[17] At least he seemed more original and daring in his thinking than the Republican president from 1953 to 1961, General Dwight Eisenhower.

Blunt-talking and incisive about the local political landscape in New York, Schoenkopf helped lead the Village Independent Democratic Club's upstart effort in 1961 to unseat Carmine DeSapio from his district leader post in Greenwich Village. DeSapio lost both the race and his hold on city and state political power as a result. The reformers' challenge to DeSapio's dominance was rooted, at least in part, in Eleanor Roosevelt's lingering animus toward DeSapio, who had supported Averell Harriman for governor over her son Franklin Jr. at the 1954 Democratic state convention, forcing the latter into an unsuccessful general election for state attorney general against Jacob Javits that fall. "I told Carmine I would get him for what he did to Franklin, and get him I did," Kempton quoted Mrs. Roosevelt, years after her November 1962 death.[18] The reformers brought the beloved former first lady's wishes to bear. Succeeding DeSapio as Greenwich Village district leader was the handsome James Lanigan, known as "Mr. Young Democrat," someone with whom Schoenkopf had run successfully in 1960 for the State Democratic Party Committee, which controlled the nomination process at the party's annual state convention.

Schoenkopf, a Vassar alumna, had initially jumped into the reform ferment by phoning Manhattan clubs she found in the yellow pages and volunteering her time. She went on to meet the peripatetic O'Dwyer at a meeting of the Council of Reform Democrats on Eighth Avenue, she recalled. Eventually, they became friends, and Paul and Kathleen were invited to the Kovners' wedding.

Did she recall being wowed by Paul's surname, famous in the midcentury story of New York? "No, no. 'O'Dwyer' meant nothing, because his brother was disgraced. He was more like an anti-O'Dwyer," she said with a chuckle in a 2021 interview. "It was just that he was a very captivating person."[19]

The future New York senator Daniel Patrick Moynihan argued after DeSapio's fall in 1961 that "liberals are not neighborhood people."[20] But their proving ground was, in fact, the neighborhood, where they inserted themselves into both the local and the national political processes and discourse. In one of the most significant early signs of influence, their activism contributed, in some measure, to the two-term mayor Robert Wagner Jr.'s head-spinning decision in 1961 to run as a Tammany *opponent* for a third term, notwithstanding his history as a Tammany *regular*. Wagner, despite the 180-degree turnabout, maintained strong ties to labor, as municipal unions were grateful for the introduction of collective bargaining on Wagner's watch (a sea change in management-labor relations set in motion by the former mayor Bill O'Dwyer's grant of bargaining rights to a transit workers' division on Staten Island). He may even have earned the reformers' grudging respect and was reelected in 1961. For his own part, Paul was able to more comfortably support Wagner's campaign than might otherwise have been the case. He did so after first renouncing a short-lived plan to run himself for city comptroller.

While the O'Dwyer name had loomed large in the postwar story of New York, Paul's involvement in the FDR-Wilson Club was welcomed, at least by some in the movement, said Manfred Ohrenstein, one of the club's initial members. Elected state senator in 1960 with its backing, Ohrenstein went on to be state senate minority leader fifteen years later and was important to the bipartisan passage of legislative funding packages to keep a cash-strapped New York City government from declaring bankruptcy in 1975 (with O'Dwyer then the city council president). But others, of course, were wary, since Bill's awkward fall from power had occurred little more than a decade before. "Paul O'Dwyer was around a lot earlier than we were," argued Ohrenstein. "He was 20 to 30 years our senior when he became a member of the club and, at least for me, it was a big deal to have Paul O'Dwyer do that. He remained with us through the anti-Vietnam War period, and was always kind of our senior statesman."[21]

———

THE SENIOR STATESMAN was not too statesman-like, however, on a hot and humid night in August 1962 when, standing up for the rights of Puerto Ricans in his neighborhood, his temper flared and he nearly came to fisticuffs with a city government lawyer named Milton Mollen. Recently appointed as chair of the city's Housing Redevelopment Board, Mollen was seeking community approval of the Wagner administration's revised blueprint to tear down old buildings and build new housing to the north and east of the site for Lincoln Center, which would open in 1965.[22] Embattlement over the future of the neighborhood and the rehousing of some of its poor citizens was running strong that night, and O'Dwyer was poised to pounce when Mollen, addressing the skeptical audience of more than 150 residents, outlined city hall's urban renewal schema with Herman Badillo, the administration's head of relocation.

The area being targeted for redevelopment stretched from Eighty-Seventh and Ninety-Seventh Streets and from Central Park West to Amsterdam Avenue. It was home to about twenty-seven thousand people, many of whom lived in overcrowded and physically neglected tenements. (O'Dwyer resided with his family in a doorman-operated apartment building on Central Park West between Ninety-Fourth and Ninety-Fifth Streets.)

Also in the audience with Paul was Harry Browne, the pastor of St. Gregory the Great Catholic Church at 144 West Ninetieth Street. Long after becoming an Upper West Side resident, Paul considered himself a natural ally of the fiery, radical priest, one of the community's most visible and vocal defenders of its Puerto Rican minority. Known as the "housing priest," Browne was the founder of Strycker's Bay Neighborhood Council. His service to poor migrants was inspired by the faith-based social activism, direct action, and civil disobedience of Dorothy Day, cofounder of the Catholic Worker movement. Puerto Rican West Siders filled his church pews along with white congregants to hear his Sunday morning homilies, in which he linked the scriptures to issues of US military spending, racial discrimination, and economic hardship.

Like Paul, the Reverend Browne's distrust of New York City government's urban reconstruction program was considerable. Mollen, however, told skeptics of urban renewal that the rehabilitation project for the West Side would not be controlled by the imperious Robert Moses or the mayor's Slum Clearance Committee. In fact, Mollen said, the Wagner administration had recently regained control of the committee from Moses, forcing him to release his files and pushing legislation in Albany to abolish it altogether.[23] Mollen and Badillo, a Puerto Rican trailblazer in city politics, said the Wagner administration intended to work collaboratively with community leaders. The goal was to ensure that anyone displaced by the project would gain a comparably sized or even larger place to live within the community.

O'Dwyer was having none of it. He made this plainly evident after the town hall meeting had nearly run its course.

"Paul at that meeting—he meant well but he was making factual mistakes and I called him on it," Mollen recalled.

> "I've always had a great deal of respect for you," I told him, "and I like you personally, and I personally believe in a lot of things you've stood for, but you're mistaken about what this plan is, the need for it, and what good will come from it." We had some wild words: Paul was accusing me of moving people around like pawns and of furthering the interest of the big-money developers and their bankers—the same things that Father Browne had been saying. We practically started going toward each other with hostile intentions, but people stepped in between us and that was the end of it.[24]

When the shouting match and meeting were over, bleary-eyed attend-ees spilled out onto the sidewalk. But the project got under way in the mid-1960s according to terms the Strycker's Bay Neighborhood Coun-cil, and O'Dwyer himself, deemed acceptable. The agreed-upon stipula-tions included a Wagner administration commitment to increase the number of low-income housing units in the original plan—from the ini-tial 400 to 2,500—and a reduction in planned luxury units from 5,000 to 1,300. The agreement preserved more than two dozen brownstones, many of which had been used as rooming houses like the one Paul had stayed in as an immigrant fresh off the boat. Also provided was a provi-sion for cash bonuses for those who found another place to live without guaranteed city relocation assistance.[25]

The episode betrayed not only O'Dwyer's intemperate side but also his suspicion of the Establishment after the Moses Slum Committee's his-tory of brusque treatment of the poor, with tens of thousands dispos-sessed in a secretive and unaccountable government process. But the confrontation with Mollen also brought out a quality for which Paul was admired in reform circles: in Kovner's words, his "Irish rebelliousness."[26] However, O'Dwyer was fighting the last war: the Wagner administration had taken urban renewal out of Moses's hands when Mollen showed up on the West Side. The project Paul objected to was in fact a test case for a more community-sensitive approach.

————

O'DWYER'S INVOLVEMENT with housing, an issue at the center of the New York left's agenda since before World War II, had gotten going in 1938, when he chaired a Brooklyn Heights–based civic group that pre-sented a blueprint to replace decrepit housing where Brooklyn Navy Yard dockworkers lived with their families. Moses himself shot it down, con-demning its advocates as naive in a "tirade," in Paul's remembrance. At the time, state law supported the city using eminent domain to clear large areas designated as slums for reconstruction, foreshadowing the federal Title I Act of 1949, a major instrument in Moses's toolbox for sweeping urban renewal.

By the time of his outburst against Mollen, O'Dwyer was known for fighting in court for equal treatment for minorities in both public and private housing. His reputation grew mainly from his involvement in a

long-running controversy centered on the refusal of Metropolitan Life Insurance Co. (MetLife) to allow Black people to live at Stuyvesant Town,
a private housing development built on eighty acres between Fourteenth
and Twenty-First Streets from First Avenue to Avenue C known as the
Gas House District. The development, featuring interior grounds laced
by greens, walking paths, and benches, resulted from a pioneering "public-
private" partnership between the La Guardia administration and the
corporation, entailing the displacement of some twelve thousand people
and the razing of their tenements, churches, schools, and the giant gas
plant. Stuyvesant Town opened in 1947. In December of 1950, Paul Ross
of the American Labor Party asked O'Dwyer to represent himself and
other Stuyvesant tenants facing eviction for opposing the color line of
MetLife there. Ross had worked for Bill O'Dwyer's election and then for
the O'Dwyer administration, only to resign over the doubling of the original subway fare to ten cents.

Paul agreed to represent three dozen tenant activists notified that their
Stuyvesant Town leases were not going to be renewed. The threat of eviction stemmed from their vocal opposition to MetLife's exclusionary
tenant-selection policies and their support for integration.

The company's explicit barriers to African Americans at Stuyvesant
Town and its adjacent Peter Cooper Village—with a combined total of
11,250 apartments in 110 brick buildings—were not then illegal. No
one was more insistent about that than Frederick Ecker, the MetLife
president, who had worked his way up from the company mailroom and
was in his late seventies when Paul took the case for the threatened
tenants.

"Negroes and whites don't mix," the executive once told a reporter
from the *New York Post*, following a 1943 city council hearing. "Maybe
they will in a hundred years, but not now."[27]

With Moses serving as liaison to Ecker under Mayor La Guardia, the
Little Flower sought a voluntary commitment from MetLife to allow
African American New Yorkers to rent apartments in Stuyvesant Town.
By the time the complex was fully occupied, O'Dwyer filed legal papers
for the members of its Tenants Committee to End Discrimination, reminding the court of the city's grant of eminent domain, multiyear tax
breaks, and other *public* incentives to MetLife—all part of the reason, he
argued, that his clients had every right to believe the company was

obliged to open the door to Black residents and that the tenants were allowed under the First Amendment to advocate for integration.[28]

For a history of Stuyvesant Town published in 2014, *New York Times* reporter Charles Bagli turned up back-channel La Guardia administration memos to MetLife seeking a change of heart from the company. And in 1944, La Guardia was able to announce something of a compromise with the developer, albeit less than he would have liked and unsatisfactory to the city's robust and interracial civil rights movement: in addition to the (segregated) Stuyvesant Town, MetLife would build Riverton in Harlem, a much smaller development with 1,232 apartments in seven thirteen-story buildings, and open to all races. Stuyvesant, however, would remain lily-white.[29]

In the fall of 1945, with the land for Stuyvesant Town's construction cleared and ready, MetLife announced that it was already receiving requests for leases from thousands of applicants and that it would give priority to white World War II veterans.[30]

MetLife's eviction notices to the activist tenants were out of step not only with public sentiment within the development (at least as reflected by the committee's two surveys of residents) but also with recent US Supreme Court rulings derailing racial segregation in railroad dining cars and challenging its existence in higher education—and with the hope that de jure separation of the races might be on the way out in America.[31] The *Amsterdam News* detected what it called "the beginning of the end of racial segregation" and a "death blow" to Jim Crow in both the North and South.[32] A city council bill by the Manhattan council members Stanley Isaacs, a Republican former Manhattan borough president, and Earl Brown, a Democrat, established a ban on local housing discrimination, though the change would not become a reality until 1957 after several legal challenges.[33]

The Stuyvesant case dragged on and on until, at the start of 1952, rallies by supporters of housing integration at Stuyvesant Town grew more frequent and larger and the date of the activist tenants' anticipated removal by a city marshal neared. Running out of options, with his First Amendment arguments unsuccessful to date, Paul contended to Magistrate George Genung that the carefully screened tenant-plaintiffs were victims of deception since MetLife did not advise them when they moved in that the basis for an eviction could extend beyond a violation of traditional

occupancy rules (noise, disruption, arrears) to the exercise of their constitutionally protected opinions and beliefs.

Finally, O'Dwyer resorted to a direct appeal to Old Man Ecker, se-
curing a sit-down in the corporation boardroom. When Paul arrived,
Ecker, nearly attired and peering through wire-rimmed spectacles, was
surrounded by company lawyers and vice presidents at a long table. The
liberal lawyer tried to appeal to the executive's better angels.

Ecker started by asking O'Dwyer to explain the reason for the meeting.
And with that, the tenants' lawyer explained that he hoped to convince
Ecker to give serious thought to rescinding the looming evictions. Paul
asked, too, why MetLife was not more interested in tapping into the African American market for modern, middle-class housing. Ecker stared
blankly, Paul later recalled. One day, perhaps, Ecker responded. For the
time being, however, the executive was certain that the general public held
similar reservations about mandating what a private company did. If he
was in error, then MetLife was not in any case legally bound to address
a social issue. Moreover, the company felt no moral compunction to do
so, he said.[34]

Seven years had passed since the final Stuyvesant Town blueprint was
first placed on the city's drawing board, based on what was then a novel
business-government partnership to address a neighborhood's physical
deterioration and the shortage of up-to-date accommodations for middle-
class city residents. Before Paul got up to leave the boardroom, Ecker gave
no indication that he would even consider heeding Paul's final request—to
allow the nineteen threatened tenants to stay in their Stuyvesant Town
apartments *without* lease renewals.

But a reprieve for the remaining activists soon did come. With a few
days to go before the forced evictions, slated for January 1952, and with
officials worried about possible violence and unrest, City Council President Rudolph Halley (the former counsel to the Kefauver Committee),
announced that MetLife had agreed to hold off on evictions. At the same
time, he allowed, MetLife reserved the legal right to exclude anyone based
on any factors the insurance company deemed pertinent, including the
color of a person's skin.[35]

———

BY 1960, housing advocates in every corner of the city were still struggling
to make a difference for the poor amid slum clearance and urban redevel-

opment. The bane of their hopes for greater government commitment to fair housing practices was Robert Moses, Ecker's ideological cousin when it came to defending the legal right of a private landlord to deny the constitutional rights of Black and Latino residents. Moses held many government titles, including chair of the mayor's Slum Clearance Committee. Though unelected, his authority was far-reaching, as were the new highways, bridges, and tunnels he sponsored for the automobile age.

From La Guardia to Wagner, successive mayors had shown no compunction to thwart Moses's projects, as he carried out what they felt needed to be done without creating a need to raise taxes or turning to borrowing to pay for them. Moses's power stemmed, too, from his dealings with a web of interests and allies across the municipal bond market, savings and loan industry, construction unions, the Democratic bosses of the city and state, and commercial builders, all profiting in one way or another from his mega projects, built with borrowing backed with toll revenue collected by the bridge authority Moses also controlled. Moses at one point folded plans for a satellite campus for Fordham University sought by the Catholic archdiocese into his plan for demolishing San Juan Hill, an adjacent lower-class neighborhood of some seven thousand Black and Latino residents and eight hundred businesses; the neighborhood was forced to make way for what was said to be the jewel in Moses's crown: Lincoln Center.[36] In keeping with his autocratic style, the promises of relocation made to those who lived or operated stores in the path of bulldozers were broken. "Moses was not making even a pretense of creating new homes for the families displaced," Robert Caro wrote in *The Power Broker*, his Pulitzer Prize–winning biography of Moses published in 1974.

Before the filming of the opening scene of the 1961 movie version of the Broadway musical *West Side Story* in the rubble of San Juan Hill, and a year before Paul's early-morning confrontation with city lawyer Mollen in 1962, Moses began to lose his luster and reputation as a proponent of "good government" dating back to his early years as an aide to Governor Al Smith. By 1960, neighborhood activists in Manhattan and even the usually supportive *New York Times* raised questions about Moses and his methods. One of the earliest dustups began when Stuart Constable, Moses's top aide in the Parks Department (Moses was then the city parks commissioner), threatened to kill the free Shakespeare in the Park festival in Central Park. When the threat to the popular summertime series arose in 1959, Moses had already lost a battle with a loosely organized group of affluent West Side mothers to pave a natural glen in order to create a parking lot for the park's upmarket Tavern on the Green restaurant.[37]

Unusually aggressive coverage by the liberal newspaper owner Dorothy Schiff's *New York Post* and its competitor the *New York World-Telegram* revealed, meanwhile, the names of housing developers to whom slum clearance sites had been assigned. Some of the stories were scathing. In one example, it was shown that one of the redevelopers was identified in testimony before the Kefauver Committee as having engaged in business deals with the reputed mobsters Frank Costello, Meyer Lansky, and Joe Adonis. The articles raised questions about the closed-door process for awarding Title I property under a financially complex process, with easily digestible headlines like "Costello Pal Got Title I Deal" (June 30, 1959, *New York Post*) and "Banker Had Warning on Costello Pal" (*New York World-Telegram*). The newspapers had been smelling a rat inside the House of Moses for months. Now it had one by the tail.[38]

The downtown neighborhood activist Jane Jacobs, at the same time, marshaled Greenwich Village activists against another Moses mega dream, a crosstown highway in the vicinity of Canal Street, taking on not only the master builder but DeSapio too, and out-organizing both. Jacobs's more human-scale vision for urban planning included tree-lined streets, stoops, and small shops, with room for automobile traffic, too, but no life-squelching highways severing older residential neighborhoods, as Moses had built in the Bronx to the demise of working-class communities like the vibrant, Jewish middle- and lower-class East Tremont section.

———

AFTER O'DWYER and other housing reformers accepted the post-Moses plan for the Upper West Side after many changes and compromises, he led sixty Reform Democrats to the September 1962 Democratic state nominating convention in Saratoga, New York. The party gathering proved to be useful to him as preparation for the Democratic presidential convention coming to Atlantic City in 1964 and the following one in Chicago in 1968, where he would play a leading role as the New York Democratic candidate for US Senate. At the Saratoga gathering of 1,200 Democratic delegates, he tried to marshal Democratic reformers and wavering regulars to obtain, for himself, the nomination to run in the 1962 primary for the Senate. (While the convention had the power to give some-one an automatic spot on the ballot, others could still get on the ballot by gathering enough signatures.) The journalist Sidney Zion would later describe Paul's 1962 effort as pure "chutzpah" since he had never won a primary or an election up to that point.[39]

Yet the same Yiddish phrase could have just as aptly described James Donovan, the party's final choice to run for the Senate after the floor fight. Though Donovan had helped to negotiate the release of the American U-2 spy-plane navigator Francis Gary Powers in exchange for a Soviet spy, the fame arising from this accomplishment was insufficient for him to overcome Jacob Javits, the liberal Republican incumbent senator, in the 1962 general election. Paul watched glumly from the sidelines as Dono-van, having won the party's nod, lost badly in November. (He, like O'Dwyer, had never been elected before.)

But O'Dwyer was interested and attentive when, after the debacle, he sat down with Hedi Piel, a West Side tenant activist and district leader, and she advised him to run in 1963 for one of the newly created Man-hattan councilman-at-large seats, "the only game in town." Paul talked it over with friends and family members and decided to try, hitching his "outsider" horse as a Democratic Reform movement participant to his "in-sider" trap—his ties to Mayor Wagner—in the coming contest.[40]

It was helpful to Paul's designs on the city council that Wagner, Paul's contemporary and twenty years Bill's junior, owed a political debt to the O'Dwyer brothers for past assistance. Not only had Paul acted as Wag-ner's labor-aligned supporter in all his races, but Bill, as mayor, had ap-pointed Wagner to his first city post: city planning commissioner. (Not that Bill admitted to being impressed by the relatively diminutive scion: spying him one day, Bill as mayor was heard to remark, "Here comes young Bob Wagner, wearing his father's pants.")[41]

But Paul also owed a debt to Wagner because in March 1960 he had appointed Paul's niece Joan O'Dwyer O'Neill to serve as magistrate on the Queens County Criminal Court.[42] Paul attended her city hall swear-ing-in, beaming with pride.[43]

———

THE AT-LARGE COUNCIL MEMBER'S seat Paul had his eye on in 1963, as suggested to him by Piel, was one of two such positions in each borough that were created to provide greater political access to members of minority groups. The at-large seats were created to broaden representation on the council of candidates sponsored by third parties. (In 1969, three Liberals would be elected this way.)

In the later remembrance of the future governor Hugh Carey, Wagner was a barnacle, attaching himself to anyone or any office willing to have him. Wagner viewed Paul as equally loyal to their party yet at the same time as someone who could be difficult to control, perhaps more determined to follow his own ideological muse than to fall in line on an important city council vote. "Keep an eye on that son of a bitch" were Wagner's supposed words to Bill O'Dwyer when the ex-mayor, recently returned from living in Mexico at the time and working at O'Dwyer & Bernstien, put in a word with Wagner for his brother's candidacy, according to Mychal McNicholas. Bill related the comment, chuckling, to McNicholas, an O'Dwyer cousin and longtime legal assistant in the law firm.[44]

Publicly, at least, Wagner lauded Paul for his principles and independence, delivering his formal endorsement at a fundraising dinner for O'Dwyer at the Americana Hotel on West Thirty-Eighth Street in Manhattan. "In fact," the mayor declared, "Paul is a fighting man. What Irishman isn't? But Paul fights with charm and wit, as well as with passion. So, if you're on the opposite side of Paul on any issue, as I have been on some, you end up by forgiving him."[45]

Attaining his party's nomination to run for the council-at-large seat was not automatic for the Wagner ally, all the same. O'Dwyer first needed to overcome two dozen candidates vying for the reform faction's nod, a goal complicated by his refusal to support every reformer who was then running against an old guard candidate.[46] He did receive the reform endorsement in the end, however, and subsequently appeared before the New York County Executive Board, or Tammany Hall. He spoke of his service as the New York State cochair of John Kennedy's 1960 presidential campaign along with his role, also at the Irish Catholic president's request, as chair of a committee that rallied public support for a national health insurance program for the aged (Medicare would be passed by Congress in 1965) and voter registration.

But there was still the delicate matter of his strong ties to the reform movement, which did not sit well with the Tammany board. Joseph Zaretzki, the New York state senate minority leader and a district leader in

Washington Heights, came to his aid. Thanks to Zaretzki speaking up for him, Paul was granted the Democratic endorsement, albeit "with little enthusiasm."[47]

So, in the 1963 councilman-at-large primary, Paul was able to ride two horses simultaneously, as when he ran for Congress in 1948. Back then, the two factions behind him were Tammany and the American Labor Party (the latter was dissolved in 1956); now they were Tammany and Reform. Mayor Wagner, in his endorsement of O'Dwyer, said Paul was "attacked by some reformers as being soft on the old guard, and by some of the old guard as being starry-eyed, and by some of both as being Wagner's personal candidate. Of course, there was a little bit of truth, but only a little, in all three of those accusations."[48]

Privately, O'Dwyer felt his future in politics depended on his succeeding in the at-large election with organizational support. If he lost, then his political career would likely be done.[49] But, helped by Kathleen, his available children, and his law associates, and the backing of Harlem's political boss J. Raymond Jones (like Wagner a former aide to Bill O'Dwyer), he pulled more votes in Harlem than his African American opponent, John Young, a politically active Harlemite whose campaign posters were plastered all over the West Side. And he performed well among Irish, Italians, and Greeks, many of them union members. His friends in the Democratic Reform movement were critical to his success.

In November, the ballot contained the names of a Liberal, a Socialist, a Republican, and Paul, a Democrat. The second at-large seat for Manhattan went to a Republican, Richard Aldrich, a cousin of Nelson Rockefeller who specialized in economic development in South America.[50]

With Paul's victory, the O'Dwyer flag would wave again at city hall, though, in truth, it did not rise very high since the city council, even as newly enlarged, would remain a weak appendage to the executive branch, serving merely as an occasional check on the mayor's powers. It did not even carry the weight of a rubber stamp, as Henry Stern, a later council member, lamented—because at least "a rubber stamp leaves an impression."[51]

Still, from his first days as a council member, O'Dwyer searched for ways to make an imprint all the same. He cast a rare Democratic vote *against* the mayor's annual expense budget after his then law associate

with some experience sitting on city and state commissions, Bernie Richland, showed him that the city plan relied on "deficit financing," an
accounting maneuver that tended to obscure and aggravate revenue
shortfalls.

What raised Richland's and then Paul's eyebrows was Wagner's intention to borrow millions of dollars in the municipal bond market to
pay for routine operating costs such as salaries and pothole repairs. Traditionally, long-term borrowing was for construction of facilities with
long life spans, like schools and hospitals. Turning to the bond market
for the cash to plug the yearly operating budget was unorthodox, burdening the annual operating budget with interest costs and bond transaction fees.[52]

Since the mayor had the power to estimate total tax revenues and set
the spending priorities for the year ahead, it was a rare Democratic council member who voted against the city budget plan proposed by the mayor,
lest it imperil an appropriation of city funds for his district, party support for his reelection, or his appointment to a public job or judgeship.
But O'Dwyer, as always, ran his own law firm with Oscar Bernstien, with
revenue mainly drawn from injury and malpractice cases and representing labor unions. He had no pressing need to cultivate city hall's patronage, nor was the counsel for the defense interested in landing a government
post or becoming a judge. So he could afford to question the mayor's
priorities.

———

BECAUSE HIS BROTHER had faced a cascade of difficulties after World
War II, Paul understood, probably better than most city council members,
that serving as mayor of New York was truly the second-hardest job in
America, after the president. It certainly had been so for Bill, who was
forced to institute a crash program to provide 7,000 housing units to accommodate returning veterans along with 1,325 Quonset huts, as well
as schools, hospitals, and incinerators left unbuilt or unfinished during
the war. In only Bill's second month in office, the city suffered a midwinter strike by 3,500 tugboat operators who delivered coal to the city; he
declared a public emergency and announced a rationing system, including brownouts, no heat in the subways, and the closing of schools to house
people lacking fuel, but the labor action ended after a week and Bill admit

ted that he had overreacted. But he had gotten his first taste of the job's enormous burdens, stakes, and complexities, which were far beyond anything he had experienced as a district attorney or judge. By the time a case of smallpox shockingly made its way by bus into Manhattan from Mexico City in 1947 (prompting his administration to roll out a mass inoculation program that became a model of success), there was no turning back from the exhaustion and difficulties of the job. "I tell you there were times when, as mayor, I truly wanted to jump," Bill O'Dwyer said several years later. "You would look over the city from some place high above it, and you would say to yourself, 'Good Jesus, it's too much for me!'"[53]

Paul had also seen his brother floundering, notably so in his final months at Gracie Mansion in the late summer of 1950. The orchestration of Bill's premature exit by the Bronx Democratic leader Edward Flynn—the same man who had talked him into running for reelection the year before—confirmed for Paul the fickleness of political allegiances. More than a decade on, Bill's youngest sibling felt sympathy for anyone brave, ambitious, or foolhardy enough to be mayor of New York. And, starting in the mid-1960s, the job grew even more complicated—due to enormous racial tensions.

———

AN EARLY INDICATION was the fatal shooting of James Powell, a fifteen-year-old Black teenager from the Bronx, by a white, off-duty police lieutenant named Tom Gilligan, thirty-six, outside an apartment building on the East Side of Manhattan, where Gilligan claimed the boy brandished a pocketknife.

Coincidentally, a Harlem protest march was set to take place that day, organized by the Congress of Racial Equality (CORE) to highlight the disappearance in Mississippi of the civil rights workers Andrew Goodman and Michael Schwerner of New York City and James Chaney of Meridian, Mississippi. As word of Powell's shooting spread, the march's focus switched to local police brutality. After two days of peaceful protests, tensions rose outside a Harlem police station, as the New York City Police Department responded to thrown objects with bully clubs and gunfire to disperse the crowd. The turmoil lasted for several days and resulted in the arrest of five hundred people, damage to seven hundred businesses, and city costs totaling about $4 million. Additional clashes also broke out in Bedford-Stuyvesant and Brownsville, earning the days of sporadic rioting the name "New York's Birmingham," a reference to the televised scenes of young people blasted with high-pressure fire hoses, clubbed by cops, and lunged at by police dogs at the nonviolent anti-segregation demonstrations that had taken place a year earlier in the segregated Alabama city.

In a letter from the Birmingham jail where he sat incarcerated after protesting unjust racial codes, the Reverend King of the Southern Christian Leadership Council related the purpose of nonviolent direct action: "to create such a crisis and foster such a tension that a community which has constantly refused to negotiate is forced to confront the issue. It seeks to dramatize the issue that it can no longer be ignored." Such was the hope of many radicalizing civil rights activists, among them the playwright Lorraine Hansberry, who, at a forum in New York a month before the Harlem uprising, questioned just how far white liberals' commitment to fighting for justice would go when the struggle reached their own neighborhoods and their children's schools. Known for her 1959 success in *A Raisin in the Sun*, Hansberry wrestled with this question in a way few white liberals, or mayors, had to date. She assailed the ambivalence of some of the well-intentioned white people appearing with her on the panel, declaring, "We have to find some way with these dialogues to show and to encourage the white liberal to stop being a liberal and become an American radical." Writing two days after the discussion, Hansberry described the town hall—convened by the Association of Artists for Freedom, a coalition of well-known Black performers and writers—as having been fraught: "Negroes are so angry and white people are so confused and sensitive to criticism," she reflected in a journal.[54]

Her sensitivity to liberal sanctimony, the acceptance of de facto racial exclusion in the communities where they lived and sent their children to school, was perhaps more widely appreciated when the Harlem disturbances erupted only two weeks after President Lyndon B. Johnson had signed the Civil Rights Act on July 2, 1964. What was more, the rioting that followed young Powell's killing marked only the first of scores of deadly urban race riots to break out around the country despite these breakthrough advances for racial equality, most tragically of all, perhaps, the August 1965 burning of the Watts section of Los Angeles in which thirty-two people lost their lives in six days and nights of rioting. The

Watts uprising was shown on TV news nearly nonstop with the aid of a "tele-copter," a novel news-gathering technique.[55]

Many Democratic elected officials reacted to the Harlem disturbances with calls for tougher policing and stiffer penalties. The reports of daily newspapers, whose coverage of Black life was often limited to stories pulled from the crime blotter, were largely superficial or sensationalized. But Jimmy Breslin, a streetwise news columnist who grew up in the Jamaica section of Queens, disappeared from his newsroom for several days and nights after the violence broke out, sending back columns depicting streets broiling with heat, rage, and alienation. A firefighter there told him his men were targeted by Black rock-throwers "trying to kill us," while, Breslin also wrote, a "black kid with a shaved head and a gold polo shirt" menaced the disheveled newspaper man, saying, "What are you looking at, you big fat bastard?"[56]

James Baldwin, who was raised in Harlem, did not feel threatened by the younger men wandering about, however. His report in *The Nation* described "frightened, little boys" running from cops who had their weapons out, people pulling back from open windows in terror, and a policeman battering a young salesman such that he lost sight in one eye. The salesman had simply asked the cop why he was pummeling a kid. "Harlem," Baldwin wrote, underscoring a familiar outrage, "is policed like occupied territory."[57]

As the Manhattan council-member-at-large, O'Dwyer called on the city to bail out merchants who suffered property damage, and he supported Wagner's plan to expand summer youth jobs in Harlem by a thousand. He spoke most positively of a bill introduced by the Upper West Side councilman—and reform movement figure—Ted Weiss to initiate a racially diverse, civilian-dominated board on a permanent basis to review complaints of police brutality, a move the Reverend King was urging in the city.

The largely white patrolmen's union and the police department stood opposed when, faced with widespread public opposition to the remedy proposed under Weiss's legislation, O'Dwyer sought a broader approach—an office of citizens' redress with the power to investigate all city agencies, not just the police department, saying of police violence that it was systemic rather than simply a question of individual conduct. He felt his measure was more likely to pass than a bill to establish civilian oversight of the New York Police Department, and he was not incorrect: In 1966, the Republican-Liberal mayor John Lindsay, Wagner's successor, proposed a police review board consisting of four civilians and three police officers, asking voters to approve it in a ballot referendum. The Patrolmen's Benevolent Association mounted a well-financed counter-offensive, with the union's president, John Cassese, insisting that public safety should not take a back seat to politics. "You won't satisfy these people until you get all Negroes and Puerto Ricans on the board and every policeman who goes in front of it is found guilty," he declared—and the *Daily News* opined that the board would "be infested sooner or later with cop-haters, professional liberals, representatives of pressure groups, and the like, to the great undermining of the police force."[58]

Many conservatives and even some liberals seemed to agree. Though several cities had already set up civilian-majority police oversight panels, New York voters, by a margin of two to one, voted "No" to the Lindsay proposal, effectively marking what Christopher Hayes, the author of a 2021 history on the Harlem uprising, described as "the end of the civil rights coalition among African Americans and white allies, particularly Jewish New Yorkers."[59] Some historians like Hayes have also seen the referendum vote as a turning point in Black-Jewish relations. Other scholars, though, have linked the breakdown in interracial cooperation on civil rights to a later clash, in 1968, between the city's largely Jewish teachers' union and African American parents and community leaders concerning the hiring and firing of white teachers in Ocean Hill–Brownsville public schools.

Considering that O'Dwyer typically drew out a historical parallel to British oppression in Ireland and the continuing resistance of the Irish Republican Army, he was neither indignant nor that surprised when some Black activists turned more strident and even militant in tone in response to discrimination and joblessness, or acted in Malcolm X's phrasing "by any means necessary"—by which he meant leaving open all available options of resistance to white oppression, including using violence. The Black Power movement in Oakland, California, was soon protecting poor Black communities from police brutality by organizing armed street patrols.

Looking for ways to bridge the racial divide constructively, O'Dwyer proposed a bill after the uptown rioting that would require all businesses in the city to pay an hourly wage of no less than $1.50 to all employees. Labor unions backed the measure strongly, helping Paul overcome the opposition by the Commerce and Industry Association, which contended that the higher wage standard would cause joblessness by saddling business owners with higher costs.

In response to the business group, Paul emphasized that the workforce citywide was predominantly nonunion and woefully low-paid. He asked whether New Yorkers really wanted to be known for living on a "noncompetitive, high-wage island" where the dishwasher, the launderer, and the confectionery worker were forced to supplement their paychecks with welfare checks and people at the bottom of the labor market were denied an income they could survive on. How could that possibly contribute to law and order? he asked.

When Mayor Wagner announced his support for the measure, it was clear that the bill had surmounted "hostility from many powerful forces in our city who seem to be devoted to the cause of starvation wages," as Paul described it. O'Dwyer also argued that the council, for a change, needed to demonstrate some muscle by pushing beyond the restrained statewide minimum wage, citing a recent state-approved expansion of the scope of municipal home rule. "Capacity for self-government can be acquired only by the practice of self-government," he told the largely Democratic chamber in the floor debate. And to Oliver Pilat of the *New York Post*, he emphasized the importance of a living wage for ghetto dwellers and new immigrants, saying, "People of color are primarily the ones that must be helped."[60]

Immediately after the minimum wage measure was signed into law in July 1964, the trade association went to court, and its appeal proved successful, preventing the law's implementation under a ruling that asserted that New York State's cities lacked legal authority to set their own wage floors. In response, prominent labor figures like A. Philip Randolph, the president of the Brotherhood of Sleeping Car Porters, and John O'Rourke, the chair of Joint Council 16 of the International Brotherhood of Teamsters, turned to Nelson Rockefeller, asking the Republican governor of New York to push through enabling legislation to get around the court's limitation. Rockefeller set up a committee to look into this, but that was as far as it went. The state minimum wage, scheduled to rise from $1.15 to $1.25 an hour at the end of 1964, remained in force for

New York City. Nonunion service and factory workers continued to contend with very low pay.

———

SURPRISINGLY, PAUL HAD NOT BEEN present for the city hall public hearing when Mayor Wagner signed the ill-fated minimum wage bill to robust applause, having sent word to New York–area unions that he, along with his friend from the National Lawyers Guild, Phil Sipser, were headed for the Appalachian hills of southeastern Kentucky. There, he said, they intended to defend eight coal miners facing charges resulting from a bitter, long-lasting strike.[61] In a "Dear Friends" letter, O'Dwyer explained that the accused miners were "framed on charges of attempting to blow up a bridge leading to a scab-operated mine." For that reason, he wrote, "I will not be present at the hearing and hope your spokesman can argue for me."[62]

Threatened by three-dollar-a-day strikebreakers and abandoned by their corruption-tainted union—the United Mine Workers once led by John L. Lewis—the accused miners were on strike against pension cuts. Their cause was taken up in New York City by the Committee for Miners, an advocacy effort organized in part by the labor organizer Stanley Aronowitz, later a City University sociology professor of note. When approached by the committee, O'Dwyer and Sipser volunteered to provide free legal counsel. Since the fund raised for the miners' defense was skimpy, Sipser went looking for contributions and got $5,000 from a notable former client: Jimmy Hoffa, the ethically challenged president of the International Association of Teamsters. Paul also convinced Leonard Boudin, who had been the first attorney to upend an espionage case fueled by one of J. Edgar Hoover's investigations (that of Judith Coplon), to write up the appellate brief at no charge.

Sipser was the Jewish son of a tomato pushcart peddler on the Lower East Side and drawn to prolabor radicalism and the trade union movement as a young lawyer. In his legal career, he was known for representing symphonic musicians in breakthrough contract negotiations with the New York Philharmonic and other major concert halls after having been effectively blacklisted during the peak of the Cold War. For him, and O'Dwyer, participation in the case far from New York was a calling. But their trip to a dirt-poor mountain community also provided them with an appreciation for the region's folkways and vernacular. Sipser's son, Bill, recalled one story told by his dad about the Kentucky case: "An FBI guy was testifying, talking about using bloodhounds to try to track these guys down, and one of the coal miners leans over to my father in the middle of his testimony and in a heavy Kentucky accent says, '*Pheel*, them dogs nearly bit my ass!'"[63]

The sentences for four of the miners were reduced in light of the violations of their constitutional rights revealed by their New York lawyers. The other four miners were acquitted of the bombing charges.[64] Sipser and O'Dwyer returned home with amusing stories and took pride in their relative success on behalf of exploited workers.

———

THE KENTUCKY AFFAIR was not the last time Paul would dash off to address an injustice. He was especially pleased when Carl Rachlin, the general counsel of CORE, asked him to head to Mississippi to represent Lois Chaffee, a white college instructor from Idaho arrested and jailed after joining with her African American students in a nonviolent civil rights memorial rally in Jackson in June 1963, the day after Medgar Evers, a Black field-worker for the National Association for the Advancement of Colored People (NAACP) and voting rights activist, was murdered in the city.

At the time of Evers's shocking killing, racial segregation in Jackson was the focus of student-led sit-ins at Woolworth's restaurant counters. A World War II veteran, Evers had been instrumental in finding witnesses and evidence of the 1955 lynching of fifteen-year-old Emmett Till, a murder followed by a miscarriage of justice that brought national attention to Mississippi's white supremacist regime. O'Dwyer confronted the state's virulently racist legal system on Chaffee's behalf, at a time when Mississippi had no white lawyers willing to accept a civil rights case and just two Black members of the state bar. Chaffee denied charges of interfering with police. She was charged with and convicted of perjury all the same, though TV news footage had showed police assaulting nonviolent protesters with impunity, not the other way around.

O'Dwyer took her appeal to the US Circuit Court in Atlanta, where every possible technicality was thrown into the path of her Northern lawyer. Still, he successfully argued that the US Constitution obligated the court to let him represent Chaffee, noting that no lawyer in the state of Mississippi had come forward to represent her. In November 1965, following a plea deal that included her paying a $500 fine, Chaffee's ordeal ended with her release.[65]

O'Dwyer also went down south to assist a US Senate bid by Victoria Gray, a Black Mississippian and the founding member of the Mississippi Freedom Democratic Party (MFDP), to unseat the staunch segregationist senator John Stennis—a bold, and risky, demonstration of Black Americans' willingness to confront their long and systematic disenfranchisement. When the then four-month-old MFDP sent delegates by bus to the Democratic presidential convention held in Atlantic City, New Jersey, in the summer of 1964, O'Dwyer offered them unqualified support for their demand to be seated in place of the segregationist state delegation.

The Mississippi activists were effectively leading an attack on the status quo in Congress, which had long bowed to States' Rights Democrats (known as Dixiecrats) whose power rested on illegal poll taxes, unfairly administered literacy tests, and rifle-toting night riders. The undemocratic authority stemmed from a grotesque Confederate history dating to the "Black Codes" at the end of the Civil War and the subsequent "Compromise of 1877" between Democratic and Republican leaders, which allowed the Republican Rutherford Hayes to become president at the price of ending Reconstruction and the presence of federal troops in the South. The Republicans in Congress freed Democrats to entrench Jim Crow and undermine the nascent rights and opportunities of the formerly enslaved.

The impact of the notorious backroom deal was not forgotten when the MFDP spokesperson Fannie Lou Hamer was born in 1917. She became a sharecropper in her hometown in Sunflower County, Mississippi, picking cotton and living in a shack two miles from the three-thousand-acre plantation of James Eastland's family. Eastland, who would become a state legislator and a US senator by the time the Atlantic City convention was held, was born in 1904. His birth followed, not by long, a notorious local incident: his father and uncle led a white mob that burned, mutilated, and lynched an African American couple on the grounds of an African American church, a double murder that attracted notoriety for its racialized lawlessness and savagery.[66]

Determined to speak truth to power, Hamer made the case at the Atlantic City convention in 1964 that Eastland and his all-white Mississippi delegation were not entitled to remain in power given their reliance on voter suppression to gain and hold power, and that the MFDP members should be installed to replace them at the convention. While news cameras rolled, with her pocketbook perched on the table in front of her, she spoke before the Credentials Committee about her hardscrabble life and the backlash against her and others for their voting rights activism. She had been thrown off her Sunflower County plantation after attempting to register to vote. Night riders had shot up their Black neighbors' homes to keep them from registering. Hamer also told of having been brutally beaten and jailed one day while on her way home from a citizenship rights training school. "All of this on account of we want to register, to become first-class citizens, and if the Freedom Party is not seated now, I question America," she said. The white delegation walked off the floor in a fit of pique.

President Lyndon Johnson, who had recently steered the landmark Civil Rights Act past the Dixiecrats during a year of negotiations, preempted the broadcast of Hamer's speech with a hastily arranged news conference of his own. But this attempt to distract viewers from Hamer's attack on the party and potential disruption to Johnson's impending nomination backfired, as her speech was rebroadcast to the nation after Johnson's statements, reaching viewers during prime time.

What Johnson feared most was a repeat of the Southern walkout from the much-remembered 1948 convention in Philadelphia over President Truman's willingness to court African American voters and to support strong civil rights legislation. To smooth things over this time, Johnson directed the Minnesota senator Hubert Humphrey, a civil rights standard-bearer in Congress who aspired to be Johnson's vice president, to offer the MFDP a compromise: it could have two at-large, nonvoting seats on the Mississippi delegation, plus a promise that things would be different come the 1968 convention.

Hamer turned both thumbs down when the group debated the proposed compromise in a church near the convention hall, pronouncing, "We didn't come all this way for no two seats." But for all her conviction, Hamer could not prevail against the president of the United States. Joseph Rauh, a noted labor lawyer and head of Americans for Democratic Action who prepared the MFDP's original argument to the convention Credentials Committee, communicated the breakaway group's reluctant acceptance of Humphrey's offer.[67]

O'Dwyer, though he had no special influence, urged a rejection of the deal and further negotiation with the Johnson forces. He had already tried, as a New York delegate-at-large, to spur a convention floor debate on Hamer's proposal, but "Hubert Humphrey was there to put out the fires," he recalled.

"The Mississippi Freedom Democratic Party has met all the requirements of the law, the law of the state of Mississippi, while those who are seated in their place have qualified by violence, arson, threats, discrimination, bigotry, tyranny, and every form of intimidation imaginable," Paul said at the key church meeting, backing Hamer. The lily-white Mississippi delegation, he added, "come with the sponsorship and approval of apostles of hate, and their presence here is a stench in the nostrils of those who dread our tradition."

But O'Dwyer's assertion of his democratic values collided with immediate political exigencies as expressed by such Democratic regulars as Averell Harriman. In 1954, Harriman had raised Paul's body temperature by suggesting to DeSapio that he and another candidate for office that year, Franklin D. Roosevelt Jr., repudiate Bill due to the lingering rumors of the former mayor's corruption. After DeSapio told Paul of the request over dinner, Bill's younger brother threatened to buy radio time and work for the pair's defeat.

This dustup was not forgotten when Harriman shook his finger in front of Paul's face in Atlantic City for opposing the Humphrey-tendered offer for what he called high-minded reasons. "It is all right for you to be taking this position," said Harriman, in Paul's recollection. "You have no regard for the president of the United States or what problems he faces, and you don't care." O'Dwyer shot back: "If Harry Truman could have risked his election in 1948 by virtue of his position, there's no reason Lyndon Johnson can't do it in 1964, when he is assured of election."

O'Dwyer rattled on: Strom Thurmond with his "States' Rights Democratic" party had taken half of the once solid South from the Democrats as well as his home state of New York, yet Truman still won that election—whereas Harriman had failed to gain a second term as governor of New York because of his refusal to take a strong stand—on anything![68]

The crossfire came to nothing. The Democratic regulars' pleas not to tie the hands of, or embarrass, Johnson over the insistently all-white composition of the Mississippi delegation or the power of the Dixiecrats in national politics won the day. But this would not be the last time the nonconformist O'Dwyer would go up against Lyndon Johnson and Hubert Humphrey.

———

WHEN THE CURTAIN FELL on the 1964 convention, O'Dwyer returned to his more mundane duties in the low-powered city council, including responding to constituent mail. To a voter who asked that his blind father be permitted to play the horses at the racetrack—his only pleasure, denied him because of long-ago association with professional gamblers—Paul sent a note of commiseration and an official's written opinion, which he had sought without prejudice, that it was impossible to change the decision given current law. When the owner of a large parking garage business sent him free parking passes as a gift, Paul returned them, writing, "Thank you anyway."

The mail was mixed—for and against—when he voted against an appropriation of $663,000 that would have increased the number of nuclear bomb fallout shelters after the October 1962 Cuban Missile Crisis. To O'Dwyer, the proposed expenditure would be a ridiculous waste of money that would be better spent on food for the city's poor and malnourished. "There are plenty of people's kitchens which I'm sure could use a little stocking," he wrote.[69]

"The police review board will demoralize our police," came another letter, its writer angry over Paul's unbending support for civilian review. "First it was discrimination. Now it's police brutality. Tell me: how many bosses is a policeman supposed to have?"[70] O'Dwyer did not bother to respond.

Constituents wrote asking O'Dwyer to consider a greater allotment of city pistol permits, a heliport and new street parking, and measures to combat taxes, litter, rats, crime, traffic, and excessive noise. With the help of a secretary, he assumed the role of a kind of municipal Dear Abby. Usually there was little he could do for constituents except to refer worthy complaints to agency heads. But he almost always got back to them with a referral, advice, or a typed note of consolation.

Nearing the end of his first term and not wanting to seek another one, O'Dwyer announced he would run for city council president. But then, after Wagner decided to retire from city hall, declining to seek a fourth term, Paul switched to running to succeed him. It was a long shot, as he had three rivals: the incumbent council president and former sanitation commissioner Paul Screvane, the city comptroller Abe Beame, and US Representative Ryan, all of them well known. Paul's own ticket mates were to include the lawyer Bernard Richland (later the author of an advice book titled *You Can Beat City Hall*, published in 1980) for city council president and William Andrews, an African American former assemblyman and NAACP special legal assistant, for comptroller.

O'Dwyer, with a shoestring campaign, was soon assailing the fiscal stewardship of Beame and Screvane. "Deficit financing for current expenses is dangerous," he said, adding, more prophetically than he probably imagined, that the city was on the road to default.

Paul also denounced local elected officials for "hysteria" and "ineptitude" after a summer of scant rain and headlines warning that the city could run out of water. He called for the allocation of land in the Brooklyn Navy Yard to subway-car manufacturers to enable them to open plants and create local jobs; criticized Robert Moses for failing to offer discount tickets to the 1964–65 World's Fair to schoolchildren; and urged adopting the British model of treating narcotics addiction as a public health issue rather than a crime (a view shared by the *Daily News*). And he explained his support for Constance Baker Motley for Mississippi district court judge. An African American lawyer and long-time NAACP counsel for civil rights protesters, Motley was borough president of Manhattan, the first woman to hold this elective post. She would be named to the federal judiciary in New York's Southern District in 1966 by President Johnson, a rare appointment of a woman, much less a Black one, to the federal bench.

On primary day in 1965, Paul and Kathleen were up early and the first to pull the lever at their neighborhood polling place. If, as some said, the tides of New Deal liberalism were already going out to Paul's detriment, and racial backlash was growing, it was not yet clearly evident. The winners of the races for the state assembly or senate in New York the year before had included Percy Sutton, Shirley Chisholm, Constance Baker Motley, and William Thompson, all African Americans.[71] Paul hoped that African Americans' and reformers' votes would help put him over the top, but his support in the 1965 primary proved thin. Lacking machine backing, he came up short—woefully so. Beame, a machine Democrat since the days when, as a youngster, he rang doorbells for election signatures in Brooklyn, scored the largest total: 336,345 votes. Paul finished last, with 28,675 votes. A total of 750,000 votes were cast.

One of O'Dwyer's few consolations was a surprise appearance by the New York senator Robert Kennedy at his midtown campaign headquarters after the polls closed. A Beame supporter, Kennedy climbed five stories (the elevator was not working) and congratulated him for a hard-fought campaign as the booze flowed and music blared from stereo speakers. Volunteers and supporters were having such a good time that someone jokingly urged Paul to delay issuing a concession statement to let the partying continue. But, already looking ahead, Paul phoned the party's just-crowned nominee and the next day began to campaign for Beame's election. He was still a Democrat—though some of his supporters lined up for the Republican-Liberal Lindsay for mayor instead.

Murray Kempton, the columnist, seemed to have supermarket produce in mind when he wrote that Lindsay, forty-three, was "fresh" and everyone else, including Beame, fifty-nine, was "tired." With movie star looks and refinement, Lindsay triumphed in November, having put the writer's compliment to good use as a campaign motto. There would be no honeymoon, however: Unpleasantness confronted Lindsay on his first day on the job. Michael Quill—Paul's personal client and perhaps the most heedless—brought the Transport Workers Union (TWU) rank and file out on strike, shutting down bus and subway service citywide. Quill contemptuously referred to the former representative of what was known as the "Silk Stocking" district as "Mayor Lindsley."

Shortly after the twelve-day-long citywide strike began, a state judge ordered Quill, who was in obvious ill health, to jail along with eight other leaders of the union. "The judge can drop dead in his black robes," Quill shot back to reporters as he awaited arrest with O'Dwyer standing at his side.[72] The ordeal proved too much for Quill, who had come of age fighting to evict the British from Ireland: he died in late January, his requiem mass held before thousands in St. Patrick's Cathedral; Paul served as an usher. The attendees were for the most part older than Paul, fifty-eight, including many Irish republicans from the TWU. As O'Dwyer walked back slowly to his car after the funeral, Breslin, of the *New York Herald Tribune*, approached. "We are losing so many of the kind we like to think we are. We're losing the individuals. There will only be the commonplace left pretty soon," O'Dwyer said.[73]

———————

IN ADDITION TO CRIPPLING STRIKES, Lindsay was confronted by neighborhood racial animosity and violence. In July, he traveled with his aides to East New York, Brooklyn, after a three-year-old African American boy was shot and critically injured on a street corner, and walked the Italian areas of the neighborhood, drawing boos and catcalls. He sat down at Frank's Restaurant, an Italian eatery, with thirty African American community leaders. Outside, members of SPONGE (which stood for Society for the Prevention of Negroes Getting Everything) picketed, shouting, "Two, four, six, eight—We don't want to integrate." The mayor's peacemaking forays to roiling communities were to become the liberal Lindsay's signature, winning him national accolades and media coverage again in 1968 when he walked through Harlem after rioting took place in many cities in the wake of Dr. Martin Luther King's murder.

Later on the night of July 21, 1966, Italian-versus-Black street disturbances flared again, with the racial battle fought at New Lots Avenue, an unofficial racial dividing line in the area, giving way to a pistol blast that instantly killed eleven-year-old Eric Dean on a street awash with restive crowds. The victim had just returned from catching a glimpse of Lindsay nearby.

The mayor, who had already left by the time of the incident, circled back from city hall and visited the shattered Dean family. He expressed his sorrow and condolences.

News of the boy's shooting raced through East New York, leading to more violence and injuries to ten officers and bystanders. Police poured into the neighborhood by the thousands with orders to keep their guns and nightsticks at their sides even as projectiles were hurled at them from rooftops. Arrested during the chaos was seventeen-year-old Ernest Gallashaw, a local Black. He was charged with having fired the .25-caliber bullet that struck and killed Eric. Police officials suggested to the press that the bullet may have been intended for a cop.

After the fatal shooting burst into headlines in the *Daily News* and the *New York Post*, O'Dwyer was enlisted by the Council for a Better East New York, the Warwick Street Block Association, and CORE to represent young Gallashaw. His parents were seeking a replacement for the less-experienced lawyer they retained for Ernest's arraignment. Paul took the case thinking the community groups would not have gone out on a limb if they lacked strong reasons to believe Ernest was innocent.[74]

O'Dwyer brought his cousin McNicholas from their office, giving him his first chance to "second" him at the defense table. It was late August, two months before testimony in the trial would begin. They went looking for neighbors who could corroborate the Gallashaws' assertion that Ernest was at home at the time of the 10 p.m. shooting. Paul found that SPONGE vigilantes had reached potential witnesses before he did, seeking to intimidate them. He appealed directly to Brooklyn District Attorney Aaron Koota, trying to convince him to return the case to the grand jury for further review. He told Koota that "the police gave you a fast one." But, O'Dwyer said, he was simply "brushed off."[75]

Growing curious, Richard Reeves, a reporter for the *New York Times*, went to the Brooklyn courthouse and read the record and initial transcripts of the case. He found that there had been several eyewitnesses and that Gallashaw's bail was set at $15,000. Reporter Sidney Zion, an ex-lawyer, explained that a judge would not grant bail in a first-degree murder case unless he had serious questions about the validity of the charges. "There's something wrong," posited Zion.[76]

Reeves's first contact in East New York was with the Gallashaw family. He knocked at the door of the family home and asked Ernest's mother, Ernestine, if she knew who the grand jury witnesses were, as he wanted to speak with them. But she said she did not have any idea.

The reporter got his hands on a tape of a WBAI-FM interview conducted with two friends of Eric Dean the night after he died. Reeves was able to find one of the boys—fourteen-year-old Nathaniel Breaker—and ended up speaking to him for four hours. Breaker said he would testify at trial that he had seen a *white* youth, an Italian named "Lou-Lou Joe," fire the shot that killed Eric.

The newsman's interview ended close to midnight. Reeves subsequently found out that the police had known all about Breaker but had not informed the district attorney's office. As a result, Nathaniel was not brought before the grand jury.

But what of the three eyewitnesses who were brought before the panel? Reeves could find just one of them: fourteen-year-old James Windley. The young Windley, in his affidavit for authorities, had blamed Gallashaw for the shooting.

Reeves, who was white, brought Tom Johnson, a Black reporter, to the Windley apartment in East New York: "I thought the young Negro witness might be willing to talk to a Negro reporter." The young prosecution witness allowed that he had been confused—he never actually saw the street corner shooting, he admitted to Johnson and Reeves. His comments were the opposite of what he had sworn to investigators.

It was a scoop; the *Post*'s ace Ted Poston, one of the first African Americans ever hired by a mainstream city daily—in 1936—and a resident of Bedford-Stuyvesant, was hot on Reeves's heels. Still, *Times* editors held the story, giving Koota another day to respond. When the prosecutor said he would reinvestigate the case, the story hit the front page. To Paul, the *Times* piece and the district attorney's announcement amounted to an unexpected bonus for his client as the trial neared.[77]

Still another grand jury witness—an eleven-year-old friend of Windley—also repudiated important parts of his grand jury statements when Reeves tracked him down to a "dingy" apartment under elevated subway tracks. Koota at that point decided to place all of the various witnesses in protective custody. They were housed in a hotel guarded by police.

The court moved up the trial date. Jury selection began. Two women and ten men—just two of them African Americans—were chosen.

As the testimony began, an assistant district attorney brought to the stand police officers who described the days of disorder on the streets and the moment that shots were fired and all hell broke loose. Three eyewitnesses also testified for the prosecution but, the *Times* reported, they provided confusing and contradictory accounts of Gallashaw's alleged culpability.[78] Dean's older sister testified for the prosecution.[79]

Paul exploited the prosecution's weaknesses thoroughly, calling no fewer than sixteen different people to the stand, each testifying that Gallashaw was at home, around the corner from the shooting, at the time of the shooting. O'Dwyer also had little difficulty casting doubt on the reliability of the prosecution's boy witnesses, such as Windley, a pupil at a school for the emotionally disturbed; another boy who spent two years in a state mental hospital and was now an outpatient; and, finally, Windley's conflicted eleven-year-old friend, who was ruled incompetent to testify under oath.

After Windley testified that Ernest was holding the gun (which was never recovered) when Eric fell, O'Dwyer had no trouble taking him apart in cross-examination. He elicited Windley's admission that he had been suspended from school three times that spring and had once threatened to beat up a fellow schoolboy who owed him money.

When Paul decided to put Ernest himself on the stand, it was a "surprise" move, according to the *Daily News*—it meant exposing the defendant to cross-examination by prosecutors. But Paul had established the defendant's credibility for the jurors, emphasizing that Ernest had never been in trouble with the law before. To O'Dwyer, and then to prosecutors, Gallashaw stated he was not present at the scene of the fatal episode.

On October 21, the jury finally came back after six and a half hours of deliberating, and the courtroom refilled to hear the verdict. Judge Julius Helfand presided.

Ernest sat next to Paul, waiting to learn whether he would be returning to school the next day or going to a detention cell to await hearings on the imposition of a potential life sentence. He pressed his fingertips together, his hands forming an arrow, his boyish face impassive.

The lead jury member was asked to rise and announce the verdict.

"Not guilty," he intoned.

After a few seconds of stunned silence, the Brooklyn State Superior Court devolved into chatter and scattered cheers. Helfand slammed down his gavel, bringing the courtroom to stillness. The judge thanked the jury for its service and sent Ernest away with his mother as a free man.

In a country where racial minorities were incarcerated at a rate five times that of white people, the jury's decision resounded like a blow for freedom, and the next day it was inscribed on the front pages and led the evening newscasts.[80] Liberal opinion writers and newspaper editors showered O'Dwyer with praise, including Harlem's *Amsterdam News*.[81] The police, the accounts stated, had apparently hoped that arresting a Black teen for the killing of a Black child might prevent more serious racial clashes that night. But as Paul's experienced lawyering demonstrated, they arrested the wrong man, "railroaded, like it was the Deep South," as McNicholas recalled.[82]

"He belongs," the *Post* executive editor James Wechsler wrote of O'Dwyer, "to an old-fashioned breed of lawyer whose favorite species of defendant is the underprivileged underdog." But, Wechsler asked, "How many other victims are rotting in jail because they were denied such special, passionate legal attention?"[83]

Many years later, Ernest's brother, Ronald, who was thirteen when the trial took place, said of O'Dwyer, "He was a blessing in disguise."[84]

In early 1968, O'Dwyer would learn that his former client had been arrested on charges of furnishing weaponry employed in a bank robbery.[85] But Gallashaw's conviction was tossed out on appeal due to a procedural technicality. (The US Court of Appeals for the Second Circuit ruled that the trial judge had provided the jury with improper instructions.) More than a decade later, Paul received a letter from Ernest stating that he had gotten his life back together, gone to college, and become a teacher in a Philadelphia public school.[86]

Of the dozens of congratulatory telegrams that poured into O'Dwyer's office in the hours and days after the October 1966 verdict, a single Western Union telegram stood out. It was from the Gallashaw family.

"At one point, we came to feel that there was no justice for Ernest because he was a black boy," the boy's parents wrote to their lawyer. "You alone have restored our faith in democracy."[87]

Campaign portrait of the New York City Council president candidate O'Dwyer in August 1973 on the steps of Federal Hall on Wall Street.
(Photo by © Jefferson Siegel.)

Paul (left) talks with the columnist Pete Hamill on November 6, 1973. Later that night, Paul will be elected as president of the city council, his highest office.
(Photo by © Jefferson Siegel.)

Paul with three generations of family members as they await election results on election night, November 6, 1973. (Photo by © Jefferson Siegel.)

Paul (center) with his longtime mentor and law partner, Oscar Bernstien (right), as they await results of the 1973 citywide elections. (Photo by © Jefferson Siegel.)

Declared the winner of the 1973 city council president race, O'Dwyer addresses news reporters and supporters at his campaign headquarters.
(Photos by © Jefferson Siegel.)

Paul O'Dwyer is sworn in at city hall in January of 1974.
(Photo by © Jefferson Siegel.)

New York City Council president Paul O'Dwyer in his office in New York's city hall in 1974. (Photo by © Jefferson Siegel.)

In city hall on March 8, 1975, Mayor Abe Beame (left, holding can) and City Council president Paul O'Dwyer (standing, popping a can) celebrate a deal that secured the Rheingold Brewery in New York City. (Photo by © Jefferson Siegel.)

Paul with Manhattan borough president (and close friend) Percy Sutton (left) and city clerk David Dinkins (third from left) in the mid-1970s. Sutton and O'Dwyer helped Dinkins recover politically from the loss of his appointment as deputy mayor two years earlier. He would go on to become mayor with their enthusiastic support, defeating Rudy Giuliani in a close 1989 contest. (NYC Municipal Archives.)

Paul walks in a memorial march in New York in September 1976, for Frank Stagg, a Provisional IRA member from County Mayo who died on hunger strike that February in Wakefield Prison, West Yorkshire, England. Paul is accompanied by the columnist Jimmy Breslin (to his right), as well as Bronx borough president Howard Golden and the Bronx congressman Mario Biaggi (to his far left). Stagg was convicted in Birmingham Crown Court of working in a unit planning attacks in Coventry. The strike lasting sixty-two days was conducted in solidarity with the convicted London bombers Marion and Dolours Price, as well as other Irish republican prisoners. Stagg's demands for an end to solitary confinement, no prison work, and repatriation to a prison in Ireland were not met. The IRA vowed to avenge Stagg's death and ignited thirteen bombs around England. (Indiana University Library/*The Irish People* archives.)

Jesse Jackson (left) with O'Dwyer during Jackson's 1988 campaign for president. O'Dwyer was early to endorse the bid by the former aide to Martin Luther King Jr., as he had in 1984. The Baptist minister and fiery political activist finished second in convention balloting behind Massachusetts governor Michael Dukakis, who Paul predicted would neither catalyze Democratic turnout nor succeed. (Indiana University Library/*The Irish People* archives.)

Bill Clinton shakes O'Dwyer's hand upon arriving at an evening forum on Irish issues at the Manhattan Sheraton Hotel two days before the 1992 Democratic primary for president in New York. The Arkansas governor said for the first time that if elected he would allow the Sinn Féin leader Gerry Adams to visit the United States and would appoint a Northern Ireland special envoy. His declaration at the grassroots-organized campaign event helped to establish the path that would lead to US-brokered negotiations to end the Troubles in Northern Ireland. Paul was ecstatic after Clinton's appearance, telling colleagues that his comments represented a major potential breakthrough.
(Indiana University Library/*The Irish People* archives.)

9

Conscience of the Party

W HEN O'DWYER first traveled to Mississippi in 1962, African Americans in the Magnolia State comprised nearly half of its population of 2.25 million people but less than 7 percent of its registered voters.[1] Thousands of nonviolent civil rights foot soldiers, mainly college students from the North, soon began flooding into the state to challenge the systematic denial of voting rights, one method of many used to perpetuate white supremacy.

Paul's experience with the Deep South saw him protesting the University of Mississippi's attempt to prevent James Meredith from attending because of his skin color. President John F. Kennedy sent federal troops to ensure Meredith's enrollment. Paul's son, Brian, then sixteen, rendezvoused with his dad in Oxford, Mississippi, joining him at nonviolent protests. Luckily, he later recalled, state troopers and sheriff's deputies exhibited rare restraint.[2]

Although the trip to the Delta region left Brian's mother feeling "desperately worried," in her youngest son's memory, Paul could not resist the chance to return in 1964 when he volunteered for the Congress of Racial Equality (CORE) and other civil rights groups for visits lasting from twelve hours to three days each. Until 1967, when he would serve as an attorney and poll watcher in Mississippi anew, O'Dwyer's trips to the South were seldom. During the three-year gap, though, he sponsored New

York City Council resolutions as Manhattan councilman-at-large and campaigned with the Mississippi Freedom Democratic Party (MFDP) as an at-large delegate to the Democratic convention in Atlantic City when its Black political activists challenged Mississippi's all-white slate of delegates.

In the fall of 1964, Paul's visit to the Magnolia State was made on behalf of Victoria Gray, cofounder of the MFDP, with Fannie Lou Hamer, a member. Gray was running for a seat in the US Senate representing her state. Her bid was doomed to fail almost from the outset because of Black disenfranchisement—something that would have surprised, least of all, Hamer, who, while confronting Mississippi's history of racial exclusion head-on, had encountered an election clerk who required her to give the meaning of "de facto law" in the state constitution in order to cast a ballot two years earlier. "I knowed as much about a facto law as a horse knows about Christmas Day," Hamer recalled. But, like Hamer, Gray asserted the constitutional right of Black Americans to run for state and local office. Her bravery in the face of harassment drew the attention of CORE, who offered her the assistance of lawyers like O'Dwyer.[3]

Born on the outskirts of Hattiesburg, Gray taught voter education classes, made a living by selling Beauty Queen cosmetics, was married to a plumber, and was among large numbers of African Americans living in the South who "swept quietly through the church world into politics" from small towns like Hattiesburg, according to Taylor Branch, a historian of the civil rights movement and biographer of the Reverend Martin Luther King Jr.[4] While Gray was college-educated, most African American boys and girls in Mississippi did not attend school past the fifth grade, relegated to picking cotton on former slave plantations to support their family. The shack-like schoolhouses for Black children testified to white authorities' indifference to the landmark US Supreme Court ruling *Brown v. Board of Education of Topeka*, which in 1954 found that state laws establishing segregation in public education violated the Constitution. (The original civil rights complaint in the case was drafted by Constance Baker Motley, a lawyer for the National Association for the Advancement of Colored People's Legal Defense and Educational Fund under the future Supreme Court justice Thurgood Marshall from the mid-1940s to the mid-1960s and the first African American woman ever to argue before the US Supreme Court, winning nine of ten cases.)

During O'Dwyer's roughly three-year period of abstention from direct action in the Deep South, thousands of "Freedom Riders," including many students from Northern colleges, carried the cause of equality and voting rights over the Mason-Dixon Line. They were "outside agitators" to the alarmed white locals who watched them arriving on buses from points north to organize citizenship training and mock elections to educate prospective Black voters about registering and running in "Freedom Schools." That these activists risked injury or death was felt most keenly by those among their number who were Black, given the virulence of cross burnings, church bombings, and attacks on demonstrators in defiance of federal efforts to speed the desegregation of schools, workplaces, and public accommodations under the 1964 Civil Rights Act. To assert "states' rights"—and deny Black Americans economic opportunity, good schools, and civic rights and dignity—white professionals, elected officials, and other racist reactionaries waged anonymous terror wearing white robes and hoods. More often than not, local law enforcement authorities condoned the violence and intimidation.

One of the most infamous episodes occurred in March 1965 during the Selma-to-Montgomery march, or Bloody Sunday. Law enforcement, many on horseback, attacked several hundred nonviolent marchers with billy clubs and tear gas on the bridge named for a goateed late nineteenth- and early twentieth-century Alabama Ku Klux Klan leader, Edmund Pettus. Broadcast nationally on the nightly news, the footage of attacks against peaceful demonstrators, who included the Nobel Peace Prize recipient King and the future congressman John Lewis, shocked millions of Americans.

Though from a former Confederate state, Johnson in 1956 had been among three Southern senators (along with Estes Kefauver and Al Gore Sr., both of Tennessee) who did not sign on with the nineteen out of one hundred senators who endorsed the "Southern Manifesto." Coming amid massive resistance to school integration across the South, the manifesto challenged the "unwarranted" authority of the federal courts to dilute "states' rights" in mandating integration nationwide under *Brown v. Board of Education*. In August 1965 Johnson further undermined the segregationist voting bloc by signing the Voting Rights Act, which made it illegal to impose restrictions on local, state, and federal elections in order to deny the franchise to Black citizens. In the well of the House of Representatives, this child of the Texas Hill Country movingly invoked the unofficial ballad of the movement, declaring, "And . . . we . . . shall . . . overcome!" The juncture marked the apotheosis of the Democrats' pro–civil rights majority, so long hog-tied by segregationist senators who had even thwarted anti-lynching legislation.

By the time Johnson signed the Voting Rights Act, O'Dwyer had been litigating for five years—since 1960—in New York to remove institutionalized encumbrances to the franchise for Spanish-speaking migrants and immigrants in New York. He first represented Jose Camacho of the Bronx in federal court, followed by Martha Cardona, who was literate in Spanish only, starting in state court. Cardona moved to New York City from Puerto Rico as a young adult in 1948; Paul represented her in a lawsuit contesting the constitutional validity of the state board of elections' English-language literacy requirement for becoming a voter. Paul's judicial activism for Spanish speakers, a fast-growing immigrant group in the city, culminated in a 1966 appearance before the US Supreme Court. The high court accepted his arguments, striking down the language barrier. The ruling was handed down two weeks after Congress adopted an amendment to the Voting Rights Act permitting citizens to demonstrate literacy in their "mother tongue" rather than in English. The New York senators Robert F. Kennedy and Jacob Javits were the amendment's cosponsors, and, to Paul's gratification, Kennedy's staff used his legal research in drafting the bill. Kennedy noted O'Dwyer's contribution in the debate on the Senate floor.

When Paul went before justices of the high court, his adversary was New York State Attorney General Louis Lefkowitz. Justice Tom Clark, the former attorney general, scribbled a note to Paul when the counselor had finished parrying the justices' questions. "Bill would have been proud of you today," the note read.[5] When Paul first picked up the mantle of bringing poor Puerto Ricans into the state Democratic Party, it was a low-priority issue for many of its leading members. But it was not for him. Indeed, one of Paul's inspirations was the late socialist congressman from East Harlem Vito Marcantonio, who argued in the 1940s and '50s that, with the rapid influx of Puerto Rican migrants to his poor district and other parts of New York, such a measure was needed to ensure access to the vote.

———

AT THE BEGINNING of November 1967, touching down in Jackson, Mississippi, O'Dwyer spent a night in a motel there before driving to the tiny hamlet of Alligator, 140 miles north along the Mississippi River. Along on this civil rights mission was fellow politician-activist-lawyer Ted Weiss, a city council member from the West Side tethered to the Democratic Reform movement centered in Manhattan. The two checked in with thirty or so of their New York colleagues who were fanned out across the Delta under the aegis of William Kunstler, a constitutional attorney known for representing radicals; he was at this time assisting the New York office of the Mississippi Freedom Democratic Party. (The MFDP's main Northern office was in Washington, DC.) In this instance, as when O'Dwyer had worked for the campaign of Victoria Gray, Paul reported in the state to Eleanor Holmes Norton. A future US Equal Employment Opportunity Commission chair and delegate to Congress for the District of Columbia, where she grew up, Norton was then a fledgling lawyer assisting the Student Nonviolent Coordinating Committee and the MFDP. O'Dwyer and Weiss had signed on to assist the Freedom Summer voter registration project and MFDP through their usual point of contact, CORE, then headed by the Black Power advocate Floyd McKissick and previously, beginning with its 1942 founding, James Farmer. After landing in Jackson, the two politicians purposely rented a car bearing Mississippi license plates; for safety reasons, too, they chose not to ride with other civil rights activists, vividly recalling the 1964 abduction and murder of James Chaney, a Black Mississippian, and Michael Schwerner and Andrew Goodman, Jewish New Yorkers. The trio of Mississippi Freedom Summer activists were killed while looking into the bombing of Mount Zion United Methodist Church in Philadelphia, Mississippi. An official investigation showed that the White Knights of the Ku Klux Klan and the local police department were involved in the murders. While at President Johnson's insistence the probe included the first locally established FBI office in the state, he simultaneously had J. Edgar Hoover continue the wiretapping of leading civil rights activists, including those working in Mississippi. The reactionary Hoover feared what he saw as the radicalism of King; he and other FBI officials wanted the reverend replaced as the de facto leader of the civil rights movement by someone (Samuel Pierce, a New York Republican lawyer) they considered pliable. The FBI's relentless eavesdropping and use of informers dated back to the Kennedy administration, with the agency becoming fixated on the influence of King and other Black leaders.[6]

Anyone venturing to the Delta was on their own—the local authorities would likely not protect a "Northern interloper" from menace or violence. The federal presence, meanwhile, was still faint, barring an incident with political implications for the president.

The morning of Election Day, 1967, O'Dwyer walked over to a "little shack" of a polling place in Alligator with a dozen or so Black men and women bent on voting. He advised them to wait outside and to stay fifty feet back until summoned to fill out a paper ballot. Wearing a dark jacket and loosened tie, O'Dwyer told the poll worker, a white man named Mr. Butler, that the first voter waiting in line would approach to vote and Paul would watch off to the side. The outsider's perceived audacity did not sit comfortably with Mr. Butler, who asked, "Would you give us your credentials—who are you?" "I'm representing this man," answered Paul.

"Well, how do I know you *are* Paul O'Dwyer?" asked Butler.

At six o'clock in the evening, all of O'Dwyer's group had voted. Butler announced he was closing the polling sites. He looked at the perspiration-dampened O'Dwyer, asking, "Now what are you going to do?" Paul, citing the relevant election statutes by numerical code, responded, "I'm going to go right in there, sir, and watch you count."

Butler went looking for his supervisor, who negotiated with the poll watcher from up north, finally letting him look over Butler's shoulder. In a little while, as the ballots were being examined and counted, someone knocked at the door: it was Weiss, his eyes goggling. Having walked hurriedly from a polling place up the road, he told O'Dwyer that a Black candidate appeared close to winning a town council seat. Paul, though, had no visible reaction. Weiss screamed, "What the hell are you doing? The rednecks are *gone off*"—they were out for vengeance. "We've got to get the hell out of here."

Paul deliberatively closed his briefcase and looked up. He and Weiss went out to their rental car and drove out of town.

Careful to observe traffic regulations, they did not head back to Jackson, choosing to steer one hundred miles north to Memphis instead, and took turns behind the wheel while checking the rearview for any sign of a trooper hot on their tail or maybe a pickup filled with yahoos clutching a Confederate flag in one hand and a hunting rifle in the other.

Some three hours later, they pulled into a roadside motel, unmolested. Far enough from the jaws of Alligator, they got some sleep, waking early, scarfing down eggs and grits with black coffee, and heading out to catch a flight home.[7]

During an earlier trip that year to Jackson, Mississippi, O'Dwyer had brought court papers to argue for a number of Black citizens blocked from running for office or casting a ballot. Each of the legal briefs had needed to be prepared in advance—there was no law office where a lawyer from another state would be allowed to borrow a desk, use a telephone, or consult a book of statutes.

O'Dwyer sought out the Hinds County district attorney, Bill Waller, to talk about his case. Waller, however, refused to meet with him at his government office and would only do so after nightfall in his Jackson law office, after everyone else had left for the day.

"How much are you getting paid for coming down here?" the district attorney, later governor, asked.

"I am not getting paid," O'Dwyer replied.

But Waller did not seem to believe it, saying, "You're not getting paid anything?"

"No, it's volunteer," said O'Dwyer.

"Well then how the hell did you get into this stuff?—You're not even a Jew."[8]

ONE OF THE IRISHMAN'S more memorable interactions with the former Confederacy centered on a special election on May 2, 1967, in the town of Sunflower, a hamlet located in the county of the same name where the White Citizens' Council, and the Mississippi senator James Eastland, were born. The MFDP-endorsed candidates filled an all-Black slate to compete with an all-white one, while another Black candidate ran to unseat the white mayor. The Sunflower election was viewed up north as an early test of the 1965 Voting Rights Act. Almost a year had passed since Mississippi's US Fifth Circuit Court of Appeals invalidated the most recent municipal elections in Sunflower and in five other state localities in an unprecedented decision. The court ordered the scheduling of new elections, with the ruling arising from a legal challenge by the MFDP based on the Voting Rights Act.[9] Responding to a petition from Gray and Hamer and other civil rights leaders as the date of the superseding elections of May 1967 neared, the Justice Department agreed to provide federal poll monitors, or registrars. However, there were far too few to cover every polling site. O'Dwyer was among those who helped fill the gap, joined by the Manhattan borough president Percy Sutton and the Harlem state assemblyman Charles Rangel—both African Americans.

Sutton had first encountered Paul from a distance, listening to him deliver a speech in northern Manhattan; they spoke for the first time at a 1947 demonstration against a blanket racial barrier established by the developer of Levittown on Long Island, a sprawling development of small, affordable homes in tac-tac-toe arrangement marketed to white World War II veterans.[10] In time, their shared social and political aspirations smoothed the way to a lasting friendship, albeit one belied by superficial differences. O'Dwyer favored heavy black shoes appropriate for working on the grounds of the house in Montgomery, New York, he and Kathleen acquired in the late 1940s, where he relaxed on occasional weekends by repairing wooden fences, clearing rocky paths, and stabling Connemara ponies. In contrast, Sutton cottoned to fine blazers and tailored shirts with cufflinks. While Sutton traveled with four pieces of luggage, Paul carried but one, as he "couldn't care less about clothes," said Brian.[11] Both blessed with the gift of gab, they hailed from rural pastures and very large families, with Paul the youngest of ten children who survived to adulthood and Sutton the fifteenth-born.

Growing up an ocean, and a world, away from tiny Bohola in San Antonio, Texas, Sutton looked up to his father, an early civil rights activist who was born in the last days of slavery. After serving as an intelligence officer with the Tuskegee Airmen during World War II, Sutton earned his law degree in New York and went on to represent Malcolm X on personal matters, among other radical figures. In an early campaign for elective office in New York managed by Paul, Sutton fell short of winning—this was the 1964 race for Manhattan borough president. But he gained the office after Constance Motley Baker left for the federal bench and fellow city council members, in September of 1966, appointed him to fill the seat. He retained the position until the end of 1977, when he ran for mayor without success.

Rounding out the intrepid trio, Charles Rangel, younger than Sutton by ten years and Paul by twenty-three, was most familiar with Sutton; the two political mavericks negotiated with and challenged the established Harlem Democratic Club in tandem on many occasions. But Rangel admitted that his own understanding of New York politics exceeded his comprehension of the politics of the Deep South. He could not keep up with the sophistication of O'Dwyer and Sutton with regard to protest politics; they had more experience with it than he did.

Brought up by a factory seamstress mother and his maternal grandfather, Rangel (who was Puerto Rican on his father's side) served as an infantry operations specialist during the Korean War. Injured in combat by shrapnel, he led his racially segregated squadron in an improbable escape through the frozen and snow-covered North Korean mountains. After his service ended, he attended St. John's Law School and, in 1960, gained admission to the New York State Bar. He worked as an assistant prosecutor for the US Attorney's Office in Manhattan, marched in Selma, and began serving in the state legislature in 1967. The dusty community of Sunflower, he said, was as far from his experience as the moon.

"Percy was from Texas and sounded like it. And Paul goddamn sounded like he was from right out of Ireland," said Rangel, who went on to challenge Adam Clayton Powell for Congress successfully and served for almost fifty years. "And I was from Manhattan. I didn't understand any of it." [12]

Black residents made up 70 percent of the town of Sunflower's population of 800, with 211 Black locals registered as voters compared to 175 white ones. [13] In recent local elections, a growing number of African Americans attempted to vote despite the presence of a white police chief and often enough a white photographer to intimidate them. Of course, illiterate African American sharecroppers received no assistance from the white people chosen to "help" them fill out their ballot. Just the opposite. After years of suffering night raids, arrests, and the loss of employment just for seeking to vote, many Black sharecroppers opted to do, and vote, as they were told. [14]

Not long before the Sunflower town government election, with the final ballot still to be formalized and printed, a few Northern experts and Southern activists addressed a gathering of Black clergy, white and Black

activists, and others in a church. They got right down to the main business: to ensure that five African American candidates ran for the five available council seats, and no more.

Assigned to help with this task, Sutton, Rangel, and O'Dwyer turned
their attention to the latest, and sixth, Black candidate for council, a
preacher-farmer from one of the houses of worship scattered throughout
the area. The three were advised that he was covertly sponsored by the
white slate of council candidates in order to dilute the vote for the previously five-person Black slate.

"He was a large, obese man who knew nothing about politics and
had little or no education," remembered O'Dwyer. And Rangel, too, remembered how the preacher parked his lumbering frame on a stool in
the middle of the room, insisting his decision to be a candidate on the
ballot was based on the teachings of the Bible. However, "it turned out
to be a matter of mortgage and money," Rangel said.[15]

The assemblyman (and future congressman) was the first to speak to
this man of the cloth, who wore overalls, saying that, no matter his devo-
tion to the Good Book, he was harming the cause of Black representation
in Mississippi.

Sutton tried next, regaling the reverend with his own experiences in
business and big-city politics. The minister, said Percy, would, if he stepped
aside, become known as a "man of justice and honor" among civil rights
activists and younger people mobilizing throughout the South. He also
promised him a Harlem parade in his honor!

Couldn't he just see it now? Sutton asked. But the minister couldn't.

It was now O'Dwyer's turn to approach, though Sutton's spiel was
certainly a tough act for anyone to follow.

"I represent a number of people in the North who have great hopes
for Mississippi," Paul began as if delivering a motion for summary judgment at trial, sounding authoritative. "Many people say that the Blacks
themselves are at fault for their failure to get along among themselves.
Many people, Blacks and whites, up north spent money in order to get
the voting rights for Blacks. They are looking to this election to decide
whether or not their money was wisely spent."

The next day, to the visiting trio's surprise, the preacher ended his candidacy. He said he had never realized that the *federal* government was
interested in the Sunflower election. Evidently, he had taken O'Dwyer to

be some kind of federal official. "I was white so he thought I represented the government," Paul later surmised.[16]

Despite that happy result, the election offered little cheer. The MFDP candidate who received the most ballots in Sunflower—the African American Otis Brown, running for mayor—drew 121 votes, not enough to overcome the incumbent, W. L. Patterson, a plantation owner Rangel remembered as an ignorant hick. Patterson received 190 votes, even though 20 more Black residents voted in the town than did white ones, a result Patterson attributed to his having ignored "radical" Black residents and sought only the votes of "good n——s."[17]

None of the Black candidates for town council were successful. Yet for the first time the white candidates had been forced to cater to Black voters, addressing them as "citizens" and telling them that "these agitators" for the MFDP-endorsed candidates wanted to "run your business" and put "your home and property" at risk.[18] In the six Mississippi towns ordered by the court to hold special elections, a total of sixty MFDP candidates ran and six prevailed, signaling at least a modicum of progress.[19]

———

THROUGHOUT THEIR MINI-ADVENTURE, Sutton and Rangel dealt with the racial hostilities, cultural differences, and heavy humidity by having a good laugh at their friend Paul's expense, as when he complained about having to stay in a home previously shot up by the Klan or White Citizens' Council (there were no motels within at least fifty miles). The dignified owner of the shack, a Black woman whose many children grew up on the Eastland farm, had been targeted for taking in Freedom Riders. When Paul stayed over at the home, the windows were still shattered because the family was dirt-poor. Percy and Charlie responded to Paul's concerns with an exaggerated drawl, calling him "Mr. Paul" and, further enjoying themselves at their white friend's expense, said it was his job in the advancing civil rights movement to beat the bushes to protect his two "African guides."[20]

Coming away from the odyssey feeling more energized than scathed, O'Dwyer returned to the Magnolia State on still another civil rights escapade in 1967, campaigning for Charles Evers for Fayette mayor—and again in 1969. Evers's victory in the latter year was a vindication of his late brother, Medgar, whose alleged assassin, Byron De La Beckwith, had the temerity to run for lieutenant governor despite the allegations. Two state trials of De La Beckwith in 1964 resulted in hung all-white juries; he would be convicted in 1994 based on new evidence.

———

O'DWYER WAS BACK in New York for a citywide garbagemen's strike in February of 1968. It was followed by a walkout of low-wage Black sanitation workers, some in their seventies, in Memphis, Tennessee, where King delivered his intense and soaring "I've Been to the Mountaintop" address shortly before he was assassinated on April 4 at the Lorraine Motel. Paul served as the lawyer for New York's Uniformed Sanitationmen's Association. As trash, and public impatience, piled up, O'Dwyer tried unsuccessfully to get the union's president John DeLury released from jail to participate in negotiations with the city—DeLury was sentenced to eighteen days behind bars under the state Taylor Law, which prohibited strikes by public employees (and which the sanitation workers' union had challenged immediately upon the law's inception in 1967). When a settlement was reached, Governor Nelson Rockefeller, the Republican rival of Mayor Lindsay for national attention on questions of urban distress, appeared with O'Dwyer in a photograph on the front page of the million-plus circulation *Daily News* under the headline, "IT'S OVER!" As garbage piled up on sidewalks, the governor had inserted himself in the talks between the public union and the Lindsay administration, making the difference. At the end of the nine-day walkout, the seven thousand or so New York City trash collectors received modest improvements in wages and job safety, and the garbagemen were appreciative of the efforts of their union president's politician-attorney.

———

AS NEW YORKERS were fretting about unkempt streets and disease-carrying rodents, the Democratic Party was turning more divisive, rent by differences over Johnson's escalatory approach to the Vietnam War and by the "Long, Hot Summer" of 1967, which included, in all, 159 separate serious incidents of violent unrest in poor, Black urban communities around the country. The 1968 uprisings reached a peak, or valley, with an astonishing spate of riots in more than one hundred cities. The explosion followed on the heels of King's assassination.

Paul did not have to travel to the South to witness ramifications of systemic racial injustice, only as far as Newark, New Jersey, where, in July 1967, looting and arson by poor residents were met by gunfire from police, National Guardsmen, and state troopers. The five days of battle began after cops brutalized a Black cabbie during an arrest and a false rumor spread that the driver had died from the beating.[21] "If you have a gun," the police director of the city, Dominick Spina, announced over every Newark patrolman's radio when the disturbances began, forty-five minutes by car from Manhattan, "whether it's a shoulder weapon or whether it is a handgun, use it."[22] The lives of 26 residents (mostly Black), a white cop, and white firefighter were lost, approximately 1,500 people were arrested, and $10 million in property was destroyed.[23]

The embers were still glowing when, in Washington, DC, the Kerner Commission was formed to study the causes of inner-city mayhem. Mayor John Lindsay was one of the independent government panel's most influential members. "The nation is moving toward two societies, one black and the other white," began the report, released February 29, 1968. King's murder during his visit to Memphis to support the strike by the city's sanitation workers came little more than a month later.

Just why Black people in urban America were in open revolt was mystifying to many middle-class white people. For many liberals in particular, the most obvious explanation, besides deep racial inequality in a nation with rising economic expectations, was Black anger over a history of humiliation and brutality at the hands of nearly all-white police departments. But as in other cities' race riots—including in Buffalo in late June 1967—the use of lethal force against unarmed Black citizens drew praise from city and state politicians. "I felt a thrill of pride in the way our state police and National Guard have conducted themselves," New Jersey Governor Richard Hughes enthused after the Newark disturbances, to which he responded by sending in heavy state artillery.[24] Hughes's indifference to the underlying causes of Black outrage and deaths of innocents revealed how compelled even a Democrat felt to slake the growing public thirst for law and order crackdowns.

Some white people were outraged, however, by the willful and unrestrained use of force by agents of the state. The *New York Post* columnist Pete Hamill (a friend of O'Dwyer's) wrote a column addressed in part to adherents of a "New Politics," a new generation less susceptible to white identity politics and fear mongering voiced by old school elected officials, the press, and the pulpit.

"Law and order," Hamill wrote in 1968, was pure "glop," a "code for letting cops shoot blacks. . . . This is nonsense. You have crime in American cities because American cities are filled with poor people." Surveying America's racial divide, Hamill underscored the impact of class disparities, drawing a lesson from past decades when, he said, his forebears from Ireland carried out much of the crime and riots.

"In the 1840s, an Irish district in New York City [the Old Brewery] averaged a murder a night for 15 years," the liberal columnist wrote. The Draft Riot of 1863, he added, involved thousands of marauders and at least one hundred deaths, with the vast majority of the violence and vandalism committed by Irish slum dwellers. For Hamill, one explanation for crime eclipsed all others: racial marginalization. Then, the Irish were disproportionately poor and discriminated against; today, in the New York City area, it was Black people who were subjugated.[25]

The war in Vietnam and the military draft also contributed to the sense that a war was developing at home—as when, at Columbia University, students occupied five administrative buildings to protest university policies they termed racist toward the adjacent Harlem community and hundreds of helmeted city police crashed the campus, unleashed on the Mayor Lindsay's watch, bloodying rebellious students whom many cops considered pampered and privileged. All the shocking images beamed into America's living rooms—the building takeovers on college campuses; the Buddhist monks self-immolating in Vietnam in witness to the war's immorality; the marines torching villagers' huts with lighters and flamethrowers—poured lighter fluid on the national flames. For President Johnson, no aerial bombings, toxic defoliant spraying, or "light at the end of the tunnel" prognostications by generals could quiet the domestic fury or the divide in his party.

Johnson's escalation of the Vietnam War, for O'Dwyer, was rooted in the kind of reflexive anti-communism that he and his associates in the National Lawyers Guild (which he had rejoined by this time, drawn by a new generation of legal activists) had begun to spotlight and resist even before the House Un-American Activities Committee (HUAC) inquisitions began and Joe McCarthy and Richard Nixon became household names. US officials asserted the notion that South Vietnam was an independent country historically devoted to freedom when it was actually half a country whose southern capital, Saigon, had been the center of French imperial rule and whose French-installed leader had collaborated with Vichy France and the Japanese during World War II. After the French were defeated by independence fighters under the Communist leader Ho Chi Minh in 1954, an armistice agreement resulted in the partition of Vietnam along the seventeenth parallel and established that whoever won an internationally monitored election in 1956—whose winner was widely expected by the Americans to be Ho Chi Minh—would run the entire country. US machinations effectively ensured neither Ho Chi Minh nor any Communist successor ever got the chance to do so until the American military finally pulled out, nineteen years later.[26]

The shaky premise for the faraway and runaway Cold War conflict undergirded O'Dwyer's own opposition, as he once explained in a four-page letter to his nephew Frank O'Dwyer Jr. in July 1966. Paul had just heard from the young San Diegan, whose father was no longer alive, that he was considering enlisting in the Marine Corps Officer Candidates School so he could serve his country. Paul suggested he proceed with caution, writing back, "Knowing how every young fellow feels, at a time when the war drums are beating and the swords are rattling and the flag is waving, I would like to point out the things which differentiate this encounter from our Revolutionary War, the War of 1812, the Civil War, or the more recent conflicts in which our country has been engaged."

In all, Paul offered nine reasons why Frank should give his decision more thought, including that Congress had never authorized the use of troops, "and so the people's representatives have never spoken"; also, "we have never before been placed in the position of fighting against a Guerrilla operation"—and "if we have any excuse for being there, it is by way of an invitation of a group, at least half of whom don't want us there, and on behalf of a makeshift government that frustrates a popular election."

Major US allies were staying out of the conflict, Paul typed on, adding that "the most optimistic hopes" of the war's supporters envisioned a ten-year slog, while retired WWII General James Gavin and other military experts were terming the war "impossible to win at all. . . . Against these cogent and irrefutable facts, the superficial argument is presented that we have to stop communism someplace. This approach is really without merit. It is impossible for us to police the whole world, and in any event, if one were to succumb to this approach, we could not have chosen a more disastrous arena in which to try it out."[27]

The only son of Paul's late brother ended up enlisting in the Coast Guard Reserve rather than the Marines, remaining for six years but seeing no action in Vietnam. Paul, however, suffered no loss of esteem in his nephew's eyes. He served as best man at Frank's San Diego wedding in 1974, about a year before the close of the war.[28]

By 1967, just over two decades after the end of World War II, the notion of shirking enlistment was unthinkable for many flag-waving Americans. But categorical denunciations of the Vietnam War voiced by the movement were making headway, both among Democratic elected officials in New York and even some Americans who had served in prior wars or had children in uniform, as the nightly news on TV showed American draftees and enlistees coming home in body bags. Indeed, the war effort was looking more bogged down than American policymakers knew or would admit. To O'Dwyer, the war was a tragic fiasco born of imperial hubris and smacking of the era of European colonialism. It was not only "dangerous" in the new age of nuclear proliferation with two superpowers going toe to toe but also a "grossly immoral act."[29]

————

ALLARD LOWENSTEIN, a Yale Law School graduate from Newark, New Jersey, thirty-eight years old in 1967, was one of the youngest members of the Americans for Democratic Action (ADA). He sought to convince his fellow liberal Democrats in the group to join his "New Politics" movement in renouncing President Johnson's escalation of bombing raids and troop levels.

Lowenstein's lobbying was mostly stymied. At least half of the organization's active members were old enough to recall the post–World War II debates over the question of whether to privilege the First Amendment rights of Communists, Socialists, and liberals (whether exercised to attack the government or merely one another) above the government's assertion of official secrecy in the name of national security. Some ADA members argued that while defiance of the Establishment might be fine for the counterculture, it would be misguided for a group that had influence with the national government. And the union leader Gus Tyler, of the International Ladies' Garment Workers' Union, warned that the path of 1960s revolutionaries threatened to lead the left into terrain unrelated to the needs of working people, later to become the raging battlegrounds of the "culture war." On such a turf, he said, Republicans would hold the upper hand. Democrats, Tyler said, needed to remain focused on jobs, union rights, and a federal minimum wage. Since the ADA enjoyed access to the White House, with many ties to Congress as well, it stood to lose from cutting too confrontational a profile.[30]

A Robert F. Kennedy enthusiast who served briefly in the late 1950s on the staff of Senator Hubert Humphrey of Minnesota, then known for championing civil rights, Lowenstein pressed the case for an uncompromising anti-war posture by joining with other liberals in organizing the "Dump Johnson" movement (something the ADA never enlisted in, though it came out against the war in 1968). The more confrontational new coalition attracted Democratic dissidents around the country, including the Democratic Reform movement in New York. Ronnie Eldridge—Manhattan Reform's unofficial liaison to Kennedy, New York's junior senator—opened her Upper West Side living room for its weekly meetings, a hub of the nationwide drive to make trouble for the war-like president. O'Dwyer assisted the anti-Johnson and antiwar activists but did not attend the meetings at Eldridge's place.[31]

Manhattan still had an array of activist Democratic Reform clubs, some of them approaching ten years old, and they joined in creating another new New York entity, the Coalition for a Democratic Alternative, to coordinate the Dump Johnson activities in advance of the upcoming August 1968 presidential convention. Nationally, yet another group, the Conference of Concerned Democrats, served as an umbrella over the "New Politics" reform groups in many states.

"One cannot speak of Black Power or the riots or even Vietnam," explained Jack Newfield, a *Village Voice* reporter who had covered O'Dwyer's entrance in the council-at-large race and wanted Kennedy to run for president, "in a departmentalized vacuum. They are all part of something larger. We have permitted political power in America to pass from the people to a technological elite. . . . Representative democracy has broken down."[32]

When both Kennedy and the South Dakota senator George McGovern declined Lowenstein's request to challenge Johnson for the nomination, the door was open for Eugene McCarthy to become the anti-war candidate. The Minnesota junior senator had made something of a splash for himself at the 1960 Democratic National Convention when he recommended that the delegates there nominate their party's "prophet," Adlai Stevenson. While still in the House of Representatives, he had also been one of the few Capitol Hill lawmakers to stand up to the *other* McCarthy in a televised debate on "American Forum of the Air," parrying Tail Gunner Joe's evidence-free claims about communist influence in government during a confrontation generally judged a draw by most TV commentators at the time.[33]

A onetime professor of economics and education, McCarthy was a pensive, Stevenson-like independent but less forceful than Adlai when it came to positing alternatives to the US foreign policy rooted in Communist containment, and not strongly associated with the movement for civil rights for Black people.

O'Dwyer's modest political base on the West Side of Manhattan, the FDR–Woodrow Wilson Democratic Club, had been the first city reform club to vote, at the end of 1965, to refuse to support Johnson if he failed by the 1968 presidential primary season to end the Vietnam War.[34] Like disaffected Democrats elsewhere in the country, they were now prepared to support a dove—virtually any dove with half a chance of success—to replace the sitting president.

Two years earlier, at the 1966 New York State Democratic Convention held in Buffalo (where New York City Council President Frank O'Connor was nominated to challenge the incumbent GOP governor Nelson Rockefeller), O'Dwyer had found himself bristling when the former governor Averell Harriman, a Johnson man with whom Paul had crossed swords at the Atlantic City convention, called Johnson a "man of peace."[35] Harriman insisted that Johnson be referred to that way in the state Democratic Party platform then being debated. O'Dwyer opposed Harriman's insertion as platitudinous, but many of his allies in reform avoided a showdown over the so-called peace plank. It seemed to Paul regrettable that anyone would be intimidated by the shadow of the Johnson machine extending over the proceedings, but it appeared that some people were.[36]

At his friend and colleague Phil Sipser's suggestion, Paul began a weekly lunch at his law office after that forum with leaders of sundry anti-war groups, providing coffee—O'Dwyer's morning, afternoon, and evening fuel—and deli sandwiches. The activists would agree that the Democratic Reform wing should sponsor and run candidates for the New York delegation to the 1968 Chicago presidential nominating convention coming in August. Sarah Kovner and Harold Ickes, the son of the former secretary of the interior for Franklin Roosevelt, took up this charge by serving as codirectors of the Coalition for a Democratic Alternative.[37]

It was late in 1967 when sixty members of the coalition, including O'Dwyer, headed to the Windy City to hear Al Lowenstein introducing potential candidates to take up the fight to prevent Johnson's nomination. This gathering of the Conference of Concerned Democrats went largely unnoticed by the national press. But the five hundred attendees, hailing from forty-two different states, felt that they were potentially making a difference—or at least they were trying to. For most, the obvious choice to run for the Democratic nomination for president was Senator Kennedy, an opponent of the war. "I was all for him," Paul recalled. But Kennedy had not yet decided to run. He was not even present at the forum.[38]

Politically, Kennedy, New York's junior senator, was at the time sandwiched between Democratic reformers and regulars. He upset many in the former faction in endorsing regular of regulars Abe Beame in the 1965 mayoral primary, in which the liberal Reform Democratic congressman Ryan and councilman-at-large O'Dwyer also ran. At the same time, Sarah Kovner and some of her allies made no secret of the fact that Kennedy's record, to them, had little to recommend it. He was once a young staff aide to Joe McCarthy and had taken until 1966 to propose unconditional peace talks with all Vietnamese parties and until 1967 to urge Johnson to cease bombing North Vietnam and scale back the war. Still, it was evident that most anti-war activists, Kovner among them, would have rallied around Kennedy if he declared himself as a candidate, since he had the best chance of any anti-war figure in the party as they saw it.

McCarthy spoke to the audience of fellow liberal office holders and party activists at the Chicago forum, explaining how he had come to see the Vietnam conflict as a civil war rather than North Vietnamese aggression fomented by Moscow or Peking, and stating that Johnson had lied about the Gulf of Tonkin incident and overstepped the congressional Tonkin resolution authorizing the president's use of military force for limited defensive purposes only. McCarthy also likened Johnson's bombings and troop deployments to a "dictatorship" in foreign affairs and said he felt that this alone begged a "showdown challenge." He offered himself up as the candidate of the anti-war movement, if it would have him. O'Dwyer hopped on board, recommending McCarthy from the floor of the Chicago assembly. "I admired his reserve," Paul wrote later, stating that

McCarthy demonstrated "obvious resolve. . . . He had everything to lose, and as of that moment, nothing to gain—not even a place in history."[39]

Subsequently, McCarthy made similar appeals to anti-war audiences around the country, accruing support from anti-war ADA members like Joseph Rauh Jr. and Arthur Schlesinger, as well as from deep-pocketed Democratic Party contributors. He positioned himself to enter some of the total fifteen anticipated presidential primaries.

In turn, the Tet Offensive in late January 1968—a coordinated series of North Vietnamese attacks, supported by the South Vietnamese Liberation Forces, on more than one hundred cities in South Vietnam—stunned many Americans who had been led by political and military leaders into thinking that victory would come shortly. There was no clear path to victory—far from it. The TV anchorman Walter Cronkite waved a dispatch about the surprise attack in the offices of CBS and asked his colleagues, "What the hell is going on? I thought we were winning the war." A month later, in his closing words on that night's broadcast, the trusted voice of the CBS Evening News pronounced the conflict "mired in stalemate."[40]

DUMP JOHNSON EMISSARIES brought back to their local chapters from Chicago a preliminary resolution supporting McCarthy. It required the approval of a majority of the state chapters' executive boards. The candidate-in-waiting addressed New York's Coalition for a Democratic Alternative that January. After he finished delivering a typically slow and measured speech—one that filled eight legal-sized typed pages when reprinted—the audience members flashed V signs.

O'Dwyer subsequently received a request from Kennedy to postpone the coalition's March 11 deadline for deciding whom to endorse for president. Kennedy, at this time still making up his mind about whether to run, said that he needed an additional week. But the matter was mooted when, on March 12, McCarthy scored a near upset over Johnson in the New Hampshire primary. The results were devastating for Johnson. The Coalition for a Democratic Alternative had already endorsed McCarthy. Four days later, Kennedy announced that he was a candidate for president.

Johnson, to nearly everyone's astonishment, announced on March 31 that he would *not* seek a second term. The entire political landscape was convulsed.

By that time, 130 coalition members had traveled to an Albany hotel for a meeting of anti-Johnson Democrats to determine the coalition's choice to run, not for president in this instance, but rather for US Senate from New York. Paul made it known that he was interested in running. The primary was set for June 18, but it was not to be a presidential primary, since New York was not slated for one in 1968. Instead, the Senate rivals would top the ballot, followed by candidates to be delegates to the Democratic National Convention. The open election of delegates, then, served as a proxy for a presidential primary, and about 150 slots in the New York delegation were up for grabs. While the Kennedy camp wanted as many of the delegates as possible to be filled by party activists pledged to supporting him, McCarthy's forces mobilized to elect pro-McCarthy delegates and let voters know, congressional district by congressional district, who they were. This required a lot of campaigning around the state, especially since there would be no indication of which presidential candidate the would-be delegates supported next to their names on the primary ballot.

As the delegate-promotion efforts by pro-McCarthy ground forces shifted into higher gear, the New York State Democratic Committee indicated its support for Nassau County executive Eugene Nickerson—a Kennedy man—for the party nomination to seek to unseat incumbent Senator Jacob Javits, a Republican-Liberal. The New York State Democratic Committee—the official party apparatus, which was headed by John Burns of Binghamton—made the choice of Nickerson official on March 30. Burns was also supporting Kennedy, New York's other senator, for president.

At the Albany meeting earlier, on March 16, 130 delegates with the Coalition for a Democratic Alternative, of which O'Dwyer was a member, made their own choice of a candidate to run against Javits. At this gathering of antiwar and reform activists, Percy Sutton's name came up as a possible compromise, as it had at many similar forums in the past; Sutton was seen as someone acceptable to regulars as well as reformers, and some felt Burns could be persuaded to give him the party nod. As debate on the floor intensified, the West Side reform leader Alex Rosenberg approached O'Dwyer to discuss this. Would Paul be willing to step aside for his friend under certain circumstances, asked Rosenberg? Of course, yes, O'Dwyer said—he would certainly accede to the consensus. Hearing that, Rosenberg and some of his reform allies apparently felt more comfortable entering the relatively untested O'Dwyer's name when the floor was opened for final nominations. Paul's name was entered with the understanding that the commitment was not necessarily binding. Nonetheless, it stuck.

Another candidate whose name had been in play even before O'Dwyer was seriously considered had been the reform movement's top choice all along: Lowenstein. He alone could count on support from both the McCarthy and Kennedy ground forces. But Lowenstein would not commit himself to making the race.

When Paul left the gathering, then, he was the consensus pick of a hard-driving coalition of liberal and left Democrats chiefly concerned with ending the Vietnam War. It was understood that one of his main purposes was to carry the flag for McCarthy. He would also push the equally long-shot goal of inserting a strongly worded peace plank for the national party platform. O'Dwyer's chances of actually beating the machine-backed Gene Nickerson were widely assumed to be low. But in a state Democratic Party storm tossed by ideological differences, raging egos, and rival strategies, he still held out hope of upsetting those expectations.[41]

―――――

A FEW DAYS after the state party nominated Gene Nickerson, John and Bobby Kennedy's brother-in-law, Steve Smith, requested a sit-down meeting with O'Dwyer and, during the tête-à-tête at a neutral venue suggested by Paul, asked him to reconsider his maverick run for senator.

In the hour-long discussion, Smith, Bobby Kennedy's campaign manager, contended that Paul's presence on the primary ballot would harm the state Democratic Committee nominee Nickerson's chances and could effectively deliver a victory to Joseph Resnick, a pro-war, pro-Johnson, and decidedly anti-Kennedy politician from Ellenville, New York, who planned to spend as much as $1 million of his own cash to mount his own maverick attempt to win the Democratic Senate primary.

Clearly, though, Smith was at least as concerned about the impact that O'Dwyer's candidacy could have on the New York senator Kennedy's potential nomination at the August national convention. But Smith trod gingerly, aware, no doubt, that any suggestion that O'Dwyer was aiming to upend a member of the revered Kennedy clan could set off his temper and stiffen his resolve.[42] O'Dwyer of course identified with the transatlantic story of the Kennedys and looked upon America's first Irish Catholic president with no small amount of ethnic pride. However, he felt an even stronger compunction to live up to the hopes of his younger allies, a generation of political activists whom he was known to advise that "the ideals should always come first." As he later wrote of his critical meeting with Smith, "I had committed myself to Senator McCarthy, and I felt that if we were to abandon him because a more powerful candidate had entered the race, I would be setting a very poor example for the young, who by then had engulfed us."[43]

———

THE NEW YORK SENATE primary was to be eclipsed by dramatic and historic events. First, Johnson announced he would not seek reelection, followed nearly a month later by Vice President Hubert Humphrey deciding to run in place of him. And then Kennedy was slain, on June 5, the night he tallied a victory over McCarthy in the California primary.

With the country reeling after the second assassination of a member of the Kennedy family in five years, McCarthy told his New York headquarters that he was suspending his campaign temporarily. But his staff had already planned a rally for him at City College's Lewisohn Stadium, where he was expected to give a speech. McCarthy was already known as a somewhat muted grand marshal for peace and equality. Frustrated with his decision, his New York headquarters told him that it was going ahead with the rally anyway, with or without him.[44] The election was about ending the war, not the fate of any single candidate, he was told. McCarthy bowed to his New York directors. They were far more energized and less philosophical than the candidate, who tended to distance himself from his campaign's frenzied ground level.

O'Dwyer was just as pained by Bobby Kennedy's death, recalled Eldridge, Kennedy's friend and ally. She was hailing a cab on Columbus Avenue one or two days after the assassination when Paul pulled over and offered her a lift. "He was quite sad," she recalled. Quite uncharacteristically, "We didn't talk about politics at all."[45]

But few were more immobilized by Kennedy's slaying than Pete Hamill. A prolific writer of magazine pieces and a *New York Post* column, he was a Bobby Kennedy stalwart who had penned a letter to the senator during the latter's period of deliberations, appealing to him to run for president. Kennedy pocketed Hamill's letter, the first of two, and carried it with him until making the fateful decision to seek the party's nomination for president.

Covering the campaign, Hamill was standing a few feet away from the candidate at the Ambassador Hotel in Los Angeles when "a pimply messenger arrived from the secret filthy heart of America. He was curly-haired, wearing a pale blue sweatshirt and blue jeans, and he was planted with his right foot forward and his right arm straight out and he was firing a gun," the columnist wrote. Traumatized by the loss of a politician friend who had appeared to be putting his ideals first, Hamill returned to his New York home and stared at the blank piece of paper in the roll of his typewriter, immobilized and depressed.[46]

Since his older brother's death, Kennedy had emerged as a tribune for migrant grape pickers in California, Native Americans, and the poor, both white and Black. To Hamill and other true believers, he was a figure of destiny and decency, poised to reunite the party and the country. As he later commented, Kennedy was the only politician he had ever trusted besides Paul O'Dwyer, and he was especially drawn to the late senator for linking Irish history to the contemporary civil rights movement—as when Kennedy spoke of Irish immigrant history at a St. Patrick's Day dinner organized by the Friendly Sons of St. Patrick in Scranton, Pennsylvania, in 1964. "As the first of the racial minorities," Kennedy said, "our forefathers were subject to every discrimination found wherever discrimination is known. . . . It is toward concern for these issues—and vigorous participation on the side of freedom—that our Irish heritage must compel us. If we are true to this heritage, we cannot stand aside."

Paul, who swore by such sentiments, sat down with Hamill over a cup of coffee and heard him say that he was having a difficult time returning to his work. They talked things over. Finally, he got through.

"You're not *important* enough to have writer's block," O'Dwyer pronounced.[47]

TO THE SURPRISE of almost everyone, and to O'Dwyer perhaps most of all, he won the largely overshadowed US Senate primary in New York following the astonishing series of coincidences, as Kennedy's murder deprived O'Dwyer's principal primary-election opponent, Gene Nickerson, of Kennedy's coattails, while Resnick was linked to an unpopular president who dropped out of contention. A manufacturing mogul, he finished third.

Even so, late on the night of the primary it had looked as if Nickerson might still eke out a win. The Establishment choice was ahead until very late results were tallied for Harlem and Bedford-Stuyvesant, where Paul was a popular figure due to his defense of Ernest Gallashaw in 1966, endorsement by *Amsterdam News*, and ties to Black politicians. But the state Democratic Committee leader John Burns, dropping in at O'Dwyer's suite at the Commodore Hotel after 3 a.m., confirmed that Paul was the winner.

"The Astonishing Mr. O'Dwyer," rang out the *New York Times* editorial on the election, while also pointing out the centrality of McCarthy's coattails to Paul's success, and that, just two weeks before, it had appeared uncertain whether O'Dwyer would even be able to gather enough signed petitions to get on the ballot.[48]

As anyone who knew O'Dwyer could have predicted, when flush with newfound success he did not go off in search of approval from the leaders of his party. Yet if he had been willing to adjust his demand for immediate military withdrawal from Vietnam even slightly, he might have improved his chances. Instead, he made no secret of his distaste for the equivocations of Johnson's stand-in, Vice President Humphrey, about how and when the latter would bring the troops home.

"Paul O'Dwyer had chosen to be a reformer in New York City politics," wrote the liberal *Post* columnist Murray Kempton after Paul's primary win and his own election as a delegate, "with all the general misfortunes a man must endure when he puts principle above convenience." O'Dwyer, continued Kempton, was known for getting two types of nominations: "those for secure offices that were beneath him, like a seat in the City Council, and those for offices that seemed beyond the power of any rebel to reach." But with Paul's Senate primary victory,

> those who had cherished O'Dwyer for years awoke—at just the same time as those who had never heard his name—to discover that he was someone to be taken seriously as a politician. And then he did what I should think no sensible—by which I mean ordinary—

politician would do when luck had cast up to him an opportunity
so eminent. He simply informed the Democrats that he would not
forgive Mr. Johnson his war or support Mr. Johnson's candidate in
November. So he was still with us, when he should in common
sense have been with those regulars whose help he needed.[49]

The Kovner- and Ickes-led drive for delegates to support McCarthy
and a strong peace plank were also highly successful following the exhaus-
tive push to make the reform delegates known to the primary voters. In
this first New York "open" primary, ordinary citizens were allowed to run
for seats on the New York delegation, independent of the state Democratic
Committee. The McCarthy forces worked overtime to highlight those they
selected or supported in every one of the state's thirty-two congressional
districts, though McCarthy himself exercised less enthusiasm, particularly
after Kennedy was killed. "McCarthy didn't throw cold water on the New
York primary—he pissed on it," Ickes recalled.[50]

With or without their candidate's active participation, the coalition
captured sixty-two delegates, plus fifteen at-large delegates provided to
the McCarthy camp by Burns at his discretion in recognition of the reform movement's success. The state Democratic Committee, however, reserved fifty at-large seats for its own reliable minions, to go along with
the sixty-two delegation seats won by candidates loyal to the Humphrey-
supportive state committee. It meant, in the end, that the state apparatus
maintained a controlling share of the New York delegation. While an additional thirty elected delegates were pledged to Kennedy, even if all of
them went over to McCarthy it would not tip the balance to the pro-
McCarthy renegades.

———

PAUL AND KATHLEEN flew out to an unsettled Chicago and were joined
by their sons Brian and Rory. Paul made ready to head to the convention
hall the next day.

Meanwhile, in a suite on a high floor of the Conrad Hilton, Humphrey began final preparations for his convention appearances, while
McCarthy, having arrived earlier, worked the phone in his Hilton room to
try to keep his followers away from Chicago. Both candidates expected an
outbreak of violence, as Mayor Richard Daley had blanketed the streets

with cops, barred the use of Soldier Field for protest rallies, and set tight restrictions for demonstrating. The powerful Democratic mayor consigned demonstrators to Lincoln and Grant Parks only while imposing a nightly curfew at each. Thousands of officers were poised to eject anyone lingering in either park at the stroke of 11 p.m.

Few were in the mood to cooperate with "the Man"—the autocratic Daley. The prevailingly anarchic spirit was symbolized by Pigasus J. Pig, the preferred presidential candidate of the Yippie revolutionaries Abbie Hoffman and Jerry Rubin. The pig raced squealing through bellbottomed pant legs in Grant Park while the foot soldiers of dissent smoked grass, burned waste canister fires, chanted "Hey, hey, LBJ, how many kids did you kill today?" and waved signs reading "Dump the Hump." Many were McCarthy supporters. He lauded them as the "government of the people in exile."[51]

In the barbed-wire-encircled International Amphitheater four miles from Lincoln and eight miles from Grant and the Hilton Hotel on Michigan Avenue, higher-profile McCarthy delegates included the film star Robert Ryan, the cartoonist Jules Feiffer, the musician-unionist Theodore Bikel, and Kempton, who described himself as a professional observer, unaccustomed to participating in the contact sport that is politics. The writer had run to be a delegate in spite of himself due largely to his high regard for O'Dwyer, but he was not the only political novice in the New York slate, as the McCarthy campaign "had not been a cause to attract practical men of experience; so many of our delegates—and I include myself in all important respects—had only the vaguest notion of how the party system functions," Kempton wrote.[52]

Political experience did not mean much at this juncture. The convention was unruly, spectacularly so. Praetorian cops traveled the aisles harassing pro-McCarthy delegates, barking commands, and using their nightsticks to bunt them back. The dissident delegates were ordered to return to their seats when seen clumped together and conferring. Many were harried about displaying their convention credentials.

When New Yorkers, Iowans, Californians, and Black Mississippians went to the dais to call for a strong peace plank in the party platform, the orchestra music suddenly swelled, drowning them out, only to subside when they left. Boss Daley's troops dragged Alex Rosenberg off the floor and hassled the TV newsman Dan Rather to show his convention credentials. O'Dwyer took a shove when he and another McCarthy delegate tried to keep burly officers from punching Rosenberg in the jaw.[53] Kempton stayed seated, despairing at the political dogma suffusing the hall like tear gas.

Paul was a reformer who did not go out of his way to antagonize regulars from his state. Others took the bait. A scene involving the Connecticut senator Abe Ribicoff, an Establishment Democrat, typified the rancor on the floor after newscasts showing police beating street protesters showed up on TV monitors in the amphitheater. "Gestapo tactics in the streets of Chicago!" Ribicoff cried from the podium as the convention neared its climax—and the anointment of Humphrey. Watching from the floor, Daley was caught on national TV mouthing back, "Fuck you, you Jew son of a bitch!"

Late Wednesday, the second-to-last night of the convention, Humphrey secured the nomination, receiving a large majority of the votes from the states' delegates, with the McCarthyites slipping on black armbands and raising their fists in protest. He had entered the race too late to run in any primaries, relying instead on powerful Democratic leaders to obtain slates of delegates on his behalf.

The playwright Arthur Miller, a Connecticut delegate, wrote afterward that "the ordinary Senator, Congressman, State committeeman, Mayor, officeholder, see politics as sort of a game in which you win sometimes and sometimes you lose. Issues are not something you feel, like morality, like good and evil, but something you succeed or fail to make use of. . . . To the amateurs—the McCarthy people and some of the Kennedy adherents—an issue is first of all moral, and embodies a vision of the country, even of man, and is not a counter game."[54]

The mayhem was much worse outside. Demonstrators threw beer cans and stink bombs as police and troopers made arrests and cracked some skulls.

Any hope that the huge police presence would protect rather than disturb the peace had been quickly dispelled before the convention had even begun. On its eve, thousands of youthful demonstrators, predominantly white college students marshaled by the Mobilization Against the War, or, simply, "the mobe," were set upon by about three hundred cops in Lincoln Park at curfew time. Many were beaten and kicked as they tried to flee through the fog of smoke, bandannas, tie-dye, and anti-war placards.

To supplement the army of blue-helmeted officers, Daley brought in the National Guard with bayonets and artillery mounted on trucks and heavily armed state troopers. Black helicopters thumped low in the skies as demonstrators raced through the streets and the defenders of law and order—the "Pigs!"—pursued them. At least twice, tear gas canisters landed near the feet of then law student Brian O'Dwyer, releasing yellowish gas.

The approval of President Johnson's hotly contested plank rejecting a unilateral withdrawal from the war sidelined a more forceful statement the McCarthy and Humphrey people had hammered out in hope of a compromise as Grant Park became the target of another police charge. It occurred on Wednesday night, as demonstrators there became aware that the McCarthy forces' peace plank had been shot down. Chanting "Peace now" and "Fuck LBJ," many cheered as a young man scaled a flagpole on one end of the park and started yanking down Old Glory. A police squadron ran full tilt at him, with the crowd of demonstrators picking up the chant, "The Whole World Is Watching." Then, police used an overturned barricade as a battering ram while National Guard troops cut off escape routes.

The violent episode that became known as the Battle of Michigan Avenue lasted just fifteen minutes but left dozens of protesters and many bystanders injured. The spilled blood included that of not only trapped demonstrators but charging officers as well. At the Hilton nearby, plate-glass lobby windows were smashed and hundreds of demonstrators arrested. The odor of stink bombs, tear gas, and disinfectant spray reached Humphrey's Suite 2225A, carrying up through the vents.

For many of those watching delayed feeds on the TV monitors in the amphitheater and the millions watching in their living rooms, Chicago evoked the vision of a fascist state. A week earlier, Soviet tanks had rumbled into Prague, quashing the democratic impulse among the youth of the Old World capital city. As a witness to the Windy City mayhem later told a national commission formed to investigate the causes of the disturbances outside the convention,

A young man and his girlfriend were both grabbed by officers. He screamed, "We're going, we're going," but they threw him into the pond. The officers grabbed the girl, knocked her to the ground, dragged her along the embankment and hit her with the batons on her head, arms, back, and legs. The boy tried to scramble up the embankment to her, but police shoved him back in the water at least twice. He finally got to her and tried to pull her in the water, away from the police. He was clubbed on the head five or six times. An officer shouted, "Let's get the fucking bastards!" but the boy pulled her in the water and the police left.

It was a typical account.[55]

Continuing until the convention adjourned on Thursday, August 29, Daley's domestic display of militarism fueled what the Walker Report from the National Commission on the Causes and Prevention of Violence came to label as a "police riot." Completed a month after the November election, the report described scene after scene of "gratuitous beating . . . often inflicted on persons who had broken no law, disobeyed no order, made no threat." It documented injuries to cops and demonstrators, as well as a total of 650 arrests, including that of the gentlemanly Kempton, who, swept up in the confusion on the streets, was detained in a holding cell.[56]

Before the thousands of street protesters headed back to their home states and college campuses, 425 of them had been treated at temporary medical facilities, over 200 others at the scene of their injury, and 400 more for tear gas exposure. One hundred and ten demonstrators went to the hospital, while an estimated eighty-three police officers were injured seriously, according to the report. Amazingly, no one was killed in what novelist Norman Mailer, on hand to cover the convention for *Harper's* magazine, called "the Siege of Chicago."

Humphrey's nomination took a back seat to the civil war embroiling his party—it was confirmed in a joyless roll call, with McCarthy finishing with 601 delegate votes, McGovern 146 votes, and Humphrey 1,760¼ votes. He left town with a 14-to-16-point polling deficit behind the Republican Party nominee, Richard Nixon.

With McCarthy no longer a candidate for president, Senate aspirant O'Dwyer emerged as one of the leading anti-war figures running for federal office. During the convention, he had gained TV exposure and vowed, like McCarthy, to continue to oppose Humphrey until and unless the vice president spelled out in detail his declared intention to draw down the troops. In the predawn hours of Thursday morning, Paul and six hundred other delegates had boarded buses that carried them to within one mile of Grant Park, where O'Dwyer advised the group to "march quietly and orderly" toward the green. Paul led the delegates from several states on foot to protest the shabby treatment they themselves endured in the amphitheater as well as the beating and harassment of demonstrators on the streets.[57] The delegates held flickering candles in Pepsi cups as a ranking police officer stopped the group.

"Now what is it you gentlemen want to do?" asked the Irish American commander. Recognizing O'Dwyer, perhaps from TV, he soon let them pass.[58]

———

RETURNING TO NEW YORK after the convention, O'Dwyer wasted no time launching the climactic next phase of his low-budget, seat-of-the-pants race to unseat the popular, moderate Jacob Javits, who had begun serving in the Senate in 1957. But it got off to a bumpy start: to avoid letting a desire for TV publicity get in the way of his principles, he refused to cross a worker picket line outside the local CBS outlet on West Fifty-Seventh Street in Manhattan, though due for his first live Sunday morning broadcast interview of the postconvention. With the show's producer waiting for him to arrive, Paul turned and walked off. Maurice Carroll of the *New York Times*, known as Mickey, ran after him.

He simply did not cross picket lines, O'Dwyer told the reporter. "I *walk* in 'em."[59]

Javits was interviewed the same day on WNBC-TV.

In the days and weeks to come, O'Dwyer barnstormed, hewing to his halt-the-war message. As he repeatedly told a skeptical reporter, Gabe Pressman, in a Sunday morning roundtable TV program, he could address no other issue while the war strained the federal budget and divided the populace. And when Humphrey showed up in Manhattan for the annual Labor Day parade, Paul made sure to keep his distance—he brought up the rear of the procession of 100,000 unionists, lest he appear to bow to the Johnson administration's war policies, to which the Democratic presidential nominee adhered.[60]

Upstate, Paul ran into pro-Humphrey Democrats who complained that by refusing to back Humphrey, O'Dwyer was effectively serving the interests of the right-wing Nixon. "Get out of the party if you cannot support the Democratic candidate," one said at the Washington County Courthouse.

"I don't know how your conscience works," Paul responded to an audience question from a local Democratic official at a Saratoga Springs luncheon, "but I know how mine does. Hubert would be just a continuation of Lyndon."[61]

But O'Dwyer was a smash on college campuses, where students were similarly in no mood for any compromise with Humphrey's carefully hedged statements over when and under what circumstances he would bring American troops back.

"So, when I hear people damning the young, I always ask them if they are still capable of listening," O'Dwyer declared at Vassar College in Poughkeepsie on September 24. "The young are trying to send us a message. Some of them are willing to risk even their bodies, to brave the ire of Mayor Daley. Others are in the streets of America, raising voices against the inhumanity and destructiveness that the leaders of my generation have given them."[62] O'Dwyer was interrupted fifteen times with applause.[63]

He tended to speak emphatically but without histrionics. "I'm not a shouter," he explained to the *Newsday* reporter Jerry Edgerton after receiving a sustained ovation at the State Agricultural and Technical College at Delhi in Delaware County. By turns bristling or solemn, he struck a chord with the younger generation, as when he told the Vassar assembly, "The old men complain about the obscenity used by a comparatively few young people on the streets of Chicago. The young people would answer, what is more obscene—some groupings of words or dropping napalm on villages, destroying crops, and bombing civilians in the name of freedom? The fact is that the young are saying things that we had better begin listening to. If we ignore them, we ignore them at our peril." The students who worked on street corners for Kennedy or McCarthy and those who risked their lives in Southeast Asia, declared O'Dwyer, "these are the best of our children. The purity of their generation and the corruption of and cynicism resting in my generation are the only basis of the much-discussed 'generation gap.'"

Sipser, who had helped O'Dwyer in the primary phase, opened campaign storefronts around the state, seeing them as critical to Paul gaining traction given his small campaign war chest. Jerry Zipper, a thirty-eight-year-old poet and activist, developed research papers on Javits's voting record, pulling out, for example, a statement from October 13, 1966, by the senator from the *Congressional Record*: "I stand squarely behind the U.S. commitment in Vietnam"—and other documents intended to link him to Nixon.[64] As usual, Paul's family members pitched in to help the campaign. Brian, then twenty-three and attending Georgetown Law School, gave more than two hundred talks for his father, at the Allegany County Fair, a Manhattan discotheque, the New York State College Debate Association, and a moms' babysitting pool in the Bedford-Stuyvesant section of Brooklyn, among all the rest. Rory, twenty-six, an electricians' union member, marshaled college students to volunteer to work in the campaign's local storefronts. William, thirty-two, a pediatrician at Albany Medical Center, helped out in his area of the state, while twenty-nine-year-old Eileen, then raising two children, kept tabs on the campaign's ups and downs through her husband, Tom Hughes Jr., a lawyer with O'Dwyer & Bernstien. Kathleen O'Dwyer stuffed envelopes, chauffeured the candidate, and offered moral support.[65]

The press secretary for the O'Dwyer team, Dick Starkey, thirty-seven, a former *International Herald Tribune* reporter in Paris, had worked for major broadcast outlets. Writing talking points and news releases for the candidate while herding reporters at press conferences, in the closing weeks of campaign he was taken aback when O'Dwyer "went through the roof" in Utica after the *New York Times* reporter Clayton Knowles Jr. asked the candidate if his refusal to endorse Humphrey was a help to Nixon—the issue most dogging Paul's candidacy.

O'Dwyer replied that it was certainly no help to Humphrey. He turned and left in a huff, Starkey following.

"Knowles—asking me that question in this racket-ridden town. I thought he was supposed to be a friend!" the candidate boiled over to his aide. Starkey pointed out as delicately as possible that the *Times* correspondent was only doing his job.[66]

Brian would recall that his father had little enthusiasm for sparring with the Fourth Estate—or pressing the flesh. Though he had genuine warmth, he loathed the heavy demands of retail politics in a state with 57 counties, 1,530 cities, towns, and villages, and 1,185 districts. In that sense, he was like McCarthy and the opposite of his oldest brother, a natural crowd-pleaser. Campaigning was simply not Paul's forte.

"Ordinarily, he'd go to a subway stop with one of the crew and he'd take about 10 minutes and then he'd say that he was going for a cup of coffee. He was legendary for that," Brian said with a chuckle.[67]

––––––

AFTER THE REPUBLICANS' no-surprises Miami convention held in early August 1968, before the Chicago debacle, Senator Javits lined up behind Nixon and the Californian's promise of a negotiated phaseout of the war. But he distanced himself from Nixon's running mate, Spiro Agnew, when the relatively unknown Maryland governor linked the anti-war movement to "Communist infiltration." While enjoying considerable advantages as an incumbent, Javits needed to avoid alienating the parents and grandparents of the movement's college students, as well as voters who distrusted Nixon-Agnew and planned to vote for Humphrey-Muskie (Senator Edmund Muskie of Maine). Javits walked a fine line as a member of the Republican team whose views on urban disorder and the growing Pentagon budget were moderate in comparison to the hawkish top of the ticket. He sought to placate New York liberals who sat to his left, and conservatives to his right, terming the war "an obsolete struggle," a phrase too ambiguous to offend anyone.[68]

On the first day of October 1968, O'Dwyer got his strongest newspaper endorsement, from the *Binghamton Sun-Bulletin*. The morning paper did so, "not because we love Mr. Javits the less, but because we love Mr. O'Dwyer the more."

The full-page endorsement continued,

> We do not suggest that the people of New York State and the nation would be ill served if Mr. Javits were to be returned for another term in the Senate, for in our judgment that would not be true. But we do suggest that, at this moment in the nation's history, what Paul O'Dwyer has to offer is uniquely—almost, indeed, peculiarly—suited to the nation's needs. . . .
>
> We yearn for the elusive quality of intelligent integrity. It is for lack of this that the nation is undergoing a melancholy sickness of disaffection, apathy, and alienation. We are surrounded by trimmers. We suffocate amid the pragmatists. We drown in platitudes. And along comes a man, by a fluke of the new primary system in our state, who refuses to trim, whose hard common sense is geared

to a genuine set of humanistic ideals, and who talks in specifics. Such a man should be supported and cherished. He does not emerge too often.[69]

Sipser began the work of disseminating tens of thousands of reprints statewide.

Like McCarthy, Paul in a sense was acting as the conscience of his party, much as Humphrey himself did, when, as Minneapolis mayor and leader of the liberal Americans for Democratic Action, he convinced the party to adopt a strong civil rights plank at the 1948 convention in Philadelphia over the objections of the Dixiecrat wing and thereby helped Truman to win the election.

Throughout the fall of 1968, New York City residents contended with mounting difficulties and polarizing public dramas. One of the most consequential was the citywide teachers' strike arising from an experimental district school board in Brooklyn's Ocean Hill–Brownsville area whose members and superintendent, supported by many of the African American school community's parents, claimed the right to fire teachers unilaterally. The position drew strong opposition from the city's teachers' union. O'Dwyer sided with parents and community advocates. But the battle aggravated Black-Jewish cooperation in the civil rights movement. The *New York Times*'s Sydney Schanberg, while covering O'Dwyer in Queens on October 7, reported his position on the pitched school battle, winning the candidate little praise and perhaps even fewer votes from the union's sizable, well-organized membership.

"Community-controlled schools can't turn out a worse-educated pupil than is being turned out now," Paul told the reporter. "Conceivably, with the mother and father having something to say about it, community control may indeed be the beginning of equality for black people." He added that it should not have to weaken teachers' contractually ensured job security.

Paul received a warmer welcome at the Robert F. Kennedy Community Center in Flushing, a former corner store. He was visibly moved when two five-year-old girls waiting for him outside held out pro-O'Dwyer signs made with crayons.

"We made this for you," one of them offered. The candidate went silent, then "swooped down and planted a big kiss on each little girl's cheek."

But during O'Dwyer's tour of Flushing's Main Street, trailed by Schanberg, he encountered a white Transit Authority employee who refused to shake his hand.

"The day is long past for you liberals. We'll be seeing you in museums," the man growled.[70]

O'Dwyer was coming off a successful fundraiser at the Hilton complemented by a Women for O'Dwyer luncheon in the grand ballroom at the Commodore. The writer Lillian Hellman—who was a client of Oscar Bernstien's and, facing a 1952 subpoena, had memorably advised HUAC Chairman John Stephens Wood (D-GA) in a letter, "I cannot and will not cut my conscience to fit this year's fashion"—introduced Eleanor Clark French, a liberal Democratic politician from the East Side, and Fannie Lou Hamer at the gathering, a "Women for O'Dwyer Day." It included a call for federal action on affordable day care and salary parity by means of a constitutional amendment, as well as "MediCorps," or sending volunteer medical professionals to impoverished Appalachian hills and Native American reservations, à la John F. Kennedy's Peace Corps.

When Alabama Governor George Wallace brought his third-party campaign for the White House to Madison Square Garden, O'Dwyer joined thousands of protesters at Seventh Avenue between Thirty-Sixth and Thirty-Seventh Streets to assail the unabashed segregationist.

O'Dwyer benefited too from favors from New York's theatrical and musical communities, including Leonard Bernstein, Leopold Stokowski, Tony Randall, Barbra Streisand, Godfrey Cambridge, and Diana Sands, as well as Jack Gilford, Judy Collins, the Peter, Paul and Mary trio, Pete Seeger, Tom Paxton, and Harry Belafonte, some of whom gave campaign benefit performances at such venues as the Palace Theater and the Philharmonic Hall or appeared with O'Dwyer and McCarthy in the weeks leading up to Election Day. Endorsing Paul were the Massachusetts senator Ted Kennedy, the UN ambassador Arthur Goldberg (newly placed in charge of the Humphrey campaign in New York), the former Robert F. Kennedy confidant William van den Heuvel, and Curtis Gans, who had worked with Lowenstein in launching "Dump Johnson." (Even Steve Smith—no fan, as a Kennedy in-law, of Johnson or his handpicked candidate for president— did not, in the end, begrudge Paul his decision to seek the Senate nomination, and even accepted a token role later on as an O'Dwyer campaign official while refusing to support Humphrey.)[71] The presence of so many testified to their anti-war stance, previous support for McCarthy, or connection to the state Democratic establishment. O'Dwyer, despite his resistance to the top of the ticket, was after all the Senate nominee.

After the dates for three different radio and TV debates were decided, Paul refused to prepare, Starkey noted—a rejection all the more striking given both the debates' high stakes and the trial lawyer's understanding of the importance of preparation. The sometimes-obstinate O'Dwyer had a habit of eschewing anything that smacked of being canned or artificial-sounding. He felt his opinions came from his long personal experience and needed no rehearsal. This was principled, perhaps, but hardly smart.

Following the first of the several debates and forums held in the last week of the campaign, reporter Knowles pulled Starkey aside to hear his estimation of how Paul had performed. The campaign press aide offered him his off-the-cuff assessment, presuming he was helping a friendly newsman with a personal perspective and would not be quoted. "I said Javits had won—he had been better-prepared," Starkey remembered.

The reporter, a familiar face on the campaign trail, did his job, including Starkey's words in his article the next morning in the *Times*. Mortified to see them in print, Starkey raced to find O'Dwyer and apologize. He was prepared, he added, to turn in his resignation.

Paul waved him off.

"The least serious mistake you can make in life," O'Dwyer assured him, "is to trust someone who doesn't deserve that trust."

In the often petty arena of electoral politics, Starkey never quite forgot it.[72]

————

HUMPHREY HAD BEEN TRAILING in the polls since the convention, but his numbers improved beginning in early October after he delivered his strongest call to date for a US bombing halt (just as long as he had evidence that the North Vietnamese would respect the demilitarized zone and enter into good-faith talks, he stated). For the vice president, the speech was a liberation from Johnson, who had been insisting all along that he not depart an inch from the administration's script concerning the war; the vice president was sheepish in response, and his failure to define himself had left him on the outs with many on the anti-war left and eating Nixon's dust. With this speech, however, things changed. The constant jeering at Humphrey campaign stops subsided; anti-Humphrey signs were replaced by posters reading "If You Mean It, We Are with You" and "Hecklers for Humphrey." And his poll numbers started to improve.[73]

By the middle of the month Humphrey had moved to within striking distance of the front-runner, according to both Gallup and Harris polls. Backers of George Wallace's third-party line began to return to the Democratic Party, and talk of an upset ensued.[74]

Fearing a possible "October surprise," Nixon resorted to campaign chicanery, tapping back-channel contacts to convince South Vietnam to walk away from the Paris peace talks on the day before the election—a day when the United States stood ready to stop bombing Hanoi, the capital of North Vietnam, in exchange for concessions.[75]

Nixon's efforts to keep the war going through Election Day were as surreptitious as they were treasonous; few, except perhaps Johnson, knew the whole story with any degree of certainty, and the legacy-fixated president opted not to allude to it—leaving Humphrey in the dark and powerless to use it to attract voters on the fence.

Nixon went on to win the election, but only by the narrowest of margins—by 0.75 percent of the popular vote, a slightly greater margin of victory than John Kennedy had captured in his victory over Nixon eight years earlier. In the electoral vote tally, Nixon's lead over Humphrey was a comfortable one (as Kennedy's had been). But in a number of states, such as New Jersey, Ohio, and Illinois, the final voting tallies were close enough to shift the complement of electoral votes to his opponent.

Under "peace-with-honor" Nixon, US involvement in the war would go on for five painful years more, the accumulated death toll from the war coming to encompass as many as 2 million Vietnamese civilians, 1.1 million North Vietnamese and Vietcong fighters, and 58,220 American servicemen.[76]

IT WAS NOT UNTIL October 29 that McCarthy endorsed Humphrey. Paul followed suit the next day, citing the solidification of Humphrey's position on bringing the war to a prompt close if elected.

On election night, O'Dwyer sat in a dimly lit suite at the Commodore. Staring at the television screen, he argued aloud with the WCBS-TV news program's early projections until, finally, he was "white with fatigue, and his anger was just as pale and washed out," observed Joe Flaherty, who was in the loser's locker room, Kempton-style, for the *Village Voice*.

The results were decisive, with Javits receiving 50 percent of the votes (3.26 million) to O'Dwyer's 33 percent (2.15 million) and the largely overshadowed Conservative Party candidate James Buckley's 17 percent (1.14 million).

There was little O'Dwyer could do except concede.[77]

———

AFTER THE ELECTION, the interpretation that the McCarthy-O'Dwyer effort had contributed to Humphrey's defeat lingered. The Socialist Party leader and political scientist Michael Harrington, for one, argued that a Humphrey victory would have ended the war sooner, even though the vice president's prescriptions for doing so were constrained by his alliance with President Johnson. If Harrington was correct, O'Dwyer's refusal to back Humphrey until almost the last possible moment could only be seen as myopic at best. That will never be known for sure. But it would be difficult to honestly hold O'Dwyer, or McCarthy, responsible for Humphrey's defeat, considering the civil war that tore apart the Democratic Party in 1968, so unmistakable in Chicago, and Humphrey's own missteps as a campaigner. In perhaps his most consequential mistake, Humphrey failed to secure McCarthy's backing at the convention, squandering what may have been his best chance to unite the warring wings of the party, according to the Humphrey biographer Arnold Offner. Instead, Humphrey remained squeezed between them.

The complaint that McCarthy and O'Dwyer should have endorsed the right-wing Nixon's principal opponent sooner falls short. It fails to consider that Humphrey allowed himself to become a spokesman for the Johnson administration's hawkishness, engendering a great deal of opposition from the anti-war left and those fighting the wartime draft.[78]

Humphrey's liberal bona fides were long-standing and well-deserved. He was a cofounder of the anti-communist Americans for Democratic Action in 1947; a Minneapolis mayor and Senate candidate who persuaded delegates to "get out of the shadow of states' rights" by adopting a strong civil rights platform with an eloquent speech at the 1948 Democratic National Convention; a senator who first introduced a bill calling for the Peace Corps; and, as Senate majority whip, the lead author of the Civil Rights Act of 1964. He had, with great foresight, warned Johnson that

1965 would be the best year for the administration to cut its losses by looking for an exit strategy in the Vietnam War. But when an unhinged Johnson took to ignoring his advice—and, in Offner's description, treating him almost as a child—Humphrey shrank back from crossing him and, to his own detriment, toed the president's line on the war. At crucial moments in the campaign, the vice president lacked a strong element of something O'Dwyer displayed in abundance—the courage of his convictions.

10

THE LIBERATED AREA OF CITY HALL

JOHN MCGETTRICK, a scruffy twenty-one-year-old peacenik, saw Paul O'Dwyer in person for the first time in the garrisoned city of Chicago in August 1968, when the Senate aspirant was making his way toward Grant Park with hundreds of candle-bearing convention delegates. While the delegates wore no protection, McGettrick had on a football helmet and a flak jacket padded with newspaper. What caught McGettrick's eye was Paul's proud bearing, pompadour, and fashionably long sideburns, a contrast to the flailing nightsticks, exploding tear gas canisters, and police cars revving and fishtailing to pin protesters.

Early in the week the rangy McGettrick entered a busy luncheonette to get away from rock-hurling rebels chanting "Pigs!" and the cops in blue helmets giving chase. But as he waited at the counter for the waitress to bring him the sixty-nine-cent breakfast special, "three or four cops came in and grabbed Abbie Hoffman on the next stool over. They were dragging him off the back of it, shoving me aside and screaming 'mad dog' and that they had a 'silver bullet' to kill him. People's eggs were going this way and that way, but definitely not into their mouths."

McGettrick, a "nobody" who knew of Hoffman's antiestablishment antics, such as tossing fistfuls of dollars onto the New York Stock Exchange trading floor and touching off a greed-fueled scramble, had left City College before graduating and thrown in his lot with the pro-peace, pro–civil rights presidential campaign of Robert Kennedy. He signed up as a Kennedy volunteer, traveling at one point to Indiana, where the candidate gave an impassioned speech to a largely African American crowd about the murder of the Reverend Martin Luther King Jr. With Bobby Kennedy himself cut down two months later, McGettrick returned to live in New York and volunteered, in Brooklyn, for O'Dwyer's Senate race while working as a cab driver and studying for a bachelor's degree in economics from St. John's University. Though O'Dwyer lost the race, he did not disappoint McGettrick, hiring the young man as his full-time driver when he ran in 1973 for New York City Council president.

Navigating the side streets and highways knowledgeably in the 1973 council race, McGettrick conversed with O'Dwyer, sharing how his father had endured World War II as a US Army medic in North Africa and Italy and "hated war." He himself was carried at six months old from New York to Ireland less than three years after the end of World War II and lived there for the next seven years. Rejected for conscientious objector status once out of college, the Vietnam War then raging, he resolved to flee to Canada if drafted. But like Paul during World War II, his number did not come up after his physical.[1]

On their way to campaign stops, O'Dwyer chatted with him about some of his legal cases, including those of Ernest Gallashaw, accused Irish Republican Army (IRA) soldiers, anti-war protesters, and many others. There was also the story of the unusual appearance Paul made before the state court system's Committee on Character and Fitness, where he vouched for the Columbia Law School graduate Gustin Reichbach, a future state supreme court judge. Reichbach's application for admission to the bar underwent scrutiny in nine hearings held over eighteen months due to his participation in campus takeovers at Columbia University and membership of Students for a Democratic Society during the campus disruptions of 1968. At that time, a cop's nightstick bloodied Reichbach's head. Adding to committee members' doubts about his eligibility to practice law, Reichbach was also one of the coauthors of *The Bust Book* with no less of a revolutionist than Kathy Boudin—daughter of the left-wing constitutional lawyer Leonard Boudin, a colleague of Paul's. The applicant's main detractor, recounted Paul, was a senior partner of a leading Manhattan law firm and a major cultural philanthropist who felt that Reichbach's invocation of poet LeRoi Jones's battle cry "Up against the wall, motherfuckers" in a law school newspaper had gone too far. "Well Mr. O'Dwyer," the lawyer-philanthropist declared at a hearing, "I thought

I had heard it all. But in my entire life, including the US Army, this is the worst language I have ever heard." Giving the corporate lawyer bonus points for priggishness, Paul shot back, "Perhaps that was the result of your having served in a segregated unit in the armed forces!"[2]

In his own application for admission in 1973—to city hall—O'Dwyer triumphed, winning the Democratic primary election by a 41-to-36 percent margin over the city council president Sanford Garelik despite the *New York Times* editorial page arguing, without providing examples, that Paul was "sometimes given to demagogy," and its endorsement of Garelik.[3] O'Dwyer was helped by Irish voters to his right who appreciated his 1972–73 defense of the Fort Worth Five (New York–area residents jailed for their refusal to talk to a Texas grand jury investigating an alleged plot to acquire guns for the IRA) and by Jewish voters who remembered how he helped raise money and run guns for Irgun rebels in the embattled British Mandate in Palestine. Transit workers, meanwhile, credited O'Dwyer for his service to "Red" Mike Quill during the 1966 bus and subway strike, if not Paul's push for collective bargaining for the transit workers' union as far back as the Fiorello La Guardia years.

Garelik, who was the first Jewish chief inspector of the police before becoming city council president, demanded a recount of the primary votes. As a result, Paul's total was winnowed, but it remained above the 40 percent plurality that would have triggered a runoff primary election, if barely so. He was virtually assured of success in the November election because Democratic voters in the city far outnumbered Republicans, and the GOP's nominee, Thomas Galvin, was little known in comparison. An architect, Galvin served as the vice president of the New York City Convention and Exhibition Corporation and positioned himself as a champion of a besieged middle class, with one advertisement accusing O'Dwyer of being "out of touch with the mainstream."

A day or two after the retallying, O'Dwyer neighbor and campaign worker Hedi Piel recounted an astonishing event to John McGettrick, who was then getting ready to join O'Dwyer's city hall staff; she said a young African American man had arrived at the O'Dwyer-for-Council-President offices at 80 Fifth Avenue. Dressed tastefully, the visitor arrived "carrying a briefcase filled with cash" and stated only, "Compliments of the Trump Organization." German-born Piel was a longtime West Side progressive. In her years as a dedicated advocate for New York newcomers and the poor, she married an heir to the Piel Brothers' Beer family, organized a group to oppose the House Un-American Activities Committee, and was elected district leader as a member of the FDR–Woodrow Wilson Reform Club. The brazen and unsolicited offer, she said, came just after Paul was declared the winner of the primary. Paul's campaign manager and financial backer, Charlie Keith, picked up on the apparent bribery-in-progress. Without missing a beat, Keith told the uninvited visitor bearing the satchel to "get the fuck out," said McGettrick.[4]

Two theories were discussed as to who had tried to buy off the presumptive council president-elect. One, based on Piel's descriptions, centered on the company owned by Fred Trump, a major builder and landlord with close ties to city Democratic leaders, including the mayoral primary winner Abe Beame. The second, a supposition as well, centered on a possible sting by Maurice Nadjari, a prosecutor designated by Governor Nelson Rockefeller to net corrupt Democratic district attorneys, judges, and politicians. Another Democratic candidate in the council president race, the New York State assemblyman Anthony DiFalco, was the son of the Manhattan surrogate justice then under investigation by a Nadjari grand jury, and O'Dwyer had dismissed talk of the surrogate supposedly asking individuals to give money to his own flesh and blood's campaign. ("What kind of father would he be if he didn't want to help his son?" said Paul.[5] The charges against the judge, centered on alleged case-fixing, were later dismissed.)

Despite having a reputation for probity, O'Dwyer was an appealing target for an unscrupulous businessman or a state prosecutor hunting big game, as the city council presidency was not without clout—not so much because of his position vis-à-vis the legislative body, over which a presiding president had no control, but rather due to the four votes the council president carried on the city's Board of Estimate. The board was far more powerful than the council, approving land-use contracts, franchises, water rates, and major expenditures. O'Dwyer in fact had the same number of votes on the board as his successful running mates, Mayor Beame and City Comptroller Harrison Goldin. The five borough presidents on the body controlled two votes each.[6]

While any council bill that O'Dwyer might come to introduce was likely to have a limited impact, Paul could, and from time to time did, withhold votes on the board for big-ticket items sought by fellow members of the panel. He used his power to stall approval of proposals in order to win support for his own priorities.

But a council president invariably needed to be wary of alienating the mayor, especially one of the same party. Beame was not known by the public for being tough, even punitive. But he could be, at times, and the council member and former Queens County Democratic chairman Matthew Troy discovered this after blurting out "Abe, fuck you" at a closed meeting concerning the mayor's planned introduction of an automobile-user tax, which would have hit his more car-dependent borough disproportionately. O'Dwyer's eyebrows went up. "Matty's going to regret that remark for the rest of his life," he whispered to the aide Jim Callaghan when the tension lifted. Troy, the former Queens borough president, lost his chairmanship on the council Finance Committee and the stipend on top of his annual council salary. (He had recently been maneuvered out of his perch as head of the voter-rich Queens County Democratic organization and replaced by the borough president, Donald Manes).[7]

Another time, O'Dwyer was steamed after Callaghan called into question a proposed Staten Island amusement park still under consideration by the mayor and estimate board. At a community rally against the proposal, Callaghan had offered his own speculation, telling a TV news reporter, "This *mob-built* amusement park will never get off the ground."

As soon as Callaghan returned from the rally, the office manager Sue Volk said, "You better go in and see Paul. He's livid," as Callaghan had flagged a possible O'Dwyer position before Beame had taken a position on the proposed project. By the end of the episode, Callaghan was relieved to still have his job. O'Dwyer harrumphed to Callaghan, whose advice he valued, that the "Nay" he later delivered on the amusement park plan was not based on the merits of the arguments (whether for or against), nor even the political sensitivities of the mayor, comptroller, or the borough presidents, but rather "so I wouldn't have to see your ugly face in here ever again, complaining." The "sometimes-given-to-demagogy" O'Dwyer was, as a political insider, more complex than many people realized. And as for the amusement proposal, backed by two of the borough presidents, it never went beyond the drawing board.[8]

———

ASSIGNED BY PAUL to attend the estimate board's regular private sessions for him, John McGettrick participated in the usually transactional discussions. He was tasked with keeping his boss informed on the proposals placed on the calendar for future public consideration.

One of the more contentious questions to face the board arose in Paul's first year in this citywide office. It centered on a 1969 contract with a consortium of contractors chosen to build a bypass water tunnel hundreds of feet beneath the surface of the city's streets, as deep, in certain parts, as the Woolworth Building down the block from city hall was tall.

Tunnel No. 3 was designed as a backup to the city's two existing water tunnels, completed in 1917 and 1937, respectively. In the absence of a third tunnel, Tunnel No. 2 would need to be disabled if and when Tunnel No. 1 needed repair (or vice versa). That would leave 7.5 million people without water for a month to a year—a calamity, to be sure.

Tunnel No. 3 was planned to extend for more than sixty miles. A marvel of engineering, it was described from the outset as the largest non-military construction program in the Western world. All the boring through bedrock and the encasement of a tunnel wide enough to accommodate two freight trains was destined to continue for more than half a century. It would ultimately carry on through eight successive mayors, take the lives of twenty-three workers, and raise the anticipated cost to $6 billion upon completion in 2026.

Initially the contractors estimated the cost for the first phase, a nearly fourteen-mile branch, as $222 million. The accepted offer, the lowest of those submitted, came up for questioning five years later, with change orders pushing it up to $382 million and O'Dwyer, alone among his elected colleagues on the panel, balking.

"You can put this thing through," he told Deputy Mayor for Intergovernmental Relations Stanley Friedman, "but it will be the scandal of our time, and I cannot remain silent."[9]

McGettrick had already triggered Paul's suspicions, flagging $6 million in change orders or add-ons to the original Tunnel No. 3 contract. "They called in the head of the Board of Water Supply," said McGettrick, and let Paul's aide ask about them. "Does anyone want coffee?" was the official's only reply. McGettrick promptly told Paul of the exchange, and it reinforced his suspicions: "He said, 'Ah, this is it.'"

O'Dwyer presided at the board's next meeting as the panel considered a Beame-offered compromise to halt tunnel work for four months and retain a consultant to look into the project's costs. When Paul began discussing the issue, hundreds of unionized tunnel workers, or sandhogs, fumed crowding the wooden pews, aisles, and rear of the chamber. Defiant, "one of them—huge guy with a brogue—shouted, 'You're a crook, just like your brother!'" recalled McGettrick.

The salvo from the worker in the restive audience was too much to bear for a loyal brother and a friend of labor who had represented the sandhogs' union. To the audience's surprise, O'Dwyer threw the gavel down and went headlong at the younger and larger laborer. ("He looked like a heavyweight boxer," Jim Callaghan recalled of the heckler.) The two antagonists nearly came to blows. But city hall police sergeants pushed through and separated the mismatched pugilists, fearing a melee. "The cops came to me, pleading, 'Please don't let that happen again. We would have had to pull out our guns, and who knows what would have happened,'" said McGettrick.[10] O'Dwyer might have been an ordinarily civil politician with legal training, but he could reach a breaking point, and on that night he showed it. As Stanley Friedman later explained, "It was hurtful to a guy like Paul that he would be accused of taking bread out of workers' mouths; he took it very personally. Here, in his own way, he was trying to help them and he was being attacked by them."[11]

The council president returned to the dais, collected his gavel, and brought the chamber to order. The measure was approved, and when the consultant's study found questionable costs, such as union featherbedding and city payments to engineers who were no longer involved, his office claimed credit for trims to the price. In the end, the first of five phases of the project, with all its many ensuing complications, would reach $1 billion and take until 1993 to complete.

McGettrick remembered that the controversy also brought demands for hearings at the city council. Contractors sent men in dark suits and shiny shoes to lobby the council and board members and especially O'Dwyer. "These guys would fly in for meetings from all over the country and say, 'What do we have to do to get O'Dwyer's support? What does he want?' My response, which was true, was always this: 'He wants you to honor the contract,'" said McGettrick.

In addition to igniting his ire at the public forum, the controversy brought out O'Dwyer's wry wit when a Roman Catholic bishop phoned him from San Antonio, Texas, to talk up the virtues of the owner of one of the tunnel-building firms and the owner's family-centered values. "Such a wonderful Catholic, and his wife has 14 children"—McGettrick recalled of the phone conversation he overheard in Paul's private office.

But the cleric's sales pitch only prompted Paul's spine to stiffen more. "That poor woman!" he told the bishop.[12]

———

SIXTY-SIX YEARS OLD upon taking office, O'Dwyer was a long-haul public figure in local politics and labor issues. By dint of his famous older sibling, Irish origins, and surviving brogue, he was something of a throwback to the era when an Irish-dominated Tammany Hall had reigned over municipal affairs. Those days were gone, and the 1969 regular election had proved it so—it was the first since the formal consolidation of the city in 1898 in which no Irish American won citywide office.[13]

The ethnic composition of Irish, Italian, Scandinavian, and Russian Jewish neighborhoods that Paul remembered from his first years in New York was also in flux, the result of the African American Great Migration from the South, farming mechanization in Puerto Rico, and a sweeping immigration law signed by President Johnson in the shadow of the Statue of Liberty in 1965, ridding the nation of racial quotas. Overall, the population of non-Hispanic white residents was rapidly declining while a poorer one, consisting of both African Americans and new arrivals from Latin American and Asian countries, was replenishing schools and main streets.

For three and a half centuries a safe harbor for poor and persecuted peoples, New York was contending by 1974 with economic doldrums that had been gathering strength for some time, largely outside of its control. Activity at deep-water ports had begun to dwindle in the 1950s with the advent of freight containerization and automated technologies that pushed the shipping industry to New Jersey and beyond. As in many other cities, expressways were projecting New York City's middle class outward to the surrounding suburbs, along with big corporations. The city's large constellation of smaller, specialized manufacturing was also receding, with federal subsidies of various kinds fueling the growth of economies in the now air-conditioned states of the South and Southwest, where both labor costs and taxes were lower. Left out were many Black New Yorkers who might have joined the outflow but for racial barriers to housing, schools, and employment in many suburban towns, and white residents who, due to age or poverty, could not relocate.

If anyone wished to persist in viewing the council presidency as merely ceremonial, O'Dwyer unsettled the perception from his first day on the job, when he assumed a civic onus outside his duties as defined in the city charter. The desk phones in his office in the east wing of city hall had not yet been activated, nor had the former police commissioner Theodore Roosevelt's old desk yet been brought out of storage for Paul's use when he hurried off to rescue 1,500 workers at the old Rheingold Brewery. The Brooklyn plant's owner, PepsiCo Inc., had announced that it could no longer afford to keep the plant open. With the mayor's office joining the discussions, a new owner, Chock Full O' Nuts, was found and the workers' jobs preserved after nine weeks of talks.

While O'Dwyer sought to cultivate warm relations with city and state leaders of both sides and avoided personalizing political differences, he was different from garden-variety politicians in other ways. These included his driving sense of public purpose coupled to an abiding interest in the city's political and social history, his fascination capable of keeping him in the office until 11 p.m. poring over the record of the common council debate on the causes of the 1832 cholera epidemic or the exact location of unmarked paupers' burial grounds.[14]

O'Dwyer also had an unusually diverse council staff, somewhat representative of the city's population at the time: there were six Irish, four Jews, four Puerto Rican New Yorkers, four African Americans, a Chinese American, a Scandinavian, two Italians, and a WASP. Most of his staff members were under thirty, many new to government service.[15]

What was just as obvious was that the new council president was closer to the left than virtually any of his counterparts serving in office. This would later prompt the Manhattan councilman Henry Stern to describe O'Dwyer's office as the "liberated area" of city hall, a humorous observation based on some truth. Paul found it flattering enough to repeat to others when discussing his accomplishments despite the inherent constraints of his office, including his making it more muscular by instituting a citywide ombudsman's office within it.[16]

But as Stern's quip also accurately reflected, O'Dwyer often used his local government platform to support democratic rights abroad and democratically elected foreign leaders undone with the help of the United States or its allies. He received at city hall, for instance, the widow of Salvador Allende of Chile, Hortensia Bussi, after she delivered a late-February appeal to the United Nations to condemn the junta that had ousted her popularly elected husband. Augusto Pinochet's coup d'état condemned Chileans to "genocidal repression . . . only comparable to that exercised by Hitler's Nazis," she said. In the UN assembly and its visitors' gallery, many people applauded, "particularly," the *New York Times* reported, "those of the Soviet bloc."[17] Mrs. Allende was barred under her US visa from speaking anywhere else in the country during her stay, so O'Dwyer offered to speak for her, bringing fifty union leaders to the second floor at city hall. He pointed to the widely suspected involvement of the CIA on behalf of American business interests in the 1973 Chilean government takeover, as well as the jailings, executions, and murders by Pinochet's de facto military government. The president's widow was a small, dignified woman with black-rimmed glasses. Standing not much taller at her side, O'Dwyer said the death of her husband (who had killed himself rather than surrender to the military) had "brought a sense of shock and pain in many parts of the world." The South American press carried this and other comments, while New York newspapers hardly noted them.[18]

In the summer of that year, O'Dwyer welcomed the Allendes' daughter, Beatriz Allende, a socialist and an activist, and he joined the Lawyers Committee on Chile, which sent a pair of legal observers (Martin Garbus, the former associate director of the American Civil Liberties Union, and Ira Lowe, a Washington-based constitutional and criminal lawyer) to bear witness to brazen constitutional violations in the South American nation's courts.[19]

O'Dwyer's use of his elective perch to support international humanitarian causes had started a month after his election and before assuming the duties of his office—he and the Manhattan borough president Percy Sutton traveled to the USSR for the New York Committee on Soviet Jewry to investigate the struggles of Jewish "refuseniks" barred from immigrating to Israel. During the trip, Paul and Percy took a twelve-hour train ride from Moscow to the Darnytskyi district of Kyiv, where they looked into the recently concluded trial and conviction of Alexander Feldman, who was active in the struggle for the right of Soviet Jews to relocate to Israel and had participated in public demonstrations in Kyiv and Moscow. O'Dwyer and Sutton learned that the proceedings were held in a makeshift factory, with great efforts made to conceal them. The charges were "hooliganism," stemming from Feldman bumping into a girl holding a cake and a scuffle with two men who turned out to be KGB agents. The defendant appealed his guilty verdict and sentence of three and a half years in a labor camp. O'Dwyer and Sutton got hold of the record of

THE LIBERATED AREA OF CITY HALL

appeal and flew back with it hidden in their trousers. They initiated an open letter on Feldman's behalf. O'Dwyer believed that the effort contributed to the reduction of the man's sentence to two years.[20]

Aided by his governmental title, Paul also traveled in early 1974 to Spain and Madrid's Tribunal of Public Order, a court created for political crimes, to protest the prison sentence of twenty years imposed on Spanish labor leaders known as the "Carabanchel Ten," who had had the temerity to start a trade union. On still another occasion, he attended the funeral procession of Frank Stagg, a Provisional IRA hunger striker from County Mayo who died in England's Wakefield Prison in February 1976. (Stagg's father had been in the IRA in the War of Independence.)[21] Paul also provided the only official, governmental greeting to a Japanese peace group that included survivors of President Truman's use of atomic bombs in Hiroshima and Nagasaki. (In this instance, the dailies in New York made no mention of the ceremony.)[22] His far-flung concerns may have been driven by his own politics but at times were seen by some fellow politicians and constituents as far removed from the traditional role of the city council president to address neighborhood-level problems, or even the Northern Ireland–centered foreign policy concerns of his fellow Irish Americans.

Still, O'Dwyer was chosen to serve as the honorary grand marshal of the 1974 St. Patrick's Day parade in New York, where he delivered a peppery address, turning attention to a pair of Belfast-born sisters who joined the Provisional IRA. Radicalized by British abuse of former civil rights protesters, the Prices were then sitting in an English prison, charged with setting car bombs in London. The bombs injured some two hundred people and caused a man's fatal heart attack, raising difficult moral questions for many in Irish America. Proudly wearing a top hat on Fifth Avenue and waving to the crowd, O'Dwyer did not delve deeply into them, nor lament the chaos caused by the explosions of less than two weeks before. The grand marshal spoke to the pooling stream of plastic green hats and cardboard shamrocks. Arrayed on the platform behind him were grandees of the Ancient Order of Hibernians, the procession's historic sponsor and guardian of Irish Catholic civic pride and propriety in New York since 1836.

"While we celebrate St. Patrick in New York, many of Patrick's people have given their lives in the continuing struggle to seek a simple justice," O'Dwyer pronounced. "Many people are in Long Kesh prison, and in their miserable dwellings they are nightly being assaulted by British troops."[23] He offered pointed reminders of British-sanctioned official violence and internments and the housing and employment discrimination facing the minority Catholic population in Northern Ireland, conditions he believed gave rise to insurrection. That did not of course prevent the two sisters from being sentenced soon after to life imprisonment plus twenty years.[24]

———

O'DWYER BEGAN his post-1968 path back to city hall after a third try for Congress in 1970, when he sought the late Robert Kennedy's former Senate seat, held by the Rockefeller appointee Charles Goodell, a Republican from Jamestown. Already notorious among friends and loved ones for his inattentive driving, Paul was admitted to Columbia-Presbyterian Hospital in Manhattan with abrasions and a possible concussion after a four-car crash on the Henry Hudson Parkway en route to a Democratic executive committee meeting on March 12.[25] Dusting himself off, he returned to the primary race against Richard Ottinger. But his luck did not improve: he came in second in the Democratic primary behind the largely self-funded congressman from Rochester. Ottinger and Goodell, both liberals, each fell short in November, defeated by James Buckley, the standard-bearer for the eight-year-old Conservative Party. (James was the brother of William Buckley, the editor of the *National Review*, with whom Paul occasionally corresponded.)[26]

Paul felt he could respect the success of James Buckley's third-party, pro-war campaign because, unlike Richard Nixon, candidate Buckley did not mince words. But the victory appeared to have a broader significance, signaling New York State voters' disenchantment—not just with liberal Republican Establishment politicians but also with Democratic candidates who supported court-ordered busing to desegregate education, former president Johnson's War on Poverty, and the feminist push for enactment of the Equal Rights Amendment. As Buckley aptly put it late in life, his victory proved that "conservatives had appeal not only to Republicans, but to what would be later be labeled Reagan Democrats."[27]

As the political center shifted rightward, O'Dwyer remained as committed as ever to the left, supporting organized as well as unorganized labor, a continued war on inner-city poverty, and changes in police practices (public hearings by the Knapp Commission would soon reveal enormous amounts of corruption in the New York City Police Department

[NYPD]). In February 1972, he called on the liberal New Democratic Co-alition to endorse Eugene McCarthy for president, though the dove's encore candidacy proved brief.

Another portent of reaction in New York politics came less than two months before the Senate primary election. It was sparked by an early-morning rally in the Wall Street area by more than a thousand college students upset over the Kent State shootings four days earlier and Nix-on's recent announcement of a US invasion of neutral Cambodia. Enraged by the protesters, hundreds of New York construction workers chanted "America, love it or leave it!" as O'Dwyer and other speakers gave brief speeches. The laborers muscled into the rally, startling people on the congested sidewalk, who pulled back or joined the fray. One hundred or so of the enraged laborers made their way up Broadway to city hall, where a US flag flapped at half-mast in memory of the four Kent State students slain by National Guard troops at a peaceful protest of the war. Fearing that the city's government seat would be overtaken, a deputy mayor, Richard Aurelio, returned the flag to full-mast. The mob broke up. But President Nixon in time welcomed the "Silent Majority" combatants to the White House, along with Peter Brennan, the president of the building trades' union. Bob Haldeman, Nixon's chief of staff, told the speechwriter Pat Buchanan to "put someone on the New York senate race" and start "really playing this up." Charles Colson, a White House aide, secretly organized "hardhat support" for James Buckley. Brennan and the head of the city's firemen's union and other city labor leaders pitched in.[28]

White Catholic ethnic groups in the construction union were not necessarily more supportive of Nixon's "Vietnamization" than Democrats with white-collar jobs. But they were more and more willing to vote for a Conservative or Republican, as was the Irish American Brennan. Their positions lined up with those of George Meany, the longtime anti-communist leader of the American Federation of Labor–Congress of Industrial Organizations and, despite some policy differences, a Nixon backer since 1970.

O'Dwyer departed from the "Hardhat Riot" unhappy but unscuffed. In the June primary, he collected 302,000 votes to Ottinger's 366,000, losing to him overall but faring better than his opponent in New York City. Two other candidates, the former JFK speechwriter Ted Sorensen, the state party leaders' designee, and congressman Max McCarthy, brought up the rear.

Since Nixon's victory over Humphrey in 1968, O'Dwyer had sought to soften the disappointment that overtook some of his progressive allies. He had, for example, managed to distill at least a modicum of encouragement from the disastrous Chicago convention. Contributing an essay to a collection titled *Law & Disorder*, he stressed that the New York delegation had voted 148–42 for a strongly worded peace plank, that New York and even Virginia had "voted to eliminate racism from the party," and that "the day of the Daleys"—and urban bosses—was "finished."[29] But others who were sympathetic to the Democratic Party were less sanguine, having seen Democrats warring with one another on the streets and in the amphitheater. Murray Kempton's lengthy piece on the convention, published in the *Saturday Evening Post* a few days before Nixon's election, did not pull hope from despair. The headline appropriately read, "The Decline and Fall of the Democratic Party."[30]

AFTER HIS SUCCESS in the city council race, Paul with his successful ticket mates stood on the steps of city hall on January 1, 1974. Wearing a mink coat, Bess Meyerson—the first Jewish Miss America, in 1945, who served as the consumer affairs commissioner in the Lindsay administration—was the mistress of ceremonies. The newly minted mayor, Beame, sixty-eight, a former city budget manager and comptroller, offered an understated speech, asserting that he wanted New Yorkers to believe in their city again. Goldin, thirty-six, a former state senator, was dramatic. He reached his arms toward the sky.[31]

Many New Yorkers watching the ceremony were no doubt dubious, however, perceiving city hall as indifferent to neighborhood-centered concerns, whether due to the delayed snow-plowing in the "outer boroughs" after a paralyzing February 1969 storm or the spread of graffiti, robberies, and shootings.

Under the day's overcast skies, O'Dwyer offered the audience a poetically seasoned ode to unsung heroes.

"Always in New York, in all of the lives that have been lived, or will be lived, always there will be a man swinging on a rope through the flames in the sky in order to save the lives of six people," he declared. "Always there will be a woman in a musty meeting hall suffering insults through a night as she pleads the unpopular cause of the afflicted and the helpless and the powerless."[32]

In accordance with public expectations, this was the new mayor's signature moment to introduce himself. He had failed to achieve a 40 percent plurality against Herman Badillo of the Bronx in the Democratic primary but overwhelmingly won a runoff and easily defeated the Republican John Marchi. A stalwart, five-foot-two friend of labor and organization man, Beame could have been mistaken for the owner of a corner deli and was stylistically almost the opposite of the more dashing, six-foot-four John Lindsay, who preceded him.

Born in London to Polish Jewish refugees who had fled Warsaw, Beame was raised on the Lower East Side of New York and cultivated by the same powerful Brooklyn Democratic clubhouse that had supported Bill O'Dwyer to magistrate and district attorney when it was led by Frank Kelly (the boss John McCooey's successor after his death in 1934): the Madison Club. Beame began his gradual climb gathering petition signatures door-to-door for candidates in service to the Brooklyn Democratic leader and state assemblyman Irwin Steingut. When Beame reached the pinnacle of city power, he was a decade and a half Lindsay's senior and a graduate of City College, while Lindsay, a WASP, had gone to Yale.

Beame's aspirations for the mayoralty appeared to go no further than to display financial competency. His campaign motto was simple: "He knows the buck." Lindsay, in contrast, had striven to address racial inequality and urban poverty writ large and grew to be distracted by his presidential ambitions.

During his rocky second term as mayor, Lindsay switched from Republican to Democrat and ran for president, failing miserably in short order. Hooted at by critics from both parties who blamed the city's problems on his liberalism, Lindsay evoked Paul's sympathy, laid out in a five-page personal letter written in February 1973. O'Dwyer's note to the then mayor centered on the experiences of his older brother when he had faced the choice of running for reelection or not. He referred to Bill's decision to run for a second term. "Disastrously," Paul wrote, Bill had listened to the then Democratic boss Edward Flynn of the Bronx and to the Brooklyn borough president John Cashmore when they both told him that they were getting too old to mount a lesser-known replacement candidate in the 1949 primary (Flynn would die in 1953, Cashmore in 1961). But the party leaders forgot the favor Bill paid them not long after he coasted on his popularity to a new term, the letter read.

"Prosecutors, seasoned and novices, will seek to use your betrayers as accusers and will not hesitate to create corroborating testimony," O'Dwyer warned Lindsay. "The writer has had the experience of witnessing the very butler of Gracie Mansion threatened with a jail sentence if he did not supply manufactured testimony."

A city leader, then, had to appreciate when it was time to exit from center stage.

"I truly hate to write to you along these lines," O'Dwyer continued, "but I saw it all personally. I witnessed a gentle, decent, cultured and sensitive human being undermined and torn to tatters, because one day in Gracie Mansion he made the wrong decision. Along in the fray he was wounded and the wolves who formed part of the pack found their lust could not be contained. It took my own skills and energies to save him from complete disaster."[33]

The advice struck a tone of concern and sincerity, but Paul risked being ignored as he had not been a consistent Lindsay supporter. In 1967, Lindsay had dismissed O'Dwyer as his special counsel to the Board of Estimate when Paul filed a lawsuit against city hall and the mayor on behalf of transit workers to preserve bus and subway funding in a show of independence Lindsay found grating. Nor had O'Dwyer supported Lindsay's presidential campaign (when the mayor had faced continual heckling from Forest Hills residents upset about a low-income housing development planned for the middle-class neighborhood). And Paul had not endorsed Lindsay for president but rather Brooklyn's US Rep. Shirley Chisholm, the first African American woman ever to serve in Congress. At that time, many allies from the McCarthy-for-President campaign of 1968 were coalescing around the anti-Vietnam war senator George McGovern of South Dakota. But Paul was upset that McGovern failed to support even a watered-down version of a congressional resolution that criticized British security policies in Northern Ireland. (One press release issued by Paul's American Committee for Ulster Justice [ACUJ] expressed his pique, beginning, "No matter how bellicose senator George McGovern has been about world conditions, this would-be President has lost his tongue when it comes to wholesale slaughter, prison torture, and the internment-without-trial policy of the British in Northern Ireland.") McGovern exhibited not merely overcommitment to a longtime US diplomatic ally but "duplicity," he fumed.[34]

In the end, Lindsay followed the advice, whether consciously or not, exiting center stage at the close of his second term, "an exile in his own city" in one journalist's words.[35]

On January 7, 1974, O'Dwyer sounded just as sincere in wishing Bcamc well while making his first appearance before the city's legislative body as its president. But he also used the occasion to underscore "the loss of 270,000 manufacturing jobs here in the last several years" and the "annual drain on the city treasury of over $1 billion." He ended by asking darkly, "At what point does this bloodletting stop?"[36]

In November of that economically uncertain year, the liberal Brooklyn congressman Hugh Carey won the race for governor, celebrating to Franklin D. Roosevelt's official campaign song, "Happy Days Are Here Again." Ironically, two months later—exactly one year after Paul's opening council address—Carey delivered his first State of the State speech amid an unprecedented state financial debacle, the looming collapse of the state Urban Development Corporation, a Rockefeller creation dating from better times. "Now the times of plenty, the days of wine and roses, are over," the Democratic governor pronounced in the televised address.[37]

City hall's appreciation of Carey's somber assessment and warning was yet to materialize, except inside the forty-story Manhattan Municipal Building. There, an astute member of Goldin's staff detected a disjuncture between the city government's incoming tax revenues and outflowing operating costs as a seismologist foretells an earthquake. The budget analyst, Steve Clifford, came to work each morning wearing a dashiki and pulling on a cigarette. Poring over the city's past and present balance sheets in the early months of 1974, he noticed successive years of dubious accounting methods and increasingly heavy reliance on high-interest short-term loans as well as long-term capital bonds, typically reserved for construction and repair costs, to pay the city's monthly operating bills.

In the middle of a national recession that had been triggered by the 1973 Arab oil embargo, Clifford pointed out to his colleagues in the comptroller's office, neither Albany nor Washington was likely to increase aid to the city, though the New York metro area generated far more federal tax revenue than any other region of the country. The analyst typed a memo to Goldin. "I see no alternative to the city's fiscal problem," he wrote, "other than a painful recognition that we are seriously overcommitted."

He banged out a follow-up memo to Roy Goodman, a Republican state senator on the East Side, concluding impiously, "This city is fucked." He titled the missive "The Fiscal Crisis."[38]

––––––––

O'DWYER, LIKE MOST PEOPLE, was not aware of the full scope and gravity of the city's cash crunch when, toward the end of 1974, he sponsored a bill that was distant from budgetary concerns, proposing to roll back the city founding date pressed on the city seal. Thinking 350 years into the past, he argued that "1625" would be a more accurate reflection of when Dutch settlers came ashore than the inscribed "1664."

But Paul's perhaps myopic desire to strip from the British the distinction of having founded New York was not hard to miss. For him, the change would mark a fitting riposte to more than three centuries of Anglophilia in many quarters, notwithstanding the years of the American Revolution or even *Common Sense*, the Tom Paine bestseller and Paul O'Dwyer's secular bible, which had galvanized public support to break with the English Crown.

The mayor was not as eager to offend the Brits. One of the internal memos for the English-born Beame cast doubt on 1625 as the city's inaugural year, noting that "the city actually became a legal Dutch entity in 1624, when a Dutch charter was given to that effect." Still, Beame decided this was not a battle worth mustering against.[39]

O'Dwyer took no small delight when the British home secretary, Roy Jenkins, stopped at city hall in early January 1975 during a ten-day visit to the United States and was told the municipal insignia, designed in 1914, was to be modified.

"Oh really," Jenkins replied, betraying no perturbation. "You've moved it back a bit."[40]

Yet given all the hints of perilous budgetary shortfalls circulating at city hall and the more palpable signs of decay (the collapse of a section of the forty-three-year-old West Side Highway less than two years before had seemed to symbolize to all a downward-spiraling state of affairs that had hardly been reversed), the council president's focus on amending the historical record was tangential, if not even gratuitous. So did it seem to Deputy Mayor Stanley Friedman the day he agreed to meet with John McGettrick just outside city hall. Paul's aide let the deputy mayor know the reason: the bill to amend the founding date on the city seal was making its way to introduction in the council. It was raining, McGettrick recalled, but the outdoor venue for the private conversation had been Friedman's choice. He was worried that the special prosecutor Maurice Nadjari might be bugging his office.

"*This* is what you wanted to talk about?" Friedman asked McGettrick incredulously.[41] (Friedman did not recall this conversation but said he eventually supported the city seal amendment out of deference to O'Dwyer.)[42]

As initial signs of the fiscal crisis percolated, O'Dwyer also brought to the council another one of his life's passions—defending the First Amendment rights of those with unpopular views. In late May 1975, he sponsored a trio of bills that would have restricted the police department's intelligence division. The Red Squad, as it was known colloquially to critics, was found to have maintained photographs, recorded conversations, personal histories, and a list of associations of radicals and activists, identifying the names of 240,000 suspect New Yorkers on as many index cards. "There can't possibly be 240,000 subversives," Franklin Siegel recalled O'Dwyer explaining. Recruited by Paul to work as a clerk at his law firm in 1971 after he graduated from New York University and from many an anti-war rally as well, Siegel drafted the legislation.[43]

The secret intelligence office was not the first of its kind in a police department that had associated radicalism with the potential for violence since at least 1904, when it established an "Italian Squad" at the height of Italian immigration to New York. The new incarnation came to light as a result of a raid and the arrest of nineteen male and two female members of the newly formed branch of the Black Panther Party in April 1969, and their lengthy trial before Judge John Murtagh on charges of planning to attack two police stations and a city education office with bombs and long-range rifles. The Panthers were represented by Gerald Lefcourt, a lawyer known for his defense of political radicals. But during the proceedings, the defendant Afeni Shakur, who was pregnant with the future rapper Tupac Shakur, cross-examined a prosecution witness and brought out that police undercover agents organized most of the unlawful activities at the heart of the lengthy trial.

Thirteen of those tried won acquittal of all charges in May 1971. In the aftermath of the Panthers' legal triumph, local civil liberties groups sued to enjoin the NYPD from conducting any noncriminal investigations of First Amendment–protected activities, such as rallies and meetings, where infiltration by undercover informants was not unusual. Plaintiffs in the class action suit were represented by a legal team that later came to include Franklin Siegel, and the lawsuit ended with the city law department signing a federal consent decree in 1985. The "Handschu agreement" included the appointment of a civilian overseer. Under the settlement, police investigations of political activities remained regulated until the 2001 terrorist attack against the World Trade Center, when Arabic-speaking immigrants' homes, community-based service organizations, and mosques drew intense scrutiny from the FBI, the federal immigration service, and the police.

O'Dwyer's recommendations for changes in police practices made other council members squeamish, both in this case and when he later suggested a residency requirement for future police recruits and subpoena power for his new city ombudsman's unit. The majority of the body viewed the Red Squad bills as akin to a poison pill. After hearings in late September by the council's Public Safety Committee, the proposals were shelved.[44]

In the background of the debate about police intelligence-gathering was the recently concluded Watergate bugging scandal and Nixon's resignation. Public concern about government lies and misuse of authority grew, too, fueled when a congressional committee chaired by the Idaho Democratic senator Frank Church exposed intelligence service abuses, among them covert assassinations of foreign leaders (the "Family Jewels" program), human experimentation involving mind control (MK-ULTRA), and infiltration of anti-war and civil rights groups (COINTELPRO) such as the Panthers, whose Illinois chapter leader, Fred Hampton, was killed in his sleep in a state attorney's office predawn raid in December 1969, planned with police and the FBI. Civil liberties lawyers at the same time were challenging police intelligence units similar to New York's in Detroit, Chicago, and LA, all of which seemed to intensify their surveillance activities as the FBI drew back.[45]

———

BY THE SECOND HALF OF 1975, it was difficult for local elected officials to focus on much of anything except the city's deepening revenue shortfalls. The cash problems exploded with the force of ordnance when national banks largely headquartered in Manhattan stopped buying or selling the city's tax-exempt debt notes in the municipal bond market.

Beame, indignant, demanded that the bankers reverse course. They refused, citing concerns about municipal red ink, although none of them had publicly questioned the city's budgetary priorities and practices before, with bond underwriting a profitable staple. Backing the mayor's objections, as many as ten thousand municipal union members picketed outside First National City Bank, whose senior executive Walter Wriston was leading what was comparable to a strike of sorts by the banks against city hall, replete with demands for deep cutbacks on behalf of bond investors.

The city's debts since former Mayor Wagner's time climbed to levels that were no longer supportable; they were greater than that of any other city in the United States by a long shot. Ever more loans became necessary just to repay the holders of the maturing ones. Even with unorthodox use of capital funds reserved for construction projects, like Water Tunnel No. 3, the city government did not have enough money to pay routine costs, whether for salaries, road repair, or keeping the lights on in municipal buildings.

Landlords were abandoning buildings all over town, and, with the middle class still decamping and local tax revenue falling, the mayor in October 1975 readied a filing for bankruptcy that would place the city's administration in the hands of a federal judge as debts were reorganized and the city's estimated 160,000 individual and institutional creditors compensated.[46] But the city was saved from these uncharted waters with just a few hours to spare when Albert Shanker, president of the teachers' union, agreed to invest millions of dollars from the union pension fund in Municipal Assistance Corporation (MAC) bonds backed by uncertain city revenues and issued by the state (the innovation of Felix Rohatyn, Carey's Wall Street adviser). Shanker feared the alternative, a bankruptcy proceeding of uncertain scope and duration, and that the union's wage and benefits contract—and retired teachers' pensions—might not survive it. The investment provided the needed stopgap revenue to keep the city at least temporarily in business.

Governor Carey and legislative leaders in both parties pushed through hundreds of millions of dollars in state aid for the city as well as the creation of an Emergency Financial Control Board (EFCB), and the EFCB began meeting in September, a month before Shanker's last-minute concession, in a windowless room in the rear of Carey's midtown office. Dominated by corporate executives and state officials, the board rode herd on

Mayor Beame to slash an eventual 69,672 workers from the 330,000-person municipal payroll and to close firehouses, dental and medical clinics, day care facilities, and public school programs. Despite Beame's attempts to evade the bludgeon, there ensued a subway and bus fare increase (to fifty cents, from thirty-five) to help the city cover its share of transit costs and a 25 percent increase in the city income tax levy. The long tradition of free tuition at the City University of New York, dating back to the 1847 founding of City College, would end. Streets became dirtier. Parks, playgrounds, subways, hospitals, and libraries grew frayed. Fear of crime, from robberies to shootings, rose.[47]

By pressing Beame for ever more draconian cuts in city services that everyday New Yorkers relied on, the Carey administration sought to show a recalcitrant Gerald Ford and Congress that New York City was capable of plugging up its own fiscal gaps and worthy of emergency assistance such as Treasury loans to help it avert a bankruptcy. While the Republican president had pardoned Nixon for misfeasance despite evidence produced in impeachment proceedings and Oval Office tape recordings, he recoiled from helping a liberal Democratic city suffering from what he termed "profligacy." His evidence of what he charged was a bloated public sector centered on the city's expansive city-run hospital system, its tuition-free colleges, and the nearly 1.2 million people on welfare. Ford and his advisers, Donald Rumsfeld, Alan Greenspan, and William Simon, acted to teach the social democratic city a lesson in the values of prudence and honest accounting the president recalled having learned as a boy in Grand Rapids, Michigan (population 138,000 at the time). He and his advisers ignored the larger causes of New York's spewing red ink that were not of its own doing: the disassembling of the urban manufacturing-based economy, the exodus of jobs to poorer states and countries, and the federally underwritten construction of expressways to the one-family homes and green lawns of suburbia.[48] That New York was the historic port of call for the most oppressed and impoverished, whether from Mayo or Mississippi, also went unmentioned by the Ford team.

"I can tell you, and tell you now," the president declared on October 29 at Washington's National Press Club, delivering his most definitive admonishment on the subject, "that I am prepared to veto any bill that has as its purpose a bailout of New York City to prevent a default." Ford's pronouncement was greeted with an instantly famous front-page headline, summarizing in 144-point type his resistance to helping the troubled metropolis ride out the storm: "FORD TO CITY: DROP DEAD."[49]

The president's stance eased soon enough, however, when several foreign leaders warned of international monetary shockwaves should America's capital city be financially kaput. In November, the president came out for seasonal Treasury loans totaling $2.3 billion at 1 percent higher than the market rate of interest.[50]

Throughout this white-knuckle period, O'Dwyer was among a handful of city officials willing to consider the possibility that a bankruptcy court might be fairer than the Wall Street–influenced EFCB to working-class, poor, and minority communities dependent on city services.

While the gubernatorially appointed control board included not just corporate leaders and state officials but also the mayor and the city comptroller, Beame resented losing control over the annual $13 billion annual city budget. While forced to remove his budget director and friend, James Cavanagh, he himself held onto his job: the bank executives stopped short of insisting that Carey give them Beame's scalp. It had been left to Carey, who like any governor did not want direct political responsibility for the troubles of the city, to tell the bankers and corporate leaders that Beame's successor would have been none other than Paul O'Dwyer, "the most wild, unpredictable, loosely organized liberal in history."[51] He was next in line, under the city charter.

In fact, the city's succession rules under the city charter had already been brought home to O'Dwyer and his staff after a police helicopter ferrying Beame in a rainstorm made an emergency landing in the Upper Bay just off the South Brooklyn shore in June 1974. The council leaders' staff hastened to prepare for a possible changing-of-the-guard until hearing from police that Beame was not injured, only shaken up.[52]

On the night of an EFCB meeting in the basement of Gracie Mansion, O'Dwyer stood close by Beame, then the subject of published reports that his ouster was imminent, with Ford at the time still opposing giving aid to the city outside of ensuring the continuation of "essential services" for its 7.5 million residents. Paul told the mayor not to be too concerned for his own job. The bankers, O'Dwyer said, would not allow someone like himself, with left-wing ideological credentials, to replace him.

"Abe, don't worry. As long as I'm alive, I'm your insurance," O'Dwyer assured Beame.[53]

He then turned to face his assistant, McGettrick.

"You get back in there," the $40,000-a-year council president scolded, referring to the basement EFCB meeting under way. "Nobody ever elected *them*!"[54]

———

WHEN FACED WITH THE state control board's demands for tax hikes and service cuts, O'Dwyer sought an alternative to turning away from the decades of urban liberalism in which he had participated, a period in which city hall, beginning in the modern era with Mayor La Guardia, had directed funds without apology toward services for the working and middle classes and the more disadvantaged. For example, he asked the Carey administration and state legislative leaders to require the national banks and insurance companies to buy the city's tax-exempt notes. Unlikely to pass muster in the courts, however, Paul's suggestion fell upon deaf ears. But in his letter, which was also signed by the borough presidents Percy Sutton of Manhattan and Robert Abrams of the Bronx, O'Dwyer framed an insistently democratic, human-scale, unionist, and neighborhood-level outlook, saying the city's and state's popularly elected leaders should not depend on "the whim of distant investors. . . . We must act like a government, not a beggar in search of funds."[55]

Like Beame himself, O'Dwyer knew he had been sidelined and saw little point (unlike the mayor) in pretending otherwise. While the mayor came around to accepting more of a business mindset for the government as demanded by the EFCB, one in which lowering corporate taxes and providing tax abatements for upscale developments were to be guiding principles and priorities, O'Dwyer sought alternatives to the recasting of decades of urban liberalism. Though he had served on the board of directors of a savings and loan association in the late 1950s, his concerns were largely dismissed. But he raised a valid concern about Donald Trump's proposal to convert the sixty-year-old Commodore Hotel on East Forty-Second Street into a pricier lodging destination: Would it generate a windfall for the brash young developer at the expense of the public? The financially strapped owner Penn Central's decision to close the Commodore after losing $1 million a year on its operation created a dilemma that Donald, and his father, Fred, used to come away in the end with an unprecedented forty-year exemption from local property taxes that was valued at $160 million. The Trump Organization had the support of trade unions, attracted by an anticipated 1,500 construction jobs. Ultimately, even a reluctant O'Dwyer, struck by the prospect of the Commodore standing vacant "in one of the busiest intersections in the city," went along with the rest of the Board of Estimate. He joined Sutton and the other members in approving the hefty tax abatement in May 1976, over the objections of Harlem US Rep. Charles Rangel and Manhattan council members Henry Stern and Bobby Wagner Jr. (the ex-mayor's son), who considered it too high, given the city's widespread deterioration. The new Grand Hyatt eventually rose at Grand Central Station, but not without at least one thing O'Dwyer and others on the board had required: developer-funded improvements to the nearby subway station.[56]

O'Dwyer continued, however, to advocate for city funds to be prioritized to support construction of hospital rooms over hotel rooms, better schoolhouses, and attention to poor- and middle-class people over wealthy ones, especially given the brutal recession and intensifying social protest over fiscal crisis cuts. But even as he resisted sweeping state-imposed layoffs and many other austerities, he felt powerful countervailing pressures. "I was advised that it would be in my own interest to take a more conciliatory stance," O'Dwyer recalled in his 1979 memoir, Counsel for the Defense. He saw little choice except to accede to "servitude" to corporate-style prerogatives, the governor's severe bottom line, and the EFCB's crude blade. When the fiscal crisis kettle blew with a vengeance in 1975, the socially democratic policies preferred by Paul were ruled immaterial by suddenly empowered financial professionals who, as the historian Kim Phillips-Fein put it, trotted out a new "language of technocratic, neutral questions about responsibility and the inevitability of the need for retrenchment in the provision of scarce resources."[57]

The marginalized council president had better luck shepherding through city council an idea from Lew Rudin to allow major property owners such as Rudin to pay their real estate taxes in advance of the due date. Rudin's civic-minded gesture won approval. But Paul's proposal for the Board of Estimate to prohibit the risking of employee pension funds to purchase additional MAC ("Big Mac") bonds on behalf of the teetering city government was ignored. To help the city pay its bills, union leaders had already agreed to the pleadings of the governor to purchase the special bonds with their members' nest eggs.[58]

————

PAUL STARTED LOOKING around to make his own exit and in June 1976, a year and a half before the end of his four-year council term, gained the state Democratic Party nod to challenge Conservative James Buckley for his Senate seat. The state party boss Joseph Crangle of Buffalo also cleared a path for Paul's fellow left-wingers Ramsey Clark and Bella Abzug to run as well in the Senate primary. Crangle's machinations were meant ultimately to help Daniel Patrick Moynihan, who later entered the race at the behest of Crangle and supporters of presidential candidate Senator Henry Jackson from the state of Washington. Moynihan stood out as a centrist, less radical than his three main Senate rivals (with Manhattan parking-garage-builder Abe Hirschfeld also running), and went on to win the September primary by the narrowest of margins. A former US ambassador to India and to the United Nations, Moynihan received 36 percent of the votes compared to 35 percent for Abzug, allowing him to square off against Buckley, running on the Republican and Conservative lines.

Clark and O'Dwyer, both of whom had little hope of ever drawing the spotlight from the more combative leading rivals, Moynihan and Abzug (or "Pat vs. the Hat"), received 10.28 and 9.02 percent, respectively, while Hirschfeld (who gained a campaign event visit from Menachem Begin while Paul didn't, very much to Paul's disappointment) got the remainder.[59]

Moynihan defeated Buckley that November.

From early in the summer, Paul's candidacy had puzzled friends and even his son Brian, not only because he was a long shot but also because of the extent to which his positions mirrored those of the more prominent Abzug. Both Paul and Abzug had long-standing ties to the National Lawyers Guild and the cause of civil rights. Both were opposed to a planned West Side Highway, or Westway (which Governor Carey supported); opponents argued that it would divert federal funds from the transit system. Having each protested the recently concluded Vietnam War and called for Nixon's impeachment (Abzug as a House at-large whip and O'Dwyer as city council president), the two additionally spoke to the democratic aspirations of postcolonial nations from Africa to South

America, as well as, of course, Israel. The huge Pentagon budget was still another shared focus of concern and complaint.

Based on the collegiality he accorded politicians in both parties in New York, Paul was perhaps more apt than Abzug to cultivate the Democratic leadership in Washington if elected to Congress—not because he was any more compromising, but he was typically less bruising in pursuit of legislative goals. But neither O'Dwyer nor Abzug had any patience for Moynihan's centrist, even conservative, politics. Moynihan was something of a reconstructed New Dealer, what the Abzug campaign aide Doug Ireland tagged as a "Tokyo Rose for Nixon and Ford." As an official in the Johnson administration, Moynihan in 1965 wrote a report on the family structure of the African American community in America, saying it suffered not only from harshly discriminatory policies arising from "the racist virus in the American bloodstream" but also from a "tangle of pathology" that dated from enslavement. Headlines over the latter phrase in particular touched off a firestorm. Later, working for President Nixon—an automatic mark against him for many on the left—he wrote a 1970 memo (leaked to the press and sparking another public outcry) that argued that "the issue of race could benefit from a period of benign neglect." (Moynihan convinced Nixon, but not Congress, of the need for a guaranteed minimum income for the poorest Americans.) His subsequent articles in *Commentary* and other "neoconservative" publications suggested, to the dismay of civil rights advocates like Paul and Abzug, that affirmative action on behalf of minorities went too far. Moynihan's positions on foreign affairs were no less distasteful to the left-leaning Democrats. As the UN ambassador in 1975–76, he said the United States needed to reassert itself in the "Third World" in the wake of its defeat in Vietnam. But many New York Jews took admiring notice when he denounced a General Assembly resolution, passed with the support of the Soviet bloc in November 1975, that asserted that "Zionism is a form of racism."

With his tweed cap, liberal iconoclasm, and expressions of humorous relief after losing a 1965 primary bid for city council president, Moynihan could not have contrasted more sharply with the fellow Irish American who was council president during the Senate primary of eleven years later. While Paul, unlike Bill, had made no attempt to soften the lingering traces of his native brogue, it was impossible to tell Moynihan's New York working-class roots, or that he had ever been a Hell's Kitchen child turned youthful longshoreman. Moynihan could have passed as a colorful don at Oxford. His background as a Harvard professor and Fulbright scholar at the London School of Economics only heightened the impression.

Paul and Bella also clashed. "Paul was motivated by the fact that, on some level, he didn't think a woman should be in the Senate, and he did not like Bella," contended Harold Holzer, who was Abzug's press spokesman in Congress.[60]

It was a view held by more than a few in the Abzug camp because Paul remained in the race with little apparent chance of winning, and perhaps, too, because he came up in an era when politics, and the law, was virtually an all-male sport. While he may have viewed the women's movement as less central than Abzug did, and as less important than the American civil rights movement, he had been one of the earliest adherents of New York City's Democratic Reform movement, whose significant female leadership broke ground in politics for women. In any case, O'Dwyer, as a left-wing male challenging the left-wing Abzug, who had a much better chance of defeating Moynihan, remained in a poor position to refute the contention that his campaign stood in the way of diversifying what Abzug had called the "stag" US Senate, and of the driven and forceful feminist and House leader herself.

Abzug campaign surrogates asked Paul's legal colleague Ramsey Clark to drop out, lest his presence on the primary ballot enable Moynihan to prevail. Abzug's allies Ronnie Eldridge and Richard Aurelio sat down with Clark's campaign manager Mark Green for breakfast at the Warwick Hotel on West Fifty-Fourth Street in Manhattan and made the case. It was of no use: Clark (who accepted contributions no larger than $100, an original statement on the need for campaign finance reform) refused to quit the race. O'Dwyer was no different.[61] The left-wing attorneys had not entered for the fun of it, and, though their financial contributions lagged behind Abzug's and Moynihan's, even from Big Labor, they no doubt entertained thoughts of pulling a rabbit out of the hat. During a five-way debate, many substantive issues that traditionally concerned liberal Democrats were eclipsed by whether Moynihan was or was not a "true Democrat" (he was), or whether Abzug was or was not a supporter of the sale of F-4 Phantom jets to Israel (she was). Housing, crime, the subways, drug addiction, and the city's uniquely heavy cost-share burden for welfare assistance stood little chance of sustained discussion as the primary election neared. Paul contended that Moynihan and Abzug, by feuding over their respective records, were "wrecking the party" and leaving "scar tissue all over the place."[62]

Abzug lost the party primary in a squeaker to Moynihan, 329,830 to 317,348.

In the aftermath, many Abzug supporters, including quite a few women's activists, were furious with both Clark and O'Dwyer. The two had been no help, certainly. But as some others accurately noted, her campaign had suffered a self-inflicted wound when she answered a routine question at a Dutchess County weekend fair by suggesting that she might not be willing to support Moynihan if he won the primary. The report of her comment was seized upon by Crangle since it buttressed the charges, however sexist, that Abzug was too abrasive and egotistical to finesse a bill through the Senate.[63]

But Abzug's chances were damaged even more when, in service to Pat Moynihan, the *New York Times* publisher Arthur Sulzberger overrode the editorial-page editor John Oakes's decision not to take sides in the primary, and Moynihan landed the paper of record's crucial support. (Oakes—who, like a majority of the editorial board, actually *favored* Abzug—was left to write a letter to the editor voicing disagreement with the endorsement.) Moynihan went on to win not only the primary but also the election and a total of four terms.

Although O'Dwyer could never abide the New York senator's anti-IRA stance, Moynihan never quite fulfilled the worst fears of left-leaning detractors nor the fondest hopes of neoconservative supporters. By the mid-1980s, Moynihan's opposition to Reagan-era policies on government secrecy, to meddling in Central American politics, and to cuts to American social programs for the poor were close to Paul's own views, while more difficult for the administration to dismiss since the senator's ideologies were harder to label.

O'Dwyer attempted to patch things up with Abzug, who, after all, had come to the aid of the Irish American Fort Worth Five in Congress, citing what she called abuses of the federal grand jury process. He phoned her to express his regrets over her narrow defeat and even the extent to which he may have contributed to it, but Abzug would not speak with him. It was unclear how far Paul might have gone in apologizing to her after her loss, given that Abzug could be faulted for the same criticism she had leveled against him. (After being gerrymandered out of her House seat in 1972, Abzug had remained in Congress only by running against the ailing fellow Reform Democrat William Fitts Ryan in a primary, then fending off a challenge that fall by Ryan's widow Priscilla on the Liberal Party line.) In

Gender Gap: Bella Abzug's Guide to Political Power for American Women,
her 1984 book, Bella merely confirmed that she did not forgive O'Dwyer
for remaining in the race against Moynihan and, along with Ramsey
Clark, funneling away potentially decisive votes.[64]

Paul, who would not run for Congress again, returned to a straitened
city hall.

———

AS IF THE FISCAL CRISIS were not bad enough, a psychotic killer known
as the Son of Sam was soon haunting young couples and lovers' lanes
with a .44-caliber gun and writing rambling letters about it to Jimmy Breslin at the *Daily News*. While he was still at large, the entire city was
plunged into darkness shortly after 9:30 p.m. on July 13, 1977, the result
of lightning striking power lines north of the city.

The blackout sparked widespread vandalism and looting just a year
after Beame had welcomed tall ships to the harbor for New York's American Bicentennial celebrations. Meanwhile, O'Dwyer had himself greeted
one hundred historians at city hall for a forum on the pertinence of Paine's
revolutionary *Common Sense* and, standing in for Beame at Bowling
Green, gave an Independence Day speech linking lyrics in the Marines'
Hymn—"From the halls of Montezuma . . ."—to the US annexation of
Texas and the Mexican-American War, an unscripted jeremiad against US
imperialism that was "received grimly, shall we say," by the approximately
fifteen military brass in bars and stars listening, according to John Mc-
Gettrick. The next month, at the Democratic National Convention at
Madison Square Garden, Mayor Beame's endorsement of Georgia Governor Jimmy Carter was also received grimly, including by leading New
York Democrats. But as the first leading elected official in the state to endorse Carter, Beame's gesture was not forgotten when New York leaders
revisited Washington after his departure from office. They wrangled from
the Carter White House approval of Treasury guarantees—or collateral—
for necessary city borrowing in the municipal bond market.

When the city's lights went out in the middle of a heat wave and subways and elevators stalled, trapping riders, the Beame administration
seemed to be no longer turning a corner but again floundering. Hospital
staff scrambled to activate backup generators. A Cubs-Mets game at
Shea Stadium was suspended with three innings to go. Baseball fans and

nonfans alike would long remember what they were doing and where they were at the time New York was inexplicably plunged into this episode of helplessness and imperilment.

Before city officials fully realized it, vandalism and looting erupted in poor neighborhoods (numbering more than thirty in all), as well as some of the wealthy ones. People poured into the streets, smashing store windows and carting off color TVs, furniture, armfuls of clothing, air conditioners, and cartons of beer. Many others who had not planned to loot yielded to the temptation. Cops, whether because of low morale over the fiscal crisis layoffs of five thousand of their number in the summer of '75 or sheer fear of confronting frenzied looters, acted as if they never heard Commissioner Michael Codd's activation of *all* available police personnel from his home in Elmhurst, Queens.[65]

The police who did respond to the emergency directive—ten thousand of the city's twenty-five thousand total officers—were ordered not to deploy their revolvers except to protect their own lives. "The weapon," Codd directed, "is to be used for self-defense only."[66]

The sometimes celebratory mania arising from the deprivations of the ghetto subsided in the gauzy dawn without a single policeman using his gun. Beame spoke before the press at noon, blasting the energy company Consolidated Edison's performance. In the late afternoon, one hundred community leaders gathered in the Blue Room in the west wing of city hall at the mayor's request. Many said they feared a resumption of disorder after nightfall. "There was a lot of sentiment for calling in the National Guard," O'Dwyer told a reporter immediately afterward. "Somebody called for a show of hands on whether to recommend a call-up."[67]

A majority of those present, Paul among them, opposed sending in the Guard as New Jersey's Governor Hughes had done in response to the Newark riots. The council leader even raised the specter of another Kent State University tragedy, the May 1970 fatal shooting of four nonviolent campus anti-war demonstrators and wounding of nine others by the Ohio National Guard. But Beame gave everyone a chance to express themselves and, according to Paul, a "common objective" emerged despite "inflammatory statements . . . on both sides." The goal of addressing the systemic causes of disorder included calls to improve police-community relations and to create recreational spaces, after-school programs, and job opportunities for disaffected teenagers, though the city was cutting and deferring public services of all kinds to pay back bondholders.[68]

Beame and Carey spoke to each other by phone after 4 p.m., with the mayor voicing concern that the looting in the powerless city would resume at nightfall and that "we might be running out of police strength." Members of O'Dwyer's staff, meanwhile, urged him strongly to hold a press conference to discourage a National Guard call-up, but Paul refused, saying it would impinge upon the mayor in a moment of crisis.[69] Governor Carey, on the phone with Beame, said mustering some thousand National Guardsmen would take eight to ten days and that he was unnerved by the prospect of "kids in uniform" rolling into unfamiliar poor neighborhoods with their rifles and bayonets at the ready.

In the end, only state troopers were provided, to help wave traffic through streets. The National Guard was held back just in case police and fireman resources ran too low, which did not occur.[70]

Power was restored at 10:39 p.m. on July 14, revealing more than 3,777 people in custody, virtually all of them Black or Latino and male— the largest mass arrest in the city's history, dwarfing even the 373 arrested in the Harlem disturbances that followed the 1964 killing of James Powell by an off-duty police officer, and the 465 detained after the Reverend King's assassination. The city reopened the decaying Manhattan House of Detention, the impermeable Tombs, to accommodate them. In total, 1,037 fires had been set during the episode and 1,616 stores were robbed and damaged, including a car lot where Pontiacs went missing.[71]

Despite the general consensus among the clergy and community advocates gathered by Beame that programs to address the roots of poverty and disorder were needed, public dismay crested in the blackout's aftermath. The *Daily News* letter pages included readers' reminders that a 1965 outage of similar proportions had brought neither looting nor arson. Discrimination was just as bad then, but, especially for those now discerning a generalized breakdown in morality, *something* was different. Some blamed so-called liberal permissiveness of disorder and others runaway materialism. None of the letter writers pointed to severe fiscal austerities as a possible culprit, nor racial inequities, nor even the diversion of tens of billions of dollars from butter to bombs during the Vietnam War.

"I have just one suggestion," a reader fulminated. "Bring back police brutality."[72]

———

IN SPITE OF THE ATMOSPHERE of racially tinged anger, O'Dwyer decided to run for reelection to his city council post.

Exhibit A was what he viewed as his signature accomplishment—approval of the city ombudsman's unit within his office. Based on similar programs in Scandinavia, the unit processed twelve thousand complaints in its first seven months of existence, in 1977, restoring heat to a Bronx apartment building after ten freezing nights, a retiree's Medicare payments, and the wages of a home attendant who faced eviction, Paul noted. His unit also sought to troubleshoot managerial problems at city agencies, once threatening to sue the housing department over a rat infestation in a public housing development. The ombudsman became the precursor of the city's public advocate position. A later holder of that office, Mark Green, would describe O'Dwyer as a "great people's advocate" who "saw the window of opportunity and moved swiftly through it"—including fending off accusations by the state senator Roy Goodman that he was setting up "an elaborate bureaucracy" not anticipated by those who elected him.[73]

As summer's shadows lengthened, O'Dwyer also spoke of pushing through a council bill that supported voting-by-mail and resulted in enactment by the state legislature. The measure encouraged or allowed more people to vote—sixty thousand more in all. He also negotiated full compensation for the family survivors of city teachers who unfairly lost their jobs and pensions under a repressive, since-nullified state statute in the McCarthy era (i.e., the "Feinberg Law"). And he orchestrated support to save Sailors' Snug Harbor, a home for retired seamen that O'Dwyer referred to as "Medicare before Medicare." The Staten Island facility was converted to a city-supported nonprofit cultural center as the few remaining residents, physically declining older men in want of a pension or adequate health insurance, moved to nursing homes for more intensive caretaking or passed away.[74]

Kitty Carlisle Hart, a philanthropist and actress known for her frequent guest appearances on the popular TV program *To Tell the Truth* who, as it happened, had been a supporter of Abzug for the Senate, approached O'Dwyer at a public event announcing city funding for the center. She was "gushing" over his speech retracing the history of the home and some of its saltier denizens, recalled Callaghan.

As was his wont, Paul endeavored to tell the truth.

"Thank *him*," he remarked, gesturing with his thumb toward the lanky Callaghan. "He wrote it."[75]

———

BUT SIGNIFICANT CREDIT for rescuing a much better-known New York entity, the Tweed Courthouse, redounded to O'Dwyer.

The brooding landmark of City Hall Park owes its unfortunate nickname to William Marcy Tweed, the Tammany boss who spared no expense or opportunity for self-enrichment during its mid-nineteenth-century construction. Little used, the building was in an advanced state of disrepair in 1970, "a noble building, monumental but eccentric, a building with a character and a past," the New York City archivist Ken Cobb later wrote. According to the *Guide to New York City Landmarks*, the courthouse held "some of the finest mid-19th century interiors in New York." The New York City Landmarks Preservation Commission came to call it "one of the city's grandest and most important civic monuments."[76] The distinctive interior included sets of cast iron stairs and faux marble pillars and was topped off by an octagonal rotunda capped by a skylight. But the interior was musty and drafty when members of O'Dwyer's staff began working there. One of them, Betsy Imholz, then a recent Columbia graduate in political science, recalled entering through massive front doors and riding a caged, freight-style elevator to the second floor, the gate closing with a clang. Even so, she enjoyed the atmosphere, including "generous, non-working fireplaces, and the feeling of old New York."[77]

O'Dwyer helped organize efforts to save the building from a replacement proposed by the Beame administration to modernize the city's administrative buildings. Luckily for Paul, the city's fiscal problems proved a fortuitous ally since the mayor's costly proposal struck many as evocative of Boss Tweed's storied excesses. The council leader's interest in historic preservation allowed him to see the building's potentially lasting value despite its notoriety as the object of one of the biggest corruption scandals in city history. He had little patience for the contemporary appetite, in many northeastern cities, to bulldoze distinctive nineteenth-century civic buildings to modernize downtown areas. At the same time, it was

Paul's brother who, as mayor, provided the impetus to create a New York City municipal archive, with its materials first coming together as of 1950. Paul, wrote Cobb, "was one of the first to recognize the unique features of the building and realize it was a solid structure."[78]

In 1979, the American-Victorian courthouse became the home of the previously itinerant city archives, which later gained a permanent home in the Surrogate's Courthouse, just across the street. O'Dwyer also arranged for revitalization of the city's Division of Archives and created an archives foundation, the New York Archival Society, which generated essential private support.

"The best thing he did, he saved the archives," said Idilio Gracia Peña, a former senior archivist whom Paul helped regain his job at the NYC Municipal Archives seven months after he lost it in the 1975–76 waves of city layoffs, and who remained there for the next twenty years.[79]

———

AS PAUL SAW IT, then, his record hardly added up to that of a "weak City Council president," as an otherwise complimentary article in the student-run *Columbia Daily Spectator* characterized him after his unsuccessful Senate primary loss in 1976 (won by Daniel Patrick Moynihan). "To me," wrote the student-reporter, Dan Janison, who became an esteemed political reporter in New York City after graduating from Columbia College, O'Dwyer's poor finish showed that "the members of my party don't really know who our leaders are."

O'Dwyer promptly typed a letter to the campus journalist, taking issue with the description and listing accomplishments of which he was proud and the causes for which he had fought.[80] The letter went on for three single-spaced, politely worded pages.

But he had difficulty broadcasting his successes effectively to distractible voters as the five-way race for the city council presidency picked up in the late summer of 1977. Doing so was neither his forte nor easily afforded by his characteristically modest campaign budget. O'Dwyer, now seeking reelection in earnest, also misread the field: like many observers, he figured his most significant opponent in the race to be the East Side councilman Carter Burden Jr., a distant descendant of robber baron Cornelius Vanderbilt. He also faced the Queens state assemblyman Leonard Stavisky, the parking-garage-builder Abe Hirschfeld, and the state senator Carol Bellamy of Brooklyn and Manhattan. Bellamy, though discounted at first as she was not well known, turned out to be the main threat.

Jack Deacy, a savvy and down-to-earth political operative, shifted from the council president's staff to the campaign to try to help turn things around. Overshadowed by the seven-way mayoral primary going on at the same time, "Paul wasn't getting any press at all," he recalled.

A former reporter, Deacy was the son of Martin Deacy, a contemporary of Paul's from Bohola who had owned Deacy's Café, a Brooklyn tavern at Fenimore Street and Flatbush Avenue where Paul bent an elbow in the 1950s. Jack's most recent political experience was working as a speech-writer for Assembly Speaker Stanley Steingut, the Democratic leader he remembered principally as a malaprop-prone public speaker and who, without the aid of Deacy's talents, had once declared, "Mr. Speaker, the ship of state must not be derailed."

Deacy was eighteen when he first met O'Dwyer at Bill O'Dwyer's 1964 wake in Manhattan; his father had brought him along. In 1968, after navy service, he cofounded Navy Men for McCarthy and joined Paul's Senate primary election race, helping filter a majority vote from the Bay Ridge/Sunset Park section of Brooklyn, where a visit by the candidate sometimes elicited racial epithets from spectators.

One day, in 1977, Deacy put a stop to a planned O'Dwyer ad shoot inside a graffiti-scrawled subway station, fearing that viewers of the spot would associate him with the troubles besetting the underground. He also struggled to highlight the small victories for average New Yorkers attrib-utable to the ombudsman's unit.

But O'Dwyer "wasn't all that good at retail politics," Deacy recalled. The sometimes-reluctant candidate did help himself, though, with a strong TV ad in which he pulled on his white strands and attributed each to participation in a different movement for justice in the twentieth century, the former aide said.

Managed by the New York theatrical lawyer Mel Altman, the cam-paign characteristically lacked financial backing from the Democratic Party in the city, so it depended on donations from old friends like Char-lie Keith, whose career as a wealthy landlord, begun in middle age, belied his consistent radicalism on the left. He had preserved it intact despite his 1946 expulsion from the new maritime union he had helped to forge, only to oppose its leadership for the sake of greater worker control. An orphan turned itinerant seaman, the loquacious and polyglot Keith, who was Jewish, had been a political officer with the Abraham Lincoln Brigade that fought the fascist Francisco Franco in 1930s Spain and spent a year in a Franco prison. After leaving the seaman's life afflicted with a case of lasting bitterness, he acquired some of the properties he worked on as a Greenwich Village house painter and rented the rooms to dock workers, starving artists, and Black tenants. Paul considered the husky, barrel-chested Keith to be one of the most idiosyncratic waterfront characters he ever encountered in New York.

While the 1977 primary race for council president was expected to end with an O'Dwyer-Burden runoff, Bellamy finished in second place, behind the incumbent but ahead of Burden. She went on to win the runoff against Paul, her success reflecting a strong public appetite for new blood, as well as the support of activists in the women's movement. Some were still rankled that O'Dwyer and Clark had gotten in the way of Bella Abzug a year earlier.

"We'd had the fiscal crisis, the blackout that turned into looting, and a city that was in tough, tough shape," said Deacy. "Now along came these younger faces—Carol Bellamy for council president and Ed Koch for mayor . . . by comparison to 'The Sunshine Boys'—O'Dwyer and Beame." (Bellamy was thirty-five years old, and Koch, her running mate, was fifty-two.)

None too surprisingly, the Bellamy-versus-O'Dwyer runoff struck a largely congenial tone. Under glasses and brown hair tending to dip toward an eyebrow, the state senator for parts of Brooklyn and Manhattan sounded more like a college instructor than a politician. Paul's often calm, reasoned campaigning style was not very different from his opponent's. The campaign's shortage of emotion or belligerence helped Bellamy amplify her appeal as a public policy wonk who was interested in improving governmental *systems* rather than mainly reaching out individually to citizens facing hardships—suggesting a limitation of Paul's ombudsman's unit.

Her criticism of the incumbent was more implied than stated.

"She killed us with kindness," summarized Deacy.[81]

In defeat, finally, O'Dwyer voiced no resentment of his comparatively inexperienced female challenger and soon delivered a farewell to his casually attired troops, asking that they always try to remember the average city worker exemplified by the police officers who watched the door to city hall.

"I cannot pass up the opportunity to talk about the cops who have been handling this situation at the front door," Paul told his staff on his final day at city hall.

> This is the center of the activities of the City of New York. This is the last place where people come, this is the place people blame, this is the place people point to hopefully for some redress. So we do attract the halt, the sick and the blind, the people who—and I mean insofar as life is concerned—the people who are mentally disturbed, the people who are irrational. And they come to the door. We can treat them with kindness and with an understanding or we can treat them in a fashion that would betray our own traditions. And that delicate job is not left to the philosophical professors in our learning institutions. It's given to our cops. And at the end of four years, I don't know of any incident that happened—either in the front door or the entrance to my office—that I have any reason to regret. And I think that's a hell of a tribute to the people that are outside.

There was applause and there were tears. And there was the admiring Kempton, who in his next *New York Post* column wrote that "so far as a definition of Paul O'Dwyer is concerned, those words"—of healing—"are all we need."[82]

The "kindly radical," as the column's headline called Paul, had already sat down with Anna Quindlen, a *New York Times* reporter, to discuss his dismaying defeat and acknowledged that Bellamy's election represented important progress for women in politics. "What happened," he told Quindlen, "is that I fought for a lot of civil rights 25, 35 years ago, including women's rights, and I'm in poor shape to complain if I find myself in the way of the machinery that I myself helped set in motion."

During the interview, O'Dwyer raised his voice when the young reporter reminded him that Councilman Burden had said he "practiced the politics of the past."

"What past?" Paul responded. "I have always moved on from one issue to another. The past I was involved in was medical care for the aged, Social Security. The Reform movement could not adjust itself to the sixties and so it died. Another movement grew up in its place. I think that has died, too. The new issues are human misery, unemployment, the toll the economy has taken on people's lives. I am involved in those issues."

He animatedly recalled the events of 1968 and his emergence then as a Democratic maverick supporting the urgent moral outcry against the Vietnam War. The year had marked the highlight of his career as a politician-activist, he said, "when we were taking a country engrossed in an immoral war. And we were changing this nation. And we made it feel ashamed."

The war was finally over, urban bossism vanquished, and the abuse of authority in the Oval Office, the FBI, and the CIA exposed. As he summed it up, the idealism of a new generation of progressive activists gave him renewed hope that the years to come would bring greater democratic dynamism.

"Mr. O'Dwyer raised one fist and brought it down heavily on the arm of his chair," Quindlen wrote. "Beneath his eyebrows, it was impossible to tell if the halting sound in his voice was reflected in his eyes. 'By God,' he finished with a growl, 'we did it. We did do it.'"[83]

O'Dwyer did not bring up that he was "livid, really livid" over the unhappy outcome of Percy Sutton's mayoral campaign, according to Jack Deacy.[84] Beame's belated entry in the primary had doomed the Manhattan borough president's chances. Sutton had been given to expect that Mayor Beame would endorse him, not run himself.

Even so, veteran liberal politicians were not then popular, and Sutton, with a Harlem base, had an uphill battle. Ed Koch in the end captured city hall after he called for rewiring the state's electric chair, then fourteen years dormant, opposing a civilian-majority oversight board for the police department, and vowing to restore the city's fiscal autonomy. The *New York Post*, owned by the Australian press baron Rupert Murdoch, endorsed and flagged his candidacy. (Beame also came to do so, in the general election.)

The liberal Sutton tried to project a crime-fighter posture, but he finished fifth among the seven mayoral contenders, one of whom was Abzug, who finished third.

For reasons he never made clear, O'Dwyer made no endorsement in the mayoral primary. He would never have endorsed Ed Koch, a betrayer of the liberal Democratic Reform movement; he might have had to work with Beame again if the mayor prevailed; Bella Abzug was still sore at him; Secretary of State of New York Mario Cuomo (another strong contender in the large field) had a sometimes grating personality; and Percy Sutton's chances were at best slim, hurt by his inability to nail down the Black vote in Brooklyn. It would be difficult, in any case, to say for sure, as O'Dwyer never commented on why he stepped back, except to say he rued his uncharacteristic failure to support his friend Sutton. In light of Sutton's poor showing, Paul stated that his party had fumbled the chance to elect the first African American mayor in New York City history and betrayed the city's long-denied Black voters.

Yielding at last to the advice that he had given to the then mayor Lindsay in view of his own brother's bruising finale as mayor, O'Dwyer, too, gave up seeking public office. Still, at seventy he was still vigorous and still an opinion maker and a firebrand, particularly when it came to the second Irish civil war of his lifetime—the Troubles in Northern Ireland.

11

CIVIL WARRIOR

D URING THE HEIGHT of the Vietnam War, FBI participants in a nationwide dragnet opened the heavy wooden doors to the Upper West Side's St. Gregory the Great Roman Catholic Church. Father Phil Berrigan and his fellow anti-war activist, David Eberhardt, were hiding in a closet in the rectory on the fourth floor, the secret guests of St. Gregory's popular pastor, Father Harry Browne.

Less than a week had passed since appeals by the "Catonsville Nine"—radicals convicted of draft board vandalism, among them Berrigan and Eberhardt—had failed. The two Catholic activists, previously released on bail, fled to continue a campaign against the war machine. They ended up taking refuge in Browne's sanctuary.

"The rectory was an aerie with a vast collection of books high above the street, and it made the perfect safe house," said Flavia Alaya, a Barnard alumna and literary scholar who surreptitiously raised three children with Browne and married him after he left the priesthood. "He would use it to protect draft-dodgers and to house people escaping to Canada."[1]

It was April 21, 1970, nearly four years before O'Dwyer became council president. As Alaya wrote in her memoir, *Under the Rose*, a battery of FBI agents "came four at a time in nine more waves. The rectory swam with them. They checked walls, poked ceilings, pounding wall paneling for secret priest-holes. The layout made for a perfect safe house—sealed staircases, blind walls—anyone who'd ever touched a nail to it seemed to have had afterthoughts."

Standing outside the closet where his guests were hidden, Browne shouted, "You can't come in here. You've got no warrant!" But the agents pushed open the door and one demanded, "Where's Father *Brannigan*?" Browne just shrugged—"Who?"[2]

J. Edgar Hoover's intelligencers found the two religious fugitives, clapped them in handcuffs, and took them out of the sanctuary into gray sedans as passersby stopped and gawked.

St. Gregory's, a community focal point of gospel-inspired acts to lift the poor, heal the sick, and empower the marginalized, soon shook with defiance, with hundreds of parishioners and other community members swaying in the aisles waving hand-scrawled messages and a student band belting out songs of rebellion.

That evening, the socially conscious Browne delivered a rousing sermon. In the center of the front pew sat O'Dwyer and the West Side politician Ruth Messinger, both of the Democratic FDR–Woodrow Wilson Reform Club. Browne, remembered Alaya, pleaded for calm and conciliation; from the pulpit, he held the churchgoers rapt and had them "laughing through their tears."[3]

O'Dwyer's next encounter with the Baltimore-based Philip Berrigan and the New Catholic Left peace movement occurred in a more conservative setting, three hours away by car: along with Ramsey Clark, Leonard Boudin, and three other lesser-known attorneys, Paul would put his shoulder to the defense of Phil Berrigan and six followers who were to be charged by the government with engaging in a criminal conspiracy. Becoming a celebrated cause of the anti-war movement, the activists were alleged to have conspired to raid draft boards, bomb government property, and kidnap none other than Henry Kissinger, President Nixon's national security adviser, though they failed to consummate the plans.

Phil Berrigan was alleged to have plotted from the federal prison in Lewisburg, Pennsylvania, where he was serving hard time as one of the Catonsville Nine. O'Dwyer, invited to participate in the defense after being interviewed by two of the defendants, accepted the challenge while making one thing clear: he would represent clients, not a cause. He had little patience for the kind of political grandstanding that the well-known radical attorney William Kunstler had facilitated in the service of the Chicago Eight trial of Abbie Hoffman, Tom Hayden, and other New Left anti-war figures.

O'Dwyer was not as famous as Kunstler, but his presence in a courtroom could have a stirring effect. Franklin Siegel, who worked for O'Dwyer & Bernstien in the late 1970s and early 1980s before going into private practice and serving as a staff attorney and on the board of the Center for Constitutional Rights, described in an interview for this book the impact that Paul could have "trying cases in the court of public opinion." His reputation for integrity preceded his appearance in many New York courthouses, said Siegel, who added, "The aisles would part, and the judge would say, 'Mr. O'Dwyer, step right up here, what are we here for today?'" Siegel, an acolyte, recalled the time Paul made a special appearance in a lower Manhattan courtroom in support of a blind man and his newspaper stand from a sidewalk near the New York Stock Exchange. The lawyer's involvement raised the case's public profile and may have contributed to the judge's decision that the vendor be allowed to stay put, at least temporarily.[4]

Public fascination with the Harrisburg case indeed stemmed, in part, from the participation of the three most recognizable barristers at the defense table: O'Dwyer, the former 1968 US Senate peace candidate from New York known for stout Irish republican—and underdog—sympathies; Clark, who in early 1968, as the then US attorney general, had overseen the prosecution of the anti-draft leaders Dr. Benjamin Spock and Rev. William Sloane Coffin of Riverside Church in Manhattan, as well as the lawyer Marcus Raskin in the Boston Five trial; and Boudin, one of the foremost constitutional lawyers on the left and the bane of Hoover. Boudin's success in challenging the constitutionality of FBI investigatory methods to snare Judith Coplon had forced Hoover to make the feeding of rumors and innuendo to his allies in Congress his bread and butter. Instead of being sent to court, Hoover's "red" targets were instead hauled before congressional committees in the late 1940s, the '50s, and into the '60s. Those who refused to answer a committee's questions about past statements, friends, and activities, invoking their rights under the Fifth or First Amendment, risked a citing for contempt of Congress, a charge bringing castigation, fines, or prison. Still amassing dirt on thousands of Americans, including successive presidents, Hoover wielded his Cold War cudgel and paranoic tendencies against the anti-war and civil rights movements.

By the start of the Harrisburg showdown, his power in Washington, DC, had endured for nearly fifty years. His infighting prowess had few peers in the Capitol other than Nixon.

In November 1970, Hoover spoke before a subcommittee of the Senate Appropriations Committee in support of a $14 million supplemental budget request by the FBI. Just two senators were present, as most of Congress had already left town for the Thanksgiving holiday, but Hoover's testimony and statement for the press made headlines with their sensationalist claims about the New Catholic Left. In seeking to buttress support for congressional funding, the director charged that Phil Berrigan and his better-known brother, Daniel, a fugitive since his conviction as a Catonsville Nine draft-files arsonist, were the pied pipers of "an anarchist group on the East Coast, the so-called East Coast Conspiracy to Save Lives." The cabal, Hoover stated, was suspected of "concocting a scheme to kidnap a highly placed government official" and blowing up subsurface electrical conduits and steam pipes in Washington, DC.

The press reported the accusation with little or no skepticism, but one member of Congress, US Rep. William Anderson of Tennessee, criticized the director, breaking the long-standing unwritten prohibition in Washington against offending him.

"Knowing the Berrigan brothers and being reasonably well acquainted with their careers as priests, theologians, scholars and their dedication to Christian principles, and having read much of their writings, it is impossible to believe that [your] allegations are true," the congressman wrote to Hoover. The letter was released to the public.

Privately, William Sullivan, thought by some to be Hoover's heir apparent at the spy agency, expressed dismay over Hoover's attack on pacifist priests and their followers. Sullivan told colleagues at the agency that the case was paper-thin. The Berrigan brothers "had no desire to hurt anyone, they just wanted to call attention to their cause," he told the director face-to-face.[5]

Even Kissinger was dubious, joking when he first heard of the alleged plot that it must have been cooked up by "sex-starved nuns" (with the impish remark provoking howls of protest from many Catholics around the country).[6]

But the Organized Crime Control Act of 1970, as Hoover knew, had enlarged the government's power to impanel grand juries and severely restricted a witness's right to invoke the Fifth Amendment safeguard against self-incrimination. The Justice Department, which would only become formally independent of the White House as a result of Watergate, investigated political opponents of President Nixon, muddling the line between crime and dissent.

And to dampen dissent, in June 1971, US Attorney General John Mitchell said in a speech to the Virginia Bar Association that domestic subversion was as serious as any threat from abroad. Between 1970 and 1973, all told, the Justice Department called about one hundred grand juries, indicting left-wing dissenters such as leaders of the Black Panthers, the Vietnam Veterans Against the War, Daniel Ellsberg and Anthony Russo of Pentagon Papers notoriety (with Boudin as the defense attorney), Students for a Democratic Society, the National Committee for a Sane Nuclear Policy (or SANE), and many other organizations with liberal-to-radical leanings.[7]

To start off 1971 the Nixon administration's Justice Department indicted Father Phil Berrigan; Sister Elizabeth McAlister of Montclair, New Jersey; a Pakistani American scholar of decolonization named Eqbal Ahmad; the radical priests Neil McLaughlin and Joseph Wenderoth; and Anthony Scoblick, a married former priest. The potential penalties for the alleged burglary and kidnapping conspiracy added up to life imprisonment.

Daniel Berrigan, whose fugitive status represented an ongoing embarrassment for Hoover, was listed as an unindicted coconspirator, as were six other movement sympathizers. But whatever the particulars of the indictment, O'Dwyer and his team of defense lawyers knew what they were up against—efforts at the highest levels of the US government to quash dissent against the Vietnam War.

The day after the indictment, the *Los Angeles Times* reported the basis for the government's counts: Boyd Douglas Jr., a recently released federal convict.

At the end of April, a year since Phil Berrigan was led away in handcuffs from St. Gregory's, a new prosecutor, William Lynch, a conservative Irish Catholic, was assigned to the case. He promptly came out with a superseding indictment, dropping reported co-mastermind Dan Berrigan from the list of alleged coconspirators, along with other individuals, while adding Mary Cain Scoblick, Anthony's wife and an ex-nun, and

John Glick, both anti-draft militants. The superseding indictment centered on a tapered-down and perhaps easier-to-prove allegation: conspiracy to destroy draft records. It carried a maximum of just five years.

Father Phil and his fellow defendants issued a joint statement disparaging the winnowed allegations as a "potpourri of false charges, absurd allegations and acts labeled as crimes by the law . . . as sane or insane as our government's Indochinese war . . . one is a stepchild of the other, legal overkill following military overkill. Both are devious, ruthless and mad."[8] At the same time, Phil Berrigan also handwrote twelve pages to Hoover from his cell in Danbury Prison in Connecticut, to which he had recently been transferred.

Berrigan asserted he had rehabilitated himself and should be allowed to walk free.

"This year," he stated, "I have counseled and befriended young prisoners, helped conduct classes in such books as *St. Matthew's Gospel*, *Gandhi's Autobiography*, *Gulliver's Travels*, Erikson's *Young Man Luther*. I have worked in the prison dental clinic, meditated on my crime and punishment, celebrated mass. . . . I have not, after all, murdered children under military order, nor tortured prisoners nor napalmed women, nor laid waste a foreign culture. . . . I have burned papers instead of children. Let us rejoice that justice can distinguish criminal priests from military heroes."[9]

His letter went unanswered. Yet the superseding indictment had arrived when the New Catholic Left was showing signs of losing faith, with the war grinding on, the corporations growing fat from the sale of child-killing munitions and toxic defoliants, and the novelty and mystique of priests attacking Selective Service files wearing thin.

Rooted in the New York–based Catholic Worker movement and its pacifist founder, Dorothy Day, as well as the writings on the spiritual roots of protest by the Trappist monk Thomas Merton, the New Catholic Left had managed to provide a moral and religious foundation for the anti-war movement. While it represented a sharp departure from the posture of the Catholic hierarchy, which was unquestioning of the state, the Berrigans and their followers forged alliances with anti-war Congress members, demonstrated in front of the homes of generals, and set fire to draft board records, capturing the attention of the broad anti-war movement as well as the warmakers in Washington.[10]

These were no minor feats, considering their small numbers. But when Father Phil was visited in prison by Francine du Plessix Gray for the *New*

York Review of Books, he was deflated. "I have absolutely no regrets about what I've done," the forty-nine-year-old priest told the writer as jury selection began in January 1972, "and no regrets about doing it twice. But would I do it again? Probably not."[11]

GREATER HARRISBURG, a 250,000-person metro area on the Susquehanna River, was a bastion of Nixon's "Silent Majority" where Republicans outnumbered Democrats by four to one. When the Justice Department selected the city, not Washington, DC, as the venue for the trial, lawyers for the defense assailed the decision, saying the government could not have chosen a region more hostile to the accused.[12] It seemed doubtful that the defendants could get a fair hearing in a region that had once been a Ku Klux Klan stronghold and where many of the churchgoers professed a literal belief in the Bible, Paul felt. On the other hand, pro-war sentiment appeared to be weakening. A Gallup poll published in June 1971 had found that a majority of Americans, 61 percent, thought the war had been a mistake.[13]

The proceedings began as planned in the federal courthouse in the Pennsylvania commonwealth's capital with an almost month-long voir dire, and with the defense trying out novel statistics-driven jury selection methods.[14] Nearly four hundred prospective jurors were pared to nine women and three men, some of whom indicated ignorance of national affairs and blind faith in authority.

Questioned by Boudin, a prospective juror in her early twenties claimed to know nothing at all about the Vietnam War, the killings at Kent State, or even Nixon's celebrated recent visit to China.[15]

O'Dwyer, meanwhile, asked a bar matron who worked in Lewistown, "Do your customers talk about My Lai?" citing the South Vietnamese village where a company of US Army soldiers had massacred twenty-two unarmed villagers in one of the worst atrocities of the war. When she replied, "No, sir," her interrogator pressed further.

"Do you know what I'm referring to?" he asked, speaking softly.

"No, I do not," the young woman said.

But then, this is what lawyers usually want: jurors who know nothing, with no preconceived opinion on current events.

Common to many of the prospective jurors in Harrisburg was the belief that war was simply a fact of life, neither wholly good nor completely evil. Many voiced uncertainty over whether the United States should wage an all-out struggle or commit to a full withdrawal of troops.

"I can't say I hate war—we will always have war—but I'd like to see our men come home. Maybe we could have followed a different policy—either total involvement or withdrawal, none of this half-and-half business," said a Pennsylvania state Health Department secretary, twenty-two and recently married.[16]

Paul declined remuneration for his work on the case, while others on the defense team, including Boudin, found it necessary to be compensated by a burgeoning defense fund, which included contributions raised by voluntary committees formed in twenty-one states. Money from the fund was also set aside for a potential appeal.

As Paul was not trusted by his family to drive attentively, and because he wanted to use the commute to pore over legal documents and notes, his middle son, Rory, agreed to be his chauffeur throughout the trial. The father-and-son pair made the trip from the West Side every Sunday night and returned home on Friday night. "I remember once leaving Manhattan and going through two or three feet of snow to make sure he got to court for the morning session," recalled Rory, an electrician at the time.[17]

———

O'DWYER DELIVERED the opening statement for the defense.

"Part of the reason for this is sinister," he told the jury, referring to the government's case.

"Oh, now, Mr. O'Dwyer—'sinister?'" Judge R. Dixon Herman responded. He paused before adding with a sigh, "All right, you'll prove it."

The exchange represented the start of a choppy dynamic between the defense team and Herman lasting the entire trial. When the judge sequestered the newly selected jurors in a hotel, O'Dwyer led a counterattack, noting that the procedure was more typical of federal trials of mobsters than of priests devoted to the scriptures. The decision risked coloring the jurors' state of mind against the defendants, he told the court, to no avail.[18]

At another point, O'Dwyer assailed the judge's apparent tolerance of Hoover's provocative statements to the press and congressional appropriations panel the year before—to which the jurist drily replied, "Well, we're not trying Mr. Hoover here."

"Yes, we are, judge," O'Dwyer came back.[19]

He would be the recipient of the only contempt motion meted out in the trial.

Jack Nelson and Ronald Ostrow, who covered the case for the *Los Angeles Times*, observed that O'Dwyer's courtroom performance was "sometimes based as much on emotional appeal as on law" and "not only antagonized Judge Herman and the prosecuting attorneys, but caused an uneasiness at the defense table."[20] In comparison to O'Dwyer, Boudin was more of a chess player, absorbed by the theory and strategy of the case. Wearing a recently installed pacemaker, he was carrying a tremendous amount of stress because his twenty-eight-year-old daughter, Kathy, a Bryn Mawr College valedictorian turned Weather Underground radical, had landed on the FBI's most-wanted list after an explosion destroyed the Greenwich Village townhouse used by the radical group as a bomb factory.[21] In comparison to Boudin and O'Dwyer, Clark came across as a laconic prairie lawyer.

But the three best-known members of the defense team were competitive and determined to win. Boudin had yet to lose a federal case, with a 10–0 record (though he had declined to defend Ethel and Julius Rosenberg), while Paul had the most trial experience. The larger legal team was not united about all the strategies attempted, but all agreed on at least one thing: the necessity of going hard at Boyd Douglas Jr., the former prisoner turned government informer.

Enlisted by the FBI as an informant, Douglas had reliably ferried love notes between Father Phil and Sister Liz and furnished copies to his FBI handler, Delmar "Molly" Mayfield. The romantic pair's correspondence, parts of which prosecutors would read aloud to the jury, betrayed not only Phil's attraction to Liz but also clues to the location of Dan Berrigan's hideout on Block Island off the Rhode Island coast.

Berrigan's and McAlister's letters were used to underpin the feds' case, especially the written references to a summer-night gathering and desultory conversation in which several of the defendants had batted around the idea of entering, disguised as workmen, a lacework of heating tunnels under the Department of Defense and going on to make a "citizen's arrest" of Henry Kissinger. The banter that evening had been freewheeling and abstract, the participants insisted, far different from the working out of any actual plot. But one of McAlister's letters, which she ended with "Right on!", referred to the conversationalists as members of a "planning group."[22] And, shut away under a six-year sentence in the same prison where the Teamsters boss Jimmy Hoffa was also confined, Father Phil had responded positively to Sister Liz.

"About the plan," he wrote to her, ". . . the project as you outlined it is brilliant, but grandiose. . . . Nonetheless, I like the plan and am just trying to weave elements of modesty into it. . . . Why not grab the Brain Child [Kissinger], treat him decently, but tell him nothing of his fate—or tell him his fate hinges on release of pol[itical] people or cessation of air strikes in Laos. . . . One thing should be implanted in that pea brain— that respectable murderers like him are no longer inviolable."[23]

———

PROSECUTORS TOOK PAINS to introduce the jury to Douglas as a sympathetic product of a difficult boyhood. Later in the case, they would sing of his "sterling character."[24]

Born in Creston, Iowa, Douglas was the son of a construction laborer who was forced to move frequently to find work. His mother disappeared when he was eight; she was presumed to have drowned, her body never found. He attended sixteen different schools in eleven states and finally, in 1953, was enrolled at Boys Town, Nebraska, an institution for wayward youth and boys from broken homes.

At nineteen, as a high school dropout who had been caught stealing forty dollars from a teacher, he joined the army but twice deserted. He was apprehended in 1962, by then having been charged with impersonating an army captain and obtaining $50,000 to $60,000 through fraudulent checks. In early 1963, Douglas pleaded guilty to both charges and was sentenced to six years. He was incarcerated in El Reno, Oklahoma, and a month later was moved to the prison at Lewisburg, where he met Phil Berrigan.[25]

Thirty-two years old by the date of the trial, Douglas was clean-cut. His straight brown hair swept back, he had a confident, articulate way of speaking and wore a pinstriped suit, wide lavender tie, and pink shirt in the witness chair, self-possessed and twenty to thirty pounds heavier than the defendants remembered.

He held the distinction of having been the only prisoner among Lewisburg's 1,400 convicts who was chosen for a study release program in late 1969. Approved by the US Bureau of Prisons, this dispensation enabled him to take classes at Bucknell, offering him, as of February 1970, his first taste of freedom in two years.

Under a secret arrangement with the Justice Department, the government paid him to carry letters between Father Phil and Sister Liz; he smuggled the letters out of the prison in a school notebook and made copies for the FBI. He also, by the FBI's design, infiltrated Bucknell's small antiwar community, posing as a peacenik flashing a V sign at rallies.

The defense brought out Douglas's two army desertions, string of aliases, and fraud convictions, eliciting, through the questioning of witnesses, how Berrigan had taken a sympathetic interest toward his fellow prisoner at Lewisburg when Berrigan was unaware that Douglas was sharing—with the FBI—his private correspondence.[26]

Not only was the witness a betrayer of the priest's trust, the defense lawyers sought to show, but he was a greedy and caddish one as well. Once, he even tried to convince coed Jane Hoover to marry him, saying he was suffering from terminal cancer. While she did not follow him to the altar, she helped him make copies of the prison letters for Mayfield.

The defense foregrounded, too, that Douglas had sued the government for scars on his arms that he claimed to have got as a voluntary experimental subject for the National Institutes of Health; he received a $10,000 settlement. Among his multiple payments for FBI piecework totaling $9,278 was $200 for the McAlister letter indicating Daniel Berrigan's whereabouts.[27]

O'Dwyer was the most aggressive of the defense counsels toward Douglas. He led him through a list of his FBI payments, sounding like "the stern cleric" according to one observer, his rapid-fire questions intended to rattle the informant. His questions helped bring out that Douglas had pushed for ever more, and ever larger, paychecks. A letter he wrote to Mayfield had included a request for $50,000, the evidence showed.[28]

In all, the defense team's cross-examination lasted seven days and was conducted by six defense lawyers. Paul betrayed no sympathy or understanding for Douglas, which Liz McAlister and Phil Berrigan reserved for him despite his personal betrayals. (Berrigan had unwisely ignored advice from Hoffa to stay away from Douglas.)[29]

O'Dwyer also was harsher toward the prosecution's star witness than his fellow counsel.

"He was merciless," Murray Polner and Jim O'Grady wrote of Paul's cross-examination of the key prosecution witness in their book *Disarmed and Dangerous: The Life and Times of Daniel and Philip Berrigan,* "tearing into Douglas, since he never saw the same Douglas as Phil and Wenderoth and Liz had." O'Dwyer treated the witness as a "paid informant" and "pathological liar," citing "over and over" his felonious record and reliance on aliases.[30]

O'Dwyer was also unsparing toward the FBI's Mayfield, asking whether he was "prepared to recommend payments to the informant for his services at the trial." After a moment of rumination, Mayfield replied, "Sitting right here in court at this time, I do not know the answer to that question."

Prosecutor Lynch at one point jumped to his feet, appealing to Judge Herman that O'Dwyer was covering the same territory "*ad nauseum*."

"*Ad nauseum* is on your table, Mr. Lynch," volleyed O'Dwyer.[31]

To O'Dwyer, at heart, Douglas was probably the basest individual imaginable, a poster child for immorality since he was willing to exploit the goodwill of friends and intimates to "take the king's shilling," as the old Irish expression went.

While Boudin told the jury that Douglas "had many of the attributes of a con man," O'Dwyer, chief among the defense lawyers, could not be so dispassionate. "I felt no scruple, as my clients and my colleagues did, in attacking his character," he recalled in his memoirs. Douglas was not a "weak person who had bad breaks as a boy and was being used by the FBI." Rather, he was "an informer who had betrayed the confidence good people had placed in him."[32]

To discourage any sympathies the jurors might have reserved for an "orphan," as the prosecutors called him, O'Dwyer focused his questioning on Douglas's manipulations of the Bucknell student Elizabeth Sandel, another "small-town girl" Douglas dated and whom, du Plessix Gray wrote, he gave peace symbol earrings for Christmas in 1970.

Paul's questions seemed well suited to the results of the social science team that had identified the ideal juror as "a female Democrat with no religious experience and a white-collar job or a skilled blue-collar job." The women who made up three-quarters of the jury would not likely be well disposed toward a government informant who acted caddishly toward well-meaning coeds.[33] So, O'Dwyer relentlessly pressed Douglas about whether he had urged Sandel to go to demonstrations featuring prominent Catholic Left protesters; whether he identified the coed to the FBI when shown pictures of demonstrators; and, most devastatingly, whether he asked Sandel to marry him "*before or after* you pointed her picture to the FBI." By the end of it, there seemed little left of what the prosecution had described as Douglas's "sterling character."[34]

Rory O'Dwyer took in most of Douglas's total fourteen days on the witness stand and saw him falter under defense cross-examination. As if at a tennis match, he sat elbow to elbow with the other spectators, with every available seat filled. The unadorned walls around him rose twenty feet to the ceiling. Fluorescent lights brightly illuminated the courtroom. A green wall-to-wall carpet blanketed the floor.

His younger brother, Brian, twenty-six, with O'Dwyer & Bernstien, did not attend but followed the case in the press and got into the legal weeds of it on weekends with his father. Brian was aware of how diligently Paul prepared before cross-examining prosecution witnesses, and how close study and extensive preparation helped increase his confidence in his ability to conduct a successful confrontation with a prosecution witness. But, Brian commented, "that wasn't unusual for him. You can prepare all you want for cross, but you never know what a witness will say or how he'll say it, and then it's the follow-up that matters. It's a very different skill than anything else in the courtroom. It involves incredible quickness. And he was good, he was excellent at cross-examination."[35]

The courtroom fell silent after Clark rose and announced that the defense would call no witnesses of its own. Unexpectedly, eschewing a closing statement, the defense rested. "The defendants will always seek peace, the defendants continue to proclaim their innocence—and the defense rests," he said, and returned to his chair.

Lynch, the prosecutor, was startled.

But the surprise had been worked out the night before. Like virtually everything in a criminal litigation, it was tactical, meant to suggest to the jury that the government's case was too far-fetched to merit their attention any further or even to put the major defendants on the stand. Importantly, this denied the prosecution the potential opportunity to cross-examine Phil, Liz, and Ahmad. What was more, the defense foreclosed a chance for prosecutors to conduct a fishing expedition to elicit the names of additional war resisters of the New Catholic Left.[36]

After fifty-nine hours of deliberations, the jurors trooped back into the courtroom. At Judge Herman's request, the jury foreperson announced that the twelve members were deadlocked. The judge declared a mistrial.

Ten of the twelve jurors had voted against the charges of conspiracy, a complex count whose subtleties they showed little sign of grasping. The case would never be tried again.

Rory drove his father home from Harrisburg for the last time, and Paul recalled his concerns about the trial's conservative venue.

The trip was "long enough," Paul later wrote, to allow himself to "silently apologize to the people in the 11 counties whom I had patronizingly doubted; long enough for me to feel proud of my adopted country."

In their book on the case, *The FBI and the Berrigans*, reporters Nelson and Ostrow weighed how historians might one day view the case—as fallout from the Vietnam War, surely, they wrote, but also as part of the government's unprecedented "counter-reaction" to domestic political resistance of a magnitude and intensity not experienced since the Civil War.

But the Harrisburg Seven's prosecution also bore the fingerprints of President Nixon, who "chose to ignore Hoover's blatant violation of the Bill of Rights" on behalf of his powerful ally.

The writers concluded with a warning: "When a nation that prides itself on being a system of laws—not men—permits itself to be so corrupted, the portents are ominous."[37]

O'Dwyer himself could not have said it better.

———

EVEN DURING the three-and-half-month trial, the most high-profile of the future New York City councilman's career, O'Dwyer was preoccupied by events in Northern Ireland. The singular hope of many Irish émigrés of his generation—an undivided Éire, free to work out its own future—drew him back to the intractable conflict. In contrast to his own abiding interest, the unending low-level war seemed to have a waning resonance with younger generations of Irish Americans.

So, with the Harrisburg case over, O'Dwyer devoted more time, not less, to activism and advocacy aimed at bringing about greater public and political awareness of the Troubles and, he felt, the urgency of US diplomatic engagement. Deep resentments lingered among both the much-subjugated Catholic minority and the Protestant majority determined to retain its power. The British used martial means to maintain the status quo arrangements, however unequal. Provisional Irish Republican Army

(IRA) guns took aim at the British security and political apparatus, and the Catholic and Protestant militants blew each other up. Euphemistically known as the Troubles, the state of affairs seemed as intractable as the patterns of paramilitary attacks and reprisals were numbing.

Carrying childhood memories of partition, which had brought an end to the Anglo-Irish War, or Irish War of Independence, of 1919–21, Paul had no interest in cheering on the contemporary physical-force movement of the IRA, despite his sympathies for the Catholic population of the north and support of Sinn Féin, the IRA's political wing. Nor did he condemn civil attacks carried out by the Protestant loyalist and unionist paramilitaries. He chose, instead, to emphasize as much as possible what he saw as the underlying economic and political inequities and deprivation setting Irishman against Irishman and the British government's well-engrained habit of divide and rule. The aim of all the various Irish and Irish American parties with an interest in setting Northern Ireland on a better and more peaceful course, he said, should be to rid it once and for all of British control.

Over the nearly thirty years of bitter strife lasting from the repression of Ulster's Catholic civil rights movement to the 1998 Good Friday Agreement, three thousand people were killed and ten times more were injured.

"I couldn't condemn the IRA unless I condemned all the others," O'Dwyer told the *Irish Times*, looking back on the Troubles.[38]

O'Dwyer worked with as many Congress members as he could—those whose ancestry intersected with Ireland or who addressed the hostilities on behalf of their Irish American constituents. Some promoted the gun, others the ballot. But O'Dwyer emphasized that the root of the problem was the continuing British presence in Ulster, arguing that the northern province must be allowed to work out its own political arrangements. Linking with Irish American organizations, he pressed for US and United Nations involvement despite the American government's deference to its World War I, World War II, and Cold War ally Great Britain.

O'Dwyer was an Irish republican, but he held the complicating view that no Irishman, whether Protestant or Catholic, was responsible for the protracted civil conflict. If his posture struck some Irish nationalists in America and Ireland as too agnostic, his law firm nonetheless represented the Irish Northern Aid Committee (Noraid), the IRA support network in

New York. By 1974, FBI reports estimated that Noraid, based in a store-front in the Bronx, had raised $1.5 million.[39] Noraid leaders said the money was for the widows and children of killed, maimed, or imprisoned IRA soldiers, not armaments used in bloody attacks on foes and installa-tions. The British and US governments found that implausible, as did IRA supporters in America who tossed fistfuls of dollars into a hat passed around in bars, sporting events, or even, it was said, at mass. Critics of Noraid's fundraising asserted that the group's claims of innocence were poppycock, including a rejoinder so commonly used by US officials that it became a cliché: "Money given to Noraid doesn't go to help widows and orphans," the comment went. "It goes to create them."[40]

In an interview for this book, Maureen Murphy, a scholar of Irish American studies at Hofstra University, saw the repeated assertions of IRA supporters as a kind of willing charade.

"Noraid," she said, "were always claiming they were helping families in Northern Ireland, but they were much more involved in sending weap-ons, and that work was consistent with O'Dwyer's view on the Troubles." O'Dwyer's firm was Noraid's go-to representative when US authorities went after the organization, starting in the 1970s.

O'Dwyer "wanted the 32 counties," a seamless Irish republic. De-spite his "very rigid" public posture on reunification in the face of the Protestant majority's palpable fear of being reduced to the status of a re-ligious minority under a reinstated republic, "privately he was very af-fable and would reach out"—even, quite controversially, to Protestant paramilitary leaders in the belief they would be willing to reach an accommodation.

All along, Murphy said, O'Dwyer placed front and center the assur-ance of full civil rights, a fairly allotted complement of good housing, and equal job opportunities for the Catholic minority—the essential, under-lying causes of the sectarian violence and hostilities, as he saw it. Paul considered the Provisional IRA's attacks as "causative" violence, she noted, "which I think is an important distinction. . . . It comes out of oppression."[41]

O'Dwyer, while well known to Irish Americans for his advocacy work as a republican, was principally a *litigator* for Irish rights, Murphy and other experts observed, and so independent that for many years he did not even hew to the path of John Hume, the nationalist politician in Northern Ireland who articulated a constitutionally driven, politicized protest agenda on behalf of the Catholic population and over time turned Edward Kennedy and Tip O'Neill to the nonviolent course he espoused.

With regard to Noraid, O'Dwyer was quick to place his free-speech principles in the service of its defense, even if doing so might complicate rather than complement his goal of a peaceful settlement across the multiple political parties and paramilitaries in the north. Irish American supporters of Noraid often confused him for a no-holds-barred supporter of the IRA, much to their liking.

Yet in 1977 O'Dwyer would diverge from Noraid and many others singularly, engaging with the Ulster Defence Association (UDA), the Protestant paramilitary responsible for the murder of many Catholics. The activist circulated among Irish organizations in the United States a UDA leader's white paper for fostering a future without British control so that both Catholics and Protestants might avoid what the brief called the danger of mutual extermination.[42] Seeking to carve out a diplomatic path, O'Dwyer felt that the militants on both sides of the sectarian chasm should not be marginalized and ignored by elected leaders in Washington, London, or Dublin, as they were. Every interested party, he argued, had blood on their hands, and only a far-reaching agreement could succeed.

But cooling the Troubles with the help of Protestant bomb-throwers and assassins was unusual and unpopular, to say the least. Not only were Ulster's armed defenders loathed by Irish America, but the possibility of a reconciliation was also remote. Bitterness in Northern Ireland was simply too deep-seated, and violent insurrection was proving too persistent— for example, the 1978 IRA bombing of a small hotel on the eastern outskirts of Belfast, in which a dozen people enjoying a dinner dance were killed and thirty were injured, all Protestant. ("People were on fire, actually burning alive," a waitress who survived the blast was reported saying.)[43] In the face of increasing horrors, O'Dwyer remained unorthodox in his republican thinking.

Whatever distaste O'Dwyer felt about Provisional IRA violence against officials and the advent of many innocent casualties, he kept it to himself. Did he think certain IRA-linked campaigns of bombing and assassination were counterproductive? Perhaps so—he was, he said, never a fan of violence. But he would also have known from Irish history that internal divisions in Ireland had long played into British hands—something borne out even before Eamon de Valera quarreled with John Devoy as well as Michael Collins. He focused his ire on the night raids, mass arrests, imprisonments without trial, and violence by the British-run security apparatus.

Paul was undeterred when the *New York Times*, traditionally approving British actions in the north, faulted him in a May 1975 editorial for supporting the IRA. The editorial cited the contention of the public intellectual and Dublin cabinet member Conor Cruise O'Brien that the expulsion of the British could be catastrophic, a danger made more real, he went on, by accommodations of attacks by the IRA with its resort to "the gun and the bomb."

O'Dwyer was by then president of the New York City Council, and the British were seeking a power-sharing agreement among the Catholic and Protestant political parties in the Parliament of Northern Ireland.[44] He did not bother responding to the editorial, nor did he or his nephew and law associate Frank Durkan stop providing legal counsel to Noraid. Paul was no more trusting of the Justice Department's motives for pressing Noraid to open its books than his mother had been when a British soldier showed up at her Bohola home, looking for her conscription-avoidant son Frank. (She dressed him down, by Paul's account.)[45]

O'Dwyer & Bernstien assisted not only Noraid unfailingly but also the weekly newspaper closely associated with the group, the *Irish People*, then put out by the staunchly republican Sister St. Hugh and later IRA stalwart Martin Galvin. The firm contested a lawsuit launched by the US Attorney General's office during the Nixon administration, the long civil litigation concluding with the two tax-exempt entities acceding to making annual financial disclosures under the US Foreign Agents Registration Act.

Though linked to Noraid and its newspaper, O'Dwyer had been an enthusiastic supporter of the nonviolent civil rights movement in Northern Ireland in the late 1960s. The early spate of resistance came together with the support of the Northern Ireland Civil Rights Association, a Belfast trade union consortium. The upsurge of protests took aim at gerrymandering and discrimination in housing and the right to vote. They were inspired by Martin Luther King Jr.'s philosophy of civil disobedience and students with black armbands flooding the streets of Paris to denounce the Vietnam War.

The Northern Irish campaign attracted thousands of younger people, with the protesters referred to as "Ulster's Negroes." Long lines of marchers traversed Protestant areas, and police and Protestant attacks ensued, marking the unofficial start of the period to become known as the Troubles.

———

IN LATE AUGUST 1969, Paul befriended and took under his wing the Irish civil rights movement's champion Bernadette Devlin during her tour of the United States. Devlin perplexed some Irish Americans, but certainly not O'Dwyer, with her attraction to the American left-wing and such groups as the Black Panthers. She was raised in a poor family in County Tyrone. Her father died when she was nine, her mother when Bernadette was attending Queen's University in Belfast. While helping raise her siblings, she also took part in a student-led organization, the People's Democracy, but, though an honors student, was forced out of the school due to her advocacy. The expulsion only fueled her pugnacity and decision to run for office. By the time of her first ever visit to America, she was twenty-two and the youngest ever member of the Westminster Parliament, elected to represent Mid-Ulster. "I will take my seat and fight for your rights," she said, signaling her disagreement with the republican tradition of dissent based on parliamentary abstentionism.

Organized by the National Association for Irish Justice (NAIJ), a progressive Irish American group founded by Brian Heron, the grandson of the Irish socialist trade union leader and Easter Rising martyr James Connolly, Devlin's tour was intended to raise as much as $1 million for families who had lost their homes to British attacks against protesters or whose breadwinner was in prison. She began the trip in New York with an evening appearance to which supporters and the merely curious arrived two hours early to get in. A socialist herself, she framed the conflict (like O'Dwyer) in class rather than sectarian terms, emphasizing sky-high unemployment and unequal housing laws. Like the NAIJ, she felt strong sympathies for the Southern Christian Leadership Conference and the Students for a Democratic Society, situating the minority Catholic population along the same continuum—a rising global movement for justice. "The Catholics are not fighting the Protestants because they're Protestants. Nor vice-versa. It's the poor against the government," she said, her straight hair parted down the middle and falling below the shoulders, with the gap between her two front teeth making her appear even younger than twenty-two.[46]

There was little question that Paul's ready service to Devlin alienated him from the many Irish Americans discomfited by her socialist views. His embrace of her was admirable, to be sure, but not necessarily wise for a politician who aspired to serve in Congress.

The day after her arrival, Mayor Lindsay presented Devlin with a key to the city—one she would redistribute, through a representative, to the Panthers in March 1970 as "a gesture of solidarity with the black liberation and revolutionary socialist movements in America." She joined a demonstration outside the Manhattan offices of the British Overseas Airways Corporation and then traveled to Philadelphia, where 350 people greeted her at the train station. Then it was on to Chicago and finally, on August 26, to a one-on-one with UN Secretary-General U Thant of Burma, a critic of US conduct in Vietnam who oversaw the entry of several independent African and Asian states into the United Nations. British officials were put off by the meeting, while Ulster unionists, including the incendiary Protestant politician and religious leader Ian Paisley, announced plans for American visits of their own.

The British Establishment assailed Devlin's politics, with W. Stratton Mills, the MP for Belfast North, labeling her "Castro in a miniskirt." Unbowed, she responded, "They've probably been sitting around for six weeks trying to think up a cute phrase about me, and that must be it." Paul, for his own part, crossed verbal swords with the Northern Irish MP for Newtownabbey Robin Bailey (Mills's travel mate) as well as Mills himself at a public forum.[47]

Devlin was pushed and pulled in every conceivable direction in America and, like O'Dwyer, cheered and jeered alike by Irish Americans. She relied on O'Dwyer to help guide her through the sensationalized press attention and the bewildering and contentious views of Irish Americans. Providing a ready ear, he proved faithful and steadying. In years to come, each time Devlin returned to the United States, they would get together. "He was a friend, mentor, protector and comrade in the broadest sense, as was his nephew, Frank. I looked to his wisdom and solidarity all of his life, like others to whom he was a source of wisdom and solidarity," she recalled to the authors.[48]

Devlin dropped plans to meet House Speaker John McCormack in Washington, DC, and went home a day early, on September 2. The FBI monitored her travels and told her that the agency had received information suggesting that the NAIJ, with which she was associated, was involved in fundraising for the IRA. It was another mine, and she side-stepped it.

British authorities showed little tolerance of MP Devlin after she re-turned. Shortly after her reelection to the Westminster Parliament in June 1970, she was imprisoned on charges of incitement to riot in con-nection with the three-day "Battle of the Bogside" of that August. She and thousands of Catholic nationalist residents of Protestant-controlled Derry clashed with the Royal Ulster Constabulary (Northern Ireland's police force) and British troops and loyalists. She was treated as if a Provisional IRA soldier.[49]

And that was not new. In 1971, Noraid sponsored a visit to the United States by Joe Cahill, a senior IRA soldier who sported a flat tweed cap. But the trip to promote the republican cause hit a snag when his visa allowing him to enter the United States, issued the year before, was sus-pended midflight, with the British sending a high-priority protest to the US State Department. When the plane landed in New York, Cahill was removed to a detention center in lower Manhattan. Paul's nephew Frank headed over promptly. He told reporters, whom he had alerted, that his IRA client "categorically denied statements attributed to him that he was coming out here to get money to buy guns to British soldiers."

But Cahill himself had publicly stated that the reason for his trip was "to raise money, guns and ammunition to fight the British Army in North-ern Ireland." Further complicating his case, he had failed to declare on his visa application a conviction for the 1942 murder of a police officer in the north. US authorities sent him to Dublin, where he was held with-out charge for twelve hours. Barred from returning to America, Cahill was retained by Noraid as a registered recipient of remittances for the rest of the year. Conor Cruise O'Brien issued an open letter, urging Paul not to assist a Cahill-linked group dedicated to IRA fundraising—the be-ginning of an extended exchange of views that would alternate between civil and acrimonious.[50]

———

PAUL WAS AS COMFORTABLE demanding UN intervention in Northern Ireland through a bullhorn as he was organizing letter-writing campaigns to Congress and the White House over British aggression. At a time when the US civil rights movement was refocusing its organizing energies to elect Black Americans to office (the first National Black Political Convention in Gary, Indiana, would draw over ten thousand African American activists in 1972, including the Reverend Jesse Jackson and the Congress member Barbara Jordan), O'Dwyer began working to use the Irish American groundswell over the deepening Troubles to build relationships with sympathetic lawmakers at the state and especially the federal levels. He formed dozens of small local chapters of the American Committee for Ulster Justice (ACUJ) around the United States by late 1971, leasing a headquarters for the new pressure group at the Henry Hudson Hotel on West Fifty-Seventh Street, hiring an executive director, and seeking donations for newspaper ads and other outreach to put the Northern Ireland crisis on the American political agenda. The State Department, in keeping with the positions of a succession of US presidents, maintained a hands-off attitude toward the UK province. But O'Dwyer's own demand for US diplomatic engagement was not much different from what it had been in 1947 when he formed the American League for an Undivided Ireland with allies like Frank Aiken, the chief of staff of the anti–Free State IRA in the 1920s.

O'Dwyer made his position on Northern Ireland clear through his ACUJ.

"Since the partition of Ireland some fifty years ago by Great Britain," read a newspaper ad for the group, paid for by a Connecticut chapter in November 1971, "the basic principles of human decency and social justice have been totally ignored in that unhappy land. The result of this can be seen in 1971 in the flames rising from Belfast to Londonderry, in the funeral processions of dead children, in ten thousand homeless families, and in the jails crowded with men detained without due process of law."

Seeking to keep the civil conflict in front of the sometimes wandering eyes of other Irish Americans, the voluntary group paid for an ad in the *New York Times*, which had yet to station a correspondent in Belfast. The group also ran a full-page message in the *Daily News*, a newspaper heavily read by conservative Catholics in the New York area.

"Must Ireland Be Britain's Vietnam?" it read.[51]

For O'Dwyer, an important impetus for spending money on such broadsides was Britain's reinstatement of internment without charges. Aimed at quashing the nationalist rebellion, the policy was as much a clampdown on rebels as a way to shake loose intelligence about the activities and membership of the IRA. Hundreds of people were dragged

from their flats and consigned to Long Kesh Detention Centre, the future
site of Her Majesty's Maze prison, with many released within forty-eight
hours after a determination that they were not in fact tied to IRA military operations.

In an attempt in part to complicate the State Department's lack of interest, Paul traveled to Derry and participated in a two-day unofficial
inquiry into the fatal wounding of two Catholic civilians by army soldiers in July 1971. Chaired by Lord Anthony Maurice Gifford, the investigation was arranged at Devlin's behest. In the late summer and fall, the
panel heard from more than a dozen eyewitnesses and military personnel, concluding that the men were shot without warning outside the scene
of stone-throwing unrest. In the final report, Paul provided this perspective: "In the United States and South Africa respectively, soldiers or police would not have been content to protect themselves with Perspex
shields and rubber bullets, and would in all probability have taken much
earlier and more drastic action against the civilians, with much greater
possible loss of life. Nevertheless, the Army in Londonderry may not wish
their actions to be evaluated by the standards applicable in parts of the
United States or South Africa, and we [Paul and the other members of
the investigative committee] do not propose to do so."[52]

The forty-page document was submitted by O'Dwyer to the UN Sub-
Commission on the Prevention of Discrimination and the Protection of
Minorities and soon forgotten.

NOT LONG AFTER PAUL RETURNED to New York from that mission,
Cormac O'Malley introduced himself at O'Dwyer's home with a knock at
the door. The son of Ernie O'Malley, one of the most famous IRA volunteers ever to have fought against the creation of the Irish Free State,
O'Malley was then twenty-nine. He had served in the US Navy in the
Western Pacific from 1965 to '67 and completed Columbia Law School
in 1970 and was a lawyer with a Manhattan firm that had an international portfolio.[53]

Riding the elevator to his own apartment in the same building where
Paul and Kathleen resided—he himself was a recent arrival—Cormac had
been surprised to hear Irish phrases spoken by the elevator operator, a
migrant from Puerto Rico.

"Where did you learn them?" the US-born O'Malley asked.

"From Paul O'Dwyer," the doorman said.

Welcomed into Paul's apartment, O'Dwyer soon told him about the ACUJ, and O'Malley agreed to attend the group's weekly breakfasts at a midtown hotel. Cormac went on to handle public relations and put out a newsletter, initially a mimeographed bulletin, which he would edit. The ACUJ helped draft legislative proposals for friendly Congress members, including Edward Kennedy, and, in late January 1972, it put together a rally. He and other lawyer members of the group went door-to-door at legislators' offices.[54]

It was three days after the lobbying trip that Bloody Sunday erupted. The Harrisburg Seven voir dire process was also just getting under way when soldiers in the British military's Parachute Regiment and UK security forces opened fire in Derry after an "unauthorized" civil rights protest march. When the smoke cleared, fourteen victims lay dead or dying. Another twelve people were seriously but not fatally injured. None had been armed.

The wanton use of state violence was vividly personalized when a Catholic priest fleeing from the soldiers, Edward Daley, saw a seventeen-year-old boy go down. "He suddenly gasped and threw his hands up in the air and fell on his face," the Reverend Daley, later the bishop of Derry, told reporters. The youth, he added, looked no more than twelve.

"He asked me: 'Am I going to die?' and I said no, but I administered the last rites," said Daley. "I can remember him holding my hand and squeezing it. We all wept. We got him to the top of the street. I knelt beside him and told him, 'Look, son, we've got to get you out,' but he was dead," the cleric said. The tragic scene, captured on camera, was soon seen around the world.

Echoing the philosophy of the late Mahatma Gandhi, the nonviolent revolutionary against Great Britain's colonial rule in India, the Reverend King had warned in a 1968 speech that responding to violence with violence only multiplied hatred and violence. But many young people turned after Bloody Sunday. As Gerry Adams, the often-imprisoned leader of Sinn Féin, recalled in his autobiographical book *Before the Dawn*, "Money, guns and recruits flooded into the IRA."[55]

Bernadette Devlin was among the people whom paratroopers fired upon in the mainly Catholic Bogside neighborhood of Derry, but she was denied the right to speak about the state assault from the floor of the

House of Commons. Growing more and more furious as she listened to the British home secretary Reginald Maudling delivering a three-minute speech devoid of contrition, she rose from her seat, rushed across the floor, and slapped him across the face.

Her maiden speech in Parliament, given on a less tempestuous day, had once been described as the best by an MP since Benjamin Disraeli more than a century earlier. Now, reporters surrounded the fierce and uncompromising debater as she walked from Parliament in a state of indignation.

A male reporter asked if she would admit that she may have been "un-ladylike," leaning in with a tape recorder.

"Un-ladylike?" Devlin retorted. "There is a young girl whose body was carried out of the Bogside this morning who was shot in the back by paratroopers. They didn't ask her if she was a lady."

But did she not, all the same, regret having struck the fifty-five-year-old home secretary?

"I'm just sorry I didn't get him by the throat," she flashed.[56]

It was only the beginning of the single most violent year of the Troubles—1972—in which nearly five hundred would be killed. As anguish grew, twining with hate, the British government supplanted the unionist-dominated Stormont parliament of the north. Britain asserted its control over major security-related operations. While, as a result, Catholics may have felt less vulnerable to violent attacks and warrantless raids, they were no less politically marginalized.

Edward Kennedy of Massachusetts held Senate hearings with Abraham Ribicoff, the Connecticut Democrat, and promoted a resolution recommending UN intervention in Northern Ireland. Though it did not pass, the debate reflected the dismay in Irish America over the events of Bloody Sunday. US Rep. James O'Hara, a Michigan Democrat, called Britain "simply an instrument of colonial suppression." Kennedy's sentiments echoed the ACUJ newspaper ads in calling Ulster "Britain's Vietnam."

British government officials adamantly termed the hearings "demagogic." Prime Minister Edward Heath condemned Kennedy's "ignorant outburst. . . . It seems not to be understood that the great majority of people in Northern Ireland are Protestants, that Northern Ireland is part of the United Kingdom, and that the majority wish to stay in the United Kingdom."[57] Based on something Cormac O'Malley said he later learned from Michael Lillis, an Irish political counselor in New York and Washington in the 1970s, Dublin viewed O'Dwyer as having "blood on his hands" for representing Noraid and refusing to call out the Provisional IRA for condemnation.[58] Lillis and others in his government evidently lumped Paul in with an Irish émigré community the counselor called, in one memo, "socially and culturally insecure" and attached to "a totem of historic myths of British repression and Irish failure which provides them with a history, an identity and a cause." Northern Ireland, Lillis wrote, provided "a heady focus for all this."

Conor Cruise O'Brien, the Fine Gael minister of posts and telegraphs, threw his anti-nationalist beliefs and worries about "a full-scale massacre" of the five-hundred-thousand-strong Catholic minority into even sharper relief a few years later when he sought to enforce Section 31 of the Irish Broadcasting Act, which banned Sinn Féin and the IRA from the airwaves—an action antithetical to O'Dwyer in New York.[59] The attempt at censorship drew denunciation, too, in southern Ireland.

Still, for more than two decades, successive governments in Dublin were content to maintain a policy of inertia vis-à-vis the north. The south rarely went further than criticizing Great Britain for failing to push more actively for a political solution and paid no penalty with voters in the Irish Republic; if all voters did not fear embroilment in the conflict, many felt that a more active role would be futile.[60]

The thinking about Northern Ireland was somewhat different at No. 10 Downing Street, where the British prime minister Harold Wilson, and his successor in 1976, James Callaghan, resented interference from Irish America, viewing pro-IRA leanings as disruptive and naive. Speaking at a dinner of the Association of American Correspondents in London, Wilson said, "Those who subscribe to the Irish Northern Aid Committee are not financing the welfare of the people, as they might delude themselves. They are financing murder. When they contribute dollars for the old country, they are not helping their much-loved shamrock to flower. They are splashing blood on it. Nor are they helping the minority Catholic population."[61]

Some of O'Dwyer's younger colleagues in the ACUJ might have concurred, though only to a limited extent, seeing Noraid's end-partition-now posture as anachronistic. The lawyers in the group's tightly knit New York circle were typically more interested in negotiations with Britain and the Protestant community. They fully agreed with O'Dwyer, though, that Washington was needed to broker a workable settlement.

Peter Murray was among the younger participants. Raised in an Irish American family in Elmhurst, a neighborhood of Queens, he married in 1969, and his wife was pregnant when he joined the ACUJ. The lawyer's father was a refrigeration mechanic and small business owner, and his mother was a homemaker. Both parents were lifetime Democrats and a little on the conservative side. As a boy, their son noticed his mother giving Joe McCarthy the benefit of the doubt as a result of his Irish surname. This was a familiar ethnic affinity, one that O'Dwyer often found himself at cross-purposes with in his campaigns for elective office.

Murray, at twenty-eight, looked up to the statesman-like chair of the ACUJ, particularly admiring his ability to combine pro bono civil rights work with a revenue-producing law practice. He had relatives who lived in Ulster, including a cousin who told him not to fret too much over the Protestants' 65 percent majority of the province's population, saying, "Don't worry—we'll outbreed them!" Murray felt IRA violence was not helpful. During a visit to a Bronx church for the ACUJ one day, his eyebrows lifted as he saw Noraid supporters passing a collection basket during worship.[62]

––––––––

NIALL O'DOWD, a Tipperary-born journalist and not a member of the group, first met O'Dwyer in New York, when Niall was thirty-two and looking to launch the *Irish Voice*, a weekly with coverage designed to interest a younger audience of Irish émigrés. The much older man offered legal assistance, free of charge. He went on to make a strong impression on the younger man, who saw him as a specimen of a particular kind of Irishman in danger of extinction. "I do think Paul came from a particularly unique group—people who had seen a revolution in Ireland and never forgot what they saw," he later observed.[63]

Just a few days after the jury deadlocked in the 1972 trial of Phil Berrigan and his cohorts on the New Catholic Left, an even looser group of potential defendants entered the aging O'Dwyer's law office, wearing worried faces. The Irish group of six, five men and one woman, had each been subpoenaed to testify before a federal grand jury in Fort Worth, Texas. The US prosecutor for that region was investigating alleged IRA arms smuggling from Mexico.

In the past, this type of case had been brought quickly to O'Dwyer's attention, as when activists were arrested for picketing the British embassy in New York or staging a sit-in at the British Overseas Airways Corporation. They had turned automatically to O'Dwyer & Bernstien, which never charged a fee to assist them. But the six New York–area residents in particular presented an escalation of the US government's efforts to keep the republican movement in check for the British.

Paul, though, had never heard of these particular Irish American individuals—average, lower-middle-class New Yorkers who were not known to be active in the cause except for Mary Kennedy, a Noraid secretary. Like Murray's parents, they were a bit on the conservative side, with no history of contact with law enforcement or courts. Ken Tierney was a hospital technician, Tom Laffey a real estate salesman, Mathias Reilly a bus driver, Danny Crawford a house painter, and Paschal Morahan a carpenter. All were US citizens or had filed papers to be naturalized.

If the visitors were, as Paul found, more conservative within the context of American politics than he was, their backgrounds and experiences were different from his. They would not, for instance, have grown up with the same degree of skepticism of religious authority that Paul developed by watching his father's struggles with Bohola's reigning cleric. And they would not have come into contact with as wide a range of ethnicities, racial minorities, and religions as Paul had in his travels with the American left.

As the visitors waited, O'Dwyer had Durkan phone the prosecutor long-distance to ask why the individuals were required to travel to Fort Worth. Durkan reported back that the prosecutors simply stated, "I want to question your clients." O'Dwyer summed up the difficulties. The recipients of a federal subpoena would be legally vulnerable if they agreed to testify, simply for having attended events in support of the IRA. "Should you testify," he said, "you will undoubtedly be called upon to testify about those in attendance at such gatherings and be required to supply names and addresses of those whom you know to have participated. Those, in turn—including your family and friends—are [in danger of being] subject to harassment."

The listeners did not interrupt.

"Should you testify but balk at listing your friends, it is the same as refusing to testify in the first place," Paul went on. "If the government then gives you immunity from prosecution in return for your testimony, and you still refuse to answer the questions put to you, you are subject to imprisonment for contempt of court."

He then delivered the clincher: the very same fate, imprisonment, would likely result if they refused to testify. But at least then they would not have been placed in a position where they might have felt compelled to inform on friends. The same trap was laid to ensnare those accused during the House Un-American Activities Committee's period of sympathy for membership in the Communist Party, when they were brought before congressional committees and asked, "Are you now or have you ever been a member of the Communist Party?" If the accused answered no, then government informers would be brought in to contradict them, likely ending with a perjury indictment. Yet they could not answer yes untruthfully in an attempt to satisfy their inquisitors. (In 1948, Alger Hiss, the US government official suspected of carrying out espionage for the Soviets, was convicted on two counts of perjury, landing him in prison three years later.)[64]

Although a total of six turned to O'Dwyer for pro bono counsel initially, they became known as the Fort Worth Five after Mary Kennedy was relieved from testifying. Consulting their spouses, and perhaps their souls, the targets opted in the end to remain silent, reasoning that they would rather spend a year, or two, in prison for contempt of court. Federal Judge Leo Brewster, however, put them away for an indefinite term.

Durkan, along with Doris Peterson and William Cunningham SJ, both colleagues of the woolly-haired William Kunstler of the Center for Constitutional Rights, launched a round of appeals (Cunningham had been part of the Harrisburg Seven defense). Paul, too, went to Texas, hoping to meet with the judge. Brewster's secretary, however, told him the judge had gone fishing. O'Dwyer managed to buttonhole the US marshal to move his clients from Tarrant County Jail, an "inhumane" lockup, to Seagoville Penitentiary. Brewster had denied them bail, and the Circuit Court of Appeals in Fort Worth sustained his decision.[65]

O'Dwyer returned to New York and set about mobilizing Irish American forces through his extensive press contacts and column-writing friends. Using language likely to resonate, he called the mistreatment of the Irish New Yorkers a Nixon administration ploy on behalf of its British client and decried the removal of law-abiding Irish citizens to an unsympathetic venue far from their jobs, homes, and families. He said they were being forced to pay a price for their ethnicity and their beliefs.

The government denied the attorney's assertions.

Soon, the Fort Worth Five became synonymous with the American government's longtime accommodation of Britain's rough handling of

Northern Ireland. And the episode was widely seen as a slap against the Irish American community. Support for the detainees came from both Republican and Democratic members of Congress and municipal and state elected officials. In August 1972, two months after the denial of bail, as many as three thousand people rallied in Gaelic Park in the Riverdale section of the Bronx, with many wearing T-shirts emblazoned with the slogan "IRA All the Way." O'Dwyer had once helped an Irish American businessman, John "Kerry" O'Donnell, obtain the license to operate the multipurpose outdoor athletic facility under a city-issued license. Now he was the star attraction at the concession. Standing before more than a thousand people, he used a microphone to recite a letter from "Her Majesty's Prison" in Fort Worth: if their sacrifice brought freedom nearer for Catholics of Northern Ireland, the letter from the Fort Worth Five read, then "we shall count the cost as nothing."

As he ended, a folk group belted out, "The Statue of Liberty weeps in the harbor, America / Now let your head hang in shame," and the crowd went wild with applause at the song's conclusion.[66] Far from the rally, an Irish-born New Yorker named John Kelly got into the spirit, making a 120-mile trudge through Death Valley Desert, California, on behalf of the Fort Worth detainees. Heralded by Kennedy and the Texas archbishop, Kelly's trek for thirty-four hours and nine minutes won the forty-three-year-old former pugilist a listing in *The Guinness Book of Records* and coverage on both sides of the Atlantic.[67] The detainees, who had been forced to appeal their jailing to the US Supreme Court, were allowed to return home when Justice William Douglas signed an emergency application from O'Dwyer and other lawyers for their release on bonds ranging from $5,000 to $15,000. The five unlikely heroes were welcomed back at LaGuardia Airport by Irish bagpipers and tearful relatives. O'Dwyer said he was overjoyed, wryly adding that he was glad to hear that the bail fund in Irish pubs around New York was "oversubscribed."[68]

The case was over—no indictment was ever brought—but the reverberations went on longer. A House subcommittee held hearings examining the implications for grand jury conduct of the five's subpoenas, with Paul, and Frank, making a presentment on the first day to go along with the ones by Kennedy, New York US Rep. Bella Abzug, and other lawmakers.[69] While the Fort Worth Five were regularly sought out for interviews, then and in years to come, O'Dwyer redeemed his own popularity in the city council presidential election in the fall of 1973. He was named the grand marshal in the St. Patrick's Day parade the following year and was wildly cheered.

———

O'DWYER AND HIS LAW firm were also cheered for defending militants who fled British jurisdiction and, captured in America, faced demands for their return to face trial in the United Kingdom. One of the firm's first such clients was Desmond Mackin, an IRA volunteer who fled to New York after British courts indicted him for the March 1978 murder of a British soldier in Belfast.[70]

Despite indications that he may have been an incidental party to the murder, US authorities arrested and remanded him back to the Metropolitan Correctional Center. During Mackin's fifteen-month confinement, the firm worked out legal arguments to free him with members of the Brehon Law Society, a professional association O'Dwyer formed in 1978 to assist with the defense of nationalists. The society grew from a handful of lawyers at first—mainly Paul and newer associates in his firm—to more than five hundred members in later decades.

The US District Court magistrate judge Naomi Reice Buchwald cleared Mackin in 1981, citing an exception for fugitives charged in political offenses under the 1976 US-Britain extradition treaty; the case established a precedent, and when the US Supreme Court declined to hear the government's appeal, it added up to a "a big victory, and it was fascinating," remembered Lawrence Downes, a lawyer in Paul's firm and volunteer with the Brehon Society.[71] The lawyers assisting in Mackin's lengthy appeal included Frank Durkan, James Gilroy (O'Dwyer & Bernstien), and the practitioners James Cullen and Sheila Donohue. Still other significant contributions to the high-profile case were made by the Brooklyn attorney and former US Marine Stephen Somerstein and Mary Boresz Pike, a labor lawyer who regularly joined a picket line with other Irish American women outside the British consulate in Manhattan.[72]

As one of the many legal satellites drawn to Paul's orbit, Cullen was relatively unusual, a successful corporate lawyer. While part of a large Manhattan real estate law firm, he had an abiding interest in the developing field of human rights law. For example, he represented the chaplain in the army's 1969 Peers Commission, which examined the factors that contributed to the My Lai massacre.

Paul admired Cullen and liked to tell the story of how he had mistaken him at first for a WASP on a routine day in Brooklyn civil court. Tall and lean, with a military bearing and slight mustache, Cullen was representing the Federation of Protestant Welfare Agencies that morning, while Paul handled another case involving members of an Italian civil rights coalition. Paul said he teased Cullen good-naturedly about his case, judging him Anglo-Saxon and "impervious to insult." But when O'Dwyer was heading out for coffee and a sandwich, "this man I had tried to goad said, 'So when have you been to Bohola last?'" Paul, as he told it, was momentarily devastated that he had even heard of the place, Cullen's way of letting him know he was a fellow Irishman. He was raised in Queens and worked his way through college as a truck driver, going on to St. John's School of Law. Cullen helped him to cofound the Brehon Law Society and became its first president.[73]

Equally important to Paul was Richard Harvey, a radical British barrister who would go on to defend, under international law and human rights obligations, the former president of Yugoslavia Slobodan Milošević, who faced charges of genocide and war crimes that occurred in Bosnia, Croatia, and Kosovo in the 1990s. Harvey also represented Greenpeace International, the environmental activism group, in the Netherlands.

Sean Downes, the younger brother of Lawrence, recalled how Harvey first became involved with Paul by the early 1980s. At the time, before Downes joined the firm, Paul was aware of Harvey's focus on humanitarian causes and human rights advocacy, most recently in South Africa. The opportunity arose for Paul to befriend him.

"He'd come to New York to get away from things," said Downes, who went on to a career in personal injury law (long a revenue-producing cornerstone of the O'Dwyer & Bernstien portfolio, with an emphasis on accident victims). "Paul got wind of that and he said to his nephew, Frank, 'C'mon, we're going to the airport.' And they met Richard at the airport. They sort of kidnapped him. They set him up in O'Dwyer & Bernstien until he got under way with his own criminal practice. Richard was helpful in all sorts of cases [involving republican defendants]."[74]

In one episode of their alliance, Harvey and Paul worked together to hold a demonstration outside the *New York Times* building on West Forty-Third Street after the March 1989 funeral of the Belfast criminal defense attorney Pat Finucane. A prominent lawyer for nationalists who challenged the British government in several prominent human rights cases, Finucane was shot fourteen times in front of his wife and their three children. The assassins were from the UDA, later (in 2011) admitted by the British prime minister David Cameron to have acted in collusion with British security services, as suspected by Harvey and his New York allies at the time.

Incensed that the *New York Times* was not covering the story, Harvey and O'Dwyer rode on a flatbed truck to the front door of the newspaper's headquarters. Paul, who was eighty-one, shouted demands through a megaphone. Surrounding him were some of New York's better-known politicians, such as the Nassau County comptroller (and future congressman) Peter King, the soon-to-be-elected mayor David Dinkins, the future Brooklyn district attorney Charles ("Joe") Hynes, and the Upper West Side council member Ruth Messinger, along with Brehon lawyers.

Ray O'Hanlon covered the irregular protest for the *Irish Echo* and wrote about it in his 1998 book on "the New Irish Americans." He recalled the frigid gale coming off the Hudson River on the day of the unusual demonstration.

"It was a raw, bitter wind, and it was appropriate," wrote O'Hanlon, who became the weekly newspaper's editor.

But the demand for coverage of the assassination and its aftermath fell on deaf ears at the newspaper of record, and Cullen initiated his own inquiry into Finucane's brazen killing, exerting pressure on British authorities.[75]

The many extradition battles O'Dwyer's firm took part in were fought with the understanding that anyone, including Desmond Mackin, a former taxi driver, would, if tried and convicted in Northern Ireland, be made to wear the prison uniform worn by *criminal* convicts; the British government had imposed this consistent dress code, including for anyone imprisoned for political violence, as of March 1976. IRA volunteers locked in Her Majesty's Maze, or H-Blocks, protested the policy by shedding the uniform, wearing only the blanket issued by prison guards, and refusing all food, the hallowed Fenian method of prisoners' protest.

The so-called British criminalization of political prisoners inspired a telegram from O'Dwyer during the New York City fiscal crisis, asking Gerald Ford to intervene with Downing Street, but the president responded as he initially did to the mayor and governor seeking emergency federal aide—with indifference.[76] Seven prisoners participated in a hunger strike at Her Majesty's Maze in 1980, ending after fifty-three days, and nine more did so in 1981, fatally. One of the prisoners, Bobby Sands, became a martyr to the cause of Irish independence and dignity. A foe of Margaret Thatcher, Sands was elected as a member of the British Parliament while wasting away.

His protest attracted worldwide interest, and so did that of another republican, Joe Doherty. After a 1980 firefight in Ulster, Doherty, a volunteer in the IRA's Belfast Brigade, escaped from prison and fled to America. He was arrested in New York, becoming the center of a nine-year legal and diplomatic battle for his freedom, led by leaders in Irish America, including O'Dwyer, his firm, and lawyers with the Brehon Law Society. Though sentenced in absentia in the United Kingdom to a minimum thirty years of confinement for the death of a member of the Special Air Service of the British Army, he was not charged with any crime in the United States and took no precaution to avoid capture. When authorities caught up with him, in June of 1983, he was tending Clancy's Bar on Third Avenue.

The long extradition battle that ensued was the longest and most celebrated. The New York congressman Gary Ackerman promptly showed up in court after Doherty's apprehension to try to convince the judge to set bail, as did Cullen, with the latter explaining that Doherty was not the type of individual "to run off with your money, because not one Irish republican had ever run after giving his word," as Sean Downes recalled. The judge asked Cullen what he did for a living: "Chief Judge of the U.S. Army Court of Criminal Appeals, your honor," he replied. Cullen's military credentials, however, failed to overcome prosecutors' determination to have Doherty labeled a potential flight risk. Doherty, after all, was a prison escapee.[77]

Paul's firm did not represent Doherty—that job fell to Pike. But O'Dwyer took a deep and abiding interest in the snail-like progress of the case and the health of the prisoner, visiting Doherty on five occasions at the Metropolitan Correctional Center and, on Christmas Day of 1986, the federal prison in Otisville, New York. Paul emerged from that visit to tell the press that the inmate, whom he described as a jailhouse poet, had endured five months of solitary confinement. Yet, Paul said, Doherty had never been charged in an American court, and he likened him to Tom Paine and George Washington, who, like the young people fighting religious discrimination in Northern Ireland, felt compelled to respond with arms to the "harsh, cruel and unjust colonial laws in their own native land."[78]

———

GRUESOME IRA ATTACKS in the 1980s received harsher condemnation from the US government than did the organized state violence of British troops and security forces; following the outrage over Sands's treatment and death, they tested Irish American support. Unlike O'Dwyer, Governor Carey and Senator Moynihan registered antipathy for the Provisional IRA, staying clear of the 1983 St. Patrick's Day parade in New York whose grand marshal was Michael Flannery, an unrepentant veteran of the anti-Treaty IRA in the Irish Civil War, once imprisoned by the British and released after a twenty-eight-day hunger strike.

Carey and Moynihan were among those American politicians lining up behind the Northern Ireland politician John Hume. Part of a new generation of Irish nationalists, Hume was a former schoolteacher who came to public attention as the leader of the Ulster civil rights movement of the late 1960s. In the early 1980s, he viewed as out of touch the aging Fenians who in their youth had taken up arms against the empire and advocated violence against England. First elected to the Parliament of Northern Ireland in 1969 as an independent nationalist, Hume stayed so until the imposition of direct rule from London in March 1972, the British government's response to the violent aftermath of Bloody Sunday. Born in Derry, he was a founding member of the nationalist Social Democratic and Labour Party of Northern Ireland, which was a rival to Sinn Féin, the pro-IRA political party headed by Gerry Adams.

Hume was then working with a good deal of success to convince key Irish American leaders to adopt a more strategic approach to Northern Ireland, arguing that harping on British intransigence on the question of reunifying Ireland only served to legitimize those using destabilizing violence to support nationalism. Ted Kennedy, for one, listened. As the *Boston Globe* noted, "having lost two brothers to assassination, Kennedy became outspoken against IRA violence, even as he criticized British policies he said drove young Catholics to join the IRA." Hume's influence with Kennedy, as well as with Tip O'Neill, helped make him a central figure, like Adams, in the future progress of talks on the status of the six counties of the north.[79]

———

O'DWYER COLLECTED NUMEROUS non-Irish American political allies of his own, like the New York congressmen Gary Ackerman and Mario Biaggi, working with them to keep pressure on the British and US governments. At the same time, he wrangled with a Jewish politician who was decidedly unsympathetic to IRA violence: Ed Koch.

"What a silly man," the then congressman said of O'Dwyer in 1976, two years before gaining the first of three terms as mayor. Koch judged Paul a "schmuck" for refusing to support Humphrey until the final approach to the 1968 presidential election. Koch evinced no respect, moreover, for what he described as Paul's legal support of IRA gunrunners.

In explaining his distaste for the latter, Koch said he had written to a constituent that he would not oppose British force-feedings of hunger strikers, a practice that he suggested had saved the lives of the 1973 London bombers the Price sisters, whose strike lasted more than two hundred days. After Koch's response, Paul had sent the New York representative a heated letter, demanding to know why he felt qualified to speak out on the history of Irish hunger strikes against British callousness. "Who the hell asked your opinion on terrorism?" wrote O'Dwyer.

Koch, however, depicted himself in his comments on O'Dwyer and the IRA as an opponent of insurrectional terror, no matter the perpetrators or the cause they asserted, also decrying O'Dwyer's past support for Irgun.[80] With Koch readying a run for mayor to the right as New York liberalism tottered, he was dismissive of one of the representatives of that movement, O'Dwyer, then the president of the city council.

Had he responded further to Koch, which he did not, O'Dwyer might have asked if Koch wore blinders concerning the immorality of Great Britain's mass arrests, internments without trial, and extrajudicial killings.

Someone else who would have agreed with Koch's reproach of the IRA had already clashed with O'Dwyer, chiefly in a 1971 article for the *New York Review of Books*—Conor Cruise O'Brien, the Irish politician, diplomat, historian, and academic. His piece in the highbrow publication discussed the bombings occurring in the north. O'Brien's critique had been similar to Koch's.

O'Dwyer responded to the article, stating that while he agreed with O'Brien's premise—that "violence is not the appropriate instrumentality to cure society's ills"—the notion that the IRA was a major cause of the Troubles was misguided because "the violence which brought them into prominence is the source of Northern Ireland's present state. If we could somehow eliminate the latter, the IRA would soon disintegrate or become irrelevant." (The passage of the years would prove O'Dwyer correct—twenty-seven more years, to be exact.)

O'Brien fired back. Was the IRA's violence defensive, which could be justified, or naked aggression?

"How," O'Brien went on, "do you know, or why do you even believe, that those whom you would help to collect money in the United States make any such differentiation? I put it to you that you have no means of knowing that such a differentiation is made and no control whatever over what is done with the money."[81]

Four years later, in an address at a US Chamber of Commerce luncheon in Dublin, O'Brien took his disagreements with O'Dwyer to a more vitriolic level. In words that the *New York Times* would cite in an editorial supporting British negotiations for "power-sharing" in the Northern Ireland Assembly, he observed that Paul was taking sides with a physical-force movement that considered itself superior to the democratic political process. Characteristically, O'Brien's language was deliberately provocative. "The late Adolf Hitler," he said, "while his political career was drawing to a close, amid the ruins which it had caused, reflected that the German people had not proved worthy of him. I am afraid there is a gentleman living in New York who seriously believes that the Irish people is not proving worthy of Paul O'Dwyer."

Reacting to the speech, Paul told the *New York Times* that O'Brien's attacks had "grown bolder—and more irrational." Paul did not address the Provisional IRA's escalating bombings nor point to recent lethal unionist and loyalist paramilitary bombings. He focused, instead, on the record of British human rights violations.

"I have no intention," he commented, "of being silent while a minority of Catholics in Northern Ireland are raided in their homes in the middle of the night by the British military; while Irish men and women are jailed without charge or trial in the face of proof by one commission after another, including Amnesty International, that Irish men and women have been tortured by British jailers."[82]

BEFORE THE SEVENTIES were over, O'Dwyer was asked to expound on the future of the Northern Ireland civil war. The interviewer was Claudia Dreifus of Long Island's *Newsday*, who had covered stories in Belfast. O'Dwyer described an evolution in his thinking, though "evolution" was not a word usually heard from radicals or dreamers:

> In 1969, I was still hopeful that the civil rights movement in Northern Ireland would have an effect. In Belfast, there was a movement that, at first, I thought could work because they were patterning themselves after Martin Luther King Jr. and Mahatma Gandhi. I felt that perhaps, through devolution [i.e., the Sunningdale power-sharing agreement of 1973], something could work out. In those days the IRA didn't mean anything; it was maybe a few hundred people who were carrying arms, no activity. They were out of business until such time as the [Catholic] ghettos of Belfast and Derry burned again.

When the civil rights movement in Northern Ireland faded, there was "no initiative—not from London, not from Dublin." But the Protestant UDA formulated some thinking around an independent, six-county government and sent it to him to consider carefully. He advocated that it be given due consideration by all parties, as it was "free of Dublin, free of London. . . . They were talking about pulling away from Great Britain. And that's where it's at."

If the Irish north was rid of British control, in other words, differences among the rival Irish factions could be ironed out over time. He went on: "Great Britain is the mischief. If that's out, these people will get together."

He acknowledged that there could be a "protective period of time when emotion may take over" in fratricidal Northern Ireland. A needed British pullout, then, might best be gradual rather than all at once.

Yet the civil strife seemed to have no end in sight, said Dreifus.

"No, I don't feel that," her subject said. "I feel this will end when people at the highest level make sure it ends. As long as Great Britain takes the position that it can't be pushed out of its last acres of empire, it won't end. As long as the Dublin government insults the total Protestant population by not passing laws for contraception and divorce, it won't end. But as soon as the United States comes in and says, 'Why don't we try to solve this thing,' it will end. If we can solve the problems between Egypt and Israel"—a reference to the recently consummated Camp David Accord—"we can solve this one."

Leaning back in his chair, O'Dwyer made clear that he was not a supporter of violence in Ulster by the IRA or anyone else but clung to the hope that Washington would launch a sustained diplomatic effort to broker a durable settlement. Let the feuding Irish finally have a chance to work out their differences without British interference, he said.

"Where is the initiative coming from?" asked O'Dwyer. "It falls into the hands of terrorists because there is a vacuum. When the day comes that it is United States policy to take Britain out of Northern Ireland, that's the day it will end."[83]

12

A HIGHER PLATEAU

THE ERSTWHILE CITY COUNCIL president represented his most
unpopular client ever in late November 1979: the Revolutionary
Republic of Iran. It was just two weeks after Muslim followers of
the successful revolution by Islamic fundamentalists, which overthrew the
US-backed puppet king Mohammad Reza Pahlavi, had taken over the
American embassy in Tehran and seized fifty-two American diplomats and
citizens as hostages. O'Dwyer & Bernstien filed the papers in a New York
courthouse on behalf of the new regime led by the country's first supreme
leader, Ayatollah Ruhollah Khomeini, seeking to recover billions of dollars
that Pahlavi and his wife, Farah, allegedly expropriated through a half-
dozen foundations when they fled into exile. The suit also sought damages
for the Iranian government. The coattorneys on the case were Thomas
Shack and James Abourezk of the firm of Abourezk, Shack & Mendenhall
in Washington, DC.[1]

Conservative Irish Americans, who were taken aback by O'Dwyer's
defense of Catholic priests who tossed bottles of their own blood on Selective Service files during the Nixon administration, could be forgiven
for questioning the former city council president's choice of clients, perhaps, as the "hostage crisis" dragged for 444 days. Until the hostages were
freed, just hours after Ronald Reagan succeeded Jimmy Carter on January 20, 1981, CBS News's Walter Cronkite and Ted Koppel's *Nightline*
provided nightly reminders of their captivity and the number of days that

had elapsed since the Americans suffered the consequences of the recent history of US hubris and miscalculation in the Middle East.

For more than fourteen years, Khomeini had lived in exile for opposing the shah's program of secularization. In mid-January 1979, Pahlavi left Iran for medical reasons, described as being "on vacation." Two weeks later, Khomeini, a mystical figure in Iran—some claimed to see his visage on the face of the moon—touched down in the country of his birth on a chartered Air France flight from Paris, accompanied by an international complement of 120 journalists. Emerging from the plane, he was greeted by a gleeful crowd the BBC estimated as up to five million strong.[2] The monarchical regime would soon collapse. While in Paris, Khomeini posited a "democratic political system" for Iran. Once hoisted to power by an appreciative Iranian public, however, he advocated the creation of a theocracy.

Support for the establishment of an Islamic republic was near universal in Iran. With a listing economy, the nation had been ruled for a quarter-century by a regime known for using secret police to torture and murder thousands of people; it was buttressed by billions of dollars of weapons from the US military-industrial complex. The US government had sponsored Pahlavi after the CIA helped overthrow his democratically elected predecessor, Premier Mohammad Mosaddegh, whom American and British officials had judged susceptible to falling into the Soviet orbit after he nationalized Iran's oil industry. At the time of Mosaddegh's death under house arrest in 1967, Iran under Pahlavi had fully signed over 40 percent of Iran's oil fields to US, French, and British petroleum companies, with more to come.[3]

Pahlavi was suffering from advanced lymphatic cancer; he and his wife secured humanitarian visas with the help of well-placed allies David Rockefeller, John McCloy, and Henry Kissinger and checked into New York Hospital in Manhattan.[4] The news of his admittance to the hospital precipitated students' taking of the American embassy in Tehran. Khomeini's government sought a full accounting of the shah's riches and the return of the money to the national treasury. With O'Dwyer's legal help, Iran's new supreme leader sought financial redress in American courts; a judicial ruling in Iran would have been unlikely to carry weight internationally.

Initiated two days after Iran's retention of Abourezk, Shack & Mendenhall, Paul's involvement stemmed from his political leanings, relatively high profile, and familiarity with the New York courts. The anti-shah Ramsey Clark may also have had something to do with it. Clark had been dispatched by President Carter to Iran to seek the release of the hostages. He said later that he advised Iran to sue for damages in US courts. But Paul's legal colleague was called home after the Carter administration froze all Iranian assets held in US-based and other financial institutions. Besides the fifty-two hostages' lives, the future of these assets, representing bank loans and corporate investment worth billions of dollars, hinged on the outcome of the hostage crisis and the lawsuit.

O'Dwyer may have been an acceptable choice to field the Iran government's case because some of the shah's most determined opponents in the United States were young Iranians, the children of Persian elites, attending American universities in the Northeast. Their family connections, coupled with their anti-imperialist activism, were potentially useful to influencing the US foreign policy establishment. Some turned to O'Dwyer & Bernstien when the federal immigration service began scrutinizing their education visas.[5]

As soon as the legal papers were filed with the state court, O'Dwyer sent his legal associate James Gilroy and his cousin McNicholas, an assistant since 1959, up to New York Hospital to serve a summons on the ailing shah. But upon the pair's arrival at the hospital, a security guard, who by happenstance knew Frank Durkan, let them know that machine-gun-toting bodyguards surrounded the VIP patient's bed. He gently turned them back.

"He said there'd be a bloodbath if we tried to go into that room," McNicholas recalled.[6]

McNicholas and Gilroy left, passing a sea of idle TV news crews, reporters, and photojournalists. But the pair's failure to have placed the summons directly into the shah's hands had little consequence. Responding to an affidavit from O'Dwyer and Shack, Judge Bentley Kassal granted a substituted service of summons, another method to deliver legal papers to start a case. Hearings before the state supreme court judge Irving Kirschenbaum would begin soon.[7]

Idilio Gracia Peña ran into Paul as the case dragged on in 1980, reminding him that he was perceived by some as the friend of a foreign adversary of the United States.

"Someone asked me about it and you owe me an answer," Gracia Peña remembered saying to O'Dwyer, lest his longtime admiration of Paul—

whose support of the Municipal Archives had helped save his job as a librarian—be complicated unwarrantedly.

"Idilio," Paul replied, "I'm not the lawyer for the ayatollah. I'm the lawyer for the Iranian people. The shah took $50 billion and it belongs to the Iranian people."

While Gracia Peña accepted the explanation, he blurted out, "Also you get a nice fee for that!"

"That too," sighed O'Dwyer.[8]

He could not go it alone. Brian served as a senior counsel at a later phase. In addition, Paul recruited O'Dwyer & Bernstien associate Franklin Siegel to assist with keeping track of the complicated financial litigation, while Gary Silverman, a lawyer who had recently started working at O'Dwyer & Bernstien, took on significant responsibilities in the case.

In early 1981, Kirschenbaum ruled—and he was to be upheld on appeal all the way to the US Supreme Court—that the New York courts, and taxpayers, were not responsible for hosting *Islamic Republic of Iran v. Mohammad Reza Pahlavi*. An international tribunal would be more appropriate, he said. The shah died in exile in Egypt in July 1980 as Iran neared the start of a ten-year war with its neighbor Iraq, with an estimated five hundred thousand deaths and up to 1.5 million wounded.[9]

Siegel's office was in the prow of the Flatiron Building at Twenty-Third Street and Broadway, with a view of Central Park. Wedge-shaped, the iconic 1902 building was popular for New York publishing houses, such as St. Martin's Press. Two years out of law school, surrounded by dozens of boxes stuffed with papers related to Western corporations' suspended investments tied up in Iran, Siegel had regular contact with Leonard Boudin at the latter's firm, which represented Iran's central bank, and an endless series of commercial attorneys from white-shoe houses in New York.

"Thrown into the deep end" was how Siegel characterized the start of this year and a half of litigation work for O'Dwyer.

But, with his declared interest in human rights law, the young attorney felt that his retention by Paul amounted to a vote of confidence from a lawyer he looked up to. Siegel previously worked on the city council president's staff for him and helped organize hearings on New York Police Department dossier collecting; his most recent job had been at the city's largest public employee union, District Council 37. Also active in the National Lawyers Guild, he had trained lawyers in Puerto Rico on conducting civil rights litigation in US district courts.

"Yes, there was blowback," Siegel said of the Iran matter and O'Dwyer's visible role for the ayatollah, speaking with the authors, "but Paul handled it professionally. His firm, as compared to the commercial firms that were litigating for assets, was representing a human rights principle: corrupt government leaders shouldn't be able to use the U.S. as a haven for their ill-gotten gains. It was a totally new human-rights principle."[10]

The uproar in the United States over the hostage crisis quieted when an international tribunal, established under the Algiers Accords, assumed responsibility for sorting out the Iranian claims and those of more than eighty Western firms. The hostages remaining (some had already been let go) were freed under the agreements, but only after a rescue attempt with military helicopters embarrassed the US military and President Carter, who approved the mission.

O'Dwyer, as Iran's outside cocounsel, stayed unruffled in interviews, avoiding political rhetoric. He reminded a British interviewer from Reuters in January 1980 that the State Department recognized the right of Tehran to press its case for reparation in US courts. He added, "I certainly would do everything I can with respect to the hostages."

According to McNicholas, Paul had hoped to play a role in freeing the hostages and made a trip to Iran to meet with government representatives on the legal case; McNicholas drove him to JFK Airport for his flight. James Gilroy concurred, saying, "It was my impression that this was his hope, to be part of the resolution of the hostage crisis," while noting that Paul never actually told him so.[11]

In any case, there was virtually no chance O'Dwyer might be able to pull a rabbit out of a hat for the hostages. He restricted himself to supporting an elemental principle of American jurisprudence—the right to have one's say in court. The Reuters reporter said, "This must be a fairly unpopular case for you to take in the United States," stating the obvious, and O'Dwyer pointed out in response, "That's nothing new in my life. I've had unpopular cases before. I've had 'em all my life. I've never taken a vote before I took a case."[12]

Paul's professionalism did not assuage all interested parties, to be sure. The conservative *Daily News* columnist Bill Reel went on the attack in an article headlined "How, Paul O'Dwyer, How Could You Do It?" Listing the questions he felt needed answering by O'Dwyer, Reel wrote, "What is your fee for representing kidnapper Khomeini, and how does it feel to be on the payroll of the mad warmonger whose anti-American ravings inflamed the mob that murdered 20-year-old Marine Steven Crowley [a Long Island soldier shot during the mob attack on the embassy]?"

O'Dwyer should "quit this foul gig immediately," stated Reel.[13]

To Earl Caldwell of the *Daily News*, an O'Dwyer admirer, Paul offered the following defense of his work for Iran: "They [the Iranians] came out of tyranny like we came out of tyranny. I couldn't possibly approve of the hostage-taking. I couldn't possibly approve of something which was not in keeping with our own ideas of government. But, by the same token, I couldn't possibly approve of [former secretary of state John] Foster Dulles and the CIA to put a tyrant on top of a people who were there 10,000 years before Christ."[14]

Beth Fallon was a rare female New York columnist. Writing for the *Daily News*, she was known for pricking the conscience of the powerful. For a 1982 piece headlined "Paul O'Dwyer, and His Right to Say It," she wrote that the lawyer "defended Khomeini when the rest of America, me included, would have been delighted to string him up. He doesn't have to agree with you to defend you."

Fallon added that O'Dwyer had recently finished representing the *conservative* WNEW-TV commentator Martin Abend after prosecutors charged him with failing to pay his taxes on a Brooklyn property for two years. Paul knocked the charges back, showing the court that Abend had brought himself up to date for his primary residence in New Jersey and emphasizing, too, that the state had never before prosecuted a property owner for tax evasion for a second home in a different state. Fallon quoted Brian saying his father had taken the case of the right-wing broadcaster even though "he hates everything Abend stands for."[15] With one exception, that is: although Abend was a conservative in the context of American politics, he was just as radical as Paul in the context of Northern Ireland politics and just as committed to ousting the British.

SIX OR SEVEN YEARS BEFORE, Paul had begun arrangements to donate his birth family's Bohola home to the Cheshire Trust for conversion to a supervised residence for physically disabled adults. The last O'Dwyer to live in the old home had been his eldest sister (and Frank Durkan's mother), Mary, known as May. A teacher in Bohola until the age of seventy, May died in 1978, leaving the property to her husband, Bernic, who survived until 1983.

Too much trouble to keep up as a private home, the house and three-and-a-half-acre property took on a new life, accommodating thirty elderly and infirm people. As a Cheshire Home, named for the Royal Air Force officer group captain Leonard Cheshire, with a foundation started in 1948, it entered a charitable constellation that would grow to include 270 homes for the physically impaired in 49 different countries during O'Dwyer's lifetime.[16]

As Paul was also involved with the Mayo Association for the Handicapped, he and Kathleen went to Dublin in late November 1980, amid the Iranian case, for a charity ball. But in the hotel, her heart gave out. She died with shocking suddenness in their private room at the Burlington Hotel. She was sixty-two.[17]

"That was a very sad time," recalled Paul's longtime secretary at the firm, Virginia Polihrom.[18]

Paul had expected Kathleen to outlive him, helping her to acquire a credit-reporting company located in New Hyde Park, New York, as a source of income after he was gone, said their son Rory.[19] Yet one acolyte said Paul's bewilderment and struggle may have included a tincture of guilt; during their marriage, he was given to long workdays extending into the night. O'Dwyer's firstborn physician son, Billy, said he was "a workaholic in a way" who frequently returned home from work well into the night-time, turned in at 2 a.m. or 3 a.m., and got out of bed around 6 a.m.—"It was a tough life," he said. Sometimes, returning at a more reasonable hour, say 8:30 p.m., he requested steak and peas—the usual—"so Mom cooked steak and peas for him. But on Sunday nights the entire family had a regular appointment at the dinner table."[20]

"That the children grew up whole and sound I owe to Kathleen," Paul wrote in his frank autobiography, *Counsel for the Defense*, assembled with the help of his 1973 council president campaign press spokeswoman Linda Fisher, who assisted Phil Sipser in the 1968 campaign. The memoir was published just a year before Kathleen's death.

Jimmy Breslin went to Kathleen's wake, held at Frank E. Campbell Funeral Chapel on Madison Avenue, and wrote in his column the next day that his friend's bereavement had lain beneath a blanket of stoicism.[21]

Some of the men who paid their respects had gathered around Paul in a half-circle, hands in their pockets, eyes cast down.

"Whiskey's no help," one offered, breaking their silence.

"Not for this," responded O'Dwyer. "It's just an excuse. It gives you false warmth, and you pay for it 10 times over."[22]

Paul started on the path to "false warmth" as an immigrant to the United States, beginning with beer before going on to red wine and ending with cocktails of various kinds. He gave up drinking in 1959, at age fifty-two, realizing that social lubricating with lawyers, clients, politicians, reporters, activists, and friends in the evening hours dulled his professional acumen in the light of day. Kathleen supported his decision.[23]

"Why did they drink so much at the wakes in Ireland?" someone else asked Paul.

"They never did," he replied, calling it a widely held myth.

Filling a brief silence, another male friend said, "Forty-five years—how do you keep a marriage together for that long?"

"The woman had the patience and the understanding. I don't know how you explain it after that," said O'Dwyer.

Breslin's column took note of Kathleen's intelligence, one of the more underrated ingredients, perhaps, of an enduring relationship. In addition to a doting grandmother, she was a good sport, evident the time Paul first took her dancing at a Harlem club, a world away from the Irish working class in the Yorkville section of the Upper East Side where she was raised by hardworking émigrés. In her marriage, Mrs. O'Dwyer dedicated herself to her children, guiding them through their Catholic private and city public schools. She also reserved a place in her home for Paul's relations who cycled through on their way to an apartment or a job in the city. She liked to relax in a rocking chair in their apartment that had been Bill O'Dwyer's favorite, and she was a friend to Bill during his bouts with tempestuous politics and ill health, escorting him to physicians' offices after his return from Mexico. To his writer friends, Paul was quick to help others in trouble, like "a rope on a wet deck," as Murray Kempton put it. But the same was true of Kathleen.[24]

Though he did not dedicate his memoir to his wife (nor to anyone), Paul indicated his enormous debt to Kathleen in the narrative, whether it was for the work of managing the household, stuffing campaign envelopes, or chauffeuring him as a candidate to Canarsie or up to Inwood (she drew the line at giving speeches, however, considering it "the man's place," as she told the *New York Times* for a July 1968 profile of her).[25] She acceded cheerfully to the customary "candidate's wife" newspaper interviews, accepting the publication of her age, the dress size of her formal knitted suits, and her preferences in mascara. While never terribly bothered by the red-baiting Paul's politics aroused, she worried about his trips down south and could not free herself of all the emotions and intense animosities that a race for office could stir. "In politics," commented Rory, "enemies are made many, many times. My father would always forgive an opposing politician. Once the race was over, he was done with all that. Like with a primary, two people might run for the same seat; my father would forget about it afterward. Well," he added, chuckling, "my mother would never forget it."[26]

O'Dwyer clung to his memories of a torchlight parade and songfest in Bohola that he and Kathleen received right after his victory in the 1973 Democratic primary for city council president, achieved with the dependable assistance and moral support of Kathleen.[27] During their last trip to Ireland, Paul felt that Kathleen had showed natural grace when she encountered a New York couple at the Burlington Hotel and discovered they were trying to sort out the circumstances surrounding the sudden death of their daughter. Kathleen spent an hour talking with the suffering pair then and a week later, when they returned to New York on the same flight. After Kathleen's death, according to Paul, the couple wrote to the widower of the caring stranger they felt lucky to have met, stating, "She was sympathetic and comforting to us in our darkest hour."

O'Dwyer recalled the latter episode at a May 1981 memorial service held for Kathleen at the Bohola Cheshire Home. A plaque in her honor was unveiled to go along with another memorial to the O'Dwyer family's late friend, Sean Keating, the Irish War of Independence veteran who worked in Bill's administration and then became the regional director of the US Post Office.[28]

"Her life was one of political campaigns that mostly lost and were composed of the poor, the blacks and Hispanics," Breslin wrote.

> Usually there were only a few Irish, for she and her husband worked the other side of the street. Oh, it could have been so easy to succeed and please. The Irish had big numbers in this town. But Kathleen O'Dwyer and her husband came the unpopular way, and

it was tough at the polls but easier on the heart. Which was the shock of her dying, for her heart was the last thing you'd expect to go. But now she was gone and Paul O'Dwyer, 73, stood in the middle of the room and knew that the things that are supposed to help the Irish at these times are merely fables.[29]

––––––––

LIFE IS BEST LIVED in the present, Paul would sometimes say. At his age, he might have added, it was best lived at his second home in Orange County, New York—though the county was named for an English royal whose 1690 victory in the Battle of the Boyne in the Irish kingdom was still celebrated by Ulster Protestants as the beginning of the "Orange" ascendancy. He relaxed on weekends amid the bucolic landscape, performing outdoor chores. Though he had made his life in the city, the memories of a childhood in not dissimilar rural surroundings and some of the hardiness of the slight, thick-boned son of the Irish west of the 1910s and '20s still adhered.

The widower courted Patricia Hanrahan, the head of Governor Mario Cuomo's upstate women's division for New York State and a Rockaways resident. A divorcée, she and Paul had renewed their acquaintance in 1981 and involved themselves in protest activities on behalf of Bobby Sands and his fellow hunger strikers. For O'Dwyer, the episode also occasioned a fruitless trip to the gates of the Maze, where he passed along to the prison guards a letter intended for one of the prisoners who was refusing food, Irish National Liberation Army soldier Kevin Lynch. The letter urged Lynch to accept a compromise that would allow himself and Provisional Irish Republican Army (IRA) members to survive. But the letter had no effect, and the hunger strikers, one by one, expired—martyrs to the historic republican cause. Peter King, the councilman for Hempstead, New York, and Nassau County comptroller candidate, and Nassau's district attorney Dennis Dillon attended a series of turbulent funerals for the young men, later recalling British military helicopters thumping overhead, security forces fringing the mourners' processions, and a group of IRA men in ski masks suddenly emerging and firing shots into the air. In the evening, after one of the interments, the two Long Island politicians returned to their room at the Greenan Lodge Hotel to be startled by IRA men banging on their doors and hustling them away for their own safety. In a few short hours, bombs exploded at the inn, part of a wave of nonlethal attacks in the area. The Greenan, King learned, was targeted because it had closed for three hours in observance of the wedding of Prince Charles and Princess Diana on July 29, 1981.[30]

Growing close through their shared activism for the hunger strikers as well as their familiarity with New York's politics and courts (Patricia's ex-husband was a lawyer), the two were wed in 1984 by the then city clerk David Dinkins. Paul was seventy-seven and Patricia forty-three. To inaugurate their "second act," the couple vacationed in Mexico. After their return, they moved into the thirty-eight-acre Orange County property, in Goshen, which Paul acquired after selling his weekend home in Montgomery nearby.

Another source of companionship for the aging O'Dwyer was also at hand, since Percy Sutton purchased the property on which the home stood, according to his son, Pierre; he subdivided it into three sections of equal size to accommodate homes for himself, Paul, "who wanted in," and Percy's brother, Oliver. The acreage was "rocky in parts," and a short walk from the main road. On warm, fragrant spring days, sitting together on Paul's porch, or on bitterly cold winter nights, reclining in front of a crackling fire, the progressive pair bantered. Paul and Percy may have been slowing, but neither felt comfortable sitting still for too long. Percy was involved in business and Paul in various philanthropic endeavors, among them the O'Dwyer Forestry Foundation, which he established in 1974 to replant forests and stimulate the timber industry for Ireland's five northwestern counties of the Connaught region. O'Dwyer was also keeping tabs on the Charles Lawrence Keith and Clara Miller Foundation, established with his late campaign manager's $11 million bequest. The foundation gave out $55,000 a year to such nonprofits as church soup kitchens, Irish arts programs, and cancer treatment centers. Paul was the executor of his friend Keith's estate and became president of the foundation, with his position as an officer of the board passing to Brian.[31]

O'DWYER FOUND his political patron, Charlie Keith, to be one of the most interesting people he ever came across in New York, including his amusing, if sometimes apocryphal, stories. One of the latter centered on one of Keith's former tenants, Jackson Pollock, and how he returned to his apartment in a drunken rage late one night and threw paint all over the walls and floor, launching the abstract expressionist movement.[32]

But Paul had brushes with New York eccentricity that he equally liked to share.

Sitting in his office one day—it was the early 1980s—he and Malachy McCourt were talking. After arriving in New York in 1952, the waggish McCourt had worked as a longshoreman, then as an actor, before becoming the owner of a Third Avenue bar in 1958. As bartender, McCourt liked to let female patrons "sit where you like," including at the bar, challenging the gender line that prevailed in the neon-and-shamrock watering holes in the shadow of the "el," or elevated railway. He went on to author *A Monk Swimming*, a ribald memoir that irreverently complemented his more famous older brother Frank's best-selling 1996 memoir, *Angela's Ashes*, about growing up amid severe poverty and hunger in Limerick.[33]

McCourt had first met Paul at the bar and long appreciated him, both for his individuality and politics and also for having written, without McCourt ever requesting it, a letter to his radio station employer after his hours were shaved; it was, for McCourt, a "spontaneous act of decency—he knew 100 bucks a week was a lot for me to lose [in 1962]. . . . But it was that amazing humor he had, and acceptance of human beings for what they are, so long as you don't go harming people, don't go vilifying people because of their beliefs. That was his whole thing—because he didn't."[34]

In O'Dwyer's office, McCourt cracked wise over a past encounter with the late *New Yorker* poet, fiction writer, and critic Dorothy Parker, a former member of the Algonquin Round Table of the 1920s renowned for her mordant wit, who once wrote that she wanted her tombstone to read, "Excuse my dust." Malachy told Paul that he flirted with the sunnily attired Parker at a 1961 cocktail party in Hollywood, California. She was in her late sixties. "Young man," she responded, "you might think you are flattering me, but you're mistaken."

Listening as McCourt related the tale, O'Dwyer asked McCourt if he would like to try again. Malachy paused. "I said, 'Yeah, but I think she's dead.'" Parker had passed away in 1967.

But Paul got up and went over to his desk. He reached into a metal filing cabinet drawer and pulled out a ten-inch-tall urn containing Parker's ashes. "Here she is again!" announced Paul. "Oh my god! How are you?" McCourt replied.[35]

Parker's "dust" had followed a circuitous path to O'Dwyer's law office. Parker, in addition to writing with rare pungency, participated as a left-wing activist who helped raise funds for the Scottsboro Boys. She was unofficially blacklisted as a Hollywood screenwriter in 1949,[36] with the damage to her reputation, coupled with the effects of heavy alcoholism and depression, proving irreparable.

Near the end of her days, Parker named another target of the anti-communist hysteria, Lillian Hellman, as the executor of her estate. (Hellman would also deliver a eulogy at Parker's funeral.) A noted playwright who in 1952 refused to name names before the House Un-American Activities Committee (HUAC), Hellman overrode her friend's last wishes, evidently peeved that she had not been left any money in Parker's will (she bequeathed her entire estate to Rev. Martin Luther King Jr., stipulating that upon his death the money would go to the National Association for the Advancement of Colored People [NAACP]). Seeing to the disposal of Parker's effects, including all her private and professional papers, Hellman ignored Parker's desire to be cremated.

Hellman had never been known as an easy O'Dwyer & Bernstien client. As much as possible, Paul left her to his patient son-in-law, Tom Hughes. Once, said Peter Quinn, who worked as a clerk/messenger at the firm in the early 1970s before going on to an acclaimed career as a writer on the Irish experience, Quinn was sent to deliver papers to the dramatist known for her truculence. (The novelist and critic Mary McCarthy would remark of Hellman on *The Dick Cavett Show*, "Every word out of her mouth is a lie, including the 'and,' 'the' and 'a.'") As Quinn recalled, his experience with Hellman at her residence was brief: "An African-American maid opened the door," and the playwright "was standing behind a chair. She threw some epithet at me. I took the papers and left. I was like, 'I'm sorry, I'm just delivering this.'"[37]

As a result of court action, Hellman eventually lost control of Parker's estate, and Parker's body was exhumed and, finally, cremated. But when her relatives failed to show up at the Westchester County crematory to collect her ashes, a clerk sent the urn to 99 Wall Street. Hellman had long been a client of Oscar Bernstien's (and a friend of both Oscar and his wife, Becky) and O'Dwyer's. Oscar had died in 1974, so when the container arrived at the office, Paul stored away the vessel in a small box. He did not know what else to do with it.

In 1988, O'Dwyer spoke to the *Daily News*'s Liz Smith. The gossip columnist wrote it up for the next day's paper, and Parker devotees responded with suggestions for a more fitting final resting place. Paul gathered a group for a cocktail party in Parker's memory at the Algonquin, where Benjamin Hooks of the NAACP suggested Parker's orphaned remains be interred and memorialized with a small monument in a grassy area behind the NAACP's Baltimore headquarters. The idea came to fruition that October. Parker's grandnieces, however, would subsequently reinter the ashes at Woodlawn Cemetery, nearer to Parker's original home. As the women had discovered, Parker's father had once acquired a gravesite in a Bronx boneyard with six places, two of them designated for her use.[38]

HAVING GIVEN THE DAY-TO-DAY reins of the law firm to Brian and Frank, O'Dwyer returned to the cause closest to his heart and mind: independence and reunification for Ireland. This tested the octogenarian's patience and fortitude, considering Washington's posture of nonintervention in the politics of the United Kingdom. Ulster was still as frozen as the Goshen fishing reservoir in the dead of winter and not much different from when a Nixon aide had stated, four days after 1972's Bloody Sunday, that it was doubtful that "Americans had any useful role in the matter." No amount of finger-wagging and overheated rhetoric from the New York spokesman for Irish America at that time had made any appreciable difference. At a 1975 hearing in Manhattan of a House Foreign Affairs subcommittee chaired by the Nassau County Democrat Lester Wolff, O'Dwyer said US entry into World War I "now require[s] us, on our honor, to intervene in the explosive situation in Northern Ireland, which, for sheer savagery, threatens to surpass the *genocidal mania of Adolf Hitler*."[39]

Congress, too, was difficult for any grassroots activist, even one as well connected as Paul, to penetrate, especially as Edward Kennedy and Tip O'Neill, the House Speaker from 1977 to 1987, were being influenced by John Hume and not Sinn Féin. Hume's impact could be seen, at least indirectly, in Kennedy, O'Neill, Hugh Carey, and Daniel Patrick Moynihan all joining forces as the "Four Horsemen" and decrying violence across the sectarian divide. The riders warned of an apocalyptic future if a decisive turn toward negotiations was not made.[40]

The Irish National Caucus (INC), headed by Father Seán McManus, turned up pressure on Washington, meanwhile, at the time Jimmy Carter sought the presidency. Even while adhering to what he called America's

policy of "impartiality" toward Northern Ireland, Carter pointedly urged
a peace process that "protects human rights and guarantees freedom from
discrimination." It was but a limited attempt to fill the longtime vacuum
of US leadership, one in which Irish American grassroots support for the
IRA flourished. But it was a start.

"Violence cannot resolve Northern Ireland's problems: it only in-
creases them, and solves nothing," President Carter stated.[41]

The stage was effectively being built for arguably another advance of
sorts: the Anglo-Irish Agreement of mid-November 1985, during Ronald
Reagan's administration. Though O'Dwyer found the agreement unsatisfactory, it secured southern Ireland's advisory involvement in pursuit of
a more durable settlement of the Troubles, while ensuring there would
be no change in constitutional arrangements in Ulster unless a majority
of its citizens voted to be absorbed by the rest of Ireland (an improbable
if not impossible event). The agreement also laid out the conditions for
one day setting up a devolved consensus government for the north.

In spite of the agreement's limitations, the British prime minister Margaret Thatcher's willingness to dilute Britain's central policymaking role
over the north, however minimally, marked a surprising turn of events. It
emerged in light of the 1984 US presidential primaries and debate between some of the candidates over the then novel idea of naming a special envoy to Ulster, a step strongly favored by O'Dwyer and greeted with
commensurate distaste by No. 10 Downing Street. The appointment of
an American envoy threatened to make the American government an ar-
biter of conflicts between political groups in Northern Ireland, which
London saw as treading on its turf and sovereignty.

———

IN SEEKING WASHINGTON'S DIRECT INTERVENTION, O'Dwyer
showed a stronger affinity for "grass rooters" than so-called tree toppers,
or established Irish organizations and their allies in the United States. He
avoided, all the same, a fight with those among them who were increasingly
uncomfortable with Provisional IRA attacks and reprisals for moral or
strategic reasons. For Paul, as always, there was no advantage to be gained
from locking horns with any Irish faction or flank, as he saw Britain—
and Dublin too, at least to the extent it passively accommodated British
policies—as the bane of Ireland's autonomy on both sides of the line of
partition. He was not deterred, however, from serving as the lawyer for

the Irish Northern Aid Committee (Noraid)—pro-IRA grass rooters led in the 1980s by Martin Galvin.

"I don't know that Paul ever said anything defending the IRA that I remember," said Peter King, the conservative Long Island Republican and IRA supporter who started collaborating with Paul as Nassau County comptroller in the 1980s and continued to do so as a member of the House of Representatives, to which he was elected in 1992. "But he wasn't going to oppose them. He understood what was going on. His remarks would be about injustice in Northern Ireland, the court system, the bias of police, the bias of the British army. From that you can conclude he supported the IRA, but I don't recall him ever calling for support of the IRA. He was very critical of the British system, that was his focus."[42]

Projecting an ecumenism to complement his ready brief against British misrule ("The physical harm done to the people was so extensive," Paul wrote in the foreword to *British Brutality in Ireland*, by Jack O'Brien, "that their survival is one of the great wonders of the world"), O'Dwyer cultivated friends and allies across the spectrum of Irish organizational life and politics. As King remarked, "I can think of no Irish organization he would march in lockstep with or take a command from, though he'd work with anyone."[43]

The attitude was at the same time associated with Father McManus, even after the well-known cleric broke with Noraid and joined forces with the Ancient Order of Hibernians president Jack Keane and the trade union labor leader Teddy Gleason to advance the INC.[44] McManus's nationalism was rooted in his native County Fermanagh. In 1971, three years before launching the INC, he was arrested for stopping a boy's beating by a policeman after an Enniskillen demonstration; fined twenty pounds for his conduct, McManus told the court it had no legitimate authority: "I never have, and never will, recognize the colonial state of British-occupied Ireland."[45] But he grew uncomfortable, too, with Provisional IRA bombings and assassinations, not only due to moral questions given the many innocent casualties of the insurrectional violence but fearing, too, that the combatants' ambushes were alienating the British, Irish, and particularly the US foreign policy establishment and segments of the Irish American public.

In contrast to the INC, and to Paul as well, Noraid and other hardline pro-IRA groups showed no inclination to seek negotiations with British officials or Ulster unionists during the 1970s and into the 1980s.

Galvin was even uncomfortable when O'Dwyer courted leaders of the Ulster Defence Association (UDA), the Protestant paramilitary force, starting in the late 1970s. O'Dwyer was the first Irish American republican of note to differentiate the UDA, with its impoverished Belfast constituency, from other loyalist and unionist paramilitaries and the Protestant, and Catholic, upper class in Ulster. Given the UDA's increasing disenchantment with British rule, and its feeling that Catholics were being favored over Protestants with new community centers built to placate Irish American politicians, O'Dwyer saw the militant UDA leader Andrew Tyrie as a potential ally.[46] Tyrie was an anti-Catholic bigot but shared with poor Catholics concerns like unemployment, deficient housing, and poor sewer and sanitation services. These conditions had a common foundation—British control—and O'Dwyer felt that extremists in the Protestant and Catholic camps might one day be willing to negotiate to lay down their arms on that basis. By comparison, Noraid, despite indebtedness to O'Dwyer for legal service, wanted no part of it, seeing the gun as the only thing the British government ever responded to.

"Paul was really a lawyer at heart, and saw things through the vision of a lawyer," said King, who abandoned the practice of law for a life in politics—he was first elected to an at-large seat on the town board of Hempstead, New York, with the backing of the Nassau County Republican machine. "Even though he was in politics, and ran for office a number of times, he had that legal direction—how can this be done, how can the law be changed, how can we put certain protections in. Even in the frenzy of a political or nationalist moment, he was at his core a lawyer."

King reflected back to the controversy surrounding Paul's unilateral outreach to Protestant militants. "Who the hell was he to bring in these type of murderers [Tyrie and his comrades in arms]—it was that kind of thing that you'd hear," the former congressman said. "But Paul was Paul. He really had his moral compass, and whether you agreed or not, you knew where he was coming from. I never heard anyone who knew Paul who ever questioned his morality or consistency."[47]

———

IRISH AMERICAN SUPPORT for the IRA was running high in the wake of the deaths of Bobby Sands and his fellow prisoners in the H-Blocks when Durkan convened a group of experienced defense attorneys to defend, in the Brooklyn federal court, five Irish nationalists arrested on gunrunning charges. Cathartic for nationalists, the 1982 case marked something of a reversion to quixotic revolutionary dreams and the Easter Rising. One of the defendants, Tom Falvey, fifty-four, a construction worker living in the Hollis section of Queens, had reached out to Durkan in the middle of the night, waking up the lawyer and his wife, Monica, at home. Before hanging up, Frank promised, as asked, to make sure his cats were taken care of during his confinement.[48]

Among the five men charged, in addition to Falvey, were Michael Flannery, eighty, a flinty veteran of the War of Independence and Irish Civil War who was retired from Metropolitan Life and living in Jackson Heights, Queens, and the Kilkelly-born New Yorker George Harrison, sixty-seven, another dyed-in the-wool nationalist. Rounding out the defendants in the much-followed trial were Daniel Gormley, thirty-three, who operated lighting and heating systems at Avery Fisher Hall, and Patrick Mullin, forty-four, who worked for the telephone company.

The five men admitted running arms for the IRA, but denied they did so with criminal intent.

"We are indicted here for the love of freedom, and the love of freedom alone," Flannery said in his opening statement. Later, Durkan, leading the defense team, rose to tell the judge of how insulted Harrison felt to hear the prosecution's accusation that he had been running guns for the last six months: "He wants the court to know that there has not been a weapon sent to Northern Ireland *in the last 25 years* without Mr. Harrison."[49]

Prosecutors laid out an astonishing array of M-60 submachine guns, Armalite rifles, thousands of bullets, a flame thrower, and numerous cannon balls (adding a nineteenth-century touch), the weaponry blanketing the top of a large table and the floor around it. FBI agents described the FBI stings that netted the Belfast-bound cache, while the defense brought up notable campaigners for Irish freedom such as Bernadette Devlin McAliskey, a survivor of a would-be assassin's fusillade the year before. She left some jurors in tears with her ringing endorsement of the five stalwarts, while Samuel O'Reilly, who was in the Dublin Post Office when the Easter Rising was launched there, lamented eight centuries of Irish self-determination denied.[50]

Even more importantly to the trial, Durkan and his team insinuated a CIA connection to the gunrunning operation, though they lacked any direct evidence. Was it or was it not customary practice for the spy agency

to respond falsely to questions about its involvement in foreign insurrections, even before Congress? The former US attorney general turned antiestablishment lawyer Ramsey Clark, appearing as an expert witness for
the defense, said the practice was not merely customary but de rigueur.

Still, another defense expert witness was asked, could the CIA really
have been oblivious to the alleged $1 million in arms transfers to the IRA?
The prosecutor objected, saying "the question had answered itself," wrote
the *New York* magazine chronicler Shana Alexander.[51] To the jury, at least,
it appeared that it had.

The jurors voted to acquit the five, who leaped from their chairs cry-
ing, "Up the IRA!"

That night, with neckties loosened and pinstriped shirts partially un-
tucked, the lawyers and dozens of their supporters crowded into the Tower
View ballroom under the Roosevelt Avenue el in Woodside and celebrated
with an outpouring of Guinness, whiskey, and song.

———

BEGINNING IN THE EARLY 1970s, Paul sought out US Rep. Mario Biaggi of the Bronx for help influencing Congress. Biaggi was invariably
receptive, his close association with the republican cause elevating his profile in the House. Like Paul's late brother, Biaggi's career was dogged by
rumors of corruption. He, too, had been a New York City cop, in his case
for twenty-three years. Wounded eleven times, he received many decora-
tions for valor and suffered a lifelong limp. On two occasions Biaggi had
shot and killed assailants, and this was something else he had in common with Bill, who, as a police officer, put a bullet in a Long Island Railroad worker during a struggle with the armed man in the home of his
estranged wife and two sons.

John McGettrick recalled pulling up at Paul's request outside a West
Side diner where, his boss somehow knew, Biaggi was sitting alone.[52] Then
running for council president, and soon to share space on the eventual
mayoral nominee Abe Beame's 1973 ticket, O'Dwyer climbed out of the
car and went into the restaurant to say hello to Biaggi. At the time, their
collaboration on Ireland was tentative, and the congressman was the target of rumors of having taken the Fifth before a grand jury looking into
public corruption, which he denied. Though no indictments were returned,
Biaggi's 1971 denial returned to haunt him in the 1973 mayor's race, when
he finally conceded that he had refused to answer the panel's questions.

Trailing Beame, Biaggi appreciated Paul's vote of confidence in him. In 1976, Biaggi and other New York politicians, Paul among them, addressed a rally after a memorial mass for the Provisional IRA leader Frank Stagg, who starved himself to death in a British prison. Reflecting the US Establishment's distaste for IRA activism, the *New York Times* op-ed columnist Anthony Lewis took O'Dwyer in particular to task for the demonstration. Writing from London, where he had previously served as bureau chief for the paper, Lewis noted the recent murder of the British ambassador to Ireland, Christopher Ewart-Biggs. "There is a particular Irish-American political strain," he opined, "whose ideas about Ireland are frozen somewhere back in 1916," and O'Dwyer was "an extreme example of the strain."[53] O'Dwyer was not too bothered by the line of attack, and stayed close to Biaggi. The congressman became the founding chair of an unofficial congressional panel, the Ad Hoc Congressional Committee on Irish Affairs, in 1977.

Going against the grain of the US-London foreign policy establishments and the columnists and editors when they toed a British-centric line, the Biaggi committee garnered attention and increasing House allies in the late 1970s and early '80s. Washington allies of Hume countered the coalition by establishing, with Kennedy's help, the more moderate Congressional Friends of Ireland (CFOI) in 1981.[54] Presenting a new flank, the CFOI was formally launched at the Irish embassy in the nation's capital after Dublin officials had become alarmed by the influence of the Ad Hoc Congressional Committee on Irish Affairs, viewing its popularity in some quarters of Irish America as, at best, nettlesome. On St. Patrick's Day of that year, the Four Horsemen, as well as President Reagan, a Thatcher Cold War ally, issued separate statements asking all Americans to join them in condemning the escalating violence in Northern Ireland.

Biaggi's Ad Hoc Committee remained focused on condemning British government policies. The committee was advisory; it could not propose legislation. But it stood out, with the House and Senate deferring action on the Troubles throughout the 1970s in deference to the US State Department. The last official House hearing of any consequence on the Troubles had occurred after Bloody Sunday in 1972, four months after Senators Kennedy and Abraham Ribicoff and then US Representative Hugh Carey cosponsored a Senate-House resolution calling for withdrawal of British troops.[55] While a variety of House and Senate committees heard testimony from Irish republican advocates in the 1970s, with

Paul among them, the hearings generated only publicity rather than successful legislation.

In one instance, public agitation produced some of the first tangible outcomes of the long-running debate over Northern Ireland: a joint effort by a wide cross section of Irish American pressure groups to support an American code of social responsibility for investment in Ulster. The long campaign proved to be a match for the British-Irish-American status quo, though the proposal faced a formidable opponent in Hume, who, like the British, expressed concern over anything that might deter corporate investment in the depressed manufacturing sector of the north. But even Hume's supporters in Congress enlisted in the concerted effort to keep US companies and government pension systems from investing capital in Northern Ireland enterprises that discriminated against Catholics. The campaign went state by state, organized by the INC in Washington and supported by Noraid. The New York City comptroller Harrison Goldin, with sole authority over the city's huge pension fund investments, got on board, and the principles came to be endorsed or enforced by eighteen American states, thirty-one cities, and eighty-eight companies, modeled after the Sullivan Principles developed in 1977 to undermine South Africa's apartheid regime. Decisively, Seán MacBride lent his name to the Northern Ireland version.

Paul had gotten behind the campaign early, but if he had developed any doubts about its chances for success, they were muted by his affinity with and respect for the Amnesty International founder and 1974 Nobel Peace Prize recipient. He and MacBride had long been in touch by letter and occasionally in person; as a result of MacBride's enlistment by the Vatican to carry a message from Paul VI to Hanoi during the Vietnam War, Paul had first discovered from his friend the disastrous truths belying US propaganda on Vietnam before running for the US Senate in 1968.

Educated in Paris and Ireland, MacBride was the child of the Anglo-Irish actress and patriot Maud Gonne and her husband Major John Mac-Bride, who was executed for his part in the 1916 Easter Rising against the British. MacBride joined the original IRA as a soldier, or volunteer, at fifteen during the Anglo-Irish War. Like Paul's own parents, he renounced the nascent Irish Free State in 1922, remaining a member of the IRA through the Irish Civil War and becoming the militant organization's chief of staff in 1936–37. He quit when, in his view (but hardly Flannery's or Harrison's), the 1937 constitution sufficiently fulfilled republican objectives, a view held by many, even most, of his countrymen. Yet in Irish politics, MacBride suffered more electoral losses than victories in the ensuing years. He definitely had that in common with his American friend, who also did not hesitate to bring matters embarrassing to his government to light. But MacBride rose to great heights as an international human rights activist, the result, as Paul noted shortly after the politician-activist's 1988 death, of his baptism by fire in the early IRA.[56]

"Without his activity as a volunteer and guerrilla leader," O'Dwyer said in the speech memorializing the former soldier turned peacemaker, "it is doubtful he would have ever reached the higher plateau."[57]

Although the MacBride Principles were not federally mandated, the unusually unified activism surrounding the campaign across the United States and the Irish American political and organizational spectrum created a lasting headwind with a far more significant impact than the familiar rallying cry, "Up the IRA!" "Irish Americans used their electoral power to wield the ultimate peaceful capital weapon, the power of the dollar, to achieve social and economic reform in Northern Ireland," wrote Kevin McNamara in his 2009 history of the MacBride Principles. "They used it to remedy a situation about which UK governments were either in denial or to which they turned a blind eye."[58]

———

JIM MULVANEY, a reporter for *Newsday*, was never far from stories of the Queens courts, not only due to his crime beat but also because his father, James, was a criminal defense lawyer in the Queens Boulevard courthouse and a true "boulevardier," interacting with some of the same Runyonesque characters—"Klein the Lawyer," "Marvin the Torch," "Shelly the Bail Bondsman"—whom Queens-bred Jimmy Breslin liked to feature in his *Daily News* and later *Newsday* columns. In 1983, Mulvaney's father represented a mortician customer who, under threat of immediate harm, extracted a slug from the head of a drug-crazed gunman's lifeless victim in a southeast Queens nudie bar. Gruesomely, the procedure required severing the head—and "Headless Body in Topless Bar" became the most famous headline ever to scream from the front page of Murdoch's *New York Post*.

Though Dan Tubridy of the Rockaways had no clear idea what Mulvaney's desired "journalism fellowship" was, he tried to help the reporter land such a position in a new beat: Belfast. He took him to meet O'Dwyer, to whom the 265-pound redhead pitched helping send Mulvaney on a reporting mission to the north, where neither the *New York Times* nor the Associated Press had a bureau at the time. "I just listened," recalled Mulvaney. "I had been told to shut up."

"You'll not be getting a fuckin' nickel out of me," said Paul (as recalled by Mulvaney).

"Oh, Mr. O'Dwyer, we're not here for money," Tubridy, who stood six-foot-five, responded respectfully.

"Just behave yourself," Paul snapped. "I've got an idea."

Holding a referral from O'Dwyer, Mulvaney was soon standing before Sister Marie Melton, the head librarian at St. John's University in Queens, explaining that *Newsday* might just be willing to contribute two-thirds of his $45,000-a-year salary if the university would provide the rest under a kind of informal international reporting fellowship. The university did have such a fellowship.

Perhaps, said the librarian. "Do you have a thesis?"

"Yes: the war in Ireland in 1984 is being covered entirely from London, there's no American outlet anywhere on the island, no nothing," Mulvaney answered. "The reporters are in London. When there's an incident worthy of their attention in Northern Ireland, they first get briefed by the Brits, then they go over there and get more information of the official sort, and they miss or slant the story." He said he would uniquely cover the stories "on the ground" for his newspaper. And at the end of a year, he said, he would conduct an analysis comparing his coverage to that of *Newsday*'s competitors based in London, "and see if it was a bias, albeit not intentional."

She seemed receptive to the idea, but money was still an issue.

"She takes out a calculator and, wearing her habit, assumes a no-nonsense posture," recalled Mulvaney. "'So, with the *vig*,' she said"—using the loan shark shorthand for *vigorish*, the interest payment on a loan—"'the amount needed for the fellowship could come out to approximately $17,500?'"

Mulvaney went looking for his employer's blessing for the proposed arrangement, but the concept hit a snag with his more cautious editors. Tubridy subsequently suggested holding a fundraiser at the Rockaways restaurant he owned, Pier 92, and went to work arranging it. The author William Kennedy was signed on to be the night's speaker, and sales of the $100 tickets really picked up when Kennedy unexpectedly received the Pulitzer Prize for his new novel, *Ironweed*. Statements from Governor Mario Cuomo and the vice-presidential candidate Geraldine Ferraro were submitted for public recitation. And Paul placed a call to a Dallas contractor, who sent $4,000 for Mulvaney.

With the money in hand, and his editors' initial concerns addressed, Mulvaney made ready to leave. First, though, he went to see O'Dwyer on his own at Neary's restaurant near Central Park. "Paul had stayed true to his word," he recalled. "He wasn't going to reach into his own pocket, which is part of the story of Paul: he did a lot for a lot of people, but, you know, he had short arms. But he came through with a rich friend."

His guidance, however, proved equally important. Mulvaney, twenty-nine, had already sought advice from King. The Nassau comptroller provided him with the phone number of Sands's mother as well as other republican contacts. An IRA man hiding out in the Rockaways offered to let him stay with his wife in the Falls Road area, the heart of Catholic Belfast. He told Paul, however, of his desire to stay on the Shankill Road in Protestant Belfast. O'Dwyer advised against the idea. "We've already gotten another fat guy from Queens"—Breslin—"who wrote all about that already," the lawyer growled.[59]

O'Dwyer sent Mulvaney off with a letter of introduction to the Protestant UDA leader Andy Tyrie to ensure he would be able to walk through Protestant areas without arousing suspicion. By living in the home of a well-connected wife of an IRA fugitive who could also vouch for his neutrality, Mulvaney was able to avoid Catholic suspicions as well. He planned to go back and forth between Dublin and Ulster.

At his first meeting with Tyrie, in 1984, Mulvaney was quick to pull out Paul's letter of introduction to the impressive militant.

He was "a big, scary guy, 6-foot-2 and almost that wide, with big, farmer's fingers, wrists like my thighs, and a steely look that'll kill you," the reporter recalled. Tyrie slowly revealed himself, though, to be something of a "jailhouse scholar," knowledgeable about Anglo and Celtic history despite little formal education and curious about how modern Catholics were different from Protestants.

In his prior discussions with Paul, Tyrie had found him surprisingly relatable. When he met Mulvaney and handed him the letter, Tyrie asked how O'Dwyer was doing. The militant's lips moved, Mulvaney later recalled, as he read Paul's letter. Then he folded it up.

"We'll take care of ya," Tyrie said, assigning a minder who carried a .38 caliber Smith & Wesson and a Black & Decker drill, known as Twister. Mulvaney accepted the bodyguard's services, understanding that he was not someone to be trifled with. One night, he would snap the arm of a Loyalists' Club patron who tried to make off with "Mr. *Mulvaneh*'s" Nikon cameras. Mulvaney told Twister he did not have to do that. "This is my place, my country, don't be telling me what I need or needn't to do," Twister replied—and Mulvaney thought better than to argue the point.

Washington's focuses lay elsewhere, with the Reagan administration covertly funding guerrilla movements on behalf of right-wing regimes from Nicaragua to the Philippines to Afghanistan, while pushing for arms talks with the Soviet "evil empire." But Mulvaney had a front-row seat to Northern Ireland's civil war and a mission: he reported on the social realities around him, the omnipresent sandbags, ribbons of barbed wire, homemade petrol bombs, and midnight police raids, a tableau of defiance, dread, and despair.

The closest Mulvaney got to the maw of numbing civil destruction was the awful day—August 12, 1984—when British security forces opened fire at a republican anti-internment rally outside Sinn Féin's headquarters. Armored police Land Rovers with grilles stretched across their windows pulled up and began firing rubber bullets as soon as the New York–born Martin Galvin pulled off his ski mask on the speaker's platform and shouted the nationalist slogan "Our day will come" into a microphone in Irish. Amid the pandemonium that then broke out, the thirty-four-year-old Noraid director, who was in the north in defiance of British authorities, made haste to the republican press center, and away. But, walking by innocently, twenty-two-year-old Sean Downes (known as John to his family) was deprived of the opportunity to even duck when a projectile caught him in the center of his pasty chest. He crumpled to the pavement on Andersonstown Road, his life snuffed out, leaving a child and wife awaiting his return to their flat from a trip to the bakery.

Mulvaney interviewed Galvin, courtesy of his IRA sources. His exclusive ran prominently back in New York. British rules of engagement, as he noted, did not permit rubber bullets to be shot above the waist, nor within twenty meters. But the rules had not mattered. The security forces had ignored the presence of the Sinn Féin leader Gerry Adams at the rally and gone right at the Noraid director to arrest him under a terrorism prevention law. He had ignored a prohibition against leading an "Irish People" bus tour in Ulster.

Mulvaney doubted O'Dwyer was pleased to find out about Galvin's role.

"He was close with Paul but there was, I think, a mutual disrespect between O'Dwyer and Galvin, as Martin was something of a poseur who liked the IRA life," the reporter speculated, adding, "He was wearing a bulletproof vest and here, this young guy, Downes, an innocent bystander, with bread and rolls, his wife at home with the baby, dies."

Pounding the pavement on both sides of the corrugated-steel wall that separated Protestant and Catholic neighborhoods, Mulvaney one day walked on the Shankill Road with George Seawright, an extremist politician in the Unionist Party and the Ulster Protestant Volunteers. The Scottish-born Seawright took him to bonfires where an image of the pope was burned in effigy.

On other days, Mulvaney walked a dog named Bugsy in the Falls Road neighborhood as a favor to his IRA-connected hostess, the alleyways piled with uncollected refuse. But whatever side of the sectarian line he found himself on, he struggled to see a glimmer of cooperation. They were few and far between, he said, but they did exist. Belfast taxi services invested jointly in the black-cab fleets, for example. And he was able to convince Peter King to meet Tyrie and friends in his stronghold, though the IRA supporter might not necessarily make it back in one piece to Catholic West Belfast, where he stayed with relatives of Sands.

King remembered the day. A cab driven by an IRA volunteer dropped him off at the far edge of the Falls Road under a persistent drizzle. There, he met up with Mulvaney, and the two walked through a no-man's-land between UDA and IRA territories, ending up at the basement bar where Tyrie hung out. The Protestant militant asked how Mr. O'Dwyer was doing—and King breathed easier, promptly recognizing he was on safe ground, notwithstanding the UDA brute's intermittently threatening language and apocalyptic rhetoric. Influenced, like Mulvaney, by O'Dwyer's thinking, King kept mum when Tyrie used threatening rhetoric and envisioned the potential for the Catholics to be wiped out, for Tyrie described, however crudely, the poor—both Protestants and Catholics—as victims of unfair political and economic arrangements favoring the wealthy and the powerful.[60]

There were no such hints of commonality in early 1985, however, when Thatcher delivered a speech before a joint session of Congress and 1,500 people protested outside the Capitol, among them Biaggi, Galvin, and O'Dwyer, along with representatives of the Ancient Order of Hibernians, the Irish American Unity Conference, and the Irish-American Labor Coalition (all groups in which Paul was a member or with which he interacted). The peaceful demonstrators protested not only the extension of a rare invitation to a foreign head of state to address both houses of Congress but also the US State Department's denial of a travel visa to Gerry Adams, and the prospect—to be realized in five months—of a new extradition treaty more amenable to Britain. This narrowing of the protection for IRA combatants was approved despite senators' questions about the legality of Britain's Diplock Courts, nonjury criminal courts used for political and terrorism-related cases in Ulster since the 1970s.

Despite Irish American complaints, Thatcher was winning. In the face of the growing carnage, the Conservative British government stepped up prosecutions with the help of "assisting offenders"—convicted defendants who turned state's evidence to avoid lifetime sentences and who were branded "supergrasses," or informers, by their own communities. In contact with O'Dwyer, King several times visited the north to gather evidence for reports condemning the state's "show trials" and use of paid informers.[61]

Previously—two months after Downes's fatal shooting at the rally where Galvin showed up in Belfast—the Provisional IRA had set off a bomb at the Grand Hotel in Brighton, where Thatcher was on hand in October 1984 with her cabinet for a British Conservative Party conference. While Thatcher avoided harm in the early-morning blast, five other people were killed, including a Member of Parliament, three wives of MPs, and a regional party chair, while thirty-one others were injured. An IRA statement addressed to Thatcher after the attack spookily read, "Today we were unlucky, but remember, we have only to be lucky once. You will have to be lucky always. Give Ireland peace and there will be no war."[62] But Thatcher, on the morning after the attack, appeared before TV news cameras undaunted, calling the bombing "an attempt to cripple Her Majesty's democratically elected government." Her popularity in England shot to heights reminiscent of the acclaim she drew after preventing Argentina's military junta from seizing the Falkland Islands, a British colonial settlement in the South Atlantic since 1776.

While remaining committed to the union between Britain and Ireland, Thatcher hashed out with Ireland's taoiseach, Garret FitzGerald, the November 1985 Anglo-Irish Agreement giving Dublin and London a formal consultative role in the running of Northern Ireland.[63] Protestant politicians strongly protested the agreement, seven years in the making. Tens of thousands of their constituents massed outside Belfast city hall to resist introduction of a more active role for the Catholic-dominated government of the Irish Republic. Pitched battles involving hundreds of participants and other security crises rooted in the deeply negative Protestant reaction arose, with killings, grenade attacks, and even the bombing of police officers' homes.[64]

The Anglo-Irish Agreement had not inspired Paul's support, as Dublin and London shared the view of the north as a powder keg. Amid Protestant overreaction and British clampdowns on both sides of the sectarian divide, the IRA received secret shipments of armaments from Libya's ruler, Colonel Muammar Gaddafi, a Soviet ally who would draw American missile attacks in April 1986, having been linked by the Reagan administration to the deadly bombing of a Berlin disco patronized by US soldiers. The IRA also staged "spectaculars," killing prominent individuals and large groups of Ulster security personnel, as when, in 1985, nine Royal Ulster Constabulary officers died from mortar bombs planted inside the grounds of the Newry police station in County Down. In a landmine attack in 1989, a judge and his wife were killed. And a heavily armed unit attempted in November 1987 to blow up a constabulary station in Enniskillen, a Count Fermanagh town, leaving eleven children and adults dead and injuring sixty others. The attack during a parade by large numbers of Protestants celebrating Remembrance Day—the yearly commemoration of the World War I armistice—was widely condemned.[65]

And so it went, with "spectaculars" coming from all sides and in all directions, often provoking severe responses by British security forces and the police. The British justified martial measures as being necessary to protect the citizenry. Irish America countered with complaints about incursions on protected rights. Through the Brehon Law Society of New York, American lawyers observed proceedings in the Diplock courts and assisted defense barristers with major cases, sometimes at the request of a defendant's parents. Among these cases were appeals of verdicts in Guildford Four and Birmingham Six pub bombings in the 1970s (the convictions of alleged IRA perpetrators were eventually scotched), as well

as the 1988 trial of the Winchester Three (a trio of IRA volunteers convicted of murdering the British politician and Northern Ireland secretary
Tom King, later quashed on appeal). Paul created the Brehon Law Society because his firm was "getting overwhelmed by cases" of IRA soldiers
facing extradition or trial and undocumented Irish facing deportation,
said Cody McCone, who served as president of the society and worked
as a lawyer at O'Dwyer & Bernstien.[66]

Not unusually, McCone was drawn to O'Dwyer's orbit through a
family tie: his mother, Sheila, who once brought Paul to speak at a meeting in Chicago of the Padraig Pearce Committee for an Undivided Ireland, of which she was vice-chair. McCone volunteered with Brehon in
1985 and joined the law firm two years later. Traveling to Ulster periodically, he felt privileged to work with O'Dwyer, he later recalled. In his
youth in the late 1960s (when his mother took him to the trial of the
Chicago Seven as Black defendant Bobby Seale sat bound and gagged),
the O'Dwyer name was esteemed by his family. "The O'Dwyer family was
more important than the Kennedy family because he [Paul] had the engagement in civil rights and human rights in Northern Ireland," he said.[67]

For all the Irish American activism of the 1980s, the impetus for compromise over the future of Northern Ireland required two main ingredients, O'Dwyer and his acolytes felt: the retirement of Thatcher and Reagan
and greater openness by all parties to working out a compromise. By this
point, Paul felt that the dream of a reunified Ireland, free of violence and
British interference, would simply have to wait. Unlike his contemporaries
Flannery and Harrison, he looked centrally to the democratic political
process to relieve the north from an abjectly deplorable and seemingly
intractable state of affairs.

13

The Mountaintop

WHILE KEYED to the Northern Ireland conflict, O'Dwyer took a flight with Percy Sutton to Nashville, and the two rode on the Jackson-for-President campaign bus with the Reverend Jesse Jackson and the civil rights leader's family to Atlanta and the 1988 Democratic National Convention. Just a few days earlier, Jackson had paid a visit to the Metropolitan Correctional Center in lower Manhattan and its most famous Irish-born detainee, Joe Doherty, whom Paul called "our country's only prisoner of war." (Jackson's visit to the lockup was made at the request of Doherty's lawyers Mary Boresz Pike and Stephen Somerstein.) Doherty had been confined without bail for nearly six years, never having been accused of a US offense. To Paul, it was prosecutorial conduct worthy of an authoritarian system, not a democracy.[1]

Consequently—and because Jackson had pledged to sign the Mac-Bride Principles into law if elected—O'Dwyer became an enthusiastic backer of Jackson's bid for president.[2] There were other reasons for it as well. Paul had never been comfortable with his party's historic shortage of Black leadership. This was Jackson's second try for the White House. In the first, which also drew O'Dwyer's vote of confidence, Jackson finished third in the primaries with 3.2 million votes or 18 percent of the total, trailing the "New Democrat" senator Gary Hart and the party's eventual nominee, the former vice president Walter Mondale. Jackson's renewed bid was better organized and financed, and O'Dwyer probably agreed with the sentiment expressed by R. W. Apple, the dean of political reporters at the *New York Times*, when Apple dubbed 1988 "the Year of Jackson." The Baptist minister and activist was the first African American presidential contender to become a significant force in the party; he drew huge numbers of voters, both Black and white, as well as members of both the middle and lower classes, to his campaign rallies and enjoyed a base of Black, student, and liberal support as he voiced fury at Ronald Reagan's attacks on the safety net and "Big Government." He was arguably one of the most radical Democratic candidates for president since William Jennings Bryan of the Progressive Era, with a similar ability to bring an audience to its feet.[3] Apple quoted the presidential scholar James David Barber as crediting Jackson with accomplishing for Black Americans what Al Smith and John Kennedy achieved for Roman Catholics, "a social and cultural shift that enables all of us to entertain the possibility of having a black president in this country."[4]

As the Jackson bus navigated around sixteen-wheelers on wide Southern highways, O'Dwyer and Sutton spoke about their days in the civil rights "emancipation movement," as Paul called it, emboldened by Rosa Parks's refusal to move to the back of a bus and the resultant bus boycott by Black residents in Montgomery, Alabama. With just "half of that effort by the 41 million Irish Americans," he added, "the freedom of Ireland could be accomplished in much less time."[5]

Paul had already introduced Jackson to Irish politicians and lawyers at a soiree close to the April 1988 primary in New York, a fundraiser the conservative Peter King recalled attending in deference to its host. Raising a toast in his Central Park West apartment, O'Dwyer told his guests he had joined Jackson's campaign to underscore the candidate's interracial vote-getting potential. He said the Democratic Party should not let the moment pass to harness the broad enthusiasm for Jackson by the working class and the poor.

In 1988 as in 1984, O'Dwyer signed on as a New York delegate for the left-wing Jackson.[6] But Michael Dukakis, the moderately liberal Greek American governor of Massachusetts, won the New York primary and secured the nomination in Atlanta, only to lose to Vice President H. W. Bush after a bare-knuckle campaign that fall. (Republican strategist Lee Atwater, fatally ill with brain cancer in 1991, apologized to Dukakis for the "naked cruelty" of his remark that he would "strip the bark off the little bastard.")[7]

The next year O'Dwyer and Percy Sutton endorsed David Dinkins for mayor. It was not at all surprising. The two had come to the Harlem leader's rescue after he was forced to give up his appointment as deputy mayor by the mayor-elect Abe Beame in 1973 after acknowledging that he had owed back taxes for four years, a past debt that he had since made good on. The public embarrassment derailed what would have been the first Black politician ever appointed to the rank of deputy mayor, laying the Harlem clubhouse politician low.

Two years on, O'Dwyer and Sutton had told him about a vacancy in the position of city clerk. "I said, 'What's a City Clerk?'" Dinkins would remember. Paul's response: "Look it up in the Green Book," the municipal directory. Dinkins gained the appointment from Beame and held the job until winning election as the Manhattan borough president in 1985.

"I owe it all to Paul and Percy," he said in an interview for this book.[8]

Encouraged to run for mayor in 1989, Dinkins threw his hat in the ring against the three-term incumbent Ed Koch, who was struggling to disassociate from corruption charges roiling important Democratic political allies charged with financial corruption—the sordid story of a "City for Sale," in the title of the 1988 book by *Village Voice* reporters Jack Newfield and Wayne Barrett.

As if to distract voters from the revelations, trials, and even a suicide (by Queens borough president Donald Manes) arising as the allegations against his administration hit the fan, Koch launched salvos against Jackson, accusing the insurgent presidential candidate of an aversion to Israel's security and adding that Jewish New Yorkers considering voting for him "have got to be crazy." (Four years earlier, Koch had flagged Jackson's ties to Minister Louis Farrakhan and Jackson's use of "Hymietown" to describe New York City, a comment for which Jackson apologized to Jewish organizations.) O'Dwyer in effect rolled his eyes when Koch, a mayor he was never particularly fond of, goaded a city already riven by two different racially motivated attacks on young Black men within three years, followed by protest marches led by the Reverend Al Sharpton through Bensonhurst and Howard Beach, the white neighborhoods where they took place. The white-haired lawyer had little patience for white politicians who demanded a kind of purity from their Black counterparts, once telling Sutton during a car ride to resist demands that he denounce the murderous Ugandan dictator Idi Amin; he suggested that his friend, instead of responding directly, make a list of people whom he would like his detractors to decry, and then respond to them by saying, "I'll do it if you go first."[9]

In the tense 1989 mayoral race, two of the three largest city dailies—all except the right-wing *New York Post*—endorsed Dinkins and his counter-message extolling New York's racial and ethnic diversity as a "gorgeous mosaic." In the general election, Dinkins faced the former Manhattan US attorney Rudy Giuliani, whose prosecutorial targets had included Stanley Friedman, a Koch political ally. (Under questioning by Giuliani in 1986, the Bronx Democratic leader and former associate of Paul's in the Beame administration admitted to having guided the Commodore Hotel package through local and state hoops with the declared hope—soon satisfied—of working for the law firm of Donald Trump's counsel Roy Cohn, Joe McCarthy's chief counsel in the Army-McCarthy hearings.)[10] Initially targeting the "crack, crime and corruption" in the Koch years, Giuliani switched after the primaries to tagging Dinkins as a "Jesse Jackson Democrat."[11] When the Yiddish-accented comedian Jackie Mason, a onetime O'Dwyer client, called Dinkins "a fancy *shvartze* with a mustache,"[12] Giuliani made no effort to rebuke his prominent supporter. Many Jewish leaders slammed the statement by Mason as racist.

Throughout the campaign season, the hope for a rainbow coalition of Democrats ran strong among Dinkins's supporters. In the heavily Republican Staten Island, though, the ideal of multiracial partnership was the least popular of any borough.

Despite that, Larry Hanley, the president of Staten Island's Division 726 of the Amalgamated Transit Union, wanted his organization's bus drivers and mechanics to see past Koch's, and Giuliani's, racial fearmongering and support Dinkins for mayor over the zealous ex-prosecutor. At the suggestion of James Callaghan, a former council aide to O'Dwyer and now communications director for the union, Hanley invited Paul to address the members with Shirley Quill, the second wife and widow of the late Transport Workers Union leader Mike Quill.

Hanley was in the trenches, his union local facing a growing threat from the expansion of nonunion bus lines supported by elected leaders in the borough and by the city Department of Transportation's bus franchise division. Nationally, urban labor unions were losing ground to deindustrialization, community disinvestment, and the anti-union mood fostered by Reagan with his 1981 firing of striking air traffic controllers.

Though they agreed the middle class was under attack from "trickle-down economics," endorsing Dinkins was not an automatic decision for members of the local, with "cigarette packs tucked in T-shirt pockets, baseball capped heads and beer-bellied middles," as the *Village Voice* writer Maria Laurino described them—"Italian and Irish men [who] admit they've never supported a Black candidate."

Introduced by Ms. Quill, Paul delivered a two-hour talk to one hundred members on the modern labor movement's highs and lows. He pulled out his longshoremen's union card, which he always carried in his wallet, and elaborated on Dinkins's prolabor views. Race, said Hanley, who was white, never entered the conversation.

The union local endorsed the Harlem Democrat at the end of the night.

Hanley gratefully drove the eighty-two-year-old O'Dwyer back to Goshen, bonding with him during the two-hour ride. Paul, to Hanley, was a rare and iconic public figure, a "working-class white ethnic who knew no prejudice." As they neared his home, the passenger was weary and quiet. "I'm just glad I will live to see it: New York will have a black mayor," Paul said, tears running down his left cheek, according to an article by Hanley recounting the evening's events.[13]

For once, at least, O'Dwyer's prediction came true, with Dinkins edging Giuliani by 47,100 votes. On the night of the historic victory, O'Dwyer stood arm in arm with the mayor-elect and his exultant supporters on the stage in the ballroom of the Manhattan Sheraton.

———

BY THE ELECTION, Paul had completed a manuscript to remind New Yorkers of Bill's forgotten achievements of four decades earlier. Published by St. John's University Press in 1987, *Beyond the Golden Door* included personal recollections by both brothers. By Paul's own description in the preface, the book was "neither a biography nor an autobiography, but rather a combination of the two" and an attempt "to tell my brother's story in somewhat unconventional form."[14]

Paul got started after leaving the city council in 1977. He completed the effort in 1986 with the help of Jill Levine, his executive secretary at city hall.

The addition of information about "his people" (i.e., the montage of Irish and Irish Americans Bill knew) complemented Paul's narrative of his late brother's life as an immigrant laborer and his meteoric political career. But the insertion of three full-length chapters on Native Americans, slavery, and religious freedom did not. As Michael O'Neill wrote for the *New York Times Book Review*, Paul "needlessly digresses to expound his own well-known political views."[15]

Yet in what the reviewer described as something of "a long lawyer's brief in defense of the former Mayor's honesty," Paul also offered new facts gleaned from requests for government records under the 1966 Freedom of Information Act, including many instances of government agencies and political leaders having colluded against Bill in his tenure as Harry Truman's ambassador to Mexico. The younger O'Dwyer sought to remind readers that, whatever Bill's foibles or transgressions, he was more sinned against than sinning, his record unblemished by even a single count of corruption though New York's powerful Democratic bosses deemed him an inconvenient ally, and both J. Edgar Hoover at the FBI and a new Republican administration in Washington swapped countless tips and clips about his past and present activities. *Beyond the Golden Door* was Paul's most sustained attempt to relitigate Bill's case before the bar of history, a last demonstration of sibling loyalty to a complicated and compelling man who rose from humble origins and the same thatched-roof home in Bohola to lead the capital city of the world at the end of World War II.

The book was but another defense of a lost cause. Although, as O'Neill further allowed, "no one ever showed [Bill] O'Dwyer to be personally dishonest," the midcentury New York mayor's reputation never reclaimed its early luster. The authoritative *American National Biography*, launched in 1999 by Oxford University Press, recalled him as a "corrupt mayor," and a 2019 article in *Smithsonian Magazine* was titled "The Mayor and the Mob."[16] Paul's 432 pages of text could not alter this perception, nor did it adequately reflect Bill's talent as a witty and incisive raconteur. All of Bill's pride and bitterness were revealed in extensive oral history interviews for Columbia University late in his life with John Kelly, a former Rhodes scholar and police officer turned University of Delaware professor. When Paul asked Sloane Simpson for her opinion of his book manuscript shortly before it was published, she responded, "So far, this is reasonably factual and incredibly dull. . . . This certainly contains none of the charm, humor or anything else I remember about Bill O'Dwyer. I suppose it is all right for the record."

In typical fashion, Paul included her critique in the preface.[17]

————

AFTER FOUR MONTHS AS MAYOR, David Dinkins thanked Paul for his support in the hard-fought campaign by appointing him to the post of New York City commissioner to the United Nations and Consular Corps. He had already spent a year, 1986, as the official Manhattan borough historian, another honorary role.

From the commission's East Forty-Fourth Street offices, O'Dwyer worked as the New York City liaison to the 44,000-person diplomatic corps, sorting out ambassadorial complaints about parking tickets (which they did not have to pay) and noisy demonstrations outside their missions. With his distinguished appearance, he was sometimes mistaken for an ambassador. Wandering the halls of the General Assembly with a *New York Times* reporter after starting in the post, he was approached by the representative of Tanzania, by Cuba's envoy, who smoked a cigar, and then by the Indian ambassador C. R. Gharekhan. The latter diplomat introduced O'Dwyer to his country's visiting army chief of staff as "former Mayor O'Dwyer, one of the greatest leaders of New York City." Rather than bothering to correct him, Paul merely bowed his head.

The obligatory habits of civility and accommodation fell to the wayside when UN cafeteria workers were dismissed for striking for union representation. O'Dwyer disclosed he would no longer be eating lunch there, firing off a letter to Secretary-General Javier Pérez de Cuéllar, of Peru.

"I cannot believe," he wrote, "that the representatives of nations, who so firmly believe in the principles and purpose of the United Nations, including those who, with the help of the U.N., have so recently thrown off the yoke of colonialism, would approve of what is happening in the dining areas."[18]

When he left the UN in December 1991, he indicated the immediate cause: he wanted to speak out freely about human rights problems on the Indonesian island of East Timor, where hundreds of pro-independence demonstrators had been massacred less than a month before. He also wanted to express himself about the Bush administration's abandonment of thousands of Kurds to brutal reprisals; the Kurds had taken up arms with the United States in the 1990–91 Persian Gulf War precipitated by the Iraq leader Saddam Hussein's invasion of Kuwait.

"Then there is Northern Ireland, also the offspring of partition," he said.[19]

———

NEW YORK HAD BY THAT TIME welcomed Nelson Mandela, the long-imprisoned leader of South Africa's anti-apartheid movement, and his activist wife, Winnie, with enormous celebrations from the streets of largely African American neighborhoods to Yankee Stadium to a city hall–sponsored ticker tape parade. The Mandelas made New York the first stop of their freedom tour because of the city's history of supporting the movement. O'Dwyer once pushed through a council resolution barring white South Africans from competing in a major city tennis tournament, while more than forty thousand New Yorkers gathered in Central Park to mark the tenth anniversary of the 1976 Soweto uprising in which upward of five hundred Black Africans were killed. The Koch administration withdrew $665 million in pension investments from banks engaged with the racist South African regime.

Then, less than a year after the huge crowds and excitement of the freedom tour, a little-known organization of Irish gay men and lesbians applied to march in the 1991 St. Patrick's Day parade, only to be rejected by the Ancient Order of Hibernians (AOH), the parade sponsor, on the grounds that the parade was oversubscribed. The Irish Lesbian and Gay Organization, known as ILGO, cried foul. Its members turned to Dinkins's city hall, and First Deputy Mayor Bill Lynch, one of the masterminds of Dinkins's election, went to work to find a compromise before the March 1991 parade kicked off on Fifth Avenue. The mayor's office proposed to extend the parade by one hour in order to make room for ILGO and other organizations. The idea went nowhere, but another one did: ILGO's 135 members could join as guests of Manhattan AOH Division 7 led by Brooklyn District Attorney Charles ("Joe") Hynes, not under their group's own banner. At the Gracie Mansion announcement, O'Dwyer approached one of the ILGO leaders, Anne Maguire, a Northern Ireland émigré with brilliant curly red hair who, as a teenager, had worked for Bernadette Devlin McAliskey's campaign for Parliament. The impromptu conversation with the lawyer, "a decent man," she later wrote, helped put her at ease.[20]

The "St. Paddy's Day Gay Furor!"—as the *New York Post* dubbed the controversy—played out in the middle of the tragic AIDS epidemic, after both Reagan and Koch had resisted demands for increased funding for experimental research and an expansion of medical services. Brendan Fay of Woodside (he was born in County Louth) helped make gay rights and public health voices heard by founding an inclusive St. Patrick's Day parade in Queens. Fay long appreciated O'Dwyer's support for gay people, saying it dated back to 1970, when the lawyer-activist embraced the Gay Activist Alliance formed in the wake of the 1969 Stonewall Uprising, considered the advent of the gay rights movement. "Ever the man of conscience," Fay would write, "he was always willing to take the unpopular stand."[21]

But Paul's upfront support of ILGO, including marching with them in Division 7, was another occasion where his conscience and politics irked conservatives in the Irish American community. Though unaffiliated with it, ILGO was often linked by detractors to the AIDS Coalition to Unleash Power (ACT-UP), as well as the "die-in" and "Stop the Church" protest that ACT-UP held at St. Patrick's Cathedral in December 1989, in which five thousand people demonstrated against the Roman Catholic hierarchy for opposing free condoms and safe-sex education for adolescents. ILGO's participation in the parade was resented for politicizing the world's largest celebration of Irish heritage, or so some felt. The dismay was expressed in homophobia, with some yelling out antigay epithets and tossing empty beer cans at the Manhattan 7 contingent. Paul, walking with a cane, left the procession after about eight blocks with the help of his wife, Patricia, and one of her friends. Then David Dinkins joined the group as planned a bit farther up Fifth Avenue, just south of St. Patrick's.

"I knew there would be deep emotions," the mayor said after police opened large umbrellas to protect him from the projectiles tossed during the parade. "But I did not anticipate the cowards in the crowd."[22]

As it happened, ILGO's twenty-six-year-old, Ireland-born lawyer was also named Paul O'Dwyer. The possibility for confusion was confirmed when the older O'Dwyer received a call at his office as the details of the group's participation were being ironed out at city hall. The caller, who did not give his name, demanded to know whether Paul was representing "these people!"

"You're damn right I do," the octogenarian responded.[23] He slammed down the receiver.

If he wore a wry smile at that moment, it would not have surprised anyone.

PAUL'S VIEW OF THE AOH, the parade sponsor first established at St. James Church near New York's Five Points slum in 1836, blended resignation and respect. The AOH and Irish county societies around the city provided welcome mats for Irish immigrants during periods of fierce anti-Catholic discrimination and condescension during the nineteenth and early twentieth centuries. O'Dwyer himself had joined one of them after arriving in New York. But the Hibernians were socially conservative. Historically, the group saw itself as a guardian of Irish civic pride and propriety, a posture it maintained under the fiercely anti-communist tenure of Francis Cardinal Spellman (1939–67) as well as the late twentieth-century discomfort of John Cardinal Connor with issues related to sexual freedom.

Dan Tubridy, the Rockaways restaurant owner, provided an earlier occasion that pitted O'Dwyer against the AOH, this one connected to the St. Patrick's Day parade of 1988.

Tubridy by that time had been exposed to O'Dwyer for twenty years, beginning at a forum at the College of Police Science (later the John Jay College of Criminal Justice) where he was then an undergraduate student. His first impression was unfavorable. "I was put off by him at first because I asked him about his position in favor of legalizing drugs," recalled Tubridy, the son and grandson of cops. Paul pointed out that opium dens were legal in the nineteenth century. "Here I'm a college kid, trying to be smart, and he slapped me down. I was frankly annoyed by it."

After graduating, Tubridy ran unsuccessfully for the state assembly and was planning to try again in his community of Rockaway Beach when, in 1977, he showed up at a sparsely attended fundraiser for Paul's reelection campaign for city council president. By this time, he had come to appreciate O'Dwyer more—for rebutting a statement at a city hall hearing to the effect that there were not any Irish poor left in New York. The then council president's research showed otherwise, leading to the creation of the United Irish Foundation (UIF), a city-funded nonprofit delivering food and other services mainly to elderly Irish immigrants on the eleven-mile peninsula. The group continued for twenty-five years.

Tubridy also put O'Dwyer in touch with additional private sources of support for the UIF because it was making a difference for isolated senior citizens despite "political whispers that implied it was a conflict of interest," he said. Paul, he continued, was not acting out of self-interest, but "really just looking to take care of his own." Dan later became its president. He also served on the board of the Irish Institute, Paul's Celtic cultural-support foundation located in Hell's Kitchen.

But the occasion that permanently bonded Tubridy to O'Dwyer was a 1981 Revolutionary-style Tea Party event at his bayside restaurant where he and other alcohol purveyors dumped British-made booze into Jamaica Bay to protest Margaret Thatcher letting Bobby Sands and his fellow hunger strikers waste away in Her Majesty's Maze. Several TV crews rolled up. Paul, whom he had consulted about the idea, advised, "Just tell him how you feel."[24] And with that, the Irish Rockaways boycott became a national, even international, story.

By that year, Paul was better known on the peninsula. In addition to checking in on the work of the foundation, he circulated at community meetings and helped Sutton generate support for his bid for a city franchise for his Queens Inner City Cable service. Sutton, who went on to win a partnership with Time Warner, paid Paul a $5,000-a-month retainer.[25]

The 1991 ILGO uproar was foreshadowed when Tubridy and his dad, John, were ordered to be excluded from marching in 1988 because the year before they were seen striding with a group of sandhogs who unfurled a banner quoting James Connolly, the Marxist labor leader executed for participating in the Easter Rising. ("Let us cast our religions aside and work together as human beings and equals," the banner read.) Tubridy called Paul even before receiving the notice, having heard through the grapevine that it was coming (organizational banners with political messages other than "England Get Out of Ireland" were traditionally frowned upon by the AOH). Paul told him not to worry. "Ah, Dan, pay no mind to it," he advised.

But four days before the parade, O'Dwyer did pay the First Amendment matter some mind, filing a civil lawsuit against the AOH chair Francis Beirne, of Yonkers, New York, and Daniel Hunt, the leader of Rockaway Beach AOH Division 21. A state supreme court judge responded favorably, delivering an order allowing the Tubridys to join the parade. The jurist cited late notification of their banishment and attempted abridgment of protected speech. The Tubridys could celebrate their Irish pride with their neighbors, in the end. Dan and his father felt redeemed, and they asked Paul over a cup of coffee after the decision how much they owed him for his law firm's services.

"'Now Paul,' my father says," recalled Dan, "'I realize there's a legal bill in here somewhere. 'Ah, yeah, yeah,' Paul says. 'Here's the bill.' He reaches over and hands my father the breakfast bill—$15!"[26]

In late 1992, O'Dwyer suffered a mild stroke at eighty-five, to be followed over the next few years by what his son Brian described as "a series of mini-strokes."[27] Paul's neurologist drafted a letter that his patient used in applying for a disability license plate following the initial one, stating that O'Dwyer now relied on a wheelchair and a walker.[28] Though his speech slowed, O'Dwyer remained engaging, telling Eileen Battersby of the *Irish Times* in June 1994, "I had a stroke a year and a half ago. The doctors said I'd be fine and would have a complete recovery. Boy were they wrong. I can't speak as well." Battersby commented in her profile of what she called the last of the Irish political power brokers of New York, "He seems more bewildered at his bad luck than bitter, and is apologetic."[29]

———

BEFORE PAUL'S FIRST mild stroke, the 1992 presidential race opened a way, as he saw it, to quell the tit-for-tat violence in Northern Ireland once and for all.

The confirmation came at a campaign forum on April 5, 1992, at the Manhattan Sheraton featuring Arkansas Governor Bill Clinton. Appearing before more than fifty politicians and lawyers of the O'Dwyer republican regiment, the candidate displayed familiarity with Irish issues such as Paul had never heard before from a serious presidential contender in either major party.

Hosted by John Dearie, a Bronx Democratic assemblyman, the half-hour question-and-answer forum took place after Clinton heard that his principal Democratic rival, California Governor Jerry Brown, would be making an appearance there later that night. Entering the small hotel function room rented for the occasion, the Arkansan made a beeline straight to Paul, seated in the front row; Clinton bent forward to shake the elder statesmen's hand.

They had first met in 1991, when O'Dwyer initiated warm contacts that contributed to Clinton's willingness to participate with the republican lawyers and lawmakers in what would come to be seen as a watershed event, coming two days before the New York primary.[30]

After greeting O'Dwyer, Clinton went over to the lectern. In the back of the room, a C-SPAN camera's red light indicated the tape was rolling, and Mayor of Boston Ray Flynn asked the first question: If elected, would Clinton appoint a peace envoy to Northern Ireland, as had been done for a variety of other countries beset by civil strife?

"I would," Clinton responded without a moment of hesitation. "I think sometimes we are too reluctant to engage in a positive way in pursuit of our clearly stated interests and values because of our long-standing special relationship with Great Britain and also because it seemed such a thorny problem. But I have a very strong feeling that in the aftermath of the Cold War, we need a governing rationale for our engagement in the world, not just in Northern Ireland."

There was loud applause.

Answering a question from Patrick Farrelly of the *Irish Voice* about recent Amnesty International and Helsinki Watch reports of extrajudicial killings by British security forces, Clinton stated he would use the envoy to investigate atrocities by all the "purveyors of death," including but not limited to the security agencies.

Then, asked by Ray O'Hanlon of the *Irish Echo* whether he would encourage Arkansas to adopt the MacBride Principles, Clinton answered in the affirmative.

Most applauded was Clinton's response when Martin Galvin asked, "If you were elected president, would you direct the State Department to allow a visa for Gerry Adams and other prominent members of Sinn Féin?" It was the most politically sensitive question of the session. Long seen by the US government as an advocate of violence, Adams had been turned down for a travel visa seven times since the early 1980s. Yet Clinton flatly answered, "I would support a visa for Gerry Adams, and I would support a visa for any other properly elected official from a government we recognize. I think it would be totally harmless to our national security interests and it might be enlightening to the political debate in this country about the issues involved."[31]

After the prewritten questions were exhausted, the forty-seven-year-old Clinton made his way—amid sustained clapping—to the exit, posing for snapshots. The Belfast-born *Irish Times* correspondent Conor O'Clery shouted one last question, wanting to know if the candidate had been aware of Galvin's affiliation with the Irish Northern Aid Committee (Noraid).

"C'mon, give me a break," the candidate responded, continuing to wade through the throng. "I'm doing the best I can."[32]

Clinton had just lost the Connecticut primary to Brown and was in danger of losing his footing in New York amid a flurry of news stories about his alleged affair with Gennifer Flowers, his participation in a real estate venture called Whitewater, allegations of draft-dodging and marijuana-smoking, and an unfortunate round of golf at an all-white Little Rock country club. After he departed from the Sheraton, Patricia and Paul, Peter King, the *Irish Voice* publisher and writer Niall O'Dowd, and a few others gathered at a table in the hotel bar. A rumpled Jimmy Breslin joined. "If these goddamn Irish don't vote for him, they don't deserve nothing," he said.[33]

They were sipping coffee, waiting for Brown to show up for the same set of questions. O'Dowd recalled that O'Dwyer, more than anyone at the table, was exultant, remarking on Clinton's keen intellect and knowledge of Irish history. Moreover, he said, his commitment to engaging on the Northern Ireland question if elected was genuine, based on Clinton's recognition of the importance of the Irish American vote.

"If this man is elected, he'll turn the Irish issue upside down," Paul said.[34]

Also bedazzled, Brian O'Dwyer and Frank Durkan wasted little time forming a Clinton-friendly pressure group in the weeks to come with the former Connecticut congressman Bruce Morrison and the New York State AFL-CIO organizer Joseph Jamison. Morrison, Clinton's former law school classmate (Yale, class of '73), assumed the chairmanship. The goal was to generate Irish American support for the Clinton-Gore ticket. Like the campaign group's postelection incarnation, dubbed Americans for a New Irish Agenda (ANIA), it was designed to ensure that Clinton kept his promises.

Immediately after Clinton was elected president, championing the middle class, the ANIA went to Little Rock and met on Irish issues with Chris Hyland, the campaign's deputy national political director. Paul joined these initial discussions.[35]

For O'Dowd, who would later serve as an unofficial go-between for Irish Republican Army (IRA) and White House negotiators, gaining access to the presidential transition team's deliberations represented a first peek at the inner sanctum of an American administration taking shape, a heady moment, especially for an immigrant born in County Tipperary and raised since the age of nine in Drogheda who had relocated to Northern California in the late 1970s, painting houses. He made a go at starting a San Francisco weekly called *The Irishman* with a $962 loan from a friend, and researched O'Dwyer's history of legal work on behalf of IRA soldiers on the run and Noraid.[36]

Moving to New York City in 1985, O'Dowd made a point to introduce himself to O'Dwyer, as he was now developing a bimonthly, *Irish America*, and wanted his legal and editorial thoughts. He was also looking to launch a new city weekly, the *Irish Voice*. "Like everybody else, I ended up down in Paul's office," he said. O'Dwyer & Bernstien had moved to Duane Street; a huge oil portrait of Bill O'Dwyer hung in the outer office. Paul said that O'Dowd "was 'very full of piss and vinegar,' and I think he saw something in that that he admired."

Two years later, when O'Dowd's *Voice* made its debut, aiming for a new generation of Irish American readers, he received Paul's help with getting the peppery newspaper incorporated—Paul indicated he was delighted to be of service because he felt the venerable *Irish Echo* could benefit from the competition. O'Dowd discovered that O'Dwyer had attended the 1928 launch of the *Echo* and known its founder, Charlie "Smash the Border" Connolly, from County Monaghan. In those days, when the paper was delivered by horse-drawn laundry cart, O'Dwyer was twenty. After following a trail of protest politics and law on behalf of the Irish community, radical unionists, and racial minorities, "he just became a fascinating character to me," said O'Dowd. "Paul was extremely influential in terms of my thinking on the broader aspects of what 'revolution' meant, and what people underwent in the civil rights movement in the American South. He was a most unusual kind of Irish American in that he was radical on everything." And, like Quill, who was a dispatch rider for the anti-British IRA in the 1919–21 War of Independence and volunteered to shoulder a gun for the anti-Treaty IRA, Paul was part of a class of Irish immigrants who were "basically extraordinary people in terms of the range and depth of their political beliefs that were probably about as close as you could get to communism. I found it very refreshing because the general community was very different from Paul."

O'Dowd picked up on something else that was true of O'Dwyer: he had acute observation skills, the ability to walk into a room and size up a situation, and the capacity to find out who the key decision-makers were. He was definitive in his recommendations and actions, making him a valuable asset to experienced and novice reporters and someone New York City's news and opinion columnists turned to for tips, pith, perspective, and, perhaps most of all, political candor.

After Clinton's appearance at the Irish-American Democratic Candidates Forum of 1992 at the Sheraton, O'Dwyer and his associates "were all so excited"—especially due to Clinton's support for issuing a visa for Adams—and acted like people who had "been kind of walking in the desert for the best part of 100 years, hoping for a president who would pay attention." All of a sudden, one had appeared, signaling with no holds barred that support by Irish American voters was more important to him than paying obligatory deference to the US-British ironclad "special relationship."

Clinton's public remarks offered Paul the one thing for which he had thirsted for a quarter-century: to involve Washington deeply in the task of remediating the second Irish civil war in his lifetime.

"He was ready to punch the ceiling," remembered O'Dowd.[37]

———

TO HIS YOUNGER COLLEAGUES in the firm, Paul's Oscar Bernstien–like legal exactitude—his insistence, for example, on spending two hours going over what Cody McCone should say in summation to a Bronx jury for a client who slipped on spilled ketchup in a supermarket and sued—was offset by their boss's moments of simply being casual and himself. In a comically absent-minded vein, Paul once drove off from a parking garage in a stranger's pink Cadillac, using the key left for the parking attendants to use and thinking the car was one of the same make and model belonging to an older law associate, Leon Hershbaum, who had said he could borrow it. On another occasion, when a recently retained lawyer in the practice, Sean Downes, drove up to Montgomery to deliver a case file, he found Paul with a shovelful of horse manure. "C'mon," Paul told the startled colleague. "This is what we all do all day long at the office!"

Another time, former police detective Joe Finn, the then council president's driver/bodyguard, arrived to pick him up in a new Oldsmobile. Approaching with a garbage can in his hands, Paul planted the metal waste bin on top of the gleaming hood, revealing how little thought he gave to material possessions.

One other story showed his guilelessness, or perhaps in this case guile: walking back with Peter King from lunch near city hall, a liberal elected official passed them on the sidewalk, and O'Dwyer blurted out (perhaps for King's sake, since he valued the Long Island Republican's collaboration on Irish issues), "What a miserable prick *he* is." The Nassau comptroller lost a step.[38]

But come 1993, well after O'Dwyer had retired from city politics and the firm, he finished putting his personal affairs in order and waited for President Clinton to make good on his promises from before the New York primary. He was eighty-six.

In 1993, he was not the only one starting to wonder if the Democrat would come through.

So, ANIA increased public pressure on the White House with lobbying that was complemented by the Congressional Friends of Ireland, led by Edward Kennedy, and hearings before the Ad Hoc Committee for Irish Affairs. The committee had lost its founding chairman, Mario Biaggi, in 1988 after he was convicted of accepting illegal gratuities and resigned from his seat in Congress. It was cochaired by the Congress members Hamilton Fish, Tom Manton, and Ben Gilman, all of New York.

As Irish American republican activists awaited action by the White House, ANIA's Bruce Morrison, Ray Flynn, Brian O'Dwyer, and Frank Durkan cobbled together the prototypical statement: it was high time, they stated, that British and American policymakers stop admonishing the IRA and Noraid; what was needed was "a policy of political and economic incentives which satisfies the entire Northern Ireland community and leads to peace," and, they added, "a special envoy appointed by President Clinton can be a catalyst to develop these incentives."[39]

But Clinton was in no rush even to appoint the regular US ambassador to Dublin. Chuck Feeney, a duty-free shop mogul and member of ANIA, pressed for the latter post to be filled, and when Jean Kennedy Smith took up these duties in June 1993, she impressed the republicans in New York and Boston with her knowledgeable and assertive efforts to move a long-stuck dial in the Irish Republic and Ulster.

If the IRA was ever going to agree to lay down its arms, Gerry Adams of course was key. But he had lost to a Social Democratic and Labour Party candidate in the 1992 election for his west Belfast seat in the British Parliament, and Nancy Soderberg, Clinton's National Security Council staff director, thought that this deprived him of legitimacy. It weighed against an Adams visa, as did renewed violence by the IRA in Ulster and in London. His ability to control the military operations was at the same time an open question.

Adams, though, had worked since the mid-1980s to soften his image to placate wary American authorities. With his voice banned from British broadcast media, he readily responded to requests for interviews from American reporters like Francis Clines of the *New York Times* and Niall O'Dowd of the *Irish Voice*, while *Times* stories revealing Britain's shoot-to-kill practices in the north in 1985 complicated the view that he and the IRA bore significant responsibility for the state of affairs in the north and should not be legitimized through a US-sanctioned visit.

Clinton twice denied Adams's application for a visa. He finally approved it over warnings from the State Department, as well as firm opposition from House of Representatives Speaker Tom Foley and the British government. The approval also came after a notorious March 1993 bombing in a shopping center in Warrington, a town in northwest England; a three-year old boy and a twelve-year-old boy lost their lives. That attack was the second in Warrington in little over a month, the first having caused extensive damage but only one injury, to a police officer. Weeks after the reprise, though, Adams and John Hume issued an unprecedented joint statement, asserting that "we accept that the most pressing issue facing the people of Ireland and Britain today is the question of a lasting peace and how it can best be achieved." Dublin officials, meanwhile, accused the British government of selective outrage, noting that it was silent when, on March 25, three Catholic civilians and one Provisional IRA volunteer were gunned down in Castlerock, the seaside Londonderry village, by members of the loyalist Ulster Defence Association.

Despite the horrific bloodshed, one striking instance of ANIA activism in particular brought forth a remarkable, if merely temporary, cessation of bombings and bullets in September 1993. The pause came at the request of a traveling delegation led by Morrison and Brian O'Dwyer and also including O'Dowd, Feeney, and the Mutual of America president Bill Flynn. The group visited major political leaders in the south and in the north, including, albeit separately, Adams and Hume, presenting them with a position paper stressing that a suspension of paramilitary hostilities during their visit would help them to make their case to the Clinton White House for an active diplomatic effort to achieve democratic reforms in the north. When the carnage actually halted (to be resumed at month's end) it was "hugely significant," wrote Andrew Sanders, a scholar of the Northern Ireland conflict. The temporary outbreak of peace foreshadowed the possibility of a more enduring resolution of the Troubles through US diplomatic engagement. O'Dowd noted that Paul "wasn't a band leader anymore but he was very much in the chorus," exchanging views on such major developments as the *New York Times* editorial that supported granting the visa to Adams.[40]

Adams came to New York on January 31, 1994, with Paul among a small crowd waving to him when he arrived on a two-day visa at the Waldorf Astoria. (He was not permitted to engage in fundraising, nor stray more than twenty-five miles from the hotel.) The following day, a kind of peace conference was convened by the National Committee on American Foreign Policy, an elite organization whose members included Henry Kissinger. During the two-hour forum, Adams avoided overtly political statements. The star attraction shared the dais with Hume and John Alderdice of Northern Ireland's Alliance Party and later appeared on *Larry King Live* on CNN.

The hastily arranged welcome that followed—organized by Lawrence Downes, a lawyer volunteer with the Brehon Law Society and later the head of US Friends of Sinn Féin—was far less controlled and far more euphoric. The Sheraton ballroom was jammed with one thousand Adams enthusiasts, with hundreds having to be turned away at the insistence of a fire marshal. Paul was hoisted to the stage in his wheelchair and Morrison joined him as the lanky, dark-bearded icon of modern Irish republicanism made his appearance, eliciting a thunderous, standing ovation. Two dozen bagpipers from the New York City Police Department (NYPD) Emerald Society Police Band, wearing kilts with city-issued revolvers strapped to their ankles, skirled "A Nation Once Again," the Irish anthem of rebellion.[41]

"I come here with a message of peace," Adams declared, launching into a short speech.[42]

The moment was unforgettable, recalled Peter King, who was elected to the House of Representatives the previous year and was on hand. "You probably won't be able to replicate anything like that in Irish American society again: Gerry Adams's first time in the country; Bill Clinton's supporting the issue; the enthusiasm that night, and having Paul on that stage. It was sort of like bringing it all together, the alpha and the omega."[43]

Niall O'Dowd also recalled the celebration as the breakthrough that showed that the most powerful government in the world was committed to supporting Irish Americans if they supported the peace process.

John Hume, in New York, was asked what good might come from the Sinn Féin leader's trip.

"He can go back home with a bit of encouragement bolstered, strong enough to risk peace," he said.[44]

And, risking peace, Adams maintained his equanimity after an egregious attack by loyalist paramilitaries in June of 1994 in which Ulster Volunteer Force gunmen burst into the Heights Bar in Loughinisland in County Down and fatally shot six people, including eighty-seven-year-old Barney Green, one of the oldest victims of the Troubles. The massacre left in its wake speculation that the town was chosen with Bill Flynn in mind because he had been involved in the efforts to bring Adams to the United States and Flynn's father, William Sr., was raised in the small village.[45]

————

IT TOOK ANOTHER YEAR before Clinton followed through on his vow to appoint a special envoy to Northern Ireland, naming the former Senate majority leader George Mitchell of Maine in December 1994. It was a relief to Paul, who had reluctantly accepted his first ever invitation to the White House state dinner on St. Patrick's Day six months earlier, telling *Newsday*'s Jim Mulvaney that he believed he was "double-crossed" by that "SOB" Clinton.[46]

But the "long peace process"—as Andrew Sanders titled his analysis of the years 1960 to 2008—began facing and clearing obstacles after Mitchell arrived in Northern Ireland in the first month of 1995. The Clinton White House and Prime Minister John Major's government made demands that the Provisional IRA lay down their arms, setting a key condition for negotiations to allow the north to govern itself more fairly across sectarian lines without either side having to face job discrimination or political suppression through future parliamentary decisions or government policies. The IRA acceded to a temporary ceasefire. Joe Cahill, the IRA veteran once turned back after attempting to tour the United States, received a visitor's visa and made another such trip, speaking to republican audiences about the importance of reduced IRA violence. Adams himself was permitted a return visit in October 1994. When it coincided with the death of Flannery, the Irish War of Independence veteran of note, Adams steered clear of the funeral in Queens, New York, for fear of inflaming republican passions and alarming the executive branch. Clinton's accommodation of the leader of Sinn Féin was a balancing act, with many domestic detractors. Five months later, though, the White House felt comfortable enough to invite the Sinn Féin leader to a St. Patrick's Day fete.[47]

The movement toward peace benefited from the formal suspension of violence announced in turn by the Provisional IRA's opposite numbers—the Ulster Volunteer Force, the Ulster Defence Association, and the Red Hand Commando; the militant groups were represented by an umbrella entity, the Combined Loyalist Military Command. Thus, the stage was set for the complex multiparty negotiations that began, brokered by the new envoy, Mitchell. Americans for a New Irish Agenda took steps to communicate to the Clinton administration through Morrison that Irish Americans had the president's back.[48]

THEIR EXPRESSION of confidence was reciprocated: after a long, halting process, the Good Friday Agreement was finally signed on April 10, 1998, and a public referendum in late May in Ulster generated an 81 percent voter turnout and 71 percent approval of the framework, which promised democratic majority rule, minority rights, and foreign investment. But confirmation of the wisdom of the Protestant and Catholic vote was not immediate, and sporadic violence resumed.[49] In addition to economic inequities, the line of partition remained—it was agreed that no change would be made to Ireland's early twentieth-century border without the consent of the majority of those living under the new arrangements in the north. But violence subsided, dramatically so with time, under a devolved system in which unionists and nationalists shared power, as fostered by the Ulster Unionist Party of David Trimble and the Social Democratic and Labour Party led by Hume (the two were cowinners of the 1998 Nobel Peace Prize). The historian Andrew Sanders wrote that the former prime minister John Major's earlier contributions to peace were largely underestimated (he was succeeded by Tony Blair in 1997), while Clinton, who had unmistakably risked his political capital, phoned his corollaries in London, Dublin, and Ulster during crucial final hours, helping bring the marathon negotiations to a successful conclusion.

Among the key participants, too, were Sinn Féin and the Alliance Party, while the Democratic Unionist Party did not support the accord and walked out of the talks. Sinn Féin and loyalist parties did assent, after the Protestant and Catholic paramilitaries took a final step of agreeing to decommission their weapons.[50]

———

PAUL WAS PHYSICALLY and cognitively feeble by the time the historic Good Friday Agreement was consummated. His family and friends doubt that he was able to appreciate that the agreement had come together. What was certain, though, was that he had seen it coming, and his famous spirit of persistence seemed to hang over the negotiations when they threatened to collapse, seeing them through. "I remember thinking," said O'Dowd, "that he was the one man who should be there when we dragged this across the finish line."[51]

Posthumous recognition of O'Dwyer's contributions to the peace came in September, at a highly enthusiastic ceremony on the South Lawn of the White House. The Emerald Isle Immigration Center, a center in Woodside, New York, for new immigrants of all nationalities that Brian helped found, awarded Clinton the first Paul O'Dwyer Peace & Justice Award, enabling the president and first lady to bask in adulation as he sought to fend off an impeachment battle over his alleged affair with a White House intern. When Bill and Hillary Clinton appeared, they received deafening applause lasting two minutes and fifteen seconds. A second round went on nearly half as long from the senators and representatives, cabinet members, mayors, state government officials, and Irish American organizational figures present with members of the O'Dwyer extended family and several of the lawyers and grassroots activists who had seen Clinton make his promises at the Manhattan Sheraton in 1992.

"Ladies and gentlemen," Vice President Al Gore declared, "welcome to the White House."[52]

———

IN THE LAST YEAR and a half of O'Dwyer's life, Sutton regularly walked over in the early evening in Goshen and read poetry and classics aloud to his friend. Patricia regulated the flow of family and friends who wanted to visit because of his fragility. When Paul died—on June 23, 1998—he was just shy of his ninety-first birthday, one year since hundreds of friends had gathered at the Waldorf Astoria to mark his ninetieth. He died surrounded by loved ones.

One of his favorite lines, from Yeats, still obtained:

That I may seem, though I die old,
A foolish, passionate man.[53]

"I would say about Paul O'Dwyer that the fire never went out," said Frank Durkan, who died just eight years later at seventy-six.[54]

———

THE FUNERAL SERVICE at Holy Trinity Roman Catholic Church on West Eighty-Second Street drew seven hundred mourners. The bagpipes and drums of the NYPD's Emerald Society played "A Nation Once Again" as pallbearers carried Paul's cortege into the sanctuary, and the Reverend Thomas P. Leonard delivered the homily to the assembled family members, friends, columnists, politicians, and activists, almost enough to fill the extra-large Rolodex his longtime secretary for the firm, Virginia Polihrom, used to manage. Quietly dropping into a pew was actor-comedian Bill Murray, an admirer.

In his eulogy, Frank Durkan turned at one point to one of his uncle's targets. "Mayor Giuliani," said Durkan, "you're lucky, in a way, that you're not in his [Paul's] line of fire at the moment"—particularly for his failure to have challenged the detention of Joe Doherty.

Sutton set a slightly different tone for the service, addressing the congregation.

"You see," he said, "Paul O'Dwyer was not just Irish. Paul O'Dwyer was Italian. Paul O'Dwyer was Jewish. Paul O'Dwyer was Greek. He was Polish. Paul O'Dwyer was also African American. In his involvement in the causes that were not necessarily his, Paul O'Dwyer was us."

Paul's niece, Judge Joan O'Dwyer Savarese, invoked the philosophical concept that at death, the deeds of one's life are replayed like a movie. "Uncle Paul," she said, "what a show you're in for!"

Patricia Hanrahan O'Dwyer recalled a Board of Estimate meeting in which a scuffle had erupted between building owners and tenants—"odd, that," she said, evoking chuckles. Paul, she recalled, leaped into the fray as a peacemaker. Her husband of more than thirteen years "is truly not dead," she said. "We have evidence of his physical passing. But that spirit and that passion—it will stay alive if we all leave here today committed to making the lives of our fellow human beings better."

In the service's closing moments, a white pall was replaced by the Irish flag. Wrapped by the tricolor, the casket was borne out of the sanctuary.[55]

The next day, Paul's nephew Adrian Flannelly was among family members accompanying Paul's ashes on a flight to Ireland. In Bohola, a mass was conducted before friends and neighbors, with a reception held at the Cheshire Home on the old three-and-a-half-acre family property. Flannelly was supposed to scatter his uncle's ashes in Bohola: Paul had indicated, though never in writing, that he wanted them scattered at his parent's Bohola burial plots. Paul's daughter Eileen, though, wanted the ashes taken back to Kathleen's gravesite in New York. With his uncle, the family bedrock, gone, Flannelly felt that he had to make the decision, as "nobody was volunteering for this."

He quietly asked the groundskeeper, someone he knew well, to pry open Paul's urn without drawing attention. The work was not easy but, once it had been accomplished, Flannelly poured a portion of the ashes into two different envelopes, one for Eileen to return with to New York and the other for himself to scatter in the Catholic cemetery. He left some ashes in the urn, to be displayed in the Cheshire Home. Call it the O'Dwyer family Good Friday Agreement, with back channels, secrecy, and an eye to weighing all sides. And luckily enough, it held.[56]

———

OVER A LIFETIME lived on both sides of the ocean, though mainly in America, O'Dwyer was not like most Irish Americans of his generation. He was deeply ambivalent about the Catholic Church, something Flannelly acknowledged while saying Paul "was much more for the church than the church ever was for him."[57] And in the long arc of his left-wing activism—a trajectory that set him apart from so many Irish in America—O'Dwyer remained close to the Carmelites, the Roman Catholic religious order with a history of favoring the Irish republican movement, including sheltering fugitives on the run, and associated with a number of New York priests with republican sympathies at least as pronounced as his own.

Though voters in the city did not always appreciate his positions on Northern Ireland and rarely saw fit to reward him for supporting labor unions, minority groups, and immigrants from around the world, Paul's voice carried weight in the left wing of the Democratic Party and among liberals. His presence was consistently welcomed in the movements for voting rights, equality of opportunity, freedom of speech, and international human rights.

Little emulated by fellow Irish Americans, O'Dwyer never set himself apart from, or above, his countrymen in the diaspora. Holy Trinity's Father Leonard, in his homily, described O'Dwyer's characteristic manner this way: "confrontation, with wit and sagacity." And if he was seen by some as a contrarian, McGettrick put the issue to rest in an interview for this book. "Oh no," said Paul's former government aide, "he strongly and honestly believed that we Americans and New Yorkers could do better in so many areas of foreign affairs, civil rights, even urban infrastructure. That was not really contrarian at all. That was somebody who hoped that things would work better."[58]

That he certainly did.

Stamped by his experiences as a boy in Ireland and as an immigrant in America, by the tribulations of his oldest brother, and by his own experiences as a perennial office-seeker, radical lawyer, and civil rights activist, O'Dwyer pledged allegiance to the United States and fought for the principles of the Constitution and Bill of Rights in eras of war and reaction. Known for confrontation, he shifted decidedly in later years toward an attitude of compromise and stimulated decisive progress toward the resolution of sectarian violence in Northern Ireland. He straddled two countries all along, ballasted by his democratic beliefs and an enduring feeling for the poor and disenfranchised.

Ending the eulogy, Reverend Leonard told mourners of a conversation between two senior citizens poring over O'Dwyer's obituary in the *New York Times* in the rectory before the service. Considering Paul's near-lifelong insistence on justice for all, the congregants' brief exchange about the subject of the article concluded on an especially apt note.

"One said, 'Wasn't he an anarchist?'" recounted the priest. "The other answered: 'No, no, no! He was Irish!'"[59]

ACKNOWLEDGMENTS

O UR INDEPENDENT BIOGRAPHY of Paul O'Dwyer, the first ever published, would not have been possible without the help of many people. We wish to thank them.

If newspapers are the first draft of history, then libraries are at least as crucial—the repositories of yellowing personal papers, transcripts of interviews and court cases, TV and radio interview snippets, and out-of-print memoirs and histories. Thus, we owe a debt, not only to the reporters and columnists who covered our subject but also to the archivists who guided us through the thicket.

Some of the most valuable oral history Q and As we read were conducted under the auspices of the Columbia University Oral History Center; the New York University (NYU) Tamiment Library and Robert F. Wagner Labor Archives and its Archives of Irish America; the New York City Municipal Archives; and the American Jewish Committee Oral History Collection. Luckily for us, too, Kate O'Callaghan Farrelly, a documentary filmmaker, kept cassette tapes capturing her long-ago interview with Paul about his youth, which she shared with us, while the New York State Archives found the records of Paul's petition to Benjamin Cardozo. The future Supreme Court justice signed a waiver allowing O'Dwyer to take the bar exam before he had officially become a US citizen.

O'Dwyer's voluminous personal and professional papers are held at NYU Tamiment, by St. John's University Special Collections, and at the

Municipal Archives. In all these libraries, the authors were permitted to comb through black-and-white photographs, letters and cards, memos preserved on notepad scraps and on wrinkly ditto paper, and many primary and secondary sources.

In addition, we also relied on documents released by the FBI under the Freedom of Information Act, which proved particularly helpful when we examined government scrutiny of Bill's and Paul's actions during the McCarthy era.

Adding to the contemporaneous and recently published accounts of Irish, American, and New York history we read, we spoke with some one hundred individuals who had intersected with Paul. We are grateful to Paul's sons, Bill, Rory, and Brian, and his nephew Adrian Flannelly for their detailed remembrances. In addition, Monica Durkan led us to a clearer understanding of her late husband and Paul's nephew, Frank Durkan, and their representation of IRA fugitives and sympathizers in the United States.

We appreciate the assistance extended by other relatives, friends, and lawyers of O'Dwyer, including those who spoke with us despite the COVID-19 pandemic. Among them were Frank O'Dwyer Jr., the devoted son of Paul's late brother of the same name, and the three children of his late niece, Joan O'Dwyer Savarese.

Among Paul's adjutants at his law firm, Mychal McNicholas, an O'Dwyer cousin, was exceedingly generous with his time. In addition, John McGettrick was among several people who told us about Paul's years at city hall. Over many phone calls, McGettrick laid out an invaluable roadmap to aspects of Paul's character and conduct as a politician. Franklin Siegel, too, offered hard-to-find records along with his recollections and interpretation of O'Dwyer's work as a lawyer and public official.

Concerning O'Dwyer's response to the Troubles in Northern Ireland, we are indebted to Niall O'Dowd, the founding publisher of the *Irish Voice* and a participant in behind-the-scenes negotiations leading to the Good Friday Peace Agreement. As our account also reflects, the former New York congressman Peter King and the decorated *Newsday* foreign correspondent Jim Mulvaney shared with us their experiences with O'Dwyer—as did the Rockaways restaurateur and community advocate Dan Tubridy.

The book's flaws are attributable to the authors and the authors alone. But, especially as O'Dwyer was something of a twentieth-century Zelig, we turned to a surfeit of thoughtful and engaging persons from law and the judiciary, local and national politics, journalism, public relations, the academy, and government to help us explore his countless instances of advocacy for underdogs on both sides of the Atlantic.

We wish to thank the following people: Ken Auletta, Charles Bagli, Kevin Baker, Mark Barrett, the late Wayne Barrett, Howard Beldock, the late Myron Beldock, Carol Bellamy, Theodore Blumberg, the late Jimmy Breslin, Jim Callaghan, the late Mickey Carroll, Marion Casey, the late Ramsey Clark, Ken Cobb, Evelyn David, Jack Deacy, Dave DiBiasio, the late David Dinkins, William Dobbs, Larry Downes, Sean Downes, Monica Durkan, the late Jim Dwyer, Ronnie Eldridge, Kate O'Callaghan Farrelly, Patrick Farrelly, Joe Finn, Adrian Flannelly, Stanley Friedman, the late Judge Louis Fusco Jr., Ronald Gallashaw, Martin Galvin, Jim Gilroy, Terry Golway, Matthew Goodman, Idilio Gracia Peña, Mark Green, Denis Hamill, Harold Holzer, David Hunt, Betsy Imholz, Dan Janison, Peter Johnson, Jeffrey Michael Kaufman, John Keenan, Douglas Kellner, Tim Keseker, Sarah Kovner, Matthew Larkin, Kelly O'Neill Levy, Mortimer Matz, Bernadette Devlin McAliskey, Cody McCone, Malachy McCourt, John McGettrick, Sheila McKenna, Rafael Medoff, Kathy Metz, Ruth Messinger, Milt Mollen, Fr. Pat Moloney, Peter Mones, Robert Moran, Kevin Morrissey, Jim Mulvaney, Maureen Murphy, Peter Murray, John Murtagh, Miriam Nyhan Grey, Keara O'Dempsey, Cormac O'Malley, Liam O'Neill, Shane O'Neill, Manfred Ohrenstein, Carol Opton, Susan Ould, Virginia Polihrom, the late Gabe Pressman, Peter Quinn, Charlie Rangel, Tom Robbins, Jeff Roth, Bob Schneider, Gary Silverman, Bill Sipser, the late Dick Starkey, the late Martin Steadman, and Pierre Sutton.

In the project's final stages, Robert Snyder, a professor emeritus of American studies and journalism at Rutgers University and the Manhattan borough historian, read and marked up the manuscript, a huge help, while historian-author Peter Eisenstadt and Dr. Rafael Medoff (David S. Wyman Institute for Holocaust Studies, Washington, DC) assisted us with comments on chapter 5. Mahinder Kingra, the editorial director of Cornell University Press, succeeded Michael McGandy (who approved our book proposal) in late 2022 and was expert in guiding the manuscript through to publication. Jane McNamara, associate dean at The New

School, introduced us at the outset to the publisher's regional imprint Three Hills Press and its then editor, McGandy.

Our literary agent, Ed Breslin, was a ready source of encouragement, believing in our project—and in us—when it stalled and we despaired. Referred to us by Tom Robbins, he secured the publishing contract and readily gave us the benefit of his knowledge.

The authors first met as students at Columbia in New York and re-connected to take on this full-scale biography. Happily, our friendship weathered, with aplomb, the typical trials of coauthorship, notwithstand-ing that Michael is Irish and Catholic and Robert is Jewish. In fact, our different backgrounds and political views combined to enhance our mu-tual understanding of our subject.

We wish to express our most profound appreciation of our respective parents: Louise, a teacher and an artist, and the memory of Murray Pol-ner, a writer and editor, who was Rob's mentor; and the memory of Nora and Michael Tubridy Sr., each of whom, Michael notes, "taught me every-thing important about being Irish."

For Rob, his spouse Monica McIntyre was, as always, an invaluable source of support and a knowledgeable sounding board. Rob also wishes to thank his daughters, Molly and Catherine, for their love and endorse-ment. Michael wishes to thank his brothers, John and Tom, and their fam-ilies, who helped carry him through.

NOTES

FRONT MATTER

Epigraph: Paul O'Dwyer quoted by Francis X. Clines, "Paul O'Dwyer, New York's Liberal Battler for Underdogs and Outsiders, Dies at 90," *New York Times*, June 25, 1998, B-9.

INTRODUCTION

1. Paul O'Dwyer, interview with Jane Conlon Miller, February 6, 1990, transcript, New York University Tamiment Library and Robert F. Wagner Labor Archives, 5.
2. Paul O'Dwyer, quoted by Francis X. Clines in "Paul O'Dwyer, New York's Liberal Battler for Underdogs and Outsiders, Dies at 90," *New York Times*, June 25, 1998, B-9.
3. Murray Kempton, "Paul O'Dwyer: A Kindly Radical Says Farewell," *New York Post*, December 29,1977, n.p.
4. Clines, "Paul O'Dwyer, New York's Liberal Battler."

1. THE BOY FROM BOHOLA

1. F. S. L. Lyons, *Ireland since the Famine* (London: Weidenfeld and Nicholson, 1971; reprinted, London, Fontana Press, 1990), 16. Also see Roy F. Foster's *Paddy and Mr. Punch* (London: Faber & Faber, 2011), in which Foster notes that "between forty and fifty percent of the future revolutionary leaders [of Ireland] had lived in Britain, or were of returned emigrant stock" (299).
2. William O'Dwyer, *Beyond the Golden Door*, ed. Paul O'Dwyer (New York: St. John's University Press, 1987), 2, 4.
3. W. O'Dwyer, *Beyond the Golden Door*, 5–7; Frank Durkan, "Eulogy for Paul O'Dwyer," *New York Irish History* 12 (1998), 7–9.
4. W. O'Dwyer, *Beyond the Golden Door*, 18.

5. W. O'Dwyer, *Beyond the Golden Door*, 8, 16; Durkan, "Eulogy for Paul O'Dwyer."

6. "The Great Famine, Bohola in Co. Mayo," Mayo Ireland, accessed October 12, 2021, https://www.mayo-ireland.ie/en/towns-villages/bohola/history/the-great-famine.html; W. O'Dwyer, *Beyond the Golden Door*, 16.

7. Paul O'Dwyer, *Counsel for the Defense: The Autobiography of Paul O'Dwyer* (New York: Simon & Schuster, 1979), 18.

8. W. O'Dwyer, *Beyond the Golden Door*, 30.

9. P. O'Dwyer, *Counsel for the Defense*, 11.

10. W. O'Dwyer, *Beyond the Golden Door*, 35.

11. P. O'Dwyer, *Counsel for the Defense*, 23–24.

12. W. O'Dwyer, *Beyond the Golden Door*, 45.

13. W. O'Dwyer, *Beyond the Golden Door*, 42–43; P. O'Dwyer, *Counsel for the Defense*, 23.

14. P. O'Dwyer, *Counsel for the Defense*, 24.

15. W. O'Dwyer, *Beyond the Golden Door*, 39–40; "How Hundreds of Irish Flocked to Healing Hands of the Tipperary Bone-Setter," *Irish Central*, May 25, 2021, https://www.irishcentral.com/roots/history/irish-flocked-healing-hands-tipperary-bonesetter.

16. Adrian Flannelly, interview by the authors, February 27, 2020.

17. "The Reminiscences of William O'Dwyer," interviews by John K. Kelly, 1960–1962, transcribed 1965, Columbia University Oral History Collection, 310–311.

18. W. O'Dwyer, *Beyond the Golden Door*, 39; Alan Francis Carthy, "The Treatment of Tuberculosis in Ireland from the 1890s to the 1970s: A Case Study of Medical Care in Leinster" (PhD diss., Maynooth University, 2015), 1, https://mural.maynoothuniversity.ie/9118/1/Alan%20Carthy%20PhD%20thesis%202015%20The%20treatment%20of%20tuberculosis%20in.pdf; Eugene O'Neill, *Long Day's Journey into Night*, 2nd ed. (New Haven, CT, and London: Yale University Press, 1984), 34; Helen O'Connor, "Tuberculosis in Ireland—A Lesson From History," TB Online, January 11, 2021, https://www.tbonline.info/posts/2021/1/11/tuberculosis-ireland-lesson-history; "The Reminiscences of William O'Dwyer," 310–311.

19. P. O'Dwyer, *Counsel for the Defense*, 22–23.

20. "The Reminiscences of William O'Dwyer," 677.

21. W. O'Dwyer, *Beyond the Golden Door*, 60.

22. James O'Donnell, "In Bohola, They Knew O'Dwyer as a Scrapper," *Daily News*, January 30, 1949, 76; Paul O'Dwyer, interview by Jill Levine, July 1980, transcript, William E. Wiener Oral History Library of the American Jewish Committee, New York Public Library ("Paul O'Dwyer Oral History Memoir").

23. P. O'Dwyer, interview, 9–13.

24. P. O'Dwyer, *Counsel for the Defense*, 18.

25. J. J. Lee, *Ireland, 1912–1985: Politics and Society* (Cambridge, UK: Cambridge University Press, 1989), 81.

26. W. O'Dwyer, *Beyond the Golden Door*, 40–41; Patsy McGarry, "An Irishman's Diary," *Irish Times*, September 16, 1996, https://www.irishtimes.com/opinion/an-irishman-s-diary-1.86511.

27. O'Donnell, "They Knew O'Dwyer as a Scrapper."

28. W. O'Dwyer, *Beyond the Golden Door*, 124–25.

29. W. O'Dwyer, *Beyond the Golden Door*, 38.

30. Tony Lyons, "'Inciting the Lawless and Profligate Adventure'—The Hedge Schools of Ireland," *History Ireland*, 24, no. 6 (November/December 2016), 28–31.

31. Lyons, *Ireland since the Famine*, 82–89.

32. W. O'Dwyer, *Beyond the Golden Door*, 20–22; Kiarmaid Ferriter, "Striking the Right Balance," review of *Kindling the Flame: 150 Years of the Irish National Teachers' Organisation*, by Niamh Puirséil, *Irish Times*, March 17, 2018, https://www.irishtimes .com/culture/books/kindling-the-flame-150-years-of-the-irish-national-teachers -organisation-by-niamh-puirseil-striking-the-right-balance-1.3417008.

33. Wesley Boyd, "Edward Carson's Long Shadow," *Irish Times*, January 14, 2014, https://www.irishtimes.com/culture/heritage/edward-carson-s-long-shadow-1 .1649952.

34. "Patrick Pearse's Graveside Panegyric for O'Donovan Rossa on 1 August 1915 at Glasnevin Cemetery in Dublin," Easter Rising 1916, accessed November 19, 2021, http://www.easter1916.net/oration.htm.

35. Mike Levine, "How Can a Blade of Grass Move the Wind?" *Times Herald-Record*, May 14, 1995, https://www.recordonline.com/article/20070115/news/70115614 (article removed from the website by August 22, 2023).

2. SECOND-CLASS PASSENGER

1. "The Reminiscences of Paul O'Dwyer," interview by John K. Kelly, 1962, transcript, Columbia University Oral History Collection, 14.

2. Paul O'Dwyer, interview by Kate O'Callaghan, documentary filmmaker, 1988, audio recording provided to the authors by O'Callaghan.

3. Most of the details in this description of Bohola are based on the recollections of Paul and Bill O'Dwyer in, respectively, *Counsel for the Defense* and *Beyond the Golden Door*. Paul mentions the three pubs and the town center in his audio interview by Kate O'Callaghan, 1988, and the church, the priest's house, and a post office in an interview by Jill Levine for the American Jewish Committee (July 9, 1989).

4. See David Leeson, *The Black and Tans: British Police and Auxiliaries in the Irish War of Independence, 1920–21* (Oxford: Oxford University Press, 2011). The following is an extrapolation from a sample of Black and Tan recruits: "The Black-and-Tans and Auxiliaries were overwhelmingly British (78.6 per cent of the sample). Almost two thirds were English, fourteen per cent were Scottish, and fewer than five per cent came from Wales and outside the UK. An unexpected finding that is at odds with popular memory is that nearly nineteen per cent of the sampled recruits (514) were Irish-born, twenty per cent of Black-and-Tans and about ten per cent of Auxiliaries. Extrapolating from the sample, more than 2,300 of all Black-and-Tans and 225 of all Auxiliaries were Irish." See W. J. Lowe, "Who Were the Black and Tans?" *History Ireland* 12, no. 3 (Autumn 2004), https://www.historyireland.com/who-were -the-black-and-tans.

5. Cormac O'Comhrai, *Revolution in Connacht: A Photographic History, 1913–23* (Cork: Mercier Press, 2012), 59.

6. Paul O'Dwyer, *Counsel for the Defense: The Autobiography of Paul O'Dwyer* (New York: Simon & Schuster, 1979), 40.

7. Paul O'Dwyer, interview by Patricia Molino, 1987, audio, Columbia University Oral History Collection.

8. P. O'Dwyer, *Counsel for the Defense*, 40.

9. P. O'Dwyer, interview, 1987.

10. P. O'Dwyer, *Counsel for the Defense*, 43.

11. Jay Dolan, *The Irish Americans* (London and New York: Bloomsbury Press, 2008), 205.

12. Daniel Mulhall, "The Anglo-Irish Treaty of December 1921," *Ambassador's Blog*, December 6, 2021, https://www.dfa.ie/irish-embassy/usa/about-us/ambassador/ambassadors-blog/the-anglo-irish-treaty-of-december-1921.html; P. O'Dwyer, *Counsel for the Defense*, 48.

13. P. O'Dwyer, *Counsel for the Defense*, 48; Tim Pat Coogan, *Eamon de Valera: The Man Who Was Ireland* (New York: Harper Perennial, 1996), 238.

14. P. O'Dwyer, interview, 1988.

15. P. O'Dwyer, interview, 1988.

16. P. O'Dwyer, *Counsel for the Defense*, 47.

17. Coogan, *The Man Who Was Ireland*, 294.

18. Coogan, *The Man Who Was Ireland*, 481–85.

19. Oscar Bernstien, interview by John K. Kelly, 1962, transcript, Columbia University Oral History Collection.

20. Frank Durkan, "Eulogy for Paul O'Dwyer," *New York Irish History* 12 (1998), 7–9.

21. William O'Dwyer, *Beyond the Golden Door* (New York: St. John's University Press, 1987), 111; P. O'Dwyer, *Counsel for the Defense*, 44.

22. P. O'Dwyer, *Counsel for the Defense*, 43.

23. "The Reminiscences of William O'Dwyer," interview by John K. Kelly, 1962, transcript, Columbia University Oral History Collection, 308; P. O'Dwyer, *Counsel for the Defense*, 47.

24. P. O'Dwyer, *Counsel for the Defense*, 46.

25. P. O'Dwyer, *Counsel for the Defense*, 44.

26. Durkan, "Eulogy for Paul O'Dwyer"; "The Reminiscences of William O'Dwyer," 364; P. O'Dwyer, *Counsel for the Defense*, 47.

27. "The Reminiscences of Paul O'Dwyer," 10.

28. "The Reminiscences of Paul O'Dwyer," 17–18.

29. P. O'Dwyer, *Counsel for the Defense*, 54.

30. P. O'Dwyer, *Counsel for the Defense*, 37; P. O'Dwyer, interview, 1987.

31. "The Paul O'Dwyer Story: From Longshoreman to Mayor?" (Part I), *Irish Echo*, September 4, 1965; P. O'Dwyer, interview, 1988; Paul O'Dwyer, oral history interview by Jane Conlon Muller, April 11, 1991, audio, CD 20, New York University Tamiment Library and Robert F. Wagner Labor Archives.

32. Liam O'Neill, interview by Robert Polner, January 26, 2021.

33. "The Reminiscences of Paul O'Dwyer," 14.

34. P. O'Dwyer, interview, 1987.

35. Dolan, *The Irish Americans*, 217–18.

36. P. O'Dwyer, *Counsel for the Defense*, 58.

37. "The Reminiscences of Paul O'Dwyer," 22.

38. "The Reminiscences of Paul O'Dwyer," 24.

39. "The Reminiscences of Paul O'Dwyer," 28

40. "The Paul O'Dwyer Story."

41. Paul O'Dwyer, quoted in Jane Conlon Muller Oral History Collection, CD #34, May 15, 1991, New York University Tamiment Library/Robert F. Wagner Labor Archives, http://dlib.nyu.edu/findingaids/html/tamwag/aia_012/scopecontent.html.

42. P. O'Dwyer, *Counsel for the Defense*, 68; "The Reminiscences of Paul O'Dwyer," 36.

43. "The Connected City: Water, Water, Everywhere," National Museum of American History, accessed December 3, 2021, https://americanhistory.si.edu/america-on-the-move/connected-city.

44. P. O'Dwyer, interview, 1987.

45. See James T. Fisher, *On the Irish Waterfront: The Crusader, the Movie, and the Soul of the Port of New York* (Ithaca, N.Y.: Cornell University Press, 2009), 37.

46. P. O'Dwyer, interview, 1987.

47. "The Reminiscences of Paul O'Dwyer," 36–50.

48. "The Reminiscences of Paul O'Dwyer," 39–40

49. P. O'Dwyer, *Counsel for the Defense*, 61.

50. P. O'Dwyer, *Counsel for the Defense*, 69.

51. P. O'Dwyer, *Counsel for the Defense*, 69. The historian Francis Russell came to change his mind about Sacco and Vanzetti's innocence in "Sacco Guilty, Vanzetti Innocent?" *American Heritage* 13, no. 4 (June 1962), https://www.americanheritage .com/sacco-guilty-vanzetti-innocent, a stance he later spelled out in greater detail in *Sacco Vanzetti: The Case Resolved* (New York: HarperCollins, 1986). The biographer of the author-activist Upton Sinclair, Tony Arthur, explained in an interview that their longtime defender Sinclair privately believed that Sacco and Vanzetti might be guilty; "Sacco and Vanzetti: Guilty After All?" interview by Debbie Elliott, March 4, 2006, NPR, https://www.npr.org/templates/story/story.php?storyId=5245754.

52. Paul O'Dwyer, interview by Jill Levine, 1980, transcript, William E. Wiener Oral History Library of the American Jewish Committee, New York Public Library ("Paul O'Dwyer Oral History Memoir"), 15.

53. Dolan, *The Irish Americans*, 217.

54. Dolan, *The Irish Americans*, 215.

55. Dolan, *The Irish Americans*, 217.

56. "The Reminiscences of Paul O'Dwyer," 26.

57. Office of the Historian, United States Department of State, "The Immigration Act of 1924 (The Johnson-Reed Act)," accessed October 2, 2022, https://history.state .gov/milestones/1921-1936/immigration-act; A. P. Lobo and J. J. Salvo, "Resurgent Irish Immigration to the US in the 1980s and 1990s: A Socio-Demographic Profile," *International Migration* 36, no. 2 (1998): 258.

58. P. O'Dwyer, *Counsel for the Defense*, 66.

59. W. O'Dwyer, *Beyond the Golden Door*, 118.

60. O'Neill, interview.

61. O'Neill, interview.

62. P. O'Dwyer, *Counsel for the Defense*, 66.

63. P. O'Dwyer, *Counsel for the Defense*, 67.

64. The "wind" quote comes from Paul's interview with Francis X. Clines in "About New York," *New York Times*, February 24, 1979, 23.

65. W. O'Dwyer, *Beyond the Golden Door*, 116.

66. "Plane Kills 2 in Coney Crowd," *Brooklyn Daily Times*, September 8, 1929, 1; "Healy Holds Trial in Air to Settle Coney Death Guilt with Defendant as Pilot," *Brooklyn Daily Eagle*, September 19, 1929, 1; "Unsafe Flying in New York," *Brooklyn Daily Eagle*, October 7, 1929, 20.

67. W. O'Dwyer, *Beyond the Golden Door*, 117.

68. Bernstien, interview; "Canton People Grieved," *Brooklyn Times-Union*, December 27, 1921.

69. "Rebecca Drucker Bernstien, Writer, 105," *New York Times*, January 2, 1996, 36.

70. Bernstien, interview.

71. Bernstien, interview.

72. P. O'Dwyer, *Counsel for the Defense*, 74–75; P. O'Dwyer, interview, 1980, 26–27.

3. AMONG THIEVES

1. Paul O'Dwyer, interview by Patricia Molino, April 16 and April 28, 1987, audio, Columbia University Oral History Collection.

2. Thomas Kessner, *Fiorello La Guardia and the Making of Modern New York* (London: Penguin Press, 1991), 170; Samantha Sokol, "On This Day in NYC History, December 11: The Bank of the United States in New York Fails in 1930," *Untapped New York*, December 11, 2013, https://untappedcities.com/2013/12/11/on-this-day-on-nyc-history-december-11-the-bank-of-the-united-states-in-new-york-fails-in-1930; Robert Caro, *The Power Broker: Robert Moses and the Fall of New York* (New York: Vintage Books, 1975), 324–27.

3. Pauline O'Toole, "Unemployment in the Great Depression," New York City Department of Records & Information Services, October 9, 2020, https://www.archives.nyc/blog/2020/10/9/9ovdpgn8lc5zxcild0ooltvzmfwx22.

4. Kessner, *Fiorello La Guardia*, 208.

5. Red Hook Waterstories Team, "'Tin City' Folks Gird for Dreariest Winter, 1932," *Red Hook Waterstories*, April 6, 2018, https://www.redhookwaterstories.org/items/show/1690.

6. Kessner, *Fiorello La Guardia*, 375.

7. William O'Dwyer, *Beyond the Golden Door*, ed. Paul O'Dwyer (New York: St. John's University Press, 1987), 80.

8. P. O'Dwyer, interview, 1987; "3 Cops Deny They Burned Youth's Wrist," *Brooklyn Daily Eagle*, June 12, 1936, 9; "Clear 7 Officers of Beating Charge," *Brooklyn Daily Eagle*, July 9, 1936, 19; "Killer of Woman Is Shot in Chase," *Brooklyn Times-Union*, April 5, 1937, 20.

9. W. O'Dwyer, *Beyond the Golden Door*, 117.

10. Eileen Battersby, "Irish—But American, Too," *Irish Times*, June 16, 1994.

11. "Fired as Mechanic He Becomes Lawyer," *Brooklyn Daily Eagle*, May 30, 1932.

12. Paul O'Dwyer, *Counsel for the Defense: The Autobiography of Paul O'Dwyer* (New York: Simon & Schuster, 1979), 80–83; W. O'Dwyer, *Beyond the Golden Door*, 124–25.

13. Bernard Whalen and Jon Whalen, *The NYPD's First Fifty Years: Politicians, Police Commissioners and Patrolmen* (Nebraska: University of Nebraska Press, 2014), 127.

14. Caro, *The Power Broker*, 338–39.

15. Herbert Mitgang, *The Man Who Rode the Tiger: The Life of Judge Samuel Seabury and the Story of the Greatest Investigation of City Corruption in This Century* (New York: Fordham University Press, 1970), 204–5; Kenneth T. Jackson, Lisa Keller, and Nancy Flood, eds., *The Encyclopedia of New York City* (New Haven, CT: Yale University Press, 2010), s.v. "Jimmy Walker."

16. "Boy, 17, Rehabilitated by Adolescents Court," *Brooklyn Daily Eagle*, March 22, 1936, 9.

17. P. O'Dwyer, *Counsel for the Defense*, 92–93.

18. P. O'Dwyer, *Counsel for the Defense*, 92–93.

19. P. O'Dwyer, *Counsel for the Defense*, 93–94.

20. Brian O'Dwyer, interview by Robert Polner (RP), April 28, 2020.

21. Brian O'Dwyer, interview.

22. Jimmy Breslin, "Irish Wake," *Sacramento Bee*, reprinted from *Daily News*, December 8, 1980.

23. Breslin, "Irish Wake."

24. Rory O'Dwyer, email to Michael Tubridy, November 1, 2021.

25. "Paul O'Dwyer's Family—Biographies," campaign press release, in the Paul O'Dwyer Papers, Box 22, Folder 286, Senate Campaign-1968 Biographical File, Department of Records and Information Services, NYC Municipal Archives.
26. Dr. William O'Dwyer, interview by RP, May 7, 2020.
27. "Young Lawyer Gets Murder Defense as a Wedding Present," *Brooklyn Times-Union*, August 22, 1935.
28. P. O'Dwyer, *Counsel for the Defense*, 93.
29. Paul O'Dwyer, interview by Jane Conlon Muller, December 7, 1990, transcript, New York University Tamiment Library and Robert F. Wagner Labor Archives (also available online: "Paul O'Dwyer, In His Own Words," *New York Irish History* 12 (1998): 11–15, https://nyirishhistory.us/article/paul-odwyer-in-his-own-words).
30. P. O'Dwyer, *Counsel for the Defense*, 27–29.
31. "O'Dwyer Slayers Fight for Lives," *Brooklyn Times-Union*, October 15, 1934, 3.
32. "Death Witness Admits Perjury," *Brooklyn Daily Eagle*, August 27, 1934, 1.
33. P. O'Dwyer, *Counsel for the Defense*, 93.
34. "O'Dwyer Slayer and Cop's Killer Walk Last Mile," *Brooklyn Times-Union*, January 11, 1935, 8.
35. Adrian Flannelly, interview by the authors, February 27, 2020.
36. Brian O'Dwyer, interview; Timothy Sullivan, "The Trials of Paul O'Dwyer," *Manhattan Lawyer*, January 10–16, 1989.
37. "Clear 7 Officers of Beating Charge," *Brooklyn Daily Eagle*, July 9, 1936, 19.
38. Michael Lumer and Nancy Tenney, "The Death Penalty in New York: An Historical Perspective," *Journal of Law and Policy* 4, no. 1 (1995): 87–91.
39. P. O'Dwyer, *Counsel for the Defense*, 91.
40. P. O'Dwyer, *Counsel for the Defense*, 91, emphasis added; "Grubee Guilty in 2nd Degree," *Brooklyn Daily Eagle*, October 1, 1937, 1–2.
41. Sullivan, "The Trials of Paul O'Dwyer."
42. Niven Busch Jr., *21 Americans: Being Profiles of Some Famous People in Our Time with Characterized Drawings* (Lake Oswego, OR: e-Net Press, 2014), 101, a collection of *New Yorker* magazine stories by the novelist/filmmaker first published in 1931.
43. Ed Reid, *The Shame of New York* (New York: Random House, 1953), 211.
44. Reid, *The Shame of New York*, 143.
45. Kessner, *Fiorello La Guardia*, 365.
46. Kessner, *Fiorello La Guardia*, 366.
47. Kessner, *Fiorello La Guardia*, 366–67.
48. Kessner, *Fiorello La Guardia*, 367.
49. Kessner, *Fiorello La Guardia*, 367.
50. "Father Curran Condemns Unfair Attacks on Boro; Defends Geoghan Record," *The Brooklyn Citizen*, October 12, 1938, 1–2.
51. Fred J. Cook, *The Secret Rulers: Criminal Syndicates and How They Control the Underworld* (New York: Duell, Sloan and Pearce, 1966), 144–45.
52. Kings County Investigation, 1938–1942, Final Public Report, Brooklyn Public Library; "The Racket-Buster," *The Chiseler*, accessed March 15, 2013, https://chiseler.org/post/36970615767/the-racket-buster.
53. Kings County Investigation, Final Public Report.
54. L. E. O'Toole, letter to the editor, *The Tablet*, June 23, 1934.
55. Clifford Evans, interview by John K. Kelly, 1962, transcript, Columbia University Oral History Collection.
56. W. O'Dwyer, *Beyond the Golden Door*, 132–33.
57. Evans, interview.

58. W. O'Dwyer, *Beyond the Golden Door*, 144.
59. W. O'Dwyer, *Beyond the Golden Door*, 146.
60. W. O'Dwyer, *Beyond the Golden Door*, 147–48.
61. W. O'Dwyer, *Beyond the Golden Door*, 148.
62. P. O'Dwyer, *Counsel for the Defense*, 94.
63. Ellen Schrecker, *Many Are the Crimes: McCarthyism in America* (Princeton, NJ: Princeton University Press, 1998), 35.
64. Joshua B. Freeman, "Irish Workers in the Twentieth Century in the United States: The Case of the Transport Workers' Union," *Saothar: Journal of Irish Labor History* 8 (1982), 24–45.
65. Freeman, "Irish Workers in the Twentieth Century."
66. Victor Rabinowitz, *Unrepentant Leftist: A Lawyer's Memoir* (Urbana and Chicago: University of Illinois Press, 1996), 21–22.
67. Philip S. Foner, *The Fur and Leather Workers Union: A Story of Dramatic Struggles and Achievements* (Newark: Nordan Press, 1950), 287.
68. "AFL Union's Agents Blasts Gold at Fur Trial," *Daily Worker*, April 5, 1940, 3.
69. Foner, *The Fur and Leather Workers Union*, 580.
70. "Gold is Acquitted in Jury Plot Trial," *New York Times*, July 12, 1940, 34.
71. "Frank Holmes Dies in Plunge," *Brooklyn Eagle*, October 29, 1938, 1.
72. Paul O'Dwyer, *Counsel for the Defense*, 100.

4. TESTS OF LOYALTY

1. The American Friends of Irish Neutrality (AFIN) records, 1938–1952, St. John's University Archives and Special Collections; Paul O'Dwyer, "The Young Fighter Who Made Good," *The Irish Press*, September 2, 1976; Ray O'Hanlon, *Unintended Consequences: The Story of Irish Immigration to the U.S. and How America's Door was Closed to the Irish* (Newbridge, County Kildare, Ireland: Merrion Press, 2021).
2. David Brundage, *Irish Nationalists in America: The Politics of Exile, 1798–1998* (Oxford: Oxford University Press, 2016), 185; Paul O'Dwyer, interview by Patricia Molino, 1987, audio, Columbia University Oral History Collection.
3. P. O'Dwyer, "The Young Fighter Who Made Good."
4. P. O'Dwyer, "The Young Fighter Who Made Good"; AFIN records.
5. Brundage, *Irish Nationalists in America*.
6. P. O'Dwyer, "The Young Fighter Who Made Good."
7. Paul O' Dwyer, *Counsel for the Defense: The Autobiography of Paul O'Dwyer* (New York: Simon & Schuster, 1979), 106.
8. Paul O'Dwyer to Ian Adamson of Farset Youth and Community Development in Belfast, April 13, 1991, correspondence, in the Paul O'Dwyer Papers, Box 3, New York University Tamiment Library and Robert F. Wagner Labor Archives.
9. P. O' Dwyer, *Counsel for the Defense*, 106–7.
10. P. O' Dwyer, *Counsel for the Defense*, 107–8.
11. Thomas Kessner, *Fiorello La Guardia and the Making of Modern New York* (London: Penguin Press, 1991), 336.
12. Kessner, *Fiorello La Guardia*, 341.
13. Kessner, *Fiorello La Guardia*, 468–70.
14. P. O'Dwyer, *Counsel for the Defense*, 102.
15. Kessner, *Fiorello La Guardia*, 496.
16. "The Reminiscences of William O'Dwyer," interview by John K. Kelly, 1962, transcript, Columbia University Oral History Collection, 622.

17. "The Reminiscences of Paul O'Dwyer," 162–63.

18. Robert Caro, *The Power Broker: Robert Moses and the Fall of New York* (New York: Vintage Books, 1975), 765.

19. Federal Bureau of Investigation, "William O'Dwyer–Information Concerning," memo, February 16, 1953, released under Freedom of Information Act to the authors.

20. P. O'Dwyer, *Counsel for the Defense*, 161.

21. P. O'Dwyer, *Counsel for the Defense*, 161.

22. Caro, *The Power Broker*, 759–60, referring to Councilman Stanley Isaacs of Manhattan.

23. "Citizens Group Raps Dewey in Albany Parley," *Brooklyn Eagle*, January 11, 1948, 4; J. H. Schmalacker, "Lawyers Ask 40 PC Income Tax for City," *Brooklyn Eagle*, January 18, 1948, 1.

24. P. O'Dwyer, *Counsel for the Defense*, 103.

25. Kessner, *Fiorello La Guardia*, 497.

26. Clifford Evans, interview by John K. Kelly, 1962, transcript, Columbia University Oral History Collection.

27. P. O'Dwyer, *Counsel for the Defense*, 103.

28. P. O'Dwyer, *Counsel for the Defense*, 103; "The Reminiscences of Paul O'Dwyer," 155.

29. "The Reminiscences of Paul O'Dwyer," 155.

30. "Will Destroy All Grafters, O'Dwyer Tells Tammany," *Brooklyn Eagle*, October 17, 1941.

31. "The Reminiscences of Paul O'Dwyer," 162–63.

32. Edward A. Cargan, "Burton B. Turkus, 80, Prosecutor of Murder Inc. in the 1940s, Dies," *New York Times*, November 24, 1982, D-21.

33. Myron Beldock, interview by Robert Polner (RP), October 12, 2013. Beldock provided the authors with a copy of the presentment from his files.

34. George Walsh, *Public Enemies: The Mayor, the Mob, and the Crime That Was* (New York: W.W. Norton, 1980), 123–24.

35. "The Reminiscences of Paul O'Dwyer," 74–76.

36. Alan A. Block, "On the Waterfront Revisited: The Criminology of Waterfront Organized Crime," *Contemporary Crises* 6 (1982), 373–96.

37. Nathan Ward, *Dark Harbor: The War for the New York Waterfront* (New York: Picador, 2011), 5, in reference to testimony given to the New York State Crime Commission, which began its work in 1953.

38. Ward, *Dark Harbor*, 5.

39. Ward, *Dark Harbor*, 7.

40. Forrest Hylton, "Labor Noir: Murders and Funerals on the Brooklyn Waterfront," Transport Workers Solidarity Committee, November 8, 2014, https://www.transportworkers.org/node/1618

41. Ward, *Dark Harbor*, 8.

42. Ward, *Dark Harbor*, 23. Stephen Schwartz, "Arthur Miller's Proletariat: The True Stories of 'On the Waterfront', Pietro Panto, and Vincenzo Longhi," *Film History* 16 (2004): 378–92.

43. Alan Block, *East Side-West Side: Organized Crime in New York 1930–1950* (Cardiff, UK: University College Cardiff Press, 1980), 189.

44. Ward, *Dark Harbor*, 200.

45. "The Reminiscences of Paul O'Dwyer," 68.

46. "The Reminiscences of Paul O'Dwyer," 51–54.

47. Walsh, *Public Enemies*, 118.

48. Block, "On the Waterfront Revisited," 379.
49. Robert Patterson to Franklin Roosevelt, February 26,1944, quoted by W. O'Dwyer, *Beyond the Golden Door*, ed. Paul O'Dwyer (New York: St. John's University Press, 1987), 182.
50. Ann Fagan Ginger and Eugene M. Tobin, eds., *The National Lawyers Guild: From Roosevelt through Reagan* (Philadelphia: Temple University Press, 1988), 11.
51. Ellen Schrecker, *Many Are the Crimes: McCarthyism in America* (Princeton, NJ: Princeton University Press, 1998), 93.
52. Larry Tye, *Demagogue: The Life and Long Shadow of Senator Joe McCarthy* (New York: Mariner Books, 2020), 127.
53. Tye, *Demagogue*, 129–30.
54. See the NLG's self-published history entitled *A History of the National Lawyers Guild, 1937–1987* (New York: National Lawyers Guild Foundation, 1987), 35, which includes the recollections of Martin Popper.
55. *A History of the National Lawyers Guild*, xix–xx.
56. P. O'Dwyer, *Counsel for the Defense*, 116–20.
57. John Keenan, retired US District Court justice for the Southern District of New York, interview by RP, December 5, 2013.
58. Schrecker, *Many Are the Crimes*, 41, 84.

5. IRISH ZIONIST

1. Jim Dwyer, interview by Robert Polner, April 22, 2020.
2. Paul O'Dwyer, interview by Jane Conlon Muller, December 7, 1990, transcript, New York University Tamiment Library and Robert F. Wagner Labor Archives.
3. Aidan Beatty, "A Long and Oddly Intertwined History—Irish Nationalism and Zionism," *The Irish Story*, January 23, 2013, https://www.theirishstory.com/2013/01/23/a-long-and-oddly-intertwined-history-irish-nationalism-and-zionism. See also Rona Fields, "Poignant Parallels in Irish Republicanism and Jewish Zionism," Frank Durkan Papers, Box 29, Folder 13, New York University Tamiment Library and Robert F. Wagner Labor Archives.
4. Rana Mitter, "Legacy of Violence: The Bloody Ends of Empire," review of *Legacy of Violence: A History of the British Empire*, by Caroline Elkins, *Financial Times*, March 17, 2022, https://www.ft.com/content/e7c4feac-7123-4e7c-8a7e-bf13107ee6f9; Sunil Khilnani, "The British Empire Was Much Worse than You Realize," review of *Legacy of Violence: A History of the British Empire*, by Caroline Elkins, *New Yorker*, March 28, 2022, https://www.newyorker.com/magazine/2022/04/04/the-british-empire-was-much-worse-than-you-realize-caroline-elkinss-legacy-of-violence. On Duff, see Douglas V. Duff, *Sword for Hire* (London: J. Murray, 1934).
5. Tom Segev, *One Palestine, Complete: Jews and Arabs under the British Mandate* (New York: Henry Holt, 1999), 414–43 in the chapter titled "Ireland in Palestine."
6. Rafael Medoff, *Militant Zionism in America: The Rise and Impact of the Jabotinsky Movement in the United States, 1926–1948* (Tuscaloosa and London: University of Alabama Press, 2002), 15.
7. Rabbi Stephen Wise, "Why Zionists Cannot Support Jabotinsky and Revisionism," excerpts of address delivered before the Free Synagogue at Carnegie Hall, March 10, 1935, 5, https://www.infocenters.co.il/jabo/jabo_multimedia/a%201/151653.pdf.
8. Medoff, *Militant Zionism in America*, 49.

9. Paul O'Dwyer, interview by Jill Levine, 1980, transcript, William E. Wiener Oral History Library of the American Jewish Committee, New York Public Library ("Paul O'Dwyer Oral History Memoir").

10. Medoff, *Militant Zionism in America*, 79.

11. Julien Gorbach, *The Notorious Ben Hecht: Iconoclastic Writer and Militant Zionist* (West Lafayette: Purdue University Press), 178.

12. Medoff, *Militant Zionism in America*, 105.

13. Gorbach, *The Notorious Ben Hecht*, 180.

14. Rebecca Erbelding, *Rescue Board: The Untold Story of America's Efforts to Save the Jews of Europe* (New York: Anchor Books, 2019), 163–76 and 273–78.

15. Paul O'Dwyer, *Counsel for the Defense: The Autobiography of Paul O'Dwyer* (New York: Simon & Schuster, 1979), 152.

16. P. O'Dwyer, interview, 1980.

17. Numbers for the casualties in the Arab-Israeli War have long been debated. Those for the number of Israeli fighters and civilians killed are from Adam M. Garfinkle, *Politics and Society in Modern Israel: Myths and Realities* (Armonk, NY: M. E. Sharpe, 2000), 61; casualties for the Arab Army and Palestinian Arabs are from Benny Morris, *The Birth of the Palestinian Refugee Problem: 1947–1949* (Cambridge: Cambridge Middle East Library, 1988), 40–46; and the Palestinian refugee data are from Kristopher J. Peterson-Overton, Johannes D. Schmidt, and Jacques Hersh, "Retooling Peace Philosophy: A Critical Look at Israel's Separation Policy," in *Peace Philosophy in Action*, ed. Candice C. Carter and Ravindra Kumar (New York: Palgrave Macmillan, 2010), 49.

18. P. O'Dwyer, *Counsel for the Defense*, 157–60.

19. Salvatore LaGumina, *New York at Mid-Century: The Impellitteri Years* (London: Greenwood Press, 1992), 74. Bill O'Dwyer was "demonstrating uncanny appreciation for ethnic politics, which other Democratic chieftains lacked," LaGumina writes.

20. P. O'Dwyer, *Counsel for the Defense*, 157.

21. National Lawyers Guild Records, Part I, Series IV: NLG committees, Box 12, Folder 5, Justice in Palestine Committee, 1948, New York University Tamiment Library and Robert F. Wagner Labor Archives.

22. Medoff, *Militant Zionism in America*, 207–9; "Two in Arms Cache for Palestine Free," *New York Times*, May 29, 1948, 2.

23. Medoff, *Militant Zionism in America*, 207–9.

24. Medoff, *Militant Zionism in America*, 207–9; "Two in Arms Cache for Palestine Free."

25. P. O'Dwyer, *Counsel for the Defense*, 154.

26. David McCullough, *Truman* (New York: Simon & Schuster, 1992), 614–18.

27. Jewish Telegraphic Agency, "Tens of Thousands Jam NY Meeting to Greet Establishment of Jewish State," Archive, May 17, 1948, https://www.jta.org/archive/tens-of-thousands-jam-new-york-meeting-to-greet-establishment-of-new-jewish-state.

28. P. O'Dwyer, interview, 1980.

29. Daniel Gordis, *Menachem Begin: The Battle for Israel's Soul* (New York: Schocken Books, 2014), 50–54.

30. P. O'Dwyer, *Counsel for the Defense*, 166.

31. P. O'Dwyer, interview, 1980.

32. P. O'Dwyer, interview, 1980.

33. Rebecca Heilweil, "'Only in America': The Jewish Lord Mayor Robert Briscoe of Dublin in the United States, 1956–1958," *Penn History Review* 25, no. 1 (May 2018): 12.

34. Jewish Telegraphic Agency, "Briscoe Likens Jews' Homeland Dream to Irish Freedom Drive," Archive, February 14, 1939, https://www.jta.org/archive/briscoe-likens-jews-homeland-dream-to-irish-freedom-drive; Yitshaq Ben-Ami, *Years of Wrath, Days of Glory: Memoirs from the Irgun*, 2nd expanded ed. (New York: Shengold, 1983), 219–20. Ben-Ami was one of the leaders of the Bergson Group.
35. Chris McNickle, *To Be Mayor of New York: Ethnic Politics in the City* (New York: Columbia University Press, 1993), 68.
36. William O'Dwyer, *Beyond the Golden Door*, ed. Paul O'Dwyer (New York: St. John's University Press, 1987), 218.
37. McNickle, *To Be Mayor of New York*, 68–69; John Cross and Dick Lee, "Only Battle Is for Surrogate as Lists Close," *Daily News*, July 28, 1948; "Brother of O'Dwyer in Congress Race," *Rochester Democrat and Chronicle*, July 27, 1948, 5; "Albert Wald, Sponsor of Key State Wage Bill," *New York Times*, February 6, 1985.
38. P. O'Dwyer, interview, 1980.
39. P. O'Dwyer, interview, 1980.
40. The district's 1940 census data are cited by Robert W. Snyder, "The Neighborhood Changed: The Irish of Washington Heights and Inwood Since 1945," in *The New York Irish*, ed. Ronald H. Bayor and Timothy J. Meagher (Baltimore: Johns Hopkins University Press, 1996), 442.
41. P. O'Dwyer, interview, 1980; Bayor and Meagher, *The New York Irish*, especially the chapter by Robert W. Snyder titled "The Neighborhood Changed," 441–42.
42. P. O'Dwyer, *Counsel for the Defense*, 133.
43. P. O'Dwyer, *Counsel for the Defense*, 134.
44. Richard Norton Smith, *Thomas E. Dewey and His Times* (New York: Simon & Schuster, 1982), 442–47.
45. John Crosson, "City Hall," *Daily News*, August 8, 1948.
46. Jacob Javits, with Rafael Steinberg, *Javits: The Autobiography of a Public Man* (New York: Houghton Mifflin Harcourt, 1981), 109–10.
47. P. O'Dwyer, *Counsel for the Defense*, 136.
48. "Red Baiters at AFL Parley Move to Bar 29," *Daily Worker*, August 3, 1948, 4.
49. George Sokolsky, "These Days," syndicated column, *Jackson Sun* (Mississippi), October 21, 1948.
50. P. O'Dwyer, *Counsel for the Defense*, 137.
51. P. O'Dwyer, *Counsel for the Defense*, 137.
52. P. O'Dwyer, *Counsel for the Defense*, 138–39.
53. Paul O'Dwyer quoted in Sidney Zion, "Says Paul O'Dwyer: 'The Times Seem to Have Caught Up with Me,'" *New York Times*, August 11, 1968, SM10.
54. Ralph Nunberg to Paul O'Dwyer, letter written soon after the election of November 2, 1948, in the records of Paul O'Dwyer, Box 1, Folder 4, NYC Municipal Archives.
55. P. O'Dwyer, interview, 1980.
56. Jim Callaghan, "When Percy and Paul Crusaded for Justice," *The Chief*, January 7, 2010; Franklin Siegel refers to O'Dwyer's involvement with the movement for fair housing and protests against racial exclusion at Levittown, New York, in an article for a journal for the "Sixty-Second Annual Dinner of the National Lawyers Guild New York City Chapter Honoring the Association of Legal Aid Attorneys-UAW Local 2325 on Its 30th Anniversary," dinner of March 26, 1999, titled "The National Lawyers Guild Remembers: Paul O'Dwyer."
57. "Education Board Bans 'Paine' Book," *New York Times*, February 27, 1947, https://www.trussel.com/hf/eduboard.htm.

58. "Vote for Brother Urged by O'Dwyer," *New York Times*, October 14, 1948.
59. "Bill Assailed for O.K. of Brother Despite ALP Link," *Brooklyn Eagle*, October 19, 1948.
60. Editorial, "Javits in the 21st," *Daily News*, October 28, 1948.

6. BROTHER'S KEEPER

1. Hoover's memo is summarized in William O'Dwyer, *Beyond the Golden Door*, ed. Paul O'Dwyer (New York: St. John's University Press, 1987), 422.
2. "Farewell To Mayor O'Dwyer—New York 1950," British Pathé, September 5, 1950, video, 0:38, https://www.britishpathe.com/video/farewell-to-mayor-odwyer-new-york/query/ODwyer; "Mayor O'Dwyer's Decision," *New York Times*, August 16, 1950, quoted in W. O'Dwyer, *Beyond the Golden Door*, 338.
3. Malcolm MacKay, "'In with Flynn': Why I Wrote the Book & How Political Levers Have Changed Since FDR," *Brooklyn Eagle*, January 21, 2021, https://brooklyneagle.com/articles/2021/01/21/in-with-flynn-why-i-wrote-the-book-how-political-levers-have-changed-since-fdr; "Ed Flynn, The Bronx Boss at FDR's Side," *Irish Echo*, March 14, 2012, https://www.irishecho.com/2012/3/ed-flynn-the-bronx-boss-at-fdrs-side; Judge Louis Fusco Jr., interview by Robert Polner (RP), April 2014. Much to his chagrin, when FDR nominated Flynn as ambassador to Australia in 1943, the appointment came a cropper because of interchangeable associations of the New York Irish with Tammany Hall. See Terrence Golway, "Machine-Made: Irish America, Tammany Hall and the Creation of Modern New York Politics" (PhD diss., Rutgers University, 2012), https://rucore.libraries.rutgers.edu/rutgers-lib/37410/PDF/1/play, 4–5.
4. W. O'Dwyer, *Beyond the Golden Door*, passim.
5. David Krajicek, "The Man Who Bought the NYPD," *Daily News*, September 22, 2018, https://www.nydailynews.com/news/ny-news-harry-gross-police-corruption-20180919-story.html, accessed August 3, 2023; David Samuels, "The Mayor and the Mob," *Smithsonian Magazine*, October 2019, https://www.smithsonianmag.com/history/mayor-william-odwyer-new-york-city-mob-180973078.
6. Samuels, "The Mayor and the Mob"; Ed Reid, "Guilty Plea May Shield Gross' Clients, Police," *Brooklyn Eagle*, December 31, 1950, 1, 2; Sidney E. Zion, "Says Paul O'Dwyer: 'The Times Seem to Have Caught Up with Me,'" *New York Times*, August 11, 1968, 45.
7. W. O'Dwyer, *Beyond the Golden Door*, 277–78; Miles McDonald, interview by the *New York Times*, cited in Samuels, "The Mayor and the Mob."
8. W. O'Dwyer, *Beyond the Golden Door*, 278; Matthew Goodman, *The City Game: Triumph, Scandal, and a Legendary Basketball Team* (New York: Ballantine Books, 2019), 379.
9. Ross Sandler, "Past Corruption in New York City: Marcus, Tweed & Gross," *CityLand*, August 23, 2016, https://www.citylandnyc.org/past-corruption-new-york-city-marcus-tweed-gross.
10. W. O'Dwyer, *Beyond the Golden Door*, 147.
11. Goodman, *The City Game*, 76; W. O'Dwyer, *Beyond the Golden Door*, 147; Robert Moran, interview by RP, May 27, 2014; "Reminiscences of Paul Crowell," interview by John K. Kelly, July 27, 1962, transcript, Columbia University Oral History Collection; Bill O'Dwyer, testimony before the Kefauver Committee.
12. Goodman, *The City Game*, 76.
13. Warren Moscow, *What Have You Done for Me Lately: The Ins and Outs of New York City Politics* (Englewood Cliffs, NJ: Prentice Hall, 1967), 32.

422 ❖ NOTES TO PAGES 138–143 ❖

14. "Reminiscences of Oscar Bernstien," interview by John K. Kelly, 1962, transcript, Columbia University Oral History Collection; "Reminiscences of Paul Crowell."
15. Goodman, *The City Game*, 157; Moran, interview.
16. Robert Walsh, "O'Dwyer's Moran Dies on IND Train," *Daily News*, January 6, 1968, 16.
17. W. O'Dwyer, *Beyond the Golden Door*, 381; Richard H. Parke, "Moran Jury Hears of 96 Weber Visits," *New York Times*, May 5, 1951, 1; Moran, interview; Myron Beldock, interview by RP, September 2013; "James J. Moran, 66, Is Dead; Jailed in '52 City Kickback Case," *New York Times*, January 6, 1968; Walsh, "O'Dwyer's Moran Dies on IND Train," 3.
18. Moran, interview.
19. Walsh, "O'Dwyer's Moran Dies on IND Train"; "N.Y.C. Scandal Figure, James Moran, 66, Dies," *Advance News* (Ogdenburg, NY), January 7, 1968, 1.
20. Zion, "The Times Seem to Have Caught Up with Me," 45.
21. Moran, interview.
22. "Reminiscences of William O'Dwyer," interview by John K. Kelly, 1962, transcript, Columbia University Oral History Collection, 434; Edmund Elmaleh, *The Canary Sang but Couldn't Fly: The Fatal Fall of Abe Reles, the Mobster Who Shattered Murder Inc.'s Code of Silence* (New York: Union Square Press, 2009), 187; Joseph Kiernan and Neal Patterson, "Paid Ex-Comm. O'Brien: Gross," *Daily News*, May 8, 1952, 3, 4, and 6.
23. "The Reminiscences of William O'Dwyer," 662.
24. "The Reminiscences of William O'Dwyer," 663.
25. Sidney Weintraub, interview by Charles Stuart Kennedy, May 13, 1996, the Association for Diplomatic Studies and Training Foreign Affairs Oral History Project, Library of Congress, https://tile.loc.gov/storage-services/service/mss/mfdip/2004/2004wei04/2004wei04.pdf.
26. Smith Simpson, interview by Charles Stuart Kennedy and John J. Crowley, May 13, 1991, the Association for Diplomatic Studies and Training Foreign Affairs Oral History Project, https://adst.org/OH%20TOCs/Simpson,%20Smith.toc.pdf.
27. David H. Stowe, oral history interview by C. T. Morrissey, December 7, 1963, Harry S. Truman Library and Museum, https://www.trumanlibrary.gov/library/oral-histories/stowe6.
28. Laurance F. Stuntz, "Bill O'Dwyer's Mexican Friends Smooth First Year as Diplomat," *Asheville Citizen-Times*, November 18, 1951, C-11.
29. W. O'Dwyer, *Beyond the Golden Door*, 342.
30. The Ambassador in Mexico (William O'Dwyer) to the Deputy Assistant Secretary of State for Inter-American Affairs (Thomas Mann), confidential memo, January 14, 1952, in *Foreign Relations of the United States, 1952–1954, The American Republics, Volume IV*, Document 567, https://history.state.gov/historicaldocuments/frus1952-54v04/d567.
31. Robert Robinson, "Taking the Fair Deal to the Fields: Truman's Commission on Migratory Labor, Public Law 78, and the Bracero Program, 1950–1952," *Agricultural History* 84, no. 3 (Summer 2010): 381.
32. Frank O'Dwyer Jr., interview by RP, March 6, 2021; W. O'Dwyer, *Beyond the Golden Door*, 385.
33. "Special Committee on Organized Crime in Interstate Commerce, Notable Senate Investigations, U.S. Senate Historical Office, Washington, D.C.," United States Senate, accessed January 23, 2022, https://www.senate.gov/about/resources/pdf/kefauver-committee-full-citations.pdf.

34. "Special Committee on Organized Crime in Interstate Commerce."
35. W. O'Dwyer, *Beyond the Golden Door*, 361.
36. The Saypol visit is discussed in a secret memo of the legal attaché at the US embassy in Mexico to J. Edgar Hoover, dated April 25, 1951.
37. Memo to Hoover.
38. Memo to Hoover; Gilbert King, "The Senator and the Gangsters," *Smithsonian Magazine*, April 18, 2012, https://www.smithsonianmag.com/history/the-senator-and-the-gangsters-69770823.
39. W. O'Dwyer, *Beyond the Golden Door*, 360–61.
40. W. O'Dwyer, *Beyond the Golden Door*, 360–63, 378; "Kefauver Committee Hearing: Ex-N.Y. Mayor O'Dwyer Faces Senate Probe," United International Newsreel, video, 02:34, accessed January 23, 2022, https://www.senate.gov/about/powers-procedures/investigations/kefauver-committee/newsreel2-1.htm. W. O'Dwyer, *Beyond the Golden Door*, 363, 378; "Kefauver Committee Hearing."
41. George Walsh, *Public Enemies: The Mayor, the Mob, and the Crime That Was* (New York: W. W. Norton, 1980), 215–16.
42. See Alan Block, *East Side-West Side: Organizing Crime in New York, 1930–50* (Cardiff, UK: University College Cardiff Press, 1980), 95–97.
43. "Excerpts from Senate Committee's Report on Crime in New York, Condemning O'Dwyer," *New York Times*, May 2, 1951, 23, https://timesmachine.nytimes.com/timesmachine/1951/05/02/89431012.html?login=smartlock&auth=login-smartlock&pageNumber=23.
44. W. O'Dwyer, *Beyond the Golden Door*, 368.
45. "Reminiscences of Clifford Evans," interview by John K. Kelly, 1962, transcript, Columbia University Oral History Collection.
46. "William O'Dwyer Would Cinch Title of 'Quizmasters Dream Man,'" *Okemah Daily Leader* (Oklahoma), January 22, 1953, 6.
47. Lester Velie, "How Does a Man Fall So Far So Fast?" *Collier's Weekly*, August 21, 1953, 37, https://www.unz.com/print/Colliers-1953aug21-00030; "The Reminiscences of William O'Dwyer."
48. Velie, "How Does a Man Fall So Far So Fast?" 37; Mimi Swartz, "Sloane, Alone," *Texas Monthly*, June 1997, http://www.texasmonthly.com/content/sloane-alone.
49. W. O'Dwyer, *Beyond the Golden Door*, 375.
50. W. O'Dwyer, *Beyond the Golden Door*, 374.
51. Memo to Hoover.
52. W. O'Dwyer, *Beyond the Golden Door*, 374.
53. Murray Kempton, "For Paul O'Dwyer," *New York Post*, September 11, 1968.
54. Ruth Montgomery, "Senate Probe Traces O'D.'s Million Credit," *Daily News*, August 1, 1951, 3; "O'Dwyer's Receipt of Funds Explained," *Binghamton Press*, August 3, 1951, 15; W. O'Dwyer, *Beyond the Golden Door*, 404.
55. J. Edgar Hoover, memo to Office of Security, State Department, October 21, 1959, 1.
56. W. O'Dwyer, *Beyond the Golden Door*, 353; "UP Press Chief Stands Firm on O'Dwyer," *Oceanside Daily Blade-Tribune,* July 30, 1952, 1, https://cdnc.ucr.edu/?a=d&d=BT19520730.1.1&e=-------en--20--1--txt-txIN--------1; "O'Dwyer Loses His Temper," *Life*, August 11, 1952, 35.
57. Ben Stephansky, interview by James Shea, 1992, Association for Diplomatic Studies and Training Foreign Affairs Oral History Project, https://adst.org/OH%20TOCs/Stephansky,%20Ben.toc.pdf.
58. Philip Hamburger, *Mayor Watching and Other Pleasures* (New York and Toronto: Rinehart, 1958); see the chapter titled "That Great Big New York Up There." The

keenly perceptive Hamburger of the *New Yorker* was fond of Bill and Frank O'Dwyer, as was the magazine's founder, Harold Ross. The piece, originally in the magazine, was one of the gentler, and more illuminating, profiles to appear in print after the end of Bill's mayoralty.

59. Lester Velie, "The Man Who Won't Come Home," *Collier's Weekly*, August 7, 1953; part II Velie, "How Does a Man Fall So Far So Fast?"
60. "The Reminiscences of William O'Dwyer," 561.

7. "A VERY PECULIAR TIME"

1. Paul O'Dwyer, oral history interview by Jane Conlon Muller, December 7, 1990, Tape 12, A, New York University Tamiment Library and Robert F. Wagner Labor Archives.
2. Franklin Siegel, interview by the authors, March 8, 2021; "Quit Bar Association, Charging Race Bias; Judge Goldstein and A. G. Hays Protest Exclusion of Negro," *New York Times*, April 9, 1943, 24, https://www.nytimes.com/1943/04/09/archives /quit-bar-association-charging-race-bias-judge-goldstein-and-ag-hays.html; *A History of the National Lawyers Guild, 1937–1987* (New York: National Lawyers Guild Foundation, 1987), 7, 10, https://www.nlg.org/wp-content/uploads/2017/06/A -History-of-the-NLG-1937-1987.pdf; Robert Kenny, "My First Forty Years in California Politics, 1922–1962" (manuscript completed under the auspices of the Oral History Program, University of California, 1962), 109, https://archive.org/stream /myfirstfortyyear00kenn/myfirstfortyyear00kenn_djvu.txt.
3. P. O'Dwyer, interview, 1990; Kenny, "My First Forty Years," 2; Alfred E. Clark, "Robert Kenny, Attorney, Dead; Led National Lawyers Guild," *New York Times*, July 22, 1976, 34, https://www.nytimes.com/1976/07/22/archives/robert-kenny-attorney-dead -led-national-lawyers-guild.html.
4. Clarence Darrow, "Argument of Clarence Darrow in the Case of the Communist Labor Party" (Chicago: Charles H. Kerr, 1920), 17, http://moses.law.umn.edu/darrow /documents/Argument_in_Defense_of_the_Communists.pdf.
5. Victor Rabinowitz, *Unrepentant Leftist: A Lawyer's Memoir* (Urbana and Chicago: University of Illinois Press, 1996), 71.
6. P. O'Dwyer, interview, 1990; *A History of the National Lawyers Guild*, 7, 10.
7. *A History of the National Lawyers Guild*, 7.
8. The NLG statement is cited in Yesol Han, "Defining American Freedoms: Jurists Respond to the American Communist Party Trial, 1948–1952" (master's thesis, Columbia University, 2011), 57, https://history.columbia.edu/wp-content/uploads/sites /20/2017/07/Yesol-Han.pdf.
9. Paul O'Dwyer, *Counsel for the Defense: The Autobiography of Paul O'Dwyer* (New York: Simon & Schuster, 1979), 98–99.
10. These conclusions, now overwhelmingly accepted after decades of debate, were based on the long-classified "VENONA transcripts"—a series of secret Moscow–Washington intelligence cables intercepted and decrypted by the US Army Signals Intelligence Service. For the products of this research, see John Earl Haynes and Harvey Klehr, *Venona: Decoding Soviet Espionage in America* (New Haven, CT, and London: Yale University Press, 1999); Allen Weinstein and Alexander Vassiliev, *The Haunted Wood: Soviet Espionage in America—The Stalin Era* (New York: Random House, 1999); and Ronald Radosh and Joyce Milton, *The Rosenberg File: Second Edition* (New Haven, CT: Yale University Press, 1997).

11. Richard Gid Powers, *Secrecy and Power: The Life of J. Edgar Hoover* (New York: The Free Press, 1987), 300.

12. Thomas C. Reeves, *The Life and Times of Joe McCarthy* (New York: Stein & Day, 1982), 225; Larry Tye, *Demagogue: The Life and Long Shadow of Senator Joe McCarthy* (New York: Mariner Books, 2020), 114–15; John Earl Haynes and Harvey Klehr, *Early Cold War Spies: The Espionage Trials That Shaped American Politics* (Cambridge: Cambridge University Press), 40.

13. P. O'Dwyer, interview, 1990.

14. Paul O'Dwyer to Clifford Forster, acting director, ACLU, April 29, 1947.

15. Hudson River Maritime Museum, "Paul Robeson and the Peekskill Riots," *History Blog*, January 18, 2021, https://www.hrmm.org/history-blog/paul-robeson-and-the -peekskill-riots.

16. Ed Sullivan, "Little Ole New York," column, *Philadelphia Inquirer*, September 7, 1949, 41, reprinted from the *Daily News*.

17. Eric Barnouw, *Tube of Plenty: The Evolution of American Television*, 2nd rev. ed. (New York: Oxford University Press, 1990), 118–21; P. O'Dwyer, *Counsel for the Defense*, 124–25.

18. P. O'Dwyer, *Counsel for the Defense*, 125; Tom Hawthorn, "Singer Leon Bibb Was the Voice of Civil Rights," *The Toronto Globe and Mail*, November 1, 2015, https:// www.theglobeandmail.com/arts/music/singer-leon-bibb-was-the-voice-of-civil -rights/article27060314.

19. "Asks Paul O'Dwyer to Give Reasons for His Stand," *The Tablet*, July 1, 1950, emphasis added.

20. "A Bad Proposal," *The Tablet*, August 18, 1948.

21. P. O'Dwyer, interview, 1990.

22. Victor Rabinowitz, "The National Lawyers Guild: Thomas Emerson and the Struggle for Survival," *Case Western Reserve Law Review* 38, no. 4 (1988): 613, https:// scholarlycommons.law.case.edu/cgi/viewcontent.cgi?article=2594&context =caselrev; Thomas I. Emerson, "Introduction: The National Lawyers Guild in 1950– 1951," *NLG Practitioner*, Spring 1976; William Glaberson, "F.B.I. Admits Bid to Disrupt Lawyers Guild," *New York Times*, October 13, 1989, B1.

23. The story of Bartley Crum, a West Coast leader of the National Lawyers Guild who killed himself in 1959 following an extensive FBI surveillance and wiretapping campaign, was told by his daughter Patricia Bosworth in "Receiving Credit Where Credit Is Long Overdue," *New York Times*, April 20, 1997, https://www.writing.upenn.edu /~afilreis/50s/crum.html, and in more detail in the 1997 biography *Anything Your Little Heart Desires: An American Family Story* (New York: Simon & Schuster, 1997).

24. Bill Sipser, interview by the authors, May 12, 2020; P. O'Dwyer, *Counsel for the Defense*, 122; Tye, *Demagogue*, 309.

25. Sipser, interview.

26. For a full account of the Nixon-Douglas campaign, see Greg Mitchell, *Tricky Dick and the Pink Lady* (New York: Random House, 1998).

27. David A. Walsh, "How the Right Wing Convinces Itself That Liberals Are Evil," *Washington Monthly*, July/August 2018, https://washingtonmonthly.com/2018/07 /15/how-the-right-wing-convinces-itself-that-liberals-are-evil.

28. C. D. Jackson, memo, December 21, 1953, Eisenhower Presidential Library, https:// www.eisenhowerlibrary.gov/sites/default/files/research/online-documents /mccarthyism/1953-12-21-cd-jackson.pdf; Robert Caro, *The Years of Lyndon Johnson: Master of the Senate* (New York: Alfred A. Knopf, 2002), 549, 552.

29. Daniel Patrick Moynihan, *Secrecy: The American Experience* (New Haven, CT: Yale University Press, 1998), 62, https://archive.nytimes.com/www.nytimes.com/books /first/m/moynihan-secrecy.html.

30. Nixon had used material resulting from Hoover's black bag jobs when he made his call for the HUAC investigation. See *A History of the National Lawyers Guild*, 28.

31. Simon Sebag Montefiore, *Stalin: The Court of the Red Tsar* (New York: Vintage Press, 2005), 629–631.

32. William Standard, "Report on Lawyers' Congress," *New York Times*, August 12, 1947, 22, https://timesmachine.nytimes.com/timesmachine/1947/08/12/87550931 .pdf; P. O'Dwyer, *Counsel for the Defense*, 129.

33. P. O'Dwyer, interview, 1990; Robert Levy, "Ana Pauker: Dilemmas of a Reluctant Stalinist," staff-prepared summary of the East European Studies discussion of the Wilson Center, May 21, 2003, https://www.wilsoncenter.org/event/ana-pauker -dilemmas-reluctant-stalinist.

34. J. Hoberman, "FILM: When Guilt Divorced the Facts," *New York Times*, September 2, 2001, Section 2, 17, https://www.nytimes.com/2001/09/02/movies/film-when -guilt-divorced-the-facts.html.

35. P. O'Dwyer, interview, 1990.

36. P. O'Dwyer, interview, 1990; Oliver Knox, *Rebels and Informers: Stirrings of Irish Independence* (New York: St. Martin's Press, 1997).

37. Shaun Richman, "A Brief History of the U.S. Government's Targeting of Left-Wing Immigrants," *In These Times* (Chicago, IL), September 30, 2020. Richman studied the Obermeier case. In this article, though, he discusses Julia Rose Kraut's *Threat of Dissent: A History of Ideological Exclusion and Deportation in the United States* (Boston: Harvard University Press, 2020), the source for the total arrests and names on the attorney general's target list.

38. P. O'Dwyer, *Counsel for the Defense*, 127; "Obermeier Convicted of Perjury in New York," *The Dispatcher* (official newspaper of the International Longshoremen's and Warehousemen's Union), August 4, 1950, 4, http://archive.ilwu.org/wp-content /uploads/2015/02/19500804.pdf; Shaun Richman, "Searching for Comrade Obermeier," March 28, 2006, https://shaunrichman.com/2006/03/28/060328obermeier; Gerald Horne, *Red Seas: Ferdinand Smith and Radical Black Sailors in the United States and Jamaica* (New York: New York University Press, 2005), 201; George Soll, Assoc. Staff Counsel, ACLU, "Conversation with Paul O'Dwyer re: Obermeier," July 24, 1950, American Civil Liberties Union Records: Subgroup 2, Subject Files Series, 1947–1995; "Michael J. Obermeier," *New York Times*, May 21, 1960.

39. P. O'Dwyer, *Counsel for the Defense*, 169.

40. Paul O'Dwyer, "Brief History of the Irish Institute 1948 to 1984," Paul O'Dwyer Papers, New York University Tamiment Library and Robert F. Wagner Archives, 4–8.

41. Kevin Morrissey, interview by Robert Polner (RP), October 11, 2020.

42. Morrissey, interview; Dan Tubridy, interview by RP, October 3, 2020.

43. P. O'Dwyer, "Brief History of the Irish Institute," 13–16.

44. "Reminiscences of Sean Keating," interview by Thomas Hogan, January 24, 1974, 38, Columbia University Oral History Collection; P. O'Dwyer, "Brief History of the Irish Institute," 11.

45. William O'Dwyer, *Beyond the Golden Door*, ed. Paul O'Dwyer (New York: St. John's University Press, 1987), 425. John Francis Fox Jr., "'In Passion and in Hope': The Pilgrimage of an American Radical, Martha Dodd Stern and Family, 1933–1990" (PhD diss., University of New Hampshire, 2001), 316–17, https://core.ac.uk /download/pdf/215514517.pdf.

46. Erik Larson, *In the Garden of Beasts* (New York: Crown Publishers, 2011), 359–60; Jennet Conant, *A Covert Affair: Julia Child and Paul Child in the OSS* (New York: Simon & Schuster, 2011), 217.

47. Fox, "In Passion and in Hope," 3; Tom Nolan, "'Hollywood Double Agent' Review: Man on a String," *Wall Street Journal*, June 26, 2020.

48. Eric A. Gordon, "Interviewing the Principals of San Francisco's Hollywood Blacklist Festival," *People's World*, April 2, 2019, https://www.peoplesworld.org/article /interviewing-the-principals-of-san-franciscos-hollywood-blacklist-festival.

49. Fox, "In Passion and in Hope," 316, 326; W. O'Dwyer, *Beyond the Golden Door*, 419; Albert Maltz, "The Citizen Writer in Retrospect Oral History," interview by Joel Gardner, January 3, 1979, Interview Tape Number: XXIII, Side One, Oral History Program, University of California, Los Angeles, 888–91, https://static .library.ucla.edu/oralhistory/text/masters/21198-zz0008zc11-4-master .html#session23a; Katrina Vanden Heuvel, "Grand Illusions," *Vanity Fair*, September 1991, https://archive.org/stream/vanityfair54sepnewy/vanityfair54sepnewy _djvu.txt.

50. W. O'Dwyer, *Beyond the Golden Door*, 425; Vanden Heuvel, "Grand Illusions."

51. Soviet intelligence memo in Weinstein and Vassiliev, 65–66; M. H. Mahoney, *Women in Espionage: A Biographical Dictionary* (Santa Barbara, CA: ABC/CLIO, 1993), 237–38; Fox, "In Passion and in Hope," 287.

52. NKVD memo cited in Larson, *In the Garden of the Beasts*, 254.

53. Mahoney, *Women in Espionage*, 203; Fox, "In Passion and in Hope," 287; Martha Dodd Stern letter March 11, 1942, in Alexander Vassiliev, "Translation of Original Notes from KGB Archive Files" (1993–1996), translated by Steve Shabad, reviewed and edited by Alexander Vassiliev and John Earl Haynes (2007), https://www .wilsoncenter.org/sites/default/files/media/documents/publication/White_Notebook _No.2_Translated1.pdf.

54. Robert Johnson memo cited in W. O'Dwyer, *Beyond the Golden Door*, 426 (emphasis in original).

55. FBI, R. R. Roach to A. H. Belmont, memo, September 12, 1957; FBI, John N. Speakes cablegrams, September 11 and 15, 1958.

56. P. O'Dwyer, *Counsel for the Defense*, 122. "Proceedings against Martin Popper," *Deschler's Precedents*, vol. 4, chapters 15–17, 2439, https://www.govinfo.gov/content /pkg/GPO-HPREC-DESCHLERS-V4/html/GPO-HPREC-DESCHLERS-V4-1.htm; "Martin Popper, 79, Lawyer in Leftist Causes," *New York Times*, January 29, 1989, 36, https://www.nytimes.com/1989/01/29/obituaries/martin-popper-79-lawyer-in -leftist-causes.html; see also comments by Benedict Wolf, Popper's law partner for four decades and member of the NLG, in an audiocassette of Popper's memorial service at Community Church, New York, February 25, 1989 (where O'Dwyer was also one of the speakers), in the Martin Popper Papers, Box 11, New York University Tamiment Library and Robert F. Wagner Labor Archives. "It was not an easy decision," said Wolf.

57. P. O'Dwyer, *Counsel for the Defense*, 122.

58. P. O'Dwyer, *Counsel for the Defense*, 123; W. O'Dwyer, *Beyond the Golden Door*, 416; "About Wolf Popper," *Wolf Popper*, accessed August 5, 2023, https://www .wolfpopperblog.com/about.

59. Brian O'Dwyer, interview by RP, April 28, 2020.

60. See "1952 Press Photo Ethel Merman Divorcing Paul O'Dwyer William Brother" (United Press telephoto, June 9, 1952, of Ethel Merman being met at airport in Mexico by lawyer Paul O'Dwyer," HistoricImages.com, https://historicimages.com /products/rse26655; "Suzy Parker Seeks to Divorce de La Salle," *New York Herald*

Tribune (Paris edition), May 6, 1960, 3; *Daily News*, "Nancy and Her Maharaja Separated," April 11, 1953, 63.

61. "Man Gets $37,500 for Crushed Foot," *Brooklyn Eagle*, September 17, 1953, 7; Harold Harris, "Politics and People," news column, *Brooklyn Eagle*, November 24, 1953, 2.

62. Jack Deacy, "The IRA, New York Brigade," *New York*, March 15, 1972, 42–43; Rafael Medoff, *Militant Zionism in America: The Rise and Impact of the Jabotinsky Movement in the United States, 1928–1948* (Tuscaloosa, AL: The University of Alabama Press, 2002), 209; Jimmy Breslin, "How They Said Goodbye to Mike Quill," *New York Herald Tribune*, February 2, 1966.

63. P. O'Dwyer, *Counsel for the Defense*, 148.

64. Dr. William O'Dwyer, interview by RP, May 7, 2020; "Kerry T. O'Dwyer to Marry in June," *New York Times*, October 16, 1988, Section 1, 50, https://www.nytimes.com/1988/10/16/style/kerry-t-o-dwyer-to-marry-in-june.html.

65. "Obituary: Eileen O'Dwyer Hughes," Dignity Memorial, July 2021, https://www.dignitymemorial.com/obituaries/new-york-ny/eileen-hughes-10257382; "Thomas Hughes, Jr. Loved Riverdale, Law," *Riverdale Press*, December 17, 2015, https://riverdalepress.com/stories/Thomas-Hughes-Jr-loved-Riverdale-law,58754; "Eileen O'Dwyer, Beaver Alumna, Becomes Bride; Niece of Ex-Mayor Is Married Upstate to Thomas Hughes Jr.," *New York Times*, July 15, 1962, 56, https://www.nytimes.com/1962/07/15/archives/eileen-odwyer-beaver-alumna-becomes-bride-niece-of-exmayor-is.html. Also, further proving that blood is thicker than water, O'Dwyer lobbied city hall for a seat on the Bronx criminal court for his Mayo-born nephew John Byrne, the son of Josephine, his sister. Mayor Beame cooperated: he included Byrne, a graduate of New York Law School, among the thirteen judicial appointments he made on his way out of office at the end of 1977.

66. Brian O'Dwyer, interview.

67. Rory O'Dwyer, interviews by Michael Tubridy (MT), May 22 and May 30, 2020.

68. R. O'Dwyer, interviews.

69. Paul O'Dwyer to Mary ("May") Durkan, January 11, 1946, New York City Department of Records and Information Services (NYC Municipal Archives).

70. Paul O'Dwyer to Mary ("May") Durkan, October 24, 1949, NYC Municipal Archives.

71. Adrian Flannelly, interview by the authors, February 27, 2020; "Irish America Top 100," *Irish America Magazine*, April–May 2008, 96, https://issuu.com/irishamerica/docs/ia_april_may_2008.

72. Judge Kelly O'Neill Levy (Joan O'Dwyer's daughter), interview by RP, January 31, 2021.

73. Levy, interview.

74. Paul O'Dwyer to Dorothy Schiff, March 27, 1960, Dorothy Schiff Files, New York Public Library; Paul O'Dwyer, interview by Jeffrey Gerson, September 2, 1993, La-Guardia & Wagner Archives, La Guardia Community College; Layhmond Robinson, "O'Dwyer's Niece Named to Bench," *New York Times*, May 6, 1960, 1; "Death of Joan O'Dwyer Savarese," *Irish Echo*, June 9, 2011, https://www.irishecho.com/2011/6/death-of-joan-odwyer-savarese; Rachel Vick, "Queens' First Female Judge Broke Ground on Bench 61 Years Ago," *Queens Daily Eagle*, March 12, 2021, https://queenseagle.com/all/queens-first-female-judge-broke-ground-on-bench-61-years-ago.

75. Monica Durkan, interview by MT, February 16, 2021; Douglas Martin, "Frank Durkan, Irish Advocate, Dies at 76," *New York Times*, November 19, 2006, https://www.nytimes.com/2006/11/19/nyregion/19durkan.html.

76. Franklin Siegel, interview by the authors, March 8, 2021; Virginia Pohlirom, interview by the authors, April 15, 2021.

77. M. Durkan, interview; Sean Downes, interview by the authors, June 14, 2021; Martin Galvin, "Way to Go for Durkan," *Irish Echo*, November 1, 2012, http://www.nuzhound.com/articles/arts2012/nov1_Frank-Durkan__MGalvin_Irish-Echo.php.

78. Paul O'Dwyer, interview by Patricia Molino, April 16 and 28, 1987, audio, Columbia University Oral History Collection.

79. Paul O'Dwyer to William and Sloane O'Dwyer, November 22, 1950, NYC Municipal Archives.

80. Flannelly, interview.

81. "The Reminiscences of William O'Dwyer," interview by John K. Kelly, 1962, transcript, Columbia University Oral History Collection, 94; W. O'Dwyer, *Beyond the Golden Door*, 384.

82. Moran, sentenced to twelve and a half to twenty-five years in prison for his role in the shakedown scheme, was paroled in 1962 after serving a combined ten years in state and federal prison. See "O'Dwyer Aide Gets Parole," *The Times-Record* (Troy, NY), April 27, 1962; Robert Walsh, "O'Dwyer's Moran Dies on IND Train," *Daily News*, January 6, 1968.

83. Joseph J. Thorndike, "Tax History: Ike's IRS Commissioner Called the Income Tax a 'Devouring Evil,'" Tax History Project, January 28, 2016, https://www.taxnotes.com/tax-history-project/tax-history-ikes-irs-commissioner-called-income-tax-devouring-evil/2016/02/02/g21x. See also Coleman Andrews, cited in Ray Tucker, "Andrews Denounces Some Judges' Leniency," *San Bernardino Sun*, September 21, 1955, 26, https://cdnc.ucr.edu/?a=d&d=SBS19550921.1.26&e=-------en--20--1--txt-txIN--------1 (California Digital Newspaper Collection, from the University of California Riverside's Center for Bibliographical Studies and Research).

84. W. O'Dwyer, *Beyond the Golden Door*, 385–86.

85. W. O'Dwyer, *Beyond the Golden Door*, 386.

86. Alexander Feinberg, "O'Dwyer Tax Case Termed 'Politics,'" *New York Times*, June 13, 1956, 28, https://timesmachine.nytimes.com/timesmachine/1956/06/13/94294316.html?pageNumber=28.

87. W. O'Dwyer, *Beyond the Golden Door*, 386.

88. W. O'Dwyer, *Beyond the Golden Door*, 386.

89. W. O'Dwyer, *Beyond the Golden Door*, 392.

90. Feinberg, "O'Dwyer Tax Case Termed 'Politics'"; Allen Drury, "Tax Court Rules O'Dwyer Got $10,000 From Crane; Brother Speaks for O'Dwyer," *New York Times*, June 28, 1957, 1, https://www.nytimes.com/1957/06/28/archives/tax-court-rules-odwyer-got-10000-from-crane-brother-speaks-for.html; "O'Dwyer v. Comm'r of Internal Revenue," Case text, June 24, 1957, https://casetext.com/case/odwyer-v-commr-of-internal-revenue.

91. Diane L. Fahey, "Is the United States Tax Court Exempt from Administrative Law Jurisprudence When Acting as a Reviewing Court?" *Cleveland State Law Review* 58, no. 603 (2010): 603–48, https://engagedscholarship.csuohio.edu/cgi/viewcontent.cgi?article=1084&context=clevstlrev.

92. P. O'Dwyer, interview, 1987.

93. W. O'Dwyer, *Beyond the Golden Door*, 407–8; Philip Hamburger, *Mayor Watching and Other Pleasures* (New York: Rinehart, 1958), 112–14.

94. W. O'Dwyer, *Beyond the Golden Door*, 407–8; Lew Rudin, interview by a family-hired archivist, undated.

95. Edward Robb Ellis, *The Epic of New York City: A Narrative History* (New York: Basic Books, 1966), 578.

96. Jimmy Breslin, "Bill O'," *Manchester Evening Herald*, March 18, 1964, 5, reprinted from the *New York Herald-Tribune*, http://www.manchesterhistory.org/News /Manchester%20Evening%20Hearld_1964-03-18.pdf.

97. W. O'Dwyer, *Beyond the Golden Door*, 412–13; McCandlish Phillips, "O'Dwyer Funeral Attended by 1,700," *New York Times*, November 28, 1964, 21, https://www .nytimes.com/1964/11/28/archives/patrolmen-carry-coffin-of-former-mayor-william -odvvyer-from-st.html.

98. "The Reminiscences of William O'Dwyer," 620, 622.

99. W. O'Dwyer, *Beyond the Golden Door*, 374.

8. MIDDLE-AGED REFORMER

1. Paul O'Dwyer, *Counsel for the Defense: The Autobiography of Paul O'Dwyer* (New York: Simon & Schuster, 1979), 191.

2. "New York Committee of Democratic Voters, Report of the Executive Director for 1962," Box 5, Folder 44, Councilman-at-Large, Correspondence, 1964–1965, NYC Municipal Archives.

3. O'Dwyer, *Counsel for the Defense*, 198; see also Arlene Kurtis, "How Upper West Side Coffee Drinkers Took Down Tammany Hall," *West Side Rag*, October 24, 2015, https://www.westsiderag.com/2015/10/24/weekend-history-how-upper-west-side -coffee-drinkers-took-down-tammany-hall.

4. O'Dwyer, *Counsel for the Defense*, 184.

5. Gail Collins, "Bella Abzug and Paul O'Dwyer: When Politics Had Passion," *New York Times*, January 3, 1999, Section 6, 31.

6. "This Day in History: April 17, 1965: Largest Anti-War Protest," Zinn Education Project, https://www.zinnedproject.org/news/tdih/largest-antiwar-protest.

7. O'Dwyer, *Counsel for the Defense*, 185.

8. O'Dwyer, *Counsel for the Defense*, 184–85.

9. Jonathan Kandell, "Carmine DeSapio, Political Kingmaker and Last Tammany Hall Boss, Dies at 95," *New York Times*, July 28, 2004, C12.

10. O'Dwyer, *Counsel for the Defense*, 208.

11. Oliver Pilat, "Council Candidate," column, *New York Post*, 1963, in the records of Paul O'Dwyer, clippings scrapbook, NYC Municipal Archives.

12. Pilat, "Council Candidate."

13. O'Dwyer, *Counsel for the Defense*, 187–88.

14. In an interview by Rob Polner (RP) on May 7, 2020, Dr. William O'Dwyer said of his mother, "She would drive because my father was an awful driver. When Third Avenue had the el [elevated railway], there were a lot of stanchions that had parts of our car on it." See also "Matriarch," an O'Dwyer family recollection about Kathleen, 1980, Paul O'Dwyer Papers, Box 1, Folder 32, New York University Tamiment Library and Robert F. Wagner Labor Archives. Lawrence Downes, lawyer with the O'Dwyer-founded Brehon Law Society, told the authors with a chuckle, "He was a terrible driver. That's one thing I can tell you" (interview, April 13, 2021).

15. Adrian Flannelly offered the anecdote about "great men"—and Kathleen's teasing response—in an interview by the authors on February 27, 2020.

16. Murray Kempton, "How to Lose," *New York Post*, 1968 [otherwise undated], in the records of Paul O'Dwyer, clippings scrapbook, NYC Municipal Archives.

17. Sarah Kovner, interview by Robert Polner (RP), June 24, 2020.

18. Kandell, "Carmine DeSapio."

19. Kovner, interview.

20. Daniel Patrick Moynihan, "'Bosses' and 'Reformers': A Profile of the New York Democrats," *Commentary*, June 1961, https://www.commentary.org/articles/daniel -moynihan/bosses-and-reformersa-profile-of-the-new-york-democrats.

21. Manfred Ohrenstein, interview by RP, March 10, 2020.

22. Milton Mollen, interview by RP, August 13, 2012.

23. Mollen, interview.

24. Mollen, interview.

25. Oksana Mironova, "The Scythe of Progress Must Move Forward: Urban Renewal on the Upper West Side," *Urban Omnibus*, June 10, 2015, https://urbanomnibus.net /2015/06/the-scythe-of-progress-must-move-northward-urban-renewal-on-the -upper-west-side; see also "The Priest Who Woke the West Side," Straus Media, January 22, 2019, https://www.nypress.com/news/local-news/the-priest-who-woke-the -west-side-GENP1020190122190129987.

26. Robert Caro, *The Power Broker: Robert Moses and the Fall of New York* (New York: Vintage Books, 1975), chap. 41; Kovner, interview.

27. Arthur Simon, *Stuyvesant Town USA: Pattern for Two Americas* (New York: New York University Press, 1970), 7; see also "Comments: Validity of Municipal Law Barring Discrimination in Private Housing," *Columbia Law Review* 58, no. 5 (May 1958): 728–35.

28. Simon, *Stuyvesant Town USA*, 95.

29. Charles V. Bagli, *Other People's Money: Inside the Housing Crisis and the Demise of the Greatest Real Estate Deal Ever Made* (New York: Plume, 2014), 21–29.

30. Simon, *Stuyvesant Town USA*, 51.

31. Simon, *Stuyvesant Town USA*, 83.

32. Simon, *Stuyvesant Town USA*, 84.

33. "Housing Bias Bill Is Reintroduced," *New York Times*, September 29, 1950, 29.

34. O'Dwyer, *Counsel for the Defense*, 146–47.

35. Simon, *Stuyvesant Town USA*, 86–88.

36. Caro, *The Power Broker*, 1013–14.

37. Caro, *The Power Broker*, 1029–31.

38. See Caro, *The Power Broker*, 1044. Also, the banker in question was Tom Shanahan, Moses's hands-on vice president of the Slum Clearance Committee and the chair of Federation Bank & Trust Co., in which the federal Title I funds were deposited to the benefit of the bank (also discussed by Caro on p. 1044–55). Sometimes known as "Tammany's banker," Shanahan was an Irish American success story in New York. In the mid-1950s, Paul sought his advice on how to start his own immigrant savings and loan institution. The idea never got too far; see also O'Dwyer, *Counsel for the Defense*, 181.

39. Sidney E. Zion, "Says Paul O'Dwyer: 'The Times Seem to Have Caught Up with Me,'" *New York Times Magazine*, August 11, 1968.

40. O'Dwyer, *Counsel for the Defense*, 200.

41. James Clarity, "Robert Wagner, Pivotal New York Mayor, Dies," *New York Times*, February 13, 1991, 1.

42. "O'Dwyer Niece Gets Praise of 28 Judges," *New York Times*, March 28, 1960, 31; Layhmond Robinson, "O'Dwyer's Niece Named to Bench," *New York Times*, May 6, 1960, 1.

43. "Joan O'Dwyer O'Neill Sworn in as City Magistrate by Wagner," *New York Times*, May 7, 1960, 9.

44. Mychal McNicholas, interview by RP, September 17, 2020.
45. Robert F. Wagner, remarks at dinner in honor of Paul O'Dwyer, October 10, 1963, in the records of Paul O'Dwyer, NYC Municipal Archives.
46. O'Dwyer, *Counsel for the Defense*, 203.
47. O'Dwyer, *Counsel for the Defense*, 202.
48. Wagner, remarks.
49. O'Dwyer, *Counsel for the Defense*, 204.
50. Harry Schlegel, "Dem Victors, GOP Take 5 Council-at-Large Seats," New York *Daily News*, November 6, 1963, 3.
51. Editorial, "Henry Stern, 1935–2019," *New York Post*, March 29, 2019, https://www .pressreader.com/usa/new-york-post/20190329/textview.
52. O'Dwyer, *Counsel for the Defense*, 205.
53. Philip Hamburger, *Mayor Watching and Other Pleasures* (New York: Rinehart, 1958), 110.
54. American RadioWorks, "Lorraine Hansberry (1930–1965): 'The Black Revolution and the White Backlash' Forum at Town Hall sponsored by the Association for Artists for Freedom, New York City, June 15, 1964," *Say It Plain–Say It Loud*, http:// americanradioworks.publicradio.org/features/blackspeech/lhansberry.html.
55. Christopher Hayes, *The Harlem Uprising: Segregation and Inequality in Postwar New York City* (New York: Columbia University Press, 2021), 110–27; see also Rick Perlstein, *Nixonland: The Rise of a President and the Fracturing of America* (New York: Scribner, 2008), 4.
56. Jimmy Breslin, "Fear and Hate—Sputtering Fuse," *New York Herald Tribune*, July 20, 1964.
57. James Baldwin, "A Report from Occupied Territory," *The Nation*, July 11, 1966.
58. Hayes, *The Harlem Uprising*, 210.
59. Hayes, *The Harlem Uprising*, 210.
60. Paul O'Dwyer, formal statement at bill signing ceremony, July 15, 1964, in the records of Paul O'Dwyer, Subject File: Minimum Wage, Box 9, Folder 96, NYC Municipal Archives; Paul O'Dwyer, press release in response to Commerce and Industry Group, undated, in the records of Paul O'Dwyer, Subject File: Minimum Wage, Box 9, Folder 96, NYC Municipal Archives; Pilat, "Council Candidate"; Paul O'Dwyer, councilman-at-large statement of June 18, 1965, in the records of Paul O'Dwyer, Subject File: Minimum Wage, Box 9, Folder 96, NYC Municipal Archives. O'Dwyer's statement about the "capacity for self-government" came from Thomas H. Reed, *Municipal Government in the United States* (New York: The Century Co., 1926), 158.
61. Paul O'Dwyer, "Dear Friends" letter addressed to the secretaries of more than one hundred union locals in Greater New York, July 15, 1964, in the records of Paul O'Dwyer, Subject File: Minimum Wage, 1964–65, Box 9, NYC Municipal Archives.
62. O'Dwyer, "Dear Friends."
63. Bill Sipser, interview by the authors, May 11, 2021.
64. O'Dwyer, *Counsel of the Defense*, 227–28.
65. O'Dwyer, *Counsel for the Defense*, 211–14
66. J. Todd Moye, *Let the People Decide: Black Freedom and White Resistant Movements in Sunflower County, Mississippi, 1945–1986* (Chapel Hill: University of North Carolina Press, 2004), 3–21.
67. J. Todd Moye, *Let the People Decide*, 134–40.
68. O'Dwyer, *Counsel for the Defense*, 215–20.
69. Paul O'Dwyer, letter, undated, in the records of Paul O'Dwyer, Subject File: Councilman at Large, 1965–66, Box 8, Folder 70, NYC Municipal Archives.

70. O'Dwyer, letter, undated.
71. See John H. Britton, "How Election Results Will Help Negroes: Benefits for Many, Not Just Select Few a Happy Prospect," *Jet*, November 19, 1964, 13. Looking at the successful African American candidates for state offices, the magazine put out the headline "Volume of Victories Overwhelm Backlash Voters." Another successful New York African American candidate in 1964 was Thomas R. Jones, who was elected to the District Civil Court. Jones was "one of the deans of Black politics in Brooklyn" according to his son David Jones, a lawyer, president and CEO of the Community Service Society of New York. O'Dwyer mounted an unsuccessful effort to get Thomas Jones elected to the state court of appeals in the early 1970s. See the younger Jones's blog entry, "Up from Poverty" (*Huffington Post*, July 22, 2009, https://huffpost.netblogpro.com/entry/up-from-poverty_b_218467), in which he recalls his father famously telling Bobby Kennedy that he was weary of study after study on urban blight, as the senator toured crumbling buildings in Bedford-Stuyvesant, and that action was needed. Kennedy soon after announced what became the Restoration Corporation, a model for community development corporations in the years to come. Jones also recounted how, when he was a boy, a distinguished cast of artists, politicians, and agitators passed through the kitchen of the family home on Dean Street in the 1940s and early 1950s, including "Eleanor Roosevelt, Dizzy Gillespie, Paul Robeson, Paul O'Dwyer, the artist Jake Lawrence who left paintings at the house on Dean Street when he couldn't pay his legal bills, and now is prominently displayed at MOMA" ("Up from Poverty").
72. Murray Schumach, "Union Chief Irate; Says that 'Judge Can Drop Dead in His Black Robes,'" *New York Times*, January 5, 1966, 1.
73. Jimmy Breslin, "How They Said Goodbye to Mike Quill," *New York Herald Tribune*, February 2, 1966.
74. James A. Wechsler, "For the Defense," *New York Post*, October 20, 1964.
75. Wechsler, "For the Defense."
76. Richard Reeves, "A Question about Gallashaw and Where It Led," *Times Talk* (*New York Times* newsroom newsletter), November 8, 1966, in the records of Paul O'Dwyer, Subject Files: Councilman-at-Large, 1965–66, Box 5, Folder 77, NYC Municipal Archives.
77. Reeves, "A Question about Gallashaw."
78. Richard Reeves, "Gallashaw Free in Boy's Slaying," *New York Times*, October 14, 1966, 1.
79. Jimmy Breslin, column (no headline), *New York Herald Tribune*, October 14, 1966.
80. Bruce Drake, "Incarceration Gap Widens between Blacks and Whites," Pew Research Center, September 6, 2013, https://www.pewresearch.org/fact-tank/2013/09/06/incarceration-gap-between-whites-and-blacks-widens.
81. Editorial, "It's Refreshing," *Amsterdam News*, October 22, 1966.
82. Mychal McNicholas, follow-up conversation with RP, July 15, 2020.
83. James Wechsler, "For the Defense," column, *New York Post*, October 20, 1964.
84. Ronald Gallashaw, interview by RP, July 15, 2020.
85. F. David Anderson, "Gallashaw Accused of Renting Out Guns," *New York Times*, January 5, 1968.
86. "United States of America, Appellee, vs. Ernest Gallishaw [*sic*], Defendant-appellant, U.S. Court of Appeals, 428 F. 2d, 760 (2nd Cir., 1970)," Justia—US Law, https://law.justia.com/cases/federal/appellate-courts/F2/428/760/172927/; Earl Caldwell, "O'Dwyer Feeling Heat Again, but It's No Sweat," *Daily News*, January 24, 1981.

87. "Mr. and Mrs. Gallashaw and Family," Western Union telegram, October 15, 1966, in the records of Paul O'Dwyer, Subject File: Councilman at Large, 1965–66, Box 5, Folder 77, NYC Municipal Archives.

9. CONSCIENCE OF THE PARTY

1. *The Voting Rights Act: Ten Years After*, US Commission on Civil Rights, January 1975, 43, Library of Congress Online Catalog; U.S. Commission on Civil Rights, *Racial and Ethnic Tensions in American Communities: Poverty, Inequality, and Discrimination, Volume VII: The Mississippi Delta Report*, chap. 3 (2001).
2. Brian O'Dwyer, interview by Robert Polner (RP) (on his mother's reaction), April 28, 2020; Paul O'Dwyer, oral history interview by Jane Conlon Muller, transcript dated August 7, 1990, New York University Tamiment Library and Robert F. Wagner Labor Archives (on the duration of visits).
3. P. O'Dwyer, interview, August 1990, 10–11; Peter Dreier, "'I Question America': Remembering Fannie Lou Hamer's Famous Speech 50 Years Ago," *Huffington Post* via *Portside*, August 26, 2014, https://portside.org/2014-08-26/i-question-america -remembering-fannie-lou-hamers-famous-speech-50-years-ago.
4. Tim Weiner, "Victoria Gray Adams, Civil Rights Leader, is Dead at 79," *New York Times*, August 19, 2006 (cites Branch Taylor's *Pillar of Fire: America in the King Years, 1963–65* [New York: Simon & Schuster, 1998]).
5. Paul O'Dwyer, *Counsel for the Defense: The Autobiography of Paul O'Dwyer* (New York: Simon & Schuster, 1979), 208–11; Marco Balestri, "The Fight to Read, Write, and Vote: The New York State Literacy Test, 1922–1965" (undergraduate senior thesis, Columbia University, 2021), https://asit-prod-web1.cc.columbia.edu /historydept/wp-content/uploads/sites/20/2022/05/Balestri-Marco_Final-Thesis .pdf.
6. See David J. Garrow, "The FBI and Martin Luther King," *The Atlantic*, July/August 2002.
7. Paul O'Dwyer, oral history interview by Jane Conlon Muller, transcript dated February 6, 1990, New York University Tamiment Library and Robert F. Wagner Labor Archives, 1–6. Paul describes "the motivating force" for his trips to the American South as his knowledge of the British against the Irish, including some of his own Bohola neighbors as a child during the Black and Tan War.
8. P. O'Dwyer, interview, February 1990, 1–7.
9. Mississippi Freedom Democratic Party, "MFDP Announces Historic Decision in Sunflower Federal Elections Case and Demands Federal Registrar for That County," press release (Washington, DC), March 16, 1966; see Bryan Dunlap, Mississippi Freedom Project, 1964–1965 (Papers, 1964–1972, 1994; Z: Accessions, M2000–007, Box 2, Folder 5) in the Freedom Summer digital collection of the Wisconsin Historical Society Online Collections, http://wisconsinhistory.org.
10. Jim Callaghan, "When Percy and Paul Crusaded for Justice," *The Chief*, January 7, 2010.
11. B. O'Dwyer, interview.
12. Charles Rangel, interview by RP, April 25, 2020.
13. Committee for Free Elections in Sunflower (New York, NY, headed by the Congress of Racial Equality's Bayard Rustin and US Rep. William Fitts Ryan, with whom O'Dwyer, Rangel, and Sutton worked to secure African American voting rights in Sunflower), "Progress Report," April 6, 1967, Fannie Lou Hamer Collection, University of Mississippi Libraries.

14. J. Todd Moye, *Let the People Decide: Black Freedom and White Resistant Movements in Sunflower County, Mississippi, 1945–1986* (Chapel Hill: University of North Carolina Press, 2004), 164.

15. Rangel, interview.

16. P. O'Dwyer, interview, August 1990, 25.

17. Moye, *Let the People Decide*, 144–45.

18. Moye, *Let the People Decide*, 163.

19. Moye, *Let the People Decide*, 162–65.

20. P. O'Dwyer, interview, August 1990, 25; P. O'Dwyer, *Counsel for the Defense*, 221–25.

21. Rick Perlstein, *Nixonland: The Rise of a President and the Fracturing of America* (New York: Scribner, 2008), 190.

22. Perlstein, *Nixonland*, 191.

23. Rick Rojas and Khorri Atkinson, "Five Days of Unrest That Shaped, and Haunted, Newark," *New York Times*, July 11, 2017, for the statistics on lives lost and property damage; the number of arrests comes from State of New Jersey Governor's Select Commission on Civil Disorder, *Report for Action: An Investigation into the Causes and Events of the 1967 Newark Race Riots*, February 1968, 129.

24. Perlstein, *Nixonland*, 190–94.

25. Pete Hamill, "What Law? What Order?" *New York Post* (reprinted in *New York Stateman*, the newspaper of the O'Dwyer-for-Senate campaign, October 12, 1968), Subject File: Paul O'Dwyer Campaign, 1968, Box 35 (New-Nixon), Folder 428 ("New Politics"), NYC Municipal Archives.

26. Perlstein, *Nixonland*, 100.

27. P. O'Dwyer to Frank O'Dwyer Jr., July 14, 1966.

28. Frank O'Dwyer Jr., interview by RP, January 19, 2022.

29. P. O'Dwyer, interview, February 1990, 5.

30. Perlstein, *Nixonland*, 218.

31. Ronnie Eldridge, interview by RP, November 15, 2019.

32. Perlstein, *Nixonland*, 219.

33. Eugene J. McCarthy, *Parting Shots from My Brittle Bow: Reflections on American Politics and Life* (Golden, CO: Fulcrum Publishing, 2004), 4.

34. P. O'Dwyer, *Counsel for the Defense*, 231.

35. *Beyond the Golden Door* relates that gubernatorial candidate Harriman and state attorney general candidate Franklin Roosevelt Jr. were so terrified that they would lose New Yorkers' votes in 1954 that they deputized the Tammany Hall leader Carmine DeSapio to tell Paul to keep Bill away from the city lest Bill's return unleash a media storm to their own detriment. Paul, incensed his brother was being treated as a political pariah, threatened to buy airtime and to work to defeat both Harriman and Roosevelt. William O'Dwyer, *Beyond the Golden Door*, ed. Paul O'Dwyer (New York: St. John's University Press, 1987), 356, 358.

36. P. O'Dwyer, *Counsel for the Defense*, 231–32.

37. P. O'Dwyer, *Counsel for the Defense*, 232.

38. P. O'Dwyer, *Counsel for the Defense*, 233.

39. P. O'Dwyer, *Counsel for the Defense*, 233.

40. Cronkite's remarks about "winning the war" come from Douglas Brinkley, "The Sage of Black Rock," *American Heritage* 62, no. 1 (Spring 2012), https://www.americanheritage.com/sage-black-rock; Cronkite's "mired in stalemate" statement comes from CBS Evening News, "Report from Vietnam," *Voices & Visions*, February 27, 1968, http://vandvreader.org/report-from-vietnam-february-27-1968/.

41. Associated Press, "Critics of War Choose O'Dwyer to Oppose Javits for Senate," *New York Times*, March 17, 1968, 71.

42. P. O'Dwyer, *Counsel for the Defense*, 236–37.

43. P. O'Dwyer, *Counsel for the Defense*, 236; Francis X. Clines, "Paul O'Dwyer, New York's Liberal Battler for Underdogs and Outsiders, Dies at 90," *New York Times*, June 25, 1998, B9.

44. Sarah Kovner, interview by RP, June 24, 2020.

45. Eldridge, interview.

46. See the interview with Pete Hamill in the documentary *Breslin & Hamill—Deadline Artists*, directed and produced by Jonathan Alter, John Block, and Steve McCarthy (New York: HBO, 2019).

47. *Breslin & Hamill—Deadline Artists*; Kennedy's St. Patrick's Day statement is taken from Robert F. Kennedy, "Address by Attorney General Robert F. Kennedy to the Friendly Sons of St. Patrick of Lackawanna County, Scranton, Pennsylvania, on March 17, 1964," US Department of Justice, https://www.justice.gov/sites/default /files/ag/legacy/2011/01/20/03-17-1964.pdf.

48. Editorial, "The Astonishing Mr. O'Dwyer," *New York Times*, June 20, 1968, 44.

49. Murray Kempton, *Rebellions, Perversities, and Main Events* (New York: Crown, 1994), 464.

50. Jules Witcover, *The Year the Dream Died: Revisiting 1968 in America* (New York: Warner, 1997), 207, https://vdoc.pub/documents/the-year-the-dream-died-revisiting -1968-in-america-1piu7iiqdtv8.

51. Daniel Walker, *Rights in Conflict: The Walker Report* (New York: Bantam, 1969), 304.

52. Murray Kempton, "The Decline and Fall of the Democratic Party," *Saturday Evening Post*, November 2, 1968, 66–79.

53. "Police Rough Up People Inside the Convention: Delegates and Newsmen Assaulted," *Washington Post* wire service, August 30, 1968.

54. Walter Schneier, ed., *Telling It Like It Was: The Chicago Riots* (New York: Signet Books–The New American Library, 1969), 44.

55. See Walker, *Rights in Conflict*, as well as excerpts published by Chicago68.com: http://chicago68.com/ricsumm.html, accessed August 7, 2023.

56. Walker, *Rights in Conflict*, 314–17.

57. Walker, *Rights in Conflict*, 297–300; also, a photograph of the candlelight process appears in the report.

58. Schneier, *Telling It Like It Was*, 41.

59. Maurice Carroll, "O'Dwyer Refuses to Pass Pickets," *New York Times*, June 24, 1968, 15.

60. Vincent Ryder, "Humphrey Leads Mass 'Victory' Parade; Enthusiasm Lacking," *Daily Telegraph*, September 3, 1968, 18.

61. Clayton Knowles, "O'Dwyer Meets Anger Upstate over Refusal to Back Humphrey," *New York Times*, August 20, 1968, 28.

62. Speech, transcript, September 24, 1968, in the records of Paul O'Dwyer, Subject File: O'Dwyer Senate Campaign, 1968, Senate Race Speeches, Box 11, Folder 124, NYC Municipal Archives.

63. Jerry Edgerton, "Independence is O'Dwyer's Big Pitch," *Newsday*, September 25, 1968.

64. Jerry Edgerton, "O'Dwyer Pursues Support of Youth," *Newsday*, September 24, 1968; speech, transcript, September 24, 1968, in the records of Paul O'Dwyer; Bill Sipser, interview by the authors, May 11, 2021.

65. Gannett News Service, "Family's Campaigning for Dad," October 28, 1968.

66. Starkey provided the authors with a brief backgrounder (a memo dated November 11, 1994) on O'Dwyer that he typed up for the then governor Mario Cuomo, for whom he was working as an aide in the 1990s. The story about Paul and the campaign is described therein.
67. Brian O'Dwyer, interview with RP.
68. Nick Thimmesch, "The Realities of Jake Javits," *New York*, November 4, 1968, 34.
69. "O'Dwyer for Senator," unsigned editorial, initialed "D. B.," *Binghamton Sun-Bulletin*, October 1, 1968, 8.
70. Sydney H. Schanberg, "O'Dwyer Favors Community Control of Schools," *New York Times*, October 8, 1968, 32.
71. James F. Clarity, "O'Dwyer Gets Aid of Stephen Smith," *New York Times*, September 20, 1968, 1, 35, https://www.nytimes.com/1968/09/20/archives/odwyer-gets-aid-of-stephen-smith-kennedy-inlaw-have-a-key-role-had.html.
72. Starkey, memo.
73. Arnold A. Offner, *Humphrey: The Conscience of the Country* (New Haven, CT: Yale University Press, 2018), 318.
74. Offner, *Humphrey*, 320.
75. Jason Daley, "Notes Indicate Nixon Interfered with 1968 Peace Talks," *Smithsonian Magazine*, January 2, 2017, https://www.smithsonianmag.com/smart-news/notes-indicate-nixon-interfered-1968-peace-talks-180961627; Offner, *Humphrey*, 323–35.
76. "Vietnam War, 1954–1975," Encyclopedia Britannica, History & Society, accessed August 24, 2023, https://www.britannica.com/event/Vietnam-War.
77. Joe Flaherty, "Ask Not What Nixon Will Do for You," *Village Voice*, November 14, 1968.
78. Offner, *Humphrey*, 334–36.

10. THE LIBERATED AREA OF CITY HALL

1. John McGettrick, interview by Robert Polner (RP), March 21, 2022.
2. Tom Robbins, "The Judge and the G-Man," *Village Voice*, October 16, 2007.
3. Editorial, "City Council President," *New York Times*, May 26, 1973, 30.
4. John McGettrick, interview by RP, February 27, 2020.
5. Andy Logan, "Will You Love Me in November," *New Yorker*, July 12, 1976.
6. In 1989 the US Supreme Court ruled that the Board of Estimate violated the constitutional principle of "one-man, one-vote," and the body was replaced by an enlarged, more empowered New York City Council. The allotment of an equal number of votes for each borough president despite the borough's varying populations led to the court's ruling. The councilman-at-large seats, two for each borough, suffered from the same defect, and were eliminated, according to the ruling.
7. Jim Callaghan, interview by RP, May 28, 2020.
8. Callaghan, interview (emphasis added).
9. Steven Marcus, "The $1-Billion Tunnel to Nowhere," *New York*, July 9–16, 1979, 40–46; Friedman received from Beame a lifetime appointment to a $25,000-a-year seat on the city Board of Water Supply. As in the case of James Moran, the recipient of a similar paid assignment from the exiting mayor Bill O'Dwyer, Friedman's selection as Beame's term wrapped up did not last. Beame's successor as mayor, Ed Koch, convinced Friedman to give up his patronage post while supporting him at the same time for the chairmanship of the Bronx Democratic organization. Friedman meanwhile became a law partner of Roy Cohn, former Senator Joe McCarthy's onetime aide. He was convicted in 1986 of civil and federal corruption charges

centered on the city Parking Violations Bureau and sentenced to a twelve-year prison term. He was released in 1992.

10. McGettrick, interview, 2020.

11. Stanley Friedman, interview by RP, May 18, 2020.

12. McGettrick, interview, 2020.

13. Andy Logan, "Irishy," *New Yorker*, February 9, 1976.

14. Idilio Gracia Peña, interview by RP, January 6, 2020.

15. Lucinda Franks, "Council Presidency Getting New Look under O'Dwyer," *New York Times*, April 8, 1974, 37; McGettrick, interview, 2020.

16. Paul O'Dwyer to Dan Janison, a student reporter with the *Columbia Daily Spectator*, October 5, 1976, listing his city council accomplishments (letter provided by the recipient).

17. Kathleen Teltsch, "Allende's Widow Appeals to U.N.," *New York Times*, February 26, 1974, 7.

18. Teltsch, "Allende's Widow Appeals to U.N.," 7. See also O'Dwyer to Janison, October 5, 1976.

19. "Statement by Paul O'Dwyer, President of the New York City Council, Welcoming Beatriz Allende (Daughter of the Former Constitutional President of Chile), To the United States," July 26, 1974 (provided by the then aide Franklin Siegel); "Lawyers' Group Sending 2 to Observe Chile Trials," *New York Times*, April 14, 1974, 22; Franklin Siegel, interview by the authors, March 3, 2021.

20. Paul O'Dwyer, interview, 1989, William E. Wiener Oral History Library (on Feldman). Also see National Conference of Soviet Jewry Records, Box 69, Folder 20, in Part 2, American Jewish Historical Society, New York, as well as "The Trial of Alexander D. Feldman, 23 November 1973," A Chronicle of Current Events for Human Rights and Freedom of Expression in the USSR, December 31, 1973, https://chronicle -of-current-events.com/2021/04/11/the-trial-of-alexander-feldman-30-5.

21. See John Gibney, "Documentary on One: Frank Stagg's Three Funerals," *History Ireland* 26, no. 1 (January/February 2018), https://www.historyireland.com/documentary -one-frank-staggs-three-funerals.

22. O'Dwyer to Janison, October 5, 1976.

23. City Council President's Office, "Statement by Paul O'Dwyer on the Meaning of St. Patrick's Day," press release, March 15, 1973, in the records of Paul O'Dwyer, Subject File: Ireland, Box. 128, NYC Municipal Archives.

24. Franks, "Council Presidency Getting New Look"; Rosemary Rogers, "Wild Irish Women: A Most Sorrowful Mystery," *Irish America*, May/June 2019 (on the Price sisters).

25. United Press International, "O'Dwyer Hurt in N.Y. Crash," printed in *Times Herald* (Middletown, NY), March 13, 1970.

26. William F. Buckley and Paul remained on good terms despite their ideological differences; Buckley's occasional tweaks of Paul's liberal views in published articles and his Tory-style hauteur seemed of a piece with his personal affluence. Correspondence in O'Dwyer's papers at the NYC Municipal Archives shows that during the 1965 mayoral race in which both men were candidates, Paul sent Bill Buckley one of the pieces of hate mail he had received, joking that Buckley should consider asking its writer for a contribution. On another occasion, Bill wrote to O'Dwyer, suggesting he try to find the time to read the works of more Irish, as well as English, poets.

27. Jack Fowler, "The Story of James L. Buckley's Historic Senate Victory," *National Review*, December 17, 2020.

28. Trevor Griffey, "The Blacks Should Not Be Administering the Philadelphia Plan: Nixon, the Hard Hats and 'Voluntary' Affirmative Action," in *Black Power at Work: Community Control, Affirmative Action, and the Construction Industry*, ed. David Goldberg and Trevor Griffey (Ithaca, NY: Cornell University Press, 2010); also in Humanities Commons, accessed August 1, 2023, https://hcommons.org/deposits /objects/hc:16488/datastreams/CONTENT/content.

29. Donald Myrus and Burtin Joseph (publishers), *Law & Disorder: The Chicago Convention and Its Aftermath* (single-issue magazine), January 1969, in the records of Paul O'Dwyer, 1968 Senate Campaign, NYC Municipal Archives.

30. Murray Kempton, "The Decline and Fall of the Democratic Party," *Saturday Evening Post*, November 2, 1968, 66–79.

31. John Corry, "About New York: First Day of an Era," *New York Times*, January 2, 1974, 52.

32. Corry, "About New York," 52.

33. Paul O'Dwyer to John Lindsay, February 21, 1973, in the records of Paul O'Dwyer, City Council President Campaign, Box 67, Folder 720 ("Correspondence"), NYC Municipal Archives.

34. Paul O'Dwyer, memo, in the records of Paul O'Dwyer, City Council President Campaign, Box 57, Folder 641 ("Shirley Chisholm"), NYC Municipal Archives; the anti-McGovern ACUJ press release is dated February 22, 1972, and is held in the Paul O'Dwyer Papers, Box 30, Folder 8 ("ACUJ Press Releases, Nov. 71–Aug.72"), St. John's University archives.

35. Harry Stein, "An Exile in His Own City," *New York Times Magazine*, January 8, 1978, SM-3.

36. Paul O'Dwyer, text of address, January 9, 1974 (provided to the authors by Franklin Siegel).

37. Seymour Lachman and Robert Polner, *The Man Who Saved New York: Hugh Carey and the Great Fiscal Crisis of 1975* (New York: SUNY Press, 2010), 82.

38. Kim Phillips-Fein, *Fear City: New York's Fiscal Crisis and the Rise of Austerity Politics* (New York: Metropolitan Books, 2017), 62–65.

39. Sam Roberts, "New York's Birth Date: Don't Go by the City Seal," *New York Times*, July 14, 2008, B1.

40. United Press International, "Briton Told That New York Is Going Dutch," January 8, 1975, printed in the *International Herald Tribune*.

41. McGettrick, interview, 2020.

42. Friedman, interview.

43. Siegel, interview.

44. City Council President's Office, "City Council Committee Holds Hearings on Intro. 781 and Intro. 782 Pertaining to Political Surveillance and Dossier Collection Activities of Intelligence Unit of Police Department," press release, September 29, 1975 (provided to the authors by Franklin Siegel).

45. Siegel, interview. See also Dorothy Plohn, "O'Dwyer's Red Squad Blues: Hearings Fizzle," *East Apple* (New York), October 7, 1975.

46. Lachman and Polner, *The Man Who Saved New York*, 142.

47. Phillips-Fein, *Fear City*, 206–7.

48. Phillips-Fein, *Fear City*, 313–14.

49. Frank Van Riper, "Ford to New York: Drop Dead," *Daily News*, October 30, 1975, p. 3. (Note that the headline for the story on page 3 differs slightly from the page 1 headline, which substitutes "City" for "New York.")

50. Lachman and Polner, *The Man Who Saved New York*, 157. President Ford's state-
    ment appears in full in his "Remarks and a Question-and-Answer Session at the
    National Press Club on the Subject of Financial Assistance to New York City," Oc-
    tober 29, 1975, *The American Presidency Project*, https://www.presidency.ucsb.edu
    /documents/remarks-and-question-and-answer-session-the-national-press-club-the
    -subject-financial.
51. Hugh Carey, interview by RP, January 16, 2009, for *The Man Who Saved New York*.
52. Jack Deacy, interview by RP, January 22, 2020; McGettrick, interview, 2020; Fran-
    cis X. Clines, "Beame Copter Forced Down Off Brooklyn in Storm," *New York Times*,
    June 22, 1974, 1, 58.
53. The "insurance" anecdote is also recalled by Jim Callaghan in his article titled
    "Beame's Revenge: He's Still Here, and He Matters," *New York Observer*, June 5,
    2000.
54. McGettrick, interview, 2020.
55. Phillips-Fein, *Fear City*, 174.
56. Frank Lombardi, "Commodore Hotel Plan Okayed after Taxing Study," *Daily News*,
    May 21, 1976, 5; see also "Estimate Board to Rule on Easing of Tax Allowing Com-
    modore Transformation," *New York Times*, March 3, 1976, 40. According to the
    Village Voice reporter Wayne Barrett, despite a Beame mayoral counsel's assertions
    that the Trump Organization had an exclusive option from Penn Central to develop
    the property while his company was negotiating with the estimate board and the
    state economic development agency for tax abatements for the project, it had not
    secured one (so Penn Central confirmed to Barrett). Barrett's 1979 article noted that
    Trump's father, Fred, who eventually put up the collateral for the project's financing,
    was a major contributor to the Brooklyn Democratic political machine and the Beame
    administration. In addition to Beame's political allies, Carey contributors also ben-
    efited from the approval of the real estate deal. See Wayne Barrett, "The Dirty Deal
    That Helped Make Donald Trump," *Village Voice*, February 26, 1979.
57. Paul O'Dwyer, *Counsel for the Defense: The Autobiography of Paul O'Dwyer* (New
    York: Simon & Schuster, 1979), 277; also, Phillips-Fein quotes Jack Offenhatz in
    "How Bankers & Technocrats Used the 1975 Fiscal Crisis to Permanently Reshape
    NYC," *Gothamist*, April 21, 2017, https://gothamist.com/arts-entertainment/how
    -bankers-technocrast-used-the-1975-fiscal-crisis-to-permanently-reshape-nyc.
58. "As City Council President: The Man and His Works: Some Highlights," Summer
    1977, in the records of Paul O'Dwyer, Box 73, Folder 797 ("Campaign Strategy"),
    NYC Municipal Archives.
59. Callaghan, interview.
60. Harold Holzer, interview by RP, May 4, 2020
61. Mark Green, interview by RP, April 10, 2022; Ronnie Eldridge, follow-up interview
    by RP, April 10, 2022.
62. Alan Levy, *The Political Life of Bella Abzug, 1920–1976* (Lanham, MD: Lexington
    Books, 2015), 259, 265–66.
63. Mark Green, *Bright, Infinite Future* (New York: St. Martin's Press, 2016), 139; Le-
    andra Ruth Zarnow, *Battling Bella: The Protest Politics of Bella Abzug* (Cambridge,
    MA: Harvard University Press, 2019), 259; *Bella Abzug: How One Tough Broad
    from the Bronx Fought Jim Crow and Joe McCarthy*, ed. Suzanne Braun Levine and
    Mary Thom (New York: Farrar, Straus and Giroux, 2007), 176.
64. Herb Goro, "Priscilla Ryan Picks Up the Pieces," *New York*, November 6, 1972,
    48–50; Bella Abzug and Mim Kelber, *Gender Gap: Bella Abzug's Guide to Political
    Power for American Women* (Boston: Houghton Mifflin, 1984), 184.

65. Phillips-Fein, *Fear City*, 272.
66. Donald Singleton, "Calm at Top & Luck Led Us Thru Dark Passage," *Daily News*, July 17, 1977.
67. Singleton, "Calm at Top."
68. Paul O'Dwyer, interview by Jill Levine, American Jewish Committee, William E. Wiener Oral History Collection, New York Public Library, July 1980, 129–130.
69. McGettrick, interview, 2020.
70. Singleton, "Calm at Top."
71. Jonathan Mahler, *Ladies and Gentlemen, The Bronx is Burning* (London: Picador, 2006), 218–19.
72. Mahler, *Ladies and Gentlemen*, 274; see also Jeffrey Bloodworth, *Losing the Center: The Decline of American Liberalism, 1968–1992* (Lexington: The University Press of Kentucky, 2013).
73. "Remarks by City Council President Paul O'Dwyer at New York City Campaign Debate Held on Thursday, Sept. 15, 1977," in the records of Paul O'Dwyer, Council Re-election Campaign, 1977, NYC Municipal Archives; Mark Green and Laurel Eisner, "The Public Advocate for New York City: An Analysis of the Country's Only Elected Ombudsman," *New York Law School Law Review* 42, no. 3 (1998): 1114, https://digitalcommons.nyls.edu/cgi/viewcontent.cgi?article=1917&context=nyls_law_review.
74. "Snug Harbor Cultural Center," NYC Parks, accessed September 4, 2021, https://www.nycgovparks.org/parks/sailors-snug-harbor/history.
75. Callaghan, interview.
76. The "noble building" quote comes from Ken Cobb, "Farewell to Tweed," *New York Archival Society Newsletter*, no. 3 (Spring 1984), https://www.archives.nyc/blog/2018/1/11/farewell-to-tweed; the comment on the "mid-19th century interiors," is from Andrew S. Dolkart and Matthew A. Postal, *Guide to New York City Landmarks* (New York: John Wiley & Sons, 2004), 27.
77. Betsy Imholz, interview by RP, May 13, 2020.
78. Cobb, "Farewell to Tweed."
79. Idilio Gracia Peña, interview by RP, January 16, 2021.
80. O'Dwyer to Janison, October 5, 1976.
81. Deacy, interview.
82. Murray Kempton, "Paul O'Dwyer: A Kindly Radical Says Farewell," *New York Post*, December 29, 1977.
83. Anna Quindlen, "Paul O'Dwyer Elects to Leave His Old Sod, Politics, and Is Moving on to New Ground," *New York Times*, September 21, 1977, 51.
84. Deacy, interview.

11. CIVIL WARRIOR

1. Douglas Feiden, "The Priest Who Woke the West Side," *Our Town* (New York), January 24–30, 2019.
2. Alaya Flavia, *Under the Rose: A Confession* (New York: Feminist Press at the City University of New York, 2001), 325–29.
3. Flavia, *Under the Rose*, 327–30.
4. Franklin Siegel, interview with the authors, March 8, 2021.
5. Murray Polner and Jim O'Grady, *Disarmed and Dangerous: The Radical Lives and Times of Daniel and Philip Berrigan; Brothers in Religious Faith and Civil Disobedience* (New York: Basic Books, 1997), 268–71.

6. Polner and O'Grady, *Disarmed and Dangerous*, 284.

7. Polner and O'Grady, *Disarmed and Dangerous*, 274.

8. Polner and O'Grady, *Disarmed and Dangerous*, 272–74.

9. Polner and O'Grady, *Disarmed and Dangerous*, 274–75.

10. Jack Nelson and Ronald Ostrow, *The FBI and the Berrigans* (New York: Coward, McCann & Geoghegan, 1972), 34.

11. Francine du Plessix Gray, "Harrisburg: The Politics of Salvation (Part I)," *New York Review of Books*, June 1, 1972.

12. Polner and O'Grady, *Disarmed and Dangerous*, 289.

13. "61% in Poll Assert Entry into the War Was U.S. 'Mistake,'" *New York Times*, June 6, 1971, 52.

14. Amy J. Posey and Lawrence S. Wrightsman, *Trial Consulting* (New York: Oxford University Press, 2005), 176.

15. William O'Rourke, *The Harrisburg 7 and the New Catholic Left, 40th Anniversary Edition* (Notre Dame, IN: University of Notre Dame Press, 2012), 57.

16. Nelson and Ostrow, *The FBI and the Berrigans*, 220.

17. Rory O'Dwyer, interview by Michael Tubridy (MT), May 30, 2020.

18. O'Rourke, *The Harrisburg 7*, 87–88.

19. Nelson and Ostrow, *The FBI and the Berrigans*, 204.

20. Nelson and Ostrow, *The FBI and the Berrigans*, 204.

21. Paul Wilkes, "Leonard Boudin: The Left's Lawyer's Lawyer," *New York Times Magazine*, November 14, 1971, SM38; Bob Ford, "Harrisburg 7 Trial Was about Vietnam War Protest," *Penn Live- Patriot News* (Mechanicsburg, PA), April 22, 2012.

22. Polner and O'Grady, *Disarmed and Dangerous*, 281.

23. Nelson and Ostrow, *The FBI and the Berrigans*, 116–22; see also "United States v. Berrigan, 482 F.2d 171 (1973)," Caselaw Access Project, Harvard Law School, accessed March 3, 2022, https://cite.case.law/f2d/482/171.

24. Michael McGovern, "Berrigan Spy Is Praised for His Character," *Daily News*, March 17, 1972.

25. Nelson and Ostrow, *The FBI and the Berrigans*, 138–40.

26. Polner and O'Grady, *Disarmed and Dangerous*, 286.

27. Nelson and Ostrow, *The FBI and the Berrigans*, 266.

28. Nelson and Ostrow, *The FBI and the Berrigans*, 266; O'Rourke, *The Harrisburg 7*, 213. Shortly after publication of the latter, O'Dwyer indicated to O'Rourke that he was peeved by the reference to Bill O'Dwyer's "fleeing the city and a *lickerous* [emphasis added] scandal," O'Rourke noted, though the book lauded Paul's character and his work on the Harrisburg case. The "lickerous" comment appears in *The Harrisburg 7*, 87, while Paul's annoyance is described in the afterword, 288–289.

29. Polner and O'Grady, *Disarmed and Dangerous*, 266–67.

30. Polner and O'Grady, *Disarmed and Dangerous*, 296; see also Nelson and Ostrow, *The FBI and the Berrigans*, 207, on the source of "pathological liar" (i.e., a doctor's report).

31. Nelson and Ostrow, *The FBI and the Berrigans*, 284.

32. Paul O'Dwyer, *Counsel for the Defense: The Autobiography of Paul O'Dwyer* (New York: Simon & Schuster, 1979), 253.

33. Saul M. Kassin and Lawrence S. Wrightsman, *The American Jury on Trial: Psychological Perspectives* (New York: Taylor & Francis, 1988), 57.

34. P. O'Dwyer, *Counsel for the Defense*, 254–55.

35. Brian O'Dwyer, interview by Robert Polner (RP), April 28, 2020.

36. Nelson and Ostrow, *The FBI and the Berrigans*, 288.

37. Nelson and Ostrow, *The FBI and the Berrigans*, 305–6.
38. Eileen Battersby, "Irish—But American, Too," *Irish Times*, June 16, 1994.
39. Andrew Sanders, *The Long Peace Process: The United States of America and Northern Ireland, 1960–2008* (Liverpool: Liverpool University Press, 2019), 74.
40. Warren Richey, "British, Irish Officials Advise against Donations to Noraid," *Christian Science Monitor*, January 21, 1985, https://www.csmonitor.com/1985/0121/anor.html.
41. Maureen Murphy, interview by the authors, July 24, 2020.
42. Claudia Dreifus, "The Long Island Interview: Paul O'Dwyer," *Newsday*, November 4, 1979.
43. David McKittrick and David McVea, *Making Sense of the Troubles: The Story of the Conflict in Northern Ireland* (Chicago: New Amsterdam Books, 2002), 129.
44. Editorial, "Ulster—One More Try," *New York Times*, May 1, 1975, 40.
45. P. O'Dwyer, *Counsel for the Defense*, 40.
46. Sanders, *The Long Peace Process*, 40.
47. Sanders, *The Long Peace Process*, 41.
48. Bernadette Devlin McAliskey, email response to RP, July 31, 2020.
49. Sanders, *The Long Peace Process*, 45.
50. Sanders, *The Long Peace Process*, 53–54; Conor Cruise O'Brien, *States of Ireland*, rev. ed. (London: Faber & Faber, 2015), 279.
51. Peter Murray, interview by the authors, March 24, 2022; in the Paul O'Dwyer Papers at St. John's University, see Box 34, Folder 17 ("Daily News ad—Dec. 22, 1971") for a copy of the full-page *Daily News* advertisement.
52. "Gifford Panel Finds Two Youth Slain by British Were Unarmed," *Irish Times*, November 20, 1971, 28, Paul O'Dwyer Papers, Box 1, Folder 1 ("Gifford Tribunal: Newspaper Clippings"), St. John's University Archives.
53. "Moira Kennedy Bride of Cormac O'Malley," *New York Times*, September 19, 1971, 76; see also "About Ernie O'Malley & Cormac O'Malley," Ernie O'Malley, accessed September 2, 2022, https://ernieomalley.com/learn/about-cormac-omalley.
54. Cormac O'Malley, email responses to MT, March 13, 2022; Mark Barrett, interview by the authors, May 20, 2021; Murray, interview.
55. McKittrick and McVea, *Making Sense of the Troubles*, 77.
56. BBC One, "Bernadette Devlin Attacks British Home Secretary," clip from *24 Hours*, January 31, 1972, uploaded January 27, 2012, https://www.bbc.co.uk/programmes /p00nm166; see also *Bernadette: Notes on a Political Journey*, a biographical film directed by Lelia Doolan (Digital Quilts, 2011), which premiered at the BFI London Film Festival in 2011.
57. Sanders, *The Long Peace Process*, 56–67.
58. O'Malley, emails, March 13 and May 12, 2022.
59. Michael Lillis is cited in John Bowman, "O'Brien Warned against NI Optimism," *The Irish Times*, December 30, 2005; O'Brien's position is discussed in Padraig Reidy, "Conor Cruise O'Brien 1917–2008," *Index on Censorship*, December 19, 2008, https://www.indexoncensorship.org/2008/12/conor-cruise-obrien-1917-2008.
60. A keen observer of the Irish question, the historian and novelist Peter Quinn wrote of the "benign indifference and active disinterest—sometimes outright hostility" on the Ulster question during a trip to Ireland in 1981 in his memoir, *Cross-Bronx* (New York: Fordham University Press, 2022), 91.
61. Sanders, *The Long Peace Process*, 81.
62. Murray, interview.
63. Niall O'Dowd, interview by the authors, November 13, 2020.
64. P. O'Dwyer, *Counsel for the Defense*, 259–60.

65. P. O'Dwyer, *Counsel for the Defense*, 261.

66. "NY Goes Wild for Texas 5 at Gaelic Park; Nixon Accused of Pandering to the British," *The Irish People*, August 19, 1972, 1.

67. "John Kelly," *The Tipperary Star*, February 15, 2021 (via ProQuest Central).

68. P. O'Dwyer, *Counsel for the Defense*, 261–62.

69. Sean Cronin, "Inquiry in US into Arms Case," *Irish Times*, March 2, 1973.

70. O'Dwyer's associate and nephew Frank Durkan worked on one such case, centered on federal charges in February 1974, of IRA gunrunning by the so-called Baltimore Four. The case began when two men were arrested in Woodside, New York, with a U-Haul truck containing seventy Colt AR-15 rifles. Including their suppliers, four men in all were found guilty in federal district court in Maryland and given six-year sentences. At the sentencing, Durkan put up no defense, arguing that the smuggling of weapons was not actually a crime under US statutes but rather a political matter that should be settled in the courts. Subsequently Ramsey Clark joined with defense attorneys in seeking, unsuccessfully, a sentence reduction for the four—Kiernan Mc-Mahon, Francis Larkin, Henry Hillick, and James Conlon. Clark's contention that the charges were the outgrowth of the ubiquity of weapons smuggling in America failed to impress the judge. See the Paul O'Dwyer Papers, Box 5, Folder 4 ("Baltimore Four Case Files, 1973–74"), St. John's University Archives.

71. Lawrence Downes, interview by the authors, April 13, 2021.

72. James Gilroy, interview by RP, June 16, 2020.

73. Paul O'Dwyer, oral history interview by Jane Conlon Muller, October 17, 1990, CD recording, New York University Tamiment Library and Robert F. Wagner Archives.

74. Sean Downes, interview with the authors, June 14, 2021.

75. Ray O'Hanlon, *The New Irish Americans* (Distributed by Publishers Group West, Niwot, CO: Roberts Reinhart Publishers, 1998), 168.

76. Sanders, *The Long Peace Process*, 85.

77. Sean Downes, interview by the authors, June 21, 2021.

78. Statement by Paul O'Dwyer to Executive Office for the Office of the Immigration Judge in Matter of Joseph Doherty, State of New York, City of New York, March 1989; see also "Otisville, New York," the text of a 1986 speech by Paul O'Dwyer. Both are in the Paul O'Dwyer Papers, Box 8, Folder 4 ("Doherty, Joseph, 1987–89"), St. John's University Archives.

79. Sanders, *The Long Peace Process*, 66–67.

80. Edward Koch, interview by Ed Erwin, transcript, Session 11, January 3, 1976, Columbia University Oral History Collection; Rosemary Rogers, "Wild Irish Women: A Most Sorrowful Mystery," *Irish America*, May/June 2019.

81. "Violence in Ireland: An Exchange" (letter by Paul O'Dwyer, response by Conor Cruise O'Brien), *New York Review of Books*, December 2, 1971.

82. "Irish Official Accuses O'Dwyer of Aiding Antidemocratic Unit," *New York Times*, April 22, 1975, 6.

83. Dreifus, "The Long Island Interview."

12. A HIGHER PLATEAU

1. Charles Kaiser, "Iran Sues Shah and Wife for $56 Billion," *New York Times*, November 29, 1979, A16.

2. "1979: Exiled Ayatollah Khomeini returns to Iran," BBC, On This Day, 1950–2005: 1 February, accessed August 18, 2023http://news.bbc.co.uk/onthisday/hi/dates/stories/february/1/newsid_2521000/2521003.stm.

3. Council on Foreign Relations, "U.S. Relations with Iran, 1953–2022," accessed August 18, 2023, https://www.cfr.org/timeline/us-relations-iran-1953-2022.

4. Gary Goldstein, "Review: Documentary 'A Dying King: The Shah of Iran' Chronicles Monarch's Strange Demise," *Los Angeles Times*, November 14, 2017, https://www.latimes.com/entertainment/movies/la-et-mn-dying-king-review-20171114-story.html.

5. "Ramsey Clark Advised Iran on Damages from Shah," *New York Times*, November 21, 1979, A12; Franklin Siegel, interview by the authors, March 8, 2021.

6. Mychal McNicholas, interview by Robert Polner (RP), June 11, 1920.

7. James Gilroy, interview by RP, June 16, 2020.

8. Idilio Gracia Peña, interview by RP, January 6, 2020.

9. Peter Kihss, "Judge Dismisses Iran's Move for Shah's NY Assets," *New York Times*, September 15, 1981, B6.

10. Siegel, interview.

11. McNicholas, interview; Gilroy, interview.

12. British PATHÉ News, broadcast interview with Paul O'Dwyer, distributed by Reuters, January 3, 1980.

13. Bill Reel, "How, Paul O'Dwyer, How Could You Do It?" *Daily News*, November 30, 1979, 44.

14. Earl Caldwell, "O'Dwyer Feeling Heat Again, but It's No Sweat," *Daily News*, January 24, 1981, 2, 4.

15. Beth Fallon, "Paul O'Dwyer, and His Right to Say It," *Daily News*, March 17, 1982; Roger Director, "The State vs. Martin Abend," *Daily News*, April 28, 1981.

16. Charity Commission for England and Wales, details for Leonard Cheshire Disability, March 31, 2021.

17. "Mrs. Paul O'Dwyer Dies during a Visit to Ireland," *New York Times*, December 1, 1980, B13.

18. Virginia Polihrom, interview by the authors, April 1, 2021.

19. Rory O'Dwyer, interview by Michael Tubridy (MT), May 30, 2020.

20. Dr. William O'Dwyer (Paul's eldest son), interview by RP, May 7, 2020.

21. Jimmy Breslin, "Irish Wake," *Sacramento Bee*, reprinted from *Daily News*, December 8, 1980.

22. Breslin, "Irish Wake."

23. Paul O'Dwyer, *Counsel for the Defense: The Autobiography of Paul O'Dwyer* (New York: Simon & Schuster, 1979), 149–50.

24. Murray Kempton, "For O'Dwyer," Letters to the Editor, *New York Times*, June 22, 1970, 36.

25. Judy Klemesrud, "Mrs. Javits and Mrs. O'Dwyer: Same Goal, Different Worlds," *New York Times*, July 31, 1968, Food Fashions Family Furnishings section, 26.

26. R. O'Dwyer, interview.

27. P. O'Dwyer, *Counsel for the Defense*, 271–72.

28. "Matriarch," an O'Dwyer family recollection, Paul O'Dwyer Papers, Box 1, Folder 32, New York University Tamiment Library and Robert F. Wagner Labor Archives.

29. Breslin, "Irish Wake."

30. Peter King, interview by the authors, August 20, 2021; Reuters, "Around the World: Bombs in Ulster Injure 7 and Block Key Railway," *New York Times*, August 7, 1981, A6.

31. Pierre Sutton, interview by RP, August 18, 2021. See also New York State Form 990 (2020 and 2021); Dennis Duggan, "Great Friends o'Goshen," *Newsday*, June 8, 1997.

32. Jeffrey Michael Kauffman, Charlie Keith's nephew, interview via email by RP, November 4, 2020. He noted that the Jackson Pollock story may have been apocryphal. In another sign of Keith's singularity, which Paul O'Dwyer would no doubt have appreciated, Kauffman said he delighted in the HUAC chair Martin Dies's description of him as the "baby-faced pinko of the New York docks," owing to Keith's history of fierce activism for fellow maritime workers. Also see Bernard Nossiter, "Charles Keith, A Seaman," *The Nation*, March 18, 1978, an appreciation.

33. Barbara Hoffman, "This 85-Year-Old Writer Invented New York's First Singles Bar," *New York Post*, August 11, 2017.

34. Malachy McCourt, interview by RP, April 4, 2020.

35. Laurie Gwen Shapiro, "The Improbable Journey of Dorothy Parker's Ashes," *New Yorker*, September 4, 2020.

36. Julia Trevino, "Dorothy Parker's FBI File Is Available to Public for First Time in a Decade," *Smithsonian Magazine*, May 10, 2018, https://www.smithsonianmag.com /smart-news/dorothy-parkers-fbi-file-available-public-first-time-decade-180969044.

37. Peter Quinn, interview by MT, January 6, 2021.

38. Shapiro, "The Improbable Journey."

39. Kevin McNamara, *The MacBride Principles: Irish America Strikes Back* (Liverpool: Liverpool University Press, 2009), 2–3; a transcript of O'Dwyer's statement of October 15, 1975 to the Wolff subcommittee can be found in "'Ulster' Nationalists— 'International' Orphans," *The Irish People*, October 25, 1975, 1, 15 (emphasis added).

40. Andrew Sanders, *The Long Peace Process: The United States of America and Northern Ireland, 1960–2008* (Liverpool: Liverpool University Press, 2019), 65–66, 142.

41. Jimmy Carter, "Northern Ireland Statement on U.S. Policy," American Presidency Project, August 30, 1977, https://www.presidency.ucsb.edu/documents/northern -ireland-statement-us-policy.

42. Peter King, interview by the authors, August 20, 2021. King's involvement with the question of Ulster's future included a 2001 novel, his first, titled *Terrible Beauty*.

43. Jack O'Brien, *British Brutality in Ireland* (Cork and Dublin: The Mercier Press, 1989)—see the foreword by Paul O'Dwyer; King, interview.

44. Sanders, *The Long Peace Process*, 110.

45. "Statement from Fr. Sean McManus to Enniskillen Court on September 8th, 1971," *The Irish People*, October 14, 1972, 10, https://indianamemory.contentdm.oclc.org /digital/collection/IP/id/26577.

46. King, interview.

47. King, interview.

48. Monica Durkan, interview by MT, February 16, 2021.

49. Flannery quoted in Shana Alexander, "The Patriot Game," *New York*, November 22, 1982; variations on Durkan's summary of Harrison's objection are in Joyce Wadler, "Unbowed, and Unashamed of His I.R.A. Role," *New York Times*, March 16, 2000, B2, https://www.nytimes.com/2000/03/16/nyregion/unbowed-and-unashamed-of-his -ira-role.html#:~:text=Harrison%2C%20in%20a%20grand%20heroic,last%20 25%20years%20without%20Mr, and Douglas Martin, "Frank Durkan, Irish Advocate, Dies at 76," *New York Times*, November 19, 2006, https://www.nytimes.com /2006/11/19/nyregion/19durkan.html.

50. Alexander, "The Patriot Game."

51. Alexander, "The Patriot Game."

52. John McGettrick, interview by RP, October 31, 2020.

53. Anthony Lewis, "Shadow of the Gunmen," *The New York Times*, July 22, 1976, 31.

54. Sanders, *The Long Peace Process*, 14–15.

55. Sanders, *The Long Peace Process*, 54.
56. "Sean MacBride, Winner of Nobel and Lenin Peace Prizes, Dies," *Associated Press*, January 15, 1988, https://apnews.com/article/a242d624638998e9396d4dc9945e88e4.
57. Paul O'Dwyer, "MacBride's American Dimension" speech, Paul O'Dwyer Papers, Special Collections, Box 3, Folder 22, New York University Tamiment Library and Robert F. Wagner Labor Archives.
58. McNamara, *The MacBride Principles*, 206–7.
59. All Mulvaney quotes from Jim Mulvaney, interview with RP, October 8, 2020.
60. King, interview.
61. Mervyn Jess, "History of the Supergrass System in Ireland," *BBC News*, February 22, 2012.
62. David McKittrick and David McVea, *Making Sense of the Troubles: The Story of the Conflict in Northern Ireland* (Chicago: New Amsterdam Books, 2002), 162.
63. Sanders, *The Long Peace Process*, 171.
64. Sanders, *The Long Peace Process*, 66.
65. McKittrick and McVea, *Making Sense of the Troubles*, 167–73.
66. Cody McCone, interview by the authors, January 21, 2021; Marcus Eliason, "Freedom for 'Winchester Three,' Britain Admits a Mistake," *Associated Press*, April 28, 1990, https://apnews.com/article/5daa927b61afb718436d1122b0df157f.
67. Cody McCone, interviews by the authors, December 29, 2020, and January 22, 2021.

13. THE MOUNTAINTOP

1. Paul O'Dwyer, "Whither Do We Go," Papers of the Irish Institute of New York, Archives of Irish America Collection, New York University Tamiment Library and Robert F. Wagner Labor Archives.
2. Andrew Sanders, *The Long Peace Process: The United States of America and Northern Ireland, 1960–2008* (Liverpool: Liverpool University Press, 2019), 186.
3. Joseph C. Harsch, "Jackson's Lure: The Gift of Oratory," *Christian Science Monitor*, April 7, 1988.
4. R. W. Apple, "Jackson Is Seen as Winning a Solid Place in History," *New York Times*, April 29, 1988, A16.
5. O'Dwyer, "Whither Do We Go."
6. Susan Heller Anderson and Maurice Carroll, "New York Day by Day," *New York Times*, January 10, 1984, B3.
7. Associated Press, "Gravely Ill, Atwater Offers Apology," *New York Times*, January 13, 1991, A16.
8. David Dinkins, interview by Robert Polner (RP), April 22, 2014.
9. Jim Callaghan, "For O'Dwyer, Principle Always Outweighed the Political Cost," *Irish Echo*, February 16, 2011.
10. Wayne Barrett, "Koch's Clan: The Way We Were," *Village Voice*, December 9, 1986.
11. Ina Jaffe, "Giuliani Struggled with Issues in First Campaign," National Public Radio, September 12, 2007.
12. Don Terry, "An Earlier Jackie Mason Racial Slur against Dinkins Is Disclosed," *New York Times*, October 2, 1989, B1.
13. Larry Hanley, "O'Dwyer to Obama: Case Still Economic; Getting Past Racial Issues," *The Chief-Leader*, October 30, 2008.
14. William O'Dwyer, *Beyond the Golden Door*, ed. Paul O'Dwyer (New York: St. John's University Press, 1987), xiii.

15. Michael J. O'Neill, "Surrounded by Rascals," *New York Times Book Review*, August 16, 1987, 7.
16. Thomas W. Devine, "O'Dwyer, William (11 July 1890–24 November 1964)," *Dictionary of National Biography* (New York: Oxford University Press, 1999); David Samuels, "The Mayor and the Mob," *Smithsonian Magazine*, October 2019, https://www.smithsonianmag.com/history/mayor-william-odwyer-new-york-city-mob-180973078/.
17. W. O'Dwyer, *Beyond the Golden Door*, xii–xiii.
18. Steven Lee Myers, "Former New York Battler Now a Peacemaker at UN," *New York Times*, August 30, 1991, B1.
19. Paul O'Dwyer, letter of resignation, December 10, 1991, in the records of Paul O'Dwyer, Special Collections, Box 3, Folders 34–35, New York University Tamiment Library and Robert F. Wagner Labor Archives.
20. Anne Maguire, *Rock The Sham! The Irish Lesbian and Gay Organization's Battle to March in New York City's St. Patrick's Day Parade* (New York: Street Level Press, 2005), 50, 60.
21. Brendan Fay (Lavender & Green Alliance), "Paul O'Dwyer: Gay Rights Champion," letter to the editor, *Irish Voice*, July 1, 1998.
22. James Barron, "Beer Shower and Boos for Dinkins at Irish Parade," *New York Times*, March 17, 1991, A1.
23. Brian O'Dwyer, interview by Robert Polner (RP), April 28, 2020.
24. Dan Tubridy, interview by RP, October 3, 2020.
25. Pierre Sutton, interview by RP, August 18, 2021; Paul's retainer fee for Percy Sutton is listed in "The Pie and the Clout," *Daily News*, September 13, 1981 (table of information listing thirteen cable companies vying for city government approval for franchise contracts to provide cable television service and the names of their politically connected outside counsel and pitchmen).
26. Tubridy, interview.
27. Brian O'Dwyer, interview by RP, April 28, 2020.
28. Dr. Jonathan Charney, letter, December 1992, in the Paul O'Dwyer collection, personal correspondence, NYC Municipal Archives.
29. Eileen Battersby, "Thursday Interview: Mayo-Born US Civil Rights Activist Paul O'Dwyer Talks to Eileen Battersby," *Irish Times*, June 16, 1994.
30. "Pres. Clinton Receiving the Paul O'Dwyer Award (1998)," September 11, 1998, White House, South Lawn, YouTube video, 1:11:02, https://www.youtube.com/watch?v=N7d9ybg_7V0—go to 54:20 for remarks on when he first met O'Dwyer.
31. "Democratic Candidates Forum," C-SPAN, April 5, 1992, video, 23:50, https://www.c-span.org/video/?25402-1/democratic-candidates-forum&playEvent.
32. Conor O'Clery, *The Greening of the White House* (Dublin: Gill & MacMillan, 1996), 9.
33. O'Clery, *The Greening of the White House*, 11.
34. Niall O'Dowd, "The Awakening: Irish-America's Key Role in the Irish Peace Process," in *The Long Road to Peace in Northern Ireland: Peace Lectures from the Institute of Irish Studies at Liverpool University, Second Edition*, ed. Marianne Elliott (Liverpool: Liverpool University Press, 2007), 73.
35. O'Dowd, interview.
36. Kevin Sullivan and Mary Jordan, "How an Undocumented Immigrant Became an Unofficial U.S. Diplomat," *Washington Post*, March 18, 2018.
37. O'Dowd, interview.

38. Cody McCone, interview by the authors, December 29, 2020; Larry Downes, interview by the authors, April 13, 2021; Sean Downes, interview by the authors, April 18, 2021; Joe Finn, interview by RP, July 14, 2020; Peter King, interview by the authors, August 20, 2021. The Bronx jury awarded $50,000 to Cody McCone's client, "a record for a fractured elbow" in the late 1980s, McCone told the authors. Finn said Paul gave a Connemara pony to each of his three young daughters and taught them to ride, a gesture he never forgot.

39. Sanders, *The Long Peace Process*, 210–11; Biaggi's gratuities, including a $3,200 vacation spa payment, came from his longtime friend Meade Esposito, since 1969 the Brooklyn Democratic political leader, whose shadowy citywide patronage system was at the eye of the "City for Sale" corruption storm of Mayor Koch's third term. Biaggi was separately charged along with others in 1988 by Manhattan US Attorney Rudy Giuliani with having pocketed bribes for helping the Wedtech Corporation in obtaining federal procurement contracts. He was sentenced to eight years in prison. Paul "made a distinction between the sins of weakness and the sins of malice," offered King, a New York Republican congressman from 1993 through 2021 who worked closely with him on Northern Ireland, in a 2021 interview with the authors.

40. Sanders, *The Long Peace Process*, 221; O'Dowd, interview.

41. O'Clery, *The Greening of the White House*, 114.

42. O'Clery, *The Greening of the White House*, 115.

43. King, interview.

44. O'Clery, *The Greening of the White House*, 115.

45. Sanders, *The Long Peace Process*, 226.

46. Jim Mulvaney, "O'Dwyer to the White House," *Newsday*, March 16, 1994, 7.

47. Sanders, *The Long Peace Process*, 230.

48. Sanders, *The Long Peace Process*, 232.

49. "Bernadette Devlin McAliskey, 2012 Scottish Ireland Republican Meeting on Political Prisoners, Part 2," July 26, 2012, YouTube video, 20:49, https://www.youtube.com/watch?v=0f2GUjfX1gA (go to 15:30). This was part of the Scottish meeting on June 14, 2012, entitled "From Belfast to Belmarsh."

50. Sanders, *The Long Peace Process*, 252–53.

51. O'Dowd, interview.

52. Introductory remarks by Al Gore at the White House ceremony in which Bill Clinton received the Paul O'Dwyer Peace & Justice Award—see "Pres. Clinton Receiving the Paul O'Dwyer Award (1998)."

53. Francis Clines, "Paul O'Dwyer, Liberal Battler for Underdogs and Outsiders, Dies at 90," *New York Times*, June 25, 1998, B9.

54. Niall O'Dowd, "The Fire That Never Died," *Irish Voice*, July 7, 1998.

55. Mike Allen, "Political Elite out in Force to Mourn Democrat O'Dwyer," *New York Times*, June 28, 1998, 29.

56. Adrian Flannelly, interview by the authors, February 27, 2020.

57. Adrian Flannelly, interview.

58. John McGettrick, interview with RP, March 19, 2023.

59. Allen, "Political Elite out in Force."

INDEX